MCSA

Windows Server 2012

Complete Study Guide

MCSA

Windows Server® 2012

Complete Study Guide

William Panek

A Wiley Brand

Senior Acquisitions Editor: Jeff Kellum
Development Editor: Gary Schwartz
Technical Editors: Rodney Fournier and John Marta
Production Editor: Eric Charbonneau
Copy Editor: Judy Flynn
Editorial Manager: Pete Gaughan
Production Manager: Tim Tate
Vice President and Executive Group Publisher: Richard Swadley
Vice President and Publisher: Neil Edde
Media Project Manager 1: Laura Moss-Hollister
Media Associate Producer: Josh Frank
Media Quality Assurance: Doug Kuhn
Book Designer: Judy Fung
Proofreader: Nancy Bell
Indexer: Jack Lewis
Project Coordinator, Cover: Katherine Crocker
Cover Designer: Ryan Sneed

ISBN: 978-1-118-54407-5
ISBN: 978-1-118-75486-3 (ebk.)
ISBN: 978-1-118-75479-5 (ebk.)

Library of Congress Control Number: 2013936336

Dear Reader,

Thank you for choosing *MCSA: Windows Server 2012 Complete Study Guide*. This book is part of a family of premium-quality Sybex books, all of which are written by outstanding authors who combine practical experience with a gift for teaching.

Sybex was founded in 1976. More than 30 years later, we're still committed to producing consistently exceptional books. With each of our titles, we're working hard to set a new standard for the industry. From the paper we print on to the authors we work with, our goal is to bring you the best books available.

I hope you see all that reflected in these pages. I'd be very interested to hear your comments and get your feedback on how we're doing. Feel free to let me know what you think about this or any other Sybex book by sending me an email at nedde@wiley.com. If you think you've found a technical error in this book, please visit http://sybex.custhelp.com. Customer feedback is critical to our efforts at Sybex.

Best regards,

Neil Edde
Vice President and Publisher
Sybex, an Imprint of Wiley

Acknowledgments

I would like to thank my wife and best friend, Crystal. She is always the light at the end of my tunnel. I want to thank my two daughters, Alexandria and Paige, for all of their love and support during the writing of all my books. They make it all worthwhile.

I want to thank my family, and especially my brothers, Rick, Gary, and Rob. They have always been there for me. I want to thank my father, Richard, who helped me become the man I am today, and my mother, Maggie, for all of her love and support.

I want to thank everyone at Green Mountain Communications for their support while I was writing this book, including Catherine, Vic, Moe, Paul, Dana, Jimmy, Jeff, Will, and all my others coworkers. I appreciate all the support they gave me.

I want to thank everyone on my Sybex team, especially my development editor, Gary Schwartz, who helped me make this the best book possible, and Rodney R. Fournier, who is the technical editor of many of my books. It's always good to have the very best technical guy backing you up.

I want to thank Eric Charbonneau, who was my production editor, and my acquisitions editor, Jeff Kellum, who was the lead for the entire book. He has always been there for me, and it is always great to write for him. Finally, I want to thank everyone else behind the scenes who helped make this book possible.

About the Author

 **William Panek** holds the following certifications: MCP, MCP+I, MCSA, MCSA+ Security and Messaging, MCSE-NT (3.51 & 4.0), MCSE 2000 and 2003, MCSE+Security and Messaging, MCDBA, MCT, MCTS, MCITP, CCNA, and CHFI.

After many successful years in the computer industry and a degree in computer programming, Will decided that he could better use his talents and his personality as an instructor. He began teaching for schools such as Boston University, Clark University, and the University of Maryland, just to name a few. In 1998, he helped found Stellacon Corporation. Stellacon has become one of New England's most respected training companies and is a four-time winner of the Best Computer School award in Portsmouth, New Hampshire.

In 2012, Will became the Director of IT for Green Mountain Communications. He currently lives in New Hampshire with his wife and two daughters. Will was also a Representative in the New Hampshire House of Representatives from 2010 to 2012. In his spare time, he likes to golf, ski, and go snowmobiling. Will is also a commercially-rated helicopter pilot.

Contents at a Glance

Introduction   *xxxi*

Assessment Test   *xlvii*

Chapter 1   Installing and Configuring Windows Server 2012   1

Chapter 2   Domain Name System   33

Chapter 3   Active Directory Planning and Installation   99

Chapter 4   Administering Active Directory   143

Chapter 5   Managing Group Policy Objects   193

Chapter 6   Configuring Active Directory Infrastructure   255

Chapter 7   Configuring Active Directory Server Roles   321

Chapter 8   Using Virtualization in Windows Server 2012   365

Chapter 9   Configuring TCP/IP   403

Chapter 10   Managing DHCP   457

Chapter 11   Managing and Maintaining Servers   507

Chapter 12   Configuring Network Access   555

Chapter 13   Understanding Security   607

Chapter 14   Managing File and Print Services   647

Chapter 15   Managing Remote Access Services   699

Chapter 16   Configuring High Availability in Windows Server 2012   761

Chapter 17   Configuring File and Storage Services   795

Chapter 18   Implementing Disaster Recovery   829

Appendix A   Answers to Review Questions   861

Appendix B   About the Additional Study Tools   881

Index   *885*

Contents

Introduction   xxxi

Assessment Test   xlvii

Chapter   1   Installing and Configuring Windows Server 2012   1

Features and Advantages of Windows Server 2012   2
Planning the Windows Server 2012 Installation   4
Server Roles in Windows Server 2012   4
   Migrating Roles and Features to Windows
     Server 2012   8
   Deciding Which Windows Server 2012 Versions
     to Use   9
   Deciding on Type of Installation   11
   Installing Windows Server 2012   14
   Using Windows Deployment Services   18
Configuring Remote Management   22
   Windows Remote Management   22
   Windows PowerShell   23
Understanding Features On Demand   27
Summary   28
Exam Essentials   29
Review Questions   30

Chapter   2   Domain Name System   33

Introducing DNS   35
   The Form of an IP Address   36
   Understanding Servers, Clients, and Resolvers   41
   Understanding the DNS Process   42
Introducing DNS Database Zones   48
   Understanding Primary Zones   49
   Understanding Secondary Zones   50
   Understanding Active Directory Integrated DNS   51
   Understanding Stub Zones   53
   GlobalName Zones   54
   Zone Transfers and Replication   54
Advantages of DNS in Windows Server 2012   58
   Background Zone Loading   58
   Support for IPv6 Addresses   58
   Support for Read-Only Domain Controllers   59
   DNS Socket Pools   59
   DNS Cache Locking   60

DNS Security Extensions (DNSSEC)   60
DNS Devolution   61
Record Weighting   61
Netmask Ordering   61
DnsUpdateProxy Group   62
Introducing DNS Record Types   62
Start of Authority (SOA) Records   62
Name Server (NS) Records   64
Host Record   64
Alias Record   65
Pointer (PTR) Record   65
Mail Exchanger (MX) Record   66
Service (SRV) Record   66
Configuring DNS   67
Installing DNS   67
Load Balancing with Round Robin   70
Configuring a Caching-Only Server   70
Setting Zone Properties   71
Configuring Zones for Dynamic Updates   75
Delegating Zones for DNS   77
DNS Forwarding   79
Manually Creating DNS Records   79
DNS Aging and Scavenging   81
Monitoring and Troubleshooting DNS   81
Monitoring DNS with the DNS Snap-In   81
Troubleshooting DNS   84
Summary   92
Exam Essentials   93
Review Questions   95

Chapter 3   Active Directory Planning and Installation   99

Verifying the File system   101
Resilient File System (ReFS)   101
NTFS   102
Verifying Network Connectivity   106
Basic Connectivity Tests   106
Tools and Techniques for Testing Network Configuration   107
Understanding Domain and Forest Functionality   109
About the Domain Functional Level   109
About Forest Functionality   111
Planning the Domain Structure   112
Installing Active Directory   113
Adprep   113
The Installation Process   114

Verifying Active Directory Installation   124
    Using Event Viewer   124
    Using Active Directory Administrative Tools   126
    Testing from Clients   127
Creating and Configuring Application Data Partitions   129
    Creating Application Data Partitions   129
    Managing Replicas   131
    Removing Replicas   132
    Using *ntdsutil* to Manage Application
       Data Partitions   132
Configuring DNS Integration with Active Directory   134
Summary   137
Exam Essentials   137
Review Questions   139

Chapter   4   Administering Active Directory   143

An Overview of OUs   144
    The Purpose of OUs   145
    Benefits of OUs   146
Planning the OU Structure   146
    Logical Grouping of Resources   146
    Understanding OU Inheritance   148
    Delegating Administrative Control   149
    Applying Group Policies   151
Creating OUs   151
Managing OUs   155
    Moving, Deleting, and Renaming OUs   156
    Administering Properties of OUs   157
    Delegating Control of OUs   159
Troubleshooting OUs   163
Creating and Managing Active Directory Objects   163
    Overview of Active Directory Objects   163
    Managing Object Properties   171
    Understanding Groups   174
    Filtering and Advanced Active Directory Features   176
    Moving, Renaming, and Deleting Active
       Directory Objects   177
    Resetting an Existing Computer Account   179
Publishing Active Directory Objects   179
    Making Active Directory Objects Available to Users 180
    Publishing Printers   180
    Publishing Shared Folders   182
    Querying Active Directory   183
    Using the Active Directory Administrative Center   184

Using the Command Prompt for Active Directory
    Configuration   185
Summary   187
Exam Essentials   187
Review Questions   189

Chapter   5   Managing Group Policy Objects   193

Introducing Group Policy   195
    Understanding Group Policy Settings   196
    The Security Settings Section of the GPO   199
    Group Policy Objects   200
    Group Policy Inheritance   201
Planning a Group Policy Strategy   202
Implementing Group Policy   203
    Creating GPOs   203
    Linking Existing GPOs to Active Directory   207
Managing Group Policy   207
    Managing GPOs   207
    Security Filtering of a Group Policy   209
    Delegating Administrative Control of GPOs   211
    Controlling Inheritance and Filtering Group Policy 212
    Assigning Script Policies   214
    Understanding the Loopback Policy   215
    Managing Network Configuration   216
    Automatically Enrolling User and Computer
        Certificates in Group Policy   217
    Redirecting Folders   219
    Managing GPOs with Windows PowerShell
        Group Policy Cmdlets   221
Deploying Software through a GPO   222
    The Software Management Life Cycle   223
    The Windows Installer   224
    Deploying Applications   228
Implementing Software Deployment   229
    Preparing for Software Deployment   230
    Software Restriction Policies   231
    Using AppLocker   231
    Group Policy Slow Link Detection   231
    Publishing and Assigning Applications   232
    Applying Software Updates   233
    Verifying Software Installation   234
    Configuring Automatic Updates in Group Policy   235
Configuring Software Deployment Settings   236
    The Software Installation Properties Dialog Box   236

Removing Programs	239
Microsoft Windows Installer Settings	241
Troubleshooting Group Policies	242
RSoP in Logging Mode	243
RSoP in Planning Mode	246
Using the *gpresult.exe* Command	247
Summary	248
Exam Essentials	249
Review Questions	251

Chapter   6   Configuring Active Directory Infrastructure   255

Overview of Network Planning	256
The Three Types of Networks	257
Exploring Network Constraints	257
Overview of Active Directory Replication and Sites	258
Replicating Active Directory	259
Understanding Active Directory Site Concepts	259
Understanding Distributed File System Replication	263
Implementing Sites and Subnets	264
Creating Sites	266
Creating Subnets	268
Configuring Sites	270
Configuring Replication	271
Intrasite Replication	272
Intersite Replication	272
Configuring Server Topology	279
Using Universal Group Membership Caching	283
Monitoring and Troubleshooting Active Directory	
Replication	284
About System Monitor	284
Troubleshooting Replication	284
Reasons for Creating Multiple Domains	287
Reasons for Using Multiple Domains	287
Drawbacks of Multiple Domains	289
Creating Domain Trees and Forests	290
Planning Trees and Forests	290
The Promotion Process	294
Creating a Domain Tree	294
Joining a New Domain Tree to a Forest	300
Adding Additional Domain Controllers	300
Demoting a Domain Controller	301
Managing Multiple Domains	303
Managing Single-Master Operations	303
Forest Operations Masters	303

	Domain Operations Masters	304
	Assigning Single-Master Roles	304
	Managing Trusts	305
	Managing UPN Suffixes	310
	Managing Global Catalog Servers	310
	Managing Universal Group Membership Caching	312
	Summary	313
	Exam Essentials	314
	Review Questions	317
Chapter 7	**Configuring Active Directory Server Roles**	**321**
	Understanding Server Manager	323
	Configuring Active Directory Certificate Services	324
	Installing Active Directory Certificate Services	326
	Enrolling User and Computer Certificates	333
	Certificate Templates	335
	Revoking Certificates	337
	Configuring Additional CA Server Settings	340
	What's New in Windows Server 2012?	342
	Understanding Active Directory Domain Services	342
	Security Features Available for Domain Services	342
	Features of Windows Server 2012	344
	Active Directory Federation Services	346
	Installing AD FS	346
	Configuring AD FS	349
	Active Directory Lightweight Directory Services	350
	Installing AD LDS	350
	Configuring AD LDS	351
	Installing AD LDS on Server Core	354
	Active Directory Rights Management Services	355
	AD RMS Templates	360
	Summary	360
	Exam Essentials	361
	Review Questions	362
Chapter 8	**Using Virtualization in Windows Server 2012**	**365**
	Hyper-V Overview	367
	What Is Virtualization?	367
	Hyper-V Features	368
	Hyper-V Architecture	370
	Hyper-V Requirements	372
	Hyper-V Installation and Configuration	373
	Install the Hyper-V Role	373
	Hyper-V in Server Manager	375

Using Hyper-V Manager 376
Configure Hyper-V Settings 377
Manage Virtual Switches 378
Managing Virtual Hard Disks 381
Configuring Virtual Machines 385
Creating and Managing Virtual Machines 385
Back Up and Restore Virtual Machines 392
Using Physical-to-Virtual (P2V) Conversion 397
Using Virtual-to-Virtual (V2V) Conversion 398
Summary 399
Exam Essentials 399
Review Questions 401

Chapter 9   Configuring TCP/IP **403**

Understanding TCP/IP 404
Details of the TCP/IP Model 404
How TCP/IP Layers Communicate 405
Understanding Port Numbers 406
Understanding IP Addressing 407
The Hierarchical IP Addressing Scheme 407
Understanding Network Classes 409
Subnetting a Network 412
Implementing Subnetting 413
An Easier Way to Apply Subnetting 420
Applying Subnetting the Traditional Way 423
Working with Classless Inter-Domain Routing 431
Understanding IPv6 434
IPv6 History and Need 435
New and Improved IPv6 Concepts 435
IPv6 Addressing Concepts 438
IPv6 Integration/Migration 443
Understanding IP Address Management (IPAM) 447
Summary 452
Exam Essentials 452
Review Questions 453

Chapter 10   Managing DHCP **457**

Overview of DHCP 458
Introducing the DORA Process 459
Advantages and Disadvantages of DHCP 460
Ipconfig Lease Options 461
Understanding Scope Details 462
Installing and Authorizing DHCP 464
Installing DHCP 464

Introducing the DHCP Snap-In   467
Authorizing DHCP for Active Directory   468
Creating and Managing DHCP Scopes   471
Creating a New Scope in IPv4   471
Creating a New Scope in IPv6   479
Changing Scope Properties (IPv4 and IPv6)   483
Changing Server Properties   484
Managing Reservations and Exclusions   487
Setting Scope Options for IPv4   490
Activating and Deactivating Scopes   493
Creating a Superscope for IPv4   493
Creating IPv4 Multicast Scopes   494
Integrating Dynamic DNS and IPv4 DHCP   497
Using Multiple DHCP Servers   499
Working with the DHCP Database Files   500
Summary   501
Exam Essentials   502
Review Questions   503

Chapter 11   Managing and Maintaining Servers   507

Configuring Windows Server Update Services   509
Windows Update   510
Windows Automatic Updates   511
Using Windows Server Update Services   512
Overview of Windows Server 2012 Performance Monitoring   524
Using Windows Server 2012 Performance Tools   526
Introducing Performance Monitor   527
Using Other Performance-Monitoring Tools   536
Summary   549
Exam Essentials   550
Review Questions   551

Chapter 12   Configuring Network Access   555

Understanding Routing   556
What Routing Does   556
How Routing Works   557
Routing in Windows Server 2012   567
Installing RRAS   568
Configuring IP Routing   573
Creating and Managing Interfaces   573
Setting IP Routing Properties   587
Managing Routing Protocols   589
Managing Static Routes   590
Configuring TCP/IP Packet Filters   592

Configuring VPN Packet Filters   595
   PPTP Packet Filters   595
   L2TP Packet Filters   597
Managing IP Routing   597
   Using the *routeprint* Command   598
   Troubleshooting IP Routing   598
   Troubleshooting Example   599
Summary   601
Exam Essentials   601
Review Questions   603

Chapter 13   Understanding Security   607

Active Directory Security Overview   609
   Understanding Security Principals   609
   Managing Security and Permissions   619
   Using ACLs and ACEs   620
Implementing Active Directory Security   622
   Using User Templates   624
   Delegating Control of Users and Groups   625
   Understanding Dynamic Access Control   627
Using Group Policy for Security   627
   Fine-Grained Password Policies   630
Understanding Smart Card Authentication   633
   Preparing a Smart Card Certificate
      Enrollment Station   633
   Configuring Group Policy Settings for Smart Cards   634
Understanding Security Configuration and Analysis Tools   635
   Using the Security Configuration and Analysis Utility   635
   Understanding the *secedit.exe* Command   636
Implementing an Audit Policy   637
   Overview of Auditing   638
   Implementing Auditing   638
   Viewing Auditing Information   640
   Using the *Auditpol.exe* Command   640
   What's New in Windows Server 2012 Auditing   641
Summary   642
Exam Essentials   643
Review Questions   644

Chapter 14   Managing File and Print Services   647

Understanding File Servers   649
Configuring File Servers   650
   Sharing Folders   650
   Making Active Directory Objects Available to Users   651

Configuring Offline Folders   653
Volume Shadow Copy Services (VSS)   656
Understanding Permissions   656
Share and Storage Management Console   663
Understanding File Server Resource Manager (FSRM)   664
Using BitLocker Drive Encryption   666
What's New in BitLocker?   667
Windows 7 & 2008 R2 vs. Windows 8 & 2012   668
Understanding BranchCache   671
Distributed Cache Mode Requirements   672
Hosted Mode Requirements   674
BranchCache and PowerShell   676
What's New in Windows Server 2012 BranchCache?   677
Configuring DirectAccess   678
DirectAccess vs. VPNs   678
Understanding How DirectAccess Works   679
Knowing the DirectAccess Infrastructure
    Requirements   679
Configuring Disk Quotas   680
Configuring Distributed File System   682
Advantages of DFS   683
Types of DFS   683
Remote Differential Compression (RDC)   685
Understanding Printing   686
Creating and Publishing Printers   686
Configuring Printers   688
Migrating Print Servers   693
Easy Print Driver   693
Summary   693
Exam Essentials   694
Review Questions   695

Chapter   15   Managing Remote Access Services   699

Overview of Dial-Up Networking   700
What DUN Does   701
How DUN Works   701
Overview of Virtual Private Networks   705
What VPNs Do   705
VPNs and Windows Server 2012   706
How VPNs Work   706
Configuring Your Remote Access Server   710
Configuring PPP Options   710
Installing a VPN   714
How VPN Works   714
Enabling RRAS as a VPN   715

Configuring a VPN   715
   Configuring VPN Ports   715
   Troubleshooting VPNs   716
Managing Your Remote Access Server   718
   Managing Remote Users with a RADIUS Server   718
   Monitoring Overall Activity   719
   Controlling Remote Access Logging   719
   Reviewing the Remote Access Event Log   722
   Monitoring Ports and Port Activity   722
Configuring a RAS or VPN Client   723
   The General Tab   724
   The Options Tab   725
   The Security Tab   726
   The Networking Tab   729
   The Sharing Tab   730
Overview of Wireless Access   730
   Configuring Wireless Access   731
Remote Access Security   732
   User Authentication   733
   Connection Security   734
   Access Control   735
Configuring User Access   736
   Setting Up User Profiles   736
   Using Network Access Policies   738
   Using Remote Access Profiles   744
   Setting Up a VPN Network Access Policy   749
Configuring Security   751
   Controlling Server Security   751
   Configuring Network Access Protection   754
Summary   755
Exam Essentials   755
Review Questions   757

**Chapter   16   Configuring High Availability in Windows
     Server 2012   761**

Components of High Availability   762
Achieving High Availability   763
   High Availability Foundation   764
Achieving High Availability with Failover Clustering   765
   Failover Clustering Requirements   767
   Cluster Quorum   768
   Validating a Cluster Configuration   770
   Creating a Cluster   775
   Clustered Application Settings   779
   Resource Properties   783

xxiv   Contents

Windows Server 2012 Clustering Features   786
Achieving High Availability with Network Load Balancing   787
    How Does Network Load Balancing Work?   787
    Creating an NLB Cluster   788
    Modifying Cluster Properties   789
    Managing NLB Clusters   790
    NIC Teaming   791
Summary   791
Exam Essentials   791
Review Questions   792

Chapter 17   Configuring File and Storage Services   795

Storage in Windows Server 2012   796
    Initializing Disks   796
    Working with Basic and Dynamic Disks   797
    Working with Volume Sets   799
    Redundant Array of Independent Disks   800
    Mount Points   804
    Microsoft MPIO   805
    iSCSI   808
    Internet Storage Name Service   810
    Fibre Channel   813
    Network Attached Storage   814
    Virtual Disk Service   814
Configuring Windows Firewall Options   816
Summary   825
Exam Essentials   825
Review Questions   826

Chapter 18   Implementing Disaster Recovery   829

Protecting the System   830
Backup and Recovery of Active Directory   831
    Overview of the Windows Server 2012 Backup Utility   833
    Setting Up an Active Directory Backup   837
    Restoring Active Directory   841
    Active Directory Recycle Bin   842
    Restartable Active Directory   843
    Offline Maintenance   843
    Monitoring Replication   845
    Using the ADSI Editor   846
    Wbadmin Command Line Utility   846
Understanding Shadow Copies   847
    VssAdmin Command   849
    Data Protection Manager   850

Using Advanced Boot Options   850
    Starting in Safe Mode   851
    Enabling Boot Logging   852
    Using Other Advanced Boot Options Menu Modes   854
    Windows Recovery Environment   855
Using the Startup Repair Tool   856
Summary   857
Exam Essentials   857
Review Questions   858

Appendix   A   Answers to Review Questions   861

Chapter 1: Installing and Configuring Windows Server 2012   862
Chapter 2: Domain Name System   862
Chapter 3: Active Directory Planning and Installation   863
Chapter 4: Administering Active Directory   864
Chapter 5: Managing Group Policy Objects   865
Chapter 6: Configuring Active Directory Infrastructure   866
Chapter 7: Configuring Active Directory Server Roles   867
Chapter 8: Using Virtualization in Windows Server 2012   868
Chapter 9: Configuring TCP/IP   869
Chapter 10: Managing DHCP   871
Chapter 11: Managing and Maintaining Servers   873
Chapter 12: Configuring Network Access   874
Chapter 13: Understanding Security   875
Chapter 14: Managing File and Print Services   876
Chapter 15: Managing Remote Access Services   877
Chapter 16: Configuring High Availability in
    Windows Server 2012   878
Chapter 17: Configuring File and Storage Services   879
Chapter 18: Implementing Disaster Recovery   880

Appendix   B   About the Additional Study Tools   881

Additional Study Tools   882
    Sybex Test Engine   882
    Electronic Flashcards   882
    Videos   882
    PDF of Glossary of Terms   882
    Adobe Reader   883
System Requirements   883
Using the Study Tools   883
Troubleshooting   883
    Customer Care   884

Index   885

Table of Exercises

Exercise **1.1** Installing Windows Server 2012 with the GUI. 15

Exercise **1.2** Installing Windows Server 2012 Using Server Core. 17

Exercise **1.3** Starting the Windows PowerShell Utility 27

Exercise **2.1** Installing and Configuring the DNS Service 68

Exercise **2.2** Configuring a Zone for Dynamic Updates. 75

Exercise **2.3** Creating a Delegated DNS Zone. 78

Exercise **2.4** Manually Creating DNS RRs 79

Exercise **2.5** Simple DNS Testing 83

Exercise **2.6** Using the nslookup Command 87

Exercise **3.1** Viewing Disk Configuration. 104

Exercise **3.2** Promoting a Domain Controller 114

Exercise **3.3** Installing AD DS on Server Core. 120

Exercise **3.4** Viewing the Active Directory Event Log. 124

Exercise **3.5** Joining a Computer to an Active Directory Domain. 128

Exercise **3.6** Configuring DNS Integration with Active Directory. 135

Exercise **4.1** Creating an OU Structure. 153

Exercise **4.2** Modifying OU Structure. 156

Exercise **4.3** Using the Delegation of Control Wizard. 159

Exercise **4.4** Delegating Custom Tasks. 160

Exercise **4.5** Creating Active Directory Objects 165

Exercise **4.6** Creating a User Template. 168

Exercise **4.7** Managing Object Properties 172

Exercise **4.8** Moving Active Directory Objects 178

Exercise **4.9** Resetting an Existing Computer Account 179

Exercise **4.10** Creating and Publishing a Printer. 180

Exercise **4.11** Creating and Publishing a Shared Folder 182

Exercise **4.12** Finding Objects in Active Directory 183

Exercise **5.1** Creating a Group Policy Object Using the GPMC. 204

Exercise **5.2** Linking Existing GPOs to Active Directory 207

Exercise **5.3** Filtering Group Policy Using Security Groups 210

Exercise **5.4** Delegating Administrative Control of Group Policy. 211

Exercise **5.5** Configuring Automatic Certificate Enrollment in Group Policy 218

Exercise **5.6** Configuring Folder Redirection in Group Policy. 220

Exercise **5.7** Creating a Software Deployment Share 230

Exercise **5.8** Publishing and Assigning Applications Using Group Policy 232

Exercise **5.9** Applying Software Updates 234

Exercise **6.1** Creating Sites 266

Exercise **6.2** Creating Subnets 269

Exercise **6.3** Configuring Sites 271

Exercise **6.4** Creating Site Links and Site Link Bridges 275

Exercise **6.5** Moving Server Objects between Sites........................ 278

Exercise **6.6** Creating a New Subdomain................................. 295

Exercise **6.7** Assigning Single-Master Operations......................... 305

Exercise **6.8** Managing Trust Relationships.............................. 309

Exercise **6.9** Adding a UPN Suffix...................................... 310

Exercise **6.10** Managing GC Servers 311

Exercise **6.11** Managing Universal Group Membership Caching 312

Exercise **7.1** Installing Active Directory Certificate Services 327

Exercise **7.2** Configuring Certificate Auto Enrollment...................... 334

Exercise **7.3** Modifying the AIA.. 338

Exercise **7.4** Revoking a Certificate 339

Exercise **7.5** Backing Up the Certification Authority Server 341

Exercise **7.6** Installing the AD FS 346

Exercise **7.7** Installing AD LDS 351

Exercise **7.8** Configuring an AD LDS Instance 352

Exercise **7.9** Installing AD RMS.. 356

Exercise **8.1** Installing Hyper-V in Full Installation Mode.................. 373

Exercise **8.2** Creating an Internal Virtual Network 380

Exercise **8.3** Creating a Differencing Hard Disk 383

Exercise **8.4** Creating a New Virtual Machine............................. 386

Exercise **8.5** Installing Hyper-V Integration Components 391

Exercise **8.6** Creating a Snapshot of a Virtual Machine.................... 394

Exercise **8.7** Applying a Snapshot 396

Subnet Mask Exercise **1** Class C, 10 Hosts per Subnet..................... 421

Subnet Mask Exercise **2** Class C, 20 Hosts per Subnet..................... 421

Subnet Mask Exercise **3** Class C, Five Subnets........................... 421

Subnet Mask Exercise **4** Class B, 1,500 Hosts per Subnet 422

Subnet Mask Exercise **5** Class B, 3,500 Hosts per Subnet 422

Exercise **9.1** Installing the IPAM feature 449

Exercise   **10.1**   Installing the DHCP Service. 464

Exercise   **10.2**   Unauthorizing a DHCP Server 469

Exercise   **10.3**   Authorizing a DHCP Server 470

Exercise   **10.4**   Creating a New Scope 478

Exercise   **10.5**   Configuring User Class Options 492

Exercise   **10.6**   Creating a Superscope. 493

Exercise   **10.7**   Creating a New Multicast Scope. 495

Exercise   **10.8**   Enabling DHCP-DNS Integration. 499

Exercise   **11.1**   Installing a WSUS Server. 514

Exercise   **11.2**   Setting WSUS Server Options 518

Exercise   **11.3**   Configuring a GPO for WSUS 524

Exercise   **11.4**   Installing SNMP. 548

Exercise   **11.5**   Configuring SNMP 548

Exercise   **12.1**   Installing RRAS for IP Routing. 568

Exercise   **12.2**   Creating a Demand-Dial Interface. 578

Exercise   **12.3**   Installing the RIP Protocols 589

Exercise   **12.4**   Adding and Removing Static Routes 591

Exercise   **12.5**   Configuring PPTP Packet Filters 596

Exercise   **12.6**   Monitoring Routing Status 598

Exercise   **12.7**   Troubleshooting Your Server 600

Exercise   **13.1**   Creating and Managing Users and Groups 622

Exercise   **13.2**   Creating and Using User Templates. 625

Exercise   **13.3**   Delegating Control of Active Directory Objects 626

Exercise   **13.4**   Applying Security Policies by Using Group Policy. 629

Exercise   **13.5**   Fine-Grained Password Policy 631

Exercise   **13.6**   Configuring Group Policy to Require Smart Card Logon. 634

Exercise   **13.7**   Enabling Auditing of Active Directory Objects 639

Exercise   **13.8**   Generating and Viewing Audit Logs. 640

Exercise   **14.1**   Creating and Publishing a Shared Network Folder. 651

Exercise   **14.2**   Configuring Offline Folder Options 654

Exercise   **14.3**   Configuring a Shared Network Folder for Offline Access 656

Exercise   **14.4**   Configuring Shared and NTFS Settings. 662

Exercise   **14.5**   Enabling BitLocker in Windows Server 2012. 670

Exercise   **14.6**   Configuring BranchCache Firewall Exceptions. 672

Exercise   **14.7**   Installing BranchCache on Windows Server 2012 675

Exercise   **14.8** Installing the DirectAccess Feature 680

Exercise   **14.9** Configuring Disk Quotas 681

Exercise   **14.10** Installing the DFS Namespace Service 684

Exercise   **14.11** Creating and Publishing a Printer 686

Exercise   **15.1** Configuring Incoming Connections 713

Exercise   **15.2** Changing Remote Access Logging Settings 721

Exercise   **15.3** Creating a Network Access Policy 741

Exercise   **15.4** Restricting a User Profile for Dial-In Access 745

Exercise   **15.5** Configuring Encryption 749

Exercise   **15.6** Creating a VPN Network Access Policy 750

Exercise   **16.1** Installing the Failover Cluster Feature 770

Exercise   **16.2** Running the Validate a Configuration Wizard .772

Exercise   **16.3** Creating a Cluster 775

Exercise   **16.4** Clustering the Print Services Role 777

Exercise   **16.5** Using the Dependency Viewer 781

Exercise   **16.6** Creating a Network Load Balancing Cluster 788

Exercise   **17.1** Initializing Disk Drives 797

Exercise   **17.2** Converting a Basic Disk to a Dynamic Disk 798

Exercise   **17.3** Creating a Volume Set 800

Exercise   **17.4** Creating Mount Points 805

Exercise   **17.5** Installing Microsoft MPIO 806

Exercise   **17.6** Configuring iSCSI Storage Connection 809

Exercise   **17.7** Installing the iSNS Feature on Windows Server 2012 811

Exercise   **17.8** Configuring Windows Firewall 821

Exercise   **18.1**   Backing Up Active Directory. 838

Exercise   **18.2** Configuring a Shadow Copy on a Volume. 848

Exercise   **18.3** Booting Your Computer to Safe Mode. 852

Exercise   **18.4** Using Boot Logging 853

Introduction

This book was written from over 20 years of IT experience. We have taken that experience and translated it into a Windows Server 2012 book that will help you not only prepare for the MCSA: Windows Server 2012 exams, but also to develop a clear understanding of how to install and configure Windows Server 2012 while avoiding all the possible configuration pitfalls.

Many Microsoft books just explain the Windows operating system, but with *MCSA: Windows Server 2012 Complete Study Guide*, I go a step further, providing many in-depth, step-by-step procedures to support my explanations of how the operating system performs at its best.

Microsoft Windows Server 2012 is the newest version of Microsoft's server operating system software. Microsoft has taken the best of Windows Server 2003 and Windows Server 2008 and combined them into the latest creation, Windows Server 2012.

Windows Server 2012 eliminates many of the problems that plagued Windows Server 2003 and Windows Server 2008, and it includes a much faster boot time and shutdown. It is also easier to install and configure, and it barely stops to ask the user any questions during installation. In this book, I will show you what features are installed during the automated installation and where you can make changes if you need to be more in charge of your operating system and its features.

This book takes you through all the ins and outs of Windows Server 2012, including installation, configuration, Group Policy Objects, auditing, backups, and so much more.

Windows Server 2012 has improved on Microsoft's desktop environment, made networking easier, enhanced search ability, improved performance—and that's only scratching the surface.

When all is said and done, this is a technical book for IT professionals who want to take Windows Server 2012 to the next step and get certified. With this book, you will not only learn Windows Server 2012 and hopefully pass the exams, you will also become a Windows Server 2012 expert.

The Microsoft Certification Program

Since the inception of its certification program, Microsoft has certified more than two million people. As the computer network industry continues to increase in both size and complexity, this number is sure to grow—and the need for proven ability will also increase. Certifications can help companies verify the skills of prospective employees and contractors.

The Microsoft certification tracks for Windows Server 2012 include:

MCSA: Windows Server 2012   The MCSA is now the lowest level certification you can achieve with Microsoft in relation to Windows Server 2012. It requires passing three exams: 70-410, 70-411 and 70-412. Or, if you quality, you can take an Upgrade exam: Exam 70-417. This book assists in your preparation for all four exams.

MCSE: Server Infrastructure or MCSE: Desktop Infrastructure   The MCSE certifications, in relation to Windows Server 2012, require that you become an MCSA first and then pass two additional exams. The additional exams will vary depending on which of the two MCSE tracks you choose. For more information, visit Microsoft's website at www.microsoft.com/learning.

MCSM: Directory Services   The MCSM certification takes things to an entirely new level. It requires passing a knowledge exam (in addition to having the MCSE in Windows Server 2012) and a lab exam. This is now the elite level certification in Windows Server 2012.

How Do You Become Certified on Windows Server 2012?

Attaining Microsoft certification has always been a challenge. In the past, students have been able to acquire detailed exam information—even most of the exam questions—from online "brain dumps" and third-party "cram" books or software products. For the new generation of exams, this is simply not the case.

Microsoft has taken strong steps to protect the security and integrity of its new certification tracks. Now prospective candidates must complete a course of study that develops detailed knowledge about a wide range of topics. It supplies them with the true skills needed, derived from working with the technology being tested.

The new generations of Microsoft certification programs are heavily weighted toward hands-on skills and experience. It is recommended that candidates have troubleshooting skills acquired through hands-on experience and working knowledge.

Fortunately, if you are willing to dedicate the time and effort to learn Windows Server 2012, you can prepare yourself well for the exam by using the proper tools. By working through this book, you can successfully meet the requirements to pass the Windows Server 2012 exams.

MCSA Exam Requirements

Candidates for MCSA certification on Windows Server 2012 must pass at least the following three Windows Server 2012 exams:

- 70-410: Installing and Configuring Windows Server 2012
- 70-411: Administering Windows Server 2012
- 70-412: Configuring Advanced Windows Server 2012 Services

NOTE For those who have a qualifying certification, they can take the Upgrading Your Skills to MCSA Windows Server 2012 exam (Exam 70-417). The exam objectives for this exam span the three individual exams. This book covers all the objectives for the Upgrade exam. For details of the exam, visit Microsoft's website at www.microsoft.com/learning.

Microsoft provides exam objectives to give you a general overview of possible areas of coverage on the Microsoft exams. Keep in mind, however, that exam objectives are subject to change at any time without prior notice and at Microsoft's sole discretion. Please visit the Microsoft Learning website (www.microsoft.com/learning) for the most current listing of exam objectives. The published objectives and how they map this book are listed later in this Introduction

 NOTE For a more detailed description of the Microsoft certification programs, including a list of all the exams, visit the Microsoft Learning website at www.microsoft.com/learning.

Tips for Taking the Windows Server 2012 Exams

Here are some general tips for achieving success on your certification exam:

- Arrive early at the exam center so that you can relax and review your study materials. During this final review, you can look over tables and lists of exam-related information.

- Read the questions carefully. Do not be tempted to jump to an early conclusion. Make sure that you know *exactly* what the question is asking.

- Answer all questions. If you are unsure about a question, mark it for review and come back to it at a later time.

- On simulations, do not change settings that are not directly related to the question. Also, assume default settings if the question does not specify or imply which settings are used.

- For questions that you're not sure about, use a process of elimination to get rid of the obviously incorrect answers first. This improves your odds of selecting the correct answer when you need to make an educated guess.

Exam Registration

You may take the Microsoft exams at any of more than 1,000 Authorized Prometric Testing Centers (APTCs) around the world. For the location of a testing center near you, call Prometric at 800-755-EXAM (800-755-3926). Outside of the United States and Canada, contact your local Prometric registration center. You may also register for your exams online at www.prometric.com.

Find out the number of the exam you want to take, and then register with the Prometric registration center nearest to you. At this point, you will be asked for advance payment for the exam. The exams are $125 each, and you must take them within one year of payment. You can schedule exams up to six weeks in advance or as late as one working day prior to the date of the exam. You can cancel or reschedule your exam if you contact the center at least two working days prior to the exam. Same-day registration is available in some locations, subject to space availability. Where same-day registration is available, you must register a minimum of two hours before test time.

When you schedule the exam, you will be provided with instructions regarding appointment and cancellation procedures, ID requirements, and information about the testing center location. In addition, you will receive a registration and payment confirmation letter from Prometric.

Microsoft requires certification candidates to accept the terms of a nondisclosure agreement before taking certification exams.

Who Should Read This Book?

This book is intended for individuals who want to earn their MCSA: Windows Server 2012 certification

This book will not only help anyone who is looking to pass the Microsoft exams, it will also help anyone who wants to learn the real ins and outs of the Windows Server 2012 operating system.

What's Inside?

Here is a glance at what's in each chapter:

Chapter 1: Installing and Configuring Windows Server 2012   In the first chapter, I explain the requirements and steps to install and configure Windows Server 2012.

Chapter 2: Domain Name System   This chapter shows you how to install and configure DNS. We also explain the different types of DNS records and DNS zone types.

Chapter 3: Active Directory Planning and Installation   I take you through the advantages and benefits of Windows Server 2012 Active Directory.

Chapter 4: Administering Active Directory   This chapter takes you through the different ways to create and manage your users and groups on the Windows Server 2012 operating system.

Chapter 5: Managing Group Policy Objects   You will see how to configure different types of Group Policy objects (GPOs) in Active Directory.

Chapter 6: Configuring Active Directory Infrastructure   I show you how to manage Active Directory Trees and Forests using the Active Directory MMC snap-ins. This chapter explains many of the services (Global Catalogs, UGMC, Operation Masters, and so on) that help make the forest operate properly.

Chapter 7: Configuring Active Directory Server Roles   This chapter explains the different server roles, such as Active Directory Lightweight Directory Services, Active Directory Rights Management Services, Active Directory Federation Services, and Active Directory Certificate Services.

Chapter 8: Using Virtualization in Windows Server 2012   This chapter will show you how to implement and configure Windows Server Hyper-V and virtual machines. You will learn about Virtual Networking, Virtual Hard Disks, migration types, and Integration Services.

Chapter 9: Configuring TCP/IP   This chapter shows you how to configure IPv4 and IPv6. You'll look at IPv4 subnetting and how to manage a TCP/IP network.

Chapter 10: Managing DHCP   In this chapter, you will learn how to implement and maintain DHCP. You'll look at how to set up and configure DHCP pools and scopes.

Chapter 11: Managing and Maintaining Servers   In this chapter, you will learn how to configure Windows Server Update Services (WSUS) server settings. You will also learn to gather network data, monitor event logs, and capture performance data.

Chapter 12: Configuring Network Access   This chapter will show you about routing, Remote Access Policy, Network Address Translation (NAT), and VPN protocols.

Chapter 13: Understanding Security   This chapter explains how to configure domain password policies, account lockout policies, fine-grain password policies, audit logon events, audit account logon events, audit policy change, and audit access privilege use to name just a few.

Chapter 14: Managing File and Print Services   This chapter dives into configuring a file and print server. We will look at file share publishing, Offline Files, share permissions, NTFS permissions, encrypting file system (EFS), BitLocker, Access-Based Enumeration (ABE), branch cache, and Share and Storage Management console.

Chapter 15: Managing Remote Access Services   You will learn about Network Policy Server (NPS) and Network Access Protection (NAP).

Chapter 16: Configuring High Availability in Windows Server 2012   In this chapter, you will explore how to configure Windows Server 2012 machines for high availability.

You will look at failover clustering, Network Load Balancing, geoclustering support, cluster service migration, and Cluster Shared Volumes (CSV).

Chapter 17: Configuring File and Storage Services   This chapter will explain how to implement and maintain RAID types, Virtual Disk Specification (VDS), iSCSI Initiator, Storage Area Networks (SANs), mount points, Multipath I/O (MPIO), VHD mounting, boot from a VHD, and N-Port Identification Virtualization (NPIV).

Chapter 18: Implementing Disaster Recovery   In this chapter, we will show you how to protect your network from a crash or disaster. We will look at how to back up and restore your servers.

What's Included with the Book

There are many helpful items intended to prepare you for the MCSA: Windows Server 2012 certification included in this book. These items include:

Assessment Test   There is a 50-question Assessment Test at the conclusion of the introduction that can be used to quickly evaluate where you are with Windows Server 2012. This test should be taken prior to beginning your work in this book, and should help you identify areas that you are either strong or weak in. Note that these questions are purposely more simple than the types of questions you may see on the exams.

Objective Map and Opening List of Objectives   Later in this intro, we include a detailed exam objective map showing you where each of the exam objectives are covered. Each chapter also includes a list of the exam objectives that are covered.

Helfpul Exercises   Throughout the book, I have included step-by-step exercises of some of the more important tasks you should be able to perform. Some of these exercises have corresponding videos that can be downloaded from the book's website. Also, below I have a recommended home lab setup which will be helpful in completing these tasks.

Exam Essentials   The end of each chapter also includes a listing of exam essentials. These are essentially repeats of the objectives, but remember that any objective on the exam blueprint could show up on the exam.

Chapter Review Questions   Each chapter includes 20 review questions each. These are used to assess your understanding of the chapter and are taken directly from the chapter. These questions are based off of the exam objectives, and are similar in difficulty to items you might actually receive on the MCSA: Windows Server 2012 exams.

The Sybex Test Engine, flashcards, videos, and glossary can be obtained at: www.sybex.com/go/mcsawin2012.

Sybex Test Engine   Readers can access the Sybex Test Engine, which includes the Assessment Test and Chapter Review Questions in electronic format. In addition are a total of three practice exams included on the Sybex test engine: one each for Exam 70-410, 70-411, and 70-412.

Electronic Flashcards   The flashcards are included for quick reference and are great tools for learning quick facts. You can even consider these as additional simple practice questions, which is essentially what they are.

Videos   Some of the exercises include corresponding videos. These videos show you how the author does the exercises. There is also a video that shows you how to set up virtualization so that you can complete the exercises within a virtualized environment. This same video also shows you how to install Windows Server 2012 Datacenter on that virtualized machine.

PDF of Glossary of Terms   There is a glossary included which covers the key terms used in this book.

Recommended Home Lab Setup

To get the most out of this book, you will want to make sure that you complete the exercises throughout the chapters. To complete the exercises, you will need one of two setups. First, you can set up a machine with Windows Server 2012 and complete the labs using a regular Windows Server 2012 machine.

The second way to set up Windows Server 2012 (the way I set up Server 2012) is by using virtualization. I set up Windows Server 2012 as a virtual hard disk (VHD) and I did all the labs this way. The advantages of using virtualization are that you can always just wipe out the system and start over without losing a real server. Plus you can set up multiple virtual servers and create a full lab environment on one machine.

I created a video for this book showing you how to set up a virtual machine and how to install Windows Server 2012 onto that virtual machine.

How to Contact Sybex

Sybex strives to keep you supplied with the latest tools and information you need for your work. Please check the website at www.sybex.com, where I'll post additional content and updates that supplement this book should the need arise. Enter **Windows Server 2012** in the Search box (or type the book's ISBN: **9781118544075**), and click Go to get to the book's update page.

Certification Objectives Maps

Tables I.1 provides objective mappings for the 70-410 exam, Table I.2 provides objective mappings for the 70-411 exam, and Table I.3 provides objective mappings for the 70-412 exam.

In addition to the book chapters, you will find coverage of exam objectives in the flash-cards, practice exams, and videos on the book's companion website, www.sybex.com/go/mcsawin12.

> The objectives that are italic are objectives that are also included in the Upgrading Your Skills to MCSA Windows Server 2012 (70-417) exam.

TABLE I.1   70-410 Exam Objectives

Objective	Chapter
Install and configure servers (15–20%)	
Install servers	1
Plan for a server installation; plan for server roles; plan for a server upgrade; install Server Core; optimize resource utilization by using Features on Demand; migrate roles from previous versions of Windows Server	
Configure servers	1, 4, 8, 16
Configure Server Core; delegate administration; add and remove features in offline images; deploy roles on remote servers; convert Server Core to/from full GUI; configure services; configure NIC teaming	
Configure local storage	17
Design storage spaces; configure basic and dynamic disks; configure MBR and GPT disks; manage volumes; create and mount virtual hard disks (VHDs); configure storage pools and disk pools	
Configure server roles and features (15–20%)	
Configure file and share access	14
Create and configure shares; configure share permissions; configure offline files; configure NTFS permissions; configure access-based enumeration (ABE); configure Volume Shadow Copy Service (VSS); configure NTFS quotas	

Configure print and document services   14

Configure the Easy Print print driver; configure Enterprise Print
Management; configure drivers; configure printer pooling; configure print
priorities; configure printer permissions

Configure servers for remote management   1, 17

*Configure WinRM; configure down-level server management; configure
servers for day-to-day management tasks; configure multi-server
management; configure Server Core; configure Windows Firewall*

Configure Hyper-V (15–20%)

Create and configure virtual machine settings   8

*Configure dynamic memory; configure smart paging; configure Resource
Metering; configure guest integration services*

Create and configure virtual machine storage   8

*Create VHDs and VHDX; configure differencing drives; modify VHDs;
configure pass-through disks; manage snapshots; implement a virtual Fibre
Channel adapter*

Create and configure virtual networks   8

*Implement Hyper-V Network Virtualization; configure Hyper-V virtual
switches; optimize network performance; configure MAC addresses;
configure network isolation; configure synthetic and legacy virtual network
adapters*

Deploy and configure core network services (15–20%)

Configure IPv4 and IPv6 addressing   9

Configure IP address options; configure subnetting; configure
supernetting; configure interoperability between IPv4 and IPv6; configure
ISATAP; configure Teredo

Deploy and configure Dynamic Host Configuration Protocol (DHCP) service   10

Create and configure scopes; configure a DHCP reservation; configure DHCP
options; configure client and server for PXE boot; configure DHCP relay
agent; authorize DHCP server

Deploy and configure DNS service   2

Configure Active Directory integration of primary zones; configure
forwarders; configure Root Hints; manage DNS cache; create A and PTR
resource records

TABLE I.1   70-410 Exam Objectives *(continued)*

Objective	Chapter
Install and administer Active Directory (15–20%)	
Install domain controllers	3
Add or remove a domain controller from a domain; upgrade a domain controller; install Active Directory Domain Services (AD DS) on a Server Core installation; install a domain controller from Install from Media (IFM); resolve DNS SRV record registration issues; configure a global catalog server	
Create and manage Active Directory users and computers	4
Automate the creation of Active Directory accounts; create, copy, configure, and delete users and computers; configure templates; perform bulk Active Directory operations; configure user rights; offline domain join; manage inactive and disabled accounts	
Create and manage Active Directory groups and organizational units (OUs)	4
Configure group nesting; convert groups including security, distribution, universal, domain local, and domain global; manage group membership using Group Policy; enumerate group membership; delegate the creation and management of Active Directory objects; manage default Active Directory containers; create, copy, configure, and delete groups and OUs	
Create and manage Group Policy (15–20%)	
Create Group Policy objects (GPOs)	5
Configure a Central Store; manage starter GPOs; configure GPO links; configure multiple local group policies; configure security filtering	
Configure security policies	13
Configure User Rights Assignment; configure Security Options settings; configure Security templates; configure Audit Policy; configure Local Users and Groups; configure User Account Control (UAC)	
Configure application restriction policies	5
Configure rule enforcement; configure Applocker rules; configure Software Restriction Policies	
Configure Windows Firewall	17
Configure rules for multiple profiles using Group Policy; configure connection security rules; configure Windows Firewall to allow or deny applications, scopes, ports, and users; configure authenticated firewall exceptions; import and export settings	

TABLE I.2   70-411 Exam Objectives

Objective	Chapter
Deploy, manage, and maintain servers (15–20%)	
Deploy and manage server images	1
Install the Windows Deployment Services (WDS) role; configure and manage boot, install, and discover images; update images with patches, hotfixes, and drivers; install features for offline images	
Implement patch management	11
Install and configure the Windows Server Update Services (WSUS) role; configure group policies for updates; configure client-side targeting; configure WSUS synchronization; configure WSUS groups	
Monitor servers	11
Configure Data Collector Sets (DCS); configure alerts; monitor real-time performance; monitor virtual machines (VMs); monitor events; configure event subscriptions; configure network monitoring	
Configure file and print services (15–20%)	
Configure Distributed File System (DFS)	14
Install and configure DFS namespaces; configure DFS Replication Targets; configure Replication Scheduling; configure Remote Differential Compression settings; configure staging; configure fault tolerance	
Configure File Server Resource Manager (FSRM)	14
Install the FSRM role; configure quotas; configure file screens; configure reports	
Configure file and disk encryption	14
Configure Bitlocker encryption; configure the Network Unlock feature; configure Bitlocker policies; configure the EFS recovery agent; manage EFS and Bitlocker certificates including backup and restore	
Configure advanced audit policies	13
Implement auditing using Group Policy and AuditPol.exe; create expression-based audit policies; create removable device audit policies	
Configure network services and access (15–20%)	
Configure DNS zones	2
Configure primary and secondary zones; configure stub zones; configure conditional forwards; configure zone and conditional forward storage in Active Directory; configure zone delegation; configure zone transfer settings; configure notify settings	

TABLE I.2 70-411 Exam Objectives *(continued)*

Objective	Chapter
Configure DNS records	2
Create and configure DNS Resource Records (RR) including A, AAAA, PTR, SOA, NS, SRV, CNAME, and MX records; configure zone scavenging; configure record options including Time To Live (TTL) and weight; configure round robin; configure secure dynamic updates	
Configure VPN and routing	12, 15
Install and configure the Remote Access role; implement Network Address Translation (NAT); configure VPN settings; configure remote dial-in settings for users; configure routing	
Configure DirectAccess	14
Implement server requirements; implement client configuration; configure DNS for Direct Access; configure certificates for Direct Access	
Configure a Network Policy Server infrastructure (10–15%)	
Configure Network Policy Server (NPS)	15
Configure multiple RADIUS server infrastructures; configure RADIUS clients; manage RADIUS templates; configure RADIUS accounting; configure certificates	
Configure NPS policies	15
Configure connection request policies; configure network policies for VPN clients (multilink and bandwidth allocation, IP filters, encryption, IP addressing); manage NPS templates; import and export NPS policies	
Configure Network Access Protection (NAP)	15
Configure System Health Validators (SHVs); configure health policies; configure NAP enforcement using DHCP and VPN; configure isolation and remediation of non-compliant computers using DHCP and VPN; configure NAP client settings	
Configure and manage Active Directory (15–20%)	
Configure service authentication	4
Create and configure Service Accounts; create and configure Group Managed Service Accounts; create and configure Managed Service Accounts; configure Kerberos delegation; manage Service Principal Names (SPNs)	

Configure Domain Controllers   6

Configure Universal Group Membership Caching (UGMC); transfer and seize operations masters; install and configure a read-only domain controller (RODC); configure Domain Controller cloning

Maintain Active Directory   18

Back up Active Directory and SYSVOL; manage Active Directory offline; optimize an Active Directory database; clean up metadata; configure Active Directory snapshots; perform object- and container-level recovery; perform Active Directory restore

Configure account policies   13

Configure domain user password policy; configure and apply Password Settings Objects (PSOs); delegate password settings management; configure local user password policy; configure account lockout settings

Configure and manage Group Policy (15–20%)

Configure Group Policy processing   5

Configure processing order and precedence; configure blocking of inheritance; configure enforced policies; configure security filtering and WMI filtering; configure loopback processing; configure and manage slow-link processing; configure client-side extension (CSE) behavior

Configure Group Policy settings   5

Configure settings including software installation, folder redirection, scripts, and administrative template settings; import security templates; import custom administrative template file; convert administrative templates using ADMX Migrator; configure property filters for administrative templates

Manage Group Policy objects (GPOs)   5

Back up, import, copy, and restore GPOs; create and configure Migration Table; reset default GPOs; delegate Group Policy management

Configure Group Policy preferences   5

Configure Group Policy Preferences (GPP) settings including printers, network drive mappings, power options, custom registry settings, Control Panel settings, Internet Explorer settings, file and folder deployment, and shortcut deployment; configure item-level targeting

TABLE I.3 70-412 Exam Objectives

Objective	Chapter
Configure and manage high availability (15–20%)	
Configure Network Load Balancing (NLB)	16
Install NLB nodes; configure NLB prerequisites; configure affinity; configure port rules; configure cluster operation mode; upgrade an NLB cluster	
Configure failover clustering	16
Configure Quorum; configure cluster networking; restore single node or cluster configuration; configure cluster storage; implement Cluster Aware Updating; upgrade a cluster	
Manage failover clustering roles	16
Configure role-specific settings including continuously available shares; configure VM monitoring; configure failover and preference settings	
Manage Virtual Machine (VM) movement	8
Perform Live Migration; perform quick migration; perform storage migration; import, export, and copy VMs; migrate from other platforms (P2V and V2V)	
Configure file and storage solutions (15–20%)	
Configure advanced file services	14
Configure NFS data store; configure BranchCache; configure File Classification Infrastructure (FCI) using File Server Resource Manager (FSRM); configure file access auditing	
Implement Dynamic Access Control (DAC)	13
Configure user and device claim types; implement policy changes and staging; perform access-denied remediation; configure file classification	
Configure and optimize storage	17
Configure iSCSI Target and Initiator; configure Internet Storage Name server (iSNS); implement thin provisioning and trim; manage server free space using Features on Demand	
Implement business continuity and disaster recovery (15–20%)	
Configure and manage backups	18
Configure Windows Server backups; configure Windows Online backups; configure role-specific backups; manage VSS settings using VSSAdmin; create System Restore snapshots	

Recover servers   18

Restore from backups; perform a Bare Metal Restore (BMR); recover servers
using Windows Recovery Environment (Win RE) and safe mode; apply System
Restore snapshots; configure the Boot Configuration Data (BCD) store

Configure site-level fault tolerance   8, 16

*Configure Hyper-V Replica including Hyper-V Replica Broker and VMs;
configure multi-site clustering including network settings, Quorum, and failover
settings*

Configure network services (15–20%)

Implement an advanced Dynamic Host Configuration Protocol (DHCP) solution   10

Create and configure superscopes and multicast scopes; implement DHCPv6;
configure high availability for DHCP including DHCP failover and split scopes;
configure DHCP Name Protection

Implement an advanced DNS solution   2, 3

Configure security for DNS including DNSSEC, DNS Socket Pool, and cache
locking; configure DNS logging; configure delegated administration; configure
recursion; configure netmask ordering; configure a GlobalNames zone

Deploy and manage IPAM   9

*Configure IPAM manually or by using Group Policy; configure server discovery;
create and manage IP blocks and ranges; monitor utilization of IP address space;
migrate to IPAM; delegate IPAM administration; manage IPAM collections*

Configure the Active Directory infrastructure (15–20%)

Configure a forest or a domain   3, 6

Implement multi-domain and multi-forest Active Directory environments
including interoperability with previous versions of Active Directory; upgrade
existing domains and forests including environment preparation and
functional levels; configure multiple user principal name (UPN) suffixes

Configure trusts   6

Configure external, forest, shortcut, and realm trusts; configure trust
authentication; configure SID filtering; configure name suffix routing

Configure sites   6

Configure sites and subnets; create and configure site links; manage site coverage;
manage registration of SRV records; move domain controllers between sites

TABLE I.3 70-412 Exam Objectives *(continued)*

Objective	Chapter
Manage Active Directory and SYSVOL replication	18
Configure replication to Read-Only Domain Controllers (RODCs); configure Password Replication Policy (PRP) for RODCs; monitor and manage replication; upgrade SYSVOL replication to Distributed File System Replication (DFSR)	
Configure identity and access solutions (15–20%)	
Implement Active Directory Federation Services 2.1 (AD FSv2.1)	7
Implement claims-based authentication including Relying Party Trusts; configure Claims Provider Trust rules; configure attribute stores including Active Directory Lightweight Directory Services (AD LDS); manage AD FS certificates; configure AD FS proxy; integrate with cloud services	
Install and configure Active Directory Certificate Services (AD CS)	7
Install an Enterprise Certificate Authority (CA); configure CRL distribution points; install and configure Online Responder; implement administrative role separation; configure CA backup and recovery	
Manage certificates	7
Manage certificate templates; implement and manage certificate deployment, validation, and revocation; manage certificate renewal; manage certificate enrollment and renewal to computers and users using Group Policies; configure and manage key archival and recovery	
Install and configure Active Directory Rights Management Services (AD RMS)	7
Install a licensing or certificate AD RMS server; manage AD RMS Service Connection Point (SCP); manage AD RMS client deployment; manage Trusted User Domains; manage Trusted Publishing Domains; manage Federated Identity support; manage RMS templates; configure Exclusion Policies	

Exam objectives are subject to change at any time without prior notice and at Microsoft's sole discretion. Please visit Microsoft's website (www.microsoft.com/learning) for the most current listing of exam objectives.

Assessment Test

1. Which of the following is a valid role for a Windows Server 2012 computer?
   A. Stand-alone server
   B. Member server
   C. Domain controller
   D. All of the above

2. Which of the following is a benefit of using Active Directory? (Choose all that apply.)
   A. Hierarchical object structure
   B. Fault-tolerant architecture
   C. Ability to configure centralized and distributed administration
   D. Flexible replication

3. Which of the following features of the Domain Name System (DNS) can be used to improve performance? (Choose all that apply.)
   A. Caching-only servers
   B. DNS forwarding
   C. Secondary servers
   D. Zone delegation

4. Which of the following pieces of information should you have before you begin the Active Directory Installation Wizard? (Choose all that apply.)
   A. Active Directory domain name
   B. Administrator password for the local computer
   C. NetBIOS name for the server
   D. DNS configuration information

5. Which of the following single-master operations apply to the entire forest? (Choose all that apply.)
   A. Schema Master
   B. Domain Naming Master
   C. RID Master
   D. Infrastructure Master

6. Trust relationships can be configured as which of the following? (Choose all that apply.)
   A. One-way and transitive
   B. Two-way and transitive
   C. One-way and nontransitive
   D. Two-way and nontransitive

7. An Active Directory environment consists of three domains. What is the maximum number of sites that can be created for this environment?

    A. Two

    B. Three

    C. Nine

    D. Unlimited

8. What is the name of the list that shows removed certificates from a certificate server?

    A. Certificate removed list

    B. Certificate revocation list

    C. Certificate revoke list

    D. Certificate released list

9. Which of the following is *not* a valid Active Directory object?

    A. User

    B. Group

    C. Organizational unit

    D. Computer

    E. None of the above

10. Which of the following is *not* considered a security principal?

    A. Users

    B. Security groups

    C. Distribution groups

    D. Computers

11. Which of the following should play the *least* significant role in planning an OU structure?

    A. Network infrastructure

    B. Domain organization

    C. Delegation of permissions

    D. Group Policy settings

12. How can the Windows Server 2003 file and printer resources be made available from within Active Directory?

    A. A system administrator can right-click the resource and select Publish.

    B. A system administrator can create Printer and Shared Folder objects that point to these resources.

    C. The Active Directory Domains and Trusts tool can be used to make resources available.

    D. Only resources on a Windows 2000 or above server can be accessed from within Active Directory.

13. The process by which a higher-level security authority assigns permissions to other administrators is known as which of the following?

    A. Inheritance

    B. Delegation

    C. Assignment

    D. Trust

14. What is the minimum amount of information you need to create a Shared Folder Active Directory object?

    A. The name of the share

    B. The name of the server

    C. The name of the server and the name of the share

    D. The name of the server, the server's IP address, and the name of the share

15. Which of the following operations is not supported by Active Directory?

    A. Assigning applications to users

    B. Assigning applications to computers

    C. Publishing applications to users

    D. Publishing applications to computers

16. Which of the following filename extensions is used primarily for Windows Installer setup programs?

    A. `.msi`

    B. `.mst`

    C. `.zap`

    D. `.aas`

17. A system administrator wants to allow a group of users to add computer accounts to a specific organizational unit (OU). What is the easiest way to grant only the required permissions?

    A. Delegate control of a user account.

    B. Delegate control at the domain level.

    C. Delegate control of an OU.

    D. Delegate control of a computer account.

    E. Create a Group Policy object (GPO) at the OU level.

18. A Group Policy object (GPO) at the domain level sets a certain option to Disabled, while a GPO at the OU level sets the same option to Enabled. All other settings are left at their default. Which setting will be effective for objects within the OU?

    A. Enabled

    B. Disabled

    C. No effect

    D. None of the above

19. Which of the following tools can be used to create Group Policy object (GPO) links to Active Directory?

    A. Active Directory Users and Computers

    B. Active Directory Domains and Trusts

    C. Active Directory Sites and Services

    D. Group Policy Management Console

20. Which of the following statements regarding auditing and Active Directory is false?

    A. Auditing prevents users from attempting to guess passwords.

    B. System administrators should regularly review audit logs for suspicious activity.

    C. Auditing information can be generated when users view specific information within Active Directory.

    D. Auditing information can be generated when users modify specific information within Active Directory.

21. You want to set up VPN access for 30 users, and the connections must be encrypted. There is a central Windows Server 2012 domain for your users. Which of the following is the most appropriate VPN solution in this case?

    A. L2TP + IPsec

    B. PPTP

    C. Either A or B

    D. None of the above

22. What is the IPsec Policy Agent?

    A. It is an optional component that's required when using IPsec with Active Directory.

    B. It is an optional component that's required when using IPsec without Active Directory.

    C. It is an optional component that's required when using IPsec with L2TP.

    D. It is a mandatory component that's required to use IPsec.

23. To test whether a DNS server is answering queries properly, you can use which of the following tools?

    A. The `ping` tool

    B. The `nslookup` tool

    C. The `tracert` tool

    D. The `ipconfig` tool

24. Which of the following is true about IPsec?

    A. Can be used by itself

    B. Can be used only with L2TP

    C. Cannot be used with L2TP

    D. Requires third-party software for Windows 2000 and newer

25. Which of the following protocols or services is not required for an Active Directory installation?

   A. TCP/IP

   B. DNS

   C. LDAP

   D. NetBEUI

26. Which of the following is true about the time to live (TTL) attached to a DNS record?

   A. It cannot be used by a resolver; it can be used only by servers making recursive queries.

   B. It is used only by resolvers.

   C. It is used to determine how long to cache retrieved results.

   D. It is refreshed each time the record is modified.

27. To enable DHCP-DNS integration, you must do which of the following?

   A. Configure the scope to allow it to use Dynamic DNS only.

   B. Configure the server to allow it to use Dynamic DNS only.

   C. Configure the scope and the server.

   D. Configure the scope or the server.

28. You have installed the DHCP server service on a member server in your domain and have configured a scope, but clients cannot lease an address. What is the most likely cause of this problem?

   A. The scope is not activated.

   B. There are too many DHCP servers.

   C. The DHCP server is not authorized in Active Directory.

   D. The DHCP server is in another subnet.

29. Which of the following statements about Windows Server 2012 Dynamic DNS (DDNS) is true?

   A. DDNS requires a Microsoft DHCP server to work.

   B. The Windows Server 2012 DDNS server can interoperate with recent versions of BIND.

   C. DDNS clients may not register their own addresses.

   D. DDNS works only with Microsoft clients and servers.

30. DHCP address range exclusions are assigned at which level?

   A. Server level

   B. Scope level

   C. Superscope level

   D. Multicast scope level

31. The DHCP relay agent serves which function on the network?

    A. It listens for DHCP messages on a network and forwards them to a DHCP server on another network.

    B. It accepts DHCP messages from multiple networks and consolidates them for a single DHCP server.

    C. It allows DHCP clients to use WINS services.

    D. It relays DHCP requests to a Dynamic DNS server.

32. Which of the following settings cannot be adjusted when using RIP?

    A. The RIP version that can be used for incoming and outgoing traffic on each interface

    B. The set of peer routers from which routes will be accepted

    C. The default announcement interval

    D. The location where received RIP routes are stored

33. RRAS allows you to create which types of routing-related filters?

    A. Route filters only

    B. Peer filters only

    C. Route and peer filters

    D. Packet filters only

34. In which two modes do RIP routers send updates? (Choose two.)

    A. Link-state database mode

    B. Autostatic update mode

    C. Periodic update mode

    D. Border mode

35. VPN connections require which of the following? (Choose two.)

    A. The Windows Server 2012 VPN add-on

    B. The name or IP address of the VPN server

    C. The phone number of the VPN server

    D. An existing TCP/IP connection

36. Which of the following are true of dynamically maintained routing tables? (Choose all that apply.)

    A. They are automatically maintained by the routing protocols.

    B. They are normally not maintained across reboots.

    C. They may be manually edited from the command line.

    D. They consist of multiple entries, each containing a network ID, a forwarding address, and a metric.

37. You can control VPN access through which of the following mechanisms? (Choose two.)

   A. Individual user account properties

   B. Remote access policies

   C. Remote access profiles

   D. Group Policy objects

38. To reject any incoming call from a client that can't use a specified level of encryption, you would do which of the following?

   A. Turn off the No Encryption check box on the Encryption tab of the remote access policy's profile.

   B. Turn off the No Encryption check box on the Security tab of the server's Properties dialog box.

   C. Create a new remote access profile named Require Encryption.

   D. Check the Require Encryption check box in each user's profile.

39. You must restore the server's configuration to before the last set of configuration changes you made. Which command should you run?

   A. `AppCmd restore backup "Last Backup"`

   B. `AppCmd restore backup "CFGHISTORY_0000000001"`

   C. `AppCmd restore backup "CFGHISTORY_0000000100"`

   D. `AppCmd add backup "CFGHISTORY_0000000100"`

40. You have been given a server with three hard disks, all with the same capacity. The first drive contains the operating system files. You must provide data redundancy while providing the most amount of capacity. To accomplish this, which of the following would you do?

   A. Select the first drive, right-click, and select New RAID 5 Volume.

   B. Select the first drive, right-click, and select New Mirrored Volume.

   C. Select the first drive, right-click, and select New Striped Volume.

   D. Select the first drive, right-click, and select New Simple Volume.

41. You have been given a server that contains three HBAs. Each card can access the storage over a separate path. The application that runs on the server can exceed the usage of a single path. Which of the following MPIO options should be selected to provide the needed bandwidth as well as minimal redundancy?

   A. Failover

   B. Dynamic Least Queue Depth

   C. Weighted path

   D. Round robin

42. You have just deployed a new .NET Web application and need to provide it with the least amount of privileges. The application needs to be able to access the registry. Which of the following .NET trust levels will provide the least amount of privileges required?

    A. Full

    B. High

    C. Medium

    D. Low

    E. Minimal

43. You have configured an SMTP server to be the smart host for a number of servers so that the server can send all outbound email to the Internet. None of the messages that have been sent have been received by the recipient. What must be done to allow email to be delivered?

    A. Enable TLS encryption.

    B. Add the sending servers to the exceptions list on the connection control.

    C. Add the sending servers to the allow list in the relay restrictions.

    D. Enable LDAP Routing.

44. You must configure a website to allow Windows user credentials based on file system permissions to provide access to a single virtual directory. Which authentication modules must you disable on the virtual directory if the IUSR_ServerName account has permissions on the site content?

    A. Basic authentication

    B. Anonymous authentication

    C. Digest authentication

    D. Integrated Windows authentication

45. You are the administrator for an engineering firm. The chief information officer (CIO) informs you that the president of the company wants to make a live broadcast to all employees. The CIO does not want the employees to be able to record the broadcast or pause it. In addition, the CIO wants you to reduce the impact that the broadcast will have on the server. What two options should you choose to meet the CIO's requirements? (Choose two.)

    A. Deliver the content with a unicast stream.

    B. Use on-demand publishing points.

    C. Deliver the content with a multicast stream.

    D. Use a broadcast publishing point.

46. When is an operating system Hyper-V hypervisor aware?

    A. Automatically if you install a Microsoft operating system

    B. When you install the VM components

    C. After you install the Integration Components

    D. When you turn on hypervisor awareness in Hyper-V

47. What types of virtual hard disks can you configure in Hyper-V Manager? (Choose all that apply.)

   A. Dynamically expanding

   B. Fixed size

   C. Differencing

   D. Pass-through

48. What statement is correct when you create an internal-only virtual network for your virtual machines on a Hyper-V server?

   A. The virtual machines can communicate with each other and with the host machine.

   B. The virtual machines can communicate with each other only.

   C. The virtual machines can communicate with each other, with the host machine, and with the network.

   D. The virtual machines cannot communicate with each other.

49. You are an IT administrator for a medium-size company. This company has 250 Windows 8 computers and 15 Windows 2012 Server machines. One of your users puts in a service request stating that he is no longer able to open certain programs or access some functions. When the user logs into another machine, he is able to access the programs and features. He also states that he has been getting a Windows Activation pop-up from time to time. What would you do to resolve this issue?

   A. Check the user's permissions in Active Directory, and assign admin rights to his machine.

   B. Scan for viruses.

   C. Activate his copy of Windows 8.

   D. Restore the machine from a backup.

50. A failover cluster contains two nodes, and a business requires the cluster's application to remain active and not have a single point of failure. Which of the following quorum models would work in a two-node failover cluster? (Choose all that apply.)

   A. No Majority: Disk Only

   B. Node Majority

   C. Node and Disk Majority

   D. Node and File Share Majority

Answers to Assessment Test

1. **D.** Based on the business needs of an organization, a Windows 2012 Server computer can be configured in any of the roles listed. See Chapter 1 for more information.

2. **A, B, C, D.** All of the options listed are benefits of using Active Directory. See Chapter 3 for more information.

3. **A, B, C, D.** One of the major design goals for DNS was support for scalability. All of the features listed can be used to increase the performance of DNS. See Chapter 2 for more information.

4. **A, B, C, D.** Before beginning the installation of a domain controller, you should have all of the information listed. See Chapter 3 for more information.

5. **A, B.** There can be only one Domain Naming Master and one Schema Master per Active Directory forest. The purpose of the Domain Naming Master is to keep track of all the domains within an Active Directory forest. The Schema Master defines the Active Directory schema, which must be consistent across all domains in the forest. The remaining roles apply at the domain level. See Chapter 6 for more information.

6. **A, B, C, D.** All of the trust configurations listed are possible. A one-way trust means that Domain A trusts Domain B but not the reverse. A two-way trust means that both Domain A and Domain B trust each other automatically. Transitive trusts are implied, meaning that if Domain A trusts Domain B, and Domain B trusts Domain C, then Domain A trusts Domain C. See Chapter 6 for more information.

7. **D.** The number of sites in an Active Directory environment is independent of the domain organization. An environment that consists of three domains may have one or more sites, based on the physical network setup. See Chapter 3 for more information.

8. **B.** The certificate revocation list (CRL) is the list that shows all certificates that have been revoked. See Chapter 7 for more information.

9. **E.** All of the choices are valid types of Active Directory objects, and all can be created and managed using the Active Directory Users and Computers tool. See Chapter 4 for more information.

10. **C.** Permissions and security settings cannot be made on distribution groups. Distribution groups are used only for sending email. See Chapter 4 for more information.

11. **A.** In general, you can accommodate your network infrastructure through the use of Active Directory sites. All of the other options should play a significant role when you design your OU structure. Permissions and Group Policy can both be applied at the domain or OU level. See Chapter 4 for more information.

12. **B.** Printer and Shared Folder objects within Active Directory can point to Windows Server 2003 file and printer resources. See Chapter 4 for more information.

13. B. Delegation is the process by which administrators can assign permissions on the objects within an OU. This is useful when administrators want to give other users more control over administrative functions in Active Directory. See Chapter 4 for more information.

14. C. The name of the server and the name of the share make up the Universal Naming Convention (UNC) information required to create a Shared Folder object. See Chapter 4 for more information.

15. D. Applications cannot be published to computers, but they can be published to users and assigned to computers. See Chapter 5 for more information.

16. A. MSI files (`.msi`) are native Windows Installer files used with Windows Installer setup programs. The other file types do not apply to this situation. See Chapter 5 for more information.

17. E. To allow this permission at the OU level, the system administrator must create a GPO with the appropriate settings and link it to the OU. See Chapter 5 for more information.

18. A. Assuming that the default settings are left in place, the Group Policy setting at the OU level will take effect. See Chapter 5 for more information.

19. D. In Windows Server 2012, you can create GPOs only by using the Group Policy Management Console. See Chapter 5 for more information.

20. A. The purpose of auditing is to monitor and record actions taken by users. Auditing will not prevent users from attempting to guess passwords (although it might discourage them from trying, if they are aware it is enabled). See Chapter 13 for more information.

21. C. L2TP + IPsec and PPTP can both be encrypted, and with the guidelines set forth in the question, either one would do the job. See Chapter 15 for more information.

22. D. The IPsec Policy Agent is the component that downloads IPsec policy settings from the local computer or Active Directory. Accordingly, presence is required for IPsec to function. See Chapter 12 for more information.

23. B. The `nslookup` tool allows you to look up name and address information. See Chapter 2 for more information.

24. A. IPsec is a stand-alone protocol included in Windows Server 2012 that can be used by itself or in conjunction with Layer 2 Tunneling Protocol (L2TP). See Chapter 15 for more information.

25. D. NetBEUI is deprecated, but the other three protocols are required for Active Directory. See Chapter 12 for more information.

26. C. The TTL indicates how long the record may be safely cached; it may or may not be modified when the record is created. See Chapter 2 for more information on TTL.

27. D. You can enable integration either on one scope only or on all scopes on a server. See Chapter 10 for more information.

28. C. If the DHCP server isn't authorized, it will not answer lease requests; therefore, the client will end up with no address. See Chapter 10 for more information.

29. B. DDNS works with BIND 8.2 and later. See Chapter 2 for more information on DDNS.

30. B. Scopes or ranges of addresses can be assigned only at the scope level. The scope range includes the exclusion range. See Chapter 10 for more information.

31. A. The DHCP relay agent allows you to use a DHCP server that resides on one network to communicate with clients that live on a separate network. See Chapter 10 for more information.

32. D. The Routing Information Protocol (RIP) implementation in Windows Server 2012 allows you to mix RIP versions, control which peer routers can send you updates, and control how often your router will broadcast updates to others. However, it does now allow you to change where the routing table data is stored. See Chapter 12 for more information.

33. C. Route filters let you accept or ignore individual routes; peer filters let you choose the routers from which your router accepts routing information. See Chapter 12 for more information.

34. B, C. In periodic update mode, a RIP router sends its list of known routes at periodic intervals (which you define). In autostatic update mode, the RRAS router broadcasts the contents of its routing table only when a remote router asks for it. See Chapter 12 for more information.

35. B, D. VPN connections piggyback on top of regular dial-up or dedicated TCP/IP connections, and you must specify the name or address of the server you're calling. See Chapter 15 for more information.

36. A, C, D. The routing engines maintain the contents of the routing table, although you can add or remove entries manually. Persistent routes, which are the default, are automatically maintained until you delete them manually. See Chapter 12 for more information.

37. A, B. You can allow users to make VPN connections by modifying individual account properties; if you're using a native mode Windows Server 2012 domain, you can also use remote access policies. See Chapter 12 for more information.

38. A. The profile associated with each remote access policy controls whether that policy will require, allow, or disallow encryption. To force encryption, create a policy that disallows using no encryption. See Chapter 14 for more information.

39. C. The highest configuration number is the latest backup, so that would be the correct backup to restore. The backup set named "Last Backup" would not be correct because it would have been manually run instead of done when a configuration change was made. When AppCmd add backup is run, it creates a new backup, not a restore, so it would also be an incorrect choice. See Chapter 18 for more information.

40. B. Using RAID-1 is the only correct option because OS files and boot files cannot reside on RAID-5 disks. Striped and simple volumes are not redundant. See Chapter 17 for more information.

41. D. A round robin configuration uses all available active paths and will distribute I/O in a balanced round robin fashion. Failover uses only primary and standby paths, allowing for link failure. Weighted path assigns requests to the path with the least weight value. Dynamic Least Queue Depth routes requests to the path with the least number of outstanding requests. See Chapter 2 for more information.

42. B. Medium and lower trust levels do not allow access to the Registry, so they would not be suitable levels for this application. High is the first level that allows the required access. Full allows too much access, so it is also not a valid answer. See Chapter 17 for more information.

43. C. The messages are not being delivered because the default setting is to not allow relaying. The sending servers must be added to be allowed to relay. Enabling TLS encryption may secure the SMTP transmission, but it will not affect message delivery. Adding the servers to the exceptions will not allow the servers to communicate to the SMTP server at all. Enabling LDAP routing will allow email address lookups but will not affect delivery of email to the Internet. See Chapter 12 for more information.

44. B. Since the IUSR_ServerName account has permission, anonymous authentication will keep the server for prompting for credentials. See Chapter 13 for more information.

45. C, D. Options C and D are correct because multicast streams reduce the impact on the server by producing a single stream to which multiple users can connect, and broadcast publishing allows the user to only play the content. Options A and B are incorrect because unicast streams would not decrease the load on the server, and on-demand publishing is for delivering content that the users can control. See Chapter 12 for more information.

46. C. An operating system running in a virtual machine becomes hypervisor aware once the Hyper-V Integration Components or Services are installed because it will support using the VMBus. See Chapter 8 for more information.

47. A, B, C, D. All options are correct. See Chapter 8 for more information.

48. A. The virtual machines can communicate with each other and with the host machine. That's the definition for an internal-only network. If they communicate only with each other, that's called a private virtual network. If the virtual machines also can communicate with the external network, that's called external. See Chapter 8 for more information.

49. C. C is the correct answer because when a Windows 8 product is not activated, it will reduce the functionality of the machine until it is activated. See Chapter 1 for more information.

50. C, D. Node and Disk Majority and Node and File Share Majority both allow for one of the nodes to be offline and still have quorum. Although No Majority: Disk Only allows for a node to be offline, the quorum shared disk is a single point of failure. Since there are only two nodes, both nodes have to be up if only Node Majority were chosen. See Chapter 16 for more information.

Chapter 1

Installing and Configuring Windows Server 2012

THE FOLLOWING 70-410 EXAM OBJECTIVES ARE COVERED IN THIS CHAPTER:

✓ **Install servers**

- This objective may include, but is not limited to: plan for a server installation; plan for server roles; plan for a server upgrade; install Server Core; optimize resource utilization by using Features On Demand; migrate roles from previous versions of Windows Server.

✓ **Configure servers**

- This objective may include, but is not limited to: configure Server Core; deploy roles on remote servers; convert Server Core to/from full GUI; configure services.

✓ **Configure servers for remote management**

- This objective may include, but is not limited to: configure WinRM; configure down-level server management; configure servers for day-to-day management tasks; configure Server Core.

THE FOLLOWING 70-411 EXAM OBJECTIVES ARE COVERED IN THIS CHAPTER:

✓ **Deploy and manage server images**

- This objective may include, but is not limited to: Install the Windows Deployment Services (WDS) role; configure and manage boot, install, and discovery images; update images with patches, hotfixes, and drivers; install features for offline images.

In this chapter, we will start with the installation of Windows Server 2012. We will install both the full version of Windows Server 2012 and the Server Core version. I will also show you how to use some PowerShell commands in Windows Server 2012 Server Core. So let's dive right into the server by talking about some of the new features and advantages of Windows Server 2012.

Features and Advantages of Windows Server 2012

Before we begin installing and configuring Windows Server 2012, let's take a look at some of the new features and the advantages they offer.

I will talk about all of these features in greater detail throughout this book. What follows are merely brief descriptions:

Active Directory Certificate Services   *Active Directory Certificate Services (AD CS)* provides a customizable set of services that allows you to issue and manage *public key infrastructure (PKI) certificates*. These certificates can be used in software security systems that employ public key technologies.

Active Directory Domain Services   *Active Directory Domain Services (AD DS)* includes new features that make deploying domain controllers simpler and let's you implement them faster. AD DS also makes the domain controllers more flexible, both to audit and to authorize for access to files. Moreover, AD DS has been designed to make performing administrative tasks easier through consistent graphical and scripted management experiences.

Active Directory Rights Management Services   *Active Directory Rights Management Services (AD RMS)* provides management and development tools that let you work with industry security technologies, including encryption, certificates, and authentication. Using these technologies allows organizations to create reliable information protection solutions.

BitLocker   *BitLocker* is a tool that allows you to encrypt the hard drives of your computer. By encrypting the hard drives, you can provide enhanced protection against data theft or unauthorized exposure of your computers or removable drives that are lost or stolen.

BranchCache   *BranchCache* allows data from files and web servers on a wide area network (WAN) to be cached on computers at a local branch office. By using BranchCache, you can improve application response times while also reducing WAN traffic. Cached data can be either distributed across peer client computers (distributed cache mode) or centrally hosted on a server (hosted cache mode). BranchCache is included with Windows Server 2012 and Windows 8.

DHCP *Dynamic Host Configuration Protocol (DHCP)* is an Internet standard that allows organizations to reduce the administration overhead of configuring hosts on a TCP/IP-based network. Some of the new features are DHCP failover, policy-based assignment, and the ability to use Windows PowerShell for DHCP Server.

DNS *Domain Name System (DNS)* services are used in TCP/IP networks. DNS will convert a computer name or fully qualified domain name (FQDN) to an IP address. DNS also has the ability to do a reverse lookup and convert an IP address to a computer name. DNS allows you to locate computers and services through user-friendly names.

Failover Clustering *Failover clustering* allows an organization to have the ability to provide high availability and scalability to networked servers. Failover clusters can include file share storage for server applications, such as Hyper-V and Microsoft SQL Server, and server applications that run on physical servers or virtual machines.

File Server Resource Manager *File Server Resource Manager* is a set of tools that allows administrators to manage and control the amount and type of data stored on the organization's servers. By using File Server Resource Manager, administrators have the ability to set up file management tasks, use quota management, get detailed reports, set up a file classification infrastructure, and configure file-screening management.

Hyper-V *Hyper-V* is one of the most changed features in Windows Server 2012. Microsoft's new slogan is "Windows Server 2012, built from the cloud up," and this has a lot to do with Hyper-V. It allows an organization to consolidate servers by creating and managing a virtualized computing environment. It does this by using virtualization technology that is built into Windows Server 2012.

Hyper-V allows you to run multiple operating systems simultaneously on one physical computer. Each virtual operating system runs in its own virtual machine environment.

IPAM *IP Address Management (IPAM)* is one of the brand-new features introduced with Windows Server 2012. IPAM allows an administrator to customize and monitor the IP address infrastructure on a corporate network.

Kerberos Authentication Windows Server 2012 uses the *Kerberos authentication* (version 5) protocol and extensions for password-based and public-key authentication. The Kerberos client is installed as a *security support provider (SSP)* and can be accessed through the *Security Support Provider Interface (SSPI).*

Managed Service Accounts Stand-alone *managed service accounts*, originally created for Windows Server 2008 R2 and Windows 7, are configured domain accounts that allow automatic password management and *service principal names* (SPNs) management, including the ability to delegate management to other administrators.

Networking There are many networking technologies and features in Windows Server 2012, including BranchCache, Data Center Bridging (DCB), NIC Teaming, and many more.

Remote Desktop Services Before Windows Server 2008, we use to refer to this as Terminal Services. *Remote Desktop Services* allows users to connect to virtual desktops,

RemoteApp programs, and session-based desktops. Using Remote Desktop Services allows users to access remote connections from within a corporate network or from the Internet.

Security Auditing   *Security auditing* gives an organization the ability to help maintain the security of an enterprise. By using security audits, you can verify authorized or unauthorized access to machines, resources, applications, and services. One of the best advantages of security audits is to verify regulatory compliance.

Smart Cards   Using *smart cards*, referred to as two-factor authentication, and their associated *personal identification numbers (PINs)* is a popular, reliable, and cost-effective way to provide authentication. When using smart cards, the user must not only have the physical card but also must know the PIN to be able to gain access to network resources. This is very effective because even if the smart card is stolen, thieves can't access the network unless they know the PIN.

TLS/SSL (Schannel SSP)   *Schannel* is a security support provider (SSP) that uses the *Secure Sockets Layer (SSL)* and *Transport Layer Security (TLS)* Internet standard authentication protocols together. The Security Support Provider Interface (SSPI) is an API used by Windows systems to allow security-related functionality, including authentication.

Windows Deployment Services   *Windows Deployment Services* allows an administrator to install Windows operating systems remotely. Administrators can use Windows Deployment Services to set up new computers by using a network-based installation.

Planning the Windows Server 2012 Installation

Before you install Windows Server 2012, you must first ask yourself these important questions: What type of server do I need? Will the server be a domain controller? What roles do I need to install on this server?

Once you have figured out what you need the server to do, you can make a game plan for the installation. So let's start by looking at some of the server roles and technologies that can be installed on a Windows Server 2012 computer.

Server Roles in Windows Server 2012

When you install Windows Server 2012, you have to decide which roles and features are going to be installed onto that server. This is a very important decision in the computer world. Many administrators not only overuse a server, they also underutilize servers in their organization.

For example, many administrators refuse to put any other roles or features on a domain controller. This may not be a good use of a server. Domain controllers help authenticate users onto the network, but after that the domain controllers are really not very busy all day long. Domain controllers have tasks that they must perform all day, but the server on which they reside it is not heavily used when compared to a SQL Server machine or an Exchange mail server. This is where monitoring your server can be very useful.

Now let's take a look at some of the roles and features that you can install onto a Windows Server 2012 machine. Knowing the different roles and features that you can install will help you to design, deploy, manage, and troubleshoot technologies in Windows Server 2012. Figure 1.1 shows the Add Roles And Features Wizard in the Server Manager. It shows you just some of the roles that can be installed on a Windows Server 2012 machine.

FIGURE 1.1   Available roles in Windows Server 2012

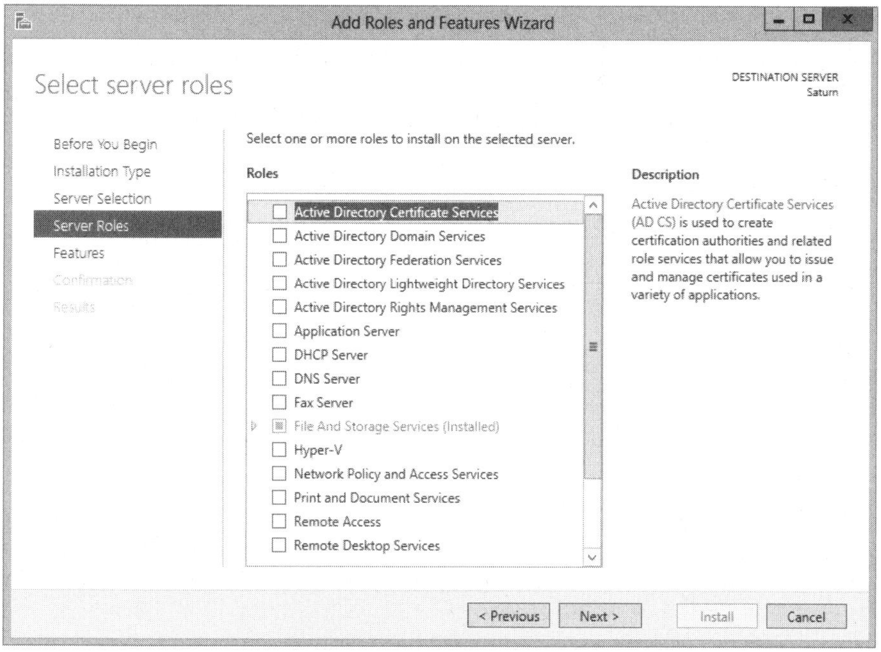

Roles and Features

Many of these features were discussed in the previous section, "Features and Advantages of Windows Server 2012." I include them here again because they are also *roles* that can also be installed on Windows Server 2012.

Active Directory Certificate Services

> **Feature**   *Active Directory Certificate Services (AD CS)* provides a customizable set of services that allows you to issue and manage *public key infrastructure (PKI)* certificates. These certificates can be used in software security systems that employ public key technologies.

> **Role**   *Active Directory Certificate Services (AD CS)* in Windows Server 2012 is the server role that allows you to build a *public key infrastructure (PKI)* and provide public key cryptography, digital certificates, and digital signature capabilities for your organization.

> The following roles are available in Windows Server 2012:

Active Directory Certificate Services   *Active Directory Certificate Services (AD CS)* in Windows Server 2012 is the server role that allows you to build a public key infrastructure (PKI) and provide public key cryptography, digital certificates, and digital signature capabilities for your organization.

Active Directory Domain Services   The *Active Directory Domain Services (AD DS)* server role allows you to create a scalable, secure, and manageable infrastructure for user and resource management and provide support for directory-enabled applications, such as Microsoft Exchange Server.

Active Directory Federation Services   *Active Directory Federation Services (AD FS)* provides Internet-based clients with a secure identity access solution that works on both Windows and non-Windows operating systems. AD FS gives users the ability to do a *single sign-on (SSO)* and access applications on other networks without needing a secondary password.

Active Directory Lightweight Directory Services   *Active Directory Lightweight Directory Services (AD LDS)* is a *Lightweight Directory Access Protocol (LDAP)* directory service that provides flexible support for directory-enabled applications, without the dependencies and domain-related restrictions of AD DS.

Active Directory Rights Management Services   *Active Directory Rights Management Services (AD RMS)* in Windows Server 2012 is the server role that provides you with management and development tools that work with industry security technologies including encryption, certificates, and authentication to help organizations create reliable information protection solutions.

Application Server   *Application Server* provides an integrated environment for deploying and running custom, server-based business applications.

Failover Clustering   The *Failover Clustering* feature provides a way to create, configure, and manage failover clusters for up to 4,000 virtual machines or up to 64 physical nodes.

File and Storage Services   *File and Storage Services* allows an administrator to set up and manage one or more file servers. These servers can provide a central location on your network where you can store files and then share those files with network users. If users require access to the same files and applications, or if centralized backup and file management are important issues for your organization, administrators should set up network servers as a file server.

Group Policy   *Group policies* are a set of rules and management configuration options that you can control through the Group Policy settings. These policy settings can be placed on users' computers throughout the organization.

Hyper-V   The *Hyper-V* role allows administrators to create and manage a virtualized environment by taking advantage of the technology built into the Windows Server 2012 operating system. When an administrator installs the Hyper-V role, all required virtualization components are installed.

Some of the required components include the Windows hypervisor, Virtual Machine Management Service, the virtualization WMI provider, the virtual machine bus (VMbus), the virtualization service provider (VSP) and the virtual infrastructure driver (VID).

Networking   This feature allows administrators to design, deploy, and maintain a Windows Server 2012 network. The networking features include 802.1X authenticated wired and wireless access, BranchCache, Data Center Bridging, low-latency workloads technologies, and many more.

Network Load Balancing   The *Network Load Balancing (NLB)* feature dispenses traffic across multiple servers by using the TCP/IP networking protocol. By combining two or more computers that are running applications in Windows Server 2012 into a single virtual cluster, NLB provides reliability and performance for mission-critical servers.

Network Policy and Access Services   Use the *Network Policy and Access Services* server role to install and configure *Network Access Protection (NAP)*, secure wired and wireless access points, and RADIUS servers and proxies.

Print and Document Services   *Print and Document Services* allows an administrator to centralize print server and network printer tasks. This role allows you also to receive scanned documents from network scanners and route the documents to a shared network resource, Windows SharePoint Services site, or email addresses. Print and Document Services also provides fax servers with the ability to send and receive faxes while also giving the administrator the ability to manage fax resources such as jobs, settings, reports, and fax devices on the fax server.

Remote Desktop Services   *Remote Desktop Services* allows for faster desktop and application deployments to any device, improving remote user effectiveness while helping to keep critical data secure. Remote Desktop Services allows for both a *virtual desktop infrastructure (VDI)* and session-based desktops, allowing users to connect from anywhere.

Security and Protection   Windows Server 2012 has many new and improved security features for your organization. These security features include Access Control, AppLocker, BitLocker, Credential Locker, Kerberos, NTLM, passwords, security auditing, smart cards, and Windows Biometric Framework (WBF).

Telemetry   The *Telemetry* service allows the Windows Feedback Forwarder to send feedback to Microsoft automatically by deploying a Group Policy setting to one or more organizational units. Windows Feedback Forwarder is available on all editions of Windows Server 2012, including Server Core.

Volume Activation   Windows Server 2012 *Volume Activation* will help your organization benefit from using this service to deploy and manage volume licenses for a medium to large number of computers.

Web Server (IIS)   The *Web Server (IIS)* role in Windows Server 2012 allows an administrator to set up a secure, easy-to-manage, modular, and extensible platform for reliably hosting websites, services, and applications.

Windows Deployment Services   *Windows Deployment Services* allow an administrator to install a Windows operating system over the network. Administrators do not have to install each operating system directly from a CD or DVD.

Windows Server Backup Feature   The *Windows Server Backup* feature gives an organization a way to back up and restore Windows servers. You can use Windows Server Backup to back up the entire server (all volumes), selected volumes, the system state, or specific files or folders.

Windows Server Update Services   *Windows Server Update Services (WSUS)* allows administrators to deploy application and operating system updates. By deploying WSUS, administrators have the ability to manage updates that are released through Microsoft Update to computers in their network. This feature is integrated with the operating system as a server role on a Windows Server 2012 system.

Windows System Resource Manager   *Windows System Resource Manager* allows you to manage server processor and memory usage with standard or custom resource policies. By managing your resources, you can ensure that all of the services provided by a single server are available. It also allows you to verify that services run on an equal basis or that your resources will always be available to high-priority applications, services, or users.

Migrating Roles and Features to Windows Server 2012

Once you decide on which roles and features you are going to install onto your Windows Server 2012 system, you then have to either install those roles and features from scratch or migrate them from a previous version of Windows server.

Windows Server 2012 includes a set of migration tools that administrators can use to help ease the process of migrating server roles, features, operating system settings, and data. Administrators can migrate this data from an existing server that is running Windows Server 2003, Windows Server 2003 R2, Windows Server 2008, Windows Server 2008 R2, or Windows Server 2012 to a computer that is running Windows Server 2012.

Using Windows Server Migration Tools to migrate roles, role services, and features can simplify deployment of new servers. You can migrate roles and features on servers running the Server Core installation option of Windows Server 2012 and virtual servers. By using Windows Server Migration Tools, an administrator can reduce migration downtime, increase the accuracy of the migration process, and help eliminate conflicts that could otherwise occur during the migration process.

One advantage of using the migration tools is that most of them support cross-architecture migrations (x86-based to x64-based computing platforms), migrations between physical and virtual environments, and migrations between both the full and Server Core installation options of the Windows Server operating system. In Windows Server 2012, Windows Server Migration Tools also supports cross-subnet migrations.

To use Windows Server Migration Tools, the feature must be installed on both the source and destination computers. Windows Server Migration Tools installation and preparation can be divided into the following stages:

1. Installing Windows Server Migration Tools on destination servers that run Windows Server 2012.

2. Creating deployment folders on destination servers that run Windows Server 2012 for copying to source servers.

3. Copying deployment folders from destination servers to source servers.

4. Registering Windows Server Migration Tools on source servers.

If you plan to use Windows Server Migration Tools, you must be a member of the Administrators group on both the source and destination servers to install, remove, or set up the tools.

Administrators can install Windows Server Migration Tools by using either the Add Roles Or Features Wizard in Server Manager or Windows PowerShell deployment cmdlets for Server Manager.

To install Windows Server Migration Tools on a Server Core installation of Windows Server 2012, you would complete the following steps:

1. Open a Windows PowerShell session by typing `powershell.exe` in the current command prompt session and then pressing Enter.

2. In the Windows PowerShell session, install Windows Server Migration Tools by using the Windows PowerShell `Install-WindowsFeature` cmdlet for Server Manager. In the Windows PowerShell session, type the following, and then press Enter. (Omit the `ComputerName` parameter if you are installing the Windows Server Migration Tools on the local server.)

```
Install-WindowsFeature Migration –ComputerName computer_name
```

Deciding Which Windows Server 2012 Versions to Use

You may be wondering which version of Windows Server 2012 is best for your organization. After all, Microsoft offers the following four versions of Windows Server 2012:

Windows Server 2012 Datacenter   *Windows Server 2012 Datacenter* was designed for organizations that are looking to migrate to a highly virtualized, private cloud environment. Windows Server 2012 Datacenter has full Windows Server functionality with unlimited virtual instances.

Windows Server 2012 Standard   *Windows Server 2012 Standard* was designed for organizations with physical or minimally virtualized environments. Windows Server 2012 Standard has full Windows Server functionality with two virtual instances.

Windows Server 2012 Essentials   *Windows Server 2012 Essentials* is ideal for small businesses that have as many as 25 users and 50 devices. Windows Server 2012 Essentials has a simpler interface and preconfigured connectivity to cloud-based services but no virtualization rights.

Windows Server 2012 Foundation   *Windows Server 2012 Foundation* was designed for smaller companies that need a Windows Server experience for as few as 15 users. Windows Server 2012 Foundation is a general-purpose server with basic functionality but no virtualization rights.

Once you choose what roles are going on your server, you must then decide how you're going to install it. There are two ways to install Windows Server 2012. You can upgrade a Windows Server 2008 or Windows Server 2008 R2 machine to Windows Server 2012, or you can do a clean install of Windows Server 2012. If you decide that you are going to upgrade, there are specific upgrade paths that you must follow.

Your choice of Windows Server 2012 version is dictated by how your current network is designed. If you are building a brand-new network from scratch, then it's pretty straightforward. Just choose the Windows Server 2012 version based on your server's tasks. However, if you already have a version of Windows Server 2008 installed, you should follow the recommendations in Table 1.1, which briefly summarizes the supported upgrade paths to Windows Server 2012.

 If your version of Microsoft Windows Server is not listed in the left column, upgrading to Windows Server 2012 is not supported. If there is more than one edition listed in the right column, you can then choose either edition.

TABLE 1.1   Supported Windows Server 2012 upgrade path recommendations

Current System	Upgraded System
Windows Server 2008 Standard with SP2 or Windows Server 2008 Enterprise with SP2	Windows Server 2012 Standard or Windows Server 2012 Datacenter
Windows Server 2008 Datacenter with SP2	Windows Server 2012 Datacenter
Windows Web Server 2008	Windows Server 2012 Standard
Windows Server 2008 R2 Standard with SP1 or Windows Server 2008 R2 Enterprise with SP1	Windows Server 2012 Standard or Windows Server 2012 Datacenter
Windows Server 2008 R2 Datacenter with SP1	Windows Server 2012 Datacenter
Windows Web Server 2008 R2	Windows Server 2012 Standard

Deciding on Type of Installation

One of the final choices that you must make before installing Windows Server 2012 is what type of installation you want. There are two ways to install Windows Server 2012:

Windows Server 2012 with the Graphical User Interface (GUI)   This is the version with which most administrators are familiar. This is the version that uses *Microsoft Management Console (MMC)* windows, and it is the version that allows the use of a mouse to navigate through the installation.

Windows Server 2012 Server Core   This is a bare-bones installation of Windows Server 2012. You can think of it this way: If Windows Server 2012 is a top-of-the-line luxury car, then Windows Server 2012 Server Core is the stripped-down model with no air-conditioning, manual windows, and cloth seats. It might not be pretty to look at, but it gets the job done.

 Real World Scenario

Server Core

Here is an explanation of Server Core that I have used ever since it was introduced in Windows Server 2008.

I am a *huge* sports fan. I love watching sports on TV, and I enjoy going to games. If you have ever been to a hockey game, you know what a hockey goal looks like. In between hockey periods, the stadium workers often bring out a huge piece of Plexiglas onto the ice. There is a tiny square cut out of the bottom of the glass. The square is just a bit bigger that a hockey puck itself.

Now they pick some lucky fan out of the stands, give them a puck at center ice, and then ask them to shoot the puck into the net with the Plexiglas in front of it. If they get it through that tiny little square at the bottom of the Plexiglas, they win a car or some such great prize.

Well, Windows Server 2012 with the GUI is the like hockey with a net and Windows Server 2012 Server Core is the Plexiglas version.

Server Core supports a limited number of roles:

- Active Directory Domain Services (AD DS)
- Active Directory Lightweight Directory Services (AD LDS)
- DHCP Server
- DNS Server

- File Services
- BITS Server
- BranchCache
- Hyper-V
- IIS
- Print and Document Services
- Streaming Media Services
- iSCSI
- Load Balancing
- MPIO
- qWave
- Telnet
- Unix Migration
- Active Directory Certificate Services

Server Core does not have the normal Windows interface or GUI. Almost everything has to be configured via the command line or, in some cases, using the Remote Server Administration Tools from a full version of Windows Server 2012. While this might scare off some administrators, it has the following benefits:

Reduced Management   Because Server Core has a minimum number of applications installed, it reduces management.

Minimal Maintenance   Only basic systems can be installed on Server Core, so it reduces the upkeep you would need in a normal server installation.

Smaller Footprint   Server Core requires only 1 GB of disk space to install and 2 GB of free space for operations.

Tighter Security   With only a few applications running on a server, it is less vulnerable to attacks.

The prerequisites for Server Core are basic. It requires the Windows Server 2012 installation media, a product key, and the hardware on which to install it.

After you install the base operating system, you use PowerShell or the remote administrative tools to configure the network settings, add the machine to the domain, create and format disks, and install roles and features. It takes only a few minutes to install Server Core, depending on hardware.

One of the new things to keep in mind is that you can upgrade or downgrade to Server Core. In Windows Server 2008 R2 and Windows Server 2008, if you wanted to switch your Windows Server GUI to Server Core or vice versa, there was no way to convert to a full Windows Server installation or a Server Core installation without reinstalling the operating system. In Windows Server 2012, the Server Core or GUI installation options are no longer an irreversible selection made during setup. An administrator now has the ability to convert between a Server Core installation and a full installation as needed.

⊕ **Real World Scenario**

Better Security

When I started in this industry more than 20 years ago, I was a programmer. I used to program computer hospital systems. When I switched over to the networking world, I continued work under contract with hospitals and doctors' offices.

One problem that I ran into is that many doctors are affiliated with hospitals but don't have offices within the hospital. Generally, they have offices either near the hospital or, in some cases, right across the street.

Here is the issue: Do we put servers into the doctors' offices or do we make the doctor log into the hospital network through a remote connection? Doctors' offices normally don't have computer rooms, and we don't want to place a domain controller or server on someone's desk. It's just unsafe!

This is where Windows Server 2012 Server Core can come into play. Since it is a slimmed-down version of Windows and there is no GUI, it makes it harder for anyone in the office to hack into the system. Also, Microsoft introduced a new domain controller in Windows Server 2008 called a *read-only domain controller (RODC)*. As its name suggests, it is a read-only version of a domain controller (explained in detail later in this book).

With Server Core and a RODC, you can feel safer placing a server on someone's desk or in any office. Server Core systems allow you to place servers in areas that you would never have placed them before. This can be a great advantage to businesses that have small, remote locations without full server rooms.

If you have a server that is running Server Core, there may be a situation in which you need to use the graphical user interfaces available only in Windows Server 2012 With A GUI mode. Windows Server 2012 allows you to switch the Server Core system to a Server With A GUI mode or vice versa.

To convert from a Windows 2012 Server Core system to Server With A GUI mode, run this code snippet (a restart is required):

```
Install-WindowsFeature Server-Gui-Mgmt-Infra,Server-Gui-Shell –Restart
```

To convert from Server Core mode to Server With A GUI mode, follow these steps when the server is initially installed in Server Core mode:

1. Determine the index number for a server with a GUI image (for example, SERVERDATACENTER, not SERVERDATACENTERCORE) using this cmdlet:

   ```
   Get-WindowsImage -ImagePath path to wim\install.wim
   ```

2. Run this line of code:

```
Install-WindowsFeature Server-Gui-Mgmt-Infra,Server-Gui-Shell –Restart ↵
-Source wim: path to wim\install.wim: Index # from step 1
```

3. Alternatively, if you want to use Windows Update as the source instead of a WIM file, use this Windows PowerShell cmdlet:

```
Install-WindowsFeature Server-Gui-Mgmt-Infra,Server-Gui-Shell –Restart
```

After you have completed the management tasks, you can switch the server back to Server Core mode whenever it is convenient (a restart is required) with this Windows PowerShell cmdlet:

```
Uninstall-WindowsFeature Server-Gui-Mgmt-Infra -restart
```

Installing Windows Server 2012

In the following sections, I am going to walk you through two different types of installs. I will show you how to do a full install of Windows 2012 Server with the GUI, and then I will show you how to install the Server Core version of the same software.

For these labs, I am using the full release of Windows Server 2012 Datacenter.

Installing with the GUI

In Exercise 1.1, I will show you how to install Windows Server 2012 Datacenter with the GUI. The GUI represents the Windows applications on the Desktop and the operating system functions that you can control and navigate with a mouse. The Server Core version is a command-line version only—you cannot use a mouse with Server Core.

Windows Installation

At the time of this writing, I used the first full release of Windows Server 2012 Datacenter. For this reason, there may be screens that have changed somewhat since the book was published.

EXERCISE 1.1

Installing Windows Server 2012 with the GUI

1. Insert the Windows Server 2012 installation DVD, and restart machine from the installation media.

2. At the first screen, Windows Server 2012 will ask you to configure your language, time and currency, and keyboard. Make your selections, and click Next.

3. At the next screen, click Install Now.

4. The Select The Operating System That You Want To Install screen then appears. Choose the Windows Server 2012 Datacenter (Server With A GUI) selection and click Next.

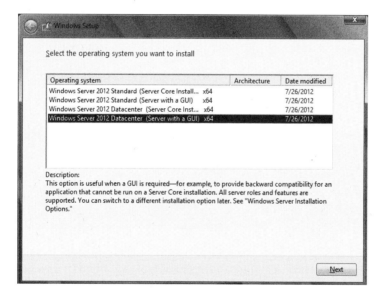

5. The license terms screen appears. After reading the Windows Server 2012 license agreement, check the I Accept The License Terms check box and click Next.

6. On the Which Type Of Installation Do You Want? screen, choose Custom: Install Windows Only (Advanced).

7. The next screen will ask you where you want to install Windows. If your hard disk is already formatted as NTFS, click on the drive and then click Next. If the hard disk is not yet set up or formatted, choose the New link and create a partition. After creating the partition, click the Format link. Once the format is done, make sure you choose the new partition and click Next.

8. The Installing Windows screen will appear next. This is where the files from your media will be installed onto the system. The machine will reboot during this installation.

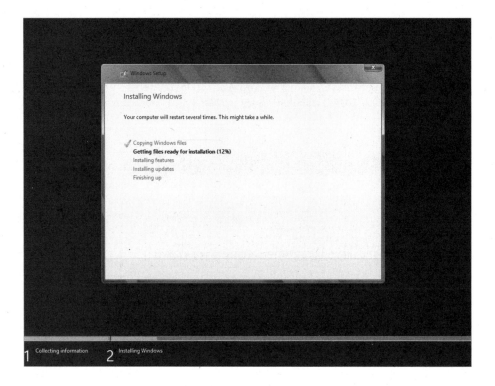

9. After the machine is finished rebooting, a screen requesting the administrator password will appear. Type in your password. (**P@ssword** is used in this exercise.) Your password must meet the password complexity requirements (one capitalized letter, one number, and/or one special character). Click Finished.

10. Next, log into the system. Press Ctrl+Alt+Del, and type in the administrator password. The machine will set up the properties of the administrator account.

11. Notice that the Server Manager dashboard automatically appears. Your Windows Server 2012 installation is now complete.

12. Close Server Manager.

After you have logged into the Windows Server 2012 Datacenter system, you will notice some big changes. The first is that there is *no Start button* in the lower-left corner of the screen. If you need to get to a Start button, click the Windows key (see Figure 1.2).

FIGURE 1.2   Windows key on a standard keyboard

Installing Windows Server 2012 Server Core

In Exercise 1.2, you will learn how to install Windows Server 2012 Server Core. You'll notice that the steps are very similar to the ones listed in Exercise 1.1, with a couple of exceptions. As mentioned earlier, Server Core is a command-line configuration of Windows Server 2012.

EXERCISE 1.2

Installing Windows Server 2012 Using Server Core

1. Insert the Windows Server 2012 installation DVD, and restart machine from the installation media.

2. At the first screen, Windows Server 2012 will prompt you to configure your language, time and currency, and keyboard. Make your selections, and click Next.

3. At the next screen, click Install Now.

4. The Select The Operating System That You Want To Install screen then appears. Choose the Windows Server 2012 Datacenter (Server Core Installation) selection and click Next.

5. The license terms screen appears. After reading the Windows Server 2012 license agreement, check the I Accept The License Terms check box and click Next.

6. At the Which Type Of Installation Do You Want? screen, choose Custom: Install Windows Only (Advanced).

7. The next screen will ask you where you want to install Windows. If your hard disk is already formatted as NTFS, click on the drive and then click Next. If the hard disk is not set up or formatted, choose the New link and create a partition. After creating the partition, click the Format link. Once the format is done, make sure you choose the new partition and click Next.

8. The Installing Windows screen appears next. This is where the files from your media will be installed onto the system. The machine will reboot during this installation.

9. After the machine is finished rebooting, a screen asking for the administrator password will appear. Click the OK button, and type in your password. (**P@ssword** for this exercise.) Your password must meet the password complexity requirements (one capitalized letter, one number, and/or one special character). Click the arrow key.

10. A screen telling you that your password has been changed appears. Click the OK button.

11. You will notice that the command prompt will automatically appear. Your Windows Server 2012 Server Core installation is now complete.

12. To log out or turn off the machine, press Ctrl+Alt+Del.

After Windows Server 2012 server is installed, you need to look at how to manage and configure the server. In the next section, you will learn how to manage a server remotely and with Windows PowerShell.

Using Windows Deployment Services

Another way that many IT departments deploy operating systems has been through the use of Remote Installation Services (RIS). RIS was a utility that allowed an administrator to deploy an operating system remotely. On the client machine that was receiving the operating system, you would use a set of disks (RIS client disks) that would automatically initiate a network card, connect to the RIS server, and download the operating system.

Starting with Windows 7 / Windows Server 2008 and continuing with Windows 8 and Windows Server 2012, a new version of RIS was developed and it's called Windows Deployment Services (WDS). WDS allows an IT administrator to install a Windows operating system without using a CD or DVD installation disk. Using WDS allows you to deploy the operating system through a network installation. WDS can deploy Windows XP, Windows Server 2003, Windows Vista, Windows 7, Windows Server 2008 / 2008 R2 and Microsoft Windows Server 2012.

The following are some of the advantages of using WDS for automated installation:

- You can remotely install Windows 7 / Windows 8.

- The procedure simplifies management of the server image by allowing you to access Windows 7 / 8 distribution files from a distribution server.

- You can quickly recover the operating system in the event of a computer failure.

Here are the basic steps of the WDS process from a PXE-enabled WDS client:

1. The WDS client initiates a special boot process through the PXE network adapter (and the computer's BIOS configured for a network boot). On a PXE client, the user presses F12 to start the PXE boot process and to indicate that they want to perform a WDS installation.

2. A list of available Windows PE boot images is displayed. The user should select the appropriate Windows PE boot image from the boot menu.

3. The Windows Welcome screen is displayed. The user should click the Next button.

4. The WDS user is prompted to enter credentials for accessing and installing images from the WDS server.

5. A list of available operating system images is displayed. The user should select the appropriate image file to install.

6. The WDS user is prompted to enter the product key for the selected image.

7. The Partition And Configure The Disk screen is displayed. This screen provides the ability to install a mass storage device driver, if needed, by pressing F6.

8. The image copy process is initiated, and the selected image is copied to the WDS client computer.

The following sections describe how to set up the WDS server and the WDS clients and how to install Windows 7 / 8 through WDS.

Preparing the WDS Server

With the WDS server, you can manage and distribute Windows 7 / 8 operating system images to WDS client computers. The WDS server contains any files necessary for PXE booting, Windows PE boot images, and the Windows 7 / 8 images to be deployed.

The following steps for preparing the WDS server are discussed in the upcoming sections:

1. Make sure the server meets the requirements for running WDS.

2. Install WDS.

3. Configure and start WDS.

4. Configure the WDS server to respond to client computers (if this was not configured when WDS was installed).

For WDS to work, the server on which you will install WDS must meet the requirements for WDS and be able to access the required network services.

WDS Server Requirements

The WDS server must meet these requirements:

- The computer must be a domain controller or a member of an Active Directory domain.

- At least one partition on the server must be formatted as NTFS.

- WDS must be installed on the server.

- The operating system must be Windows Server 2003, Windows Server 2008 / 2008 R2, or Windows Server 2012.

- A network adapter must be installed.

Network Services

The following network services must be running on the WDS server or be accessible to the WDS server from another network server:

- TCP/IP installed and configured
- A DHCP server, which is used to assign DHCP addresses to WDS clients (Ensure that your DHCP scope has enough addresses to accommodate all the WDS clients that will need IP addresses.)
- A DNS server, which is used to locate the Active Directory controller
- Active Directory, which is used to locate WDS servers and WDS clients as well as authorize WDS clients and manage WDS configuration settings and client installation options

Installing the WDS Server Components

You can configure WDS on a Windows Server 2003 / 2008 / 2008 R2 or Windows Server 2012 computer by using the Windows Deployment Services Configuration Wizard or by using the WDSUTIL command-line utility. Table 1.2 describes the WDSUTIL command-line options.

TABLE 1.2   WDSUTIL command-line options

WDSUTIL Option	Description
/initialize-server	Initializes the configuration of the WDS server
/uninitialized -server	Undoes any changes made during the initialization of the WDS server
/add	Adds images and devices to the WDS server
/convert-ripimage	Converts Remote Installation Preparation (RIPrep) images to WIM images
/remove	Removes images from the server
/set	Sets information in images, image groups, WDS servers, and WDS devices
/get	Gets information from images, image groups, WDS servers, and WDS devices
/new	Creates new capture images or discover images
/copy- image	Copies images from the image store
/export-image	Exports to WIM files images contained within the image store

WDSUTIL Option	Description
`/start`	Starts WDS services
`/stop`	Stops WDS services
`/disable`	Disables WDS services
`/enable`	Enables WDS services
`/approve-autoadddevices`	Approves Auto-Add devices
`/reject-autoadddevices`	Rejects Auto-Add devices
`/delete-autoadddevices`	Deletes records from the Auto-Add database
`/update`	Uses a known good resource to update a server resource

The first step in setting up WDS to deploy operating systems to the clients is to install the WDS role. You do this by using Server Manager.

One of the advantages of using the Windows deployment server is that WDS can work with Windows image (.wim) files. As stated earlier in this chapter, Windows image files can be created through the use of the Windows Sysprep utility.

One component that you need to pay attention to when using the Windows deployment server is Preboot Execution Environment (PXE) network devices. PXE boot devices are network interface cards (NICs) that can talk to a network without the need for an operating system. PXE boot NIC adapters are network adapters that have a set of preboot commands within the boot firmware.

This is important when using WDS because PXE boot adapters connect to a WDS server and request the data needed to load the operating system remotely. Remember, most of these machines that you are using WDS for do not have an operating system on the computer. You need NIC adapters that can connect to a network without the need for an operating system for WDS to work properly.

For the same reason, you must set up DHCP to accept PXE machines. Those machines need a valid TCP/IP address so that they can connect to the WDS server.

Preparing the WDS Client

The WDS client is the computer on which Windows 7 / 8 will be installed. WDS clients rely on a technology called PXE, which allows the client computer to remotely boot and connect to a WDS server.

To act as a WDS client, the computer must meet all the hardware requirements for Windows 7 / Windows 8 and have a PXE-capable network adapter installed, and a WDS server must be present on the network. Additionally, the user account used to install the image must be a member of the Domain Users group in Active Directory.

After the WDS server has been installed and configured, you can install Windows 7 / Windows 8 on a WDS client that uses a PXE-compliant network card.

To install Windows 7 / Windows 8 on the WDS client, follow these steps:

1. Start the computer. When prompted, press F12 for a network service boot. The Windows PE appears.

2. The Windows Welcome screen appears. Click the Next button to start the installation process.

3. Enter the username and password of an account that has permissions to access and install images from the WDS server.

4. A list of available operating system images stored on the WDS server appears. Select the image to install, and click Next.

5. Enter the product key for the selected Windows 7 / 8 image, and click Next.

6. The Partition And Configure The Disk screen appears. Select the desired disk-partitioning options, or click OK to use the default options.

7. Click Next to initiate the image-copying process. The Windows Setup process will begin after the image is copied to the WDS client computer.

Configuring Remote Management

As an administrator, there may be times you need to manage a server remotely. There are a few different tools that you can use to do this task. You can use remote administration to help configure services on a Windows Server 2012 system. In the following sections, we will look at Windows Remote Management and Windows PowerShell.

 Windows PowerShell does not always have to be used remotely. For example, you can use Windows PowerShell when configuring a Windows Server 2012 Server Core installation locally.

Windows Remote Management

The *Windows Remote Management (WinRM) utility* is Microsoft's version of the WS-Management protocol, an industry-standard protocol that allows different vendors' operating systems and hardware to work together. There are three main ways to access the WinRM utility:

- WinRM command-line tool
- WinRM scripting objects
- Windows Remote Shell command-line tool

The WinRM utility allows you to execute commands remotely and obtain management data from local and remote computers. You can use the WinRM utility on both Windows-based operating systems and non-Windows-based operating systems.

When using the WinRM utility, you can use the `-machine` switch to indicate the remote machine to which you are connecting. When connecting to a machine, you can connect using the localhost name, the NetBIOS name, the fully qualified domain name (FQDN), or the IP address of the remote machine. The following is an example of a WinRM command using a FQDN name on the secure port 443:

```
winrm get -machine:server.stellacon.local -port:443
```

Table 1.3 shows the command-line WinRM commands and descriptions of what each command does.

TABLE 1.3   WinRM commands and descriptions

Command	Description
`WinRM g` or `WinRM get`	Retrieves management information
`WinRM s` or `WinRM set`	Modifies management information
`WinRM c` or `WinRM create`	Creates a new instance on the managed resources
`WinRM d` or `WinRM delete`	Removes an instance from a managed resource
`WinRM e` or `WinRM enumerate`	Lists all instances of a managed resource
`WinRM i` or `WinRM invoke`	Executes a method on a managed resource
`WinRM id` or `WinRM identity`	Determines whether a WS-Management implementation is running on a remote machine
`WinRM quickconfig`	Configures a machine to accept WS-Management commands from a remote machine
`WinRM configSDDL`	Modifies an existing security descriptor for a Uniform Resource Identifier (URI)
`WinRM helpmsg`	Displays error messages for an error code

Now that you have looked at WinRM, let's take a look at how to use the Windows PowerShell utility.

Windows PowerShell

Windows PowerShell is a task-based, command-line scripting utility that allows you to execute commands locally or remotely on a Windows Server 2012 machine. It was specifically designed for system administrators to allow for local or remote administration.

Microsoft asks a lot of questions on the exam about Windows PowerShell. Therefore, I will be discussing PowerShell throughout this book due to its importance on all of the Windows Server 2012 exams.

Most operating system shells, including Cmd.exe and the SH, KSH, CSH, and BASH Unix shells, work by running a command or utility in a new process and then presenting the results to the user as text. These system shells also have commands that are built into the shell and execute in the shell process. In most system shells, because there are only a few built-in commands, many utilities have been created over the years to complete tasks.

Windows PowerShell contains an interactive prompt and a scripting environment that can be used independently or in combination. Unlike the previously mentioned system shells, which accept and return text, Windows PowerShell is built using the *.NET Framework common language runtime (CLR)* and the .NET Framework. Because of this, Windows PowerShell accepts and returns .NET Framework objects. This important change in the shell allows you to use entirely new tools and methods to manage and configure Windows.

Windows PowerShell introduced the concept of using cmdlets (pronounced "command-lets"). Cmdlets are simple, single-function command-line tools built into the shell. Administrators can either use the cmdlets independently or they can combine these tools to execute complex tasks and harness the true power of PowerShell. Windows PowerShell includes more than one hundred core cmdlets, but the true advantage of PowerShell is that anyone can write their own cmdlets and share them with other users.

Administrators often automate the management of their multicomputer environments by running sequences of long-running tasks, or *workflows*, which can affect multiple managed computers or devices at the same time. Windows PowerShell can help administrators accomplish workflows in a more effective way. Windows PowerShell includes some of the following advantages:

Windows PowerShell Scripting Syntax   Administrators can use Windows PowerShell scripting expertise to create script-based tasks by using the extensible Windows PowerShell language. Windows PowerShell script-based tasks are easy to create, and IT members can share them easily by entering them into an email or publishing them on a web page.

Multidevice Management   Administrators can concurrently apply workflow tasks to hundreds of managed computers. Windows PowerShell includes common parameters to set workflows automatically, such as PSComputerName, to enable multicomputer administrative scenarios.

Single Task to Manage Complex, End-to-End Processes   Administrators can combine related scripts or commands that act upon an entire scenario into a single workflow. The status of activities within the workflow can be viewed at any time.

Automated Failure Recovery   Using Windows PowerShell allows workflows to survive both planned and unplanned interruptions, such as computer restarts. Administrators have the ability to suspend workflow operations and then restart or resume the workflow from the exact point at which it was suspended. Administrators can then create checkpoints as part of their workflow process so that they can resume the workflow from the last persisted task (or checkpoint) instead of restarting the workflow from the beginning.

Activity Retries   Administrators can create workflows that also specify activities that must rerun if the activity does not get completed on one or more managed computers (for example, if a target node was not online at the time the activity was running).

Connect and Disconnect   Administrators can connect and disconnect from the node that is executing the workflow, but the workflow will continue to run.

Task Scheduling   Workflow tasks have the ability to be scheduled and started when specific conditions are met. This is also true for any other Windows PowerShell cmdlet or script.

Table 1.4 defines a few of the cmdlets that are available in Windows PowerShell. Again, there are hundreds of cmdlets, and the ones listed in the table are just some of the more common ones. You can retrieve a list of all of the cmdlets starting here:

http://technet.microsoft.com/en-us/scriptcenter/dd772285.aspx

TABLE 1.4   Windows PowerShell cmdlets

Cmdlet	Definition
Clear-History	Deletes entries from the command history
Invoke-command	Runs commands on local or remote computers
Start-job	Starts a Windows PowerShell background job
Stop-job	Stops a Windows PowerShell background job
Remove-job	Deletes a Windows PowerShell background job
Import-Module	Adds modules to the current session
Receive-job	Gets the results of a Windows PowerShell background job
Format-table	Shows the results in a table format
Out-file	Sends the job results to a file
Get-Date	Gets the date and time
Set-Date	Sets the system time and date on a computer

TABLE 1.4   Windows PowerShell cmdlets *(continued)*

Cmdlet	Definition
Get-event	Gets an event in the event queue
New-event	Creates a new event
Trace-command	Configures and starts a trace of a command on a machine
Get-WindowsFeature	Gets a list of available and installed roles and features on the local server
Get-WindowsFeature -ServerName	Gets a list of available and installed roles and features on a remote server
Get-Help Install-WindowsFeature	Gets the syntax and accepted parameters for the Install-WindowsFeature cmdlet
Uninstall-WindowsFeature	Removes a role or feature
Get-NetIPAddress	Gets information about IP address configuration
Set-NetIPAddress	Modifies IP address configuration properties of an existing IP address
Set-NetIPv4Protocol	Modifies information about the IPv4 protocol configuration

---

Windows PowerShell Commands

I will show you Windows PowerShell commands throughout this entire book. If I show you how to install a role or feature in Server Manager, I will also include the Windows PowerShell equivalent.

Another advantage of Windows PowerShell is that it allows you to gain access to a file system on a computer and to access the Registry, digital certificate stores, and other data stores.

Complete Exercise 1.3 to start the Windows PowerShell utility in the Windows Server 2012 Server Core machine installed in the previous exercise.

EXERCISE 1.3

Starting the Windows PowerShell Utility

1. Type **PowerShell** at the Windows Server 2012 Server Core command prompt.

2. When the Windows PowerShell utility starts, type **Help** and press Enter. This will show you the Windows PowerShell syntax and some of the commands included in Windows PowerShell.

3. At the Windows PowerShell command prompt, type **Get-Date**. This will show you the system's date and time.

4. At the Windows command prompt, type **Help** *. This will show you all the cmdlets that you can use.

5. Close the Windows PowerShell utility by typing **Exit**.

Now that you understand how to manage a server remotely, we will look at how Windows Server 2012 stores roles and features on the system.

Understanding Features On Demand

One of the problems in previous versions of Windows Server was how roles and features were stored on the hard disk. Before the introduction of Windows Server 2012, even if a server role or feature was disabled on a server, the binary files for that role or feature were still present on the disk. The problem with this approach is that, even if you disable the role, it still consumes space on your hard drive.

Features On Demand in Windows Server 2012 solves this issue because not only can administrators disable a role or feature, they can also completely remove the role or feature's files.

Once this is done, the state of "removed" is shown in Server Manager or the state of "disabled with payload removed" is shown in the Dism.exe utility. To reinstall a role or feature that has been completely removed, you must have access to the installation files.

If you want to remove a role or feature completely from the system, use -Remove with the Uninstall-WindowsFeature cmdlet of Windows PowerShell. For example, if you want to remove Windows Explorer, Internet Explorer, and all dependent components completely, run the following Windows PowerShell command:

```
Uninstall-WindowsFeature Server-Gui-Shell -Remove
```

If you want to reinstall a role or feature that has been removed completely, use the Windows PowerShell -Source option of the Install-WindowsFeature Server Manager cmdlet. Using the -Source option states the path where the WIM image files and the index number of the image will be located. If an administrator decides not to use the -Source option, Windows will use Windows Update by default.

When you're using the Features On Demand configuration, if feature files are not available on the server computer and the installation requires those feature files, Windows Server 2012 can be directed to get those files from a side-by-side feature store, which is a shared folder that contains feature files. It is available to the server on the network, from Windows Update, or from installation media. This can be overwritten by using the `-Source` option in the Windows PowerShell utility.

Source Files for Roles or Features

Offline virtual hard disks (VHDs) cannot be used as a source for installing roles or features that have been completely removed. Only sources for the exact same version of Windows Server 2012 are supported.

To install a removed role or feature using a WIM image, follow these steps:

1. Run the following command:

   ```
   Get-windowsimage -imagepath \install.wim
   ```

2. Then run this command:

   ```
   Install-WindowsFeature featurename -Source wim: path:index
   ```

In step 1, *imagepath* is the path where the WIM files are located. In step 2, *featurename* is the name of the role or feature from `Get-WindowsFeature`. *Path* is the path to the WIM mount point, and *index* is the index of the server image from step 1.

To add or remove a role or feature, you must have administrative rights to the Windows Server 2012 machine.

Summary

In this chapter, you studied the latest advantages of using Windows Server 2012. You also learned about the different roles and features that you can install on a Windows Server 2012 machine. We also explored how to migrate those roles and features from a Windows Server 2008 and 2008 R2 machine to a Windows Server 2012 machine.

We discussed the different upgrade paths that are available and which upgrades are best for your current network setup. You learned that another important issue to decide when installing Windows Server 2012 is whether to use Server Core or the GUI installation.

You learned how to install Windows Server 2012 Datacenter with GUI and you installed the Windows Server 2012 Server Core. Remember, Server Core is a slimmed-down version of Windows Server. With no GUI desktop available, it's a safer alternative to a normal

Windows install. As we discussed, a nice advantage of Windows Server 2012 is that you can change from Server Core to the GUI version and back again.

We then took a look at remote configuration and two tools that allow us to configure servers:

- Windows Remote Management allows you to configure a server remotely from another machine.

- PowerShell is an important tool in the Windows Server 2012 arsenal. Microsoft has been moving the industry toward PowerShell, and there will be many questions on the exam about PowerShell.

We finished the chapter by discussing a brand-new feature called Features On Demand. This feature not only allows you to remove roles and features from the operating system but also to remove the associated files completely from the hard drive, thus saving disk space.

In the next chapter, we will look at one of the most important services on a network: *Domain Name System (DNS)*. This is one of the services that even many IT people truly don't understand. They set it up, and never look at it again. You will learn how to get the most out of your DNS server.

Exam Essentials

Understand the upgrade paths.   It's very important to make sure that you understand the different upgrade paths from Windows Server 2008 and Windows Server 2008 R2 to Windows Server 2012.

Understand Windows Server 2012 server roles.   Understand what the Windows Server 2012 server roles do for an organization and its users.

Understand Windows Server 2012 GUI vs. Server Core.   Understand the difference between the Windows Server 2012 GUI version and the Windows Server 2012 Server Core version. Know the benefits of using Server Core, and know that you can convert between the two different versions.

Understand Windows PowerShell.   Understanding Windows PowerShell is not only important for the exam, it will also allow you to configure Server Core more efficiently. Windows PowerShell is a command-line utility that allows you not only to run single cmdlets but also to run complex tasks to exploit the full power from PowerShell.

Understand Features On Demand.   Understand the brand-new feature called Features On Demand. Microsoft loves to ask exam questions about their new features, and this will be no exception. Understand how features and roles stay on the system until you physically remove them from the hard drive.

Review Questions

1. You are the administrator for the ABC Company. You are looking to install Windows Server 2012, and you need to decide which version to install. You need to install a version of Windows that is just for logon authentication and nothing else. You want the most secure option. What should you install?

   A. Windows Server 2012 Datacenter with GUI

   B. Windows Server 2012 Datacenter Server Core

   C. Windows Server 2012 Standard with GUI

   D. Windows Server 2012 Web Server Core

2. You are the IT manager for a large organization. One of your coworkers installed a new Windows Server 2012 Datacenter Server Core machine, but now the IT team has decided that it should be a Windows Server 2012 Datacenter with GUI. What should you do?

   A. Reinstall Windows Server 2012 Datacenter Server Core on the same machine.

   B. Install a new machine with Windows Server 2012 Datacenter Server Core.

   C. Convert the current Windows Server 2012 Datacenter Server Core to the Windows Server 2012 Datacenter with GUI version.

   D. Dual-boot the machine with both Windows Server 2012 Datacenter Server Core and Windows Server 2012 Datacenter with GUI.

3. You are the administrator for your company, and you are looking at upgrading your Windows Server 2008 web server to Windows Server 2012. Which version of Windows Server 2012 does Microsoft recommend that you use?

   A. Windows Server 2012 Datacenter

   B. Windows Server 2012 Standard

   C. Windows Server 2012 Essentials

   D. Windows Server 2012 Foundation

4. You are looking at upgrading your Windows Server 2008 R2 Enterprise with SP2 machine to Windows Server 2012. Your organization is considering virtualizing its entire server room, which has 25 servers. To which version of Windows Server 2012 would you upgrade?

   A. Windows Server 2012 Datacenter

   B. Windows Server 2012 Standard

   C. Windows Server 2012 Essentials

   D. Windows Server 2012 Foundation

5. You have been hired to help a small company set up its first Windows network. It has had the same 13 users for the entire two years it has been open, and the company has no plans to expand. What version of Windows Server 2012 would you recommend?

   A. Windows Server 2012 Datacenter

   B. Windows Server 2012 Standard

   C. Windows Server 2012 Essentials

   D. Windows Server 2012 Foundation

6. You have been hired to help a small company set up their Windows network. They have 20 users, and they have no plans to expand. What version of Windows Server 2012 would you recommend?

   A. Windows Server 2012 Datacenter

   B. Windows Server 2012 Standard

   C. Windows Server 2012 Essentials

   D. Windows Server 2012 Foundation

7. Which of the following are benefits of using Windows Server 2012 Server Core? (Choose all that apply.)

   A. Reduced management

   B. Minimal maintenance

   C. Smaller footprint

   D. Tighter security

8. You have been asked to configure a Windows Server 2012 Datacenter Server Core machine. Which remote configuration applications can you use to configure this server from your machine? (Choose all that apply.)

   A. Windows Remote Management

   B. Command prompt

   C. Windows PowerShell

   D. Microsoft Remote Admin (MRA)

9. You are a server administrator, and you are trying to save hard drive space on your Windows Server 2012 Datacenter machine. Which feature can help you save hard disk space?

   A. HDSaver.exe

   B. Features On Demand

   C. ADDS

   D. WinRM

10. You are working on a Windows Server 2012 Datacenter Server Core system. You need to view which roles and services are installed on the machine. Which PowerShell cmdlet can you use to see this?

   A. `Get-event`

   B. `New-event`

   C. `Trace-command`

   D. `Get-WindowsFeature`

Chapter

2

Domain Name System

THE FOLLOWING EXAM 70-410 EXAM OBJECTIVES ARE COVERED IN THIS CHAPTER:

✓ **Deploy and configure DNS service**

  ▪ This objective may include, but is not limited to: Configure Active Directory integration of primary zones; configure forwarders; configure Root Hints; manage DNS cache; create A and PTR resource records.

THE FOLLOWING EXAM 70-411 EXAM OBJECTIVES ARE COVERED IN THIS CHAPTER:

✓ **Configure DNS zones**

  ▪ This objective may include, but is not limited to: Configure primary and secondary zones; configure stub zones; configure conditional forwards; configure zone and conditional forward storage in Active Directory; configure zone delegation; configure zone transfer settings; configure notify settings.

✓ **Configure DNS records**

  ▪ This objective may include, but is not limited to: Create and configure DNS Resource Records (RR) including A, AAAA, PTR, SOA, NS, SRV, CNAME, and MX records; configure zone scavenging; configure record options including Time To Live (TTL) and weight; configure round robin; configure secure dynamic updates.

THE FOLLOWING EXAM 70-412 EXAM OBJECTIVES ARE COVERED IN THIS CHAPTER:

✓ **Implement an advanced DNS solution**

- ▪ This objective may include, but is not limited to: Configure security for DNS including DNSSEC, DNS Socket Pool, and cache locking; configure DNS logging; configure delegated administration; configure recursion; configure netmask ordering; configure a GlobalNames zone.

The Domain Name System (DNS) is one of the key topics that you'll need to understand if you plan to take any of the Microsoft Windows Server 2012 administration exams (70-410, 70-411, 70-412, and so forth). As you can see from the exam objectives at the beginning of this chapter, DNS knowledge will be required for all three MCSA exams, so we are going to cover all of the DNS exam objectives for exams 70-410, 70-411, and 70-412 in this chapter.

It's also imperative that you understand DNS to work with Active Directory because it requires DNS to function properly and many important system functions (including Kerberos authentication and finding domain controllers) are handled through DNS lookups. Windows 2000, Windows XP, Windows Vista, Windows 7, and Windows 8 clients use DNS for name resolution and to find Kerberos key distribution centers (KDCs), global catalog servers, and other services that may be registered in DNS.

By the time you complete this chapter, you will have a deeper understanding of how DNS works and how to set up, configure, manage, and troubleshoot DNS in Microsoft Windows Server 2012.

Introducing DNS

The *Domain Name System (DNS)* is a service that allows you to resolve a hostname to an Internet Protocol (IP) address. One of the inherent complexities of operating in networked environments is working with multiple protocols and network addresses. Owing largely to the tremendous rise in the popularity of the Internet, however, most environments have transitioned to use *TCP/IP (Transmission Control Protocol/Internet Protocol)* as their primary networking protocol. Microsoft is no exception when it comes to supporting TCP/IP in its workstation and server products. All current versions of Microsoft's operating systems support TCP/IP, as do most other modern operating systems.

A very easy way to understand DNS is to think about making a telephone call. If you wanted to call Microsoft and did not know the phone number, you could call information, tell them the name (Microsoft), and get the telephone number. You would then make the call. Now think about trying to connect to Server1. You don't know the TCP/IP number (the computer's telephone number), so your computer asks DNS (information) for the number of Server1. DNS returns the number, and your system makes the connection (call). DNS is your network's 411, or information, and it returns the TCP/IP data for your network.

TCP/IP is actually a collection of different technologies (protocols and services) that allow computers to function together on a single, large, and heterogeneous network. Some of the major advantages of this protocol include widespread support for hardware, software, and network devices; reliance on a system of standards; and scalability. TCP handles tasks like sequenced acknowledgments. IP involves many jobs, such as logical subnet assignment and routing.

The Form of an IP Address

To understand DNS, you must first understand how TCP/IP addresses are formed. Because DNS is strictly on a network to support TCP/IP, understanding the basics of TCP/IP is extremely important.

> **NOTE** Microsoft exams cover TCP/IP in depth. The TCP/IP material will be covered in Chapter 9, "Understanding TCP/IP."

An *IP address* is a logical number that uniquely identifies a computer on a TCP/IP network. TCP/IP allows a computer packet to reach the correct host. Windows Server 2012 works with two versions of TCP/IP: IPv4 and IPv6. An IPv4 address takes the form of four octets (eight binary bits), each of which is represented by a decimal number between 0 and 255. The four numbers are separated by decimal points. For example, all of the following are valid IP addresses:

- 128.45.23.17
- 230.212.43.100
- 10.1.1.1

The dotted decimal notation was created to make it easier for users to deal with IP addresses, but this idea did not go far enough. As a result, another abstraction layer was developed, which used names to represent the dotted decimal notation—the domain name. For example, the IP address 11000000 10101000 00000001 00010101 maps to 192.168.1.21, which in turn might map to server1.company.org, which is how the computer's address is usually presented to the user or application.

As stated earlier, IPv4 addresses are made up of octets, or the decimal (base 10) representation of 8 bits. It takes four octets to add up to the 32 bits required. IPv6 expands the address space to 128 bits. The address is usually represented in hexadecimal notation as follows:

```
2001:0DB8:0000:0000:1234:0000:A9FE:133E
```

You can tell that the implementation of DNS would make life a lot easier for everyone; even those of us who like to use alphanumeric values. (For example, some of us enjoy pinging the address in lieu of the name.) Fortunately, DNS already has the ability to handle IPv6 addresses using an AAAA record. An A record in IPv4's addressing space is 32 bits, and an AAAA record (4 As) in IPv6's is 128 bits.

Nowadays, most computer users are quite familiar with navigating to DNS-based resources, such as www.microsoft.com. In order to resolve these "friendly" names to TCP/IP addresses that the network stack can use, you need a method for mapping them. Originally, ASCII flat files (often called HOSTS files, as shown in Figure 2.1) were used for this purpose. In some cases, they are still used today in very small networks, and they can be useful in helping to troubleshoot name resolution problems.

FIGURE 2.1   HOSTS file

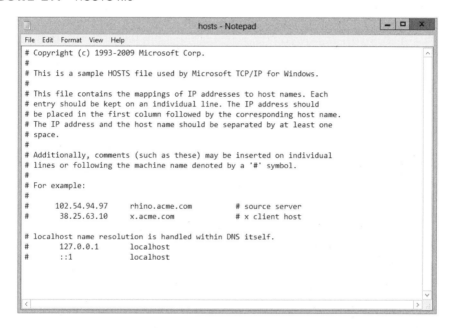

As the number of machines and network devices grew, it became unwieldy for administrators to manage all of the manual updates required to enter new mappings to a master HOSTS file and distribute it. Clearly, a better system was needed.

As you can see from the sample HOSTS file in Figure 2.1, you can conduct a quick test of the email server's name resolution as follows:

1. Open the HOSTS file: C:\Windows\Systems32\drivers\etc.

2. Add the IP-address-to-hostname mapping.

3. Try to ping the server using the hostname to verify that you can reach it using an easy-to-remember name.

Following these steps should drive home the concept of DNS for you because you can see it working to make your life easier. Now you don't have to remember 10.0.0.10; you only need to remember exchange03. However, you can also see how this method can become unwieldy if you have many hosts that want to use easy-to-remember names instead of IP addresses to locate resources on your network.

When dealing with large networks, users and network administrators must be able to locate the resources they require with minimal searching. Users don't care about the actual physical or logical network address of the machine; they just want to be able to connect to it using a simple name that they can remember.

From a network administrator's standpoint, however, each machine must have its own logical address that makes it part of the network on which it resides. Therefore, some scalable and easy-to-manage method for resolving a machine's logical name to an IP address and then to a domain name is required. DNS was created just for this purpose.

DNS is a hierarchically distributed database. In other words, its layers are arranged in a definite order, and its data is distributed across a wide range of machines, each of which can exert control over a portion of the database. DNS is a standard set of protocols that defines the following:

- A mechanism for querying and updating address information in the database

- A mechanism for replicating the information in the database among servers

- A schema of the database

 DNS is defined by a number of Requests for Comments (RFCs), though primarily by RFC 1034 and RFC 1035.

DNS was originally developed in the early days of the Internet (called ARPAnet at the time) when it was a small network created by the Department of Defense for research purposes. Before DNS, computer names, or hostnames, were manually entered into a HOSTS file located on a centrally administered server. Each site that needed to resolve hostnames outside of its organization had to download this file. As the number of computers on the Internet grew, so did the size of this HOSTS file—and along with it the problems of its management. The need for a new system that would offer features such as scalability, decentralized administration, and support for various data types became more and more obvious. DNS, introduced in 1984, became this new system.

With DNS, the hostnames reside in a database that can be distributed among multiple servers, decreasing the load on any one server and providing the ability to administer this naming system on a per-partition basis. DNS supports hierarchical names and allows for the registration of various data types in addition to the hostname-to-IP-address mapping used in HOSTS files. Database performance is ensured through its distributed nature as well as through caching.

The DNS distributed database establishes an inverted logical tree structure called the *domain namespace*. Each node, or domain, in that space has a unique name. At the top of the tree is the root. This may not sound quite right, which is why the DNS hierarchical model is described as being an inverted tree, with the root at the top. The root is represented by the null set "". When written, the root node is represented by a single dot (.).

Each node in the DNS can branch out to any number of nodes below it. For example, below the root node are a number of other nodes, commonly referred to as *top-level domains (TLDs)*. These are the familiar .com, .net, .org, .gov, .edu, and other such names. Table 2.1 lists some of these TLDs.

TABLE 2.1 Common top-level DNS domains

Common Top-Level Domain Names	Type of Organization
com	Commercial (for example, stellacon.com for Stellacon Training Corporation).
edu	Educational (for example, gatech.edu for the Georgia Institute of Technology)
gov	Government (for example, whitehouse.gov for the White House in Washington, D.C.).
int	International organizations (for example, nato.int for NATO); this top-level domain is fairly rare.
mil	Military organizations (for example, usmc.mil for the Marine Corps); there is a separate set of root name servers for this domain.
net	Networking organizations and Internet providers (for example, hiwaay.net for HiWAAY Information Systems); many commercial organizations have registered names under this domain too.
org	Noncommercial organizations (for example, fidonet.org for FidoNet).
au	Australia
uk	United Kingdom
ca	Canada
us	United States
jp	Japan

Each of these nodes then branches out into another set of domains, and they combine to form what we refer to as *domain names*, such as microsoft.com. A domain name identifies the domain's position in the logical DNS hierarchy in relation to its parent domain by separating each branch of the tree with a dot. Figure 2.2 shows a few of the top-level domains, where the Microsoft domain fits, and a host called Tigger within the microsoft.com domain. If someone wanted to contact that host, they would use the *fully qualified domain name (FQDN)*, tigger.microsoft.com.

FIGURE 2.2 The DNS hierarchy

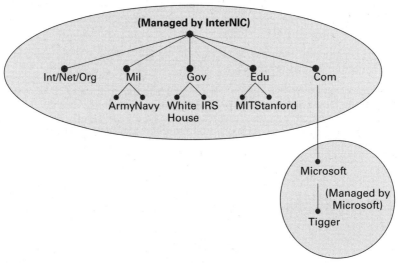

An FQDN includes the trailing dot (.) to indicate the root node, but it's commonly left off in practice.

As previously stated, one of the strengths of DNS is the ability to delegate control over portions of the DNS namespace to multiple organizations. For example, the Internet Corporation for Assigned Names and Numbers (ICANN) assigns the control over TLDs to one or more organizations. In turn, those organizations delegate portions of the DNS namespace to other organizations. For example, when you register a domain name, let's call it example.com, you control the DNS for the portion of the DNS namespace within example.com. The registrar controlling the .com TLD has delegated control over the example.com node in the DNS tree. No other node can be named example directly below the .com within the DNS database.

Within the portion of the domain namespace that you control (example.com), you could create host and other records (more on these later). You could also further subdivide example.com and delegate control over those divisions to other organizations or departments. These divisions are called *subdomains*. For example, you might create subdomains named for the cities in which the company has branch offices and then delegate control over those subdomains to the branch offices. The subdomains might be named losangeles.example.com, chicago.example.com, portsmouth.example.com, and so on.

Each domain (or delegated subdomain) is associated with DNS name servers. In other words, for every node in the DNS, one or more servers can give an authoritative answer to queries about that domain. At the root of the domain namespace are the root servers. More on these later.

Domain names and hostnames must contain only characters a to z, A to Z, 0 to 9, and - (hyphen). Other common and useful characters, like the & (ampersand), / (slash), . (period), and _ (underscore) characters, are not allowed. This is in conflict with NetBIOS's naming restrictions. However, you'll find that Windows Server 2012 is smart enough to take a NetBIOS name, like Server_1, and turn it into a legal DNS name, like server1 .example.com.

DNS servers work together to resolve hierarchical names. If a server already has information about a name, it simply fulfills the query for the client. Otherwise, it queries other DNS servers for the appropriate information. The system works well because it distributes the authority over separate parts of the DNS structure to specific servers. A DNS zone is a portion of the DNS namespace over which a specific DNS server has authority (DNS zone types are discussed in detail later in this chapter).

There is an important distinction to make between DNS zones and Active Directory (AD) domains. Although both use hierarchical names and require name resolution, DNS zones do not map directly to AD domains.

Within a given DNS zone, resource records (RRs) contain the hosts and other database information that make up the data for the zone. For example, an RR might contain the host entry for www.example.com, pointing it to the IP address 192.168.1.10.

Understanding Servers, Clients, and Resolvers

You will need to know a few terms and concepts in order to manage a DNS server. Understanding these terms will make it easier to understand how the Windows Server 2012 DNS server works:

DNS Server   Any computer providing domain name services is a *DNS name server*. No matter where the server resides in the DNS namespace, it's still a DNS name server. For example, 13 root name servers at the top of the DNS tree are responsible for delegating the TLDs. The *root servers* provide referrals to name servers for the TLDs, which in turn provide referrals to an authoritative name server for a given domain.

The Berkeley Internet Name Domain (BIND) was originally the only software available for running the root servers on the Internet. However, a few years ago the organizations responsible for the root servers undertook an effort to diversify the software running on these important machines. Today, root servers run multiple types of name server software. BIND is still primarily on Unix-based machines, and it is also the most popular for Internet providers. None of the root servers run Windows DNS.

Any DNS server implementation supporting Service Location Resource Records (see RFC 2782) and Dynamic Updates (RFC 2136) is sufficient to provide the name service for any operating system running Windows 2003 software and above.

DNS Client   A *DNS client* is any machine that issues queries to a DNS server. The client hostname may or may not be registered in a DNS database. Clients issue DNS requests through processes called *resolvers*. You'll sometimes see the terms *client* and *resolver* used synonymously.

Resolver   *Resolvers* are software processes, sometimes implemented in software libraries, that handle the actual process of finding the answers to queries for DNS data. The resolver is also built into many larger pieces of software so that external libraries don't have to be called to make and process DNS queries. Resolvers can be what you'd consider client computers or other DNS servers attempting to resolve an answer on behalf of a client (for example, Internet Explorer).

Query   A *query* is a request for information sent to a DNS server. Three types of queries can be made to a DNS server: recursive, inverse, and iterative. We'll discuss the differences between these query types in the section "DNS Queries" a bit later in the chapter.

Understanding the DNS Process

To help you understand the DNS process, we will start by covering the differences between Dynamic DNS and Non-Dynamic DNS. During this discussion, you will learn how Dynamic DNS populates the DNS database. You'll also see how to implement security for Dynamic DNS. We will then talk about the workings of different types of DNS queries. Finally, we will discuss caching and time to live (TTL). You'll learn how to determine the best setting for your organization.

Dynamic DNS and Non-Dynamic DNS

To understand Dynamic DNS and Non-Dynamic DNS, you must go back in time (here is where the TV screen always used to get wavy). Many years ago when we all worked on NT 3.51 and NT 4.0, most networks used Windows Internet Name Service (WINS) to do their TCP/IP name resolution. Windows versions 95/98 and NT 4.0 Professional were all built on the idea of using WINS. This worked out well for administrators because WINS was dynamic (which meant that once it was installed, it automatically built its own database). Back then, there was no such thing as Dynamic DNS; administrators had to enter DNS records into the server manually. This is important to know even today. If you have clients still running any of these older operating systems (95/98 or NT 4), these clients cannot use Dynamic DNS.

Now let's move forward in time to the release of Windows Server 2000. Microsoft announced that DNS was going to be the name resolution method of choice. Many administrators (me included) did not look forward to the switch. Because there was no such thing as Dynamic DNS, most administrators had nightmares about manually entering records. However, luckily for us, when Microsoft released Windows Server 2000, DNS had the ability to operate dynamically. Now when you're setting up Windows Server 2012 DNS, you can choose what type of dynamic update you would like to use, if any. Let's talk about why you would want to choose one over the other.

The *Dynamic DNS (DDNS) standard*, described in RFC 2136, allows DNS clients to update information in the DNS database files. For example, a Windows Server 2012 DHCP server can automatically tell a DDNS server which IP addresses it has assigned to what machines. Windows 2000, 2003, 2008, XP Pro, Vista, Windows 7, and Windows 8 DHCP clients can do this too. For security reasons, however, it's better to let the DHCP server do it. The result: IP addresses and DNS records stay in sync so that you can use DNS and DHCP together seamlessly. Because DDNS is a proposed Internet standard, you can even use the Windows Server 2012 DDNS-aware parts with Unix/Linux based DNS servers.

Non-Dynamic DNS (NDDNS) does not automatically populate the DNS database. The client systems do not have the ability to update to DNS. If you decide to use Non-Dynamic DNS, an administrator will need to populate the DNS database manually. Non-Dynamic DNS is a reasonable choice if your organization is small-to-midsize and you do not want extra network traffic (clients updating to the DNS server) or if you need to enter the computer's TCP/IP information manually because of strict security measures.

 Dynamic DNS has the ability to be secure, and the chances are slim that a rogue system (a computer that does not belong in your DNS database) could update to a secure DNS server. Nevertheless, some organizations have to follow stricter security measures and are not allowed to have dynamic updates.

The major downside to entering records into DNS manually occurs when the organization is using the *Dynamic Host Configuration Protocol (DHCP)*. When using DHCP, it is possible for users to end up with different TCP/IP addresses every day. This means that an administrator has to update DNS manually each day to keep it accurate.

If you choose to allow Dynamic DNS, you need to decide how you want to set it up. When setting up dynamic updates on your DNS server, you have three choices (see Figure 2.3):

None   This means your DNS server is Non-Dynamic.

Nonsecure and Secure   This means that any machine (even if it does not have a domain account) can register with DNS. Using this setting could allow rogue systems to enter records into your DNS server.

Secure Only   This means that only machines with accounts in Active Directory can register with DNS. Before DNS registers any account in its database, it checks Active Directory to make sure that account is an authorized domain computer.

FIGURE 2.3   Setting the Dynamic Updates option

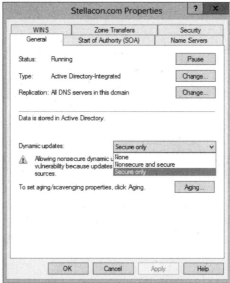

How Dynamic DNS Populates the DNS Database

TCP/IP is the protocol used for network communications on a Microsoft Windows Server 2012 network. Users have two ways to receive a TCP/IP number:

- Static (administrators manually enter the TCP/IP information)

- Dynamic (using DHCP)

When an administrator sets up TCP/IP, DNS can also be configured.

Once a client gets the address of the DNS server, if that client is allowed to update with DNS, the client sends a registration to DNS or requests DHCP to send the registration. DNS then does one of two things, depending on which Dynamic Updates option is specified:

- Check with Active Directory to see if that computer has an account (Secure Only updates), and if it does, enter the record into the database.

- Enter the record into its database (Nonsecure and Secure updates).

What if you have clients (95/98 and NT 4) that cannot update DNS? Well, there is a solution—DHCP. In the DNS tab of the IPv4 Properties window, check the option labeled "Dynamically update DNS A and PTR records for DHCP clients that do not request updates (for example, clients running Windows NT 4.0)," which is shown in Figure 2.4.

FIGURE 2.4   DHCP settings for DNS

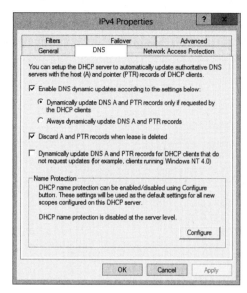

DHCP, along with Dynamic DNS clients, allows an organization to update its DNS database dynamically without the time and effort of having an administrator manually enter DNS records.

DNS Queries

As stated earlier, a client can make three types of queries to a DNS server: recursive, inverse, and iterative. Remember that the client of a DNS server can be a resolver (what you'd normally call a client) or another DNS server.

Iterative Queries

Iterative queries are the easiest to understand: A client asks the DNS server for an answer, and the server returns the best answer. This information likely comes from the server's cache. The server never sends out an additional query in response to an iterative query. If the server doesn't know the answer, it may direct the client to another server through a referral.

Recursive Queries

In a *recursive query*, the client sends a query to a name server, asking it to respond either with the requested answer or with an error message. The error states one of two things:

- The server can't come up with the right answer.
- The domain name doesn't exist.

In a recursive query, the name server isn't allowed to just refer the client to some other name server. Most resolvers use recursive queries. In addition, if your DNS server uses a forwarder, the requests sent by your server to the forwarder will be recursive queries.

Figure 2.5 shows an example of both recursive and iterative queries. In this example, a client within the Microsoft Corporation is querying its DNS server for the IP address for www.whitehouse.gov.

FIGURE 2.5 A sample DNS query

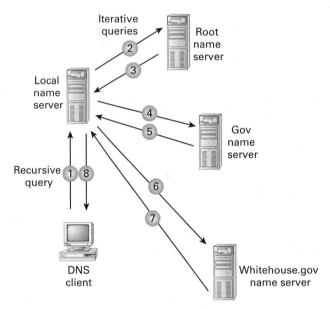

Here's what happens to resolve the request:

1. The resolver sends a recursive DNS query to its local DNS server asking for the IP address of www.whitehouse.gov. The local name server is responsible for resolving the name, and it cannot refer the resolver to another name server.

2. The local name server checks its zones, and it finds no zones corresponding to the requested domain name.

3. The root name server has authority for the root domain and will reply with the IP address of a name server for the .gov top-level domain.

4. The local name server sends an iterative query for www.whitehouse.gov to the Gov name server.

5. The Gov name server replies with the IP address of the name server servicing the whitehouse.gov domain.

6. The local name server sends an iterative query for www.whitehouse.gov to the whitehouse.gov name server.

7. The whitehouse.gov name server replies with the IP address corresponding to www.whitehouse.gov.

8. The local name server sends the IP address of www.whitehouse.gov back to the original resolver.

Inverse Queries

Inverse queries use pointer (PTR) records. Instead of supplying a name and then asking for an IP address, the client first provides the IP address and then asks for the name. Because there's no direct correlation in the DNS namespace between a domain name and its associated IP address, this search would be fruitless without the use of the in-addr.arpa domain. Nodes in the in-addr.arpa domain are named after the numbers in the dotted-octet representation of IP addresses. However, because IP addresses get more specific from left to right and domain names get less specific from left to right, the order of IP address octets must be reversed when building the in-addr.arpa tree. With this arrangement, administration of the lower limbs of the DNS in-addr.arpa tree can be given to companies as they are assigned their Class A, B, or C subnet address or delegated even further down thanks to Variable Length Subnet Masking (VLSM).

Once the domain tree is built into the DNS database, a special PTR record is added to associate the IP addresses with the corresponding hostnames. In other words, to find a hostname for the IP address 206.131.234.1, the resolver would query the DNS server for a PTR record for 1.234.131.206.in-addr.arpa. If this IP address is outside the local domain, the DNS server will start at the root and sequentially resolve the domain nodes until arriving at 234.131.206.in-addr.arpa, which would contain the PTR record for the desired host.

Caching and Time to Live

When a name server is processing a recursive query, it may be required to send out several queries to find the definitive answer. Name servers, acting as resolvers, are allowed to cache all the received information during this process; each record contains information called *time to live (TTL)*. The TTL specifies how long the record will be held in the local cache until it must be resolved again. If a query comes in that can be satisfied by this cached data, the TTL that's returned with it equals the current amount of time left before the data is flushed.

There is also a negative cache TTL. The *negative cache TTL* is used when an authoritative server responds to a query indicating that the record queried doesn't exist, and it indicates the amount of time that this negative answer may be held. Negative caching is quite helpful in preventing repeated queries for names that don't exist.

The administrator for the DNS zone sets TTL values for the entire zone. The value can be the same across the zone, or the administrator can set a separate TTL for each RR within the zone. Client resolvers also have data caches and honor the TTL value so that they know when to flush.

Choosing Appropriate TTL Values

For zones that you administer, you can choose the TTL values for the entire zone, for negative caching, and for individual records. Choosing an appropriate TTL depends on a number of factors, including the following:

- Amount of change you anticipate for the records within the zone

- Amount of time that you can withstand an outage that might require changing an IP address

- Amount of traffic that you believe the DNS server can handle

Resolvers query the name server every time the TTL expires for a given record. A low TTL, say 60 seconds, can burden the name server, especially for popular DNS records. (DNS queries aren't particularly intensive for a server to handle, but they can add up quickly if you mistakenly use 60 seconds instead of 600 seconds for the TTL on a popular record.) Set a low TTL only when you need to respond quickly to a changing environment.

A high TTL, say 604,800 seconds (that's one week), means that if you need to make a change to the DNS record, clients might not see the change for up to a week. This consideration is especially important when making changes to the network, and it's one that's all too frequently overlooked. I can't count the times I've worked with clients who have recently made a DNS change to a new IP for their email or website only to ask why it's not working for some clients. The answer can be found in the TTL value. If the record is being cached, then the only thing that can solve their problem is time.

You should choose a TTL that's appropriate for your environment. Take the following factors into account:

- The amount of time that you can afford to be offline if you need to make a change to a DNS record that's being cached

- The amount of load that a low TTL will cause on the DNS server

In addition, you should plan well ahead of any major infrastructure changes and change the TTL to a lower value to lessen the effect of the downtime by reducing the amount of time that the record(s) can be cached.

Introducing DNS Database Zones

As mentioned earlier in this chapter, a DNS zone is a portion of the DNS namespace over which a specific DNS server has authority. Within a given DNS zone, there are resource records (RRs) that define the hosts and other types of information that make up the database for the zone. You can choose from several different zone types. Understanding the characteristics of each will help you choose which is right for your organization.

The DNS zones discussed in this book are all Microsoft Windows Server 2012 zones. Non-Windows (for example, Unix) systems set up their DNS zones differently.

In the following sections, I will discuss the different zone types and their characteristics.

Understanding Primary Zones

When you're learning about zone types, things can get a bit confusing. But it's really not difficult to understand how they work and why you would want to choose one type of zone over the other. Zones are databases that store records. By choosing one zone type over another, you are basically just choosing how the database works and how it will be stored on the server.

The primary zone is responsible for maintaining all of the records for the DNS zone. It contains the primary copy of the DNS database. All record updates occur on the primary zone. You will want to create and add primary zones whenever you create a new DNS domain.

There are two types of primary zones:

- Primary zone
- Primary zone with Active Directory Integration (Active Directory DNS)

From this point forward, I refer to a primary zone with Active Directory Integration as an *Active Directory DNS*. When I use only the term *primary zone,* Active Directory is not included.

To install DNS as a primary zone, first you must install DNS using the Server Manager MMC. Once DNS is installed and running, you create a new zone and specify it as a primary zone.

The process of installing DNS and its zones will be discussed later in this chapter. In addition, there will be step-by-step exercises to walk you through how to install these components.

Primary zones have advantages and disadvantages. Knowing the characteristics of a primary zone will help you decide when you need the zone and when it fits into your organization.

Local Database

Primary DNS zones get stored locally in a file (with the suffix .dns) on the server. This allows you to store a primary zone on a domain controller or a member server. In addition, by loading DNS onto a member server, you can help a small organization conserve resources. Such an organization may not have the resources to load DNS on an Active Directory domain controller.

Unfortunately, the local database has many disadvantages:

Lack of Fault Tolerance   Think of a primary zone as a contact list on your smartphone. All of the contacts in the list are the records in your database. The problem is that, if you lose your phone or the phone breaks, you lose your contact list. Until your phone gets fixed or you swap out your phone card, the contacts are unavailable.

It works the same way with a primary zone. If the server goes down or you lose the hard drive, DNS records on that machine are unreachable. An administrator can install a secondary zone (explained later in the next section), and that provides temporary fault tolerance. Unfortunately, if the primary zone is down for an extended period of time, the secondary server's information will no longer be valid.

Additional Network Traffic   Let's imagine that you are looking for a contact number for John Smith. John Smith is not listed in your cell phone directory, but he is listed in your partner's cell phone. You have to contact your partner to get the listing. You cannot directly access your partner's cell contacts.

When a resolver sends a request to DNS to get the TCP/IP address for Jsmith (in this case Jsmith is a computer name) and the DNS server does not have an answer, it does not have the ability to check the other server's database directly to get an answer. Thus it forwards the request to another DNS. When DNS servers are replicating zone databases with other DNS servers, this causes additional network traffic.

No Security   Staying with the cell phone example, let's say that you call your partner looking for John Smith's phone number. When your partner gives you the phone number over your wireless phone, someone with a scanner can pick up your conversation. Unfortunately, wireless telephone calls are not very secure.

Now a resolver asks a primary zone for the Jsmith TCP/IP address. If someone on the network has a packet sniffer, they can steal the information in the DNS packets being sent over the network. The packets are not secure unless you implement some form of secondary security. Also, the DNS server has the ability to be dynamic. A primary zone accepts all updates from DNS servers. You cannot set it to accept secure updates only.

Understanding Secondary Zones

In Windows Server 2012 DNS, you have the ability to use secondary DNS zones. Secondary zones are noneditable copies of the DNS database. You use them for *load balancing* (also referred to as *load sharing*), which is a way of managing network overloads on a single server. A secondary zone gets its database from a primary zone.

A *secondary zone* contains a database with all of the same information as the primary zone, and it can be used to resolve DNS requests. Secondary zones have the following advantages:

- A secondary zone provides fault tolerance, so if the primary zone server becomes unavailable, name resolution can still occur using the secondary zone server.

- Secondary DNS servers can also increase network performance by offloading some of the traffic that would otherwise go to the primary server.

Secondary servers are often placed within the parts of an organization that have high-speed network access. This prevents DNS queries from having to run across slow wide area network (WAN) connections. For example, if there are two remote offices within the `stellacon.com` organization, you may want to place a secondary DNS server in each remote office. This way, when clients require name resolution, they will contact the nearest server for this IP address information, thus preventing unnecessary WAN traffic.

> Having too many secondary zone servers can actually cause an increase in network traffic because of replication (especially if DNS changes are fairly frequent). Therefore, you should always weigh the benefits and drawbacks and properly plan for secondary zone servers.

Understanding Active Directory Integrated DNS

Windows Server 2000 introduced *Active Directory Integrated DNS* to the world. This zone type was unique and was a separate choice during setup. In Windows Server 2003, this zone type became an add-on to a primary zone. In Windows Server 2012, it works the same way. After choosing to set up a primary zone, you check the box labeled Store The Zone In Active Directory (see Figure 2.6).

FIGURE 2.6 Setting up an Active Directory Integrated zone

```
┌─────────────────────────────────────────────────────────────┐
│                      New Zone Wizard                      ☒   │
├─────────────────────────────────────────────────────────────┤
│  Zone Type                                                    │
│      The DNS server supports various types of zones and storage.   │
│                                                               │
│     Select the type of zone you want to create:               │
│     ● Primary zone                                            │
│         Creates a copy of a zone that can be updated directly on this server.   │
│                                                               │
│     ○ Secondary zone                                          │
│         Creates a copy of a zone that exists on another server. This option helps balance   │
│         the processing load of primary servers and provides fault tolerance.   │
│     ○ Stub zone                                               │
│         Creates a copy of a zone containing only Name Server (NS), Start of Authority   │
│         (SOA), and possibly glue Host (A) records. A server containing a stub zone is not   │
│         authoritative for that zone.                          │
│                                                               │
│     ☑ Store the zone in Active Directory (available only if DNS server is a writeable domain   │
│        controller)                                            │
│                                                               │
│                              [ < Back ]  [ Next > ]  [ Cancel ]   │
└─────────────────────────────────────────────────────────────┘
```

Disadvantages of Active Directory Integrated DNS

The main disadvantage of Active Directory Integrated DNS is that it has to reside on a domain controller because the DNS database is stored in Active Directory. As a result, you cannot load this zone type on a member server, and small organizations might not have the resources to set up a dedicated domain controller.

Advantages of Active Directory Integrated DNS

The advantages of using an Active Directory Integrated DNS zone well outweigh the disadvantage just discussed. Following are some of the major advantages to an Active Directory Integrated zone:

Full Fault Tolerance   Think of an Active Directory Integrated zone as a database on your server that stores contact information for all your clients. If you need to retrieve John Smith's phone number, as long as it was entered, you can look it up on the software.

If John Smith's phone number was stored only on your computer and your computer stopped working, no one could access John Smith's phone number. But since John Smith's phone number is stored in a database to which everyone has access, if your computer stops working, other users can still retrieve John Smith's phone number.

An Active Directory Integrated zone works the same way. Since the DNS database is stored in Active Directory, all Active Directory DNS servers can have access to the same data. If one server goes down or you lose a hard drive, all other Active Directory DNS servers can still retrieve DNS records.

No Additional Network Traffic   As previously discussed, an Active Directory Integrated zone is stored in Active Directory. Since all records are now stored in Active Directory, when a resolver needs a TCP/IP address for Jsmith, any Active Directory DNS server can access Jsmith's address and respond to the resolver.

When you choose an Active Directory Integrated zone, DNS zone data can be replicated automatically to other DNS servers during the normal Active Directory replication process.

DNS Security   An Active Directory Integrated zone has a few security advantages over a primary zone:

- An Active Directory Integrated zone can use secure dynamic updates.
- As explained earlier, the Dynamic DNS standard allows secure-only updates or dynamic updates, not both.
- If you choose secure updates, then only machines with accounts in Active Directory can register with DNS. Before DNS registers any account in its database, it checks Active Directory to make sure that it is an authorized domain computer.
- An Active Directory Integrated zone stores and replicates its database through Active Directory replication. Because of this, the data gets encrypted as it is sent from one DNS server to another.

Background Zone Loading   Background zone loading (discussed in more detail later in this chapter) allows an Active Directory Integrated DNS zone to load in the background. As a result, a DNS server can service client requests while the zone is still loading into memory.

Understanding Stub Zones

Stub zones work a lot like secondary zones—the database is a noneditable copy of a primary zone. The difference is that the stub zone's database contains only the information necessary (three record types) to identify the authoritative DNS servers for a zone (see Figure 2.7). You should not use stub zones to replace secondary zones, nor should you use them for redundancy and load balancing.

FIGURE 2.7 DNS stub zone type

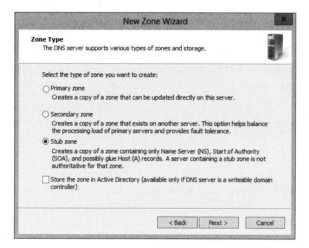

 Stub zone databases contain only three record types: name server (NS), start of authority (SOA), and glue host (A) records. Understanding these records will help you on the Microsoft certification exams. Microsoft asks many questions about stub zones on all DNS-related exams.

When to Use Stub Zones

Stub zones become particularly useful in a couple of different scenarios. Consider what happens when two large companies merge: example.com and example.net. In most cases, the DNS zone information from both companies must be available to every employee. You could set up a new zone on each side that acts as a secondary for the other side's primary zone, but administrators tend to be very protective of their DNS databases and they probably wouldn't agree to this plan.

A better solution is to add to each side a stub zone that points to the primary server on the other side. When a client in example.com (which you help administer) makes a request for a name in example.net, the stub zone on the example.com DNS server would send the client to the primary DNS server for example.net without actually resolving the name. At this point, it would be up to example.net's primary server to resolve the name.

An added benefit is that, even if the administrators over at example.net change their configuration, you won't have to do anything because the changes will automatically replicate to the stub zone, just as they would for a secondary server.

Stub zones can also be useful when you administer two domains across a slow connection. Let's change the previous example a bit and assume that you have full control over example.com and example.net but they connect through a 56 Kbps line. In this case, you wouldn't necessarily mind using secondary zones because you personally administer the entire network. However, it could get messy to replicate an entire zone file across that slow line. Instead, stub zones would refer clients to the appropriate primary server at the other site.

GlobalName Zones

Earlier in this chapter, I talked about organizations using WINS to resolve NetBIOS names (also referred to as *computer names*) to TCP/IP addresses. Even today, many organizations still use WINS along with DNS for name resolution. Unfortunately, WINS is slowly becoming obsolete.

To help organizations move forward with an all-DNS network, Microsoft Windows Server 2012 DNS supports *GlobalName zones*. These use single-label names (DNS names that do not contain a suffix such as .com, .net, and so on). GlobalName zones are not intended to support peer-to-peer networks and workstation name resolution, and they don't support dynamic DNS updates.

GlobalName zones are designed to be used with servers. Because GlobalName zones are not dynamic, an administrator has to enter the records into the zone database manually. In most organizations, the servers have static TCP/IP addresses, and this works well with the GlobalName zone design. GlobalName zones are usually used to map single-label CNAME (alias) resource records to an FQDN.

Zone Transfers and Replication

DNS is such an important part of the network that you should not just use a single DNS server. With a single DNS server, you also have a single point of failure, and in fact, many domain registrars encourage the use of more than two name servers for a domain. Secondary servers or multiple primary Active Directory Integrated servers play an integral role in providing DNS information for an entire domain.

As previously stated, secondary DNS servers receive their zone databases through zone transfers. When you configure a secondary server for the first time, you must specify the primary server that is authoritative for the zone and will send the zone transfer. The primary server must also permit the secondary server to request the zone transfer.

Zone transfers occur in one of two ways: *full zone transfers (AXFR)* and *incremental zone transfers (IXFR)*.

When a new secondary server is configured for the first time, it receives a full zone transfer from the primary DNS server. The full zone transfer contains all of the information in the DNS database. Some DNS implementations always receive full zone transfers.

After the secondary server receives its first full zone transfer, subsequent zone transfers are incremental. The primary name server compares its zone version number with that of the secondary server, and it sends only the changes that have been made in the interim. This significantly reduces network traffic generated by zone transfers.

The secondary server typically initiates zone transfers when the refresh interval time for the zone expires or when the secondary or stub server boots. Alternatively, you can configure notify lists on the primary server that send a message to the secondary or stub servers whenever any changes to the zone database occur.

When you consider your DNS strategy, you must carefully consider the layout of your network. If you have a single domain with offices in separate cities, you want to reduce the number of zone transfers across the potentially slow or expensive WAN links, although this is becoming less of a concern because of continuous increases in bandwidth.

Active Directory Integrated zones do away with traditional zone transfers altogether. Instead, they replicate across Active Directory with all of the other AD information. This replication is secure and encrypted because it uses the Active Directory security.

How DNS Notify Works

Windows Server 2012 supports DNS Notify. *DNS Notify* is a mechanism that allows the process of initiating notifications to secondary servers when zone changes occur (RFC 1996). DNS Notify uses a push mechanism for communicating to a select set of secondary zone servers when their zone information is updated. (DNS Notify does not allow you to configure a notify list for a stub zone.)

After being notified of the changes, secondary servers can then start a pull zone transfer and update their local copies of the database.

Many different mechanisms use the push/pull relationship. Normally, one object pushes information to another, and the second object pulls the information from the first. Most applications push replication on a change value and pull it on a time value. For example, a system can push replication after 10 updates, or it can be pulled every 30 minutes.

To configure the DNS Notify process, you create a list of secondary servers to notify. List the IP address of the server in the primary master's Notify dialog box (see Figure 2.8).

The Notify dialog box is located under the Zone Transfers tab, which is located in the zone Properties dialog box (see Figure 2.9).

FIGURE 2.8 DNS Notify dialog box

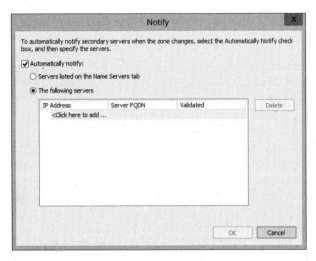

FIGURE 2.9 DNS Zone Transfers tab

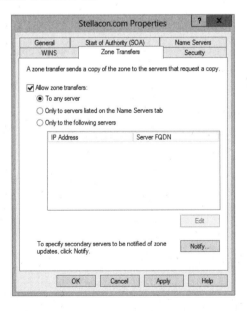

Configuring Stub Zone Transfers with Zone Replication

In the preceding section, I talked about how to configure secondary server zone transfers. What if you wanted to configure settings for stub zone transfers? This is where zone replication scope comes in.

Only Active Directory–integrated primary and stub zones can configure their replication scope. Secondary servers do not have this ability.

You can configure zone replication scope configurations in two ways. An administrator can set configuration options through the DNS snap-in or through a command-line tool called DNSCmd.

To configure zone replication scope through the DNS snap-in, follow these steps:

1. Click Start ➢ Administrative Tools ➢ DNS.

2. Right-click the zone that you want to set up.

3. Choose Properties.

4. In the Properties dialog box, click the Change button next to Replication (see Figure 2.10).

FIGURE 2.10   DNS zone replication scope

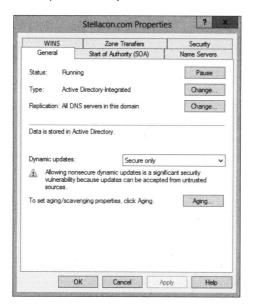

5. Choose the replication scope that fits your organization.

Advantages of DNS in Windows Server 2012

DNS in Microsoft Windows Server 2012 has some great advantages over many other versions of Microsoft DNS. Here are some of the improvements of DNS in Windows Server 2012 (some of these became available in Windows Server 2008):

- Background zone loading
- Support for TCP/IP version 6 (IPv6)
- Read-only domain controllers
- GlobalName zone
- DNS Socket Pool
- DNS Cache Locking
- DNS Security Extensions (DNSSEC)
- DNS Devolution
- Record Weighting
- Netmask Ordering
- DnsUpdateProxy Group

Background Zone Loading

If an organization had to restart a DNS server with an extremely large Active Directory Integrated DNS zones database in the past, DNS had a common problem with an Active Directory Integrated DNS zone. After the DNS restart, it could take hours for DNS data to be retrieved from Active Directory. During this time, the DNS server was unable to service any client requests.

Microsoft Windows Server 2008 DNS addressed this problem by implementing background zone loading, and Windows Server 2012 has taken it a step further. As the DNS restarts, the Active Directory zone data populates the database in the background. This allows the DNS server to service client requests for data from other zones almost immediately after a restart.

Background zone loading accomplishes this task by loading the DNS zone using separate threads. This allows a DNS server to service requests while still loading the rest of the zone. If a client sends a request to the DNS server for a computer that has not yet loaded into memory, the DNS server retrieves the data from Active Directory and updates the record.

Support for IPv6 Addresses

Over the past few years, the Internet has starting running into a problem that was not foreseen when it was first created—it started running out of TCP/IP addresses. As you probably know, when the Internet was created, it was used for government and academic purposes only. Then, seemingly overnight, it grew to be the information superhighway. Nowadays, asking someone for their email address is almost as common as asking for their phone number.

Version 4 (IPv4) was the common version of TCP/IP. The release of TCP/IP version 6 (IPv6) has solved the lack-of-IP-addresses problem. IPv4 addresses are 32 bits long, but IPv6 addresses are 128 bits in length. The longer lengths allow for a much greater number of globally unique TCP/IP addresses.

Microsoft Windows Server 2012 DNS has built-in support to accommodate both IPv4 and IPv6 address records (DNS records are explained later in this chapter). DHCP can also issue IPv6 addresses, which lets administrators allow DHCP to register the client with DNS, or the IPv6 client can register their address with the DNS server.

Support for Read-Only Domain Controllers

Windows Server 2008 introduced a new type of domain controller called the *read-only domain controller (RODC)*. This is a full copy of the Active Directory database without the ability to write to Active Directory. The RODC gives an organization the ability to install a domain controller in a location (onsite or offsite) where security is a concern.

Microsoft Windows Server 2012 DNS has implemented a type of zone to help support an RODC. A primary read-only zone allows a DNS server to receive a copy of the application partition (including ForestDNSZones and DomainDNSZones) that DNS uses. This allows DNS to support an RODC because DNS now has a full copy of all DNS zones stored in Active Directory.

A primary, read-only zone is just what it says—a read-only zone; so to make any changes to it, you have to change the primary zones located on the Active Directory Integrated DNS server.

DNS Socket Pools

If your server is running Windows Server 2012, you will be able to take advantage of DNS socket pools. *DNS socket pools* allow source port randomization to protect against DNS cache-poisoning attacks.

If you choose to use source port randomization, when the DNS service starts, the DNS server will randomly pick a source port from a pool of available sockets. This is an advantage because instead of DNS using a well-known source port when issuing queries, the DNS server uses a random port selected from the socket pool. This helps guard against attacks because a hacker must correctly access the source port of the DNS query. The socket pool is automatically enabled in DNS with the default settings.

When using the DNS Socket Pool, the default size of the DNS socket pool is 2,500. When configuring the socket pool, you have the ability to choose a size value from 0 to 10,000. The larger the value, the greater the protection you will have against DNS spoofing attacks. If you decide to configure your socket pool size with a zero value, only a single socket for remote DNS queries will be used.

DNS Cache Locking

Windows Server 2012 *DNS cache locking* allows cached DNS records to remain safe for the duration of the record's time to live (TTL) value. This means that the cached DNS records cannot be overwritten or changed. Because of this new DNS feature, it's tougher for hackers to perform cache-poisoning attacks against your DNS server.

DNS administrators can set how long a record will remain safe in cache. The configuration is based on a percent value. For example, if you set your cache locking value to 50 percent, then the cached records cannot be overwritten until half of the TTL has been reached. DNS cache locking is set to 100 percent by default. This means that the cached records never get overwritten.

DNS Security Extensions (DNSSEC)

One major issue that you must always look at is keeping your DNS safe. Think about it, DNS is a database of computer names and IP addresses. As a hacker, if I control DNS, I can control your company. In organizations that do not support extra security like IPSec, DNS security is even more important. This is where DNSSEC can help.

Windows Server 2012 can use a suite of extensions that will help add security to DNS, and that suite is called *Domain Name System Security Extensions (DNSSEC)*, which was introduced in Windows Server 2008 R2. The DNSSEC protocol allows your DNS servers to be secure by validating DNS responses. DNSSEC secures your DNS resource records by accompanying the records with a digital signature.

To allow your DNS resource records to receive digital signatures, DNSSEC is applied to your DNS server by a procedure called *zone signing*. This process begins when a DNS resolver initiates a DNS query for a resource record in a signed DNS zone. When a response is returned, a digital signature (RRSIG) accompanies the response and this allows the response to be verified. If the verification is successful, then the DNS resolver knows that the data has not been modified or tampered with in any way.

Once you implement a zone with DNSSEC, all the records that are contained within that zone get individually signed. Since all of the records in the zone get individually signed, this gives administrators the ability to add, modify, or delete records without resigning the entire zone. The only requirement is to resign any updated records.

Trust Anchors

Trust anchors are an important part of the DNSSEC process because trust anchors allow the DNS servers to validate the DNSKEY resource records. *Trust anchors* are preconfigured public keys that are linked to a DNS zone. For a DNS server to perform validation, one or more trust anchors must be configured. If you are running an Active Directory Integrated zone, trust anchors can be stored in the Active Directory Domain Services directory partition of the forest. If you decide to store the trust anchors in the directory partition, then all DNS servers that reside on a domain controller get a copy of this trust anchor. On DNS servers that reside on stand-alone servers, trust anchors are stored in a file called TrustAnchors.dns.

If your servers are running Windows Server 2012, then you can view trust anchors in the DNS Manager Console tree in the Trust Points container. You can also use Windows PowerShell or Dnscmd.exe to view trust anchors. Windows PowerShell is the recommended command-line method for viewing trust anchors. The following line is a PowerShell command to view the trust anchors for Contoso.com.

```
get-dnsservertrustanchor sec.contoso.com
```

DNSSEC Clients

Windows 7, Windows 8, Windows Server 2008 R2, and Windows Server 2012 are all DNS clients that receive a response to a DNS query, examine the response, and then evaluate whether or not the response has been validated by a DNS server. The DNS client itself is nonvalidating, and the DNS client relies on the local DNS server to indicate that validation was successful. If the server doesn't perform validation, then the DNS client service can be configured to return no results.

DNS Devolution

Using *DNS devolution*, if a client computer is a member of a child namespace, the client computer will be able to access resources in the parent namespace without the need to explicitly provide the fully qualified domain name (FQDN) of the resource. DNS devolution removes the leftmost label of the namespace to get to the parent suffix. DNS devolution allows the DNS resolver to create the new FQDNs. DNS devolution works by appending the single-label, unqualified domain name with the parent suffix of the primary DNS suffix name.

Record Weighting

Weighting DNS records will allow an administrator to place a value on DNS SRV records. Clients will then randomly choose SRV records proportional to the weight value assigned.

Netmask Ordering

If round robin is enabled, when a client requests name resolution, the first address entered in the database is returned to the resolver, and it is then sent to the end of the list. The next time a client attempts to resolve the name, the DNS server returns the second name in the database (which is now the first name) and then sends it to the end of the list, and so on. Round robin is enabled by default.

Netmask ordering is a part of the round robin process. When an administrator configures netmask ordering, the DNS server will detect the subnet of the querying client. The DNS server will then return a host address available for the same subnet. Netmask ordering is enabled through the DNS Manager console on the Advanced tab of the server Properties dialog box.

DnsUpdateProxy Group

As mentioned previously, the DHCP server can be configured to register host (A) and pointer (PTR) resource records dynamically on behalf of DHCP clients. Because of this, the DNS server can end up with stale resources. To help solve this issue, an administrator can use the built-in security group called *DnsUpdateProxy*.

To use the DnsUpdateProxy group, an administrator must first create a dedicated user account and configure the DHCP servers with its credentials. This will protect against the creation of unsecured records. Also, when you create the dedicated user account, members of the DnsUpdateProxy group will be able to register records in zones that allow only secured dynamic updates. Multiple DHCP servers can use the same credentials of one dedicated user account.

Now that we have looked at some of the new features of Windows Server 2012 DNS, let's take a look at some of the DNS record types.

Introducing DNS Record Types

No matter where your zone information is stored, you can rest assured that it contains a variety of DNS information. Although the DNS snap-in makes it unlikely that you'll ever need to edit these files by hand, it's good to know exactly what data is contained there.

As stated previously, zone files consist of a number of resource records (RRs). You need to know about several types of resource records to manage your DNS servers effectively. They are discussed in the following sections.

Part of the resource record is its class. *Classes* define the type of network for the resource record. There are three classes: Internet, Chaosnet, and Hesoid. By far, the Internet class is the most popular. In fact, it's doubtful that you'll see either Chaosnet or Hesoid classes in the wild.

The following are some of the more important resource records in a DNS database. For a complete listing of records in a Microsoft DNS database, visit Microsoft's website at `http://technet.microsoft.com/en-us/library/cc958958.aspx`.

Start of Authority (SOA) Records

The first record in a database file is the *start of authority (SOA) record*. The SOA defines the general parameters for the DNS zone, including the identity of the authoritative server for the zone.

The SOA appears in the following format:

```
@ IN SOA primary_mastercontact_e-mailserial_number
refresh_timeretry_timeexpiration_timetime_to_live
```

Here is a sample SOA from the domain example.com:

```
@ IN SOA win2k3r2.example.com. hostmaster.example.com. (
                        5               ; serial number
                        900             ; refresh
                        600             ; retry
                        86400           ; expire
                        3600            ) ; default TTL
```

Table 2.2 lists the attributes stored in the SOA record.

TABLE 2.2   The SOA record structure

Field	Meaning
Current zone	The current zone for the SOA. This can be represented by an @ symbol to indicate the current zone or by naming the zone itself. In the example, the current zone is example.com. The trailing dot (.com.) indicates the zone's place relative to the root of the DNS.
Class	This will almost always be the letters *IN* for the Internet class.
Type of record	The type of record follows. In this case, it's SOA.
Primary master	The primary master for the zone on which this file is maintained.
Contact email	The Internet email address for the person responsible for this domain's database file. There is no @ symbol in this contact email address because @ is a special character in zone files. The contact email address is separated by a single dot (.). So the email address of root@example.com would be represented by root.example.com in a zone file.
Serial number	This is the "version number" of this database file. It increases each time the database file is changed.
Refresh time	The amount of time (in seconds) that a secondary server will wait between checks to its master server to see if the database file has changed and a zone transfer should be requested.
Retry time	The amount of time (in seconds) that a secondary server will wait before retrying a failed zone transfer.
Expiration time	The amount of time (in seconds) that a secondary server will spend trying to download a zone. Once this time limit expires, the old zone information will be discarded.
Time to live	The amount of time (in seconds) that another DNS server is allowed to cache any resource records from this database file. This is the value that is sent out with all query responses from this zone file when the individual resource record doesn't contain an overriding value.

Name Server (NS) Records

Name server (NS) records list the name servers for a domain. This record allows other name servers to look up names in your domain. A zone file may contain more than one name server record. The format of these records is simple:

```
example.com.    IN    NS    Hostname.example.com
```

Table 2.3 explains the attributes stored in the NS record.

TABLE 2.3   The NS record structure

Field	Meaning
Name	The domain that will be serviced by this name server. In this case I used example.com.
AddressClass	Internet (IN)
RecordType	Name server (NS)
Name Server Name	The FQDN of the server responsible for the domain

Any domain name in the database file that is not terminated with a period will have the root domain appended to the end. For example, an entry that just has the name *sales* will be expanded by adding the root domain to the end whereas the entry sales.example.com. won't be expanded.

Host Record

A *host record* (also called an *A record* for IPv4 and *AAAA record* for IPv6) is used to associate statically a host's name to its IP addresses. The format is pretty simple:

```
host_nameoptional_TTL IN  A  IP_Address
```

Here's an example from my DNS database:

```
www  IN  A  192.168.0.204
SMTP IN  A  192.168.3.144
```

The A or AAAA record ties a hostname (which is part of an FQDN) to a specific IP address. This makes these records suitable for use when you have devices with statically assigned IP addresses. In this case, you create these records manually using the DNS snap-in. As it turns out, if you enable DDNS, your DHCP server can create these for you. This automatic creation is what enables DDNS to work.

Notice that an optional TTL field is available for each resource record in the DNS. This value is used to set a TTL that is different from the default TTL for the domain. For example, if you wanted a 60-second TTL for the www A or AAAA record, it would look like this:

```
www 60 IN  A  192.168.0.204
```

Alias Record

Closely related to the host record is the *alias record*, or *canonical name (CNAME) record*. The syntax of an alias record is as follows:

```
aliasoptional_TTL  IN  CNAME  hostname
```

Aliases are used to point more than one DNS record toward a host for which an A record already exists. For example, if the hostname of your web server was actually chaos, you would likely have an A record such as this:

```
chaos IN A 192.168.1.10
```

Then you could make an alias or CNAME for the record so that www.example.com would point to chaos:

```
www IN CNAME chaos.example.com.
```

Note the trailing dot (.) on the end of the CNAME record. This means the root domain is not appended to the entry.

Pointer (PTR) Record

A or AAAA records are probably the most visible component of the DNS database because Internet users depend on them to turn FQDNs like www.microsoft.com into the IP addresses that browsers and other components require to find Internet resources. However, the host record has a lesser-known but still important twin: the *pointer (PTR) record*. The format of a PTR record appears as follows:

```
reversed_address.in-addr.arpa. optional_TTL IN PTR targeted_domain_name
```

The A or AAAA record maps a hostname to an IP address, and the PTR record does just the opposite—mapping an IP address to a hostname through the use of the in-addr.arpa zone.

The PTR record is necessary because IP addresses begin with the least-specific portion first (the network) and end with the most-specific portion (the host), whereas hostnames begin with the most-specific portion at the beginning and the least-specific portion at the end.

Consider the example 192.168.1.10 with a subnet mask 255.255.255.0. The portion 192.168.1 defines the network and the final .10 defines the host, or the most-specific portion of the address. DNS is just the opposite: The hostname www.example.com. defines the most-specific portion, www, at the beginning and then traverses the DNS tree to the least-specific part, the dot (.), at the root of the tree.

Reverse DNS records, therefore, need to be represented in this most-specific-to-least-specific manner. The PTR record for mapping 192.168.1.10 to www.example.com would look like this:

```
10.1.168.192.in-addr.arpa. IN PTR www.example.com.
```

Now a DNS query for that record can follow the logical DNS hierarchy from the root of the DNS tree all the way to the most-specific portion.

Mail Exchanger (MX) Record

The *mail exchanger (MX) record* is used to specify which servers accept mail for this domain. Each MX record contains two parameters—a preference and a mail server, as shown in the following example:

```
domain IN MX preference mailserver_host
```

The MX record uses the preference value to specify which server should be used if more than one MX record is present. The preference value is a number. The lower the number, the more preferred the server. Here's an example:

```
example.com.    IN  MX  0   mail.example.com.
example.com.    IN  MX  10  backupmail.example.com.
```

In the example, mail.example.com is the default mail server for the domain. If that server goes down for any reason, the backupmail.example.com mail server is used by emailers.

Service (SRV) Record

Windows Server 2012 depends on some other services, like the Lightweight Directory Access Protocol (LDAP) and Kerberos. Using a service record, which is another type of DNS record, a Windows 2000, XP, Vista, Windows 7, or Windows 8 client can query DNS servers for the location of a domain controller. This makes it much easier (for both the client and the administrator) to manage and distribute logon traffic in large-scale networks. For this approach to work, Microsoft has to have some way to register the presence of a service in DNS. Enter the service (SRV) record.

Service (SRV) records tie together the location of a service (like a domain controller) with information about how to contact the service. SRV records provide seven items of information. Let's review an example to help clarify this powerful concept. (Table 2.4 explains the fields in the following example.)

```
ldap.tcp.example.com.    86400 IN SRV   10   100   389   hsv.example.com
ldap.tcp.example.com.    86400 IN SRV   20   100   389   msy.example.com
```

TABLE 2.4   The SRV record structure

Field	Meaning
Domain name	Domain for which this record is valid (`ldap.tcp.example.com.`).
TTL	Time to live (86,400 seconds).
Class	This field is always `IN`, which stands for Internet.
Record type	Type of record (SRV).
Priority	Specifies a preference, similar to the Preference field in an MX record. The SRV record with the lowest priority is used first (`10`).
Weight	Service records with equal priority are chosen according to their weight (`100`).
Port number	The port where the server is listening for this service (`389`).
Target	The FQDN of the host computer (`hsv.example.com` and `msy.example.com`).

You can define other types of service records. If your applications support them, they can query DNS to find the services they need.

Configuring DNS

In the following sections, you'll begin to learn about the actual DNS server. You will start by installing DNS. Then I will talk about different zone configuration options and what they mean. Finally, you'll complete an exercise that covers configuring Dynamic DNS, delegating zones, and manually entering records.

Installing DNS

Let's start by installing DNS. Installing DNS is an important part of running a network. Exercise 2.1 walks you through the installation of a DNS server.

EXERCISE 2.1

Installing and Configuring the DNS Service

1. Open the Server Manager.

2. On the Server Manager dashboard, click the Add Roles And Features link.

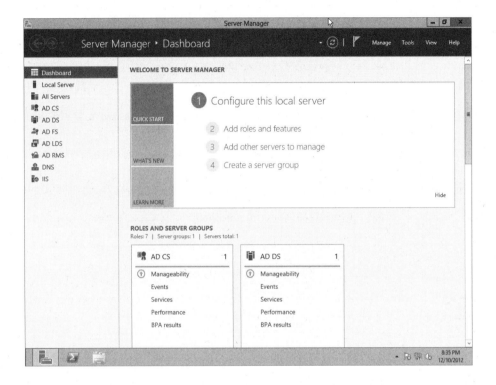

3. If a Before You Begin screen appears, click Next.

4. On the Selection type page, choose Role-Based Or Feature-Based Installation and click Next.

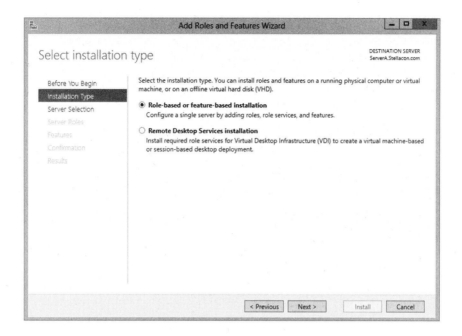

5. Click the Select A Server From The Server Pool radio button, and choose the server under the Server Pool section. Click Next.

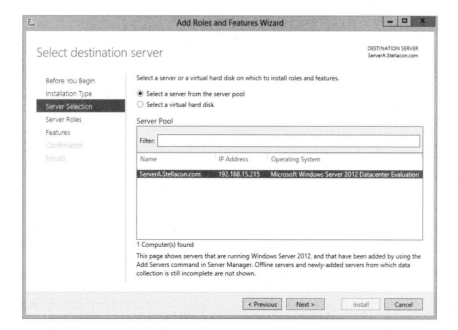

6. Click the DNS Server Item in the Server Role list. If a pop-up window appears telling you that you need to add additional features, click the Add Features button. If a window appears stating that you need a static TCP/IP address, just click the Continue button to bypass the error. Click Next to continue.

7. On the Add Features page, just click Next.

8. Click Next on the DNS Server information screen.

9. On the Confirm Installation screen, choose the Restart The Destination Server Automatically If Required check box and then click the Install button.

10. At the Installation progress screen, click Close after the DNS server is installed.

11. Close Server Manager.

Load Balancing with Round Robin

Like other DNS implementations, the Windows Server 2012 implementation of DNS supports load balancing through the use of round robin. Load balancing distributes the network load among multiple network hosts if they are available. You set up round robin load balancing by creating multiple resource records with the same hostname but different IP addresses for multiple computers. Depending on the options that you select, the DNS server responds with the addresses of one of the host computers.

If round robin is enabled, when a client requests name resolution, the first address entered in the database is returned to the resolver and is then sent to the end of the list. The next time a client attempts to resolve the name, the DNS server returns the second name in the database (which is now the first name) and then sends it to the end of the list, and so on. Round robin is enabled by default.

Configuring a Caching-Only Server

Although all DNS name servers cache queries that they have resolved, caching-only servers are DNS name servers that only perform queries, cache the answers, and return the results. They are not authoritative for any domains, and the information that they contain is limited to what has been cached while resolving queries. Accordingly, they don't have any zone files, and they don't participate in zone transfers. When a caching-only server is first started, it has no information in its cache; the cache is gradually built over time.

Caching-only servers are very easy to configure. After installing the DNS service, simply make sure the root hints are configured properly:

1. Right-click your DNS server, and choose the Properties command.

2. When the Properties dialog box appears, switch to the Root Hints tab (see Figure 2.11).

FIGURE 2.11   The Root Hints tab of the DNS server's Properties dialog box

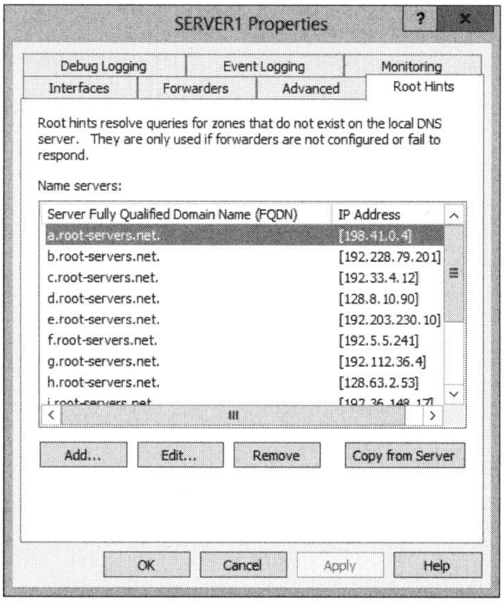

| | SERVER1 Properties | ? | x |

| Debug Logging | Event Logging | Monitoring |
| Interfaces | Forwarders | Advanced | Root Hints |

Root hints resolve queries for zones that do not exist on the local DNS server. They are only used if forwarders are not configured or fail to respond.

Name servers:

Server Fully Qualified Domain Name (FQDN)	IP Address	
a.root-servers.net.	[198.41.0.4]	
b.root-servers.net.	[192.228.79.201]	
c.root-servers.net.	[192.33.4.12]	
d.root-servers.net.	[128.8.10.90]	
e.root-servers.net.	[192.203.230.10]	
f.root-servers.net.	[192.5.5.241]	
g.root-servers.net.	[192.112.36.4]	
h.root-servers.net.	[128.63.2.53]	
i.root-servers.net.	[192.36.148.17]	

[Add...] [Edit...] [Remove] [Copy from Server]

[OK] [Cancel] [Apply] [Help]

3. If your server is connected to the Internet, you should see a list of root hints for the root servers maintained by ICANN and the Internet Assigned Numbers Authority (IANA). If not, click the Add button to add root hints as defined in the cache.dns file.

    You can obtain current cache.dns files on the Internet by using a search engine. Just search for "cache.dns" and download one. (I always try to get cache.dns files from a university or a company that manages domain names.)

Setting Zone Properties

There are six tabs on the Properties dialog box for a forward or reverse lookup zone (see Figure 2.10). You only use the Security tab to control who can change properties and to make dynamic updates to records on that zone. The other tabs are discussed in the following sections.

NOTE   Secondary zones don't have a Security tab, and their SOA tab shows you the contents of the master SOA record, which you can't change.

General Tab

The General tab (see Figure 2.10) includes the following:

- The Status indicator and the associated Pause button let you see and control whether this zone can be used to answer queries. When the zone is running, the server can use it to answer client queries; when it's paused, the server won't answer any queries it gets for that particular zone.

- The Type indicator and its Change button allow you to select the zone type. The options are Standard Primary, Standard Secondary, and AD-Integrated. (See "Introducing DNS Database Zones" earlier in this chapter.) As you change the type, the controls you see below the horizontal dividing line change too. For primary zones, you'll see a field that lets you select the zone filename; for secondary zones, you'll get controls that allow you to specify the IP addresses of the primary servers. But the most interesting controls are the ones you see for AD Integrated zones. When you change to the AD Integrated zones, you have the ability to make the dynamic zones Secure Only.

- The Replication indicator and its Change button allow you to change the replication scope if the zone is stored in Active Directory. You can choose to replicate the zone data to any of the following:

  - All DNS servers in the Active Directory forest

  - All DNS servers in a specified domain

  - All domain controllers in the Active Directory domain (required if you use Windows 2000 domain controllers in your domain)

  - All domain controllers specified in the replication scope of the application directory partition

- The Dynamic Updates field gives you a way to specify whether you want to support Dynamic DNS updates from compatible DHCP servers. As you learned earlier in the section "Dynamic DNS and Non-Dynamic DNS," the DHCP server or DHCP client must know about and support Dynamic DNS in order to use it, but the DNS server has to participate too. You can turn dynamic updates on or off, or you can require that updates be secured.

Start Of Authority (SOA) Tab

The following options in the Start Of Authority (SOA) tab, shown in Figure 2.12, control the contents of the SOA record for this zone:
- The Serial Number field indicates which version of the SOA record the server currently holds. Every time you change another field, you should increment the serial number so that other servers will notice the change and get a copy of the updated record.

FIGURE 2.12   The Start Of Authority (SOA) tab of the zone Properties dialog box

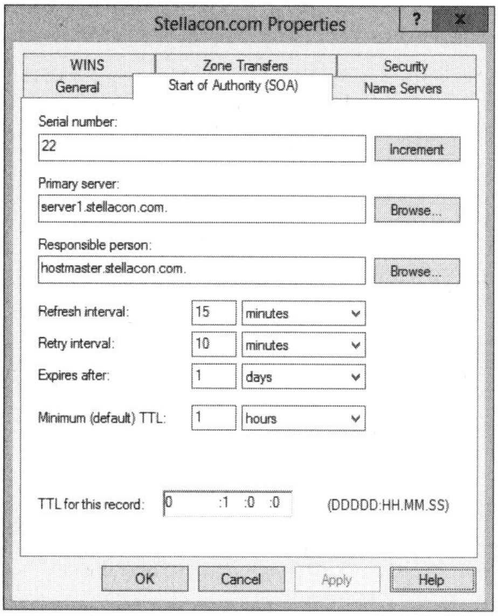

- The Primary Server and Responsible Person fields indicate the location of the primary name server (NS) for this zone and the email address of the administrator responsible for the maintenance of this zone, respectively. The standard username for this is hostmaster.

- The Refresh Interval field controls how often any secondary zones of this zone must contact the primary zone server and get any changes that have been posted since the last update.

- The Retry Interval field controls how long secondary servers will wait after a zone transfer fails before they try again. They'll keep trying at the interval you specify (which should be shorter than the refresh interval) until they eventually succeed in transferring zone data.

- The Expires After field tells the secondary servers when to throw away zone data. The default of 1 day (24 hours) means that a secondary server that hasn't gotten an update in 24 hours will delete its local copy of the zone data.

- The Minimum (Default) TTL field sets the default TTL for all RRs created in the zone. You can assign specific TTLs to individual records if you want.

- The TTL For This Record field controls the TTL for the SOA record itself.

Name Servers Tab

The *name server (NS) record* for a zone indicates which name servers are authoritative for the zone. That normally means the zone primary server and any secondary servers you've configured for the zone. (Remember, secondary servers are authoritative read-only copies of the zone.) You edit the NS record for a zone using the Name Servers tab (see Figure 2.13). The tab shows you which servers are currently listed, and you use the Add, Edit, and Remove buttons to specify which name servers you want included in the zone's NS record.

FIGURE 2.13   The Name Servers tab of the zone Properties dialog box

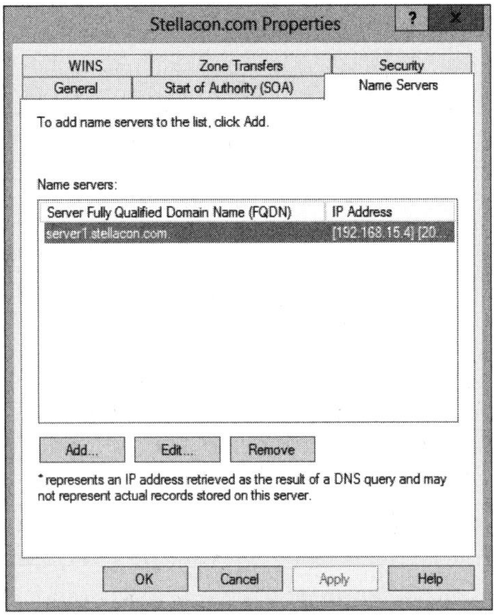

WINS Tab

The WINS tab allows you to control whether this zone uses WINS forward lookups or not. These lookups pass on queries that DNS can't resolve to WINS for action. This is a useful setup if you're still using WINS on your network. You must explicitly turn this option on with the Use WINS Forward Lookup check box in the WINS tab for a particular zone.

Zone Transfers Tab

Zone transfers are necessary and useful because they're the mechanism used to propagate zone data between primary and secondary servers. For primary servers (whether AD Integrated or not), you can specify whether your servers will allow zone transfers (see Figure 2.9) and, if so, to whom.

You can use the following controls on the Zone Transfers tab to configure these settings per zone:

- The Allow Zone Transfers check box controls whether the server answers zone transfer requests for this zone at all—when it's not checked, no zone data is transferred. The Allow Zone Transfers selections are as follows:

    - To Any Server allows any server anywhere on the Internet to request a copy of your zone data.

    - Only To Servers Listed On The Name Servers Tab (the default) limits transfers to servers you specify. This is a more secure setting than To Any Server because it limits transfers to other servers for the same zone.

    - Only To The Following Servers allows you to specify exactly which servers are allowed to request zone transfers. This list can be larger or smaller than the list specified on the Name Servers tab.

- The Notify button is for setting up automatic notification triggers that are sent to secondary servers for this zone. Those triggers signal the secondary servers that changes have occurred on the primary server so that the secondary servers can request updates sooner than their normally scheduled interval. The options in the Notify dialog box are similar to those in the Zone Transfers tab. You can enable automatic notification and then choose either Servers Listed On The Name Servers Tab or The Following Servers.

Configuring Zones for Dynamic Updates

In Exercise 2.2, you will create and then modify the properties of a forward lookup zone. In addition, you'll configure the zone to allow dynamic updates.

EXERCISE 2.2

Configuring a Zone for Dynamic Updates

1. Open the DNS management snap-in by selecting Server Manager. Once in Server Manager, click DNS on the left-hand side. In the Servers window (center screen), right-click your server name and choose DNS Manager.

2. Click the DNS server to expand it, and then click the Forward Lookup Zones folder. Right-click the Forward Lookup Zones folder, and choose New Zone.

EXERCISE 2.2 *(continued)*

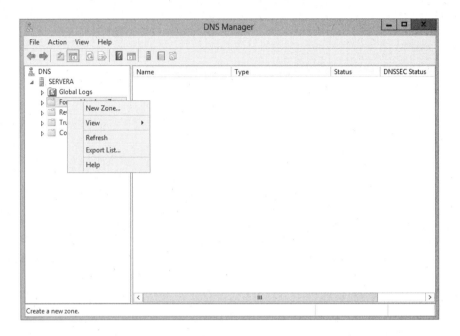

3. At the New Zone Welcome screen, click Next.

4. At the Zone Type screen, choose the Primary Zone option. If your DNS server is also a domain controller, do not check the box to store the zone in Active Directory. Click Next when you are ready.

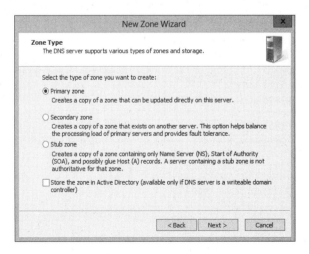

5. Enter a new zone name in the Zone Name field and click Next. (I used my last name— Panek.com.)

6. Leave the default zone filename and click Next.

7. Select the Do Not Allow Dynamic Updates radio button and click Next.

8. Click Finish to end the wizard.

9. Right-click the zone you just created, and choose the Properties command.

10. Click the down arrow next to Dynamic Updates. Notice that there are only two options (None and Nonsecure And Secure). The Secure Only option is not available because we are not using Active Directory Integrated. Make sure Nonsecure And Secure is chosen.

11. Click OK to close the Properties box.

12. Close the DNS management snap-in.

13. Close the Server Manager snap-in.

Delegating Zones for DNS

DNS provides the ability to divide the namespace into one or more zones, which can then be stored, distributed, and replicated to other DNS servers. When deciding whether to divide your DNS namespace to make additional zones, consider the following reasons to use additional zones:

- A need to delegate management of part of your DNS namespace to another location or department within your organization

- A need to divide one large zone into smaller zones for distributing traffic loads among multiple servers, for improving DNS name-resolution performance, or for creating a more fault-tolerant DNS environment

- A need to extend the namespace by adding numerous subdomains at once, such as to accommodate the opening of a new branch or site

Each newly delegated zone requires a primary DNS server just as a regular DNS zone does. When delegating zones within your namespace, be aware that for each new zone you create, you need to place delegation records in other zones that point to the authoritative DNS servers for the new zone. This is necessary both to transfer authority and to provide correct referral to other DNS servers and clients of the new servers being made authoritative for the new zone.

In Exercise 2.3, you'll create a delegated subdomain of the domain you created back in Exercise 2.2. Note that the name of the server to which you want to delegate the subdomain must be stored in an A or CNAME record in the parent domain.

EXERCISE 2.3

Creating a Delegated DNS Zone

1. Open the DNS management snap-in by selecting Server Manager. Once in Server Manager, click DNS on the left-hand side. In the Servers window (center screen), right-click your server name and choose DNS Manager.

2. Expand the DNS server, and locate the zone you created in Exercise 2.2.

3. Right-click the zone, and choose the New Delegation command.

4. The New Delegation Wizard appears. Click Next to dismiss the initial wizard page.

5. Enter **ns1** (or whatever other name you like) in the Delegated Domain field of the Delegated Domain Name page. This is the name of the domain for which you want to delegate authority to another DNS server. It should be a subdomain of the primary domain (for example, to delegate authority for farmington.example.net, you'd enter **farmington** in the Delegated Domain field). Click Next to complete this step.

6. When the Name Servers page appears, click the Add button to add the name(s) and IP address(es) of the servers that will be hosting the newly delegated zone. For the purpose of this exercise, enter the server name you used in Exercise 2.2. Click the Resolve button to resolve this domain name's IP address automatically into the IP address field. Click OK when you are finished. Click Next to continue with the wizard.

7. Click the Finish button. The New Delegation Wizard disappears, and you'll see the new zone you just created appear beneath the zone you selected in step 3. The newly delegated zone's folder icon is drawn in gray to indicate that control of the zone is delegated.

DNS Forwarding

If a DNS server does not have an answer to a DNS request, it may be necessary to send that request to another DNS server. This is called *DNS forwarding*. You need to understand the two main types of forwarding:

External Forwarding   When a DNS server forwards an external DNS request to a DNS server outside your organization, this is considered *external forwarding*. For example, a resolver requests the host www.microsoft.com. Most likely, your internal DNS server is not going to have Microsoft's web address in its DNS database. So your DNS server is going to send the request to an external DNS (most likely your ISP).

Conditional Forwarding   *Conditional forwarding* is a lot like external forwarding except that you are going to forward requests to specific DNS servers based on a condition. Usually this is an excellent setup for internal DNS resolution. For example, let's say that you have two companies, stellacon.com and stellatest.com. If a request comes in for Stellacon.com, it gets forwarded to the Stellacon DNS server, and any requests for Stellatest.com will get forwarded to the Stellatest DNS server. Requests are forwarded to a specific DNS server depending on the condition that an administrator sets up.

Manually Creating DNS Records

From time to time you may find it necessary to add resource records manually to your Windows Server 2012 DNS servers. Although Dynamic DNS frees you from the need to fiddle with A and PTR records for clients and other such entries, you still have to create other resource types (including MX records, required for the proper flow of SMTP email) manually. You can manually create A, PTR, MX, SRV, and many other record types.

There are only two important things to remember for manually creating DNS records:

- You must right-click the zone and choose either the New Record command or the Other New Records command.

- You must know how to fill in the fields of whatever record type you're using.

  For example, to create an MX record, you need three pieces of information (the domain, the mail server, and the priority). To create an SRV record, however, you need several more pieces of information.

In Exercise 2.4, you will manually create an MX record for a mailtest server in the zone you created back in Exercise 2.2.

EXERCISE 2.4

Manually Creating DNS RRs

1. Open the DNS management snap-in by selecting Server Manager. Once in Server Manager, click DNS on the left-hand side. In the Servers window (center screen), right-click your server name and choose DNS Manager.

2. Expand your DNS server, right-click its zone, and choose New Host (A record).

3. Enter **mailtest** in the Name field. Enter a TCP/IP number in the IP Address field. (You can use any number for this exercise, for example, 192.168.1.254.) Click the Add Host button.

4. A dialog box appears stating that the host record was created successfully. Click OK. Click Done.

5. Right-click your zone name, and choose New Mail Exchanger (MX).

6. Enter **mailtest** in the Host Or Child Domain field, and enter **mailtest.yourDomain.com** (or whatever domain name you used in Exercise 2.2) in the Fully-Qualified Domain Name (FQDN) Of Mail Server field, and then click OK. Notice that the new record is already visible.

7. Next create an alias (or CNAME) record to point to the mail server. (It is assumed that you already have an A record for mailtest in your zone.) Right-click your zone, and choose New Alias (CNAME).

8. Type **mail** into the Alias Name field.

9. Type **mailtest.yourDomain.com** into the Fully-Qualified Domain Name (FQDN) For Target Host field.

10. Click the OK button.

11. Close the DNS management snap-in.

DNS Aging and Scavenging

When using dynamic updates, computers (or DHCP) will register a resource record with DNS. These records get removed when a computer is shut down properly. A major problem in the industry is that laptops are frequently removed from the network without a proper shutdown. Therefore, their resource records continue to live in the DNS database.

Windows Server 2012 DNS supports two features called *DNS aging* and *DNS scavenging*. These features are used to clean up and remove stale resource records. DNS zone or DNS server aging and scavenging flag old resource records that have not been updated in a certain amount of time (determined by the scavenging interval). These stale records will be scavenged at the next cleanup interval. DNS uses time stamps on the resource records to determine how long they have been listed in the DNS database.

Monitoring and Troubleshooting DNS

Now that you have set up and configured your DNS name server and created some resource records, you will want to confirm that it is resolving and replying to client DNS requests. A couple of tools allow you to do some basic monitoring and managing. Once you are able to monitor DNS, you'll want to start troubleshooting.

The simplest test is to use the ping command to make sure the server is alive. A more thorough test would be to use nslookup to verify that you can actually resolve addresses for items on your DNS server.

In the following sections, we'll look at some of these monitoring and management tools and how to troubleshoot DNS.

Monitoring DNS with the DNS Snap-In

You can use the DNS snap-in to do some basic server testing and monitoring. More important, you use the snap-in to monitor and set logging options. On the Event Logging tab of the server's Properties dialog box (see Figure 2.14), you can pick which events you want logged. The more events you select, the more logging information you'll get. This is useful when you're trying to track what's happening with your servers, but it can result in a very, very large log file if you're not careful.

The Monitoring tab (see Figure 2.15) gives you some testing tools. When the check box labeled A Simple Query Against This DNS Server is checked, a test is performed that asks for a single record from the local DNS server. It's useful for verifying that the service is running and listening to queries, but not much else. When the check box labeled A Recursive Query To Other DNS Servers is checked, the test is more sophisticated—a recursive query checks whether forwarding is working okay. The Test Now button and the Perform Automatic Testing At The Following Interval check box allow you to run these tests now or later as you require.

FIGURE 2.14   The Event Logging tab of the server's Properties dialog box

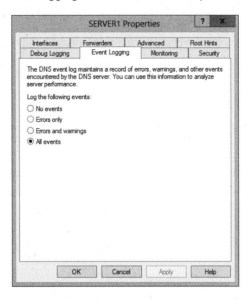

FIGURE 2.15   The Monitoring tab of the server's Properties dialog box

Another tab in the server's properties that allows you to monitor the activity of the DNS server is the Debug Logging tab. The Debug Logging tab allows you to monitor all outbound and inbound DNS traffic, packet content, packet type, and which transport protocol (TCP or UDP) that you want to monitor on the DNS server.

If the simple query fails, check that the local server contains the zone `1.0.0.127.in-addr.arpa`. If the recursive query fails, check that your root hints are correct and that your root servers are running.

In Exercise 2.5, you will enable logging, use the DNS MMC to test the DNS server, and view the contents of the DNS log.

EXERCISE 2.5

Simple DNS Testing

1. Open the DNS management snap-in by selecting Server Manager. Once in Server Manager, click DNS on the left-hand side. In the Servers window (center screen), right-click your server name and choose DNS Manager.

2. Right-click the DNS server name on the top left, and select Properties.

3. Switch to the Debug Logging tab, check all the debug logging options except Filter Packets By IP Address, and enter a full path and filename in the File Path And Name field. Click the Apply button.

4. Switch to the Monitoring tab, and check both A Simple Query Against This DNS Server and A Recursive Query To Other DNS Servers.

5. Click the Test Now button several times, and then click OK.

6. Press the Windows key on the keyboard (left side between the Ctrl and Alt keys), and then choose Computer. Navigate to the folder that you specified in step 3, and use WordPad or Notepad to view the contents of the log file.

Troubleshooting DNS

When troubleshooting DNS problems, ask yourself the following basic questions:

- What application is failing? What works? What doesn't work?

- Is the problem basic IP connectivity, or is it name resolution? If the problem is name resolution, does the failing application use NetBIOS names, DNS names, or hostnames?

- How are the things that do and don't work related?

- Have the things that don't work ever worked on this computer or network? If so, what has changed since they last worked?

Windows Server 2012 provides several useful tools, discussed in the following sections, that can help you answer these questions:

- Nslookup is used to perform DNS queries and to examine the contents of zone files on local and remote servers.

- DNSLint is a command-line utility used for troubleshooting many common DNS issues.

- Ipconfig allows you to perform the following tasks:

  - View DNS client settings.

  - Display and flush the resolver cache.

  - Force a dynamic update client to register its DNS records.

- The DNS log file monitors certain DNS server events and logs them for your edification.

Using *Nslookup*

Nslookup is a standard command-line tool provided in most DNS server implementations, including Windows Server 2012. Windows Server 2012 gives you the ability to launch nslookup from the DNS snap-in.

> **NOTE** When nslookup is launched from the DNS snap-in, a command prompt window opens automatically. You enter nslookup commands in this window.

Nslookup offers you the ability to perform query testing of DNS servers and to obtain detailed responses at the command prompt. This information can be useful for diagnosing and solving name resolution problems, for verifying that resource records are added or updated correctly in a zone, and for debugging other server-related problems. You can do a number of useful things with nslookup:

- Use it in noninteractive mode to look up a single piece of data.
- Enter interactive mode, and use the debug feature.
- Perform the following from within interactive mode:
    - Set options for your query.
    - Look up a name.
    - Look up records in a zone.
    - Perform zone transfers.
    - Exit nslookup.

When you are entering queries, it is generally a good idea to enter FQDNs so that you can control what name is submitted to the server. However, if you want to know which suffixes are added to unqualified names before they are submitted to the server, you can enter nslookup in debug mode and then enter an unqualified name.

Using *Nslookup* on the Command Line

To use nslookup in plain-old command-line mode, enter the following in the command prompt window:

nslookup DNS_name_or_IP_address server_IP_address

This command will look up a DNS name or address using a server at the IP address you specify.

Using *Nslookup* in Interactive Mode

Nslookup is a lot more useful in interactive mode because you can enter several commands in sequence. Entering **nslookup** by itself (without specifying a query or server) puts it in interactive mode, where it will stay until you type **exit** and press Enter. Before that point, you can look up lots of useful stuff. Following are some of the tasks you can perform with nslookup in interactive mode:

Setting Options with the set Command   While in interactive mode, you can use the set command to configure how the resolver will carry out queries. Table 2.5 shows a few of the options available with set.

TABLE 2.5 Command-line options available with the `set` command

Option	Purpose
set all	Shows all the options available.
set d2	Puts nslookup in debug mode so that you can examine the query and response packets between the resolver and the server.
set domain=*domain name*	Tells the resolver what domain name to append for unqualified queries.
set timeout=*timeout*	Tells the resolver how long to keep trying to contact the server. This option is useful for slow links where queries frequently time out and the wait time must be lengthened.
set type=*record type*	Tells the resolver which type of resource records to search for (for example, A, PTR, or SRV). If you want the resolver to query for all types of resource records, type **settype=all**.

Looking Up a Name   While in interactive mode, you can look up a name just by typing it: **stellacon.com**. In this example, `stellacon` is the owner name for the record for which you are searching, and `.com` is the server that you want to query.

You can use the wildcard character (*) in your query. For example, if you want to look for all resource records that have *k* as the first letter, just type **k*** as your query.

Looking Up a Record Type   If you want to query a particular type of record (for instance, an MX record), use the `set type` command. The command `set type=mx` tells nslookup that you're interested only in seeing MX records that meet your search criteria.

Listing the Contents of a Domain   To get a list of the contents of an entire domain, use the `ls` command. To find all the hosts in your domain, you'd type **set type=a** and then type **ls -t yourdomain.com**.

Troubleshooting Zone Transfers   You can simulate zone transfers by using the `ls` command with the -d switch. This can help you determine whether the server you are querying allows zone transfers to your computer. To do this, type the following: **ls -d domain__name**.

Nslookup Responses and Error Messages

A successful nslookup response looks like this:

```
Server: Name_of_DNS_server
Address: IP_address_of_DNS_server
Response_data
```

Nslookup might also return an error message. Some common messages are listed in Table 2.6:

TABLE 2.6   Common nslookup error messages

Error Message	Meaning

`DNS request timed out.`
`Timeout was x seconds.`
`*** Can't find server name for`
`address IP_Address: Timed out`
`*** Default servers are not available`
`Default Server: Unknown`
`Address: IP_address_of_DNS_server`
	The resolver did not locate a PTR resource record (containing the hostname) for the server IP address you specified. Nslookup can still query the DNS server, and the DNS server can still answer queries.

`*** Request to Server timed-out`	A request was not fulfilled in the allotted time. This might happen, for example, if the DNS service was not running on the DNS server that is authoritative for the name.

`*** Server can't find Name_or_IP_`
`address_queried_for: No response from`
`server`
	The server is not receiving requests on UDP (User Datagram Protocol) port 53.

`*** Server can't find Name_or_IP_`
`address_queried_for: Non-existent`
`domain`
	The DNS server was unable to find the name or IP address in the authoritative domain. The authoritative domain might be on the remote DNS server or on another DNS server that this DNS server is unable to reach.

`*** Server can't find Name_or_IP_` `address_queried_for: Server failed`	The DNS server is running, but it is not working properly. For example, it might include a corrupted packet, or the zone in which you are querying for a record might be paused. However, this message can also be returned if the client queries for a host in a domain for which the DNS server is not authoritative. You will also receive the error if the DNS server cannot contact its root servers, it is not connected to the Internet, or it has no root hints.

In Exercise 2.6, you'll get some hands-on practice with the nslookup tool.

EXERCISE 2.6

Using the nslookup Command

1. Press the Windows key on the keyboard (left side between the Ctrl and Alt keys), and then choose Computer. Navigate to the C:\Windows\System32 folder, and double-click

CMD.exe. (When you get to this file, you can right-click the file and choose Send To Desktop. The shortcut will then always be available on the desktop.)

2. Type **nslookup**, and press the Enter key. (For the rest of the exercise, use the Enter key to terminate each command.)

3. Try looking up a well-known address: Type **www.microsoft.com**.

4. Try looking up a nonexistent host: Type **www.example.ccccc**. Notice that your server indicates that it can't find the address and times out. This is normal behavior.

5. Type **Exit** at the prompt. Type **Exit** again to leave the command prompt.

Using *DNSLint*

Microsoft Windows Server 2012 DNS can use the DNSLint command-line utility to help diagnose some common DNS name-resolution issues and to help diagnose potential problems of incorrect delegation. You need to download DNSLint from the Microsoft Download Center.

DNSLint uses three main functions to verify DNS records and to generate a report in HTML:

dnslint /d   This function helps diagnose the reasons for "lame delegation" and other related DNS problems.

dnslint /ql   This function helps verify a user-defined set of DNS records on multiple DNS servers.

dnslint /ad   This function helps verify DNS records pertaining to Active Directory replication.

Here is the syntax for DNSLint:

```
dnslint /d domain_name | /ad [LDAP_IP_address] | /ql input_file
[/c [smtp,pop,imap]] [/no_open] [/r report_name]
[/t] [/test_tcp] [/s DNS_IP_address] [/v] [/y]
```

The following are some sample queries:

```
dnslint /d stellacon.com
dnslint /ad /s 192.168.36.201
dnslint /ql dns_server.txt
dnslint /ql autocreate
dnslint /v /d stellacon.com
dnslint /r newfile /d stellacon.com
dnslint /y /d stellacon.com
dnslint /no_open /d stellacon.com
```

Table 2.7 explains the command options.

TABLE 2.7 DNSLint command options

Command Option	Meaning
/d	Domain name that is being tested.
/ad	Resolves DNS records that are used for Active Directory forest replication.
/s	TCP/IP address of host.
/ql	Requests DNS query tests from a list. This switch sends DNS queries specified in an input file.
/v	Turns on verbose mode.
/r *filename*	Allows you to create a report file.
/y	Overwrites an existing report file without being prompted.
/no_open	Prevents a report from opening automatically.

Using *Ipconfig*

You can use the command-line tool ipconfig to view your DNS client settings, to view and reset cached information used locally for resolving DNS name queries, and to register the resource records for a dynamic update client. If you use the ipconfig command with no parameters, it displays DNS information for each adapter, including the domain name and DNS servers used for that adapter. Table 2.8 shows some command-line options available with ipconfig.

TABLE 2.8 Command-line options available for the ipconfig command

Command	What It Does
ipconfig /all	Displays additional information about DNS, including the FQDN and the DNS suffix search list.
ipconfig /flushdns	Flushes and resets the DNS resolver cache. For more information about this option, see the section "Configuring DNS" earlier in this chapter.
ipconfig /displaydns	Displays the contents of the DNS resolver cache. For more information about this option, see "Configuring DNS" earlier in this chapter.
ipconfig /registerdns	Refreshes all DHCP leases and registers any related DNS names. This option is available only on Windows 2000 and newer computers that run the DHCP client service.

NOTE   You should know and be comfortable with the `ipconfig` commands related to DNS for the exam.

Using *DNSCmd*

DNSCmd allows you to display and change the properties of DNS servers, zones, and resource records through the use of command-line commands. The DNSCmd utility allows you to modify, create, and delete resource records and/or zones manually, and it allows you to force replication between two DNS servers.

Table 2.9 lists some of the DNSCmd commands and their explanations.

TABLE 2.9   DNSCmd command-line options

Command	Explanation
dnscmd /clearcache	Clears the DNS server cache
dnscmd /config	Resets DNS server or zone configuration
dnscmd /createdirectorypartition	Creates a DNS application directory partition
dnscmd /deletedirectorypartition	Deletes a DNS application directory partition
dnscmd /enumrecords	Shows the resource records in a zone
dnscmd /exportsettings	Creates a text file of all server configuration information
dnscmd /info	Displays server information
dnscmd /recordadd	Adds a resource record to a zone
dnscmd /recorddelete	Deletes a resource record from a zone
dnscmd /zoneadd	Creates a new DNS zone
dnscmd /zonedelete	Deletes a DNS zone
dnscmd /zoneexport	Creates a text file of all resource records in the zone
dnscmd /zoneinfo	Displays zone information
dnscmd /zonerefresh	Forces replication of the master zone to the secondary zone

Using the DNS Log File

You can configure the DNS server to create a log file that records the following information:

- Queries
- Notification messages from other servers
- Dynamic updates
- Content of the question section for DNS query messages
- Content of the answer section for DNS query messages
- Number of queries this server sends
- Number of queries this server has received
- Number of DNS requests received over a UDP port
- Number of DNS requests received over a TCP port
- Number of full packets sent by the server
- Number of packets written through by the server and back to the zone

The DNS log appears in `systemroot\System32\dns\Dns.log`. Because the log is in RTF format, you must use WordPad or Word to view it.

Once the log file reaches the maximum size, Windows Server 2012 writes over the beginning of the file. You can change the maximum size of the log. If you increase the size value, data persists for a longer time period, but the log file consumes more disk space. If you decrease the value, the log file uses less disk space, but the data persists for a shorter time period.

Do not leave DNS logging turned on during normal operation because it sucks up both processing and hard disk resources. Enable it only when diagnosing and solving DNS problems.

Troubleshooting the .*(root)* Zone

The *DNS root zone* is the top-level DNS zone in the DNS hierarchy. Windows Server 2012–based DNS servers will build a `.(root)` zone when a connection to the Internet can't be found.

Because of this, the `.(root)` zone may prevent access to the Internet. The DNS forwarding option and DNS root hints will not be configurable. If you want your DNS to work as a DNS forwarder or you want to use root hints, you must remove the `.(root)` zone.

Issues with Non-Microsoft DNS Servers

Another troubleshooting problem that you may run into is working with both Microsoft DNS servers and non-Microsoft DNS servers. One of the most common non-Microsoft DNS servers is the Unix-based BIND DNS server.

If you need to complete a zone transfer from Microsoft DNS to a BIND DNS server, you need to enable BIND Secondaries on the Microsoft DNS server (see Figure 2.16).

FIGURE 2.16   Enabling BIND Secondaries

If you need to enable Bind Secondaries, complete the following steps:

1. Open DNS management.
2. Right-click the server name, and choose Properties.
3. Click the Advanced tab.
4. Check the Enable BIND Secondaries box.
5. Click OK.

Summary

DNS was designed to be a robust, scalable, and high-performance system for resolving friendly names to TCP/IP host addresses. The chapter presented an overview of the basics of DNS and how DNS names are generated. We then looked at the many new features available in the Microsoft Windows Server 2012 version of DNS, and we focused on how to install, configure, and manage the necessary services. Microsoft's DNS is based on a widely accepted set of industry standards. Because of this, Microsoft's DNS can work with both Windows- and non-Windows-based networks.

Exam Essentials

Understand the purpose of DNS.   DNS is a standard set of protocols that defines a mechanism for querying and updating address information in the database, a mechanism for replicating the information in the database among servers, and a schema of the database.

Understand the different parts of the DNS database.   The SOA record defines the general parameters for the DNS zone, including who is the authoritative server. NS records list the name servers for a domain; they allow other name servers to look up names in your domain. A host record (also called an address record or an A record) statically associates a host's name with its IP addresses. Pointer records (PTRs) map an IP address to a hostname, making it possible to do reverse lookups. Alias records allow you to use more than one name to point to a single host. The MX record tells you which servers can accept mail bound for a domain. SRV records tie together the location of a service (like a domain controller) with information about how to contact the service.

Know how DNS resolves names.   With iterative queries, a client asks the DNS server for an answer, and the client, or resolver, returns the best kind of answer it has. In a recursive query, the client sends a query to one name server, asking it to respond either with the requested answer or with an error. The error states either that the server can't come up with the right answer or that the domain name doesn't exist. With inverse queries, instead of supplying a name and then asking for an IP address, the client first provides the IP address and then asks for the name.

Understand the differences among DNS servers, clients, and resolvers.   Any computer providing domain name services is a DNS server. A DNS client is any machine issuing queries to a DNS server. A resolver handles the process of mapping a symbolic name to an actual network address.

Know how to install and configure DNS.   DNS can be installed before, during, or after installing the Active Directory service. When you install the DNS server, the DNS snap-in is installed too. Configuring a DNS server ranges from very easy to very difficult, depending on what you're trying to make it do. In the simplest configuration, for a caching-only server, you don't have to do anything except to make sure the server's root hints are set correctly. You can also configure a root server, a normal forward lookup server, and a reverse lookup server.

Know how to create new forward and reverse lookup zones.   You can use the New Zone Wizard to create a new forward or reverse lookup zone. The process is basically the same for both types, but the specific steps and wizard pages differ somewhat. The wizard walks you through the steps, such as specifying a name for the zone (in the case of forward lookup zones) or the network ID portion of the network that the zone covers (in the case of reverse lookup zones).

Know how to configure zones for dynamic updates.   The DNS service allows dynamic updates to be enabled or disabled on a per-zone basis at each server. This is easily done in the DNS snap-in.

Know how to delegate zones for DNS.   DNS provides the ability to divide the namespace into one or more zones; these can then be stored, distributed, and replicated to other DNS servers. When delegating zones within your namespace, be aware that for each new zone you create, you need delegation records in other zones that point to the authoritative DNS servers for the new zone.

Understand the tools that are available for monitoring and troubleshooting DNS.   You can use the DNS snap-in to do some basic server testing and monitoring. More important, you use the snap-in to monitor and set logging options. Windows Server 2012 automatically logs DNS events in the event log under a distinct DNS server heading. Nslookup offers the ability to perform query testing of DNS servers and to obtain detailed responses at the command prompt. You can use the command-line tool ipconfig to view your DNS client settings, to view and reset cached information used locally for resolving DNS name queries, and to register the resource records for a dynamic update client. Finally, you can configure the DNS server to create a log file that records queries, notification messages, dynamic updates, and various other DNS information.

Review Questions

 Microsoft continually updates its question pool. We occasionally will add new and updated questions online. Please check the Sybex website at www.sybex.com/go/mcsawin2012.

1. You are the network administrator for the ABC Company. Your network consists of two DNS servers named *DNS1* and *DNS2*. The users who are configured to use DNS2 complain because they are unable to connect to Internet websites. The following table shows the configuration of both servers.

    The users connected to DNS2 need to be able to access the Internet. What needs to be done?

DNS1	DNS2
_msdcs.abc.comabc.com	.(root)_msdcs.abc.comabc.com

    A. Build a new Active Directory Integrated zone on DNS2.

    B. Delete the .(root) zone from DNS2, and configure conditional forwarding on DNS2.

    C. Delete the current cache.dns file.

    D. Update your cache.dns file and root hints.

2. You are the network administrator for a large company that has one main site and one branch office. Your company has a single Active Directory forest, ABC.com. You have a single domain controller (ServerA) in the main site that has the DNS role installed. ServerA is configured as a primary DNS zone. You have decided to place a domain controller (ServerB) in the remote site and implement the DNS role on that server. You want to configure DNS so that, if the WAN link fails, users in both sites can still update records and resolve any DNS queries. How should you configure the DNS servers?

    A. Configure ServerB as a secondary DNS server. Set replication to occur every 5 minutes.

    B. Configure ServerB as a stub zone.

    C. Configure ServerB as an Active Directory Integrated zone, and convert ServerA to an Active Directory Integrated zone.

    D. Convert ServerA to an Active Directory Integrated zone, and configure ServerB as a secondary zone.

3. You are the network administrator for a midsize computer company. You have a single Active Directory forest, and your DNS servers are configured as Active Directory Integrated zones. When you look at the DNS records in Active Directory, you notice that there are many records for computers that do not exist on your domain. You want to make sure only domain computers register with your DNS servers. What should you do to resolve this issue?

    A. Set dynamic updates to None.

    B. Set dynamic updates to Nonsecure And Secure.

    C. Set dynamic updates to Domain Users Only.

    D. Set dynamic updates to Secure Only.

4. Your company consists of a single Active Directory forest. You have a Windows Server 2012 domain controller that also has the DNS role installed. You also have a Unix-based DNS server at the same location. You need to configure your Windows DNS server to allow zone transfers to the Unix-based DNS server. What should you do?

    A. Enable BIND secondaries.

    B. Configure the Unix machine as a stub zone.

    C. Convert the DNS server to Active Directory Integrated.

    D. Configure the Microsoft DNS server to forward all requests to the Unix DNS server.

5. You are the network administrator for Stellacon Corporation. Stellacon has two trees in its Active Directory forest, stellacon.com and abc.com. Company policy does not allow DNS zone transfers between the two trees. You need to make sure that when anyone in abc.com tries to access the stellacon.com domain, all names are resolved from the stellacon.com DNS server. What should you do?

    A. Create a new secondary zone in abc.com for stellacon.com.

    B. Configure conditional forwarding on the abc.com DNS server for stellacon.com.

    C. Create a new secondary zone in stellacon.com for abc.com.

    D. Configure conditional forwarding on the stellacon.com DNS server for abc.com.

6. You are the network administrator for your organization. A new company policy states that all inbound DNS queries need to be recorded. What can you do to verify that the IT department is compliant with this new policy?

    A. Enable Server Auditing - Object Access.

    B. Enable DNS debug logging.

    C. Enable server database query logging.

    D. Enable DNS Auditing - Object Access.

7. You are the network administrator for a small company with two DNS servers: DNS1 and DNS2. Both DNS servers reside on domain controllers. DNS1 is set up as a standard primary zone, and DNS2 is set up as a secondary zone. A new security policy was written stating that all DNS zone transfers must be encrypted. How can you implement the new security policy?

   A. Enable the Secure Only setting on DNS1.

   B. Enable the Secure Only setting on DNS2.

   C. Configure Secure Only on the Zone Transfers tab for both servers.

   D. Delete the secondary zone on DNS2. Convert both DNS servers to use Active Directory Integrated zones.

8. You are responsible for DNS in your organization. You look at the DNS database and see a large number of older records on the server. These records are no longer valid. What should you do?

   A. In the zone properties, enable Zone Aging and Scavenging.

   B. In the server properties, enable Zone Aging and Scavenging.

   C. Manually delete all the old records.

   D. Set Dynamic Updates to None.

9. Your IT team has been informed by the compliance team that they need copies of the DNS Active Directory Integrated zones for security reasons. You need to give the Compliance department a copy of the DNS zone. How should you accomplish this goal?

   A. Run dnscmd /zonecopy.

   B. Run dnscmd /zoneinfo.

   C. Run dnscmd /zoneexport.

   D. Run dnscmd /zonefile.

10. You are the network administrator for a Windows Server 2012 network. You have multiple remote locations connected to your main office by slow satellite links. You want to install DNS into these offices so that clients can locate authoritative DNS servers in the main location. What type of DNS servers should be installed in the remote locations?

   A. Primary DNS zones

   B. Secondary DNS zones

   C. Active Directory Integrated zones

   D. Stub zones

Chapter 3

Active Directory Planning and Installation

THE FOLLOWING 70-410 EXAM OBJECTIVES ARE COVERED IN THIS CHAPTER:

✓ **Install domain controllers**

- This objective may include, but is not limited to: Add or remove a domain controller from a domain; upgrade a domain controller; install Active Directory Domain Services (ADDS) on a Server Core installation; install a domain controller from Install from Media (IFM); resolve DNS SRV record registration issues; configure a global catalog server.

THE FOLLOWING 70-412 EXAM OBJECTIVES ARE COVERED IN THIS CHAPTER:

✓ **Configure a forest or a domain**

- This objective may include, but is not limited to: Implement multi-domain and multi-forest Active Directory environments including interoperability with previous versions of Active Directory; upgrade existing domains and forests including environment preparation and functional levels.

In previous chapters, you learned about factors that you need to take into account when planning for Active Directory. Such factors include your company's physical and logical structure and the need for centralized or decentralized administration. The time you spend learning these concepts is very important because the success of your Active Directory implementation depends on them.

Now that you are familiar with Domain Name System (DNS), you need to verify that the computer you upgrade to a domain controller (DC) meets the basic file system and network connectivity requirements so that Active Directory runs smoothly and efficiently in your organization.

Next, you'll explore the concept of *domain functional levels*, which essentially determine what sorts of domain controllers you can use in your environment. For instance, in the Windows Server 2003 domain functional level, you can include Server 2012, Server 2008 R2, Server 2008, and Server 2003 domain controllers, but the functionality of the domain is severely limited.

Once you understand how to plan properly for your domain environment, you will learn how to install Active Directory, which you will accomplish by promoting a Windows Server 2012 computer to a domain controller. I will also discuss a feature in Windows Server 2012 called a *read-only domain controller (RODC)*.

After you become familiar with the initial Active Directory installation, you will learn how to install and configure Application Directory partitions. These partitions provide replicable data repositories using the Active Directory paradigm, but they don't actually store any security principals, such as users or groups. As the name implies, you use Application Directory partitions primarily to store data generated by applications that need to be replicated throughout your network environments independent of the rest of Active Directory.

The final section of this chapter deals with integrating DNS with Active Directory. You learned about DNS in Chapter 2, "Domain Name System," but in this chapter I will review how DNS implements with Active Directory.

For these exercises, I assume that you are creating a Windows Server 2012 machine in a test environment and not on a live network. If this Windows Server 2012 machine is being added into a Windows Server 2008 R2 domain, you will need to prep the domain (explained in the section "Adprep" later in this chapter).

Verifying the File system

When you're planning your Active Directory deployment, the file system that the operating system uses is an important concern for two reasons. First, the file system can provide the ultimate level of security for all of the information stored on the server itself. Second, it is responsible for managing and tracking all of this data. The Windows Server 2012 platform supports two file systems:

- Windows NT File System (NTFS)
- Resilient File System (ReFS)

Although ReFS is new to Windows Server 2012, NTFS has been around for many years and NTFS in Windows Server 2012 has been improved for better performance.

If you have been working with servers for many years, you may have noticed a few changes to the server file system choices. For example, in Windows Server 2003, you could choose between FAT, FAT32, and NTFS. In Windows Server 2008 R2, you could choose between FAT32 and NTFS. In Windows Server 2012, you will notice that all versions of FAT have been removed (see Figure 3.1).

FIGURE 3.1   Format options on Windows 2012 Server

Resilient File System (ReFS)

Windows Server 2012 now includes a brand-new file system called *Resilient File System (ReFS)*. ReFS was created to help Windows Server 2012 maximize the availability of data and online operation. ReFS allows the Windows Server 2012 system to continue to function despite some errors that would normally cause data to be lost or for the system to be down. ReFS uses Data integrity to protect your data from errors and also to make sure that all of your important data is online when that data is needed.

One of the issues that IT members have had to face over the years is the problem of rapidly growing data sizes. As we continue to rely more and more on computers, our data continues to get larger and larger. This is where ReFS can help out an IT department. ReFS was designed specifically with the issues of scalability and performance in mind, and this resulted in some of the following ReFS features:

Availability   If your hard disk becomes corrupt, ReFS has the ability to implement a salvage strategy that removes the data that has become corrupted. This feature allows the healthy data to continue to be available while unhealthy data is removed. All of this can be done without taking the hard disk offline.

Scalability   One of the main advantages of ReFS is the ability to support volume sizes up to 2^{78} bytes using 16 KB cluster sizes, while Windows stack addressing allows 2^{64} bytes. ReFS also supports file sizes of $2^{64}-1$ bytes, 2^{64} files in a directory, and the same number of directories in a volume.

Robust Disk Updating   ReFS uses a disk updating system referred to as an *allocate-on-write transactional model* (also known as *copy on write*). This model helps to avoid many hard disk issues while data is written to the disk because ReFS updates data using disk writes to multiple locations in an atomic manner instead of updating data in place.

Data Integrity   ReFS uses a check-summed system to verify that all data that is being written and stored is accurate and reliable. ReFS always uses allocate-on-write for updates to the data, and it uses checksums to detect disk corruption.

Application Compatibility   ReFS allows for most NTFS features and also supports the Win32 API. Because of this, ReFS is compatible with most Windows applications.

NTFS

Let's start with some of the features of NTFS. There are many benefits to using NTFS, including support for the following:

Disk Quotas   To restrict the amount of disk space used by users on the network, system administrators can establish *disk quotas*. By default, Windows Server 2012 supports disk quota restrictions at the volume level. That is, you can restrict the amount of storage space a specific user uses on a single disk volume. Third-party solutions that allow more granular quota settings are also available.

File System Encryption   One of the fundamental problems with network operating systems (NOSs) is that system administrators are often given full permission to view all files and data stored on hard disks, which can be a security and privacy concern. In some cases, this is necessary. For example, to perform backup, recovery, and disk management functions, at least one user must have all permissions. Windows Server 2012 and NTFS address these issues by allowing for *file system encryption*. Encryption essentially scrambles all of the data stored within files before they are written to the disk. When an authorized user requests the files, they are transparently decrypted and provided. By using encryption, you can prevent the data from being used in case it is stolen or intercepted by an unauthorized user—even a system administrator.

Dynamic Volumes   Protecting against disk failures is an important concern for production servers. Although earlier versions of Windows NT supported various levels of Redundant Array of Independent Disks (RAID) technology, software-based solutions had some shortcomings. Perhaps the most significant was that administrators needed to perform server reboots to change RAID configurations. Also, you could not make some configuration changes without completely reinstalling the operating system. With Windows Server 2012's support for *dynamic volumes*, system administrators can change RAID and other disk configuration settings without needing to reboot or reinstall the server. The result is greater data protection, increased scalability, and increased uptime. Dynamic volumes are also included with ReFS.

Mounted Drives   By using *mounted drives*, system administrators can map a local disk drive to an NTFS directory name. This helps them organize disk space on servers and increase manageability. By using mounted drives, you can mount the C:\Users directory to an actual physical disk. If that disk becomes full, you can copy all of the files to another, larger drive without changing the directory pathname or reconfiguring applications.

Remote Storage   System administrators often notice that as soon as they add more space, they must plan the next upgrade. One way to recover disk space is to move infrequently used files to tape. However, backing up and restoring these files can be quite difficult and time consuming. System administrators can use the *remote storage* features supported by NTFS to off-load seldom-used data automatically to tape or other devices. The files, however, remain available to users. If a user requests an archived file, Windows Server 2012 can automatically restore the file from a remote storage device and make it available. Using remote storage like this frees up system administrators' time and allows them to focus on tasks other than micromanaging disk space.

Self-Healing NTFS   In previous versions of the Windows Server operating system, if you had to fix a corrupted NTFS volume, you used a tool called Chkdsk.exe. The disadvantage of this tool is that the Windows Server's availability was disrupted. If this server was your domain controller, that could stop domain logon authentication.

To help protect the Windows Server 2012 NTFS file system, Microsoft now uses a feature called self-healing NTFS. *Self-healing* NTFS attempts to fix corrupted NTFS file systems without taking them offline. Self-healing NTFS allows an NTFS file system to be corrected without running the Chkdsk.exe utility. New features added to the NTFS kernel code allow disk inconsistencies to be corrected without system downtime.

Security   NTFS allows you to configure not only folder-level security but also file-level security. NTFS security is one of the biggest reasons most companies use NTFS. ReFS also allows folder- and file-level security.

> NTFS/ReFS security and shared permissions will be discussed in greater detail in Chapter 13, "Understanding Security."

Setting Up the NTFS Partition

Although the features mentioned in the previous section likely compel most system administrators to use NTFS, additional reasons make using it mandatory. The most important reason is that the Active Directory data store must reside on an NTFS partition. Therefore, before you begin installing Active Directory, make sure you have at least one NTFS partition available. Also, be sure you have a reasonable amount of disk space available (at least 4 GB). Because the size of the Active Directory data store will grow as you add objects to it, also be sure you have adequate space for the future.

Exercise 3.1 shows you how to use the administrative tools to view and modify disk configuration.

> Before you make any disk configuration changes, be sure that you completely understand their potential effects; then perform the test in a lab environment and make sure you have good, verifiable backups handy. Changing partition sizes and adding and removing partitions can result in a total loss of all information on one or more partitions.

If you want to convert an existing partition from FAT or FAT32 to NTFS, you need to use the CONVERT command-line utility. For example, the following command converts the C: partition from FAT to NTFS:

```
CONVERT c: /fs:ntfs
```

EXERCISE 3.1

Viewing Disk Configuration

1. Press the Windows key on the keyboard (left side between the Ctrl and Alt keys), and then choose Administrative Tools.

2. Double-click Computer Management.

3. Under Storage, click Disk Management.

   The Disk Management program shows you the logical and physical disks that are currently configured on your system. Note that information about the size of each partition is also displayed (in the Capacity column).

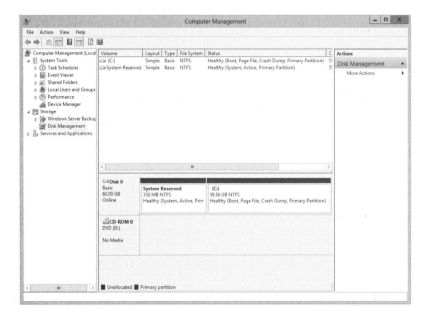

EXERCISE 3.1 *(continued)*

4. Use the View menu to choose various depictions of the physical and logical drives in your system.

5. To see the available options for modifying partition settings, right-click any of the disks or partitions. This step is optional.

6. Close Computer Management.

Verifying Network Connectivity

Although a Windows Server 2012 computer can be used by itself without connecting to a network, you will not harness much of the potential of the operating system without network connectivity. Because the fundamental purpose of a network operating system is to provide resources to users, you must verify network connectivity.

Basic Connectivity Tests

Before you begin to install Active Directory, you should perform several checks of your current configuration to ensure that the server is configured properly on the network. You should test the following:

Network Adapter At least one network adapter should be installed and properly configured on your server. A quick way to verify that a network adapter is properly installed is to use the Computer Management administrative tool. Under Device Manager, Network Adapters branch, you should have at least one network adapter listed. If you do not, use the Add Hardware icon in Control Panel to configure hardware.

TCP/IP Make sure that TCP/IP is installed, configured, and enabled on any necessary network adapters. The server should also be given a valid IP address and subnet mask. Optionally, you may need to configure a default gateway, DNS servers, WINS servers, and other network settings. If you are using DHCP, be sure that the assigned information is correct. It is always a good idea to use a static IP address for servers because IP address changes can cause network connectivity problems if they are not handled properly.

You must understand TCP/IP to use Windows Server 2012 and Active Directory. TCP/IP will be covered in greater detail in Chapter 9 "Understanding TCP/IP."

Internet Access   If the server should have access to the Internet, verify that it is able to connect to external web servers and other machines outside the local area network (LAN). If the server is unable to connect, you might have a problem with the TCP/IP configuration.

LAN Access   The server should be able to view other servers and workstations on the network. You can quickly verify this type of connectivity by clicking Start ➤ Network. If other machines are not visible, make sure the network and TCP/IP configuration are correct for your environment.

Client Access   Network client computers should be able to connect to your server and view any shared resources. A simple way to test connectivity is to create a share and test whether other machines are able to see files and folders within it. If clients cannot access the machine, ensure that both the client and server are configured properly.

Wide Area Network Access   If you're working in a distributed environment, you should ensure that you have access to any remote sites or users that will need to connect to this machine. Usually, this is a simple test that can be performed by a network administrator.

Tools and Techniques for Testing Network Configuration

In some cases, verifying network access can be quite simple. You might have some internal and external network resources with which to test. In other cases, it might be more complicated. You can use several tools and techniques to verify that your network configuration is correct:

Using the `Ipconfig` Utility   By typing `ipconfig/all` at the command prompt, you can view information about the TCP/IP settings of a computer. Figure 3.2 shows the types of information you'll receive.

FIGURE 3.2   Viewing TCP/IP information with the `ipconfig` utility

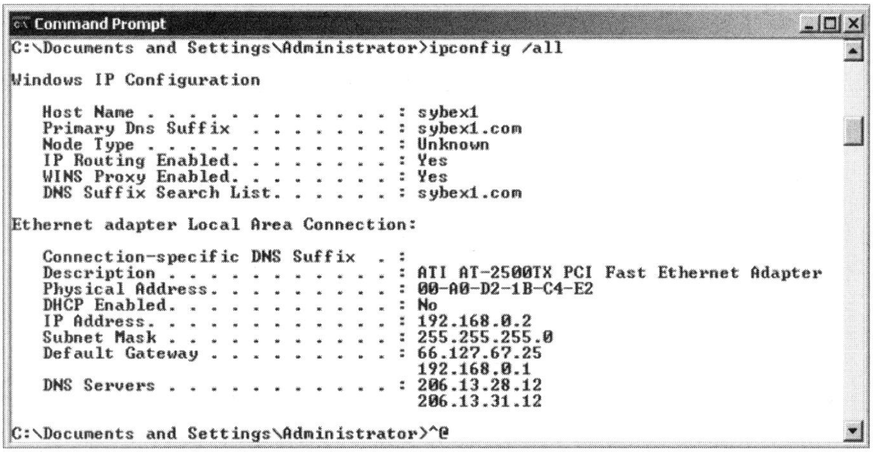

Using the Ping Command The ping command was designed to test connectivity to other computers. You can use the command simply by typing ping and then an IP address or hostname at the command line. The following are some steps for testing connectivity using the ping command.

Ping Other Computers on the Same Subnet You should start by pinging a known active IP address on the network to check for a response. If you receive one, then you have connectivity to the network.

Next check to see if you can ping another machine using its hostname. If this works, then local name resolution works properly.

Ping Computers on Different Subnets To ensure that routing is set up properly, you should attempt to ping computers that are on other subnets (if any exist) on your network. If this test fails, try pinging the default gateway. Any errors may indicate a problem in the network configuration or a problem with a router.

When You Don't Receive a Response

Some firewalls, routers, or servers on your network or on the Internet might prevent you from receiving a successful response from a ping command. This is usually for security reasons (malicious users might attempt to disrupt network traffic using excessive pings as well as redirects and smurf attacks). If you do not receive a response, do not assume that the service is not available. Instead, try to verify connectivity in other ways. For example, you can use the TRACERT command to demonstrate connectivity beyond your subnet, even if other routers ignore Internet Control Message Protocol (ICMP) responses. Because the display of a second router implies connectivity, the path to an ultimate destination shows success even if it does not display the actual names and addresses.

Browsing the Network To ensure that you have access to other computers on the network, be sure that they can be viewed by clicking Libraries Folder ➢ Network. This verifies that your name resolution parameters are set up correctly and that other computers are accessible. Also, try connecting to resources (such as file shares or printers) on other machines.

 By default, Network Discovery is turned off. To browse the network, you must first enable Network Discovery from Control Panel.

Browsing the Internet   You can quickly verify whether your server has access to the Internet by visiting a known website, such as www.microsoft.com. Success ensures that you have access outside of your network. If you do not have access to the Web, you might need to verify your proxy server settings (if applicable) and your DNS server settings.

By performing these simple tests, you can ensure that you have a properly configured network connection and that other network resources are available.

Understanding Domain and Forest Functionality

Windows Server 2012 Active Directory uses a concept called *domain and forest functionality*. The functional level that you choose during the Active Directory installation determines which features your domain can use.

Windows Server 2008, Windows Server 2008 R2, and Windows Server 2012 include additional forest functionality compared to Windows 2003. Forest functionality applies to all of the domains in a forest.

About the Domain Functional Level

Windows Server 2012 will support the following domain functional levels:

- Windows 2003
- Windows Server 2008
- Windows Server 2008 R2
- Windows Server 2012

Which function level you use depends on the domain controllers you have installed on your network. This is an important fact to remember. You can use Windows 2003 Server, Windows Server 2008, and Windows 2008 R2 member servers in the Windows Server 2012 function level as long as all domain controllers are running Windows Server 2012.

When you are deciding which function level you will use in your organization, you must choose the function level of your lowest domain controller. For example, if you have a Windows Server 2003 domain controller, your function levels must be Windows 2003. If you choose a higher level, the Windows Server 2003 domain controller will not function. Be careful; once a forest function level is upgraded, it cannot be downgraded.

Table 3.1 shows the features available in Windows 2003, Windows Server 2008, Windows Server 2008 R2, and Windows Server 2012 domain function levels.

TABLE 3.1 Comparing domain functional levels

Domain Functional Feature	Windows Server 2003	Windows Server 2008	Windows Server 2008 R2	Windows Server 2012
Authentication assurance	Disabled	Disabled	Enabled	Enabled
Fine-grained password policies	Disabled	Enabled	Enabled	Enabled
Last interactive logon information	Disabled	Enabled	Enabled	Enabled
Advanced Encryption Services (AES 128 and 256) support for the Kerberos protocol	Disabled	Enabled	Enabled	Enabled
Distributed File System replication support for Sysvol	Disabled	Enabled	Enabled	Enabled
Read-only domain controller (RODC)	Enabled	Enabled	Enabled	Enabled
Ability to redirect the Users and Computers containers	Enabled	Enabled	Enabled	Enabled
Ability to rename domain controllers	Enabled	Enabled	Enabled	Enabled
Logon time stamp updates	Enabled	Enabled	Enabled	Enabled
Kerberos KDC key version numbers	Enabled	Enabled	Enabled	Enabled
Passwords for InetOrgPerson objects	Enabled	Enabled	Enabled	Enabled
Converts NT groups to domain local and global groups	Enabled	Enabled	Enabled	Enabled
SID history	Enabled	Enabled	Enabled	Enabled
Group nesting	Enabled	Enabled	Enabled	Enabled
Universal groups	Enabled	Enabled	Enabled	Enabled

About Forest Functionality

Windows Server 2012 forest functionality applies to all of the domains in a forest. All domains have to be upgraded to Windows Server 2012 before the forest can be upgraded to Windows Server 2012.

There are four levels of forest functionality:

- Windows Server 2003
- Windows Server 2008
- Windows Server 2008 R2
- Windows Server 2012

Windows Server 2003, Windows Server 2008, Windows Server 2008 R2, and Windows Server 2012 have many of the same forest features. Some of these features are described in the following list:

Global Catalog Replication Enhancements   When an administrator adds a new attribute to the Global Catalog, only those changes are replicated to other Global Catalogs in the forest. This can significantly reduce the amount of network traffic generated by replication.

Defunct Schema Classes and Attributes   You can never permanently remove classes and attributes from the Active Directory schema. However, you can mark them as defunct so that they cannot be used. With Windows Server 2003, Windows Server 2008, Windows Server 2008 R2, and Windows Server 2012 forest functionality, you can redefine the defunct schema attribute so that it occupies a new role in the schema.

Forest Trusts   Previously, system administrators had no easy way of granting permission on resources in different forests. Windows Server 2003, Windows Server 2008, Windows Server 2008 R2, and Windows Server 2012 resolve some of these difficulties by allowing trust relationships between separate Active Directory forests. Forest trusts act much like domain trusts, except that they extend to every domain in two forests. Note that all forest trusts are intransitive.

Linked Value Replication   Windows Server 2003, Windows Server 2008, Windows Server 2008 R2, and Windows Server 2012 use a concept called *linked value replication*. With linked value replication, only the user record that has been changed is replicated (not the entire group). This can significantly reduce network traffic associated with replication.

Renaming Domains   Although the Active Directory domain structure was originally designed to be flexible, there were several limitations. Because of mergers, acquisitions, corporate reorganizations, and other business changes, you may need to rename domains. In Windows Server 2003, Windows Server 2008, Windows Server 2008 R2, and Windows Server 2012, you can change the DNS and NetBIOS names for any domain. Note that this operation is not as simple as just issuing a rename command. Instead, there's a specific process that you must follow to make sure the operation is successful. Fortunately, when you properly follow the procedure, Microsoft supports domain renaming even though not all applications support it.

Other Features   Windows Server 2003, Windows Server 2008, Windows Server 2008 R2, and Windows Server 2012 also support the following features:

- Improved replication algorithms and dynamic auxiliary classes are designed to increase performance, scalability, and reliability.

- *Active Directory Federation Services (ADFS)*, also known as *Trustbridge*), handles federated identity management. *Federated identity management* is a standards-based information technology process that enables distributed identification, authentication, and authorization across organizational and platform boundaries. The ADFS solution in Windows Server 2003 (Release 2), Windows Server 2008, Windows Server 2008 R2, and Windows Server 2012 helps administrators address these challenges by enabling organizations to share a user's identity information securely.

- *Active Directory Application Mode (ADAM)* was developed by Microsoft as part of Windows Server 2012 Active Directory for organizations that require flexible support for directory-enabled applications. ADAM, which uses the Lightweight Directory Access Protocol (LDAP), is a directory service that adds flexibility and helps organizations avoid increased infrastructure costs.

Many of the concepts related to domain and forest functional features are covered in greater detail later in this book.

Planning the Domain Structure

Once you have verified the technical configuration of your server for Active Directory, it's time to verify the Active Directory configuration for your organization. Since the content of this chapter focuses on installing the first domain in your environment, you really need to know only the following information prior to beginning setup:

- The DNS name of the domain

- The computer name or the NetBIOS name of the server (which will be used by previous versions of Windows to access server resources)

- In which domain function level the domain will operate

- Whether other DNS servers are available on the network

- What type of and how many DNS servers are available on the network

However, if you will be installing additional domain controllers in your environment or will be attaching to an existing Active Directory structure, you should also have the following information:

- If this domain controller will join an existing domain, you should know the name of that domain. You will also either require a password for a member of the Enterprise Administrators group for that domain or have someone with those permissions create a domain account before promotion.

- You should know whether the new domain will join an existing tree and, if so, the name of the tree it will join.

- You should know the name of a forest to which this domain will connect (if applicable).

Installing Active Directory

Installing Active Directory is an easy and straightforward process as long as you planned adequately and made the necessary decisions beforehand. In the following sections, you'll look at the required steps to install the first domain controller in a given environment.

Adprep

When you are adding a new user to Windows Server 2008 R2, you fill in fields in Active Directory like First Name, Last Name, and so on. These fields are called *attributes*. The problem is that when you go to install Windows Server 2012, its version of Active Directory has some newer attributes. Thus you need to set your current version of Active Directory up so that it can accept the installation of Windows Server 2012 Active Directory. This is why we use ADPrep.exe. Adprep is required to run in order to add the first Windows Server 2012 domain controller to an existing domain or forest.

You would need to run Adprep /forestprep to add the first Windows Server 2012 domain controller to an existing forest. Adprep /forestprep must be run by an administrator who is a member of the Enterprise Admins group, the Schema Admins group, and the Domain Admins group of the domain that hosts the schema master.

You would need to run Adprep /domainprep to add the first Windows Server 2012 domain controller to an existing domain. Again, to achieve this command, you must be a member of the Domain Admins group of the domain where you are installing the Windows Server 2012 domain controller.

Adprep /rodcprep must be run to add the first Windows Server 2012 RODC to an existing forest. The administrator who runs this command must be a member of the Enterprise Admins group.

One feature that is new to the Windows Server 2012 Active Directory installation process is that, if needed, Adprep will automatically be executed during the normal Active Directory Domain Services installation.

The Installation Process

With early versions of the Windows NT operating system, you had to determine during installation the role of your server as it related to the domain controller or member server. Choices included making the machine a primary domain controller (PDC), a backup domain controller (BDC), or a member server. This was an extremely important decision because, even though you could promote a BDC to a PDC, you had to reinstall the operating system completely to make any changes to the server's role between a domain controller and a member server.

Instead of forcing you to choose during setup whether the machine will participate as a domain controller, Windows Server 2012 allows you to promote servers after you install Active Directory. Therefore, at the end of the setup process, all Windows Server 2012 computers are configured as either member servers (if they are joined to a domain) or stand-alone servers (if they are part of a workgroup). The process of converting a server to a domain controller is known as *promotion*. Through the use of a simple and intuitive wizard, system administrators can quickly configure servers to be domain controllers after installation.

The first step in installing Active Directory is promoting a Windows Server 2012 computer to a domain controller. The first domain controller in an environment serves as the starting point for the forest, trees, domains, and the operations master roles.

Exercise 3.2 shows the steps you need to follow to promote an existing Windows Server 2012 to a domain controller. To complete the steps in this exercise, you must have already installed and configured a Windows Server 2012 computer. You also need a DNS server that supports SRV records. If you do not have a DNS server available, the Active Directory Installation Wizard automatically configures one for you.

EXERCISE 3.2

Promoting a Domain Controller

1. Install the Active Directory Domain Services by clicking the Add Roles And Features link in Server Manager.

2. At the Before You Begin screen, click Next.

3. The Select installation Type screen will be next. Make sure the Role-Based radio button is selected and click Next.

4. At the Select Destination Server screen, choose the local machine. Click Next.

5. At the Select Server Roles screen, click the check box for Active Directory Domain Services.

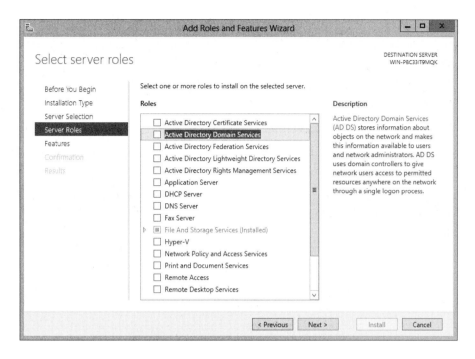

6. After you check the Active Directory Domain Services box, a pop-up menu will appear asking you to install additional features. Click the Add Features button.

EXERCISE 3.2 *(continued)*

7. Click Next.

8. At the Select Features screen, accept the defaults and click Next.

9. Click Next at the information screen.

10. Click the Install button at the Confirmation Installation screen.

11. The Installation Progress screen will show you how the installation is progressing.

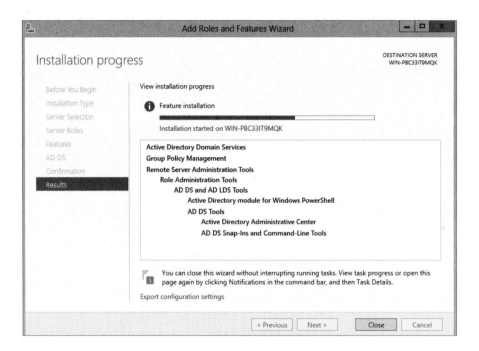

12. After the installation is complete, click the Close button.

13. Close Server Manager, and reboot the server.

14. After the machine restarts, log in as the Administrator. Server Manager will automatically start.

15. On the left side window, click the AD DS link.

16. Click the More link next to Configuration Required for Active Directory Domain Services.

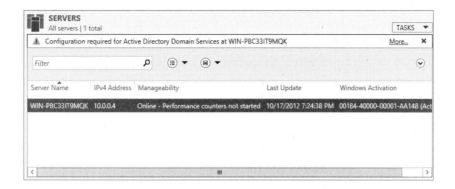

17. Under the Post-Deployment Configuration section, click the Promote This Server To A Domain Controller link.

18. At this point, you will configure this domain controller. You are going to install a new domain controller on a new domain in a new forest. At the Deployment Configuration screen, choose the Add A New Forest radio button. You then need to add a root domain name. In this exercise, I will use Sybex.com. Click Next.

EXERCISE 3.2 *(continued)*

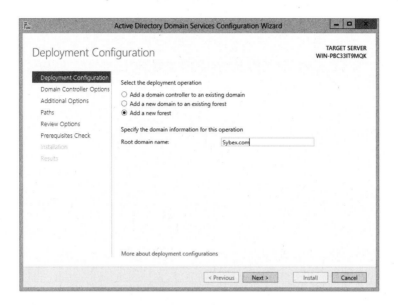

19. At the Domain Controller Options screen, set the following options;

   ▪ Function levels: Windows Server 2008 R2 (for both)

   ▪ Verify that DNS and Global Catalog check boxes are checked

   ▪ Password: **P@ssw0rd**

   ▪ Click Next.

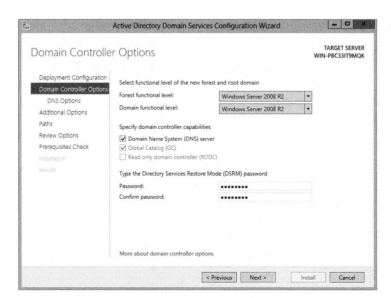

20. At the DNS screen, click Next.

21. At the additional options screen, accept the default NetBIOS domain name and click Next.

22. At the Paths screen, accept the default file locations and click Next.

23. At the Review Options screen, verify your settings and click Next.

24. At the Prerequisites Check screen, click the Install button (as long as there are no errors).

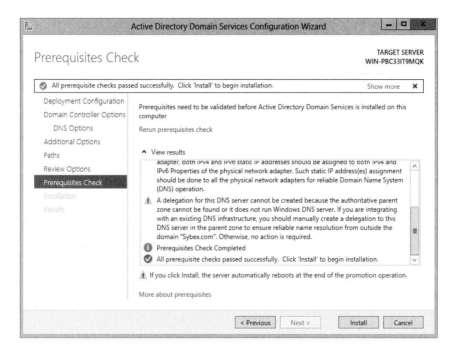

25. After the installation completes, the machine will automatically reboot. Log in as the Administrator.

26. Close Server Manager.

27. Click the Start button on the keyboard, and choose Administrative Tools.

28. You should see new MMC snap-ins for Active Directory.

EXERCISE 3.2 *(continued)*

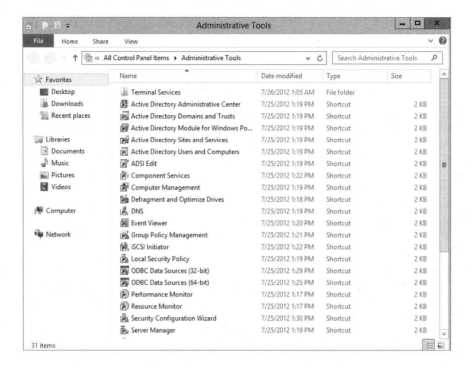

29. Close the Administrative Tools window.

In Exercise3.3, you will learn how to install Active Directory on a Server Core installation. We will use Windows Server 2012 Datacenter Server Core. Before actually installing AD DS, you will learn how to configure the computer name, the time, the administrator password, a static TCP/IP address, and install DNS.

EXERCISE 3.3

Installing AD DS on Server Core

1. At the Server Core command prompt, type cd\windows\system32 and press the Enter Key.

2. Type timedate.cpl and set your date, local time zone, and time. Click OK.

3. Type Netsh, and press Enter

4. Type Interface, and press Enter

5. Type IPv4, and press Enter

6. Type Show IP, and press Enter. This will show you the current TCP/IP address and the interface to which the TCP/IP address is associated.

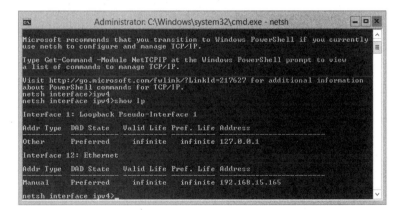

7. As you can see, interface 12 is my Ethernet interface. So to change this interface, type the following command and press Enter:

    Set address name="12" source=static address=192.168.15.165 mask=255.255.255.0
    gateway=192.168.15.1

I used 192.168.15.*x* for my address. You can replace the address, mask, and gateway based on your local settings.

8. Type Show IP, and press Enter. You should see that the new address is now manual and set to the IP address you set.

9. Type Exit, and press Enter.

10. Type Net User Administrator *, and press Enter.

11. Type in your password, and then confirm the password. I used P@ssw0rd for my password.

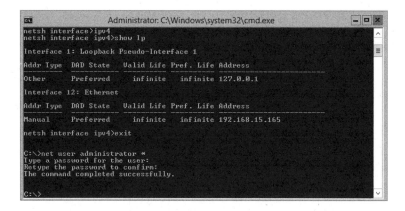

12. Type the following command and press Enter:

Netdom renamecomputer %computername% /newname:ServerA

13. Type Y, and press Enter.

14. Type Shutdown /R /T 0, and press Enter. This will reboot the machine. After the reboot, log back into the system.

15. Type PowerShell, and press Enter.

16. At the PowerShell prompt, type Add-WindowsFeature DNS and press Enter. This will add DNS to the server.

17. At the PowerShell prompt, type `Add-WindowsFeature AD-Domain-Services` and press Enter.

18. At the PowerShell prompt, type `Import-Module ADDSDeployment`.

19. At the PowerShell prompt, type `Install-ADDSForest`.

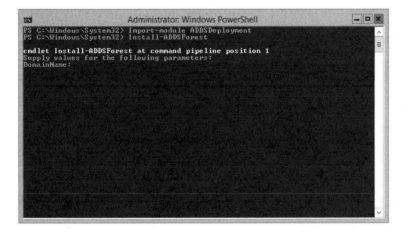

20. Type in your domain name, and press Enter. I used `Sybex.com`.

21. Next you will be asked for your Safe mode administrator password. Type in `P@ssw0rd`, and then confirm it.

22. Type `Y`, and press Enter.

Active Directory will install, and the machine will automatically reboot.

Verifying Active Directory Installation

Once you have installed and configured Active Directory, you'll want to verify that you have done so properly. In the following sections, you'll look at methods for doing this.

Using Event Viewer

The first (and perhaps most informative) way to verify the operations of Active Directory is to query information stored in the Windows Server 2012 event log. You can do this using the Windows Server 2012 Event Viewer. Exercise 3.4 walks you through this procedure. Entries seen with the Event Viewer include errors, warnings, and informational messages.

To complete the steps in Exercise 3.4, you must have configured the local machine as a domain controller.

EXERCISE 3.4

Viewing the Active Directory Event Log

1. Open Administrative tools by clicking the Windows key and choosing Administrative Tools.

2. Open the Event Viewer snap-in from the Administrative Tools program group.

3. In the left pane, under Applications And Services Logs, select Directory Service.

4. In the right pane, you can sort information by clicking column headings. For example, you can click the Source column to sort by the service or process that reported the event.

5. Double-click an event in the list to see the details for that item. Note that you can click the Copy button to copy the event information to the Clipboard. You can then paste the data into a document for later reference. Also, you can move between items using the up and down arrows. Click OK when you have finished viewing an event.

6. Filter an event list by right-clicking the Directory Service item in the left pane and selecting Filter Current Log. Note that filtering does not remove entries from the event logs—it only restricts their display.

7. To verify Active Directory installation, look for events related to the proper startup of Active Directory, such as Event ID 1000 (Active Directory Startup Complete) and 1394 (Attempts To Update The Active Directory Database Are Succeeding). Also, be sure to examine any error or warning messages because these could indicate problems with DNS or other necessary services.

8. When you've finished viewing information in the Event Viewer, close the application.

Gaining Insight through Event Viewer

Despite its simple user interface and somewhat limited GUI functionality, the Event Viewer tool can be your best ally in isolating and troubleshooting problems with Windows Server 2012. The Event Viewer allows you to view information that is stored in various log files that are maintained by the operating system. This includes information from the following logs:

Application   Stores messages generated by programs running on your system. For example, SQL Server 2012 might report the completion of a database backup job within the Application log.

Security   Contains security-related information as defined by your auditing settings. For example, you could see when users have logged onto the system or when particularly sensitive files have been accessed.

System   Contains operating system–related information and messages. Common messages might include a service startup failure or information about when the operating system was last rebooted.

Directory Service   Stores messages and events related to how Active Directory functions. For example, details related to replication might be found here.

DNS Server   Contains details about the operations of the DNS service. This log is useful for troubleshooting replication or name-resolution problems.

Other Log Files   Contain various features of Windows Server 2012 and the applications that may run on this operating system, which can create additional types of logs. These files allow you to view more information about other applications or services through the familiar Event Viewer tool.

Additionally, developers can easily send custom information from their programs to the Application log. Having all of this information in one place really makes it easy to analyze operating system and application messages. Also, many third-party tools and utilities are available for analyzing log files.

Although the Event Viewer GUI does a reasonably good job of letting you find the information you need, you might want to extract information to analyze other systems or applications. One especially useful feature of the Event Viewer is its ability to save a log file in various formats. You can access this feature by clicking Action ➢ Save As. You'll be given the option of saving in various formats, including tab- and comma-delimited text files. You can then open these files in other applications (such as Microsoft Excel) for additional data analysis.

Overall, in the real world, the Event Viewer can be an excellent resource for monitoring and troubleshooting your important servers and workstations.

In addition to providing information about the status of events related to Active Directory, the Event Viewer shows you useful information about other system services and applications. You should routinely use this tool.

Using Active Directory Administrative Tools

After a server has been promoted to a domain controller, you will see various tools added to the Administrative Tools program group , including these:

Active Directory Administrative Center   This is a *Microsoft Management Console (MMC)* snap-in that allows you to accomplish many Active Directory tasks from one central location. This MMC snap-in allows you to manage your directory services objects, including the following:

- Reset user passwords.
- Create or manage user accounts.
- Create or manage groups.
- Create or manage computer accounts.
- Create or manage organizational units (OUs) and containers.
- Connect to one or several domains or domain controllers in the same instance of Active Directory Administrative Center.
- Filter Active Directory data.

Active Directory Domains and Trusts   Use this tool to view and change information related to the various domains in an Active Directory environment. This MMC snap-in also allows you to set up shortcut trusts.

Active Directory Sites and Services   Use this tool to create and manage Active Directory sites and services to map to an organization's physical network infrastructure. Sites and services are covered in detail in Chapter 4, "Administering Active Directory."

Active Directory Users and Computers   User and computer management is fundamental for an Active Directory environment. The Active Directory Users and Computers tool allows you to set machine- and user-specific settings across the domain. This tool is discussed throughout this book.

Active Directory Module for Windows PowerShell   *Windows PowerShell* is a command-line shell and scripting language. The Active Directory Module for Windows PowerShell is a group of cmdlets used to manage your Active Directory domains, Active Directory Lightweight Directory Services (AD LDS) configuration sets, and Active Directory Database Mounting Tool instances in a single, self-contained package.

A good way to make sure Active Directory is accessible and functioning properly is to run the Active Directory Users And Computers tool. When you open the tool, you should see a configuration similar to that shown in Figure 3.3. Specifically, you should make sure the name of the domain you created appears in the list. You should also click the

`Domain Controllers` folder and make sure the name of your local server appears in the right pane. If your configuration passes these two checks, Active Directory is present and configured.

FIGURE 3.3 Viewing Active Directory information using the Active Directory Users and Computers tool

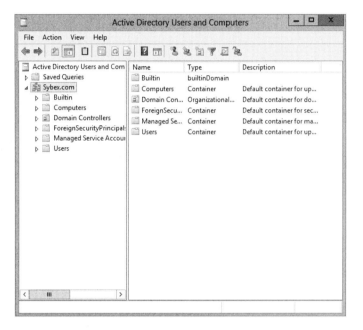

Testing from Clients

The best test of any solution is simply to verify that it works the way you had intended in your environment. When it comes to using Active Directory, a good test is to ensure that clients can view and access the various resources presented by Windows Server 2012 domain controllers. In the following sections, you'll look at several ways to verify that Active Directory is functioning properly.

Verifying Client Connectivity

If you are unable to see the recently promoted server on the network, there is likely a network configuration error. If only one or a few clients are unable to see the machine, the problem is probably related to client-side configuration. To fix this, make sure that the client computers have the appropriate TCP/IP configuration (including DNS server settings) and that they can see other computers on the network.

If the new domain controller is unavailable from any of the other client computers, you should verify the proper startup of Active Directory using the methods mentioned earlier in this chapter. If Active Directory has been started, ensure that the DNS settings are correct. Finally, test network connectivity between the server and the clients by accessing My Network Places.

Joining a Domain

If Active Directory has been properly configured, clients and other servers should be able to join the domain. Exercise 3.5 outlines the steps you need to take to join a Windows 7 or Windows 8 computer to the domain.

To complete this exercise, you must have already installed and properly configured at least one Active Directory domain controller and a DNS server that supports SRV records in your environment. In addition to the domain controller, you need at least one other computer, not configured as a domain controller, running one of the following operating systems: Windows 2000, Windows XP Professional (Windows XP Home Edition cannot join a domain), Vista, Windows 7, Windows 8, Windows Server 2003, Windows Server 2008, Windows Server 2008 R2, or Windows Server 2012.

Once clients are able to join the domain successfully, they should be able to view Active Directory resources using the My Network Places icon. This test validates the proper functioning of Active Directory and ensures that you have connectivity with client computers.

 Exercise 3.5 is being done from a Windows 7 Enterprise computer.

EXERCISE 3.5

Joining a Computer to an Active Directory Domain

1. Right-click the Computer icon on the Start menu, and click Properties.

2. Go to the section called Computer Name. On the right-hand side, click the Change Settings link.

3. Next to the section To Rename This Computer Or Change Its Domain Or Workgroup, click the Change button.

4. In the Member Of section, choose the Domain option. Type the name of the Active Directory domain that this computer should join. Click OK.

5. When prompted for the username and password of an account that has permission to join computers to the domain, enter the information for an administrator of the domain. Click OK to commit the changes. If you successfully joined the domain, you will see a dialog box welcoming you to the new domain.

6. You will be notified that you must reboot the computer before the changes take place. Select Yes when prompted to reboot.

Creating and Configuring Application Data Partitions

Organizations store many different kinds of information in various places. For the IT departments that support this information, it can be difficult to ensure that the right information is available when and where it is needed. Windows Server 2012 uses a feature called *application data partitions*, which allows system administrators and application developers to store custom information within Active Directory. The idea behind application data partitions is that, since you already have a directory service that can replicate all kinds of information, you might as well use it to keep track of your own information.

Developing distributed applications that can, for example, synchronize information across an enterprise is not a trivial task. You have to come up with a way to transfer data between remote sites (some of which are located across the world), and you have to ensure that the data is properly replicated. By storing application information in Active Directory, you can take advantage of its storage mechanism and replication topology. Application-related information stored on domain controllers benefits from having fault-tolerance features and availability.

Consider the following simple example to understand how this can work. Suppose your organization has developed a customer Sales Tracking and Inventory application. The company needs to make the information that is stored by this application available to all of its branch offices and users located throughout the world. However, the goal is to do this with the least amount of IT administrative effort. Assuming that Active Directory has already been deployed throughout the organization, developers can build support into the application for storing data within Active Directory. They can then rely on Active Directory to store and synchronize the information among various sites. When users request updated data from the application, the application can obtain this information from the nearest domain controller that hosts a replica of the Sales Tracking and Inventory data.

Other types of applications can also benefit greatly from the use of application data partitions. Now that you have a good understanding of the nature of application data partitions, let's take a look at how you can create and manage them using Windows Server 2012 and Active Directory.

Creating Application Data Partitions

By default, after you create an Active Directory environment, you will not have any customer application data partitions. Therefore, the first step in making this functionality available is to create a new application data partition. You can use several tools to do this:

Third-Party Applications or Application-Specific Tools   Generally, if you are planning to install an application that can store information in the Active Directory database, you'll receive some method of administering and configuring that data along with the application. For example, the setup process for the application might assist you in the steps you need to take to set up a new application data partition and to create the necessary structures for storing data.

NOTE The creation and management of application data partitions is an advanced Active Directory–related function. Be sure that you have a solid understanding of the Active Directory schema, Active Directory replication, LDAP, and your applications' needs before you attempt to create new application data partitions in a live environment.

Active Directory Service Interfaces ADSI is a set of programmable objects that can be accessed through languages such as Visual Basic Scripting Edition (VBScript), Visual C#, Visual Basic .NET, and many other language technologies that support the Component Object Model (COM) standard. Through the use of ADSI, developers can create, access, and update data stored in Active Directory and in any application data partitions.

The LDP Tool You can view and modify the contents of the Active Directory schema using LDAP-based queries. The LDP tool allows you to view information about application data partitions.

Ldp.exe is a graphical user interface (GUI) tool that allows an administrator to configure Lightweight Directory Access Protocol (LDAP) directory service. Administrators have the ability to use the LDP tool to administer an Active Directory Lightweight Directory Services (AD LDS) instance. To use the LDP tool, you must be an Administrator or equivalent.

Figure 3.4 shows an example of connecting to a domain controller and browsing Active Directory information.

FIGURE 3.4 Using the LDP tool to view Active Directory schema information

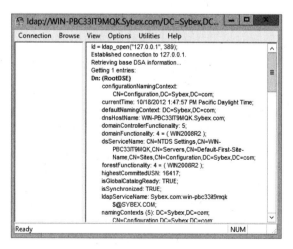

ntdsutil The ntdsutil utility is the main method by which system administrators create and manage application data partitions on their Windows Server 2012 domain controllers. This utility's specific commands are covered later in this chapter.

Creating and managing application data partitions can be fairly complex. Such a project's success depends on the quality of the architecture design. This is a good example of where IT staff and application developers must cooperate to ensure that data is stored effectively and that it is replicated efficiently.

You can create an application data partition in one of three different locations within an Active Directory forest:

- As a new tree in an Active Directory forest
- As a child of an Active Directory domain partition

  For example, you can create an Accounting application data partition within the Finance.MyCompany.com domain.

- As a child of another application data partition

  This method allows you to create a hierarchy of application data partitions.

As you might expect, you must be a member of the Enterprise Admins or Domain Admins group to be able to create application data partitions. Alternatively, you can be delegated the appropriate permissions to create new partitions.

Now that you have a good idea of the basic ways in which you can create application data partitions, let's look at how replicas (copies of application data partition information) are handled.

Managing Replicas

A *replica* is a copy of any data stored within Active Directory. Unlike the basic information that is stored in Active Directory, application partitions cannot contain security principals. Also, not all domain controllers automatically contain copies of the data stored in an application data partition. System administrators can define which domain controllers host copies of the application data. This is a very important feature because, if replicas are used effectively, administrators can find a good balance between replication traffic and data consistency. For example, suppose that 3 of your organization's 30 locations require up-to-date accounting-related information. You might choose to replicate the data only to domain controllers located in the places that require the data. Limiting replication of this data reduces network traffic.

Replication is the process by which replicas are kept up-to-date. Application data can be stored and updated on designated servers in the same way basic Active Directory information (such as users and groups) is synchronized between domain controllers. Application data partition replicas are managed using the *Knowledge Consistency Checker (KCC)*, which ensures that the designated domain controllers receive updated replica information. Additionally, the KCC uses all Active Directory sites and connection objects (covered in Chapter 4) that you create to determine the best method to handle replication.

Removing Replicas

When you perform a *demotion* on a domain controller, that server can no longer host an application data partition. If a domain controller contains a replica of application data partition information, you must remove the replica from the domain controller before you demote it. If a domain controller is the machine that hosts a replica of the application data partition, then the entire application data partition is removed and will be permanently lost. Generally, you want to do this only after you're absolutely sure that your organization no longer needs access to the data stored in the application data partition.

Using *ntdsutil* to Manage Application Data Partitions

The primary method by which system administrators create and manage application data partitions is through the ntdsutil command-line tool. You can launch this tool simply by entering **ntdsutil** at a command prompt. The ntdsutil command is both interactive and context sensitive. That is, once you launch the utility, you'll see an ntdsutil command prompt. At this prompt, you can enter various commands that set your context within the application. For example, if you enter the domain management command, you'll be able to use domain-related commands. Several operations also require you to connect to a domain, a domain controller, or an Active Directory object before you perform a command.

> For complete details on using ntdsutil, see the Windows Server 2012 Help and Support Center.

Table 3.2 provides a list of the domain management commands supported by the ntdsutil tool. You can access this information by typing the following sequence of commands at a command prompt.

```
ntdsutil
domain management
help
```

TABLE 3.2 ntdsutil domain management commands

ntdsutil Domain Management Command	Purpose
Help or ?	Displays information about the commands that are available within the Domain Management menu of the ntdsutil command.
Connection or Connections	Allows you to connect to a specific domain controller. This will set the context for further operations that are performed on specific domain controllers.

ntdsutil Domain Management Command	Purpose
Create NC *Partition DistinguishedName DNSName*	Creates a new application directory partition.
Delete NC *Partition DistinguishedName*	Removes an application data partition.
List NC Information *PartitionDistinguishedName*	Shows information about the specified application data partition.
List NC Replicas *PartitionDistinguishedName*	Returns information about all replicas for the specific application data partition.
Precreate *Partition "DistinguishedNameServer DNSName*	Pre-creates cross-reference application data partition objects. This allows the specified DNS server to host a copy of the application data partition.
Remove NC Replica *Partition DistinguishedName DCDNSName*	Removes a replica from the specified domain controller.
Select Operation Target	Selects the naming context that will be used for other operations.
Set NC Reference Domain *PartitionDistinguishedName DomainDistinguishedName*	Specifies the reference domain for an application data partition.
Set NC Replicate NotificationDelay *PartitionDistinguishedName FirstDCNotificationDelay OtherDCNotificationDelay*	Defines settings for how often replication will occur for the specified application data partition.

NOTE
The ntdsutil commands are all case insensitive. Mixed-case was used in the table to make them easier to read. NC in commands stands for "naming context," referring to the fact that this is a partition of the Active Directory schema.

Figure 3.5 provides an example of working with ntdsutil. The following commands were entered to set the context for further operations:

```
ntdsutil
domain management
connections
```

```
connect to server localhost
connect to domain ADTest
quit
list
```

FIGURE 3.5   Viewing naming contexts on the local domain controller

Configuring DNS Integration with Active Directory

There are many benefits to integrating Active Directory and DNS services:

- You can configure and manage replication along with other Active Directory components.

- You can automate much of the maintenance of DNS resource records through the use of dynamic updates.

- You will be able to set specific security options on the various properties of the DNS service.

Exercise 3.6 shows the steps that you must take to ensure that these integration features are enabled. You'll look at the various DNS functions that are specific to interoperability with Active Directory.

Before you begin this exercise, make sure that the local machine is configured as an Active Directory domain controller and that DNS services have been properly configured. If you instructed the Active Directory Installation Wizard to configure DNS automatically, many of the settings mentioned in this section may already be enabled. However, you should verify the configuration and be familiar with how the options can be set manually.

EXERCISE 3.6

Configuring DNS Integration with Active Directory

1. Open Administrative tools by clicking the Windows key and choosing Administrative Tools.

2. Open the DNS snap-in from the Administrative Tools program group.

3. Right-click the icon for the local DNS server, and select Properties. Click the Security tab. Notice that you can now specify which users and groups have access to modify the configuration of the DNS server. Make any necessary changes, and click OK.

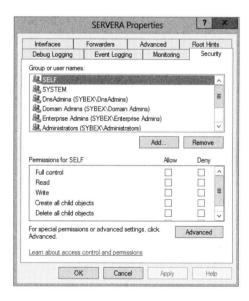

4. Expand the local server branch and the Forward Lookup Zones folder.

5. Right-click the name of the Active Directory domain you created, and select Properties.

6. On the General tab, verify that the type is Active Directory–Integrated and that the Data Is Stored In Active Directory message is displayed. If this option is not currently selected, you can change it by clicking the Change button next to Type and choosing the Store The Zone In Active Directory check box on the bottom.

7. Verify that the Dynamic Updates option is set to Secure Only. This ensures that all
    updates to the DNS resource records database are made through authenticated Active
    Directory accounts and processes.

    The other options are Nonsecure And Secure (accepts all updates) and None (to disal-
    low dynamic updates).

8. Finally, notice that you can define the security permissions at the zone level by clicking
    the Security tab. Make any necessary changes, and click OK.

Summary

This chapter covered the basics of implementing an Active Directory forest and domain structure, creating and configuring application data partitions, and setting the functional level of your domain and forest.

You are now familiar with how you can implement Active Directory. We carefully examined all the necessary steps and conditions you need to follow to install Active Directory on your network. First you need to prepare for the Domain Name System (DNS) because Active Directory cannot be installed without the support of a DNS server.

You also need to verify that the computer you upgrade to a domain controller (DC) meets some basic file system and network connectivity requirements so that Active Directory can run smoothly and efficiently in your organization. These are some of the most common things you will have to do when you deploy Active Directory.

We also covered the concept of domain functional levels, which essentially determine the kinds of domain controllers you can use in your environment. For instance, in the Windows 2003 functional level, you can include Windows Server 2012, Windows Server 2008 R2, Windows Server 2008, and Windows Server 2003 domain controllers, but the functionality of the domain is severely limited.

In this chapter, you also learned how to install Active Directory, which you accomplish by promoting a Windows Server 2012 computer to a domain controller using Server Manager. You also learned how to verify the installation by testing Active Directory from a client computer.

This chapter was limited in scope to examining the issues related to installing and configuring the first domain in an Active Directory environment. In later chapters, you'll see how to create and manage more complex configurations.

Exam Essentials

Know the prerequisites for promoting a server to a domain controller.   You should understand the tasks that you must complete before you attempt to upgrade a server to a domain controller. Also, you should have a good idea of the information you need in order to complete the domain controller promotion process.

Understand the steps of the Active Directory Installation Wizard.   When you run the Active Directory Installation Wizard, you'll be presented with many different choices. You should understand the effects of the various options provided in each step of the wizard.

Be familiar with the tools that you will use to administer Active Directory.   Three main administrative tools are installed when you promote a Windows Server 2012 to a domain controller. Be sure that you know which tools to use for which types of tasks.

Understand the purpose of application data partitions.   The idea behind application data partitions is that, since you already have a directory service that can replicate all kinds of security information, you can also use it to keep track of application data. The main benefit of storing application information in Active Directory is that you can take advantage of its storage mechanism and replication topology. Application-related information stored on domain controllers benefits from having fault-tolerance features and availability.

Review Questions

1. You are the system administrator of a large organization that has recently implemented Windows Server 2012. You have a few remote sites that do not have very tight security. You have decided to implement read-only domain controllers (RODCs). What forest and function levels does the network need for you to do the install? (Choose all that apply.)

    A. Windows 2000 Mixed

    B. Windows 2008 R2

    C. Windows 2003

    D. Windows 2008

2. What is the maximum number of domains that a Windows Server 2012 computer configured as a domain controller may participate in at one time?

    A. Zero

    B. One

    C. Two

    D. Any number of domains

3. A system administrator is trying to determine which file system to use for a server that will become a Windows Server 2012 file server and domain controller. The company has the following requirements:

    - The file system must allow for file-level security from within Windows 2012 Server.

    - The file system must make efficient use of space on large partitions.

    - The domain controller SYSVOL must be stored on the partition.

    Which of the following file systems meets these requirements?

    A. FAT

    B. FAT32

    C. HPFS

    D. NTFS

4. For security reasons, you have decided that you must convert the system partition on your removable drive from the FAT32 file system to NTFS. Which of the following steps must you take in order to convert the file system? (Choose two.)

    A. Run the command CONVERT /FS:NTFS from the command prompt.

    B. Rerun Windows Server 2008 R2 Setup, and choose to convert the partition to NTFS during the reinstallation.

    C. Boot Windows Server 2008 R2 Setup from the installation CD-ROM, and choose Rebuild File System.

    D. Reboot the computer.

5.   Windows Server 2012 requires the use of which of the following protocols or services in order to support Active Directory? (Choose two.)

   A.   DHCP

   B.   TCP/IP

   C.   NetBEUI

   D.   IPX/SPX

   E.   DNS

6.   You are promoting a Windows Server 2012 computer to an Active Directory domain controller for test purposes. The new domain controller will be added to an existing domain. While you are using the Active Directory Installation Wizard, you receive an error message that prevents the server from being promoted. Which of the following might be the cause of the problem? (Choose all that apply.)

   A.   The system does not contain an NTFS partition on which the SYSVOL directory can be created.

   B.   You do not have a Windows Server 2012 DNS server on the network.

   C.   The TCP/IP configuration on the new server is incorrect.

   D.   The domain has reached its maximum number of domain controllers.

7.   Your network contains a single Active Directory domain. The domain contains five Windows Server 2008 R2 domain controllers. You plan to install a new Windows Server 2012 domain controller. Which two actions would you need to perform? (Each correct answer presents part of the solution. Choose two.)

   A.   `adprep.exe /rodcprep`

   B.   `adprep.exe /forestprep`

   C.   `adprep.exe /domainprep`

   D.   From Active Directory Domains and Trusts, raise the functional level of the domain.

   E.   From Active Directory Users and Computers, pre-stage the RODC computer account.

8.   You are the network administrator for a large company that creates widgets. You are asked by management to implement a new Windows Server 2012 system. You need to implement federated identity management. Which of the following will help you do this?

   A.   Active Directory Federation Services

   B.   Active Directory DNS Services

   C.   Active Directory IIS Services

   D.   Active Directory IAS Services

9. You are the system administrator responsible for your company's infrastructure. You think you have an issue with name resolution and you need to verify that you are using the correct hostname. You want to test DNS on the local system, and need to see if the hostname server-1 resolves to the IP address 10.1.1.1. Which of the following actions provides a solution to the problem?

A. Add a DNS server to your local subnet.

B. Add the mapping for the hostname server-1 to the IP address 10.1.1.1 in the local system's HOSTS file.

C. Add an A record to your local WINS server.

D. Add an MX record to your local DNS server.

10. You have one Active Directory forest in your organization that contains one domain named Stellacon.com. You have two domain controllers configured with the DNS role installed. There are two Active Directory Integrated zones named stellacon.com and stellatest.com. One of your IT members (who is not an administrator) needs to be able to modify the Stellacon.com DNS server, but you need to prevent this user from modifying the Stellatest.com SOA record. How do you accomplish this?

A. Modify the permissions of the stellacon.com zone from the DNS Manager snap-in.

B. Modify the permissions of the stellatest.com zone from the DNS Manager snap-in.

C. Run the Delegation of Control Wizard in Active Directory.

D. Run the Delegation of Control Wizard in the DNS snap-in.

Chapter

4

Administering
Active Directory

THE FOLLOWING 70-410 EXAM OBJECTIVES ARE COVERED IN THIS CHAPTER:

✓ **Create and manage Active Directory users and computers**

- May include, but is not limited to: Automate the creation of Active Directory accounts; create, copy, configure, and delete users and computers; configure templates; perform bulk Active Directory operations; configure user rights; offline domain join; manage inactive and disabled accounts.

✓ **Configure service authentication**

- This objective may include but is not limited to: Create and configure Service Accounts; create and configure Group Managed Service Accounts; create and configure Managed Service Accounts; configure Kerberos delegation; manage Service Principal Names (SPNs).

✓ **Create and manage Active Directory groups and organizational units (OUs)**

- May include, but is not limited to: Configure group nesting; convert groups including security, distribution, universal, domain local, and domain global; manage group membership using Group Policy; enumerate group membership; delegate the creation and management of Active Directory objects; manage default Active Directory containers; create, copy, configure, and delete groups and OUs; automate creation of Active Directory accounts.

In previous chapters, you learned how to install Domain Name Service (DNS) and Active Directory, but you still haven't been introduced to the lower-level objects that exist in Active Directory.

In this chapter, you will look at the structure of the various components within a domain. You'll see how an organization's business structure can be mirrored within Active Directory through the use of organizational units (OUs) for ease of use and to create a seamless look and feel. Because the concepts related to OUs are quite simple, some system administrators may underestimate their importance and not plan to use them accordingly. Make no mistake: One of the fundamental components of a successful Active Directory installation is the proper design and deployment of OUs.

You'll also see in this chapter the actual steps you need to take to create common Active Directory objects and then learn how to configure and manage them. Finally, you'll look at ways to publish resources and methods for creating user accounts automatically.

User, Group, and Service Account permissions are discussed in detail in Chapter 13 "Understanding Security."

An Overview of OUs

An *organizational unit (OU)* is a logical group of Active Directory objects, just as the name implies. OUs serve as containers within which Active Directory objects can be created, but they do not form part of the DNS namespace. They are used solely to create organization within a domain.

OUs can contain the following types of Active Directory objects:

- Users
- Groups
- Computers
- Shared Folder objects
- Contacts
- Printers
- InetOrgPerson objects
- MSMQ (Microsoft Message Queuing) Queue aliases
- Other OUs

Perhaps the most useful feature of OUs is that they can contain other OU objects. As a result, system administrators can hierarchically group resources and objects according to business practices. The OU structure is extremely flexible and, as you will see later in this chapter, can easily be rearranged to reflect business reorganizations.

Another advantage of OUs is that each can have its own set of policies. Administrators can create individual and unique Group Policy objects (GPOs) for each OU. GPOs are rules or policies that can apply to all of the objects within the OU. GPOs are discussed in detail in Chapter 5, "Managing Group Policy Objects."

Each type of object has its own purpose within the organization of Active Directory domains. Later in this chapter, you'll look at the specifics of User, Computer, Group, and Shared Folder objects. For now, let's focus on the purpose and benefits of using OUs.

The Purpose of OUs

OUs are mainly used to organize the objects within Active Directory. Before you dive into the details of OUs, however, you must understand how OUs, users, and groups interact. Most important, you should understand that OUs are simply containers that you can use to group various objects logically. They are not, however, groups in the classical sense. That is, they are not used for assigning security permissions. Another way of stating this is that the user accounts, computer accounts, and group accounts that are contained in OUs are considered security principals while the OUs themselves are not.

OUs do not take the place of standard user and group permissions (covered in Chapter 13, "Understanding Security"). A good general practice is to assign users to groups and then place the groups within OUs. This enhances the benefits of setting security permissions and of using the OU hierarchy for making settings. Figure 4.1 illustrates this concept.

FIGURE 4.1   Relationships of users, groups, and OUs

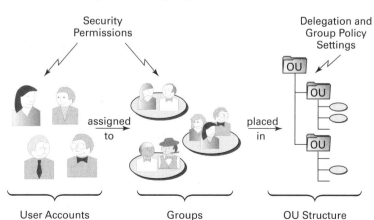

An OU contains objects only from within the domain in which it resides. As you'll see in the section "Delegating Administrative Control" later in this chapter, the OU is the finest level of granularity used for group policies and other administrative settings.

Benefits of OUs

There are many benefits to using OUs throughout your network environment:

- OUs are the smallest unit to which you can assign directory permissions.
- You can easily change the OU structure, and it is more flexible than the domain structure.
- The OU structure can support many different levels of hierarchy.
- Child objects can inherit OU settings.
- You can set Group Policy settings on OUs.
- You can easily delegate the administration of OUs and the objects within them to the appropriate users and groups.

Now that you have a good idea of why you should use OUs, take a look at some general practices you can use to plan the OU structure.

Planning the OU Structure

One of the key benefits of Active Directory is the way in which it can bring organization to complex network environments. Before you can begin to implement OUs in various configurations, you must plan a structure that is compatible with business and technical needs. In this section, you'll learn about several factors that you should consider when planning for the structure of OUs.

Logical Grouping of Resources

The fundamental purpose of using OUs is to group resources (which exist within Active Directory) hierarchically. Fortunately, hierarchical groups are quite intuitive and widely used in most businesses. For example, a typical manufacturing business might divide its various operations into different departments as follows:

- Sales
- Marketing
- Engineering
- Research and Development
- Support
- Information Technology (IT)

Each of these departments usually has its own goals and mission. To make the business competitive, individuals within each of the departments are assigned to various roles. The following role types might be used:

- Managers
- Clerical staff
- Technical staff
- Planners

Each of these roles usually entails specific job responsibilities. For example, managers should provide direction to general staff members. Note that the very nature of these roles suggests that employees may fill many different positions. That is, one employee might be a manager in one department and a member of the technical staff in another. In the modern workplace, such situations are quite common.

All of this information helps you plan how to use OUs. First the structure of OUs within a given network environment should map well to the business's needs, including the political and logical structure of the organization as well as its technical needs. Figure 4.2 shows how a business organization might be mapped to the OU structure within an Active Directory domain.

FIGURE 4.2 Mapping a business organization to an OU structure

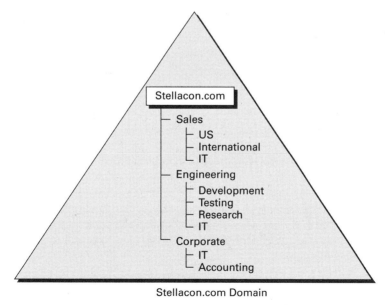

Stellacon.com Domain

When naming OUs for your organization, you should keep several considerations and limitations in mind:

Keep the Names and Descriptions Simple The purpose of OUs is to make administering and using resources simple. Therefore, it's always a good idea to keep the names of your objects simple and descriptive. Sometimes finding a balance between these two goals can be a challenge. For example, although a printer name like "The LaserJet located near Bob's cube" might seem descriptive, it is certainly difficult to type. Also, imagine the naming changes that you might have to make if Bob moves (or leaves the company)!

Pay Attention to Limitations The maximum length for the name of an OU is 64 characters. In most cases, this should adequately describe the OU. Remember, the name of an OU does not have to describe the object uniquely because the OU is generally referenced only as part of the overall hierarchy. For example, you can choose to create an OU named "IT" within two different parent OUs. Even though the OUs have the same name, users and administrators are able to distinguish between them based on their complete pathname.

Pay Attention to the Hierarchical Consistency The fundamental basis of an OU structure is its position in a hierarchy. From a design standpoint, this means that you cannot have two OUs with the same name at the same level. However, you can have OUs with the same name at different levels. For example, you could create an OU named "Corporate" within the North America OU and another one within the South America OU. This is because the fully qualified domain name includes information about the hierarchy. When an administrator tries to access resources in a Corporate OU, they must specify which Corporate OU they mean.

For example, if you create a North America OU, the Canada OU should logically fit under it. If you decide that you want to separate the North America and Canada OUs into completely different containers, then you might want to use other, more appropriate names. For example, you could change North America to U.S. Users and administrators depend on the hierarchy of OUs within the domain, so make sure it remains logically consistent.

Based on these considerations, you should have a good idea of how best to organize the OU structure for your domain.

Understanding OU Inheritance

When you rearrange OUs within the structure of Active Directory, you can change several settings. When they are moving and reorganizing OUs, system administrators must pay careful attention to automatic and unforeseen changes in security permissions and other configuration options. By default, OUs inherit the permissions of their new parent container when they are moved.

By using the built-in tools provided with Windows Server 2012 and Active Directory, you can move or copy OUs only within the same domain. You cannot use the Active Directory Users and Computers tool to move OUs between domains. To do this, use the *Active Directory Migration Tool (ADMT)*. This is one of the many Active Directory support tools.

Delegating Administrative Control

I already mentioned that OUs are the smallest component within a domain to which administrative permissions and group policies can be assigned by administrators. Now you'll take a look specifically at how administrative control is set on OUs.

Real World Scenario

Delegation occurs when a higher security authority assigns permissions to a lesser security authority. As a real-world example, assume that you are the director of IT for a large organization. Instead of doing all of the work yourself, you would probably assign roles and responsibilities to other individuals. For example, if you worked within a multidomain environment, you might make one system administrator responsible for all operations within the Sales domain and another responsible for the Engineering domain. Similarly, you could assign the permissions for managing all printers and print queues objects within your organization to one individual user while allowing another individual user to manage all security permissions for users and groups. In this way, you can distribute the various roles and responsibilities of the IT staff throughout the organization.

Businesses generally have a division of labor that handles all of the tasks involved in keeping the company's networks humming. Network operating systems (NOSs), however, often make it difficult to assign just the right permissions, or in other words, they do not support very granular permission assignments. Sometimes fine granularity is necessary to ensure that only the right permissions are assigned. A good general rule of thumb is to provide users and administrators with the minimum permissions they require to do their jobs. This way, you can ensure that accidental, malicious, and otherwise unwanted changes do not occur.

 You can use auditing to log events to the Security log in the Event Viewer. This is a way to ensure that if accidental, malicious, and otherwise unwanted changes do occur, they are logged and traceable.

In the world of Active Directory, you delegate to define responsibilities for OU administrators. As a system administrator, you will occasionally be tasked with having to delegate responsibility to others—you can't do it all, although sometimes administrators believe that they can. You understand the old IT logic of doing all the tasks yourself for job security, but this can actually make you look worse.

You can delegate control only at the OU level and not at the object level within the OU.

If you do find yourself in a role where you need to delegate, remember that Windows Server 2012 was designed to offer you the ability to do so. In its simplest definition, delegation allows a higher administrative authority to grant specific administrative rights for containers and subtrees to individuals and groups. What this essentially does is to eliminate the need for domain administrators with sweeping authority over large segments of the user population. You can break up this control over branches within your tree, within each OU you create.

 To understand delegation and rights, you should first understand the concept of access control entries (ACEs). ACEs grant specific administrative rights on objects in a container to a user or group. The containers' access control list (ACL) is used to store ACEs.

When you are considering implementing delegation, keep these two concerns in mind:

Parent-Child Relationships   The OU hierarchy you create will be very important when you consider the maintainability of security permissions. OUs can exist in a parent-child relationship, which means that permissions and group policies set on OUs higher up in the hierarchy (parents) can interact with objects in lower-level OUs (children). When it comes to delegating permissions, this is extremely important. You can allow child containers to inherit the permissions set on parent containers automatically. For example, if the North America division of your organization contains 12 other OUs, you could delegate permissions to all of them at once (saving time and reducing the likelihood of human error) by placing security permissions on the North America division. This feature can greatly ease administration, especially in larger organizations, but it is also a reminder of the importance of properly planning the OU structure within a domain.

Inheritance Settings   Now that you've seen how you can use parent-child relationships for administration, you should consider *inheritance*, the process in which child objects take on the permissions of a parent container. When you set permissions on a parent container, all of the child objects are configured to inherit the same permissions. You can override this behavior, however, if business rules do not lend themselves well to inheritance.

Applying Group Policies

One of the strengths of the Windows operating system is that it offers users a great deal of power and flexibility. From installing new software to adding device drivers, users can make many changes to their workstation configurations. However, this level of flexibility is also a potential problem. For instance, inexperienced users might inadvertently change settings, causing problems that can require many hours to fix.

In many cases (and especially in business environments), users require only a subset of the complete functionality the operating system provides. In the past, however, the difficulty associated with implementing and managing security and policy settings has led to lax security policies. Some of the reasons for this are technical—it can be very tedious and difficult to implement and manage security restrictions. Other problems have been political—users and management might feel that they should have full permissions on their local machines, despite the potential problems this might cause.

That's where the idea of group policies comes in. Simply defined, *group policies* are collections of rules that you can apply to objects within Active Directory. Specifically, Group Policy settings are assigned at the site, domain, and OU levels, and they can apply to user accounts and computer accounts. For example, a system administrator can use group policies to configure the following settings:

- Restricting users from installing new programs

- Disallowing the use of the Control Panel

- Limiting choices for display and Desktop settings

Creating OUs

Now that you have looked at several different ways in which OUs can be used to bring organization to the objects within Active Directory, it's time to look at how you can create and manage them.

Through the use of the *Active Directory Users and Computers administrative tool*, also called the *MMC (Microsoft Management Console)*, you can quickly and easily add, move, and change OUs. This graphical tool makes it easy to visualize and create the various levels of hierarchy an organization requires.

Figure 4.3 shows a geographically based OU structure that a multinational company might use. Note that the organization is based in North America and that it has a corporate office located there. In general, the other offices are much smaller than the corporate office located in North America.

FIGURE 4.3   A geographically-based OU structure

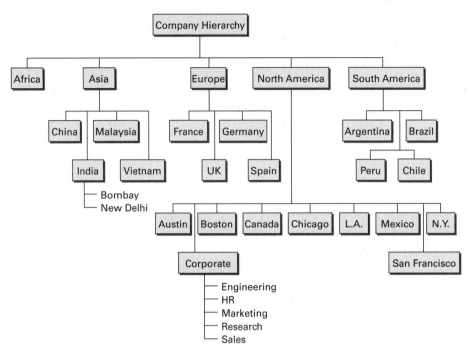

It's important to note that this OU structure could have been designed in several different ways. For example, I could have chosen to group all of the offices located in the United States within an OU named "U.S." However, because of the large size of these offices, I chose to place these objects at the same level as the Canada and Mexico OUs. This prevents an unnecessarily deep OU hierarchy while still logically grouping the offices.

One nice feature when creating an OU is the ability to protect the OU from being accidentally deleted. When you create an OU, you can check the Protect Container From Accidental Deletion check box. This check box protects against an administrator deleting the OU. To delete the OU, you must go into the advanced view of the OU and uncheck the box.

Exercise 4.1 walks you through the process of creating several OUs for a multinational business. You'll be using this OU structure in later exercises within this chapter.

To perform the exercises included in this chapter, you must have administrative access to a Windows Server 2012 domain controller.

EXERCISE 4.1

Creating an OU Structure

1. Click the Windows key on the keyboard, and choose Administrative Tools.

2. Open the Active Directory Users and Computers administrative tool.

3. Right-click the name of the local domain, and choose New ➤ Organizational Unit. You will see the dialog box shown in the following screen shot. Notice that this box shows you the current context within which the OU will be created. In this case, you're creating a top-level OU, so the full path is simply the name of the domain.

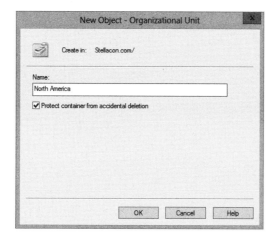

4. Type **North America** for the name of the first OU. Uncheck the box Protect Container From Accidental Deletion, and click OK to create this object.

5. Create the following top-level OUs by right-clicking the name of the domain and choosing New ➤ Organizational Unit. Also make sure to uncheck Protect Container From Accidental Deletion for all OUs in these exercises because you'll be deleting some of these OUs in later ones.

    Africa

    Asia

    Europe

    South America

    Note that the order in which you create the OUs is not important. In this exercise, you are simply using a method that emphasizes the hierarchical relationship.

EXERCISE 4.1 *(continued)*

6. Create the following second-level OUs within the North America OU by right-clicking the North America OU and selecting New ➢ Organizational Unit:

    Austin

    Boston

    Canada

    Chicago

    Corporate

    Los Angeles

    Mexico

    New York

    San Francisco

7. Create the following OUs under the Asia OU:

    China

    India

    Malaysia

    Vietnam

8. Create the following OUs under the Europe OU:

    France

    Germany

    Spain

    UK

9. Create the following OUs under the South America OU:

    Argentina

    Brazil

    Chile

    Peru

10. Create the following third-level OUs under the India OU by right-clicking India within the Asia OU and selecting New ➢ Organizational Unit:

    Bombay

    New Delhi

11. Within the North America Corporate OU, create the following OUs:

    Engineering

    HR

    Marketing

    Research

    Sales

12. When you have completed creating the OUs, you should have a structure that looks similar to the one in the left pane of the following screen shot.

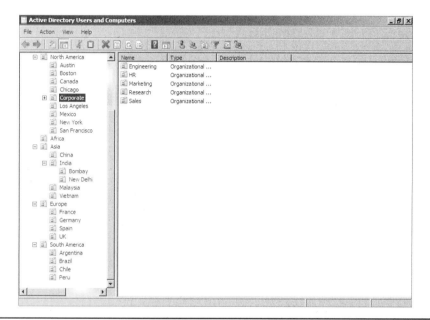

Managing OUs

Managing network environments would still be challenging even if things rarely changed. However, in the real world, business units, departments, and employee roles change frequently. As business and technical needs change, so should the structure of Active Directory.

Fortunately, changing the structure of OUs within a domain is a relatively simple process. In the following sections, you'll look at ways to delegate control of OUs and make other changes.

Moving, Deleting, and Renaming OUs

The process of moving, deleting, and renaming OUs is a simple one. Exercise 4.2 shows how you can easily modify and reorganize OUs to reflect changes in the business organization. The specific scenario covered in this exercise includes the following changes:

- The Research and Engineering departments have been combined to form a department known as Research and Development (RD).

- The Sales department has been moved from the Corporate headquarters office to the New York office.

- The Marketing department has been moved from the Corporate headquarters office to the Chicago office.

  This exercise assumes that you have already completed the steps in Exercise 4.1.

EXERCISE 4.2

Modifying OU Structure

1. Click the Windows key on the keyboard, and choose Administrative Tools.

2. Open the Active Directory Users and Computers administrative tool.

3. Right-click the Engineering OU (located within North America ➢ Corporate) and click Delete. When you are prompted for confirmation, click Yes. Note that if this OU contained objects, they have all been automatically deleted as well.

4. Right-click the Research OU, and select Rename. Type **RD** to change the name of the OU and press Enter.

5. Right-click the Sales OU and select Move. In the Move dialog box, expand the North America branch and click the New York OU. Click OK to move the OU.

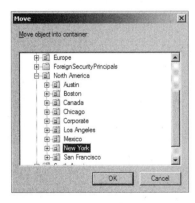

6. You will use an alternate method to move the Marketing OU. Drag the Marketing OU, and drop it onto the Chicago OU.

7. When you have finished, you should see an OU structure similar to the one shown in the following screen shot. Close the Active Directory Users and Computers administrative tool.

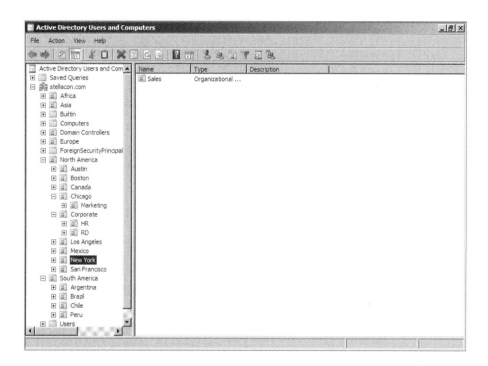

Administering Properties of OUs

Although OUs are primarily created for organizational purposes within the Active Directory environment they have several settings that you can modify. To modify the properties of an OU using the Active Directory Users and Computers administrative tool, right-click the name of any OU and select Properties. When you do, the OU Properties dialog box appears. In the example shown in Figure 4.4, you'll see the options on the General tab.

FIGURE 4.4   The General tab of the OU's Properties dialog box

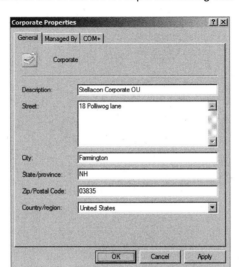

In any organization, it helps to know who is responsible for managing an OU. You can set this information on the Managed By tab (see Figure 4.5). The information specified on this tab is very convenient because it is automatically pulled from the contact information on a user record. You should consider always having a contact for each OU within your organization so that other system administrators know who to contact if they need to make any changes.

FIGURE 4.5   The Managed By tab of the OU's Properties dialog box

Delegating Control of OUs

In simple environments, one or a few system administrators may be responsible for managing all of the settings within Active Directory. For example, a single system administrator could manage all users within all OUs in the environment. In larger organizations, however, roles and responsibilities may be divided among many different individuals. A typical situation is one in which a system administrator is responsible for objects within only a few OUs in an Active Directory domain. Alternatively, one system administrator might manage User and Group objects while another is responsible for managing file and print services.

Fortunately, using the Active Directory Users and Computers tool, you can quickly and easily ensure that specific users receive only the permissions they need. In Exercise 4.3, you will use the Delegation of Control Wizard to assign permissions to individuals. To complete these steps successfully, first you must have created the objects in the previous exercises of this chapter.

EXERCISE 4.3

Using the Delegation of Control Wizard

1. Click the Windows key on the keyboard, and choose Administrative Tools.

2. Open the Active Directory Users and Computers administrative tool.

3. Right-click the Corporate OU within the North America OU, and select Delegate Control. This starts the Delegation of Control Wizard. Click Next to begin configuring security settings.

4. In the Users Or Groups page, click the Add button. In the Enter The Object Names To Select field, enter **Account Operators** and click the Check Names button. Click OK. Click Next to continue.

5. In the Tasks To Delegate page, select Delegate The Following Common Tasks and place a check mark next to the following items:

    Create, Delete, And Manage User Accounts

    Reset User Passwords And Force Password Change At Next Logon

    Read All User Information

    Create, Delete, And Manage Groups

    Modify The Membership Of A Group

    Click Next to continue.

EXERCISE 4.3 *(continued)*

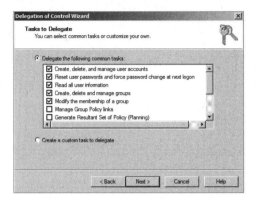

6. The Completing The Delegation Of Control Wizard page then provides a summary of the operations you have selected. To implement the changes, click Finish.

Although the common tasks available through the wizard are sufficient for many delegation operations, you may have cases in which you want more control. For example, you might want to give a particular system administrator permissions to modify only Computer objects. Exercise 4.4 uses the Delegation of Control Wizard to assign more granular permissions. To complete these steps successfully, you must have completed the previous exercises in this chapter.

EXERCISE 4.4

Delegating Custom Tasks

1. Click the Windows key on the keyboard, and choose Administrative Tools.

2. Open the Active Directory Users and Computers administrative tool.

3. Right-click the Corporate OU within the North America OU and select Delegate Control. This starts the Delegation of Control Wizard. Click Next to begin making security settings.

4. In the Users Or Groups page, click the Add button. In the Enter The Object Names To Select field, enter **Server Operators** and click the Check Names button. Click OK, and then click Next to continue.

5. In the Tasks To Delegate page, select the Create A Custom Task To Delegate radio button and click Next to continue.

6. In the Active Directory Object Type page, choose Only The Following Objects In The Folder, and place a check mark next to the following items. (You will have to scroll down to see them all.)

    User Objects

    Computer Objects

Contact Objects

Group Objects

Organizational Unit Objects

Printer Objects

Click Next to continue.

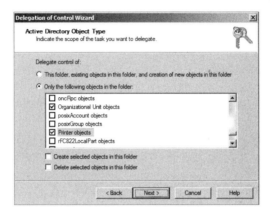

7. In the Permissions page, place a check mark next to the General option and make sure the other options are not checked. Note that if the various objects within your Active Directory schema had property-specific settings, you would see those options here. Place a check mark next to the following items:

Create All Child Objects

Read All Properties

Write All Properties

This gives the members of the Server Operators group the ability to create new objects within the Corporate OU and the permissions to read and write all properties for these objects.

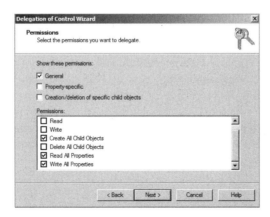

EXERCISE 4.4 *(continued)*

8. Click Next to continue.

9. The Completing The Delegation Of Control Wizard page provides a summary of the operations you have selected. To implement the changes, click Finish.

 **Real World Scenario**

Delegation: Who's Responsible for What?

You're the IT director for a large, multinational organization. You've been with the company for quite a while; that is, since the environment had only a handful of offices and a few network and system administrators. Times have changed, however. Now system administrators must coordinate the efforts of hundreds of IT staffers in 14 countries.

When the environment was a Windows NT 4 domain environment, the network was set up with many domains. For security, performance, and distribution of administration reasons, the computing resources in each major office were placed in their own domain. You have recently decided to move to Active Directory and to consolidate the numerous Windows NT domains into a single Active Directory domain. However, securely administering a distributed environment is still an important concern. Thus, the challenge involves determining how to coordinate the efforts of different system administrators.

Fortunately, through the proper use of OUs and delegation, you are given a lot of flexibility in determining how to handle the administration. You can structure the administration in several ways. First, if you choose to create OUs based on a geographic business structure, you could delegate control of these OUs based on the job functions of various system administrators. For example, you could use one user account to administer the Europe OU. Within the Europe OU, this system administrator could delegate control of offices represented by the Paris and London OUs. Within these OUs, you could further break down the administrative responsibilities for printer queue operators and security administrators.

Alternatively, the OU structure may create a functional representation of the business. For example, the Engineering OU might contain other OUs that are based on office locations such as New York and Paris. A system administrator of the Engineering domain could delegate permissions based on geography or job functions to the lower OUs. Regardless of whether you build a departmental, functional, or geographical OU model, keep in mind that each model excludes other models. This is one of the most important decisions you need to make. When you are making this decision or modifying previous decisions, your overriding concern is how it will affect the management and administration of the network. The good news is that, because Active Directory has so many features, the model you choose can be based on specific business requirements rather than imposed by architectural constraints.

Troubleshooting OUs

In general, you will find using OUs to be a relatively straightforward and painless process. With adequate planning, you'll be able to implement an intuitive and useful structure for OU objects.

The most common problems with OU configuration are related to the OU structure. When troubleshooting OUs, pay careful attention to the following factors:

Inheritance By default, Group Policy and other settings are transferred automatically from parent OUs to child OUs and objects. Even if a specific OU is not given a set of permissions, objects within that OU might still get them from parent objects.

Delegation of Administration If you allow the wrong user accounts or groups to perform specific tasks on OUs, you might be violating your company's security policy. Be sure to verify the delegations you have made at each OU level.

Organizational Issues Sometimes, business practices do not easily map to the structure of Active Directory. A few misplaced OUs, user accounts, computer accounts, or groups can make administration difficult or inaccurate. In many cases, it might be beneficial to rearrange the OU structure to accommodate any changes in the business organization. In others, it might make more sense to change business processes.

If you regularly consider each of these issues when troubleshooting problems with OUs, you will be much less likely to make errors in the Active Directory configuration.

Creating and Managing Active Directory Objects

Now that you are familiar with the task of creating OUs, you should find creating and managing other Active Directory objects quite simple. The following sections will examine the details.

Overview of Active Directory Objects

When you install and configure a domain controller, Active Directory sets up an organizational structure for you, and you can create and manage several types of objects.

Active Directory Organization

When you are looking at your Active Directory structure, you will see objects that look like folders in Windows Explorer. These objects are containers, or *organizational units (OUs)*. The difference is that an OU is a container to which you can link a GPO. Normal containers cannot have a GPO linked to it. That's what makes an OU a special container.

By default, after you install and configure a domain controller, you will see the following organizational sections within the Active Directory Users and Computers tool (they look like folders):

Built-In   The *Built-In container* includes all of the standard groups that are installed by default when you promote a domain controller. You can use these groups to administer the servers in your environment. Examples include the Administrators group, Backup Operators group, and Print Operators group.

Computers   By default, the *Computers container* contains a list of the workstations in your domain. From here, you can manage all of the computers in your domain.

Domain Controllers   The *Domain Controllers OU* includes a list of all of the domain controllers for the domain.

Foreign Security Principals   *Foreign security principals* containers are any objects to which security can be assigned and that are not part of the current domain. *Security principals* are Active Directory objects to which permissions can be applied, and they can be used to manage permissions in Active Directory.

Managed Service Accounts   The *Managed Service Accounts container* is a new Windows Server 2012 container. Service accounts are accounts created to run specific services like Exchange and SQL Server. Having a Managed Service Accounts container allows you to control the service accounts better and thus allows for better service account security.

Users   The *Users container* includes all of the security accounts that are part of the domain. When you first install the domain controller, there will be several groups in this container. For example, the Domain Admins group and the administrator account are created in this container.

You want to be sure to protect the administrator account. You should rename the admin account and make sure the password is complex. Protected admin accounts can make your network safer. Every hacker knows that there is an administrator account on the server by default. Be sure to make your network safer by protecting the admin account.

Active Directory Objects

You can create and manage several different types of Active Directory objects. The following are specific object types:

Computer   *Computer objects* represent workstations that are part of the Active Directory domain. All computers within a domain share the same security database, including user and group information. Computer objects are useful for managing security permissions and enforcing Group Policy restrictions.

Contact   *Contact objects* are usually used in OUs to specify the main administrative contact. Contacts are not security principals like users. They are used to specify information about individuals outside the organization.

Group   *Group objects* are logical collections of users primarily for assigning security permissions to resources. When managing users, you should place them into groups and then assign permissions to the group. This allows for flexible management without the need to set permissions for individual users.

InetOrgPerson The *InetOrgPerson object* is an Active Directory object that defines attributes of users in Lightweight Directory Access Protocol (LDAP) and X.500 directories.

MSIMaging-PSPs *MSIMaging-PSPs* is a container for all Enterprise Scan Post Scan Process objects.

MSMQ Queue Alias An *MSMQ Queue Alias object* is an Active Directory object for the MSMQ-Custom-Recipient class type. The MSMQ (Microsoft Message Queuing) Queue Alias object associates an Active Directory path and a user-defined alias with a public, private, or direct single-element format name. This allows a queue alias to be used to reference a queue that might not be listed in Active Directory Domain Services (AD DS).

Organizational Unit An *OU object* is created to build a hierarchy within the Active Directory domain. It is the smallest unit that can be used to create administrative groupings, and it can be used to assign group policies. Generally, the OU structure within a domain reflects a company's business organization.

Printer *Printer objects* map to printers.

Shared Folder *Shared Folder objects* map to server shares. They are used to organize the various file resources that may be available on file/print servers. Often, Shared Folder objects are used to give logical names to specific file collections. For example, system administrators might create separate shared folders for common applications, user data, and shared public files.

User A *User object* is the fundamental security principal on which Active Directory is based. User accounts contain information about individuals as well as password and other permission information.

Creating Objects Using the Active Directory Users and Computers Tool

Exercise 4.5 walks you through the steps necessary to create various objects within an Active Directory domain. In this exercise, you create some basic Active Directory objects. To complete this exercise, you must have access to at least one Active Directory domain controller, and you should have also completed the previous exercises in this chapter.

EXERCISE 4.5

Creating Active Directory Objects

1. Click the Windows key on the keyboard, and choose Administrative Tools.

2. Open the Active Directory Users and Computers tool.

3. Expand the current domain to list the objects currently contained within it. For this exercise, you will use the second- and third-level OUs contained within the North America top-level OU, as shown in the following screen shot.

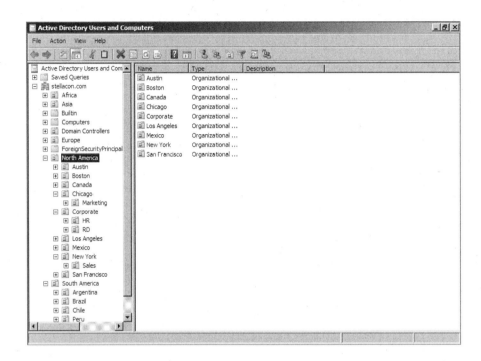

4. Right-click the Corporate OU, and select New ➤ User. Fill in the following information:

   First Name: **Maria**

   Initial: **D**

   Last Name: **President**

   Full Name: (leave as default)

   User Logon Name: **mdpresident** (leave default domain)

   Click Next to continue.

5. Enter **P@ssw0rd** for the password for this user, and then confirm it. Note that you can also make changes to password settings here. Click Next.

6. You will see a summary of the user information. Click Finish to create the new user.

7. Click the RD container, and create another user in that container with the following information:

   First Name: **John**

   Initial: **Q**

   Last Name: **Admin**

Full Name: (leave as default)

User Logon Name: **jqadmin** (leave default domain)

Click Next to continue.

8. Assign the password **P@ssw0rd**. Click Next, and then click Finish to create the user.

9. Right-click the RD OU, and select New ➢ Contact. Use the following information to fill in the properties of the Contact object:

   First Name: **Jane**

   Initials: **R**

   Last Name: **Admin**

   Display Name: **jradmin**

   Click OK to create the new Contact object.

10. Right-click the RD OU, and select New ➢ Shared Folder. Enter **Software** for the name and **\\server1\applications** for the network path (also known as the Universal Naming Convention [UNC] path). Note that you can create the object even though this resource (the physical server) does not exist. Click OK to create the Shared Folder object.

11. Right-click the HR OU, and select New ➢ Group. Type **All Users** for the group name. Do not change the value in the Group Name (Pre–Windows 2000) field. For Group Scope, select Global. and for Group Type, select Security. To create the group, click OK.

12. Right-click the Sales OU and select New ➢ Computer. Type **Workstation1** for the name of the computer. Notice that the pre–Windows 2000 name is automatically populated and that, by default, the members of the Domain Admins group are the only ones who can add this computer to the domain. Place a check mark in the Assign This Computer Account As A Pre-Windows 2000 Computer box, and then click OK to create the Computer object.

13. Close the Active Directory Users and Computers tool.

Configuring the User Principal Name

When you log into a domain, your logon name looks like an email address (for example, wpanek@willpanek.com): This is called your *user principal name (UPN)*. A UPN is the username followed by the @ sign and the domain name. At the time that the user account is created, the UPN suffix is generated by default. The UPN is created as *userName@DomainName*, but an administrator can alter or change the default UPN. If your forest has multiple domains and you need to change the UPN to a different domain, you have that ability. To change the UPN suffix, in Active Directory Users and Computers, choose a user and go into their properties. Choose the Attribute Editor tab. Scroll down to the userPrincipalName attribute and make your changes. These changes then get replicated to the global catalog.

If your organization has multiple forests set up by a trust, you can't change the UPN to a domain in the other forest. Global catalogs are used to log on users. Because UPNs get replicated to the local forest global catalog servers, you cannot log onto other forests using the UPN.

Using Templates

Now we are going to dive into user templates. *User templates* allow an Active Directory administrator to create a default account (for example, template_sales) and use that account to create all the other users that match it (all the salespeople).

If you are creating multiple accounts, this can save you a lot of time and resources. For example, if you need to add 35 new salespeople to your company, you'll create one template for sales and use a copy of that template for all the other new accounts. This saves you the trouble of filling out many of the same fields over and over again. When you copy a template, some of the information does *not* get copied over. This is because it is user-specific information. Here are some of the fields that do not get copied over from a template:

- Name
- Logon Name
- Password
- Email
- Phone Numbers
- Description
- Office
- Web Page

Many of the important fields like Member Of (groups to which the user belongs), Profile Path, Department, and Company all get copied over. There is one very important item that needs to be done when creating a template: The template account needs to be disabled after creation. You do not want anyone using this account to access your network. In Exercise 4.6, you will create a Sales template to use for your Sales department.

EXERCISE 4.6

Creating a User Template

1. Click the Windows key on the keyboard, and choose Administrative Tools.

2. Open the Active Directory Users and Computers snap-in.

3. Expand the current domain to list the objects contained within it. For this exercise, you will use the Sales OU. Right-click the Sales OU, and choose New ➢ User.

4. Use the following properties:

   First Name: **Sales**

   Last Name: **Template**

   Username: **sales_template**

   Password: **P@ssw0rd**

5. Click Next and then click Finish.

6. In the right-hand window, double-click the Sales Template user to open the properties.

7. Under the General tab, complete the following items:

   Description: **Template Account**

   Office: **Corporate**

   Telephone: **999-999-9999**

   Email: **Salet@abc.com**

   Web: **www.abc.com**

8. Click the Profile tab. In the Profile Path field, type **\\ServerA\%username%.**

9. On the Members Of tab, click the Add button. At the Enter The Object Name To Select box, type **Administrator**, and click the Check Names button. (Normally you would not add salespeople to the Administrators group, but we are doing so just for this exercise.) Click OK.

10. Click the Account tab. Scroll down in the Account Options box, and check the Account Is Disabled check box.

11. Click OK on the user's Properties window to go back to the Sales OU.

12. Right-click the Sales Template account and choose Copy.

13. Enter the following information:

    First Name: **Jenny**

    Last Name: **Sales**

    Username: **jsales**

    Password: **P@ssw0rd**

    Uncheck the Account Is disabled check box.

14. In the right-hand window, double-click the Jenny Sales user to open the properties.

15. Take a look at the Members Of tab, the General tab, and the Profile tab, and you will see that some of the fields are prefilled (including the Administrators group).

16. Close Jenny Sales Properties, and exit Active Directory Users and Computers.

Importing Objects from a File

In Exercise 4.5, you created an account using the Active Directory Users and Computers tool. But what if you need to bulk import accounts? There are two main applications for doing bulk imports of accounts: the ldifde.exe utility and the csvde.exe utility. Both utilities import accounts from files.

The ldifde utility imports from line-delimited files. This utility allows an administrator to export and import data, thus allowing batch operations like Add, Modify, and Delete to be performed in Active Directory. Windows Server 2012 includes ldifde.exe to help support batch operations.

The csvde.exe utility performs the same export functions as ldifde.exe, but csvde.exe uses a comma-separated value file format. The csvde.exe utility does not allow administrators to modify or delete objects. It supports only adding objects to Active Directory.

Active Directory Migration Tool v3.2

Another tool you can use to help import and migrate users is the *Active Directory Migration Tool (ADMT)* v3.2. ADMT v3.2 allows an administrator to migrate users, groups, and computers from a Microsoft Server 2003 domain (or Windows Server 2008, 2008 R2, or 2012) to a Windows Server 2012 Active Directory domain.

Administrators can also use the ADMT v3.2 to migrate users, groups, and computers between Active Directory domains in different forests (interforest migration) and between Active Directory domains in the same forest (intraforest migration). ADMT v3.2 also helps administrators perform security translations from a Windows Server 2003 domain (or Windows Server 2008, 2008 R2, or 2012) to a Windows Server 2012 Active Directory domain. ADMT v3.2 allows security translations between Active Directory domains in different forests.

Offline Domain Join of a Computer

Offline domain join gives administrators the ability to preprovision computer accounts in the domain to prepare operating systems for deployments. At startup, computers can then join the domain without the need to contact a domain controller. This helps reduce the time it takes to deploy computers in a datacenter.

Let's say your datacenter needs to have multiple virtual machines deployed. This is where offline domain join can be useful. Upon initial startup after the operating system is installed, offline domain join allows the virtual machines to join the domain automatically. No additional steps or restart are needed.

The following are some of the benefits of using offline domain join:

- No additional network traffic for Active Directory state changes.
- No additional network traffic for computer state changes to the domain controller.
- Changes for both the Active Directory state and the computer state can be completed at a different times.

Managing Object Properties

Once you've created the necessary Active Directory objects, you'll probably need to make changes to their default properties. In addition to the settings you made when you were creating Active Directory objects, you can configure several more properties. You can also access object properties by right-clicking any object and selecting Properties from the pop-up menu.

Each object type contains a unique set of properties.

User Object Properties

The following list describes some of the properties of a User object:

General   General account information about this user.

Address   Physical location information about this user.

Account   User logon name and other account restrictions, such as workstation restrictions and logon hours.

Profile   Information about the user's roaming profile settings.

Telephones   Telephone contact information for the user.

Organization   The user's title, department, and company information.

Member Of   Group membership information for the user.

Dial-In   Remote Access Service (RAS) permissions for the user.

Environment   Logon and other network settings for the user.

Sessions   Session limits, including maximum session time and idle session settings.

Remote Control   Remote control options for this user's session.

Remote Desktop Services Profile   Information about the user's profile for use with Remote Desktop Services.

Personal Virtual Desktop   Allows you to assign a user a specific virtual machine to use as a personal virtual desktop.

COM+   Specifies a COM+ partition set for the user.

Computer Object Properties

Computer objects have different properties than User objects. Computer objects refer to the systems that clients are operating to be part of a domain. The following list describes some Computer object properties:

General   Information about the name of the computer, the role of the computer, and its description.

You can enable an option to allow the Local System account of this machine to request services from other servers. This is useful if the machine is a trusted and secure computer.

Operating System   The name, version, and service pack information for the operating system running on the computer.

Member Of   Active Directory groups of which this Computer object is a member.

Delegation   Allows you to set services that work on behalf of another user.

Location   A description of the computer's physical location.

Managed By   Information about the User or Contact object that is responsible for managing this computer.

Dial-In   Sets dial-in options for the computer.

Setting Properties for Active Directory Objects

Now that you have seen the various properties that can be set for the Active Directory objects, let's complete an exercise on how to configure some of these properties. Exercise 4.7 walks you through how to set various properties for Active Directory objects. To complete the steps in this exercise, first you must have completed Exercise 4.5.

Although it may seem a bit tedious, it's always a good idea to enter as much information as you know about Active Directory objects when you create them. Although the name Printer1 may be meaningful to you, users will appreciate the additional information, such as location, when they are searching for objects.

EXERCISE 4.7

Managing Object Properties

1. Click the Windows key on the keyboard, and choose Administrative Tools.

2. Open the Active Directory Users and Computers tool.

3. Expand the name of the domain, and select the RD container. Right-click the John Q. Adams user account, and select Properties.

4. Here you will see the various Properties tabs for the User account. Make some configuration changes based on your personal preferences. Click OK to continue.

5. Select the HR OU. Right-click the All Users group, and click Properties. In the All Users Properties dialog box, you will be able to modify the membership of the group.

   Click the Members tab, and then click Add. Add the Maria D. President and John Q. Admin user accounts to the group. Click OK to save the settings, and then OK to accept the group modifications.

6. Select the Sales OU. Right-click the Workstation1 Computer object. Notice that you can choose to disable the account or reset it (to allow another computer to join the domain under that same name). From the context menu, choose Properties. You'll see the properties for the Computer object.

   Examine the various options, and make changes based on your personal preference. After you have examined the available options, click OK to continue.

7. Select the Corporate OU. Right-click the Maria D. President user account, and choose Reset Password. You will be prompted to enter a new password, and then you'll be asked to confirm it. Note that you can also force the user to change this password upon the next logon, and you can also unlock the user's account from here. For this exercise, do not enter a new password; just click Cancel.

8. Close the Active Directory Users and Computers tool.

By now you have probably noticed that Active Directory objects have a lot of common options. For example, Group and Computer objects both have a Managed By tab.

Windows Server 2012 allows you to manage many User objects at once. For instance, you can select several User objects by holding down the Shift or Ctrl key while selecting. You can then right-click any one of the selected objects and select Properties to display the properties that are available for multiple users. Notice that not every user property is available because some properties are unique to each user. You can configure the Description field for multiple object selections that include both users and nonusers, such as computers and groups.

A very important thing to think about when it comes to accounts is the difference between disabling an account and deleting an account. When you delete an account, the security ID (SID) gets deleted. Even if you later create an account with the same username, it will have a different SID number, and therefore it will be a different account. It is sometimes better to disable an account and place it into a nonactive OU called *Disabled*. This way, if you ever need to reaccess the account, you can do so.

Another object management task is the process of deprovisioning. *Deprovisioning* is the management of Active Directory objects in the container. When you remove an object from an Active Directory container, the deprovisioning process removes the object and synchronizes the container to stay current.

Understanding Groups

Now that you know how to create user accounts, it's time to learn how to create group accounts. As an instructor, I am always amazed when students (who work in the IT field) have no idea why they should use groups. This is something every organization should be using.

To illustrate their usefulness, let's say you have a Sales department user by the name of wpanek. Your organization has 100 resources shared on the network for users to access. Because wpanek is part of the Sales department, he has access to 50 of the resources. The Marketing department uses the other 50. If the organization is not using groups and wpanek moves from Sales to Marketing, how many changes do you have to make? The answer is 100. You have to move him out of the 50 resources he currently can use and place his account into the 50 new resources that he now needs.

Now let's say that you use groups. The Sales group has access to 50 resources and the Marketing group has access to the other 50. If wpanek moves from Sales to Marketing, you only need to make two changes. You just have to take wpanek out of the Sales group and place him in the Marketing group. Once this is done, wpanek can access everything he needs to do his job.

Group Properties

Now that you understand why you should use groups, let's go over setting up groups and their properties. When you are creating groups, it helps to understand some of the options that you need to use.

Group Type   You can choose from two group types: security groups and distribution groups.

> **Security Groups**   These groups can have rights and permissions placed on them. For example, if you want to give a certain group of users access to a particular printer but you want to control what they are allowed to do with this printer, you'd create a security group and then apply certain rights and permissions to this group.
>
> Security groups can also receive emails. If someone sent an email to the group, all users within that group would receive it (as long as they have a mail system that allows for mail-enabled groups, like Exchange).
>
> **Distribution Groups**   These groups are used for email *only* (as long as they have a mail system that allows for mail-enabled groups, like Exchange). You cannot place permissions and rights for objects on this group type.

Group Scope   When it comes to group scopes, you have three choices:

> **Domain Local Groups**   Domain local groups are groups that remain in the domain in which they were created. You use these groups to grant permissions within a single domain. For example, if you create a domain local group named HPLaser, you cannot use that group in any other domain, and it has to reside in the domain in which you created it.
>
> **Global Group**   Global groups can contain other groups and accounts from the domain in which the group is created. In addition, you can give them permissions in any domain in the forest.
>
> **Universal Groups**   Universal groups can include other groups and accounts from any domain in the domain tree or forest. You can give universal groups permissions in any domain in the domain tree or forest.

Creating Group Strategies

When you are creating a group strategy, think of this acronym that Microsoft likes to use in the exam: *AGDLP* (or *AGLP*). This acronym stands for a series of actions you should perform. Here is how it expands:

A   Accounts (Create your user accounts.)

G   Global groups (Put user accounts into global groups.)

DL   Domain local groups (Put global groups into domain local groups.)

P   Permissions (Assign permissions like Deny or Apply on the domain local group.)

Another acronym that stands for a strategy you can use is *AGUDLP* (or *AULP*). Here is how it expands:

A   Accounts (Create your user accounts.)

G   Global groups (Put user accounts into global groups.)

U   Universal groups (Put the global groups into universal groups.)

DL   Domain local groups (Put universal groups into domain local groups.)

P   Permissions (Place permissions on the local group.)

Creating a Group

To create a new group, open the Active Directory Users and Computers snap-in. Click the OU where the group is going to reside. Right-click and choose New and then Group. After you create the group, just click the Members tab and choose Add. Add the users that you want to reside in that group, and that's all there is to it.

Filtering and Advanced Active Directory Features

The Active Directory Users and Computers tool has a couple of other features that come in quite handy when you are managing many objects. You can access the Filter Options dialog box by clicking the View menu in the MMC and choosing Filter Options. You'll see a dialog box similar to the one shown in Figure 4.6. Here you can choose to filter objects by their specific types within the display. For example, if you are an administrator who works primarily with user accounts and groups, you can select those specific items by placing check marks in the list. In addition, you can create more complex filters by choosing Create Custom. Doing so provides you with an interface that looks similar to that of the Find command.

FIGURE 4.6   The Filter Options dialog box

Another option in the Active Directory Users and Computers tool is to view advanced options. You can enable the advanced options by choosing Advanced Features in the View menu. This adds some top-level folders to the list under the name of the domain. Let's take a look at a couple of the new top-level folders.

The System folder (shown in Figure 4.7) provides additional features that you can configure to work with Active Directory. You can configure settings for the Distributed File System (DFS), IP Security (IPSec) policies, the File Replication Service (FRS), and more. In addition to the System folder, you'll see the LostAndFound folder. This folder contains any files that may not have been replicated properly between domain controllers. You should check this folder periodically for any files so that you can decide whether you need to move them or copy them to other locations.

FIGURE 4.7 Advanced Features in the System folder of the Active Directory Users and Computers tool

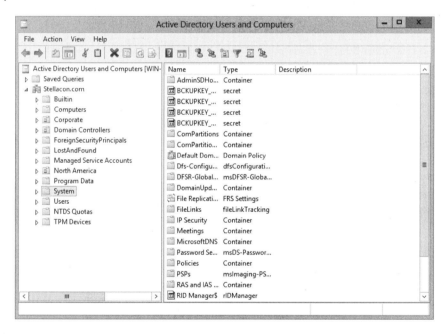

As you can see, managing Active Directory objects is generally a simple task. The Active Directory Users and Computers tool allows you to configure several objects. Let's move on to look at one more common administration function—moving objects.

Moving, Renaming, and Deleting Active Directory Objects

One of the extremely useful features of the Active Directory Users and Computers tool is its ability to move users and resources easily.

Exercise 4.8 walks you through the process of moving Active Directory objects. In this exercise, you will make several changes to the organization of Active Directory objects. To complete this exercise, first you must have completed Exercise 4.5.

EXERCISE 4.8

Moving Active Directory Objects

1. Click the Windows key on the keyboard, and choose Administrative Tools.

2. Open the Active Directory Users and Computers tool, and expand the name of the domain.

3. Select the Sales OU (under the New York OU), right-click Workstation1, and select Move. A dialog box appears. Select the RD OU, and click OK to move the Computer object to that container.

4. Click the RD OU, and verify that Workstation1 was moved.

5. Close the Active Directory Users and Computers tool.

In addition to moving objects within Active Directory, you can easily rename them by right-clicking an object and selecting Rename. Note that this option does not apply to all objects. You can remove objects from Active Directory by right-clicking them and choosing Delete.

WARNING Deleting an Active Directory object is an irreversible action. When an object is destroyed, any security permissions or other settings made for that object are removed as well. Because each object within Active Directory contains its own security identifier (SID), simply re-creating an object with the same name does not place any permissions on it. Before you delete an Active Directory object, be sure that you will never need it again. Windows Server 2012 has an Active Directory Recycle Bin to allow an administrator to retrieve a deleted object, but in case the Recycle Bin gets cleared, it's better to be safe than sorry. Don't delete AD objects unless you are absolutely sure.

TIP Windows Server 2012 has a check box called Protect Container From Accidental Deletion for all OUs. If this check box is checked, to delete or move an OU you must go into the Active Directory Users and Computers advanced options. Once you are in the advanced options, you can uncheck the box to move or delete the OU.

Resetting an Existing Computer Account

Every computer on the domain establishes a discrete channel of communication with the domain controller at logon time. The domain controller stores a randomly selected password (different from the user password) for authentication across the channel. The password is updated every 30 days.

Sometimes the computer's password and the domain controller's password don't match, and communication between the two machines fails. Without the ability to reset the computer account, you wouldn't be able to connect the machine to the domain. Fortunately, you can use the Active Directory Users and Computers tool to reestablish the connection.

Exercise 4.9 shows you how to reset an existing computer account. You should have completed the previous exercises in this chapter before you begin this exercise.

EXERCISE 4.9

Resetting an Existing Computer Account

1. Click the Windows key on the keyboard, and choose Administrative Tools.

2. Open the Active Directory Users and Computers tool, and expand the name of the domain.

3. Click the RD OU, and then right-click the Workstation1 computer account.

4. Select Reset Account from the context menu. Click Yes to confirm your selection. Click OK at the success prompt.

5. When you reset the account, you break the connection between the computer and the domain. So after performing this exercise, reconnect the computer to the domain if you want it to continue working on the network.

Publishing Active Directory Objects

One of the main goals of Active Directory is to make resources easy to find. Two of the most commonly used resources in a networked environment are server file shares and printers. These are so common, in fact, that most organizations have dedicated file and print servers. When it comes to managing these types of resources, Active Directory makes it easy to determine which files and printers are available to users.

With that being said, take a look at how Active Directory manages to publish shared folders and printers.

Making Active Directory Objects Available to Users

An important aspect of managing Active Directory objects is that a system administrator can control which objects users can see. The act of making an Active Directory object available is known as *publishing*. The two main types of publishable objects are Printer objects and Shared Folder objects.

The general process for creating server shares and shared printers has remained unchanged from previous versions of Windows: You create the various objects (a printer or a file system folder) and then enable them for sharing. To make these resources available via Active Directory, however, there's an additional step: You must publish the resources. Once an object has been published in Active Directory, clients will be able to use it.

When you publish objects in Active Directory, you should know the server name and share name of the resource. When system administrators use Active Directory objects, they can change the resource to which the object points without having to reconfigure or even notify clients. For example, if you move a share from one server to another, all you need to do is update the Shared Folder object's properties to point to the new location. Active Directory clients still refer to the resource with the same path and name they used before.

Publishing Printers

Printers can be published easily within Active Directory. This makes them available to users in your domain.

Exercise 4.10 walks you through the steps you need to take to share and publish a Printer object by having you create and share a printer. To complete the printer installation, you need access to the Windows Server 2012 installation media (via the hard disk, a network share, or the CD-ROM drive).

EXERCISE 4.10

Creating and Publishing a Printer

1. Click the Windows key on the keyboard, and choose Control Panel.

2. Click Devices And Printers ➢ Add A Printer. This starts the Add Printer Wizard. Then click the Next button.

3. In the Choose A Local Or Network Printer page, select Add A Local Printer. This should automatically take you to the next page. If it does not, click Next.

4. In the Choose A Printer Port page, select Use An Existing Port. From the drop-down list beside that option, make sure LPT1: (Printer Port) is selected. Click Next.

5. On the Install The Printer Driver page, select Generic for the manufacturer. For the printer, highlight Generic/Text Only. Click Next.

6. On the Type A Printer Name page, type **Text Printer**. Uncheck the Set As The Default Printer box, and then click Next.

7. The Installing Printer screen appears. After the system is finished, the Printer Sharing page appears. Make sure the box labeled "Share this printer so that others on your

network can find and use it" is selected, and accept the default share name of Text Printer.

8. In the Location section, type **Building 203**, and in the Comment section, add the following comment: **This is a text-only Printer**. Click Next.

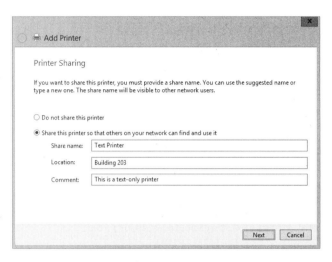

9. On the You've Successfully Added Text Printer page, click Finish.

10. Next you need to verify that the printer will be listed in Active Directory. Right-click the Text Printer icon, and select Printer Properties.

11. Select the Sharing tab, and ensure that the List In The Directory box is checked. Note that you can also add additional printer drivers for other operating systems using this tab. Click OK to accept the settings.

Note that when you create and share a printer this way, an Active Directory Printer object is not displayed within the Active Directory Users and Computers tool. The printer is actually associated with the Computer object to which it is connected.

Publishing Shared Folders

Now that you've created and published a printer, you'll see how the same thing can be done to shared folders.

Exercise 4.11 walks through the steps required to create a folder, share it, and then publish it in Active Directory. This exercise assumes that you are using the C: partition; however, you may want to change this based on your server configuration. This exercise assumes that you have completed Exercise 4.5.

EXERCISE 4.11

Creating and Publishing a Shared Folder

1. Create a new folder in the root directory of your C: partition, and name it Test Share. To do this, click the File Explorer link on the toolbar.

2. Right-click the Test Share folder. Choose Share With ➢ Specific People.

3. In the File Sharing dialog box, enter the names of users with whom you want to share this folder. In the upper box, enter **Everyone** and then click Add. Note that Everyone appears in the lower box. Click in the Permission Level column next to Everyone, and choose Read/Write from the pop-up menu. Then click Share.

4. You'll see a message that your folder has been shared. Click Done.

5. Click the Windows key on the keyboard, and choose Administrative Tools.

6. Open the Active Directory Users and Computers tool. Expand the current domain, and right-click the RD OU. Select New ➢ Shared Folder.

7. In the New Object - Shared Folder dialog box, type **Shared Folder Test** for the name of the folder. Then type the UNC path to the share (for example, **\\server1\Test Share**). Click OK to create the share.

Once you have created and published the Shared Folder object, clients can use the My Network Places icon to find it. The Shared Folder object will be organized based on the OU in which you created it. When you use publication, you can see how this makes it easy to manage shared folders.

Querying Active Directory

So far you've created several Active Directory resources. One of the main benefits of having all of your resource information in Active Directory is that you can easily find what you're looking for using the Find dialog box. Recall that I recommended that you always enter as much information as possible when creating Active Directory objects. This is where that extra effort begins to pay off.

Exercise 4.12 walks you through the steps to find specific objects in Active Directory. To complete this exercise, you must have completed Exercise 4.5.

Finding Objects in Active Directory

1. Click the Windows key on the keyboard, and choose Administrative Tools.

2. Open the Active Directory Users and Computers tool.

3. Right-click the name of the domain and select Find.

4. In the Find Users, Contacts, And Groups dialog box, select Users, Contacts, And Groups from the Find drop-down list. For the In setting, choose Entire Directory. This searches the entire Active Directory environment for the criteria you enter.

   Note that if this is a production domain and there are many objects, searching the whole directory may be a time-consuming and network-intensive operation.

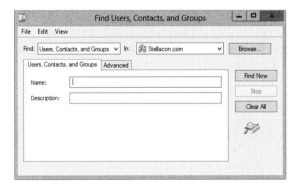

5. In the Name field, type **admin** and then click Find Now to obtain the results of the search.

6. Now that you have found several results, you can narrow down the list. Click the Advanced tab of the Find Users, Contacts, And Groups dialog box.

In the Field drop-down list, select User ➤ Last Name. For Condition, select Starts With, and for Value, type **admin**. Click Add to add this condition to the search criteria. Click Find Now. Now only the users that have the last name Admin are shown.

7.   When you have finished searching, close the Find Users, Contacts, And Groups dialog box and exit the Active Directory Users and Computers tool.

Using the many options available in the Find dialog box, you can usually narrow down the objects for which you are searching quickly and efficiently. Users and system administrators alike find this tool useful in environments of any size. Now that you have seen how to create objects in Active Directory, let's take a look at a new Windows Server 2012 feature called Active Directory Administrative Center.

Using the Active Directory Administrative Center

Windows Server 2012 has a feature called the *Active Directory Administrative Center* (see Figure 4.8). This feature allows you to manage many Active Directory tasks from one central location (see Figure 4.9).

FIGURE 4.8   Active Directory Administrative Center

FIGURE 4.9   Administrative Center Overview screen

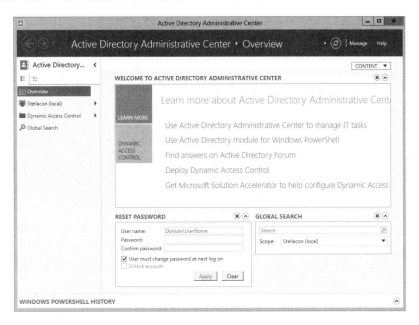

Using the Active Directory Administrative Center, here are some of the tasks that an administrator can perform:

- Reset passwords.
- Create new objects.
- Delete objects.
- Move objects.
- Perform global searches.
- Configure properties for Active Directory objects.

In Windows Server 2012, the Active Directory Administrative Center is just another tool in your Active Directory tool belt. It does not matter which way you create your Active Directory objects as long as you have a good understanding of how to create them.

Using the Command Prompt for Active Directory Configuration

Many IT administrators like to use command-line commands to configure and maintain their Active Directory environment. One advantage to using command-line commands is the ability to do multiple changes at once using batch files.

Another advantage to knowing how to manipulate Active Directory using the command prompt is working with Windows Server 2012 Server Core. Server Core is an installation of Windows Server 2012 that has no GUI windows. One of the ways to configure Server Core is to use commands in the command prompt window.

Table 4.1 shows you many of the command prompt commands and explains how each command affects Active Directory.

TABLE 4.1 Command prompt commands

Command	Explanation
Csvde	This command allows you to import and export data from Active Directory. The data gets stored in a comma-separated value (CSV) format.
Dcdiag	This troubleshooting command checks the state of your domain controllers in your forest and sends back a report of any problems.
Dsacls	This command allows you to see and change permissions in the access control list (ACL) for objects in Active Directory Domain Services (AD DS).
Dsadd	This command allows you to add an object to the AD DS directory.
Dsamain	This command shows the Active Directory data stored in either a snapshot or a backup as if it were in a Lightweight Directory Access Protocol (LDAP) server.
Dsdbutil	This command provides database utilities for Active Directory Lightweight Directory Services (AD LDS).
Dsget	This command shows the properties of an object in the AD DS directory.
Dsmgmt	This command gives an administrator management utilities for AD LDS.
Dsmod	This command allows you to modify an AD DS object.
Dsmove	This command allows you to move an object in an Active Directory domain from its current OU to a new OU within the same forest.
Dsquery	This command allows you to query AD DS.
Dsrm	This command removes an object from the AD DS directory.
Ldifde	This command allows you to import and export data from Active Directory. The data is stored as LDAP Data Interchange Format (LDIF).
Ntdsutil	This is one of the most important commands for Active Directory. It allows you to do maintenance on the Active Directory database.
Repadmin	This command allows administrators to diagnose Active Directory replication problems between domain controllers.

Summary

This chapter covered the fundamentals of administering Active Directory. The most important part of administering Active Directory is learning about how to work with OUs. Therefore, you should be aware of the purpose of OUs; that is, they help you to organize and manage the directory. For instance, think of administrative control. If you wanted to delegate rights to another administrator (such as a sales manager), you could delegate that authority to that user within the Sales OU. As the system administrator, you would retain the rights to the castle.

We also looked at how to design an OU structure from an example. The example showed you how to design proper OU layout. You can also create, organize, and reorganize OUs if need be.

In addition, we took a look at groups and group strategies. There are different types of groups—domain local, global, and universal groups and you should know when each group is available and when to use each group.

Last, this chapter covered how to use the Active Directory Users and Computers tool to manage Active Directory objects. If you're responsible for day-to-day system administration, there's a good chance that you are already familiar with this tool; if not, you should be now. Using this tool, you learned how to work with Active Directory objects such as User, Computer, and Group objects. You also learned how to import users by doing a bulk import, and you studied the two different file types that work for bulk imports. Bulk imports allow you to import multiple users without the need to add one user at a time.

Exam Essentials

Understand the purpose of OUs.   OUs are used to create a hierarchical, logical organization for objects within an Active Directory domain.

Know the types of objects that can reside within OUs.   OUs can contain Active Directory User, Computer, Shared Folder, and other objects.

Understand how to use the Delegation of Control Wizard.   The Delegation of Control Wizard is used to assign specific permissions at the level of OUs.

Understand the concept of inheritance.   By default, child OUs inherit permissions and Group Policy assignments set for parent OUs. However, these settings can be overridden for more granular control of security.

Know groups and group strategies.   You can use three groups in Native mode: domain local, global, and universal. Understand the group strategies and when they apply.

Understand how Active Directory objects work.   Active Directory objects represent some piece of information about components within a domain. The objects themselves have attributes that describe details about them.

Understand how Active Directory objects can be organized.   By using the Active Directory Users and Computers tool, you can create, move, rename, and delete various objects.

Understand how to import bulk users.   You can import multiple accounts by doing a bulk import. Bulk imports use files to import the data into Active Directory. Know the two utilities (`ldifde.exe` and `csvde.exe`) you need to perform the bulk imports and how to use them.

Learn how resources can be published.   A design goal for Active Directory was to make network resources easier for users to find. With that in mind, you should understand how using published printers and shared folders can simplify network resource management.

Review Questions

1. You are the administrator of an organization with a single Active Directory domain. A user who left the company returns after 16 weeks. The user tries to log onto their old computer and receives an error stating that authentication has failed. The user's account has been enabled. You need to ensure that the user is able to log onto the domain using that computer. What do you do?

   A. Reset the computer account in Active Directory. Disjoin the computer from the domain, and then rejoin the computer to the domain.

   B. Run the ADadd command to rejoin the computer account.

   C. Run the MMC utility on the user's computer, and add the Domain Computers snap-in.

   D. Re-create the user account, and reconnect the user account to the computer account.

2. You are the administrator of an organization with a single Active Directory domain. One of your senior executives tries to log onto a machine and receives the error "This user account has expired. Ask your administrator to reactivate your account." You need to make sure that this doesn't happen again to this user. What do you do?

   A. Configure the domain policy to disable account lockouts.

   B. Configure the password policy to extend the maximum password age to 0.

   C. Modify the user's properties to set the Account Never Expires setting.

   D. Modify the user's properties to extend the maximum password age to 0.

3. You need to create a new user account using the command prompt. Which command would you use?

   A. dsmodify

   B. dscreate

   C. dsnew

   D. dsadd

4. Maria is a user who belongs to the Sales distribution global group. She is not able to access the laser printer that is shared on the network. The Sales global group has full access to the laser printer. How do you fix the problem?

   A. Change the group type to a security group.

   B. Add the Sales global group to the Administrators group.

   C. Add the Sales global group to the Printer Operators group.

   D. Change the Sales group to a local group.

5. You are a domain administrator for a large domain. Recently, you have been asked to make changes to some of the permissions related to OUs within the domain. To restrict security for the Texas OU further, you remove some permissions at that level. Later, a junior system administrator mentions that she is no longer able to make changes to objects within the Austin OU (which is located within the Texas OU). Assuming that no other changes have been made to Active Directory permissions, which of the following characteristics of OUs might have caused the change in permissions?

   A. Inheritance

   B. Group Policy

   C. Delegation

   D. Object properties

6. Isabel, a system administrator, created a new Active Directory domain in an environment that already contains two trees. During the promotion of the domain controller, she chose to create a new Active Directory forest. Isabel is a member of the Enterprise Administrators group and has full permissions over all domains. During the organization's migration to Active Directory, many updates were made to the information stored within the domains. Recently, users and other system administrators have complained about not being able to find specific Active Directory objects in one or more domains (although the objects exist in others). To investigate the problem, Isabel wants to check for any objects that have not been properly replicated among domain controllers. If possible, she would like to restore these objects to their proper place within the relevant Active Directory domains.

   Which two of the following actions should she perform to be able to view the relevant information? (Choose two.)

   A. Change Active Directory permissions to allow object information to be viewed in all domains.

   B. Select the Advanced Features item in the View menu.

   C. Promote a member server in each domain to a domain controller.

   D. Rebuild all domain controllers from the latest backups.

   E. Examine the contents of the LostAndFound folder using the Active Directory Users and Computers tool.

7. You are a consultant hired to evaluate an organization's Active Directory domain. The domain contains over 200,000 objects and hundreds of OUs. You begin examining the objects within the domain, but you find that the loading of the contents of specific OUs takes a very long time. Furthermore, the list of objects can be very large. You want to do the following:

   ▪ Use the built-in Active Directory administrative tools, and avoid the use of third-party tools or utilities.

   ▪ Limit the list of objects within an OU to only the type of objects that you're examining (for example, only Computer objects).

   ▪ Prevent any changes to the Active Directory domain or any of the objects within it.

   Which one of the following actions meets these requirements?

   A. Use the Filter option in the Active Directory Users and Computers tool to restrict the display of objects.

   B. Use the Delegation of Control Wizard to give yourself permissions over only a certain type of object.

   C. Implement a new naming convention for objects within an OU and then sort the results using this new naming convention.

   D. Use the Active Directory Domains and Trusts tool to view information from only selected domain controllers.

   E. Edit the domain Group Policy settings to allow yourself to view only the objects of interest.

8. Your organization is currently planning a migration from a Windows NT 4 environment that consists of several domains to an Active Directory environment. Your staff consists of 25 system administrators who are responsible for managing one or more domains. The organization is finalizing a merger with another company. Will, a technical planner, has recently provided you with a preliminary plan to migrate your environment to several Active Directory domains. He has cited security and administration as major justifications for this plan. Crystal, a consultant, has recommended that the Windows NT 4 domains be consolidated into a single Active Directory domain. Which of the following statements provide a valid justification to support Crystal's proposal? (Choose all that apply.)

   A. In general, OU structure is more flexible than domain structure.

   B. In general, domain structure is more flexible than OU structure.

   C. It is possible to create a distributed system administration structure for OUs by using delegation.

   D. The use of OUs within a single domain can greatly increase the security of the overall environment.

9. Miguel is a junior-level system administrator, and he has basic knowledge about working with Active Directory. As his supervisor, you have asked Miguel to make several security-related changes to OUs within the company's Active Directory domain. You instruct Miguel to use the basic functionality provided in the Delegation of Control Wizard. Which of the following operations are represented as common tasks within the Delegation of Control Wizard? (Choose all that apply.)

    A. Reset passwords on user accounts.

    B. Manage Group Policy links.

    C. Modify the membership of a group.

    D. Create, delete, and manage groups.

10. You are the primary system administrator for a large Active Directory domain. Recently, you have hired another system administrator upon whom you intend to offload some of your responsibilities. This system administrator will be responsible for handling help desk calls and for basic user account management. You want to allow the new employee to have permissions to reset passwords for all users within a specific OU. However, for security reasons, it's important that the user not be able to make permissions changes for objects within other OUs in the domain. Which of the following is the best way to do this?

    A. Create a special administration account within the OU, and grant it full permissions for all objects within Active Directory.

    B. Move the user's login account into the OU that the new employee is to administer.

    C. Move the user's login account to an OU that contains the OU (that is, the parent OU of the one that the new employee is to administer).

    D. Use the Delegation of Control Wizard to assign the necessary permissions on the OU that the new employee is to administer.

Chapter

5

Managing Group Policy Objects

THE FOLLOWING 70-410 EXAM OBJECTIVES ARE COVERED IN THIS CHAPTER:

✓ **Create Group Policy Objects (GPOs)**

 ▪ This objective may include, but is not limited to: Configure a Central Store; manage starter GPOs; configure GPO links; configure multiple local group policies; configure security filtering.

✓ **Configure application restriction policies**

 ▪ This objective may include, but is not limited to: Configure rule enforcement; configure AppLocker rules; configure Software Restriction Policies.

THE FOLLOWING 70-411 EXAM OBJECTIVES ARE COVERED IN THIS CHAPTER:

✓ **Configure Group Policy processing**

 ▪ This objective may include, but is not limited to: Configure processing order and precedence; configure blocking of inheritance; configure enforced policies; configure security filtering and WMI filtering; configure loopback processing; configure and manage slow-link processing; configure client-side extension (CSE) behavior.

✓ **Configure Group Policy settings**

 ▪ This objective may include, but is not limited to: Configure settings including software installation, folder redirection, scripts, and administrative template settings; import security templates; import custom administrative template file; convert administrative templates using ADMX

Migrator; configure property filters for administrative templates.

✓ Manage Group Policy Objects (GPOs)

- This objective may include, but is not limited to: Back up, import, copy, and restore GPOs; create and configure Migration Table; reset default GPOs; delegate Group Policy management.

✓ Configure Group Policy Preferences

- This objective may include, but is not limited to: Configure Group Policy Preferences (GPP) settings including printers, network drive mappings, power options, custom registry settings, Control Panel settings, Internet Explorer settings, file and folder deployment, and shortcut deployment; configure item-level targeting.

For many years, making changes to computer or user environments was a time-consuming process. If you wanted to install a service pack or a piece of software, unless you had a third-party utility, you had to use the so-called *sneak-ernet* (that is, you had to walk from one computer to another with a disk containing the software).

Installing any type of software was one of the biggest challenges faced by system administrators. It was difficult enough to deploy and manage workstations throughout the environment. Combined with the fact that users were generally able to make system configuration changes, it quickly became a management nightmare!

For example, imagine that a user noticed that they did not have enough disk space to copy a large file. Instead of seeking assistance from the IT help desk, they may have decided to do a little cleanup on their own. Unfortunately, this cleanup operation may have resulted in deleting critical system files! Or, consider the case of users who changed system settings "just to see what they did." Relatively minor changes, such as modifying TCP/IP bindings or Desktop settings, could cause hours of support headaches. Now multiply these (or other common) problems by hundreds (or even thousands) of end users. Clearly, system administrators needed to have a way to limit the options available to users of client operating systems.

How do you prevent problems like these from occurring in a Windows Server 2012 environment? Fortunately, there's a readily available solution delivered with the base operating system that's easy to implement. One of the most important system administration features in Windows Server 2012 and Active Directory is *Group Policy*. By using *Group Policy objects (GPOs)*, administrators can quickly and easily define restrictions on common actions and then apply them at the site, domain, or organizational unit (OU) level. In this chapter, you will see how group policies work, and then you will look at how to implement them within an Active Directory environment.

Introducing Group Policy

One of the strengths of Windows-based operating systems is their flexibility. End users and system administrators can configure many different options to suit the network environment and their personal tastes. However, this flexibility comes at a price—generally, end users on a network should not change many of these options. For example, TCP/IP configuration and security policies should remain consistent for all client computers. In fact, end users really don't need to be able to change these types of settings in the first place because many of them do not understand the purpose of these settings.

Windows Server 2012 *group policies* are designed to provide system administrators with the ability to customize end-user settings and to place restrictions on the types of actions that users can perform. Group policies can be easily created by system administrators and then later applied to one or more users or computers within the environment. Although they ultimately do affect Registry settings, it is much easier to configure and apply settings through the use of Group Policy than it is to make changes to the Registry manually. To make management easy, Microsoft has set up Windows Server 2008, Windows Server 2008 R2, and Windows Server 2012 so that Group Policy settings are all managed from within the Microsoft Management Console (MMC) in the Group Policy Management Console (GPMC).

Group policies have several potential uses. We'll cover the use of group policies for software deployment, and we'll also focus on the technical background of group policies and how they apply to general configuration management.

Let's begin by looking at how group policies function.

Understanding Group Policy Settings

Group Policy settings are based on *Group Policy administrative templates*. These templates provide a list of user-friendly configuration options and specify the system settings to which they apply. For example, an option for a user or computer that reads Require A Specific Desktop Wallpaper Setting would map to a key in the Registry that maintains this value. When the option is set, the appropriate change is made in the Registry of the affected user(s) and computer(s).

By default, Windows Server 2012 comes with several administrative template files that you can use to manage common settings. Additionally, system administrators and application developers can create their own administrative template files to set options for specific functionality.

Most Group Policy items have three different settings options:

Enabled   Specifies that a setting for this GPO has been configured. Some settings require values or options to be set.

Disabled   Specifies that this option is disabled for client computers. Note that disabling an option *is* a setting. That is, it specifies that the system administrator wants to disallow certain functionality.

Not Configured   Specifies that these settings have been neither enabled nor disabled. Not Configured is the default option for most settings. It simply states that this group policy will not specify an option and that other policy settings may take precedence.

The specific options available (and their effects) will depend on the setting. Often, you will need additional information. For example, when setting the Account Lockout policy, you must specify how many bad login attempts may be made before the account is locked out. With this in mind, let's look at the types of user and computer settings that can be managed.

Group Policy settings can apply to two types of Active Directory objects: User objects and Computer objects. Because both users and computers can be placed into groups and organized within OUs, this type of configuration simplifies the management of hundreds, or even thousands, of computers.

The main options you can configure within user and computer group policies are as follows:

Software Settings   *Software Settings* options apply to specific applications and software that might be installed on the computer. System administrators can use these settings to make new applications available to end users and to control the default configuration for these applications.

Windows Settings   *Windows Settings* options allow system administrators to customize the behavior of the Windows operating system. The specific options that are available here are divided into two types: user and computer. User-specific settings let you configure Internet Explorer (including the default home page and other settings). Computer settings include security options, such as Account Policy and Event Log options.

Administrative Templates   *Administrative Templates* are used to configure user and computer settings further. In addition to the default options available, system administrators can create their own administrative templates with custom options.

Group Policy Preferences   The Windows Server 2012 operating system includes *Group Policy Preferences (GPPs)*, which give you more than 20 new Group Policy extensions. These extensions, in turn, give you a vast range of configurable settings within a Group Policy object. Included in the new Group Policy preference extensions are settings for folder options, mapped drives, printers, the Registry, local users and groups, scheduled tasks, services, and the Start menu.

Besides providing easier management, Group Policy preferences give an administrator the ability to deploy settings for client computers without restricting the users from changing the settings. This gives an administrator the flexibility needed to decide which settings to enforce and which not to enforce.

Figure 5.1 shows some of the options that you can configure with Group Policy.

FIGURE 5.1   Group Policy configuration options

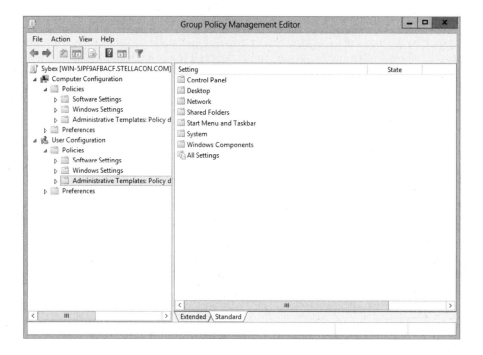

ADMX Central Store   Another consideration in GPO settings is whether to set up an *ADMX Central Store*. GPO administrative template files are saved as ADMX (.admx) files and AMXL (.amxl) for the supported languages. To get the most benefit out of using administrative templates, you should create an ADMX Central Store.

You create the Central Store in the SYSVOL folder on a domain controller. The Central Store is a repository for all of your administrative templates, and it is checked by the Group Policy tools. The Group Policy tools then use any ADMX files that they find in the Central Store. These files then replicate to all domain controllers in the domain.

If you want your clients to be able to edit domain-based GPOs by using the ADMX files that are stored in the ADMX Central Store, you must be using Windows Vista, Windows 7, Windows 8, Server 2008, Server 2008 R2, or Server 2012.

Security Template   *Security templates* are used to configure security settings through a GPO. Some of the security settings that can be configured are settings for account policies, local policies, event logs, restricted groups, system services, and the Registry.

Starter GPOs   *Starter Group Policy objects* give administrators the ability to store a collection of Administrative Template policy settings in a single object. Administrators then have the ability to import and export Starter GPOs to distribute the GPOs easily to other environments. When a GPO is created from a Starter GPO, as with any template, the new GPO receives the settings and values that were defined from the Administrative Template policy in the Starter GPO.

 Group Policy settings do not take effect immediately. You must run the gpupdate command at the command prompt or wait for the regular update cycle in order for the policy changes to take effect.

The Security Settings Section of the GPO

One of the most important sections of a GPO is the Security Settings section. The Security Settings section, under the Windows Settings section, allows an administrator to secure many aspects of the computer and user policies. The following are some of the configurable options for the Security Settings section.

Computer Section Only of the GPO

- Account Policies
- Local Policies
- Event Policies
- Restricted Groups
- System Services
- Registry
- File System
- Wired Network
- Windows Firewall with Advanced Security
- Network List Manager Policies
- Wireless Networks
- Network Access Protection
- Application Control Policies
- IP Security Policies
- Advanced Audit Policy Configuration

Computer and User Sections of the GPO

- Public Key Policies
- Software Restriction Policy

Restricted Groups   *Restricted Groups* allows you to control group membership by using a GPO. The group membership I am referring to is the normal Active Directory groups (domain local, global, and universal). Restricted Groups offers two configurable properties: Members and Members Of.

The users on the Members list do not belong to the restricted group. The users on the Members Of list do belong to the restricted group. When you configure a Restricted Group policy, members of the restricted group that are not on the Members list are removed. Users who are on the Members list who are not currently a member of the restricted group are added.

Software Restriction Policy   *Software restriction policies* allow administrators to iden-tify software and to control its ability to run on the user's local computer, organizational unit, domain, or site. This prevents users from installing unauthorized software. Software Restriction Policy is discussed in greater detail in this chapter in the "Implementing Soft-ware Deployment" section.

Group Policy Objects

So far, I have discussed what group policies are designed to do. Now it's time to drill down to determine exactly how you can set up and configure them.

To make them easier to manage, group policies may be placed in items called *Group Policy objects (GPOs)*. GPOs act as containers for the settings made within Group Policy files, which simplifies the management of settings. For example, as a system administrator, you might have different policies for users and computers in different departments. Based on these requirements, you could create a GPO for members of the Sales department and another for members of the Engineering department. Then you could apply the GPOs to the OU for each department. Another important concept you need to understand is that Group Policy settings are hierarchical; that is, system administrators can apply Group Policy set-tings at four different levels. These levels determine the GPO processing priority:

Local   Every Windows operating system computer has one Group Policy object that is stored locally. This GPO functions for both the computer and user Group Policy processing.

Sites   At the highest level, system administrators can configure GPOs to apply to entire sites within an Active Directory environment. These settings apply to all of the domains and servers that are part of a site. Group Policy settings managed at the site level may apply to more than one domain within the same forest. Therefore, they are useful when you want to make settings that apply to all of the domains within an Active Directory tree or forest.

For more information on sites, see Chapter 6, "Configuring Active Direc-tory Infrastructure."

Domains   Domains are the third level to which system administrators can assign GPOs. GPO settings placed at the domain level will apply to all of the User and Computer objects within the domain. Usually, system administrators make master settings at the domain level.

Organizational Units   The most granular level of settings for GPOs is the OU level. By configuring Group Policy options for OUs, system administrators can take advantage of the hierarchical structure of Active Directory. If the OU structure is planned well, you will find it easy to make logical GPO assignments for various business units at the OU level.

Based on the business need and the organization of the Active Directory environment, system administrators might decide to set up Group Policy settings at any of these four levels. Because the settings are cumulative by default, a User object might receive policy settings from the site level, from the domain level, and from the OUs in which it is contained.

 You can also apply Group Policy settings to the local computer (in which case Active Directory is not used at all), but this limits the manageability of the Group Policy settings.

Group Policy Inheritance

In most cases, Group Policy settings are cumulative. For example, a GPO at the domain level might specify that all users within the domain must change their password every 60 days, and a GPO at the OU level might specify the default Desktop background for all users and computers within that OU. In this case, both settings apply and users within the OU are forced to change their password every 60 days and have the default Desktop setting.

So what happens if there's a conflict in the settings? For example, suppose you create a scenario where a GPO at the site level specifies that users are to use red wallpaper and another GPO at the OU level specifies that they must green wallpaper. The users at the OU layer would have green wallpaper by default. Although hypothetical, this raises an important point about *inheritance*. By default, the settings at the most specific level (in this case, the OU that contains the User object) override those at more general levels. As a friend of mine from Microsoft always says, "Last one to apply wins."

Although the default behavior is for settings to be cumulative and inherited, system administrators can modify this behavior. They can set two main options at the various levels to which GPOs might apply:

Block Policy Inheritance   The *Block Policy Inheritance* option specifies that Group Policy settings for an object are not inherited from its parents. You might use this, for example, when a child OU requires completely different settings from a parent OU. Note, however, that you should manage blocking policy inheritance carefully because this option allows other system administrators to override the settings made at higher levels.

Force Policy Inheritance   The *Enforced option* (sometimes referred as the *No Override*) can be placed on a parent object and ensures that all lower-level objects inherit these settings. In some cases, system administrators want to ensure that Group Policy inheritance is not blocked at other levels. For example, suppose it is corporate policy that all network accounts are locked out after five incorrect password attempts. In this case, you would not want lower-level system administrators to override the option with other settings.

System administrators generally use this option when they want to enforce a specific setting globally. For example, if a password expiration policy should apply to all users and computers within a domain, a GPO with the *Force Policy Inheritance* option enabled could be created at the domain level.

We must consider one final case: If a conflict exists between the computer and user settings, the user settings take effect. If, for instance, a system administrator applies a default Desktop setting for the Computer policy and a different default Desktop setting for the User policy, the one they specify in the User policy takes effect. This is because the user settings are more specific, and they allow system administrators to make changes for individual users regardless of the computer they're using.

Planning a Group Policy Strategy

Through the use of Group Policy settings, system administrators can control many different aspects of their network environment. As you'll see throughout this chapter, system administrators can use GPOs to configure user settings and computer configurations. Windows Server 2012 includes many different administrative tools for performing these tasks. However, it's important to keep in mind that, as with many aspects of using Active Directory, a successful Group Policy strategy involves planning.

Because there are hundreds of possible Group Policy settings and many different ways to implement them, you should start by determining the business and technical needs of your organization. For example, you should first group your users based on their work functions. You might find, for example, that users in remote branch offices require particular network configuration options. In that case, you might implement Group Policy settings best at the site level. In another instance, you might find that certain departments have varying requirements for disk quota settings. In this case, it would probably make the most sense to apply GPOs to the appropriate department OUs within the domain.

The overall goal should be to reduce complexity (for example, by reducing the overall number of GPOs and GPO links) while still meeting the needs of your users. By taking into account the various needs of your users and the parts of your organization, you can often determine a logical and efficient method of creating and applying GPOs. Although it's rare that you'll come across a right or wrong method of implementing Group Policy settings, you will usually encounter some that are either better or worse than others.

By implementing a logical and consistent set of policies, you'll also be well prepared to troubleshoot any problems that might come up or to adapt to your organization's changing requirements. Later in this chapter, you'll learn about some specific methods for determining effective Group Policy settings before you apply them.

Implementing Group Policy

Now that I've covered the basic layout and structure of group policies and how they work, let's look at how you can implement them in an Active Directory environment. In the following sections, you'll start by creating GPOs. Then you'll apply these GPOs to specific Active Directory objects, and you'll take a look at how to use administrative templates.

Creating GPOs

In Windows Server 2000 and 2003, you could create GPOs from many different locations. For example, you could use Active Directory Users and Computers to create GPOs on your OUs along with other GPO tools. In Windows Server 2012, things are simpler. You can create GPOs for OUs in only one location: the Group Policy Management Console (GPMC). You have your choice of three applications for setting up policies on your Windows Server 2012 computers:

Local Computer Policy Tool   This administrative tool allows you to access quickly the Group Policy settings that are available for the local computer. These options apply to the local machine and to users who access it. You must be a member of the local administrators group to access and make changes to these settings.

Group Policy Management Console   You must use the GPMC to manage Group Policy deployment. The GPMC provides a single solution for managing all Group Policy–related tasks, and it is also best suited to handle enterprise-level tasks, such as forest-related work.

The GPMC allows administrators to manage Group Policy and GPOs all from one easy-to-use console whether their enterprise solution spans multiple domains and sites within one or more forests or it is local to one site. The GPMC adds flexibility, manageability, and functionality. Using this console, you can also perform other functions, such as backup and restore, importing, and copying.

Auditpol.exe   Auditpol.exe is a command-line utility that works with Windows Vista, Windows 7, Windows 8, Windows Server 2008, Windows Server 2008 R2, and Windows Server 2012. An administrator has the ability to display information about policies and also to perform some functions to manipulate audit policies. Table 5.1 shows some of the switches available for auditpol.exe.

TABLE 5.1 Auditpol.exe switches

Switch	Explanation
/?	This is the auditpol.exe help command.
/get	Allows you to display the current audit policy.
/set	Allows you to set a policy.
/list	Displays selectable policy elements.
/backup	Allows you to save the audit policy to a file.
/restore	Restores a policy from previous backup.
/clear	Clears the audit policy.
/remove	Removes all per-user audit policy settings and disables all system audit policy settings.
/ResourceSACL	Configures the Global Resource SACL.

Exercise 5.1 walks you through the process of installing the Group Policy Management MMC snap-in for editing Group Policy settings and creating a GPO.

WARNING You should be careful when making Group Policy settings because certain options might prevent the proper use of systems on your network. Always test Group Policy settings on a small group of users before you deploy them throughout your organization. You'll probably find that some settings need to be changed to be effective.

EXERCISE 5.1

Creating a Group Policy Object Using the GPMC

1. Click the Windows button and choose Administrative Tools ➢ Group Policy Management. The Group Policy Management tool opens.

2. Expand the Forest, Domains, *your domain name*, and North America containers. Right-click the Corporate OU, and then choose Create A GPO In This Domain, And Link It Here.

3. When the New GPO dialog box appears, type **Warning Box** in the Name field. Click OK.

4. The New GPO will be listed on the right side of the Group Policy Management window. Right-click the GPO, and choose Edit.

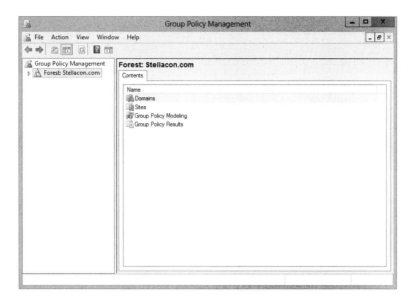

5. In the Group Policy Management Editor, expand the following: Computer Configuration ➢ Policies ➢ Windows Settings ➢ Security Settings ➢ Local Policies ➢ Security Options. On the right side, scroll down and double-click Interactive Logon: Message Text For Users Attempting To Log On.

6. Click the box labeled Define This Policy Setting In The Template. In the text box, type **Unauthorized use of this machine is prohibited** and then click OK. Close the GPO, and return to the GPMC main screen.

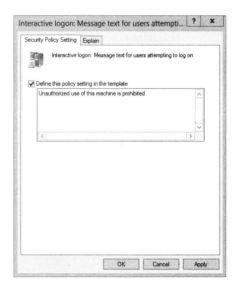

7. Under the domain name (in the GPMC), right-click Group Policy Objects and choose New.

8. When the New GPO dialog box appears, type **Unlinked Test GPO** in the Name field. Click OK.

9. On the right side, the new GPO will appear. Right-click Unlinked Test GPO and choose Edit.

10. Under the User Configuration section, click Policies ➤ Administrative Templates ➤ Desktop. On the right side, double-click Hide And Disable All Items On The Desktop and then click Enabled. Click OK, and then close the GPMC.

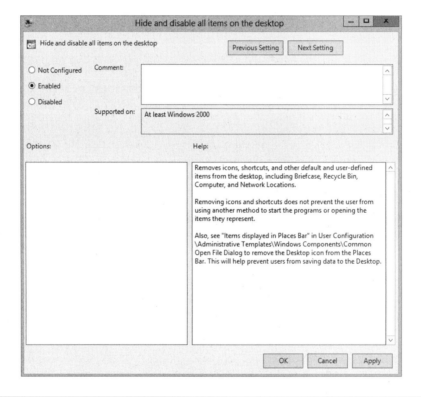

 Note that Group Policy changes may not take effect until the next user logs in (some settings may even require that the machine be rebooted). That is, users who are currently working on the system will not see the effects of the changes until they log off and log in again. GPOs are reapplied every 90 minutes with a 30-minute offset. In other words, users who are logged in will have their policies reapplied every 60 to 120 minutes. Not all settings are reapplied (for example, software settings and Password policies).

Linking Existing GPOs to Active Directory

Creating a GPO is the first step in assigning group policies. The second step is to link the GPO to a specific Active Directory object. As mentioned earlier in this chapter, GPOs can be linked to sites, domains, and OUs.

Exercise 5.2 walks you through the steps you must take to assign an existing GPO to an OU within the local domain. In this exercise, you will link the Test Domain Policy GPO to an OU. To complete the steps in this exercise, you must have completed Exercise 5.1.

EXERCISE 5.2

Linking Existing GPOs to Active Directory

1. Open the Group Policy Management Console.

2. Expand the Forest and Domain containers, and right-click the Africa OU.

3. Choose Link An Existing GPO.

4. The Select GPO dialog box appears. Click Unlinked Test GPO and click OK.

5. Close the Group Policy Management Console.

Note that the GPMC tool offers a lot of flexibility in assigning GPOs. You can create new GPOs, add multiple GPOs, edit them directly, change priority settings, remove links, and delete GPOs all from within this interface. In general, creating new GPOs using the GPMC tool is the quickest and easiest way to create the settings you need.

To test the Group Policy settings, you can simply create a user account within the Africa OU that you used in Exercise 5.2. Then, using another computer that is a member of the same domain, you can log on as the newly created user.

Managing Group Policy

Now that you have implemented GPOs and applied them to sites, domains, and OUs within Active Directory, it's time to look at some ways to manage them. In the following sections, you'll look at how multiple GPOs can interact with one another and ways that you can provide security for GPO management. Using these features is a very important part of working with Active Directory, and if you properly plan Group Policy, you can greatly reduce the time the help desk spends troubleshooting common problems.

Managing GPOs

One of the benefits of GPOs is that they're modular and can apply to many different objects and levels within Active Directory. This can also be one of the drawbacks of GPOs if they're not managed properly. A common administrative function related to using GPOs is finding all of the Active Directory links for each of these objects. You can do this when you are viewing the Linked Group Policy Objects tab of the site, domain, or OU in the GPMC (shown in Figure 5.2).

FIGURE 5.2 Viewing GPO links to an Active Directory OU

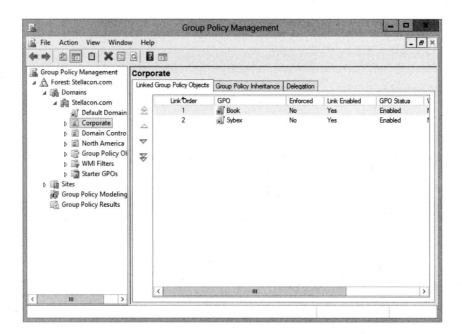

In addition to the common action of delegating permissions on OUs, you can set permissions regarding the modification of GPOs. The best way to accomplish this is to add users to the Group Policy Creator/Owners built-in security group. The members of this group are able to modify security policy. You saw how to add users to groups back in Chapter 4, "Administering Active Directory."

Windows Management Instrumentation

Windows Management Instrumentation (WMI) scripts are used to gather information or to help GPOs deploy better. The best way to explain this is to give an example. Let's say that you wanted to deploy Microsoft Office 2013 to everyone in the company. You would first set up a GPO to deploy the Office package (explained later in the section "Deploying Software through a GPO").

You can then place a WMI script on the GPO stating that only computers with 10 GB of hard disk space actually deploy Office. Now if a computer has 10 GB of free space, the Office GPO would get installed. If the computer does not have the 10 GB of hard disk space, the GPO will not deploy. You can use WMI scripts to check for computer information such as MAC addresses. WMI is a powerful tool because, if you know how to write scripts, the possibilities are endless. The following script is a sample of a WMI that is checking for at least 10 GB of free space on the C: partition/volume:

```
Select * from Win32_LogicalDisk where FreeSpace > 10737418240 AND Caption = "C:"
```

Security Filtering of a Group Policy

Another method of securing access to GPOs is to set permissions on the GPOs themselves. You can do this by opening the GPMC, selecting the GPO, and clicking the Advanced button in the Delegation tab. The Unlinked Test GPO Security Settings dialog box appears (see Figure 5.3).

FIGURE 5.3   A GPO's Security Settings dialog box

The following permissions options are available:

- Full Control
- Read
- Write
- Create All Child Objects
- Delete All Child Objects
- Apply Group Policy

You might have to scroll the Permissions window to see the Apply Group Policy item. Of these, the Apply Group Policy setting is particularly important because you use it to filter the scope of the GPO. *Filtering* is the process by which selected security groups are included or excluded from the effects of the GPOs. To specify that the settings should apply to a GPO, you should select the Allow check box for both the Apply Group Policy setting and the Read setting. These settings will be applied only if the security group is also contained within a site, domain, or OU to which the GPO is linked. To disable GPO access for a group, choose Deny for both of these settings. Finally, if you do not want to specify either Allow or Deny, leave both boxes blank. This is effectively the same as having no setting.

In Exercise 5.3, you will filter Group Policy using security groups. To complete the steps in this exercise, you must have completed Exercises 5.1 and 5.2.

EXERCISE 5.3

Filtering Group Policy Using Security Groups

1. Open the Active Directory Users and Computers administrative tool.

2. Create a new OU called **Group Policy Test**.

3. Create two new global security groups within the Group Policy Test OU, and name them **PolicyEnabled** and **PolicyDisabled**.

4. Exit Active Directory Users and Computers and open the GPMC.

5. Right-click the Group Policy Test OU, and select Link An Existing GPO.

6. Choose Unlinked Test GPO and click OK.

7. Expand the Group Policy Test OU so that you can see the GPO (Unlinked Test GPO) underneath the OU.

8. Click the Delegation tab, and then click the Advanced button in the lower-right corner of the window.

9. Click the Add button, and type **PolicyEnabled** in the Enter The Object Names To Select field. Click the Check Names button. Then click OK.

10. Add a group named **PolicyDisabled** in the same way.

11. Highlight the PolicyEnabled group, and select Allow for the Read and Apply Group Policy permissions. This ensures that users in the PolicyEnabled group will be affected by this policy.

12. Highlight the PolicyDisabled group, and select Deny for the Read and Apply Group Policy permissions. This ensures that users in the PolicyDisabled group will not be affected by this policy.

13. Click OK. You will see a message stating that you are choosing to use the Deny permission and that the Deny permission takes precedence over the Allow entries. Click the Yes button to continue.

14. When you have finished, close the GPMC tool.

Delegating Administrative Control of GPOs

So far, you have learned about how to use Group Policy to manage user and computer settings. What you haven't done yet is to determine who can modify GPOs. It's very important to establish the appropriate security on GPOs themselves for two reasons:

- If the security settings aren't set properly, users and system administrators can easily override them. This defeats the purpose of having the GPOs in the first place.

- Having many different system administrators creating and modifying GPOs can become extremely difficult to manage. When problems arise, the hierarchical nature of GPO inheritance can make it difficult to pinpoint the problem.

Fortunately, through the use of delegation, determining security permissions for GPOs is a simple task. Exercise 5.4 walks you through the steps you must take to grant the appropriate permissions to a user account. Specifically, the process involves delegating the ability to manage Group Policy links on an Active Directory object (such as an OU). To complete this exercise, you must have completed Exercises 5.1 and 5.2.

EXERCISE 5.4

Delegating Administrative Control of Group Policy

1. Open the Active Directory Users and Computers tool.

2. Expand the local domain, and create a user named **Policy Admin** within the Group Policy Test OU.

3. Exit Active Directory Users and Computers, and open the GPMC.

4. Click the Group Policy Test OU, and select the Delegation tab.

5. Click the Add button. In the field labeled Enter The Object Name To Select, type **Policy Admin**, and click the Check Names button.

6. The Add Group Or User dialog box appears. In the Permissions drop-down list, make sure the item labeled Edit Settings, Delete, Modify Security is chosen. Click OK.

7. At this point you should be looking at the Group Policy Test Delegation window. Click the Advanced button in the lower-right corner.

8. Highlight the Policy Admin account, and check the Allow Full Control box. This user now has full control of these OUs and all child OUs and GPOs for these OUs. Click OK.

   If you just want to give this user individual rights, then in the Properties window (step 8), click the Advanced button and then the Effective Permissions tab. This is where you can also choose a user and give them only the rights that you want them to have.

9. When you have finished, close the GPMC tool.

Understanding Delegation

Although I have talked about delegation throughout the book, it's important to discuss it again in the context of OUs, Group Policy, and Active Directory.

Once configured, Active Directory administrative delegation allows an administrator to delegate tasks (usually administration related) to specific user accounts or groups. What this means is that if you don't manage it all, the user accounts (or groups) you choose will be able to manage their portions of the tree.

It's very important to be aware of the benefits of Active Directory Delegation (AD Delegation). *AD Delegation* will help you manage the assigning of administrative control over objects in Active Directory, such as users, groups, computers, printers, domains, and sites. AD Delegation is used to create more administrators, which essentially saves time.

For example, let's say that you have a company whose IT department is small and situated in the central location. The central location connects three other smaller remote sites. These sites do not each warrant a full-time IT person, but the manager on staff (for example) at each remote site can become an administrator for their portion of the tree. If the user accounts for the staff at the remote site are managed by that manager, this reduces the burden on the system administrator of trivial administrative work, such as unlocking user accounts or changing passwords, and thus it reduces costs.

Controlling Inheritance and Filtering Group Policy

Controlling inheritance is an important function when you are managing GPOs. Earlier in this chapter, you learned that, by default, GPO settings flow from higher-level Active Directory objects to lower-level ones. For example, the effective set of Group Policy settings for a user might be based on GPOs assigned at the site level, the domain level, and in the OU hierarchy. In general, this is probably the behavior you would want.

In some cases, however, you might want to block Group Policy inheritance. You can accomplish this easily by selecting the object to which a GPO has been linked. Right-click the object, and choose Block Inheritance (see Figure 5.4). By enabling this option, you are effectively specifying that this object starts with a clean slate; that is, no other Group Policy settings will apply to the contents of this Active Directory site, domain, or OU.

FIGURE 5.4   Blocking GPO inheritance

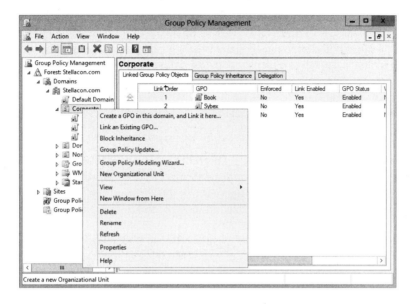

System administrators can also force inheritance. By setting the Enforced option, they can prevent other system administrators from making changes to default policies. You can set the Enforced option by right-clicking the GPO and choosing the Enforced item (see Figure 5.5).

FIGURE 5.5   Setting the Enforced GPO option

Assigning Script Policies

System administrators might want to make several changes and implement certain settings that would apply while the computer is starting up or the user is logging on. Perhaps the most common operation that logon scripts perform is mapping network drives. Although users can manually map network drives, providing this functionality within login scripts ensures that mappings stay consistent and that users only need to remember the drive letters for their resources.

Script policies are specific options that are part of Group Policy settings for users and computers. These settings direct the operating system to the specific files that should be processed during the startup/shutdown or logon/logoff processes. You can create the scripts by using the *Windows Script Host (WSH)* or with standard batch file commands. WSH allows developers and system administrators to create scripts quickly and easily using Visual Basic Scripting Edition (VBScript) or JScript (Microsoft's implementation of JavaScript). Additionally, WSH can be expanded to accommodate other common scripting languages.

To set script policy options, you simply edit the Group Policy settings. As shown in Figure 5.6, there are two main areas for setting script policy settings.

FIGURE 5.6   Viewing Startup/Shutdown script policy settings

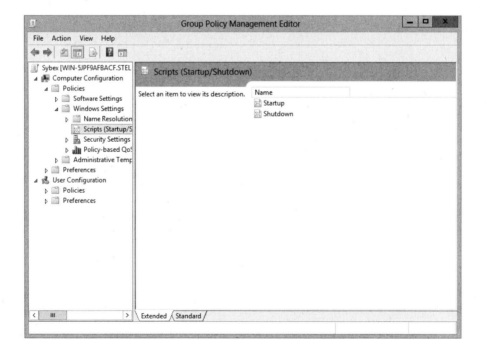

Startup/Shutdown Scripts   These settings are located within the Computer Configuration ➤ Windows Settings ➤ Scripts (Startup/Shutdown) object.

Logon/Logoff Scripts   These settings are located within the User Configuration ➤ Windows Settings ➤ Scripts (Logon/Logoff) object.

To assign scripts, simply double-click the setting and its Properties dialog box appears. For instance, if you double-click the Startup setting, the Startup Properties dialog box appears (Figure 5.7). To add a script filename, click the Add button. When you do, you will be asked to provide the name of the script file (such as `MapNetworkDrives.vbs` or `ResetEnvironment.bat`).

FIGURE 5.7   Setting scripting options

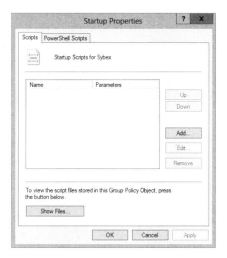

Note that you can change the order in which the scripts are run by using the Up and Down buttons. The Show Files button opens the directory folder in which you should store the Logon script files. To ensure that the files are replicated to all domain controllers, you should be sure that you place the files within the SYSVOL share.

Understanding the Loopback Policy

There may be times when the user settings of a Group Policy object should be applied to a computer based on its location instead of the user object. Usually, the user Group Policy processing dictates that the GPOs be applied in order during computer startup based on the computers located in their organizational unit. User GPOs, on the other hand, are applied in order during logon, regardless of the computer to which they log on.

In some situations, this processing order may not be appropriate. A good example is a kiosk machine. You would not want applications that have been assigned or published to a user to be installed when the user is logged on to the kiosk machine. *Loopback Policy* allows two ways to retrieve the list of GPOs for any user when they are using a specific computer in an OU:

Merge Mode The GPOs for the computer are added to the end of the GPOs for the user. Because of this, the computer's GPOs have higher precedence than the user's GPOs.

Replace Mode In Replace mode, the user's GPOs are not used. Only the GPOs of the Computer object are used.

Managing Network Configuration

Group policies are also useful in network configuration. Although administrators can handle network settings at the protocol level using many different methods, such as Dynamic Host Configuration Protocol (DHCP), Group Policy allows them to set which functions and operations are available to users and computers.

Figure 5.8 shows some of the features that are available for managing Group Policy settings. The paths to these settings are as follows:

Computer Network Options These settings are located within Computer Configuration ➢ Administrative Templates ➢ Network ➢ Network Connections folder.

User Network Options These settings are located within User Configuration ➢ Administrative Templates ➢ Network.

FIGURE 5.8 Viewing Group Policy User network configuration options

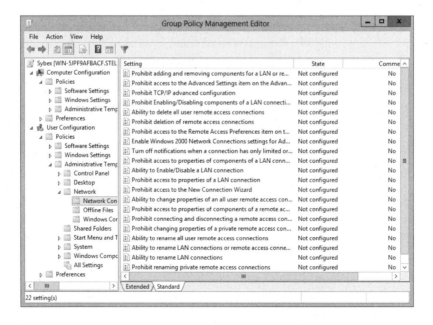

Here are some examples of the types of settings available:

- The ability to allow or disallow the modification of network settings.

  In many environments, the improper changing of network configurations and protocol settings is a common cause of help desk calls.

- The ability to allow or disallow the creation of Remote Access Service (RAS) connections.

  This option is very useful, especially in larger networked environments, because the use of modems and other WAN devices can pose a security threat to the network.

- The ability to set offline files and folders options.

  This is especially useful for keeping files synchronized for traveling users, and it is commonly configured for laptops.

Each setting includes detailed instructions in the description area of the GPO Editor window. By using these configuration options, system administrators can maintain consistency for users and computers and avoid many of the most common troubleshooting calls.

Automatically Enrolling User and Computer Certificates in Group Policy

You can also use Group Policy to enroll user and computer certificates automatically, making the entire certificate process transparent to your end users. Before proceeding further, you should understand what certificates are and why they are an important part of network security.

Think of a digital certificate as a carrying case for a public key. A certificate contains the public key and a set of attributes, including the key holder's name and email address. These attributes specify something about the holder: their identity, what they're allowed to do with the certificate, and so on. The attributes and the public key are bound together because the certificate is digitally signed by the entity that issued it. Anyone who wants to verify the certificate's contents can verify the issuer's signature.

Certificates are one part of what security experts call a *public-key infrastructure (PKI)*. A PKI has several different components that you can mix and match to achieve the desired results. Microsoft's PKI implementation offers the following functions:

Certificate Authorities CAs issue certificates, revoke certificates they've issued, and publish certificates for their clients. Big CAs like Thawte and VeriSign do this for millions of users. If you want, you can also set up your own CA for each department or workgroup in your organization. Each CA is responsible for choosing which attributes it will include in a certificate and what mechanism it will use to verify those attributes before it issues the certificate.

Certificate Publishers They make certificates publicly available, inside or outside an organization. This allows widespread availability of the critical material needed to support the entire PKI.

PKI-Savvy Applications   These allow you and your users to do useful things with certificates, like encrypt email or network connections. Ideally, the user shouldn't have to know (or even be aware of) what the application is doing—everything should work seamlessly and automatically. The best-known examples of PKI-savvy applications are web browsers like Internet Explorer and Firefox and email applications like Outlook and Outlook Express.

Certificate Templates   These act like rubber stamps. By specifying a particular template as the model you want to use for a newly issued certificate, you're actually telling the CA which optional attributes to add to the certificate as well as implicitly telling it how to fill some of the mandatory attributes. Templates greatly simplify the process of issuing certificates because they keep you from having to memorize the names of all the attributes you may potentially want to put in a certificate.

Learn More about PKI

When discussing certificates, it's also important to mention PKI and its definition. The exam doesn't go deeply into PKI, but I recommend that you do some extra research on your own because it is a very important technology and shouldn't be overlooked. PKI is actually a simple concept with a lot of moving parts. When broken down to its bare essentials, PKI is nothing more than a server and workstations utilizing a software service to add security to your infrastructure. When you use PKI, you are adding a layer of protection. The auto-enrollment Settings policy determines whether or not users and/or computers are automatically enrolled for the appropriate certificates when necessary. By default, this policy is enabled if a certificate server is installed, but you can make changes to the settings, as shown in Exercise 5.5.

In Exercise 5.5, you will learn how to configure automatic certificate enrollment in Group Policy. You must have first completed the other exercises in this chapter in order to proceed with Exercise 5.5.

EXERCISE 5.5

Configuring Automatic Certificate Enrollment in Group Policy

1. Open the Group Policy Management Console tool.

2. Right-click the North America OU that you created in the previous exercises in this book.

3. Choose Create A GPO In This Domain And Link It Here, and name it **Test CA**. Click OK.

4. Right-click the Test CA GPO, and choose Edit.

5. Open Computer Configuration ➤ Policies ➤ Windows Settings ➤ Security Settings ➤ Public Key Policies.

6. Double-click Certificate Services Client - Auto-Enrollment in the right pane.

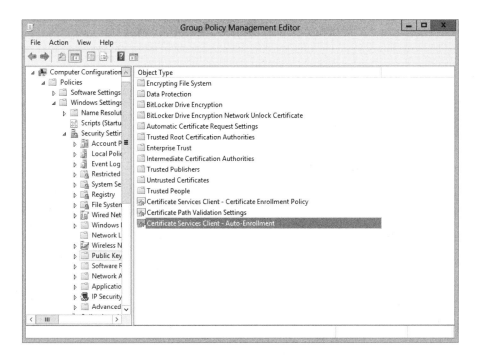

7. The Certificate Services Client - Auto-Enrollment Properties dialog box will appear.

8. For now, don't change anything. Just become familiar with the settings in this dialog box. Click OK to close it.

Redirecting Folders

Another set of Group Policy settings that you will learn about are the *folder redirection settings*. Group Policy provides a means for redirecting the Documents, Desktop, and Start Menu folders, as well as cached application data, to network locations. Folder redirection is particularly useful for the following reasons:

- When they are using roaming user profiles, a user's Documents folder is copied to the local machine each time they log on. This requires high bandwidth consumption and time if the Documents folder is large. If you redirect the Documents folder, it stays in the redirected location, and the user opens and saves files directly to that location.

- Documents are always available no matter where the user logs on.

- Data in the shared location can be backed up during the normal backup cycle without user intervention.

- Data can be redirected to a more robust server-side administered disk that is less prone to physical and user errors.

When you decide to redirect folders, you have two options: basic and advanced:

- Basic redirection redirects everyone's folders to the same location (but each user gets their own folder within that location).

- Advanced redirection redirects folders to different locations based on group membership. For instance, you could configure the Engineers group to redirect their folders to //Engineering1/Documents/ and the Marketing group to //Marketing1/Documents/. Again, individual users still get their own folder within the redirected location.

To configure folder redirection, follow the steps in Exercise 5.6. You must have completed the other exercises in this chapter to proceed with this exercise.

EXERCISE 5.6

Configuring Folder Redirection in Group Policy

1. Open the GPMC tool.

2. Open the North America OU, and then edit the Test CA GPO.

3. Open User Configuration ➢ Policies ➢ Windows Settings ➢ Folder Redirection ➢ Documents.

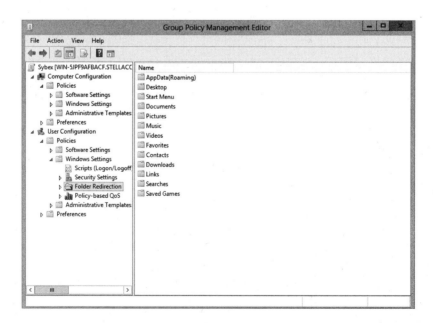

4. Right-click Documents, and select Properties.

5. On the Target tab of the Documents Properties dialog box, choose the Basic - Redirect Everyone's Folder To The Same Location selection from the Setting drop-down list.

6. Leave the default option for the Target Folder Location drop-down list, and specify a network path in the Root Path field.

7. Click the Settings tab. All of the default settings are self-explanatory and should typically be left at the default setting. Click OK when you have finished.

Folder Redirection Facts

Try not to mix up the concepts of *folder redirection* and *offline folders*, especially in a world with ever-increasing numbers of mobile users. Folder redirection and offline folders are different features.

Windows Server 2008 R2 folder redirection works as follows: The system uses a pointer that moves the folders you want to a location you specify. Users do not see any of this—it is transparent to them. One problem with folder redirection is that it does not work for mobile users (users who will be offline and who will not have access to files they may need).

Offline folders, however, are copies of folders that were local to you. Files are now available locally to you on the system you have with you. They are also located back on the server where they are stored. The next time you log in, the folders are synchronized so that both folders contain the latest data. This is a perfect feature for mobile users, whereas folder redirection provides no benefit for the mobile user.

Managing GPOs with Windows PowerShell Group Policy Cmdlets

As stated earlier in this book, *Windows PowerShell* is a Windows command-line shell and scripting language. Windows PowerShell can also help an administrator automate many of the same tasks that you perform using the Group Policy Management Console.

Windows Server 2012 helps you perform many of the Group Policy tasks by providing more than 25 cmdlets. Each of these cmdlets is a simple, single-function command-line tool.

The Windows PowerShell Group Policy cmdlets can help you perform some of the following tasks for domain-based Group Policy objects:

- Maintain, create, remove, back up, and import GPOs.

- Create, update, and remove GPO links to Active Directory containers.

- Set Active Directory OUs and domain permissions and inheritance flags.

- Configure Group Policy Registry settings.

- Create and edit Starter GPOs.

The requirement for Windows PowerShell Group Policy cmdlets is Windows Server 2012 on either a domain controller or a member server that has the GPMC installed. Windows 7 and Windows 8 also have the ability to use Windows PowerShell Group Policy cmdlets if it has Remote Server Administration Tools (RSAT) installed. RSAT includes the GPMC and its cmdlets. PowerShell is also a requirement.

Deploying Software through a GPO

It's difficult enough to manage applications on a stand-alone computer. It seems that the process of installing, configuring, and uninstalling applications is never finished. Add in the hassle of computer reboots and reinstalling corrupted applications and the reduction in productivity can be substantial.

Software administrators who manage software in network environments have even more concerns:

- First and foremost, they must determine which applications specific users require.

- Then IT departments must purchase the appropriate licenses for the software and acquire any necessary media.

- Next the system administrators need to install the applications on users' machines. This process generally involves help desk staff visiting computers, or it requires end users to install the software themselves. Both processes entail several potential problems, including installation inconsistency and lost productivity from downtime experienced when applications were installed.

- Finally, software administrators still need to manage software updates and remove unused software.

One of the key design goals for Active Directory was to reduce some of the headaches involved in managing software and configurations in a networked environment. To that end, Windows Server 2012 offers several features that can make the task of deploying software easier and less error prone. Before you dive into the technical details, however, you need to examine the issues related to software deployment.

The Software Management Life Cycle

Although it may seem that the use of a new application requires only the installation of the necessary software, the overall process of managing applications involves many more steps. When managing software applications, there are three main phases to their life cycle:

Phase 1: Deploying Software   The first step in using applications is to install them on the appropriate client computers. Generally, some applications are deployed during the initial configuration of a PC, and others are deployed when they are requested. In the latter case, this often used to mean that system administrators and help desk staffs have to visit client computers and manually walk through the installation process. With Windows Server 2012 and GPOs, the entire process can be automated.

Before You Install, Stop

It is very important to understand that just because you can easily deploy software does not necessarily mean that you have the right to do so. Before you install software on client computers, you must make sure you have the appropriate licenses for the software. Furthermore, it's very important to take the time to track application installations. As many system administrators have discovered, it's much more difficult to inventory software installations after they've been performed. Another issue that you may encounter is that you lack available resources (for instance, your system does not meet the minimum hardware requirements) and face problems such as limited hard disk space or memory that may not be able to handle the applications that you want to load and use. You may also find that your user account does not have the permission to install software. It's important to consider not only how you will install software but also whether you can or not.

Phase 2: Maintaining Software   Once an application is installed and in use on client computers, you need to ensure that the software is maintained. You must keep programs up-to-date by applying changes due to bug fixes, enhancements, and other types of updates. This is normally done with service packs, hot fixes, and updates. As with the initial software deployment, software maintenance can be tedious. Some programs require older versions to be uninstalled before updates are added. Others allow for automatically upgrading over existing installations. Managing and deploying software updates can consume a significant amount of the IT staff's time.

Using Windows Update

Make sure that you learn about Windows Update, a service that allows you to connect to Microsoft's website and download what your system may need to bring it up to compliance. This tool is very helpful if you are running a stand-alone system, but if you want to deploy software across the enterprise, the best way to accomplish this is first to test the updates you are downloading and make sure that you can use them and that they are not bug ridden. Then you can use a tool such as the Windows Server Update Service (WSUS), which was formerly called the Software Update Services (SUS).

You can check for updates at Microsoft's website (http://update.microsoft.com). Microsoft likes to ask many types of questions about WSUS on its certification exams. WSUS is described in detail in other Sybex certification series books.

Phase 3: Removing Software   The end of the life cycle for many software products involves the actual removal of unused programs. Removing software is necessary when applications become outdated or when users no longer require their functionality. One of the traditional problems with uninstalling applications is that many of the installed files may not be removed. Furthermore, the removal of shared components can sometimes cause other programs to stop functioning properly. Also, users often forget to uninstall applications that they no longer need, and these programs continue to occupy disk space and consume valuable system resources.

The Microsoft Windows Installer (MSI) manages each of these three phases of the software maintenance life cycle. Now that you have an overview of the process, let's move forward to look at the steps involved in deploying software using Group Policy.

 The *Microsoft Windows Installer* (sometimes referred to *as Microsoft Installer* or *Windows Installer*) is an application installation and configuration service. An instruction file (the Microsoft Installer package) contains information about what needs to be done to install a product. It's common to confuse the two.

The Windows Installer

If you've installed newer application programs (such as Microsoft Office 2013), you've probably noticed the updated setup and installation routines. Applications that comply with the updated standard use the *Windows Installer specification* and MSI software packages for deployment. Each package contains information about various setup options and the files required for installation. Although the benefits may not seem dramatic on the surface, there's a lot of new functionality under the hood.

The Windows Installer was created to solve many of the problems associated with traditional application development. It has several components, including the Installer service (which runs on Windows 2000, XP, Vista, Windows 7, Windows 8, Windows Server 2003, Windows Server 2008, Windows Server 2008 R2, and Windows Server 2012 computers), the Installer program (`msiexec.exe`) that is responsible for executing the instructions in a *Windows Installer package*, and the specifications third-party developers use to create their own packages. Within each installation package file is a relational structure (similar to the structure of tables in databases) that records information about the programs contained within the package.

To appreciate the true value of the Windows Installer, you'll need to look at some of the problems with traditional software deployment mechanisms and then at how the Windows Installer addresses many of them.

Application Installation Issues

Before the Windows Installer, applications were installed using a setup program that managed the various operations required for a program to operate. These operations included copying files, changing Registry settings, and managing any other operating system changes that might be required (such as starting or stopping services). However, this method had several problems:

- The setup process was not robust, and aborting the operation often left many unnecessary files in the file system.

- The process included uninstalling an application (this also often left many unnecessary files in the file system) and remnants in the Windows Registry and operating system folders. Over time, these remnants would result in reduced overall system performance and wasted disk space.

- There was no standard method for applying upgrades to applications, and installing a new version often required users to uninstall the old application, reboot, and then install the new program.

- Conflicts between different versions of *dynamic link libraries (DLLs)*—shared program code used across different applications—could cause the installation or removal of one application to break the functionality of another.

Benefits of the Windows Installer

Because of the many problems associated with traditional software installation, Microsoft created the *Windows Installer*. This system provides for better manageability of the software installation process and allows system administrators more control over the deployment process. Specifically, the Windows Installer provides the following benefits:

Improved Software Removal   The process of removing software is an important one because remnants left behind during the uninstall process can eventually clutter up the Registry and file system. During the installation process, the Windows Installer keeps track of all of the changes made by a setup package. When it comes time to remove an application, all of these changes can then be rolled back.

More Robust Installation Routines   If a typical setup program is aborted during the software installation process, the results are unpredictable. If the actual installation hasn't yet begun, then the installer generally removes any temporary files that may have been created. However, if the file copy routine starts before the system encounters an error, it is likely that the files will not be automatically removed from the operating system. In contrast, the Windows Installer allows you to roll back any changes when the application setup process is aborted.

Ability to Use Elevated Privileges   Installing applications usually requires the user to have Administrator permissions on the local computer because file system and Registry changes are required. When installing software for network users, system administrators have two options. First, they can log off of the computer before installing the software and then log back on as a user who has Administrator permissions on the local computer. This method is tedious and time consuming. The second option is to give users Administrator permissions temporarily on their own machines. This method could cause security problems and requires the attention of a system administrator.

Through the use of the Installer service, the Windows Installer is able to use temporarily elevated privileges to install applications. This allows users, regardless of their security settings, to execute the installation of authorized applications. This saves time and preserves security.

Support for Repairing Corrupted Applications   Regardless of how well a network environment is managed, critical files are sometimes lost or corrupted. Such problems can prevent applications from running properly and can cause crashes. Windows Installer packages provide you with the ability to verify the installation of an application and, if necessary, replace any missing or corrupted files. This support saves time and lessens end-user headaches associated with removing and reinstalling an entire application to replace just a few files.

Prevention of File Conflicts   Generally, different versions of the same files should be compatible with each other. In the real world, however, this isn't always the case. A classic problem in the Windows world is the case of one program replacing DLLs that are used by several other programs. Windows Installer accurately tracks which files are used by certain programs and ensures that any shared files are not improperly deleted or overwritten.

Automated Installations   A typical application setup process requires end users or system administrators to respond to several prompts. For example, a user may be able to choose the program group in which icons will be created and the file system location to which the program will be installed. Additionally, they may be required to choose which options are installed. Although this type of flexibility is useful, it can be tedious when you are rolling out multiple applications. By using features of the Windows Installer, however, users are able to specify setup options before the process begins. This allows system administrators to ensure consistency in installations, and it saves users' time.

Advertising and On-Demand Installations   One of the most powerful features of the Windows Installer is its ability to perform on-demand software installations. Prior to the Windows Installer, application installation options were quite basic—either a program was installed or it was not. When setting up a computer, system administrators would be required to guess which applications the user might need and install all of them.

The Windows Installer supports a function known as advertising. *Advertising* makes applications appear to be available via the Start menu. However, the programs themselves may not actually be installed on the system. When a user attempts to access an advertised application, the Windows Installer automatically downloads the necessary files from a server and installs the program. The result is that applications are installed only when they are needed, and the process requires no intervention from the end user. We'll cover the details of this process later in this chapter.

To anyone who has managed many software applications in a network environment, all of these features of the Windows Installer are likely welcome ones. They also make life easier for end users and application developers; they can focus on the "real work" that their jobs demand.

Windows Installer File Types

When performing software deployment with the Windows Installer in Windows Server 2012, you may encounter several different file types:

Microsoft Windows Installer Packages   To take full advantage of Windows Installer functionality, applications must include Microsoft Windows Installer (MSI) packages. Third-party application vendors and software developers normally create these packages, and they include the information required to install and configure the application and any supporting files.

Microsoft Transformation Files   *Microsoft Transformation (MST) files* are useful when you are customizing the details of how applications are installed. When a system administrator chooses to assign or publish an application, they may want to specify additional options for the package. For example, if a system administrator wants to allow users to install only the Microsoft Word and Microsoft PowerPoint components of Office 2013, they could specify these options within a transformation file. Then, when users install the application, they will be provided only with the options related to these components.

Microsoft Patches   To maintain software, patches are often required. Patches may make Registry and/or file system changes. *Patch files (MSP)* are used for minor system changes and are subject to certain limitations. Specifically, a patch file cannot remove any installed program components and cannot delete or modify any shortcuts created by the user.

Initialization Files   To provide support for publishing non–Windows Installer applications, *initialization files* can be used. These files provide links to a standard executable file that is used to install an application. An example might be \\server1\software\program1\setup .exe. These files can then be published and advertised, and users can access the *Add Or Remove Programs* icon to install them over the network.

Application Assignment Scripts   *Application assignment scripts (AAS)* store information regarding assigning programs and any settings that the system administrator makes. These files are created when Group Policy is used to create software package assignments for users and computers.

Each of these types of files provides functionality that allows the system administrator to customize software deployment. Windows Installer packages have special properties that you can view by right-clicking the file in Windows Explorer and choosing Properties (see Figure 5.9).

FIGURE 5.9   Viewing the properties of an MSI package file

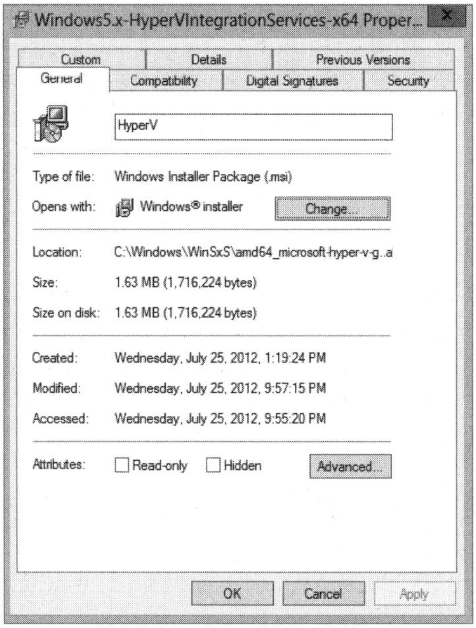

Deploying Applications

The functionality provided by Windows Installer offers many advantages to end users who install their own software. However, that is just the beginning in a networked environment. As you'll see later in this chapter, the various features of Windows Installer and compatible packages allow system administrators to determine centrally applications that users will be able to install.

There are two main methods of making programs available to end users using Active Directory: assigning and publishing. Both assigning and publishing applications greatly ease the process of deploying and managing applications in a network environment.

In the following sections, you'll look at how the processes of assigning and publishing applications can make life easier for IT staff and users alike. The various settings for assigned and published applications are managed through the use of GPOs.

Assigning Applications

Software applications can be assigned to users and computers. *Assigning* a software package makes the program available for automatic installation. The applications advertise their availability to the affected users or computers by placing icons within the Programs folder of the Start menu.

When applications are assigned to a user, programs will be advertised to the user regardless of which computer they are using. That is, icons for the advertised program will appear within the Start menu regardless of whether the program is installed on that computer. If the user clicks an icon for a program that has not yet been installed on the local computer, the application will automatically be accessed from a server and it will be installed.

When an application is assigned to a computer, the program is made available to any users of the computer. For example, all users who log on to a computer that has been assigned Microsoft Office 2013 will have access to the components of the application. If the user did not previously install Microsoft Office 2013, they will be prompted for any required setup information when the program first runs.

Generally, applications that are required by the vast majority of users should be assigned to computers. This reduces the amount of network bandwidth required to install applications on demand and improves the end-user experience by preventing the delay involved when installing an application the first time it is accessed. Any applications that may be used by only a few users (or those with specific job tasks) should be assigned to users.

Publishing Applications

When applications are *published*, they are advertised, but no icons are automatically created. Instead, the applications are made available for installation using the Add Or Remove Programs icon in Control Panel.

 Windows Vista, Windows 7, and Windows 8 do not have the Add Or Remove Programs feature. They use the Programs icon in Control Panel to install the software.

Implementing Software Deployment

So far, you have become familiar with the issues related to software deployment and management from a theoretical level. Now it's time to drill down into the actual steps required to deploy software using the features of Active Directory and the GPMC. In the following sections, you will walk through the steps required to create an application distribution share point, to publish and assign applications, to update previously installed applications, to verify the installation of applications, and to update Windows operating systems.

Preparing for Software Deployment

Before you can install applications on client computers, you must make sure the necessary files are available to end users. In many network environments, system administrators create shares on file servers that include the installation files for many applications. Based on security permissions, either end users or system administrators can then connect to these shares from a client computer and install the needed software. The efficient organization of these shares can save the help desk from having to carry around a library of CD-ROMs, and it allows you to install applications easily on many computers at once.

One of the problems in network environments is that users frequently install applications whether or not they really need them. They may stumble upon applications that are stored on common file servers and install them out of curiosity. These actions can often decrease productivity and may violate software licensing agreements. You can help avoid this by placing all of your application installation files in hidden shares (for example, software$).

Exercise 5.7 walks you through the process of creating a software distribution share point. In this exercise, you will prepare for software deployment by creating a directory share and placing certain types of files in this directory. To complete the steps in this exercise, you must have access to the Microsoft Office 2010 or Microsoft Office 2013 installation files (via CD-ROM or through a network share) and have 2000 MB of free disk space. For this exercise, I used Microsoft Office 2010.

EXERCISE 5.7

Creating a Software Deployment Share

1. Using Windows Explorer, create a folder called **Software** that you can use with application sharing. Be sure that the volume on which you create this folder has at least 2000 MB of available disk space.

2. Create a folder called **Office 2010** within the Software folder.

3. Copy all of the installation files for Microsoft Office 2010 from the CD-ROM or network share containing the files to the Office 2010 folder that you created in step 2. If you prefer, you can use switches to install all of the Office 2010 installation files. You can find these switches at http://technet.microsoft.com/en-us/library/ff521767 .aspx.

4. Right-click the Software folder (created in step 1), and select Share. In the Choose People On Your Network To Share With dialog box, type **Everyone**, and click the Add button. Next click the Share button. When you see a message that the sharing process is complete, click Done.

Once you have created an application distribution share, it's time to publish and assign the applications. This topic is covered next.

Software Restriction Policies

One of the biggest problems that we face as IT managers is users downloading and installing software. Many software packages don't cause any issues and are completely safe. Unfortunately, many software packages do have viruses and can cause problems. This is where software restriction policies can help. Software restriction policies help to identify software and to control its ability to run on a local computer, organizational unit, domain, or site.

Software restriction policies give administrators the ability to regulate unknown or untrusted software. Software restriction policies allow you to protect your computers from unwanted software by identifying and also specifying what software packages are allowed to be installed.

When configuring software restriction policies, an administrator is able to define a default security level of Unrestricted (software is allowed) or Disallowed (software is not allowed to run) for a GPO. Administrators can make exceptions to this default security level. They can create software restriction policy rules for specific software.

To create a software policy using the Group Policy Management Console, create a new GPO. In the GPO, expand the Windows Settings for either the user or computer configuration section, expand Security, right-click Software Restriction Policy, and choose New Software Restriction Policy. Set the policy for the level of security that you need.

Using AppLocker

AppLocker is a feature in Windows 7, Windows 8, and Windows Server 2012. It is the replacement for Software Restriction Policies. *AppLocker* allows you to configure a Denied list and an Accepted list for applications. Applications that are configured on the Denied list will not run on the system, whereas applications on the Accepted list will operate properly.

The new capabilities and extensions of the AppLocker feature help reduce administrative overhead and help administrators control how users can access and use files, such as EXE files, scripts, Windows Installer files (MSI and MSP files), and DLLs.

Group Policy Slow Link Detection

When setting up GPOs, most of us assume that the connection speeds between servers and clients are going to be fast. In today's world, it is very unlikely to see slow connections between locations, but they are still out there. Sometimes connection speeds can cause issues with the deployment of GPOs, specifically ones that are deploying software.

A setting in the Computer and User section of the GPO called *Group Policy Slow Link Detection* defines a slow connection for the purposes of applying and updating GPOs. If the data transfer rate from the domain controller providing the GPO to the computer is slower than what you have specified in this setting, the connection is considered to be a slow connection. If a connection is considered slow, the system response will vary depending on the policy. For example, if a GPO is going to deploy software and the connection is considered slow, the software may not be installed on the client computer. If you configure this option as 0, all connections are considered fast connections.

Publishing and Assigning Applications

As mentioned earlier in this section, system administrators can make software packages available to users by using publishing and assigning operations. Both of these operations allow system administrators to leverage the power of Active Directory and, specifically, GPOs to determine which applications are available to users. Additionally, OUs can provide the organization that can help group users based on their job functions and software requirements.

The general process involves creating a GPO that includes software deployment settings for users and computers and then linking this GPO to Active Directory objects.

Exercise 5.8 walks you through the steps required to publish and assign applications. In this exercise, you will create applications and assign them to specific Active Directory objects using GPOs. To complete the steps in this exercise, you must have completed Exercise 5.7.

EXERCISE 5.8

Publishing and Assigning Applications Using Group Policy

1. Open the Active Directory Users and Computers tool from the Administrative Tools program group (using the Windows key).

2. Expand the domain, and create a new top-level OU called **Software**.

3. Within the Software OU, create a user named **Jane User** with a login name of **juser** (choose the defaults for all other options).

4. Exit Active Directory Users and Computers, and open the Group Policy Management Console.

5. Right-click the Software OU, and choose Create A GPO In This Domain And Link It Here.

6. For the name of the new GPO, type **Software Deployment**.

7. To edit the Software Deployment GPO, right-click it and choose Edit. Expand the Computer Configuration ➢ Policies ➢ Software Settings object.

8. Right-click the Software Installation item, and select New ➢ Package.

9. Navigate to the Software share that you created in Exercise 5.7.

10. Within the Software share, double-click the Office 2010 folder and select the appropriate MSI file depending on the version of Office 2010 that you have. Office 2010 Professional is being used in this example, so you'll see that the OFFICEMUI.MSI file is chosen. Click Open.

11. In the Deploy Software dialog box, choose Advanced. (Note that the Published option is unavailable because applications cannot be published to computers.) Click OK to return to the Deploy Software dialog box.

12. To examine the deployment options of this package, click the Deployment tab. Accept the default settings by clicking OK.

13. Within the Group Policy Object Editor, expand the User Configuration ➢ Software Settings object.

14. Right-click the Software Installation item, and select New ➢ Package.

15. Navigate to the Software share that you created in Exercise 5.7.

16. Within the Software share, double-click the Office 2010 folder, and select the appropriate MSI file. Click Open.

17. For the Software Deployment option, select Published in the Deploy Software dialog box and click OK.

18. Close the GPMC.

The overall process involved with deploying software using Active Directory is quite simple. However, you shouldn't let the intuitive graphical interface fool you—there's a lot of power under the hood of these software deployment features! Once you've properly assigned and published applications, it's time to see the effects of your work.

Applying Software Updates

The steps described in the previous section work only when you are installing a brand-new application. However, software companies often release updates that you need to install on top of existing applications. These updates usually consist of bug fixes or other changes that are required to keep the software up-to-date. You can apply software updates in Active Directory by using the Upgrades tab of the software package Properties dialog box found in the Group Policy Object Editor.

In Exercise 5.9, you will apply a software update to an existing application. You should add the upgrade package to the GPO in the same way that you added the original application in steps 8 through 12 of Exercise 5.8. You should also have completed Exercise 5.8 before attempting this exercise.

EXERCISE 5.9

Applying Software Updates

1. Open the Group Policy Management Console from the Administrative Tools program group.

2. Click the Software OU, right-click the Software Deployment GPO, and choose Edit.

3. Expand the Computer Configuration ➢ Policies ➢ Software Settings ➢ Software Installation object.

4. Right-click the software package, and select Properties from the context menu to bring up the Properties dialog box.

5. Select the Upgrades tab, and click the Add button.

6. Click the Current Group Policy Object (GPO) radio button in the Choose A Package From section of the dialog box, or click the Browse button to select the GPO to which you want to apply the upgrade. Consult your application's documentation to see if you should choose the Uninstall The Existing Package, Then Install The Upgrade Package radio button or the Package Can Upgrade Over The Existing Package radio button.

7. Click Cancel to close the Add Upgrade Package dialog box.

8. Click Cancel, and exit the GPMC.

You should understand that not all upgrades make sense in all situations. For instance, if the Stellacon 2010 files are incompatible with the Stellacon 2013 application, then your Stellacon 2012 users might not want you to perform the upgrade without taking additional steps to ensure that they can continue to use their files. In addition, users might have some choice about which version they use when it doesn't affect the support of the network.

Regardless of the underlying reason for allowing this flexibility, you should be aware that there are two basic types of upgrades that are available for administrators to provide to the users:

Mandatory Upgrade   Forces everyone who currently has an existing version of the program to upgrade according to the GPO. Users who have never installed the program for whatever reason will be able to install only the new upgraded version.

Nonmandatory Upgrade   Allows users to choose whether they would like to upgrade. This upgrade type also allows users who do not have their application installed to choose which version they would like to use.

Verifying Software Installation

To ensure that the software installation settings you make in a GPO have taken place, you can log into the domain from a Windows 8, Windows 7, or Windows Vista computer that is within the OU to which the software settings apply. When you log in, you will notice two changes. First the application is installed on the computer (if it was not installed already). In order to access the application, a user needs to click one of the icons within the Program group of the Start menu. Note also that applications are available to any of the users who log on to this machine. Second, the settings apply to any computers that are contained within the OU and to any users who log on to these computers.

If you publish an application to users, the change may not be as evident, but it is equally useful. When you log on to a Windows 8, Windows 7, or Windows Vista computer that is a member of the domain, and when you use a user account from the OU where you published the application, you will be able to install any of the published applications automatically. On a Windows 8 or Windows 7 computer, you can do this by accessing the Programs icon in Control Panel. By clicking Add New Programs, you access a display of the applications available for installation. By clicking the Add button in the Add New Programs section of the Programs dialog box, you will automatically begin the installation of the published application.

Configuring Automatic Updates in Group Policy

So far you've seen the advantages of deploying application software in a group policy. Group policies also provide a way to install operating system updates across the network for Windows 2000, XP, Vista, Windows 7, Windows 8, Windows Server 2003, Windows Server 2008, Windows Server 2008 R2, and Windows Server 2012 machines using Windows Update in conjunction with Windows Server Update Service. WSUS is the newer version of SUS, and it is used on a Windows Server 2012 system to update systems. As you may remember, WSUS and SUS are patch-management tools that help you deploy updates to your systems in a controlled manner.

Windows Update is available through the Microsoft website, and it is used to provide the most current files for Windows operating systems. Examples of updates include security fixes, critical updates, updated help files, and updated drivers. You can access Windows Update by clicking the Windows Update icon in the system tray.

We will discuss WSUS in greater detail in Chapter 11, "Deploying, Managing, and Maintaining Servers."

WSUS is used to leverage the features of Windows Update within a corporate environment by downloading Windows updates to a corporate server, which in turn provides the updates to the internal corporate clients. This allows administrators to test and have full control over what updates are deployed within the corporate environment.

Within an enterprise network that is using Active Directory, you would typically see automatic updates configured through Group Policy. Group policies are used to manage configuration and security settings via Active Directory. Group Policy is also used to specify what server a client will use for automatic updates.

If the WSUS client is a part of an enterprise network that is using Active Directory, you would configure the client via a group policy.

Configuring Software Deployment Settings

In addition to the basic operations of assigning and publishing applications, you can use several other options to specify the details of how software is deployed. In the following sections, you will examine the various options that are available and their effects on the software installation process.

The Software Installation Properties Dialog Box

The most important software deployment settings are contained in the Software Installation Properties dialog box, which you can access by right-clicking the Software Installation item and selecting Properties from the context menu. The following sections describe the features contained on the various tabs of the dialog box.

Managing Package Defaults

On the Deployment tab of the Software Installation Properties dialog box, you'll be able to specify some defaults for any packages that you create within this GPO. Figure 5.10 shows the Deployment options for managing software installation settings.

FIGURE 5.10 Deployment tab of the Software Installation Properties dialog box

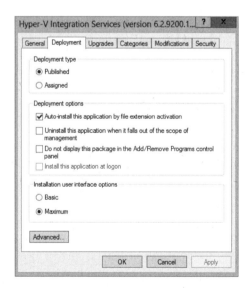

The following options are used for managing software installation settings:

Default Package Location   This setting specifies the default file system or network location for software installation packages. This is useful if you are already using a specific share on a file server for hosting the necessary installation files.

New Packages   These settings specify the default type of package assignment that will be used when you add a new package either to the user or computer settings. If you'll be assigning or publishing multiple packages, you may find it useful to set a default here. Selecting the Advanced option enables Group Policy to display the package's Properties dialog box each time a new package is added.

FIGURE 5.11   Advanced Deployment dialog box

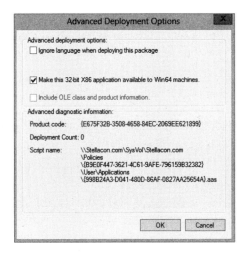

Installation User Interface Options   When installing an application, system administrators may or may not want end users to see all of the advanced installation options. If Basic is chosen, the user will only be able to configure the minimal settings (such as the installation location). If Maximum is chosen, all of the available installation options will be displayed. The specific installation options available will depend on the package itself.

Uninstall Applications When They Fall Out of the Scope of Management   So far, you have seen how applications can be assigned and published to users or computers. But what happens when effective GPOs change? For example, suppose User A is currently located within the Sales OU. A GPO that assigns the Microsoft Office 2013 suite of applications is linked to the Sales OU. You decide to move User A to the Engineering OU, which has no software deployment settings. Should the application be uninstalled or should it remain?

If the "Uninstall this application when it falls out of the scope of management" option is checked, applications will be removed if they are not specifically assigned or published within GPOs. In this example, this means that Office 2013 would be uninstalled for User A. If this box is left unchecked, however, the application will remain installed.

Managing File Extension Mappings

One of the potential problems associated with using many different file types is that it's difficult to keep track of which applications work with which files. For example, if you received a file with the filename extension .abc, you would have no idea which application you would need to view it.

Fortunately, through software deployment settings, system administrators can specify mappings for specific *filename extensions*. For example, you could specify that whenever users attempt to access a file with the extension .vsd, the operating system should attempt to open the file using Visio diagramming software. If Visio is not installed on the user's machine, the computer can automatically download and install it (assuming that the application has been properly advertised).

This method allows users to have applications automatically installed when they are needed. The following is an example of a sequence of events that might occur:

1. A user receives an email message that contains a PDF (.pdf) file attachment.

2. The computer realizes that the PDF file does not have the appropriate viewing application for this type of file installed. However, it also realizes that a filename extension mapping is available within the Active Directory software deployment settings.

3. The client computer automatically requests the PDF software package from the server, and it uses the Microsoft Windows Installer to install the application automatically.

4. The computer opens the attachment for the user.

Notice that all of these steps were carried out without any further interaction with the user.

You can manage filename extension mappings by right-clicking the Software Installation item, selecting Properties, and then clicking the File Extensions tab.

Creating Application Categories

In many network environments, the list of supported applications can include hundreds of items. For users who are looking for only one specific program, searching through a list of all of these programs can be difficult and time consuming.

Fortunately, methods for categorizing the applications are available on your network. You can easily manage the application categories for users and computers by right-clicking the Software Installation item, selecting Properties, and then clicking the Categories tab.

Figure 5.12 shows you the categories tab of the Software Installation package. When creating categories, it is a good idea to use category names that are meaningful to users because it will make it easier for them to find the programs they're seeking.

FIGURE 5.12   The Categories tab of the Software Installation Properties dialog box

Once the software installation categories have been created, you can view them by clicking the Programs or Programs And Features icon in Control Panel. When you click Add New Programs, you'll see that several options appear in the Category drop-down list. Now when you select the properties for a package, you will be able to assign the application to one or more of the categories.

Removing Programs

As discussed in the beginning of the chapter, an important phase in the software management life cycle is the removal of applications. Fortunately, if you use the GPMC and the Windows Installer packages, the process is simple. To remove an application, you can right-click the package within the Group Policy settings and select All Tasks ➢ Remove (see Figure 5.13).

FIGURE 5.13 Removing a software package

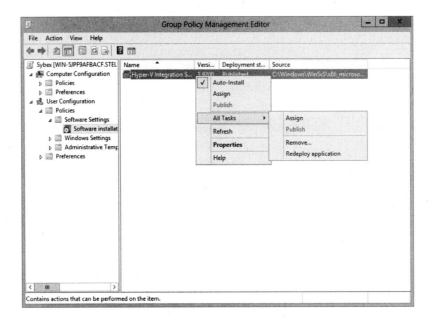

When choosing to remove a software package from a GPO, you have two options:

Immediately Uninstall The Software From Users And Computers   System administrators can choose this option to ensure that an application is no longer available to users who are affected by the GPO. When this option is selected, the program will be uninstalled automatically from users and/or computers that have the package. This option might be useful, for example, if the license for a certain application has expired or if a program is no longer on the approved applications list.

Allow Users To Continue To Use The Software, But Prevent New Installations   This option prevents users from making new installations of a package, but it does not remove the software if it has already been installed for users. This is a good option if the company has run out of additional licenses for the software, but the existing licenses are still valid.

Figure 5.14 shows these two removal options.

FIGURE 5.14 Software removal options

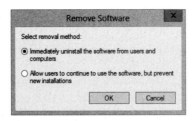

If you no longer require the ability to install or repair an application, you can delete it from your software distribution share point by deleting the appropriate Windows Installer package files. This will free up additional disk space for newer applications.

Microsoft Windows Installer Settings

Several options influence the behavior of the Windows Installer; you can set them within a GPO. You can access these options by navigating to User Configuration ➢ Administrative Templates ➢ Windows Components ➢ Windows Installer (see Figure 5.15). The options are as follows:

FIGURE 5.15   GPO settings for Windows Installer

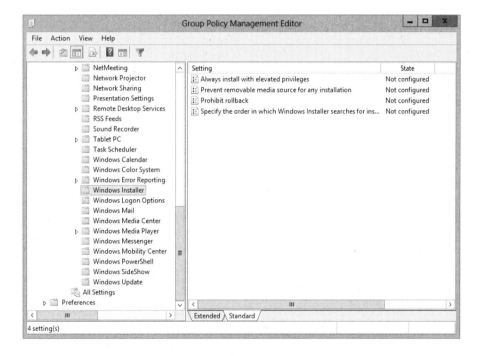

Always Install With Elevated Privileges   This policy allows users to install applications that require elevated privileges. For example, if a user does not have the permissions necessary to modify the Registry but the installation program must make Registry changes, this policy will allow the process to succeed.

Prevent Removable Media Source For Any Install   This option disallows the installation of software using removable media (such as CD-ROM or DVD-ROM). It is useful for ensuring that users install only approved applications.

Prohibit Rollback   When this option is enabled, the Windows Installer does not store the system state information that is required to roll back the installation of an application. System administrators may choose this option to reduce the amount of temporary disk space required during installation and to increase the performance of the installation operation. However, the drawback is that the system cannot roll back to its original state if the installation fails and the application needs to be removed.

Specify The order In Which Windows Installer Searches   This setting specifies the order in which the Windows Installer will search for installation files. The options include *n* (for network shares), *m* (for searching removal media), and *u* (for searching the Internet for installation files).

With these options, system administrators can control how the Windows Installer operates for specific users who are affected by the GPO.

Troubleshooting Group Policies

Because of the wide variety of configurations that are possible when you are establishing GPOs, you should be aware of some common troubleshooting methods. These methods will help isolate problems in policy settings or GPO links.

One possible problem with GPO configuration is that logons and system startups may take a long time. This occurs especially in large environments when the Group Policy settings must be transmitted over the network and, in many cases, slow WAN links. In general, the number of GPOs should be limited because of the processing overhead and network requirements during logon. By default, GPOs are processed in a synchronous manner. This means that the processing of one GPO must be completed before another one is applied (as opposed to asynchronous processing, where they can all execute at the same time).

When a group policy gets processed on a Windows-based operating system, client-side extensions are the mechanisms that interpret the stored policy and then make the appropriate changes to the operating system environment. When an administrator is troubleshooting a given extension's application of policy, the administrator can view the configuration parameters for that extension in the operating system's Registry. To view the extension in the Registry, you would view the following key:

```
HKEY_LOCAL_MACHINE\Software\Microsoft\Windows ↵
NT\CurrentVersion\Winlogon\GPExtensions
```

The most common issue associated with Group Policy is the unexpected setting of Group Policy options. In Windows Server 2000, administrators spent countless hours analyzing inheritance hierarchy and individual settings to determine why a particular user or computer was having policy problems. For instance, say a user named wpanek complains that the Run option is missing from his Start menu. The wpanek user account is stored in the New Hampshire OU, and you've applied group policies at the OU, domain, and site levels. To determine the source of the problem, you would have to sift through each GPO manually to find the Start menu policy as well as to figure out the applicable inheritance settings.

Windows Server 2012 has a handy feature called *Resultant Set of Policy (RSoP)* that displays the exact settings that actually apply to individual users, computers, OUs, domains, and sites after inheritance and filtering have taken effect. In the example just described, you could run RSoP on the wpanek account and view a single set of Group Policy settings that represent the settings that apply to the wpanek account. In addition, each setting's Properties dialog box displays the GPO from which the setting is derived as well as the order of priority, the filter status, and other useful information, as you will see a bit later.

RSoP actually runs in two modes:

Logging Mode   *Logging mode* displays the actual settings that apply to users and computers, as seen in the example in the preceding paragraph.

Planning Mode   *Planning mode* can be applied to users, computers, OUs, domains, and sites, and you use it before you apply any settings. As its name implies, planning mode is used to plan GPOs.

Additionally, you can run the command-line utility gpresult.exe to get a quick snapshot of the Group Policy settings that apply to a user and/or computer. Let's take a closer look at the two modes and the gpresult.exe command.

RSoP in Logging Mode

RSoP in logging mode can query policy settings only for users and computers. The easiest way to access RSoP in logging mode is through the Active Directory Users and Computers tool, although you can run it as a stand-alone MMC snap-in if you wish.

To analyze the policy settings for wpanek from the earlier example, you would right-click the user icon in Active Directory Users and Computers and select All Tasks ➢ Resultant Set of Policy (Logging). The Group Policy Results Wizard appears. The wizard walks you through the steps necessary to view the RSoP for wpanek.

The Computer Selection page, shown in Figure 5.16, requires you to select a computer for which to display settings. Remember that a GPO contains both user and computer settings, so you must choose a computer to which the user is logged on in order to continue with the wizard. If the user has never logged on to a computer, then you must run RSoP in planning mode because there is no logged policy information yet for that user.

The User Selection page, shown in Figure 5.17, requires you to select a user account to analyze. Because I selected a user from the Active Directory Users and Computers tool, the username is filled in automatically. This page is most useful if you are running RSoP in MMC mode and don't have the luxury of selecting a user contextually.

FIGURE 5.16   The Computer Selection page of the Group Policy Results Wizard

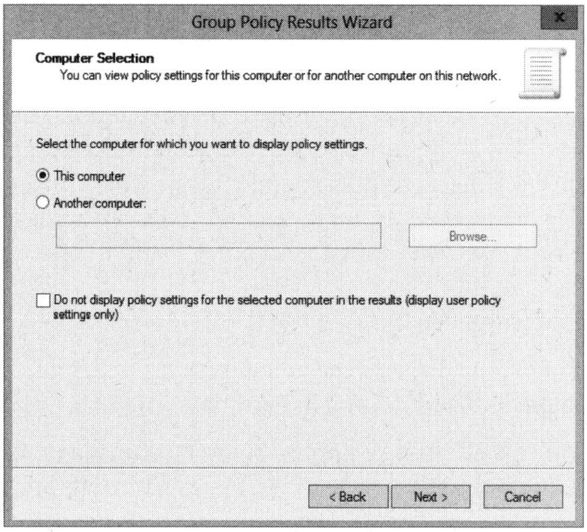

FIGURE 5.17   The User Selection page of the Group Policy Results Wizard

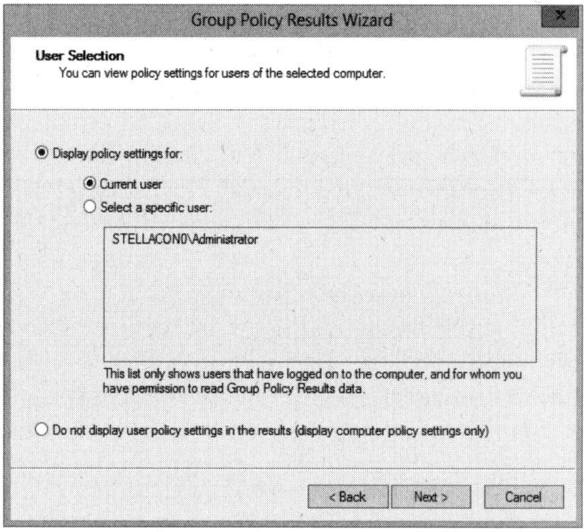

The Summary Of Selections page, shown in Figure 5.18, displays a summary of your choices and provides an option for gathering extended error information. If you need to make any changes before you begin to analyze the policy settings, you should click the Back button on the Summary screen. Otherwise, click Next.

FIGURE 5.18   The Summary Of Selections page of the Group Policy Results Wizard

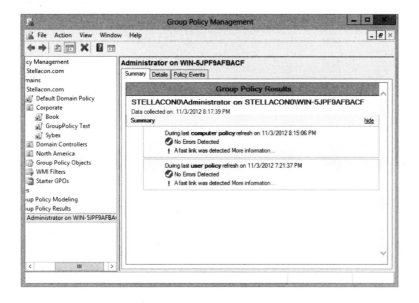

After the wizard is complete, you will see the window shown in Figure 5.19. This window displays only the policy settings that apply to the user and computer that you selected in the wizard. You can see these users and computers at the topmost level of the tree.

FIGURE 5.19   The User Selection page for the administrator on computer SERVER1

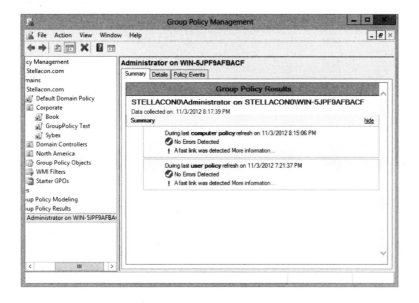

Any warnings or errors appear as a yellow triangle or red X over the applicable icon at the level where the warning or error occurred. To view more information about the warning or error, right-click the icon, select Properties, and select the Error Information tab. An error message is shown in Figure 5.20.

FIGURE 5.20   Details of event pertaining to the administrator account on computer SERVER1

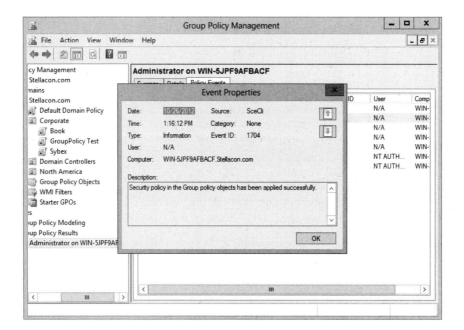

You cannot make changes to any of the individual settings because RSoP is a diagnostic tool and not an editor, but you can get more information about settings by clicking a setting and selecting Properties from the context menu.

The Details tab of the user's Properties window, shown in Figure 5.21, displays the actual setting that applies to the user in question based on GPO inheritance.

RSoP in Planning Mode

Running RSoP in planning mode isn't much different from running RSoP in logging mode, but the RSoP Wizard asks for a bit more information than you saw earlier.

FIGURE 5.21   The Details tab of the object's Properties window

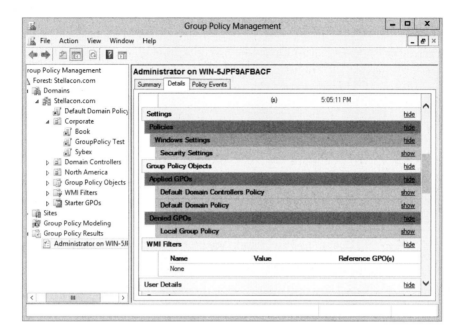

In the former example, wpanek couldn't see the Run option in the Start menu because his user account is affected by the New Hampshire GPO in the San Jose OU. As an administrator, you could plan to move his user account to the North America OU. Before doing so, you could verify his new policy settings by running RSoP in planning mode. Run the RSoP on the user wpanek under the scenario that you've already moved him from the San Jose OU to the North America OU. At this point, you haven't actually moved the user, but you can see what his settings would be if you did.

Using the *gpresult.exe* Command

The command-line utility gpresult.exe is included as part of the RSoP tool. Running the command by itself without any switches returns the following Group Policy information about the local user and computer:

- The name of the domain controller from which the local machine retrieved the policy information

- The date and time in which the policies were applied

- Which policies were applied
- Which policies were filtered out
- Group membership

You can use the switches shown in Table 5.2 to get information for remote users and computers and to enable other options.

 Table 5.2 is not a complete list. To see a complete list of the gpresult.exe command, visit Microsoft at www.microsoft.com.

TABLE 5.2   gpresult switches

Switch	Description
/S *systemname*	Generates RSoP information for a remote computer name.
/USER *username*	Generates RSoP information for a remote username.
/x /h *filename*	Generates a report in either XML (/x) or HTML (/h) format. The file-name and location is specified by the *filename* parameter.
/V	Specifies verbose mode, which displays more verbose information such as user rights information.
/Z	Specifies an even greater level of verbose information.
/SCOPE MACHINE	Displays maximum information about the computer policies applied to this system.
/SCOPE USER	Displays maximum information about the user policies applied to this system.
>*textfile.txt*	Writes the output to a text file.

For example, to obtain information about user wpanek in a system called STELLA-CON, you would use the command gpresult/S STELLACON/USERwpanek.

Through the use of these techniques, you should be able to track down even the most elusive Group Policy problems. Remember, however, that good troubleshooting skills do not replace planning adequately and maintaining GPO settings!

Summary

In this chapter, we examined Active Directory's solution to a common headache for many systems administrators: policy settings. Specifically, we discussed topics that covered Group Policy.

We covered the fundamentals of Group Policy including its fundamental purpose. You can use Group Policy to enforce granular permissions for users in an Active Directory environment. Group policies can restrict and modify the actions allowed for users and computers within the Active Directory environment.

Certain Group Policy settings may apply to users, computers, or both. Computer settings affect all users who access the machines to which the policy applies. User settings affect users regardless of the machines to which they log on.

You learned that you can link Group Policy objects to Active Directory sites, domains, or OUs. This link determines to which objects the policies apply. GPO links can interact through inheritance and filtering to result in an effective set of policies.

The chapter covered inheritance and how GPOs filter down. I showed you how to use the Enforced option on a GPO issued from a parent and how to block a GPO from a child.

You can also use administrative templates to simplify the creation of GPOs. There are some basic default templates that come with Windows Server 2012.

In addition, administrators can delegate control over GPOs in order to distribute administrative responsibilities. Delegation is an important concept because it allows for distributed administration.

You can also deploy software using GPOs. This feature can save time and increase productivity throughout the entire software management life cycle by automating software installation and removal on client computers. The Windows Installer offers a more robust method for managing installation and removal, and applications that support it can take advantage of new Active Directory features. Make sure you are comfortable using the Windows Installer.

You learned about publishing applications via Active Directory and the difference between publishing and assigning applications. You can assign some applications to users and computers so that they are always available. You can also publish them to users so that the user can install them with minimal effort when required.

You also learned how to prepare for software deployment. Before your users can take advantage of automated software installation, you must set up an installation share and provide the appropriate permissions.

The final portion of the chapter covered the Resultant Set of Policy (RSoP) tool, which you can use in logging mode or planning mode to determine exactly which set of policies apply to users, computers, OUs, domains, and sites.

Exam Essentials

Understand the purpose of Group Policy.   System administrators use Group Policy to enforce granular permissions for users in an Active Directory environment.

Understand user and computer settings.   Certain Group Policy settings may apply to users, computers, or both. Computer settings affect all users that access the machines to which the policy applies. User settings affect users, regardless of which machines they log on to.

Know the interactions between Group Policy objects and Active Directory. GPOs can be linked to Active Directory objects. This link determines to which objects the policies apply.

Understand filtering and inheritance interactions between GPOs. For ease of administration, GPOs can interact via inheritance and filtering. It is important to understand these interactions when you are implementing and troubleshooting Group Policy.

Know how Group Policy settings can affect script policies and network settings. You can use special sets of GPOs to manage network configuration settings.

Understand how delegation of administration can be used in an Active Directory environment. Delegation is an important concept because it allows for distributed administration.

Know how to use the Resultant Set of Policy (RSoP) tool to troubleshoot and plan Group Policy. Windows Server 2012 includes the RSoP feature, which you can run in logging mode or planning mode to determine exactly which set of policies applies to users, computers, OUs, domains, and sites.

Identify common problems with the software life cycle. IT professionals face many challenges with client applications, including development, deployment, maintenance, and troubleshooting.

Understand the benefits of the Windows Installer. Using the Windows Installer is an updated way to install applications on Windows-based machines. It offers a more robust method for making the system changes required by applications, and it allows for a cleaner uninstall. Windows Installer–based applications can also take advantage of new Active Directory features.

Understand the difference between publishing and assigning applications. Some applications can be assigned to users and computers so that they are always available. Applications can be published to users so that the user may install the application with a minimal amount of effort when it is required.

Know how to prepare for software deployment. Before your users can take advantage of automated software installation, you must set up an installation share and provide the appropriate permissions.

Know how to configure application settings using Active Directory and Group Policy. Using standard Windows Server 2012 administrative tools, you can create an application policy that meets your requirements. You can use automatic, on-demand installation of applications as well as many other features.

Create application categories to simplify the list of published applications. It's important to group applications by functionality or the users to whom they apply, especially in organizations that support a large number of programs.

Review Questions

1. You are the network administrator for a large organization that uses Windows Server 2012 domain controllers and DNS servers. All of your client machines currently have the Windows XP operating system. You want to be able to have client computers edit the domain-based GPOs by using the ADMX files that are located in the ADMX Central Store. How do you accomplish this task? (Choose all that apply.)

   A. Upgrade your clients to Windows 8.

   B. Upgrade your clients to Windows 7.

   C. Add the client machines to the ADMX edit utility.

   D. In the ADMX store, choose the box Allow All Client Privileges.

2. You work for an organization with a single Windows Server 2012 Active Directory domain. The domain has OUs for Sales, Marketing, Admin, R&D, and Finance. You need the users in the Finance OU only to get Windows Office 2010 installed automatically onto their computers. You create a GPO named OfficeApp. What is the next step in getting all the Finance users Office 2010?

   A. Edit the GPO, and assign the Office application to the user's account. Link the GPO to the Finance OU.

   B. Edit the GPO, and assign the Office application to the user's account. Link the GPO to the domain.

   C. Edit the GPO, and assign the Office application to the computer account. Link the GPO to the domain.

   D. Edit the GPO, and assign the Office application to the computer account. Link the GPO to the Finance OU.

3. You are hired as a consultant to the ABC Company. The owner of the company complains that she continues to have Desktop wallpaper that she did not choose. When you speak with the IT team, you find out that a former employee created 20 GPOs and they have not been able to figure out which GPO is changing the owner's Desktop wallpaper. How can you resolve this issue?

   A. Run the RSoP utility against all forest computer accounts.

   B. Run the RSoP utility against the owner's computer account.

   C. Run the RSoP utility against the owner's user account.

   D. Run the RSoP utility against all domain computer accounts.

4. You are the network administrator for a large organization that has multiple sites and multiple OUs. You have a site named SalesSite that is for the sales building across the street. In the domain, there is an OU for all salespeople called Sales. You set up a GPO for the SalesSite, and you need to be sure that it applies to the Sales OU. The Sales OU GPOs cannot override the SalesSite GPO. What do you do?

    A. On the GPO, disable the Block Child Inheritance setting.

    B. On the GPO, set the Enforce setting.

    C. On the GPO, set the priorities to 1.

    D. On the Sales OU, set the Inherit Parent Policy settings.

5. You are the administrator for an organization that has multiple locations. You are running Windows Server 2012, and you have only one domain with multiple OUs set up for each location.

    One of your locations, Boston, is connected to the main location by a 256 Kbps ISDN line. You configure a GPO to assign a sales application to all computers in the entire domain. You have to be sure that Boston users receive the GPO properly. What should you do?

    A. Disable the Slow Link Detection setting in the GPO.

    B. Link the GPO to the Boston OU.

    C. Change the properties of the GPO to publish the application to the Boston OU.

    D. Have the users in Boston run the `GPResult/force` command.

6. To disable GPO settings for a specific security group, which of the following permissions should you apply?

    A. Deny Write

    B. Allow Write

    C. Enable Apply Group Policy

    D. Deny Apply Group Policy

7. GPOs assigned at which of the following level(s) will override GPO settings at the domain level?

    A. OU

    B. Site

    C. Domain

    D. Both OU and site

8. A system administrator wants to ensure that only the GPOs set at the OU level affect the Group Policy settings for objects within the OU. Which option can they use to do this (assuming that all other GPO settings are the defaults)?

    A. The Enforced option

    B. The Block Policy Inheritance option

    C. The Disable option

    D. The Deny permission

9. A system administrator is planning to implement Group Policy objects in a new Windows Server 2012 Active Directory environment. In order to meet the needs of the organization, he decides to implement a hierarchical system of Group Policy settings. At which of the following levels is he able to assign Group Policy settings? (Choose all that apply.)

A. Sites

B. Domains

C. Organizational units

D. Local system

10. Ann is a system administrator for a medium-sized Active Directory environment. She has determined that several new applications that will be deployed throughout the organization use Registry-based settings. She would like to do the following:

- Control these Registry settings using Group Policy.

- Create a standard set of options for these applications, and allow other system administrators to modify them using the standard Active Directory tools.

Which of the following options can she use to meet these requirements? (Choose all that apply.)

A. Implement the inheritance functionality of GPOs.

B. Implement delegation of specific objects within Active Directory.

C. Implement the No Override functionality of GPOs.

D. Create administrative templates.

E. Provide administrative templates to the system administrators who are responsible for creating Group Policy for the applications.

Chapter

6

Configuring Active Directory Infrastructure

THE FOLLOWING 70-411 EXAM OBJECTIVES ARE COVERED IN THIS CHAPTER:

✓ **Configure Domain Controllers**

  ▪ This objective may include, but is not limited to: Configure Universal Group Membership Caching (UGMC); transfer and seize operations masters; install and configure a read-only domain controller (RODC); configure Domain Controller cloning.

THE FOLLOWING 70-412 EXAM OBJECTIVES ARE COVERED IN THIS CHAPTER:

✓ **Configure a forest or a domain**

  ▪ This objective may include, but is not limited to: Implement multi-domain and multi-forest Active Directory environments including interoperability with previous versions of Active Directory; upgrade existing domains and forests including environment preparation and functional levels; configure multiple user principal name (UPN) suffixes.

✓ **Configure trusts**

  ▪ This objective may include, but is not limited to: Configure external, forest, shortcut, and realm trusts; configure trust authentication; configure SID filtering; configure name suffix routing.

✓ **Configure sites**

  ▪ This objective may include, but is not limited to: Configure sites and subnets; create and configure site links; manage site coverage; manage registration of SRV records; move domain controllers between sites.

Microsoft has designed Active Directory to be an enterprise-wide solution for managing network resources. In previous chapters, you saw how to create Active Directory objects based on an organization's logical design. Domain structure and organizational unit (OU) structure, for example, should be designed based primarily on an organization's business needs.

Now it's time to learn how Active Directory can map to an organization's *physical* requirements. Specifically, you must consider network connectivity between sites and the flow of information between domain controllers (DC) under less-than-ideal conditions. These constraints determine how domain controllers can work together to ensure that the objects within Active Directory remain synchronized no matter how large and geographically dispersed the network.

Fortunately, through the use of the Active Directory Sites and Services administrative tool, you can quickly and easily create the various components of an Active Directory replication topology. Using this tool, you can create objects called sites, place servers in sites, and create connections between sites. Once you have configured Active Directory replication to fit your current network environment, you can sit back and allow Active Directory to make sure information remains consistent across domain controllers.

This chapter covers the features of Active Directory that allow system administrators to modify the behavior of replication based on their physical network design. Through the use of sites, system and network administrators will be able to leverage their network infrastructure best to support Windows Server 2012 and Active Directory.

So far, you have learned the steps necessary to install the Domain Name System (DNS) and to implement the first Active Directory domain. Although I briefly introduced multidomain Active Directory structures earlier, I focused on only a single domain and the objects within it.

Many businesses find that using a single domain provides an adequate solution to meet their business needs. By working with *trees* and *forests*, however, organizations can use multiple domains to organize their environments better.

Overview of Network Planning

Before discussing sites and replication, you need to understand some basic physical and network concepts.

The Three Types of Networks

When designing networks, system and network administrators use the following terms to define the types of connectivity between locations and servers:

Local Area Networks   A *local area network (LAN)* is usually characterized as a high-bandwidth network. Generally, an organization owns all of its LAN network hardware and software. Ethernet is by far the most common networking standard. Ethernet speeds are generally at least 10 Mbps and can scale to multiple gigabits per second. Currently, the standard for Ethernet is the 10 Gigabit Ethernet, which runs at 10 times the speed of Gigabit Ethernet (1 GB). Several LAN technologies, including routing and switching, are available to segment LANs and to reduce contention for network resources.

Wide Area Networks   The purpose of a *wide area network (WAN)* is similar to that of a LAN; that is, to connect network devices. Unlike LANs, however, WANs are usually leased from third-party telecommunications carriers and Internet service providers (ISPs). Although extremely high-speed WAN connections are available, they are generally costly for organizations to implement through a distributed environment. Therefore, WAN connections are characterized by lower-speed connections and, sometimes, nonpersistent connections.

The Internet   The *Internet* is a worldwide public network infrastructure based on the *Internet Protocol (IP)*. Access to the Internet is available through organizations known as *Internet service providers (ISPs)*. Because it is a public network, there is no single "owner" of the Internet. Instead, large network and telecommunications providers constantly upgrade the infrastructure of this network to meet growing demands.

Organizations use the Internet regularly to sell and market their products and services. For example, it's rare nowadays to see advertisements that don't direct you to one website or another. Through the use of technologies such as *virtual private networks (VPNs)*, organizations can use encryption and authentication technology to enable secure communications across the Internet.

Exploring Network Constraints

In an ideal situation, a high-speed network would connect all computers and networking devices. In such a situation, you would be able to ensure that any user of your network, regardless of location, would be able to access resources quickly and easily. When you are working in the real world, however, you have many other constraints to keep in mind, including network bandwidth and network cost.

Network Bandwidth

Network bandwidth generally refers to the amount of data that can pass through a specific connection in a given amount of time. For example, in a WAN situation, a T1 may have 1.544 Mbps (megabits per second), while a DSL might have a bandwidth of 56 or 57.6 Kbps (kilobits per second) or more. On the other hand, your LAN's Ethernet connection may have a bandwidth of 100 Mbps. Different types of networks work at different speeds. Therefore, it's imperative that you always consider network bandwidth when thinking about how to deploy domain controllers in your environment.

Network Cost

Cost is perhaps the single largest factor in determining a network design. If cost were not a constraint, organizations would clearly elect to use high-bandwidth connections for all of their sites. Realistically, trade-offs in performance must be made for the sake of affordability. Some factors that can affect the cost of networking include the distance between networks and the types of technology available at locations throughout the world. In remote or less-developed locations, you may not even be able to get access through an ISP or telecom beyond a satellite connection or dial-up, and what is available can be quite costly. Network designers must keep these factors in mind, and they must often settle for less-than-ideal connectivity.

We have considered the monetary value of doing business. Now let's consider another aspect of cost. When designing and configuring networks, you can require certain devices to make data transport decisions automatically based on an assigned network cost. These devices are commonly known as *routers*, and they use routing protocols to make routing decisions. One of the elements a router uses to configure a routing protocol is its ability to adjust the cost of a route. For example, a router may have multiple ways to connect to a remote site, and it may have multiple interfaces connected to it, each with different paths out of the network to which it is connected locally. When two or more routes are available, you can set up a routing protocol that states that the route with the lower cost is automatically used first.

Another cost is personnel. Do you have the personnel to do the job, or do you need to hire a consultant? Remember that even if you use individuals already on staff, they will be spending time on these projects. When your IT team is working on a project, this is a cost because they cannot also be working on day-to-day tasks.

All of these factors play an important role when you make your Active Directory implementation decisions.

Overview of Active Directory Replication and Sites

I now need to address two topics that not only are covered heavily on the Microsoft exams but are two areas that all IT administrators should understand. Understanding Active Directory replication and sites can help you fine-tune a network to run at peak performance.

Replicating Active Directory

Regardless of the issues related to network design and technological constraints, network users have many different requirements and needs that must be addressed. First and foremost, network resources, such as files, printers, and shared directories, must be made available. Similarly, the resources stored within Active Directory—and, especially, its security information—are required for many operations that occur within domains.

With these issues in mind, take a look at how you can configure Active Directory to reach connectivity goals using replication.

Active Directory was designed as a scalable, distributed database that contains information about an organization's network resources. In previous chapters, you saw how you can create and manage domains and how you can use domain controllers to store Active Directory databases.

Even in the simplest of network environments, you generally need more than one domain controller. The major reasons for this are *fault tolerance* (if one domain controller fails, others can still provide services as needed) and performance (the workload can be balanced between multiple domain controllers). Windows Server 2012 domain controllers have been designed to contain read-write copies as well as read-only copies of the Active Directory database. However, the domain controllers must also remain current when objects are created or modified on other domain controllers.

To keep information consistent between domain controllers, you use *Active Directory replication*. Replication is the process by which changes to the Active Directory database are transferred between domain controllers. The result is that all of the domain controllers within an Active Directory domain contain up-to-date information and achieve convergence. Keep in mind that domain controllers may be located very near to each other (for example, within the same server rack), or they may be located across the world from each other. Although the goals of replication are quite simple, the real-world constraints of network connections between servers cause many limitations that you must accommodate. If you have a domain controller on your local LAN, you may find that you have Gigabit Ethernet, which runs at 1000 Mbps between your server connections, whereas you may have a domain controller on the other side or a WAN where the network link runs at a fraction of a T1, 56 Kbps. Replication traffic must traverse each link to ensure convergence no matter what the speed or what bandwidth is available.

Throughout this chapter, you will study the technical details of Active Directory replication. You will also learn how to use the concept of sites and site links to map the logical structure of Active Directory to a physical network topology to help it work efficiently, no matter the type of link with which you are working.

Understanding Active Directory Site Concepts

One of the most important aspects of designing and implementing Active Directory is understanding how it allows you to separate the logical components of the directory service from the physical components.

The logical components—Active Directory domains, OUs, users, groups, and computers —map to the organizational and business requirements of a company.

The physical components, on the other hand, are designed based on technical issues involved in keeping the network synchronized (that is, making sure that all parts of the network have the same up-to-date information). Active Directory uses the concept of sites to map to an organization's physical network. Stated simply, a *site* is a collection of well-connected subnets. The technical implications of sites are described later in this chapter.

It is important to understand that no specified relationship exists between Active Directory domains and Active Directory sites. An Active Directory site can contain many domains. Alternatively, a single Active Directory domain can span multiple sites. Figure 6.1 illustrates this very important characteristic of domains and sites.

FIGURE 6.1   Potential relationships between domains and sites

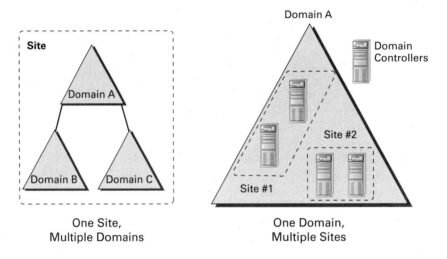

One Site,
Multiple Domains

One Domain,
Multiple Sites

There are two main reasons to use Active Directory sites: service requests and replication.

Service Requests

Clients often require the network services of a domain controller. One of the most common reasons for this is that they need the domain controller to perform network authentication. If your Active Directory network is set up with sites, clients can easily connect to the domain controller that is located closest to them. By doing this, they avoid many of the inefficiencies associated with connecting to distant domain controllers or to those that are located on the other side of a slow network connection. For example, by connecting to a local domain controller, you can avoid the problems associated with a saturated network link that might cause two domain controllers to be out of synch with each other.

Other network services that clients might access include the Licensing service (for tracking licenses associated with Microsoft and other compatible products) and the services used by messaging applications (such as Exchange Server). All of these functions depend on the availability of network services.

Replication

As mentioned earlier, the purpose of Active Directory replication is to ensure that the information stored on all domain controllers within a domain remains synchronized. In environments with many domains and domain controllers, multiple communication paths usually connect them, which makes the synchronization process more complicated. A simple method of transferring updates and other changes to Active Directory involves all of the servers communicating directly with each other as soon as a change occurs; they can all update with the change and reach convergence again. This is not ideal, however, because it places high requirements on network bandwidth and is inefficient for many network environments that use slower and more costly WAN links, especially if all environments update at the same time. Such simultaneous updating could cause the network connection at the core of your network to become saturated and decrease performance of the entire WAN.

Using sites, Active Directory can automatically determine the best methods for performing replication operations. Sites take into account an organization's network infrastructure, and Active Directory uses these sites to determine the most efficient method for synchronizing information between domain controllers. System administrators can make their physical network design map to Active Directory objects. Based on the creation and configuration of these objects, the Active Directory service can then manage replication traffic in an efficient way.

Whenever a change is made to the Active Directory database on a domain controller, the change is given an update sequence number. The domain controller can then propagate these changes to other domain controllers based on replication settings.

Windows Server 2012 uses a feature called *linked value replication* that is active only when the domain is in the Windows Server 2003, Windows Server 2008, Windows Server 2008 R2, or Windows Server 2012 domain functional level. With linked value replication, only the group member is replicated. This greatly enhances replication efficiency and cuts down on network traffic utilization. Linked value replication is automatically enabled in Windows Server 2003, Windows Server 2008, Windows Server 2008 R2, or Windows Server 2012 functional-level domains.

Planning Your Sites

Much of the challenge of designing Active Directory is related to mapping a company's business processes to the structure of a hierarchical data store. So far, you've seen many of these requirements. What about the existing network infrastructure, however? Clearly, when you plan for and design the structure of Active Directory, you must take into account your LAN and WAN characteristics. Let's see some of the ways you can use Active Directory sites to manage replication traffic.

Synchronizing Active Directory is extremely important. To keep security permissions and objects within the directory consistent throughout the organization, you must use replication. The Active Directory data store supports *multimaster replication*; that is, data can be modified at any domain controller within the domain because replication ensures that information remains consistent throughout the organization.

Ideally, every site within an organization has reliable, high-speed connections with the other sites. A much more realistic scenario, however, is one in which bandwidth is limited and connections are sometimes either sporadically available or completely unavailable.

Using sites, network and system administrators can define which domain controllers are located on which areas of the network. These settings can be based on the bandwidth available between the areas of the network. Additionally, these administrators can define *subnets*—logically partitioned areas of the network—between areas of the network. Subnets are designed by subdividing IP addresses into usable blocks for assignment, and they are also objects found within the Sites and Services Microsoft Management Console (MMC) in the Administrative Tools folder. The Windows Server 2012 Active Directory services use this information to decide how and when to replicate data between domain controllers.

Directly replicating information between all domain controllers might be a viable solution for some companies. For others, however, this might result in a lot of traffic traveling over slow or undersized network links. One way to efficiently synchronize data between sites that have slow connections is to use a *bridgehead server*. Bridgehead servers are designed to accept traffic between two remote sites and to then forward this information to the appropriate servers. Figure 6.2 provides an example of how a bridgehead server can reduce network bandwidth requirements and improve performance. Reduced network bandwidth requirements and improved performance can also be achieved by configuring replication to occur according to a predefined schedule if bandwidth usage statistics are available.

FIGURE 6.2 Using a bridgehead server

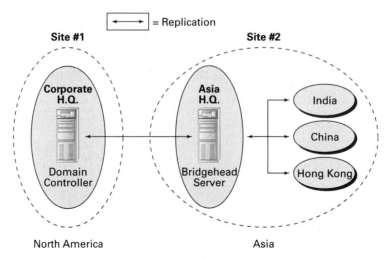

Bridgehead servers do not fit a normal hub-and-spoke WAN topology. Such a topology usually involves a core site (for example, company headquarters) with remote sites as links one off from the core. However, you can use a bridgehead server design to fit a distributed star, where you have a hub-and-spoke topology design with additional spokes coming out of the first set of spokes. Doing so would make some of your spoke sites into smaller core sites. It is at these sites that you would place your bridgehead servers. In Figure 6.2, you can see that your Asia headquarters site is also where you can connect to India, China, and Hong Kong, thus making the Asia headquarters the ideal site for the bridgehead server.

In addition to managing replication traffic, sites offer the advantage of allowing clients to access the nearest domain controller. This prevents problems with user authentication across slow network connections, and it can help find the shortest and fastest path to resources such as files and printers. Therefore, Microsoft recommends that you place at least one domain controller at each site that contains a slow link. Preferably, this domain controller also contains a copy of the global catalog so that logon attempts and resource search queries do not occur across slow links. The drawback, however, is that deploying more copies of the global catalog to servers increases replication traffic.

Through proper planning and deployment of sites, organizations can best use the capabilities of the network infrastructure while keeping Active Directory synchronized.

Understanding Distributed File System Replication

DFS Replication (DFSR) was created to replace the File Replication Service (FRS) that was introduced in the Windows 2000 Server operating systems. DFSR is a state-based, multimaster replication engine that supports replication scheduling and bandwidth throttling. DFSR has the ability to detect insertions, removals, and rearrangements of data in files. This allows DFS Replication to replicate only the changed file blocks when files are updated.

The DFS Replication component uses many different processes to keep data synchronized on multiple servers. To understand the DFSR process, it is helpful to understand some of the following concepts:

- DFSR is a multimaster replication engine, and changes that occur on one of the members are then replicated to all of the other members of the replication group.

- DFSR uses the update sequence number (USN) journal to detect changes on the volume, and then DFSR replicates the changes only after the file is closed.

- Before sending or receiving a file, DFSR uses a staging folder to stage the file.

- When a file is changed, DFSR replicates only the changed blocks and not the entire file. The RDC protocol is what helps determine the blocks that have changed in the file.

- One of the advantages of DFSR is that it is self-healing and can automatically recover from USN journal wraps, USN journal loss, or loss of the DFS Replication database.

- Windows Server 2012 DFSR includes the ability to add a failover cluster as a member of a replication group.

- Windows Server 2012 DFSR allows for read-only replicated folders on a particular member in which users cannot add or change files.
- In Windows Server 2012, it is possible to make changes to the SYSVOL folder of an RODC.

The Dfsrdiag.exe command-line tool includes three new Windows Server 2012 command-line switches that provide enhanced diagnostic capabilities for DFSR:

Dfsrdiag.exe ReplState   When you use the ReplState switch, a summary of the replication status across all connections on the specified replication group member is provided. The ReplState switch takes a snapshot of the internal state of the DFSR service, and the updates that are currently being processed (downloaded or served) by the service are shown in a list.

Dfsrdiag.exe IdRecord   The DFSR service, when replicating a file or folder, creates an ID record, and an administrator can use this ID record to determine if a file has replicated properly to a specific member. The IdRecord switch returns the DFSR ID record for the file or folder that you specify by using its path or its unique identifier (UID).

Dfsrdiag.exe FileHash   The FileHash switch, when used against a particular file, will compute and display the hash value that is generated by the DFSR service. An administrator can then look at the hash values to compare two files. If the hash values for the two files are the same, then the two files are the same.

Implementing Sites and Subnets

Now that you have a good idea of the goals of replication, take a look at the following quick overview of the various Active Directory objects, which are related to physical network topology.

The basic objects that are used for managing replication include the following:

Subnets   A *subnet* is a partition of a network. As I started to discuss earlier, subnets are logical IP blocks usually connected to other IP blocks through the use of routers and other network devices. All of the computers that are located on a given subnet are generally well connected with each other.

It is extremely important to understand the concepts of TCP/IP and the routing of network information when you are designing the topology for Active Directory replication. TCP/IP is covered in detail in Chapter 9, "Understanding TCP/IP."

Sites   An Active Directory site is a logical object that can contain servers and other objects related to Active Directory replication. Specifically, a *site* is a grouping of related subnets. Sites are created to match the physical network structure of an organization. Sites are primarily used for slow WAN links. If your network is well connected (using fiber optics, Category 5 Ethernet, and so on), then sites are not needed.

Site Links A *site link* is created to define the types of connections that are available between the components of a site. Site links can reflect a relative cost for a network connection and can reflect the bandwidth that is available for communications.

All of these components work together to determine how information is used to replicate data between domain controllers. Figure 6.3 provides an example of the physical components of Active Directory.

FIGURE 6.3 Active Directory replication objects

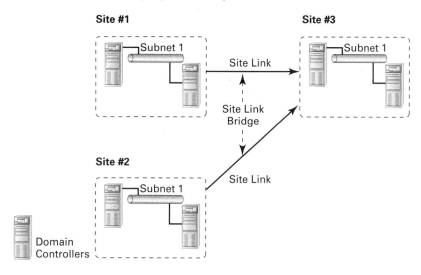

Many issues are related to configuring and managing sites; all are covered in this chapter. Overall, using sites allows you to control the behavior of Active Directory replication between domain controllers. With this background and goal in mind, let's look at how you can implement sites to control Active Directory replication so that it is efficient and in synch.

If you do not have replication set up properly, after a while you will experience problems with your domain controllers. An example of a common replication problem is Event Log event ID 1311, which states that the Windows NT Directory Services (NTDS) Knowledge Consistency Checker (KCC) has found (and reported) a problem with Active Directory replication. This error message states that the replication configuration information in Active Directory does not accurately reflect the physical topology of the network. This error is commonly found on ailing networks that have replication problems for one reason or another.

Creating Sites

The primary method for creating and managing Active Directory replication components is to utilize the Active Directory Sites and Services tool or the MMC found within the Administrative Tools folder. Using this administrative component, you can graphically create and manage sites in much the same way that you create and manage OUs.

Exercise 6.1 walks you through the process of creating Active Directory sites. In order for you to complete this exercise, the local machine must be a domain controller. Also, this exercise assumes that you have not yet changed the default domain site configuration.

 Do not perform any testing on a production system or network. Make sure you test site configuration in a lab setting only.

EXERCISE 6.1

 Creating Sites

1. Open the Active Directory Sites and Services tool from the Administrative Tools program group.

2. Expand the Sites folder.

3. Right-click the Default-First-Site-Name item, and choose Rename. Rename the site **CorporateHQ**.

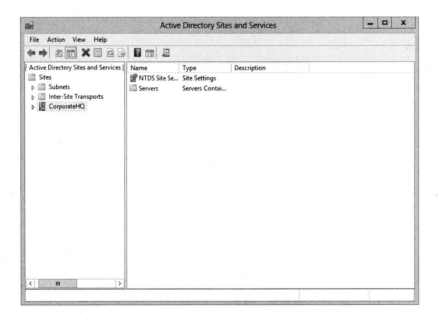

4. Create a new site by right-clicking the Sites object and selecting New Site.

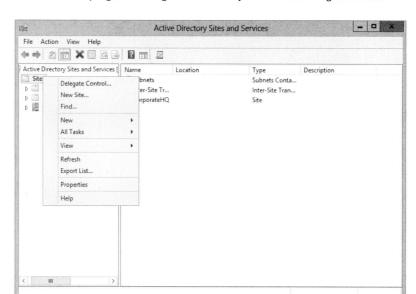

5. On the New Object - Site dialog box, type **Farmington** for the site name. Click the DEFAULTIPSITELINK item, and an information screen pops up. Then click OK to create the site. Note that you cannot include spaces or other special characters in the name of a site.

6. Notice that the Farmington site is now listed under the Sites object.

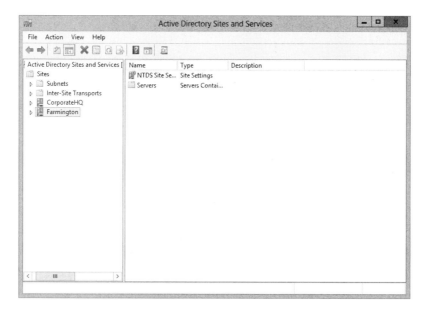

7. Create another new site, and name it **Portsmouth**. Again, choose the DEFAULTIPSITE-LINK item. Notice that the new site is listed under the `Sites` object.

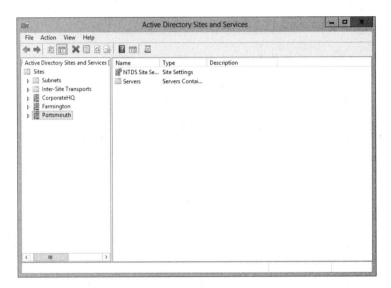

8. When you have finished, close the Active Directory Sites and Services tool.

Creating Subnets

Once you have created the sites that map to your network topology, it's time to define the subnets that define the site boundaries.

Subnets are based on TCP/IPv4 or TCP/IPv6 address information. For example, the IPv4 address may be 10.10.0.0, and the subnet mask may be 255.255.0.0. This information specifies that all of the TCP/IP addresses that begin with the first two octets are part of the same TCP/IP subnet. All of the following TCP/IP addresses would be within this subnet:

- 10.10.1.5
- 10.10.100.17
- 10.10.110.120

The Active Directory Sites and Services tool expresses these subnets in a somewhat different notation. It uses the provided subnet address and appends a slash followed by the number of bits in the subnet mask. In the example in the previous paragraph, the subnet would be defined as 10.1.0.0/16.

Remember that sites typically represent distinct physical locations, and they almost always have their own subnets. The only way for a domain controller (DC) in one site to reach a DC in another site is to add subnet information about the remote site. Generally, information regarding the definition of subnets for a specific network environment will be available from a network designer. Exercise 6.2 walks you through the steps you need to take to create subnets and assign subnets to sites. To complete the steps in this exercise, you must have completed Exercise 6.1.

EXERCISE 6.2

Creating Subnets

1. Open the Active Directory Sites and Services tool from the Administrative Tools program group.

2. Expand the Sites folder. Right-click the Subnets folder, and select New Subnet.

3. In the New Object - Subnet dialog box, you are prompted for information about the IPv4 or IPv6 details for the new subnet. For the prefix, type **10.10.1.0/24** (we are staying with the more commonly used IPv4). This actually calculates out to 10.10.1.0 with the mask of 255.255.255.0. Click the Farmington site, and then click OK to create the subnet.

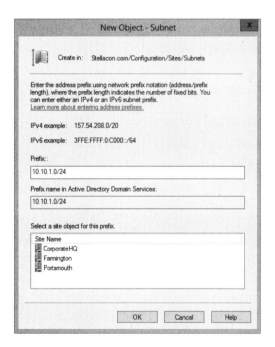

4. In the Active Directory Sites and Services tool, right-click the newly created 10.10.1.0/24 subnet object, and select Properties.

5. On the subnet's Properties dialog box, type **Farmington 100MB LAN** for the description. Click OK to continue.

6. Create a new subnet using the following information:

   Address: **160.25.0.0/16**

   Site: **Portsmouth**

   Description: **Portsmouth 100Mbit LAN**

7. Finally, create another subnet using the following information:

   Address: **176.33.0.0/16**

   Site: **CorporateHQ**

   Description: **Corporate 100Mbit switched LAN**

8. When finished, close the Active Directory Sites and Services tool.

So far, you have created the basic components that govern Active Directory sites and subnets. You also linked these two components by defining which subnets belong in which sites. These two steps—creating sites and creating subnets—form the basis of mapping the physical network infrastructure of an organization to Active Directory. Now look at the various settings that you can make for sites.

Configuring Sites

Once you have created Active Directory sites and have defined which subnets they contain, it's time to make some additional configuration settings for the site structure. Specifically, you'll need to assign servers to specific sites and configure the site-licensing options. By placing servers in sites, you tell Active Directory replication services how to replicate information for various types of servers. Later in this chapter you'll examine the details of working with replication within and between sites.

In Exercise 6.3, you will add servers to sites and configure CorpDC1 options. To complete the steps in this exercise, you must have completed Exercise 6.1 and Exercise 6.2.

EXERCISE 6.3

Configuring Sites

1. Open the Active Directory Sites and Services tool from the Administrative Tools program group.

2. Expand the Sites folder, and click and expand the Farmington site.

3. Right-click the Servers container in the Farmington site, and select New ➣ Server. Type **FarmingtonDC1** for the name of the server, and then click OK.

4. Create a new Server object within the CorporateHQ site, and name it **CorpDC1**. Note that this object also includes the name of the local domain controller.

5. Create two new Server objects within the Portsmouth site, and name them **PortsmouthDC1** and **PortsmouthDC2**.

6. Right-click the CorpDC1 server object and select Properties. In the General tab of the CorpDC1 Properties box, select SMTP in the Transports Available For Inter-site Data Transfer box, and click Add to make this server a preferred IP bridgehead server. Click OK to accept the settings.

7. When you have finished, close the Active Directory Sites and Services tool.

With the configuration of the basic settings for sites out of the way, it's time to focus on the real details of the site topology—creating site links and site link bridges.

Configuring Replication

Sites are generally used to define groups of computers that are located within a single geographic location. In most organizations, machines that are located in close physical proximity (for example, within a single building or branch office) are well connected. A typical example is a LAN in a branch office of a company. All of the computers may be connected using Ethernet, and routing and switching technology may be in place to reduce network congestion.

Often, however, domain controllers are located across various states, countries, and even continents. In such a situation, network connectivity is usually much slower, less reliable, and more costly than that for the equivalent LAN. Therefore, Active Directory replication must accommodate accordingly. When managing replication traffic within Active Directory sites, you need to be aware of two types of synchronization:

Intrasite *Intrasite replication* refers to the synchronization of Active Directory information between domain controllers that are located in the same site. In accordance with the concept of sites, these machines are usually well connected by a high-speed LAN.

Intersite *Intersite replication* occurs between domain controllers in different sites. Usually, this means that there is a WAN or other type of low-speed network connection between the various machines. Intersite replication is optimized for minimizing the amount of network traffic that occurs between sites.

In the following sections, you'll look at ways to configure both intrasite and intersite replication. Additionally, you'll see features of Active Directory replication architecture that you can use to accommodate the needs of almost any environment.

Intrasite Replication

Intrasite replication is generally a simple process. One domain controller contacts the others in the same site when changes to its copy of Active Directory are made. It compares the update sequence numbers in its own copy of Active Directory with those of the other domain controllers, then the most current information is chosen by the DC in question, and all domain controllers within the site use this information to make the necessary updates to their database.

Because you can assume that the domain controllers within an Active Directory site are well connected, you can pay less attention to exactly when and how replication takes place. Communications between domain controllers occur using the *Remote Procedure Call (RPC) protocol*. This protocol is optimized for transmitting and synchronizing information on fast and reliable network connections. The RPC protocol provides for fast replication at the expense of network bandwidth, which is usually readily available because most LANs today are running on Fast Ethernet (100 Mbps) at a minimum.

Intersite Replication

Intersite replication is optimized for low-bandwidth situations and network connections that have less reliability. Intersite replication offers several features that are tailored toward these types of connections. To begin with, two different protocols may be used to transfer information between sites:

RPC over IP When connectivity is fairly reliable, IP is a good choice. IP-based communications require you to have a live connection between two or more domain controllers in different sites and let you transfer Active Directory information. RPC over IP was originally designed for slower WANs in which packet loss and corruption may often occur.

Simple Mail Transfer Protocol *Simple Mail Transfer Protocol (SMTP)* is perhaps best known as the protocol that is used to send and receive email messages on the Internet. SMTP was designed to use a store-and-forward mechanism through which a server receives a copy of a message, records it to disk, and then attempts to forward it to another email server. If the destination server is unavailable, it holds the message and attempts to resend it at periodic intervals.

This type of communication is extremely useful for situations in which network connections are unreliable or not always available. For example, if a branch office in Peru is connected to the corporate office through a dial-up connection that is available only during certain hours, SMTP would be a good choice for communication with that branch.

SMTP is an inherently insecure network protocol. Therefore, if you would like to ensure that you transfer replication traffic securely and you use SMTP for Active Directory replication, you must take advantage of Windows Server 2012's Certificate Services functionality.

Other intersite replication characteristics are designed to address low-bandwidth situations and less-reliable network connections. These features give you a high degree of flexibility in controlling replication configuration. They include the following:

- Compression of Active Directory information. This compression is helpful because changes between domain controllers in remote sites may include a large amount of information and also because network bandwidth tends to be less available and more costly.

- Site links and site link bridges help determine intersite replication topology.

- Replication can occur based on a schedule defined by system administrators.

You can configure intersite replication by using the Active Directory Sites and Services tool. Select the name of the site for which you want to configure settings. Then right-click the NTDS Site Settings object in the right window pane, and select Properties. By clicking the Change Schedule button in the NTDS Site Settings Properties dialog box, you'll be able to configure how often replication occurs between sites (see Figure 6.4).

FIGURE 6.4   Configuring intersite replication schedules

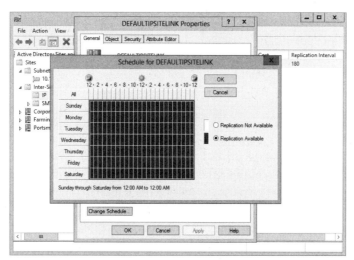

You will see how to set the replication schedule in Exercise 6.4.

In the following sections, you will see how to configure site links and site link bridges as well as how to manage connection objects and bridgehead servers.

Creating Site Links and Site Link Bridges

The overall topology of intersite replication is based on the use of site links and site link bridges. *Site links* are logical connections that define a path between two Active Directory sites. Site links can include several descriptive elements that define their network characteristics. *Site link bridges* are used to connect site links so that the relationship can be transitive. Figure 6.5 provides an example of site links and site link bridges.

FIGURE 6.5   An example of site links and site link bridges

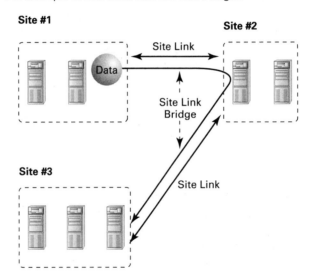

Both of these types of logical connections are used by Active Directory services to determine how information should be synchronized between domain controllers in remote sites. This information is used by the Knowledge Consistency Checker (KCC), which forms a replication topology based on the site topology created. The KCC service is responsible for determining the best way to replicate information within sites.

When creating site links for your environment, you'll need to consider the following factors:

Transporting Information   You can choose to use either RPC over IP or SMTP for transferring information over a site link. You will need to determine which is best based on your network infrastructure and the reliability of connections between sites.

Assigning a Cost Value   You can create multiple site links between sites and assign site links a cost value based on the type of connection. The system administrator determines the cost value, and the relative costs of site links are then used (by the system) to determine the optimal path for replication. The lower the cost, the more likely the link is to be used for replication.

For example, a company may primarily use a T1 link between branch offices, but it may also use a slower and circuit-switched dial-up ISDN connection for redundancy (in case the T1 fails). In this example, a system administrator may assign a cost of 25 to the T1 line and a cost of 100 to the ISDN line. This ensures that the more reliable and higher-bandwidth T1 connection is used whenever it's available but that the ISDN line is also available.

Determining a Replication Schedule   Once you've determined how and through which connections replication will take place, it's time to determine when information should be replicated. Replication requires network resources and occupies bandwidth. Therefore, you need to balance the need for consistent directory information with the need to conserve bandwidth. For example, if you determine that it's reasonable to have a lag time of six hours between when an update is made at one site and when it is replicated to all others, you might schedule replication to occur once in the morning, once during the lunch hour, and more frequently after normal work hours.

Based on these factors, you should be able to devise a strategy that allows you to configure site links.

Exercise 6.4 walks you through the process of creating site links and site link bridges. To complete the steps in this exercise, you must have completed Exercises 6.1, 6.2, and 6.3.

EXERCISE 6.4

Creating Site Links and Site Link Bridges

1. Open the Active Directory Sites and Services tool from the Administrative Tools program group.

2. Expand the Sites, Inter-site Transports, and IP objects. Right-click the DEFAULTIPSITE-LINK item in the right pane, and select Rename. Rename the object **CorporateWAN**.

3. Right-click the CorporateWAN link, and select Properties. In the General tab of the CorporateWAN Properties dialog box, type **T1 Connecting Corporate and Portsmouth Offices** for the description. Remove the Farmington site from the link by highlighting Farmington in the Sites In This Site Link box and clicking Remove. For the Cost value, type **50**, and specify that replication should occur every **60** minutes. To create the site link, click OK.

4. Right-click the IP folder, and select New Site Link. On the New Object - Site Link dialog box, name the link **CorporateDialup**. Add the Farmington and CorporateHQ sites to the site link and then click OK.

5. Right-click the CorporateDialup link, and select Properties. In the General tab of the CorporateDialup Properties dialog box, type **ISDN Dialup between Corporate and Farmington** for the description. Set the Cost value to **100**, and specify that replication should occur every **120** minutes. To specify that replication should occur only during certain times of the day, click the Change Schedule button.

6. On the Schedule ForCorporateDialup dialog box, highlight the area between 8:00 a.m. and 6:00 p.m. for the days Monday through Friday, and click the Replication Not Available option. This will ensure that replication traffic is minimized during normal work hours.

7. Click OK to accept the new schedule, and then click OK again to create the site link.

8. Right-click the IP object, and select New Site Link Bridge. On the New Object - Site Link Bridge dialog box, name the site link bridge **CorporateBridge**. Note that the Corporate Dialup and CorporateWAN site links are already added to the site link bridge. Because there must be at least two site links in each bridge, you will not be able to remove these links. Click OK to create the site link bridge.

9. When finished, close the Active Directory Sites and Services tool.

Creating Connection Objects

Generally, it is a good practice to allow Active Directory's replication mechanisms to schedule and manage replication functions automatically. In some cases, however, you may want to have additional control over replication. Perhaps you want to replicate certain changes on demand (for example, when you create new accounts). Or you may want to specify a custom schedule for certain servers.

Connection objects provide you with a way to set up these different types of replication schedules. You can create connection objects with the Active Directory Sites and Services tool by expanding a server object, right-clicking the NTDS Settings object, and selecting New Active Directory Domain Services Connection (see Figure 6.6).

FIGURE 6.6   Creating a new Active Directory Domain Services connection

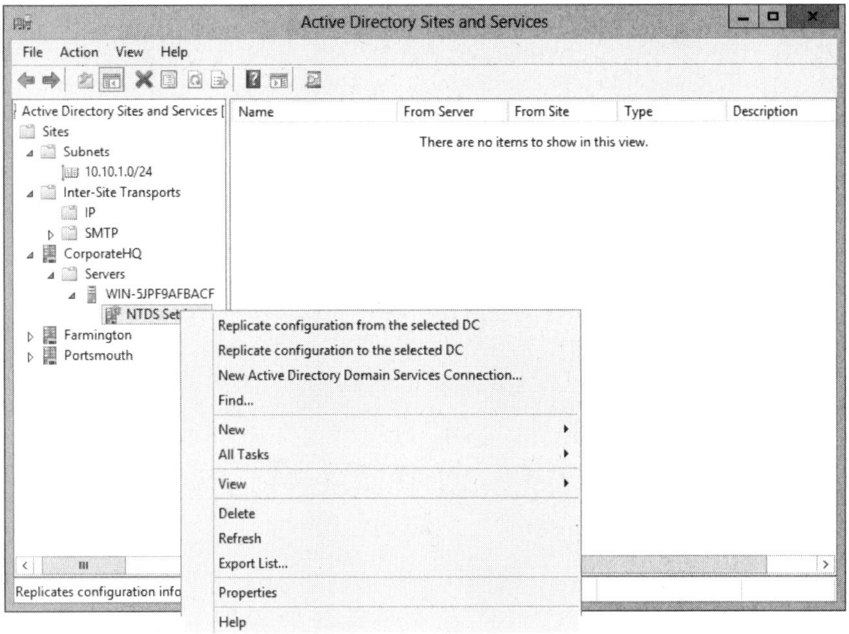

Within the properties of the connection object, which you can see in the right pane of the Active Directory Sites and Services tool, you can specify the type of transport to use for replication (RPC over IP or SMTP), the schedule for replication, and the domain controllers that participate in the replication. Additionally, you can right-click the connection object and select Replicate Now.

> **WARNING**   Make sure that if you kick off a manual replication, you don't do it during business hours if you think you do not have the bandwidth available to accomplish it. If you do it during business hours, you will most likely create a network slowdown if you do not plan properly. It's safer to plan a test during nonbusiness hours or during times of very little activity on the network.

Moving Server Objects between Sites

Using the Active Directory Sites and Services tool, you can easily move servers between sites. To do this, simply right-click the name of a domain controller and select Move. You can then select the site to which you want to move the domain controller object.

Figure 6.7 shows the Move Server dialog box. After the server is moved, all replication topology settings are updated automatically. If you want to choose custom replication settings, you'll need to create connection objects manually (as described earlier).

FIGURE 6.7   Choosing a new site for a specific server

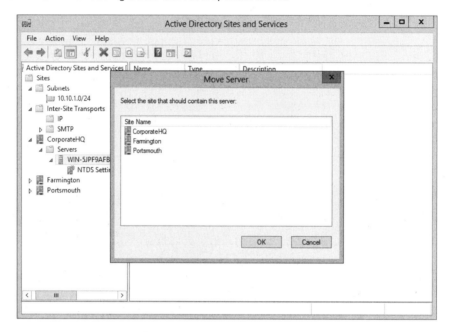

In Exercise 6.5, you move a server object between sites. To complete the steps in this exercise, you must have completed the previous exercises in this chapter.

EXERCISE 6.5

Moving Server Objects between Sites

1.   Open the Active Directory Sites and Services administrative tool.

2.   Right-click the server named PortsmouthDC1, and select Move.

3.   In the Move Server dialog box, select the Farmington site and then click OK. This moves this server to the Farmington site.

4.   To move the server back, right-click PortsmouthDC1 (now located in the Farmington site) and then click Move. Select Portsmouth for the destination site.

5.   When finished, close the Active Directory Sites and Services administrative tool.

Creating Bridgehead Servers

By default, all of the servers in one site communicate with all of the servers in another site. You can, however, further control replication between sites by using bridgehead servers. As mentioned earlier in the chapter, using bridgehead servers helps minimize replication traffic, especially in larger distributed star network topologies, and it allows you to dedicate machines that are better connected to receive replicated data. Figure 6.8 provides an example of how bridgehead servers work.

FIGURE 6.8   A replication scenario using bridgehead servers

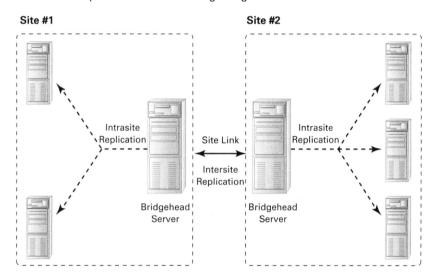

You can use a bridgehead server to specify which domain controllers are preferred for transferring replication information between sites. Different bridgehead servers can be selected for RPC over IP and SMTP replication, thus allowing you to balance the load. To create a bridgehead server for a site, simply right-click a domain controller and select Properties, which brings up the bridgehead server's Properties dialog box (see Figure 6.9). To make the server a bridgehead server, just select one or both replication types (called *transports*) from the left side of the dialog box and click the Add button to add them to the right side of the dialog box.

Configuring Server Topology

When you are using environments that require multiple sites, you must carefully consider where you place your servers. In doing so, you can greatly improve performance and the end user's experience by reducing the time they must spend performing common operations, such as authentication or searching Active Directory for resources.

FIGURE 6.9 Specifying a bridgehead server

There are two main issues to consider when you are designing a distributed Active Directory environment. The first is how you should place domain controllers within the network environment. The second is how to manage the use of global catalog servers. Finding the right balance between servers, server resources, and performance can be considered an art form for network and system administrators. In the following sections, you'll look at some of the important considerations you must take into account when you design a replication server topology.

Placing Domain Controllers

Microsoft highly recommends that you have at least two domain controllers in each domain of your Active Directory environment. As mentioned earlier in this chapter, using additional domain controllers provides the following benefits:

- Increased network performance:

  - The servers can balance the burden of serving client requests.

  - Clients can connect to the server closest to them instead of performing authentication and security operations across a slow WAN link.

- Fault tolerance (in case one domain controller fails, the other still contains a valid and usable copy of the Active Directory database).

- In Windows Server 2012, RODCs help increase security when users connect to a domain controller in an unsecured remote location.

As just mentioned, having too few domain controllers can be a problem. However, you can also have *too many* domain controllers. Keep in mind that the more domain controllers you choose to implement, the greater the replication traffic among them. Because each domain controller must propagate any changes to all of the others, compounding services can result in increased network traffic.

Placing Global Catalog Servers

A *global catalog (GC)* server is a domain controller that contains a copy of all of the objects contained in the forest-wide domain controllers that compose the Active Directory database. Making a domain controller a GC server is very simple, and you can change this setting quite easily. That brings us to the harder part—determining which domain controllers should also be GC servers.

Where you place domain controllers and GC servers and how many you deploy are very important network planning decisions. Generally, you want to make GC servers available in every site that has a slow link. This means that the most logical places to put GC servers are in every site and close to the WAN link for the best possible connectivity. However, having too many GC servers is a bad thing. The main issue is associated with replication traffic—you must keep each GC server within your environment synchronized with the other servers. In a very dynamic environment, using additional GC servers causes a considerable increase in network traffic. Therefore, you will want to find a good balance between replication burdens and GC query performance in your own environment.

To create a GC server, simply expand the Server object in the Active Directory Sites and Services tool, right-click NTDS Settings, and select Properties to bring up the NTDS Settings Properties dialog box (see Figure 6.10). To configure a server as a GC server, simply place a check mark in the Global Catalog box.

FIGURE 6.10   Enabling the global catalog on an Active Directory domain controller

Real World Scenario

Accommodating a Changing Environment

You're a system administrator for a medium-sized business that consists of many offices located throughout the world. Some of these offices are well connected because they use high-speed, reliable links, while others are not so fortunate. Overall, things are going well until your CEO announces that the organization will be merging with another large company and that the business will be restructured. The restructuring will involve opening new offices, closing old ones, and transferring employees to different locations. Additionally, changes in the IT budget will affect the types of links that exist between offices. Your job as the system administrator is to ensure that the network environment and, specifically, Active Directory keep pace with the changes and ultimately outperform them.

An important skill for any technical professional is the ability to adapt quickly and efficiently to a changing organization. When a business grows, restructures, or forms relationships with other businesses, often many IT-related changes must also occur. You may have to create new network links, for example.

Fortunately, Active Directory was designed with these kinds of challenges in mind. For example, you can use the Active Directory Sites and Services administrative tool to reflect physical network changes in Active Directory topology. If a site that previously had 64 Kbps of bandwidth is upgraded to a T1 connection, you can change those characteristics for the site link objects. Conversely, if a site that was previously well connected is reduced to a slow, unreliable link, you can reconfigure the sites, change the site link transport mechanisms (perhaps from IP to SMTP to accommodate a nonpersistent link), and create connection objects (which would allow you to schedule replication traffic to occur during the least busy hours).

Suppose further that many of your operations move overseas to a European division. This might call for designating specific domain controllers as preferred bridgehead servers to reduce the amount of replication traffic over costly and slow overseas links.

Sweeping organizational changes inevitably require you to move servers between sites. For example, an office may close and its domain controllers may move to another region of the world. Again, you can accommodate this change by using Active Directory administrative tools. You may change your OU structure to reflect new logical and business-oriented changes, and you can move server objects between sites to reflect physical network changes.

Rarely can the job of mapping a physical infrastructure to Active Directory be "complete." In most environments, it's safe to assume that you will always need to make changes based on business needs. Overall, however, you should feel comfortable that the physical components of Active Directory are at your side to help you accommodate these changes.

Using Universal Group Membership Caching

To understand how Universal Group Membership Caching (UGMC) works, you must first understand how authentication works. When a user tries to authenticate with a domain controller, the first action that takes place is that the domain controller checks with the global catalog to see to which domain the user belongs.

If the domain controller (the one to which the user is trying to authenticate) is not a GC, then the domain controller sends a request to the GC to verify the user's domain. The GC responds with the user's information, and the domain controller authenticates the user (if the user belongs to the same domain as the domain controller).

There are two ways to speed up the authentication process. First, you can make all of the domain controllers global catalogs. But then you end up with a lot of GC replication traffic. This becomes even more of an issue if you have multiple sites. Now replication traffic can be too large for your site link connections.

Thus, if you have a slower site link connection or multiple domains, you can use Universal Group Membership Caching. If you are using UGMC, after a domain controller communicates with the global catalog, the domain controller will then cache the user's credentials for eight hours by default. Now if the user logs off the domain and then logs back into the domain, the domain controller will use the cached credentials and not ask the global catalog. The downside to using UGMC is that it is for authentication only. Global catalogs help speed up Active Directory searches, and they work with Directory Service–enabled applications (applications that have to work with Active Directory) like Exchange and SQL.

Domain Controller Cloning

In Chapter 8, "Using Virtualization in Windows Server 2012," I will start to explain why so many organizations are switching to Virtualization in their server rooms. Virtualization allows an administrator to take one physical server and turn it into multiple virtual servers. Well, Windows Server 2012 helps you do this exact task.

New to Windows Server 2012, administrators can now easily and safely create replica domain controllers by copying an existing virtual domain controller. Before Windows Server 2012, an administrator would have to deploy a server image that they prepared by using sysprep.exe. After going through the process of using Sysprep.exe, the administrator would then have to promote this server to a domain controller and then complete additional configuration requirements for deploying each replica domain controller.

Domain controller cloning allows an administrator to rapidly deploy a large number of domain controllers. To setup domain controller cloning, you must be a member of the domain admins group or have the equivalent permissions. The administrator must then run Windows PowerShell from an elevated command prompt.

Only Windows Server 2012 domain controllers that are hosted on a VM compatible hypervisor can be used as a source for cloning. You should also make sure that the domain controller that you choose to clone is in a healthy state (use computer management to see the computers state).

The following example is used to create a clone domain controller named TestClone with a static IP address of 10.0.0.5 and a subnet mask of 255.255.0.0. This command also configures the DNS Server and WINS server configurations.

```
New-ADDCCloneConfigFile -CloneComputerName "TestClone" -Static -IPv4Address
"10.0.0.5" -IPv4DNSResolver "10.0.0.1" -IPv4SubnetMask "255.255.0.0" -
PreferredWinsServer "10.0.0.1" -AlternateWinsServer "10.0.0.2"
```

When you are ready to clone a domain controller, I recommend that you visit Microsoft's technet site for all of the PowerShell commands needed to complete this entire process.

Monitoring and Troubleshooting Active Directory Replication

For the most part, domain controllers handle the replication processes automatically. However, system administrators still need to monitor the performance of Active Directory replication because failed network links and incorrect configurations can sometimes prevent the synchronization of information between domain controllers.

You can monitor the behavior of Active Directory replication and troubleshoot the process if problems occur.

About System Monitor

The Windows Server 2012 System Monitor administrative tool was designed so that you can monitor many performance statistics associated with using Active Directory. Included within the various performance statistics that you can monitor are counters related to Active Directory replication.

Troubleshooting Replication

A common symptom of replication problems is that information is not updated on some or all domain controllers. For example, a system administrator creates a user account on one domain controller, but the changes are not propagated to other domain controllers. In most environments, this is a potentially serious problem because it affects network security and can prevent authorized users from accessing the resources they require.

You can take several steps to troubleshoot Active Directory replication. These are discussed in the following sections.

Verifying Network Connectivity

In order for replication to work properly in distributed environments, you must have network connectivity. Although ideally all domain controllers would be connected by high-speed LAN links, this is rarely the case for larger organizations. In the real world, dial-up connections and slow connections are common. If you have verified that your replication topology is set up properly, you should confirm that your servers are able to communicate. Problems such as a failed dial-up connection attempt can prevent important Active Directory information from being replicated.

Verifying Router and Firewall Configurations

Firewalls are used to restrict the types of traffic that can be transferred between networks. They are mainly used to increase security by preventing unauthorized users from transferring information. In some cases, company firewalls may block the types of network access that must be available for Active Directory replication to occur. For example, if a specific router or firewall prevents data from being transferred using SMTP, replication that uses this protocol will fail.

Examining the Event Logs

Whenever an error in the replication configuration occurs, the computer writes events to the Directory Service and File Replication Service event logs. By using the Event Viewer administrative tool, you can quickly and easily view the details associated with any problems in replication. For example, if one domain controller is unable to communicate with another to transfer changes, a log entry is created.

Verifying That Information Is Synchronized

It's often easy to forget to perform manual checks regarding the replication of Active Directory information. One of the reasons for this is that Active Directory domain controllers have their own read/write copies of the Active Directory database. Therefore, if connectivity does not exist, you will not encounter failures while creating new objects.

It is important to verify periodically that objects have been synchronized between domain controllers. This process might be as simple as logging on to a different domain controller and looking at the objects within a specific OU. This manual check, although it might be tedious, can prevent inconsistencies in the information stored on domain controllers, which, over time, can become an administration and security nightmare.

Verifying Authentication Scenarios

A common replication configuration issue occurs when clients are forced to authenticate across slow network connections. The primary symptom of the problem is that users complain about the amount of time it takes them to log on to Active Directory (especially during a period when there's a high volume of authentications, such as at the beginning of the workday).

Usually, you can alleviate this problem by using additional domain controllers or reconfiguring the site topology. A good way to test this is to consider the possible scenarios for the various clients that you support. Often, walking through a configuration, such as, "A client in Domain1 is trying to authenticate using a domain controller in Domain2, which is located across a slow WAN connection," can be helpful in pinpointing potential problem areas.

Verifying the Replication Topology

The Active Directory Sites and Services tool allows you to verify that a replication topology is logically consistent. You can quickly and easily perform this task by right-clicking NTDS Settings within a Server object and choosing All Tasks ➤ Check Replication. If any errors are present, a dialog box alerts you to the problem.

Another way to verify replication is by using the command-line utility `Repadmin`. Table 6.1 shows some of the `Repadmin` commands.

TABLE 6.1   Repadmin commands

Command	Description
Repadmin Bridgeheads	Lists the bridgehead servers for a specified site.
Repadmin dsaguid	Returns a server name when given a GUID.
Repadmin failcache	Shows a list of failed replication events.
Repadmin istg	Returns the server name of the Inter-Site Topology Generator (ISTG) server for a specified site. The ISTG manages the inbound replication connection objects for the bridgehead servers in a site.
Repadmin kcc	Forces the Knowledge Consistency Checker (KCC) to recalculate replication topology for a specified domain controller. The KCC modifies data in the local directory in response to system-wide changes.
Repadmin latency	Shows the amount of time between replications.
Repadmin queue	Shows tasks waiting in the replication queue.
Repadmin querysites	Uses routing information to determine the cost of a route from a specified site to another specified site or to other sites.
Repadmin replicate	Starts a replication event for the specified directory partition between domain controllers.
Repadmin replsummary	Displays the replication state and relative health of a forest.
Repadmin showrepl	Displays replication partners for each directory partition on a specified domain controller.

Reasons for Creating Multiple Domains

Before you look at the steps you must take to create multiple domains, become familiar with the reasons an organization might want to create them.

In general, you should always try to reflect your organization's structure within a single domain. By using organizational units (OUs) and other objects, you can usually create an accurate and efficient structure within one domain. Creating and managing a single domain is usually much simpler than managing a more complex environment consisting of multiple domains.

That said, you should familiarize yourself with some real benefits and reasons for creating multiple domains and some drawbacks of using them.

Reasons for Using Multiple Domains

You might need to implement multiple domains for several reasons. These reasons include the following considerations:

Scalability   Although Microsoft has designed Active Directory to accommodate millions of objects, this may not be practical for your current environment. Supporting thousands of users within a single domain requires more disk space, greater CPU (central processing unit) usage, and additional network burdens on your domain controllers (computers containing Active Directory security information). To determine the size of the Active Directory domain your network can support, you need to plan, design, test, and analyze within your own environment.

Reducing Replication Traffic   All of the domain controllers in a domain must keep an up-to-date copy of the entire Active Directory database. For small to medium-sized domains, this is generally not a problem. Windows Server 2012 and Active Directory manage all of the details of transferring the database behind the scenes. Other business and technical limitations might, however, affect Active Directory's ability to perform adequate replication. For example, if you have two sites that are connected by a very slow network link (or a sporadic link, or no link at all), replication is not practical. In this case, you would probably want to create separate domains to isolate replication traffic. Sporadic coverage across the wide area network (WAN) link would come from circuit-switching technologies such as Integrated Services Digital Network (ISDN) technologies. If you didn't have a link at all, then you would have a service provider outage or some other type of disruption. Separate domains mean separate replication traffic, but the amount of administrative overhead is increased significantly.

Because it's common to have WAN links in your business environment, you will always need to consider how your users authenticate to a domain controller (DC). DCs at a remote site are commonly used to authenticate users locally to their local area network (LAN). The most common design involves putting a DC at each remote site to keep authentication traffic from traversing the WAN. If it is the other way around, the authentication traffic may cause users problems if WAN utilization is high or if the link is broken and no other way to the central site is available. The design you are apt to see most often is one in which each server replicates its database of information to each other server so that the network and its systems converge.

However, it's important to realize that the presence of slow WAN links alone is *not* a good reason to break an organization into multiple domains. The most common solution is to set up site links with the Sites and Services Microsoft Management Console (MMC). When you use this MMC, you can manage replication traffic and fine-tune independently of the domain architecture.

You would want to use a multidomain architecture, such as when two companies merge through an acquisition, for the following reasons:

Meeting Business Needs   Several business needs might justify the creation of multiple domains. Business needs can be broken down even further into organizational and political needs.

One of the organizational reasons for using multiple domains is to avoid potential problems associated with the Domain Administrator account. At least one user needs to have permissions at this level. If your organization is unable or unwilling to trust a single person to have this level of control over all business units, then multiple domains may be the best answer. Because each domain maintains its own security database, you can keep permissions and resources isolated. Through the use of trusts, however, you can still share resources.

A political need for separate domains might arise if you had two companies that merged with two separate but equal management staffs and two sets of officers. In such a situation, you might need to have Active Directory split into two separate databases to keep the security of the two groups separate. Some such organizations may need to keep the internal groups separate by law. A multidomain architecture provides exactly this type of pristinely separate environment.

Many Levels of Hierarchy   Larger organizations tend to have very complex internal and external business structures that dictate the need for many different levels of organization. For example, two companies might merge and need to keep two sets of officers who are managed under two different logical groupings. In Chapter 4, "Administering Active Directory," I showed you that you can use OUs to help group different branches of the company so that you can assign permissions, or delegations, or whatever else you can think of without affecting anyone else. Managing data becomes much easier when you're using OUs, and if you design them correctly, OUs will help you control your network right from one console. You may need only one level of management—your company may be small enough to warrant the use of the default OU structure you see when Active Directory is first installed. If, however, you find that you need many levels of OUs to manage resources (or if large numbers of objects exist within each OU), it might make sense to create additional domains. Each domain would contain its own OU hierarchy and serve as the root of a new set of objects.

Decentralized Administration   Two main models of administration are commonly used: a centralized administration model and a decentralized administration model. In the centralized administration model, a single IT organization is responsible for managing all of the users, computers, and security permissions for the entire organization. In the decentralized administration model, each department or business unit might have its own IT department. In both cases, the needs of the administration model can play a significant role in whether you decide to use multiple domains.

Consider, for example, a multinational company that has a separate IT department for offices in each country. Each IT department is responsible for supporting only the users and computers within its own region. Because the administration model is largely decentralized, creating a separate domain for each of these major business units might make sense from a security and maintenance standpoint.

Multiple DNS or Domain Names   Another reason you may need to use a multidomain architecture is if you want or plan to use multiple DNS names within your organization. If you use multiple DNS names or domain names, you must create multiple Active Directory domains. Each AD domain can have only one *fully qualified domain name (FQDN)*. An FQDN is the full name of a system that consists of a local host, a second-level domain name, and a top-level domain (TLD). For example, `corp.stellacon.com.` is an FQDN, `.com` is the TLD, `www` is the host, and `stellacon` is the second-level domain name.

Legality   One final reason you may need to use a multidomain architecture is legality within your organization. Some corporations have to follow state or federal regulations and laws. For this reason, they may have to have multiple domains.

Drawbacks of Multiple Domains

Although there are many reasons it makes sense to have multiple domains, there are also reasons you should not break an organizational structure into multiple domains, many of which are related to maintenance and administration. Here are some of the drawbacks to using multiple domains:

Administrative Inconsistency   One of the fundamental responsibilities of most system administrators is implementing and managing security. When you are implementing Group Policy and security settings in multiple domains, you want to be careful to ensure that the settings are consistent. In Windows Server 2012, security policies can be different between and within the same domains. If this is what the organization intended, then it is not a problem. However, if an organization wishes to make the same settings apply to all users, then each domain requires a separate GPO with similar security settings.

Increased Management Challenges   Managing servers, users, and computers can become a considerable challenge when you are also managing multiple domains because many more administrative units are required. In general, you need to manage all user, group, and computer settings separately for the objects within each domain. The hierarchical structure provided by OUs, on the other hand, provides a much simpler and easier way to manage permissions.

Decreased Flexibility   Creating a domain involves the *promotion* of a DC to the new domain. Although the process is quite simple, it is much more difficult to rearrange the domain topology within an Active Directory environment than it is simply to reorganize OUs. When planning domains, you should ensure that the domain structure will not change often, if at all.

Now that you have examined the pros and cons related to creating multiple domains, it is time to see how to create trees and forests.

Creating Domain Trees and Forests

So far this chapter has covered some important reasons for using multiple domains in a single network environment. Now it's time to look at how to create multidomain structures like domain trees and domain forests.

Regardless of the number of domains you have in your environment, you always have a tree and a forest. This might surprise those of you who generally think of domain trees and forests as belonging only to Active Directory environments that consist of multiple domains. However, recall that when you install the first domain in an Active Directory environment, that domain automatically creates a new forest and a new tree.

In the following sections, you will learn how to plan trees and forests and how to promote domain controllers to establish a tree and forest environment.

Planning Trees and Forests

You have already seen several reasons you might want to have multiple domains within a single company. What you haven't yet seen is how multiple domains can be related to each other and how their relationships can translate into domain forests and trees.

A fundamental commonality between the various domains that exist in trees and forests is that they all share the same Active Directory global catalog (GC). This means that if you modify the Active Directory schema, these changes must be propagated to all of the domain controllers in all of the domains. This is an important point because adding and modifying the structure of information in the GC can have widespread effects on replication and network traffic. Also, you need to ensure that any system you use in the GC role can handle it—you might need to size up the system's hardware requirements. This is especially true if there are multiple domains.

Every domain within an Active Directory configuration has its own unique name. For example, even though you might have a sales domain in two different trees, the complete names for each domain will be different (such as sales.stellacon1.com and sales.stellacon2.com).

In the following sections, you'll look at how you can organize multiple Active Directory domains based on business requirements.

Using a Single Tree

The concept of domain trees was created to preserve the relationship between multiple domains that share a common contiguous namespace. For example, you might have the following DNS domains (based on Internet names):

- `mycompany.com`
- `sales.mycompany.com`
- `engineering.mycompany.com`
- `europe.sales.mycompany.com`

Note that all of these domains fit within a single contiguous namespace. That is, they are all direct or indirect children of the `mycompany.com` domain. In this case, `mycompany.com` is called the *root domain*. All of the direct children (such as `sales.mycompany.com` and `engineering.mycompany.com`) are called *child domains*. Finally, *parent domains* are the domains that are directly above one domain. For example, `sales.mycompany.com` is the parent domain of `europe.sales.mycompany.com`. Figure 6.11 provides an example of a domain tree.

FIGURE 6.11   A domain tree

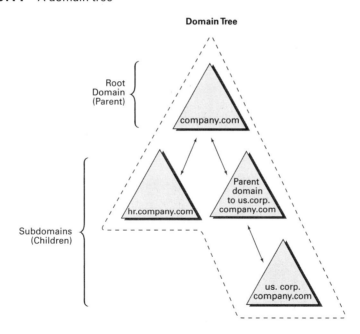

To establish a domain tree, you must first create the root domain for the tree. Then you can add child domains off this root. These child domains can then serve as parents for further subdomains. Each domain must have at least one domain controller, and domain controllers can participate in only one domain at a time. However, you can move a domain controller from one domain to another. To do this, you must first demote a domain controller to a member server and then promote it to a domain controller in another domain.

 You will learn how to demote a domain controller later in this chapter in the section titled "Demoting a Domain Controller."

Domains are designed to be logical boundaries. The domains within a tree are, by default, automatically bound together using a two-way transitive trust relationship, which allows resources to be shared among domains through the use of the appropriate user and group assignments. Because trust relationships are transitive, all of the domains within the tree trust each other. Note, however, that a trust by itself does not automatically grant any security permissions to users or objects between domains. Trusts are designed only to *allow* resources to be shared; you must still go through the process of sharing and managing them. Enterprise Administrators must explicitly assign security settings to resources before users can access resources between domains.

Using a single tree makes sense when your organization maintains only a single contiguous namespace. Regardless of the number of domains that exist within this environment and how different their security settings are from each other, they are related by a common name. Although domain trees make sense for many organizations, in some cases the network namespace may be considerably more complicated. You'll look at how forests address these situations next.

Using a Forest

Active Directory forests are designed to accommodate multiple noncontiguous namespaces. That is, they can combine domain trees together into logical units. An example might be the following tree and domain structure:

- Tree: Organization1.com
  - Sales.Organization1.com
  - Marketing.Organization1.com
  - Engineering.Organization1.com
  - NorthAmerica.Engineering.Organization1.com
- Tree: Organization2.com
  - Sales.Organization2.com
  - Engineering.Organization2.com.

Figure 6.12 provides an example of how multiple trees can fit into a single forest. Such a situation might occur in the acquisition and merger of companies or if a company is logically divided into two or more completely separate and autonomous business units.

FIGURE 6.12   A single forest consisting of multiple trees

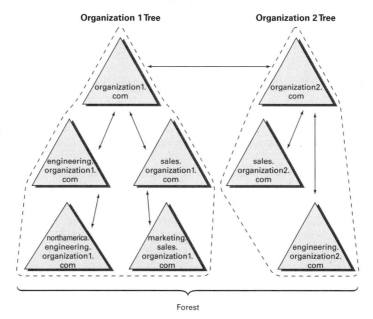

All of the trees within a forest are related through a single forest root domain. This is the first domain that was created in the Active Directory environment. The root domain in each tree creates a transitive trust with the forest root domain. The result is a configuration in which all of the trees within a domain and all of the domains within each tree trust each other. Again, as with domain trees, the presence of a trust relationship does not automatically signify that users have permissions to access resources across domains. It only allows objects and resources to be shared. Authorized network administrators must set up specific permissions.

All of the domains within a single Active Directory forest have the following features in common:

Schema   The *schema* is the Active Directory structure that defines how the information within the data store is structured. For the information stored on various domain controllers to remain compatible, all of the domain controllers within the entire Active Directory environment must share the same schema. For example, if you add a field for an employee's benefits plan number, all domain controllers throughout the environment need to recognize this information before you can share information among them.

Global Catalog   One of the problems associated with working in large network environments is that sharing information across multiple domains can be costly in terms of network and server resources. Fortunately, Active Directory uses the global catalog (GC), which serves as a repository for information about a subset of all objects within *all* Active Directory domains in a forest. System administrators can determine what types of information should be added to the defaults in the GC. Generally, they decide to store commonly used information, such as a list of all of the printers, users, groups, and computers. In addition, they can configure specific domain controllers to carry a copy of the GC. Now if you have a question about where to find all the color printers in the company, for example, all you need to do is to contact the nearest GC server.

Configuration Information   Some roles and functions must be managed for the entire forest. When you are dealing with multiple domains, this means that you must configure certain domain controllers to perform functions for the entire Active Directory environment. I will discuss some specifics of this later in this chapter.

The main purpose of allowing multiple domains to exist together is to allow them to share information and other resources. Now that you've seen the basics of domain trees and forests, take a look at how domains are actually created.

The Promotion Process

A domain tree is created when a new domain is added as the child of an existing domain. This relationship is established during the promotion of a Windows Server 2012 computer to a domain controller. Although the underlying relationships can be quite complicated in larger organizations, the Server Manager's Active Directory Installation Wizard makes it easy to create forests and trees.

Using the Active Directory Installation Wizard, you can quickly and easily create new domains by promoting a Windows Server 2012 stand-alone server or a member server to a domain controller. When you install a new domain controller, you can choose to make it part of an existing domain, or you can choose to make it the first domain controller in a new domain. In the following sections and exercises, you'll become familiar with the exact steps you need to take to create a domain tree and a domain forest when you promote a server to a domain controller.

Creating a Domain Tree

In Chapter 3, "Active Directory Planning and Installation," you saw how to promote the first domain controller in the first domain in a forest, also known as the root. If you don't promote any other domain controllers, then that domain controller simply controls that one domain and only one tree is created. To create a new domain tree, you need to promote a Windows Server 2012 computer to a domain controller. In the Active Directory Installation Wizard, you select the option that makes this domain controller the first machine in a new domain that is a child of an existing domain. As a result, you will have a domain tree that contains two domains—a parent and a child.

Before you can create a new child domain, you need the following information:

- The name of the parent domain (For the exercises, you'll use the one you created in the previous chapter.)
- The name of the child domain (the one you are planning to install)

- The file system locations for the Active Directory database, logs, and shared system volume

- DNS configuration information

- The NetBIOS name for the new server

- A domain administrator username and password

   Exercise 6.6 walks you through the process of creating a new child domain using Server Manager. This exercise assumes that you have already created the parent domain and that you are using a server in the domain that is not a domain controller.

EXERCISE 6.6

Creating a New Subdomain

1. Open Server Manager.

2. Click item 2, Add Roles And Features.

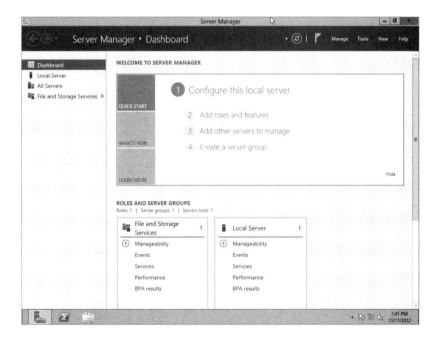

3. Make sure the Role-Based Or Feature-Based Installation button is selected and click Next.

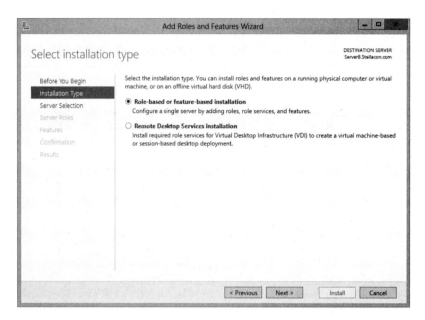

4. At the Select Destination screen, click Next.

5. At the Select Server Roles screen, check the Active Directory Domain Services check box. A box will appear stating that you need to install additional roles. Click the Add Features button. Then click Next.

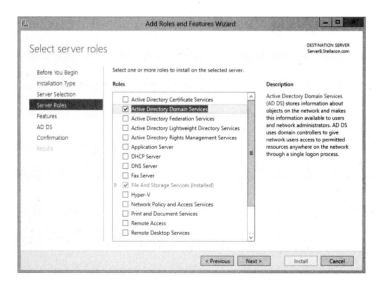

6. At the Add Roles And Features Wizard screen, click Next.

7. At the Confirmation screen, click the Install button.

8. When the installation is complete, click the Close button.

9. Close Server Manager, and restart the machine.

10. Log in and restart Server Manager.

11. In the Roles And Server Groups area, click the AD DS link.

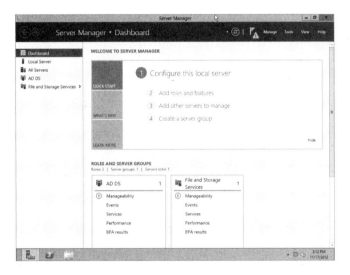

12. In the Servers section, click the More link next to Configuration Required For Active Directory Domain Services.

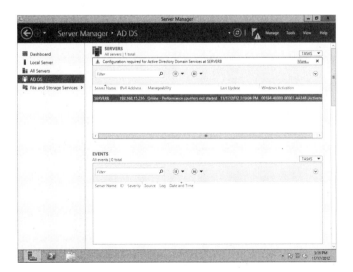

13. At the All Servers Task Details screen, click the Promote This Server To A Domain Controller link.

14. At the Deployment Configuration screen, click the radio button Add A New Domain To An Existing Forest. In the Select Domain Type drop-down, chose Child Domain and then choose your parent domain. In the New Domain Name box, type in the name of your new domain. I used NewHampshire. Click the Next button.

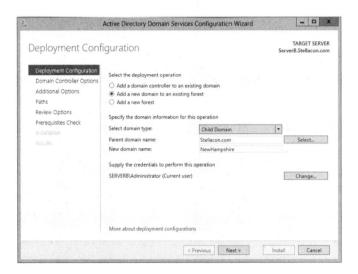

15. At the Domain Controller Options screen, I set the following options;

Domain Functional Level: Windows Server 2012

Domain Name System (DNS) Server: Checked

Global Catalog (GC): Checked

Site Name: CorporateHQ

Password: **P@ssw0rd**

Click Next.

16. At the DNS screen, click Next.

17. At the Additional Options screen, accept the default NetBIOS domain name and click Next.

18. At the Paths screen, accept the default file locations and click Next.

19. At the Review Options screen, verify your settings and click Next.

20. At the Prerequisites Check screen, click the Install button (as long as there are no errors).

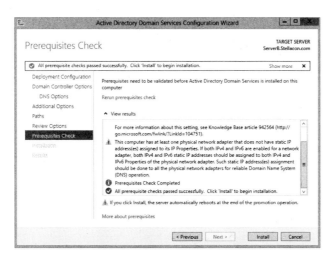

21. After the installation completes, the machine will automatically reboot. Log in as the administrator.

22. Close Server Manager.

Joining a New Domain Tree to a Forest

A *forest* is one or more trees that do not share a contiguous namespace. For example, you could join the `organization1.com` and `organization2.com` domains together to create a single Active Directory environment.

Any two trees can be joined together to create a forest, as long as the second tree is installed after the first and the trees have noncontiguous namespaces. (If the namespaces were contiguous, you would actually need to create a new domain for an existing tree.) The process of creating a new tree to form or add to a forest is as simple as promoting a server to a domain controller for a new domain that does *not* share a namespace with an existing Active Directory domain.

 The command-line tool `adprep.exe` is used to prepare a Microsoft Windows 2003, 2008, or 2008 R2 forest or a Windows 2003, 2008, or 2008 R2 domain for the installation of Windows Server 2012 domain controllers.

To add a new domain to an existing forest, you must already have at least one other domain, which is the root domain. Keep in mind that the entire forest structure is destroyed if the original root domain is ever removed entirely. Therefore, you should have at least two domain controllers in the Active Directory root domain; the second serves as a backup in case you have a problem with the first, and it can also serve as a backup solution for disaster recovery and fault tolerance purposes. Such a setup provides additional protection for the entire forest in case one of the domain controllers fails. In order to complete this exercise, you must have already installed another domain controller that serves as the root domain for a forest, and you must use a server in the domain that is not a domain controller.

Adding Additional Domain Controllers

In addition to the operations you've already performed, you can use the Active Directory Installation Wizard to create additional domain controllers for any of your domains. There are two main reasons to create additional domain controllers:

Fault Tolerance and Reliability   You should always consider the theory of *disaster recovery (DR)* and have a plan, sometimes referred to as a *disaster recovery plan (DRP)*. If you're part of one of those organizations that rely upon their network directory services infrastructures, you need Active Directory to provide security and resources for all users.

For this reason, downtime and data loss are very costly. Through the use of multiple domain controllers, you can ensure that if one of the servers goes down, another one is available to perform the necessary tasks, such as user authentication and resource browsing. Additionally, data loss (perhaps from hard disk drive failure) will not result in the loss or unavailability of network security information because you can easily recover Active Directory information from the remaining, still-functional domain controller.

Performance   The burden of processing login requests and serving as a repository for security permissions and other information can be quite extensive, especially in larger businesses. By using multiple domain controllers, you can distribute this load across multiple systems. Additionally, by strategically placing domain controllers, you can greatly increase response times for common network operations, such as authentication and browsing for resources.

As a rule of thumb, you should always plan and design your infrastructure to have at least two domain controllers per domain. For many organizations, this provides a good balance between the cost of servers and the level of reliability and performance. For larger or more distributed organizations, however, additional domain controllers greatly improve performance.

Demoting a Domain Controller

In addition to being able to promote member servers to domain controllers, the Active Directory Installation Wizard can do the exact opposite; that is, demote domain controllers.

You might choose to demote a domain controller for a couple of reasons. First, if you have determined that the role of a server should change (for example, from a domain controller to a member or stand-alone server that you might make into a web server), you can easily demote it to make this happen. Another common reason to demote a domain controller is if you wish to move the machine from one domain to another. You cannot do this in a single step: First you need to demote the existing domain controller to remove it from the current domain and then promote it into a new domain. The result is that the server is now a domain controller for a different domain.

To demote a domain controller, you simply access the Active Directory Installation Wizard. The wizard automatically notices that the local server is a domain controller, and it asks you to verify each step you take, as with most things you do in Windows. You are prompted to decide whether you really want to remove this machine from the current domain. Note that if the local server is a global catalog (GC) server, you will be warned that at least one copy of the GC must remain available so that you can perform logon authentication.

By default, at the end of the demotion process, the server is joined as a member server to the domain for which it was previously a domain controller. If you demote the last domain controller in the domain, the server becomes a stand-alone server.

Real World Scenario

Planning for Domain Controller Placement

You are the senior system administrator for a medium-sized Active Directory environment. Currently the environment consists of only one Active Directory domain. Your company's network is spread out over 40 different sites throughout North America. Recently, you've received complaints from users and other system administrators about the performance of Active Directory–related operations. For example, users report that it takes several minutes to log on to their machines in the morning between the hours of 9 a.m. and 10 a.m., when activity is at its highest. Simultaneously, system administrators complain that updating user information within the OUs for which they are responsible can take longer than expected.

Fortunately, Active Directory's distributed domain controller architecture allows you to optimize performance for this type of situation without making dramatic changes to your environment. You decide that the quickest and easiest solution is to deploy additional domain controllers throughout the organization. The domain controllers are generally placed within areas of the network that are connected by slow or unreliable links. For example, a small branch office in Des Moines, Iowa, receives its own domain controller. The process is quite simple: You install a new Windows Server 2012 computer and then run the Active Directory Installation Wizard in Server Manager to make the new machine a domain controller for an existing domain. Once the initial directory services data is copied to the new server, it is ready to service requests and updates of your domain information.

Note that there are potential drawbacks to this solution; for instance, you have to manage additional domain controllers and the network traffic generated from communications between the domain controllers. It's important that you monitor your network links to ensure that you've reached a good balance between replication traffic and overall Active Directory performance. In later chapters, you'll see how you can configure Active Directory sites to map Active Directory operations better to your physical network structure.

 Removing a domain from your environment is not an operation that you should take lightly. Before you plan to remove a domain, make a list of all the resources that depend on the domain and the reasons the domain was originally created. If you are sure that your organization no longer requires the domain, then you can safely continue. If you are not sure, think again, because the process cannot be reversed and you could lose critical information!

Managing Multiple Domains

You can easily manage most of the operations that must occur *between* domains by using the Active Directory Domains and Trusts administrative tool. On the other hand, if you want to configure settings *within* a domain, you should use the Active Directory Users and Computers tool. In the following sections, we'll look at ways to perform two common domain management functions with the tools just mentioned: managing *single-master operations* and managing *trusts*. We'll also look at ways to manage UPN suffixes in order to simplify user accounts, and we'll examine GC servers in more detail.

Managing Single-Master Operations

For the most part, Active Directory functions in what is known as multimaster replication. That is, every domain controller within the environment contains a copy of the Active Directory database that is both readable and writable. This works well for most types of information. For example, if you want to modify the password of a user, you can easily do this on *any* of the domain controllers within a domain. The change is then automatically propagated to the other domain controllers.

However, some functions are not managed in a multimaster fashion. These operations are known as *operations masters*. You must perform single-master operations on specially designated domain controllers within the Active Directory forest. There are five main single-master functions: two that apply to an entire Active Directory forest and three that apply to each domain.

Forest Operations Masters

You use the Active Directory Domains and Trusts tool to configure forest-wide roles. The following single-master operations apply to the entire forest:

Schema Master   Earlier you learned that all of the domain controllers within a single Active Directory environment share the same schema. This ensures information consistency. However, developers and system administrators can modify the Active Directory schema by adding custom information. A trivial example might involve adding a field to employee information that specifies a user's favorite color.

When you need to make these types of changes, you must perform them on the domain controller that serves as the *Schema Master* for the environment. The Schema Master is then responsible for propagating all of the changes to all of the other domain controllers within the forest.

Domain Naming Master   The purpose of the *Domain Naming Master* is to keep track of all the domains within an Active Directory forest. You access this domain controller whenever you need to add/remove new domains to a tree or forest.

Domain Operations Masters

You use the Active Directory Users and Computers snap-in to administer roles within a
domain. Within each domain, at least one domain controller must fulfill each of the following roles:

Relative ID (RID) Master   Every security object within Active Directory must be assigned
a unique identifier so that it is distinguishable from other objects. For example, if you have
two OUs named IT that reside in different domains, you must have some way to distinguish
easily between them. Furthermore, if you delete one of the IT OUs and then later re-create
it, the system must be able to determine that it is not the same object as the other IT OU.
The unique identifier for each object is made up of a domain identifier and a relative identifier (RID). RIDs are always unique within an Active Directory domain and are used for
managing security information and authenticating users. The *RID Master* is responsible for
creating these values within a domain whenever new Active Directory objects are created.

PDC Emulator Master   Within a domain, the *PDC Emulator Master* is responsible for
maintaining backward compatibility with Windows 95, 98, and NT clients.

The PDC Emulator Master serves as the default domain controller to process authentication requests if another domain controller is unable to do so. The PDC Emulator Master
also receives preferential treatment whenever domain security changes are made.

Infrastructure Master   Whenever a user is added to or removed from a group, all of the
other domain controllers should be made aware of this change. The role of the domain controller that acts as an *Infrastructure Master* is to ensure that group membership information stays synchronized within an Active Directory domain.

Unless there is only one domain controller, you should not place the Infrastructure Master on a global catalog server. If the Infrastructure Master
and global catalog are on the same domain controller, the Infrastructure
Master will not function.

  Another service that a server can control for the network is the Windows Time service.
The Windows Time service uses a suite of algorithms in the Network Time Protocol (NTP).
This helps to ensure that the time on all computers throughout a network is as accurate
as possible. All client computers within a Windows Server 2012 domain are synchronized
with the time of an authoritative computer.

Assigning Single-Master Roles

Now that you are familiar with the different types of single-master operations, take a look
at Exercise 6.7. This exercise shows you how to assign these roles to servers within the
Active Directory environment. In this exercise, you will assign single-master operations

roles to various domain controllers within the environment. To complete the steps in this exercise, you need one Active Directory domain controller.

EXERCISE 6.7

Assigning Single-Master Operations

1. Open the Active Directory Domains and Trusts administrative tool.

2. Right-click Active Directory Domains And Trusts, and choose Operations Masters.

3. In the Operations Masters dialog box, note that you can change the operations master by clicking the Change button. If you want to move this assignment to another computer, first you need to connect to that computer and then make the change. Click Close to continue without making any changes.

4. Close the Active Directory Domains and Trusts administrative tool.

5. Open the Active Directory Users and Computers administrative tool.

6. Right-click the name of a domain, and select Operations Masters. This brings up the RID tab of the Operations Masters dialog box.

Notice that you can change the computer that is assigned to the role. To change the role, first you need to connect to the appropriate domain controller. Notice that the PDC and Infrastructure roles have similar tabs. Click Close to continue without making any changes.

7. When you have finished, close the Active Directory Users and Computers tool.

 Remember that you manage single-master operations with three different tools. You use the Active Directory Domains and Trusts tool to configure the Domain Name Master role, while you use the Active Directory Users and Computers snap-in to administer roles within a domain. Although this might not seem intuitive at first, it can help you remember which roles apply to domains and which apply to the whole forest. The third tool, the Schema Master role, is a bit different than these other two. To change the Schema Master role, you must install the Active Directory Schema MMS snap-in and change it there.

Managing Trusts

Trust relationships make it easier to share security information and network resources between domains. As was already mentioned, standard transitive two-way trusts are automatically created between the domains in a tree and between each of the trees in a forest. Figure 6.13 shows an example of the default trust relationships in an Active Directory forest.

FIGURE 6.13 Default trusts in an Active Directory forest

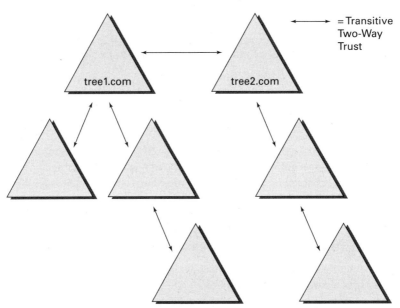

When configuring trusts, there are two main characteristics you need to consider:

Transitive Trusts By default, Active Directory trusts are *transitive trusts*. The simplest way to understand transitive relationships is through this example: If Domain A trusts Domain B and Domain B trusts Domain C, then Domain A implicitly trusts Domain C. If you need to apply a tighter level of security, trusts can be configured as intransitive.

One-Way vs. Two-Way Trusts can be configured as one-way or two-way relationships. The default operation is to create *two-way trusts* or *bidirectional trusts*. This makes it easier to manage trust relationships by reducing the trusts you must create. In some cases, however, you might decide against two-way trusts. In one-way relationships, the trusting domain allows resources to be shared with the trusted domain but not the other way around.

When domains are added together to form trees and forests, an automatic transitive two-way trust is created between them. Although the default trust relationships work well for most organizations, there are some reasons you might want to manage trusts manually:

- You may want to remove trusts between domains if you are absolutely sure that you do not want resources to be shared between domains.
- Because of security concerns, you may need to keep resources isolated.

In addition to the default trust types, you can configure the following types of special trusts:

External Trusts   You use *external trusts* to provide access to resources on a Windows NT 4 domain or forest that cannot use a forest trust. Windows NT 4 domains cannot benefit from the other trust types that are used in Windows Server 2012. So in some cases, external trusts could be your only option. External trusts are always nontransitive, but they can be established in a one-way or two-way configuration.

Default SID Filtering on External Trusts   When you set up an external trust, remember that it is possible for hackers to compromise a domain controller in a trusted domain. If this trust is compromised, a hacker can use the security identifier (SID) history attribute to associate SIDs with new user accounts, granting themselves unauthorized rights (this is called an *elevation-of-privileges attack*). To help prevent this type of attack, Windows Server 2012 automatically enables SID filter quarantining on all external trusts. SID filtering allows the domain controllers in the trusting domain (the domain with the resources) to remove all SID history attributes that are not members of the trusted domain.

Realm Trusts   *Realm trusts* are similar to external trusts. You use them to connect to a non-Windows domain that uses Kerberos authentication. Realm trusts can be transitive or nontransitive, one-way or two-way.

Cross-Forest Trusts   *Cross-forest trusts* are used to share resources between forests. They have been used since Windows Server 2000 domains and cannot be nontransitive, but you can establish them in a one-way or a two-way configuration. Authentication requests in either forest can reach the other forest in a two-way cross-forest trust. If you want one forest to trust another forest, you must set it (at a minimum) to at least the forest function level of Windows Server 2003.

Selective Authentication vs. Forest-wide Authentication   Forest-wide authentication on a forest trust means that users of the trusted forest can access all the resources of the trusting forest. Selective authentication means that users cannot authenticate to a domain controller or resource server in the trusting forest unless they are explicitly allowed to do so. Exercise 6.8 will show you the steps necessary to change forest-wide authentication to selective authentication.

Shortcut Trusts   In some cases, you may actually want to create direct trusts between two domains that implicitly trust each other. Such a trust is sometimes referred to as a *shortcut trust*, and it can improve the speed at which resources are accessed across many different domains. Let's say that you have a forest, as shown in Figure 6.14.

FIGURE 6.14   Example of a forest

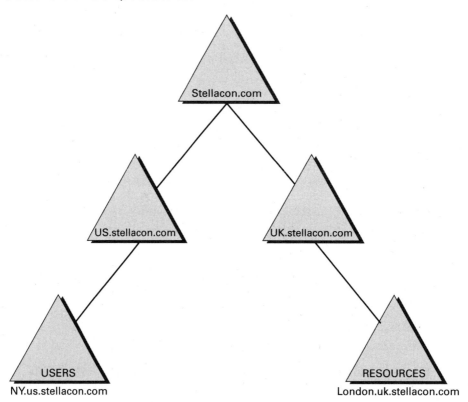

Users in the NY.us.stellacon.com domain can access resources in the London.uk.stellacon .com domain, but the users have to authenticate using the parent domains to gain access (NY.us.stellacon.com to us.stellacon.com to stellacon.com to uk.stellacon.com to finally reach London.uk.stellacon.com). This process can be slow. An administrator can set up a one-way trust from London.uk.stellacon.com (trusting domain) to NY.us .stellacon.com (trusted domain) so that the users can access the resources directly.

Perhaps the most important aspect to remember regarding trusts is that creating them only *allows* you to share resources between domains. The trust does not grant any permissions between domains by itself. Once a trust has been established, however, system administrators can easily assign the necessary permissions.

Exercise 6.8 walks you through the steps necessary to manage trusts. In this exercise, you will see how to assign trust relationships between domains. To complete the steps in this exercise, you must have domain administrator access permissions.

EXERCISE 6.8

Managing Trust Relationships

1. Open the Active Directory Domains and Trusts administrative tool.

2. Right-click the name of a domain and select Properties.

3. Select the Trusts tab. You will see a list of the trusts that are currently configured. To modify the trust properties for an existing trust, highlight that trust and click Properties.

4. The Properties window for the trust displays information about the trust's direction, transitivity, and type along with the names of the domains involved in the relationship. Click Cancel to exit without making any changes.

5. To create a new trust relationship, click the New Trust button on the Trusts tab. The New Trust Wizard appears. Click Next to proceed with the wizard.

6. On the Trust Name page, you are prompted for the name of the domain with which the trust should be created. Enter the name of the domain and click Next.

7. On the Trust Type page, you would normally choose the Trust With A Windows Domain option if you know that the other domain uses a Windows domain controller. Choose Realm Trust. Click Next when you have finished.

8. On the Transitivity Of Trust page, you choose whether the trust is transitive or nontransitive. Choose the Nontransitive option, and click Next to continue.

9. On the Direction Of Trust page, you select the direction of the trust. If you want both domains to trust each other, you select the Two-Way option. Otherwise, you select either One-Way: Incoming or One-Way: Outgoing, depending on where the affected users are located. For the sake of this exercise, choose One-Way: Incoming and then click Next.

10. On the Trust Password page, you need to specify a password that should be used to administer the trust. Type **P@ssw0rd** and confirm it. Note that if there is an existing trust relationship between the domains, the passwords must match. Click Next to continue.

11. Now you see the Trust Selections Complete page that recaps the selections you have made. Because this is an exercise, you don't actually want to establish this trust. Click Cancel to cancel the wizard without saving the changes.

12. Exit the trust properties for the domain by clicking Cancel.

To Enable Selective Authentication

1. In the console tree, right-click the name of a domain and select Properties.

2. Select the Trusts tab. Under either Domains Trusted By This Domain (Outgoing Trusts) or Domains That Trust This Domain (Incoming Trusts), click the forest trust that you want to administer, and then click Properties.

3. On the Authentication tab, click Selective Authentication and then click OK.

Managing UPN Suffixes

User principal name (UPN) suffixes are the part of a user's name that appears after the @ symbol. For example, the UPN suffix of wpanek@stellacon.com would be stellacon.com. By default, the UPN suffix is determined by the name of the domain in which the user is created. In this example, the user wpanek was created in the domain stellacon.com, so the two pieces of the UPN logically fit together. However, you might find it useful to provide an alternative UPN suffix to consolidate the UPNs forest wide.

For instance, if you manage a forest that consists of stellacon.com and stellacon2 .com, you might want all of your users to adopt the more generally applicable stellacon .com UPN suffix. By adding additional UPN suffixes to the forest, you can easily choose the appropriate suffix when it comes time to create new users. Exercise 6.9 shows you how to add additional suffixes to a forest.

EXERCISE 6.9

Adding a UPN Suffix

1. Open the Active Directory Domains and Trusts administrative tool.

2. Right-click Active Directory Domains And Trusts in the left side of the window and select Properties.

3. On the UPN Suffixes tab of the Active Directory Domains And Trusts Properties dialog box, enter an alternative UPN suffix in the Alternative UPN Suffixes field. Click the Add button to add the suffix to the list.

4. To remove a UPN suffix, select its name in the list and click the Remove button.

Managing Global Catalog Servers

One of the best features of a distributed directory service like Active Directory is that you can store different pieces of information in different places within an organization. For example, a domain in Japan might store a list of users who operate within a company's Asian operations business unit, while one in New York would contain a list of users who operate within its North American operations business unit. This architecture allows system administrators to place the most frequently accessed information on domain controllers in different domains, thereby reducing disk space requirements and replication traffic.

However, you may encounter a problem when you deal with information that is segmented into multiple domains. The issue involves querying information stored within Active Directory. For example, what would happen if a user wanted a list of all of the printers available in all domains within the Active Directory forest? In this case, the search would normally require information from at least one domain controller in each of the domains within the environment. Some of these domain controllers may be located across slow WAN links or may have unreliable connections. The result would include an extremely long wait while retrieving the results of the query; that is, if any results came up without the query timing out.

Fortunately, Active Directory has a mechanism that speeds up such searches. You can configure any number of domain controllers to host a copy of the GC. The GC contains all of the schema information and a subset of the attributes for all domains within the Active Directory environment. Although a default set of information is normally included with the GC, system administrators can choose to add additional information to this data store if it is needed. To help reduce replication traffic and to keep the GC's database small, only a limited subset of each object's attributes is replicated. This is called the *partial attribute set (PAS)*. You can change the PAS by modifying the schema and marking attributes for replication to the GC.

Servers that contain a copy of the GC are known as *GC servers*. Now whenever a user executes a query that requires information from multiple domains, they need only contact the nearest GC server for this information. Similarly, when users must authenticate across domains, they do not have to wait for a response from a domain controller that may be located across the world. The result is that the overall performance of Active Directory queries improves.

Exercise 6.10 walks you through the steps that you need to take to configure a domain controller as a GC server. Generally, GC servers are useful only in environments that use multiple Active Directory domains.

EXERCISE 6.10

Managing GC Servers

1. Open the Active Directory Sites and Services administrative tool.

2. Find the name of the local domain controller within the list of objects, typically under Default First Site Name ➢ Servers, and expand this object. Right-click NTDS Settings, and select Properties.

3. In the NTDS Settings Properties dialog box, type **Primary GC Server for Domain** in the Description field. Note that there is a check box that determines whether this computer contains a copy of the global catalog. If the box is checked, then this domain controller contains a subset of information from all other domains within the Active Directory environment. Select the Global Catalog check box, and then click OK to continue.

4. When you have finished, close the Active Directory Sites and Services administrative tool.

Managing Universal Group Membership Caching

Many networks run into problems with available network bandwidth and server hardware limitations. For this reason, it may not be wise to install a GC in smaller branch offices. Windows Server 2012 can help these smaller sites by deploying domain controllers that use *Universal Group Membership Caching (UGMC)*.

Once enabled, Universal Group Membership Caching stores information locally when a user attempts to log on for the first time. With the use of a GC, the domain controller retains the universal group membership for that logged-on user.

The next time that user attempts to log on, the authenticating domain controller running Windows Server 2012 will obtain the universal group membership information from its local cache without the need to contact a GC. By default, the universal group membership information is retained on the domain controller for eight hours.

There are several advantages of using Universal Group Membership Caching:

Faster Logon Times   Because the domain controller does not need to contact a global catalog, logon authentication is faster.

Reduced Network Bandwidth   The domain controller does not have to handle object replication for all of the objects located in the forest.

Ability to Use Existing Hardware   There is no need to upgrade hardware to support a GC.

Exercise 6.11 shows you the steps necessary to configure Universal Group Membership Caching.

EXERCISE 6.11

Managing Universal Group Membership Caching

1. Open the Active Directory Sites and Services administrative.

2. Click Sites, and then click CorporateHQ. In the right pane, right-click NTDS Settings and choose Properties.

3. In the NTDS Site Settings Properties dialog box, check the box labeled Enable Universal Group Membership Caching, and then click OK to continue.

4. When you have finished, close the Active Directory Sites and Services administrative tool.

Summary

In this chapter, we discussed the purpose of Active Directory replication. As you have learned, replication is used to keep domain controllers synchronized and it is important in Active Directory environments of all sizes. Replication is the process by which changes to the Active Directory database are transferred between domain controllers.

This chapter also covered the concepts of sites, site boundaries, and subnets. In addition to learning how to configure them, you learned that subnets define physical portions of your network environment, and that sites are defined as collections of well-connected IP subnets. Site boundaries are defined by the subnet or subnets that you include in your site configuration.

We also covered the basics of replication and the differences between intrasite and intersite replication. We also covered the purpose and use of bridgehead servers in depth. Although replication is a behind-the-scenes type of task, the optimal configuration of sites in distributed network environments results in better use of bandwidth and faster response by network resources. For these reasons, you should be sure that you thoroughly understand the concepts related to managing replication for Active Directory.

We covered the placement of domain controllers and Global Catalog servers in the network and how, when placed properly, they can increase the performance of Active Directory operations.

We also showed how to monitor and troubleshoot replication. The Windows Server 2012 System Monitor administrative tool was designed so that you can monitor many performance statistics associated with using Active Directory.

The chapter also covered the basics of linking multiple domains in trees and forests. You now know why you would want to plan for them and the benefits and drawbacks of using only one domain or of having a multidomain environment. For example, you might decide to have multiple domains if you have an acquisitions-and-mergers situation where you need to keep multiple administrators. In addition, by using multiple domains, organizations can retain separate security databases; however, in such cases, they are also able to share resources between domains.

You can use multiple domains to provide two major benefits for the network directory services—security and availability. These benefits are made possible through Active Directory and the administrative tools that can be used to access it.

System administrators can simplify operations while still ensuring that only authorized users have access to their data. Multiple domains can interact to form Active Directory trees and forests, and you can use the Active Directory Installation Wizard to create new Active Directory trees and forests.

Exam Essentials

Understand the reasons for using multiple domains.   There are seven primary reasons for using multiple domains: They provide additional scalability, they reduce replication traffic, they help with political and organizational issues, they provide many levels of hierarchy, they allow for decentralized administration, they preserve legality, and they allow for multiple DNS or domain names.

Understand the drawbacks of using multiple domains.   With multiple domains, maintaining administrative consistency is more difficult. The number of administrative units multiplies as well, which makes it difficult to keep track of network resources. Finally, it is much more difficult to rearrange the domain topology within an Active Directory environment than it is simply to reorganize OUs.

Know how to create a domain tree.   To create a new domain tree, you need to promote a Windows Server 2012 computer to a domain controller, select the option that makes this domain controller the first machine in a new domain, and make that domain the first domain of a new tree. The result is a new domain tree.

Know how to join a domain tree to a forest.   Creating a new tree to form or add to a forest is as simple as promoting a server to a domain controller for a new domain that does *not* share a namespace with an existing Active Directory domain. To add a domain to an existing forest, you must already have at least one other domain. This domain serves as the root domain for the entire forest.

Understand how to manage single-master operations.   Single-master operations must be performed on specially designated machines within the Active Directory forest. There are five main single-master functions: two that apply to an entire Active Directory forest (Schema Master and Domain Naming Master) and three that apply to each domain (RID Master, PDC Emulator Master, and Infrastructure Master).

Understand how to manage trusts.   When configuring trusts, you'll need to consider two main characteristics: transitivity and direction. The simplest way to understand transitive relationships is through this example: If Domain A trusts Domain B and Domain B trusts Domain C, then Domain A implicitly trusts Domain C. Trusts can be configured as nontransitive so that this type of behavior does not occur. In one-way relationships, the trusting domain allows resources to be shared with the trusted domain. In two-way relationships, both domains trust each other equally. Special trusts include external trusts, realm trusts, cross-forest trusts, and shortcut trusts.

Understand how to manage UPN suffixes.   By default, the name of the domain in which the user is created determines the UPN suffix. By adding additional UPN suffixes to the forest, you can easily choose more manageable suffixes when it comes time to create new users.

Understand how to manage global catalog servers.   You can configure any number of domain controllers to host a copy of the global catalog. The GC contains all of the schema information and a subset of the attributes for all domains within the Active Directory environment. Servers that contain a copy of the GC are known as GC servers. Whenever a user executes a query that requires information from multiple domains, they need only contact the nearest GC server for this information. Similarly, when users must authenticate across domains, they will not have to wait for a response from a domain controller that may be located across the world. The result is increased overall performance of Active Directory queries.

Understand universal group membership caching.   You can enable a domain controller as a Universal Group Membership Caching server. The Universal Group Membership Caching machine will then send a request for the logon authentication of a user to the GC server. The GC will then send the information back to the Universal Group Membership Caching server to be cached locally for eight hours (by default). The user can then authenticate without the need to contact the GC again.

Understand the purpose of Active Directory replication.   Replication is used to keep domain controllers synchronized, and it is important in Active Directory environments of all sizes. Replication is the process by which changes to the Active Directory database are transferred between domain controllers.

Understand the concept of sites, site boundaries, and subnets.   Subnets define physical portions of your network environment. Sites are defined as collections of well-connected IP subnets. Site boundaries are defined by the subnet or subnets that you include in your site configuration.

Understand the differences between intrasite and intersite replication.   Intrasite replication is designed to synchronize Active Directory information to machines that are located in the same site. Intersite replication is used to synchronize information for domain controllers that are located in different sites.

Understand the purpose of bridgehead servers.   Bridgehead servers are designed to accept traffic between two remote sites and to then forward this information to the appropriate servers. One way to synchronize data between sites that are connected with slow connections efficiently is to use a bridgehead server.

Implement site links, site link bridges, and connection objects.   You can use all three of these object types to finely control the behavior of Active Directory replication and to manage replication traffic. Site links are created to define the types of connections that are available between the components of a site. Site links can reflect a relative cost for a network connection and can reflect the bandwidth that is available for communications. You can use site link bridges to connect site links so that the relationship can be transitive. Connection objects provide you with a way to set up special types of replication schedules such as immediate replication on demand or specifying a custom schedule for certain servers.

Configure replication schedules and site link costs.   You can create multiple site links between sites, and you can assign site links a cost value based on the type of connection.

The system administrator determines the cost value, and the relative costs of site links are then used to determine the optimal path for replication. The lower the cost, the more likely the link is to be used for replication. Once you've determined how and through which connections replication will take place, it's time to determine *when* information should be replicated. Replication requires network resources and occupies bandwidth. Therefore, you need to balance the need for consistent directory information with the need to conserve bandwidth.

Determine where to place domain controllers and global catalog servers based on a set of requirements. Where you place domain controllers and global catalog servers can positively affect the performance of Active Directory operations. However, to optimize performance, you need to know the best places to put these servers in a network environment that consists of multiple sites.

Monitor and troubleshoot replication. The Windows Server 2012 System Monitor administrative tool is designed so that you can monitor many performance statistics associated with using Active Directory. In addition to this monitoring, you should always verify basic network connectivity and router and firewall connections and also examine the event logs.

Review Questions

1. You need to deactivate the UGMC option on some of your domain controllers. At which level in Active Directory would you deactivate UGMC?

    A. Server

    B. Site

    C. Domain

    D. Forest

2. You work for an organization with a single domain forest. Your company has one main location and two branch locations. All locations are configured as Active Directory sites and all sites are connected with the DEFAULTIPSITELINK object. Your connections are running slower than the company policy allows. You want to decrease the replication latency between all domain controllers in the various sites. What should you do?

    A. Decrease the Replication interval for the DEFAULTIPSITELINK object.

    B. Decrease the Replication interval for the site.

    C. Decrease the Replication schedule for the site.

    D. Decrease the Replication schedule for all domain controllers.

3. You need to enable three of your domain controllers as global catalog servers. Where would you configure the domain controllers as global catalogs?

    A. Forest, NTDS settings

    B. Domain, NTDS settings

    C. Site, NTDS settings

    D. Server, NTDS settings

4. Daniel is responsible for managing Active Directory replication traffic for a medium-sized organization that has deployed a single Active Directory domain. Currently, the environment is configured with two sites and the default settings for replication. Each site consists of 15 domain controllers. Recently, network administrators have complained that Active Directory traffic is using a large amount of available network bandwidth between the two sites. Daniel has been asked to meet the following requirements:

    - Reduce the amount of network traffic between domain controllers in the two sites.

    - Minimize the amount of change to the current site topology.

    - Require no changes to the existing physical network infrastructure.

    Daniel decides that it would be most efficient to configure specific domain controllers in each site that will receive the majority of replication traffic from the other site. Which of the following solutions meets the requirements?

    A. Create additional sites that are designed only for replication traffic, and move the existing domain controllers to these sites.

   B. Create multiple site links between the two sites.

   C. Create a site link bridge between the two sites.

   D. Configure one server at each site to act as a preferred bridgehead server.

5. Which of the following does not need to be created manually when you are setting up a replication scenario involving three domains and three sites?

   A. Sites

   B. Site links

   C. Connection objects

   D. Subnets

6. Which of the following services of Active Directory is responsible for maintaining the replication topology?

   A. File Replication Service

   B. Knowledge Consistency Checker

   C. Windows Internet Name Service

   D. Domain Name System

7. A system administrator for an Active Directory environment that consists of three sites wants to configure site links to be transitive. Which of the following Active Directory objects is responsible for representing a transitive relationship between sites?

   A. Additional sites

   B. Additional site links

   C. Bridgehead servers

   D. Site link bridges

8. You have configured your Active Directory environment with multiple sites and have placed the appropriate resources in each of the sites. You are now trying to choose a protocol for the transfer of replication information between two sites. The connection between the two sites has the following characteristics:

- The link is generally unavailable during certain parts of the day because of an unreliable network provider.

- The replication transmission must be attempted whether the link is available or not. If the link was unavailable during a scheduled replication, the information should automatically be received after the link becomes available again.

- Replication traffic must be able to travel over a standard Internet connection.

Which of the following protocols meets these requirements?

   A. IP

   B. SMTP

   C. RPC

   D. DHCP

9. A system administrator suspects that there is an error in the replication configuration. How can the system administrator look for specific error messages related to replication?

A. By using the Active Directory Sites and Services administrative tool

B. By using the Computer Management tool

C. By going to Event Viewer ➤ System Log

D. By going to Event Viewer ➤ Directory Service Log

10. Christina is responsible for managing Active Directory replication traffic for a medium-sized organization. Currently, the environment is configured with a single site and the default settings for replication. The site contains more than 50 domain controllers, and the system administrators are often making changes to the Active Directory database. Recently, network administrators have complained that Active Directory traffic is consuming a large amount of network bandwidth between portions of the network that are connected by slow links. Ordinarily, the amount of replication traffic is reasonable, but recently users have complained about slow network performance during certain hours of the day.

Christina has been asked to alleviate the problem while meeting the following requirements:

- Be able to control exactly when replication occurs.

- Be able to base Active Directory replication on the physical network infrastructure.

- Perform the changes without creating or removing any domain controllers.

Which two of the following steps can Christina take to meet these requirements? (Choose two.)

A. Create and define Connection objects that specify the hours during which replication will occur.

B. Create multiple site links.

C. Create a site link bridge.

D. Create new Active Directory sites that reflect the physical network topology.

E. Configure one server at each of the new sites to act as a bridgehead server.

Chapter

7

Configuring Active Directory Server Roles

THE FOLLOWING 70-412 EXAM OBJECTIVES ARE COVERED IN THIS CHAPTER:

✓ **Implement Active Directory Federation Services 2.1 (AD FSv2.1)**

- This objective may include, but is not limited to: Implement claims-based authentication including Relying Party Trusts; configure Claims Provider Trust rules; configure attribute stores including Active Directory Lightweight Directory Services (AD LDS); manage AD FS certificates; configure AD FS proxy; integrate with Cloud Services.

✓ **Install and configure Active Directory Certificate Services (AD CS)**

- This objective may include, but is not limited to: Install an Enterprise Certificate Authority (CA); configure CRL distribution points; install and configure Online Responder; implement administrative role separation; configure CA backup and recovery.

✓ **Manage certificates**

- This objective may include, but is not limited to: Manage certificate templates; implement and manage certificate deployment, validation, and revocation; manage certificate renewal; manage certificate enrollment and renewal to computers and users using Group Policies; configure and manage key archival and recovery.

✓ **Install and configure Active Directory Rights Management Services (AD RMS)**

- This objective may include, but is not limited to: Install a licensing or certificate AD RMS server; manage AD RMS Service Connection Point (SCP); manage AD RMS client deployment; manage Trusted User Domains; manage Trusted Publishing Domains; manage Federated Identity support; manage RMS templates; configure Exclusion Policies.

So far, you have learned how to install the main components of Active Directory. At this point, you should be able to install Domain Name System (DNS) and Active Directory. You should also understand what domains, sites, and trees can do for your organization.

In this chapter, you'll take your domain a step further. First I am going to talk about the Server Manager application, which allows you to install the many different server roles. Then we are going to dive into the five main Active Directory server roles and talk about what they can do to make your network run more securely and efficiently.

Understanding Server Manager

In Windows Server 2003, there were many different tools available to install and configure Active Directory components, including Manage Your Server, Configure Your Server, and Add/Remove Windows Components.

Windows Server 2012 combines many of these tools in a Microsoft Management Console (MMC) snap-in called *Server Manager*. Server Manager was first installed with Windows Server 2008. Server Manager allows an administrator to view the server configuration and installed roles. Server Manager also includes links for adding and removing features and roles (see Figure 7.1).

Server Manager is your one-stop-shopping MMC snap-in. By that I mean that you can take care of all your server management needs in one easy interface. You can use Server Manager to install and manage the following roles.

- Active Directory Certificate Services
- Active Directory Domain Services
- Active Directory Federation Services
- Active Directory Lightweight Directory Services
- Active Directory Rights Management Services

FIGURE 7.1 Server Manager showing Windows Server 2012 server roles

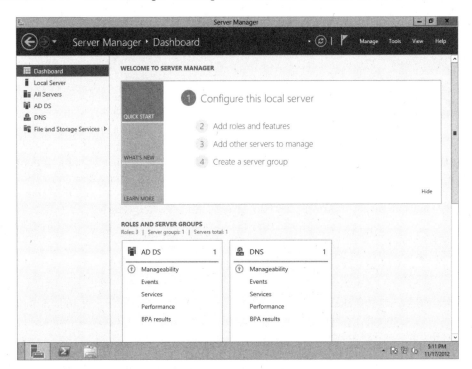

Configuring Active Directory Certificate Services

Using *Active Directory Certificate Services (AD CS)*, administrators can configure public key certificate services. AD CS security allows a private key to be combined with objects (such as users and computers), devices (such as routers), or services. The public key infrastructure greatly increases data security.

In Windows Server 2012, AD CS provides services for creating and managing public key certificates used in software security systems that employ public key technologies. Organizations can use AD CS to enhance security by binding the identity of a user, device, or service to a corresponding private key. AD CS also includes features that allow you to manage certificate enrollment and revocation in a variety of environments.

Think of a digital certificate as a carrying case for a public key. A certificate contains the public key and a set of attributes, like the key holder's name and email address. These attributes specify something about the holder: their identity, what they're allowed to do with the certificate, and so on. The attributes and the public key are bound together because the certificate is digitally signed by the entity that issued it. Anyone who wants to verify the certificate's contents can verify the issuer's signature.

Certificates are one part of what security experts call a *public key infrastructure (PKI)*. A PKI has several different components that you can mix and match to achieve the desired results.

Applications supported by AD CS include Secure/Multipurpose Internet Mail Extensions (S/MIME), secure wireless networks, virtual private networks (VPNs), Internet Protocol Security (IPSec), Encrypting File System (EFS), smart card logon, Secure Sockets Layer/Transport Layer Security (SSL/TLS), and digital signatures.

The following are some of the AD CS components:

Cert Publishers Group   *Certificates* are used to increase security by allowing for strong authentication methods. User accounts are placed within the Cert Publishers group if they need to be able to publish security certificates. Generally, these accounts are used by Active Directory security services.

PKI-Savvy Applications   *PKI-savvy applications* allow you and your users to do useful things with certificates, like encrypt email or network connections. Ideally, the user shouldn't have to know (or even necessarily be aware of) what the application is doing—everything should work seamlessly and automatically. The best-known examples of PKI-savvy applications are web browsers like Internet Explorer and Firefox and email applications like Outlook and Outlook Express.

Online Responder Service   Some applications, including S/MIME, SSL, EFS, and smart cards, need to validate the status of certificates. The Online Responder Service authoritatively responds to such requests.

Certification Practice Statement   A *Certification Practice Statement (CPS)* is a statement that is issued by a certificate creator. It represents the creator's practices for issuing and validating certificates. The CPS represents the technical, procedural, and personnel policies and practices of the issuing certification authority (CA) organization.

Enrollment Agents   *Enrollment agents* are administrators who have the ability to enroll users into the certificate services program. Enrollment agents can issue and manage certificate requests. Windows Server 2012 includes three certificate templates that allow different types of enrollment agents. (Templates are explained later in the section "Certificate Templates.")

- Enrollment Agent
- Enrollment Agent (Computer)
- Exchange Enrollment Agent (Offline Request)

Network Device Enrollment Service   Network devices such as routers do not have accounts in the Active Directory Domain. The *Network Device Enrollment Service (NDES)* allows such network devices to obtain certificates.

Web Enrollment   With the *Certificate Authority Web Enrollment Role Service*, users can easily request certificates and retrieve certificate revocation lists (CRLs) through a web browser. It is a good practice to load this service on a member server and not a domain controller. This machine can issue certificates to web users and, for security reasons, you do not want a domain controller talking to web-based users.

Certificate Mapping   Administrators have the ability to configure domain user accounts to use *certificate mapping* to control access to network resources. Administrators also can use certificate mapping to control access to website resources for Internet Information Services.

Authentication Mechanism Assurance   *Authentication mechanism assurance* allows applications to control resource access. The resource access control is based on authentication strength and method. Administrators have the ability to configure properties of a resource, including authentication type and authentication strength. This feature is enabled at the Windows Server 2012 domain functional level.

Installing Active Directory Certificate Services

When you are installing AD CS, the Installation Wizard will walk you through the installation process and you will need to answer some configuration questions. If at any time during installation you do not know how to configure an option, you can click the help link for explanations. Here are some of the AD CS options that you can configure during the installation:

Certificate Authorities   *Certificate authorities (CAs)* issue, revoke, and publish certificates for their clients. Big CAs like Thawte and VeriSign may do this for millions of users. If you wish, you can also set up your own CA for each department or workgroup in your organization.

Each CA is responsible for choosing what attributes it will include in a certificate and what mechanism it will use to verify those attributes before it issues the certificate.

There are three types of CA:

>   **Enterprise Root CAs**   These are automatically integrated with Active Directory, and they are the most trusted CAs of the hierarchy. They hold the certificates that you issue to the users within your organization.

>   **Stand-Alone Root CAs**   These hold the certificates that you issue to Internet users.

>   **Subordinate CAs**   These are below the enterprise and stand-alone root CAs in the hierarchy. The enterprise or stand-alone root CAs give certificates to the subordinate CAs, which in turn issue certificates to objects and services.

Cryptographic Service Provider   The *cryptographic service provider (CSP)* is the mechanism that is responsible for authentication, encoding, and encryption services that Windows-based applications access through the Microsoft Cryptography application programming interface (CryptoAPI). Every CSP offers a unique implementation of the CryptoAPI. Some CSPs offer a strong cryptographic algorithm, while others use hardware components, such as smart cards.

Hash Algorithm   An algorithm that produces a hash value of some piece of data, such as a message or session key, is called a *hash algorithm*. If you use a well-designed hash algorithm, the hash value changes when the data changes. Because of this characteristic, hash values are useful when you are trying to detect whether any modifications have been made to data (such as a message). Also, a well-designed hash algorithm makes it almost impossible for two independent inputs to have the same hash value.

Exercise 7.1 shows you the steps that you need to follow to install the AD CS server. You need to complete the exercises in Chapter 3, "Active Directory Planning and Installation," before you attempt Exercise 7.1.

EXERCISE 7.1

Installing Active Directory Certificate Services

1. Open Server Manager by selecting the Server Manager link on the toolbar (it looks like a toolbox in front of a server).

2. Under the Configure This Local Server link, click the number 2 link, Add Roles And Features.

3. At the Before You Begin screen, click the Skip This Page By Default check box. Click Next.

4. Choose the role-based or feature-based installation radio button. Click Next.

5. On the Select Destination screen, choose your local server name and click Next.

6. On the Select Server Roles screen, check the box next to Active Directory Certificate Services.

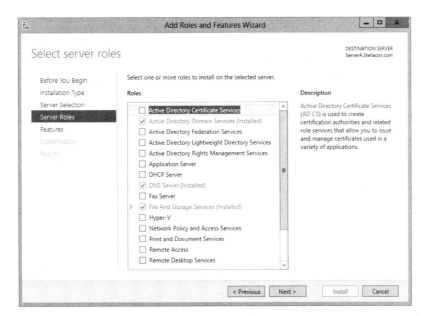

7. An add features box appears. Choose the defaults and click the Add Features button. When the Select Server Roles screen reappears, click Next.

8. At the Select Features screen, just click Next.

9. At the Active Directory Certificates Screen, click Next.

10. At the Select Role Services screen, make sure the Certification Authority and Certification Authority Web Enrollment boxes are both checked.

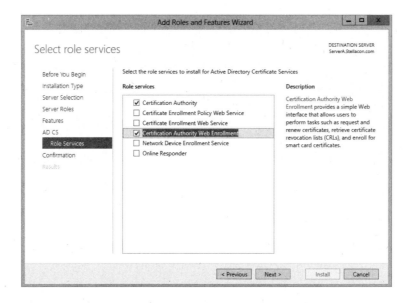

11. An add features box appears. Choose the defaults, and click the Add Features button. When the Select Role Services screen reappears, click Next.

12. When the Web Server Role (IIS) screen appears, just click Next.

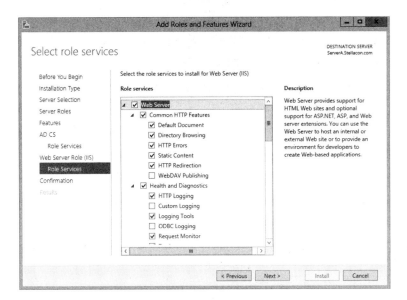

13. At the confirmation screen, check the box for restarting the computer and click the Install button.

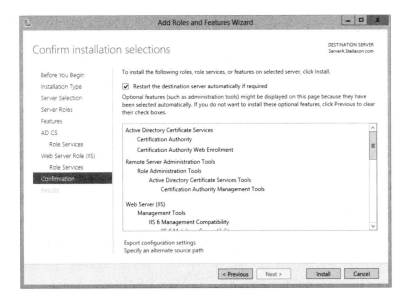

14. When the installation is complete, click the Close button. Make sure the system reboots.

EXERCISE 7.1 *(continued)*

15. Log in and restart Server Manager.

16. On the left side, click on the AD CS link.

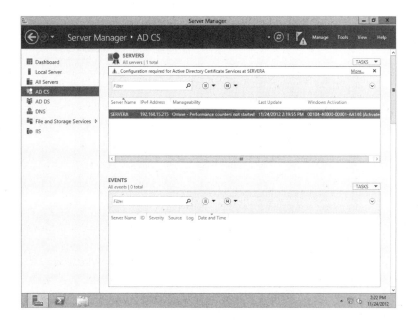

17. On the top bar, click the More link next to Configuration Required For Active Directory Certificate Services.

18. The All Servers Task Details and Notifications screen appears. Click the Configure Active Directory Certificates link under Action.

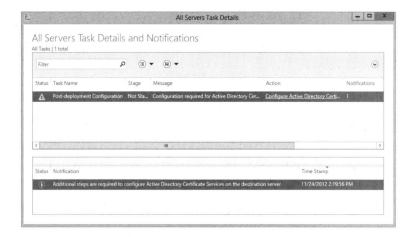

19. At the Credentials screen, make sure the administrator account is listed and click Next.

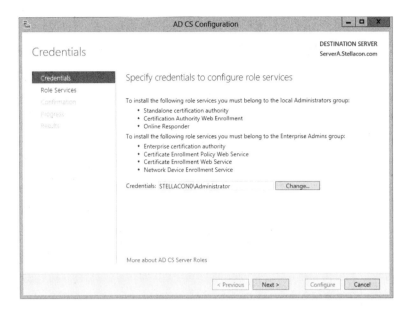

20. At the Role Services screen, check the Certificate Authority and Certificate Authority Web Enrollment check boxes. Click Next.

21. At the Setup Type screen, choose Enterprise CA and click Next.

22. At the CA Type screen, choose Root CA and click Next.

23. At the Private Key screen, choose Create A New Private Key, and then click Next.

This option allows you to create a new key for your certificate server. You would choose Use Existing Private Key if you were reinstalling or using previously issued keys.

24. When the Cryptography For CA screen appears, you must select a CSP. Choose RSA#Microsoft Software Key Storage Provider. Make sure the Key Character Length value is 2048, and choose SHA1 for the hash algorithm. Click Next.

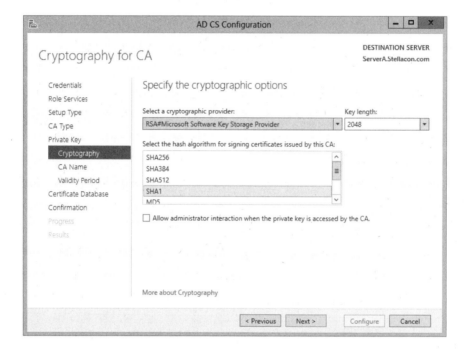

25. At the CA Name screen, accept the defaults and click Next. The common name is the general name that is used to help identify the CA, and the common name is also added to all issued certificates.

26. At the Validity Period screen, change the default to 1 Years and click Next.

27. The CA Database screen will prompt you to enter the storage location for your database files. Accept the defaults and click Next.

28. At the Confirm Installation Selections screen, click Configure.

29. At the Results screen, you will see the status of the installation. You should see an Installation Succeeded message. Click Close, and exit Server Manager.

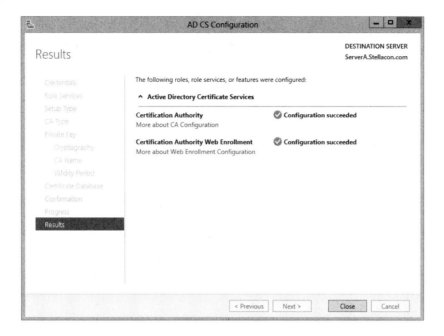

 If you need to set up the Active Directory certificate authority using PowerShell, you would need to use the `Install-CertificationAuthority` command.

Enrolling User and Computer Certificates

Now that you have installed the AD CS, it's time for your users and computers to receive certificates. Users can receive their certificates multiple ways:

Group Policy Objects (GPOs)   You can use group policies to enroll user and computer certificates automatically, making the entire certificate process transparent to your end users. See Chapter 5, "Managing Group Policy Objects."

Web Enrollment   You can request a certificate by using http://servername/certsrv.

Extranet Enrollment   The Certificate Enrollment Web Service enables users and computers to perform certificate enrollment by using the HTTPS protocol.

Smart Card Enrollment   The enrollment agent capability, also referred to as the *smart card enrollment station*, allows an authorized user to issue smart cards from a centralized workstation.

Certificate Auto Enrollment   To set up certificate auto enrollment, you configure the local security policy (see Figure 7.2 and Exercise 7.2).

FIGURE 7.2 Configuring auto enrollment through the Local Security Policy application

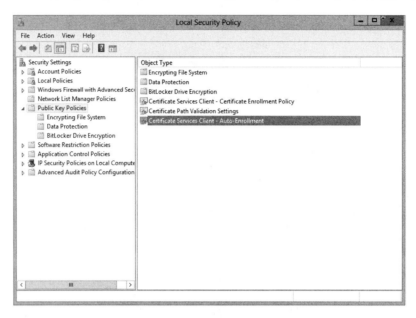

![Real World Scenario icon] **Real World Scenario**

User Enrollment through Auto Enrollment

For an IT administrator, security is always a major concern on any network. When deciding to implement certificates, you must decide how you want to issue them. It is always a good practice to auto-enroll your end users. The fewer steps that an end user has to do, the better the chance that it will get done. I am not saying this in a bad way. Your end users are not as concerned with network security as you are as an administrator. End users start doing their day-to-day tasks and, before you know it, they forget to implement the certificate. Try to make a practice of auto enrolling your end users to make sure that the certificate gets issued and the network is secure.

Exercise 7.2 shows the steps necessary to configure auto enrollment.

EXERCISE 7.2

Configuring Certificate Auto Enrollment

1. Open Local Security Policy in Administrative Tools.

2. In the left pane, click Public Key Policies. In the right pane, right-click Certificate Services Client - Auto-Enrollment and choose Properties.

3. In the Configuration Model drop-down list, choose Enabled and click OK.

Certificate Templates

Certificate templates act like rubber stamps. By specifying a particular template as the model you want to use for a newly issued certificate, you're actually telling the CA which optional attributes to add to the certificate as well as implicitly telling it how to fill in some of the mandatory attributes. Templates greatly simplify the process of issuing certificates because they keep you from having to memorize the names of all of the attributes you might potentially want to put into a certificate. In Windows Server 2012, multiple templates are available, and you also have the ability to secure templates using template permissions.

Version 4 certificate templates are new templates that have been added to Windows Server 2012 (see figure 7.3). Windows Server 2012 supports *Cryptography Next Generation (CNG)*. CNG introduces support for Suite B cryptographic algorithms such as elliptic curve cryptography (ECC).

Version 4 certificate templates include the following new features:

- Renewing with the same key
- Support for both CSP and KSP as well as the ability to organize providers in order of preference
- Allowing key-based renewal
- Enabling requestor-specified issuance

FIGURE 7.3 Certificate template properties

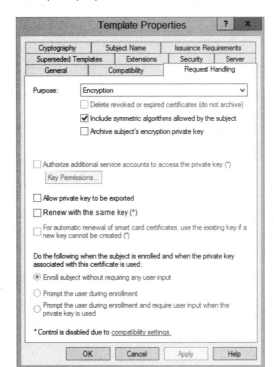

Certificate templates are categorized in different certificate template types:

CA Certificate When this certificate is present on the client and server computers, the certificate notifies the client or server that it can trust other certificates that are issued by this CA. This type of certificate is required for deployments of certificate-based authentication methods.

Client Computer Certificate This certificate type is issued to client computers, and the certificate is used when the client computer needs to prove its identity to a server during the authentication process.

Server Certificate This certificate type is issued to Network Policy Server (NPS) servers, and the certificate is used during the authentication process to prove its identity to client computers.

User Certificate This is the certificate type that is issued to individuals by the certificate server. This is also the certificate type typically distributed to smart cards.

Table 7.1 shows some of the default Windows Server 2012 templates that are available.

TABLE 7.1 Some of the default Windows Server 2012 templates

Template	Description	Type
Administrator	Allows trust list signing and user authentication	User
Authenticated Session	Allows subjects to authenticate to a web server	User
Basic EFS	Used by EFS to encrypt data	User
CA Exchange	Used to protect private keys as they are sent to the CA for private key archival	Computer
Code Signing	Used to digitally sign software	User
Computer	Allows a computer to authenticate itself on the network	Computer
Domain Controller Authentication	Used to authenticate Active Directory computers and users	Computer
EFS Recovery Agent	Allows the subject to decrypt files that are encrypted with EFS	User
Enrollment Agent	Used to request certificates on behalf of another user	User
Enrollment Agent (Computer)	Used to request certificates on behalf of another computer	Computer
Exchange Enrollment Agent (Offline request)	Used to request certificates on behalf of another user and supply the username in the request; used by the Network Device Enrollment Service for its enrollment agent certificate	User
IPSec	Used by IP Security (IPSec) to digitally sign, encrypt, and decrypt network communication	Computer
Smart Card Logon	Allows the holder to authenticate its identity by using a smart card	User
User	Used by users for email, EFS, and client authentication	User

Revoking Certificates

Occasionally, you will need to remove a certificate from a user or computer. This is known as *certificate revocation*. For example, if a user gets terminated from your organization, as an administrator you have the ability to revoke this user's certificate so that they cannot access any data or confidential information after they leave the company.

The following are some of the certificate revocation components:

Certificate Revocation List   When certificates get revoked, they are listed in the *certificate revocation list (CRL)*. When configured properly by an administrator, all the certificate servers use this list. The CRL helps validate certificates and helps prevent revoked certificates from being used.

CRL Distribution Point   You need to publish your CRL to a shared location called a *CRL distribution point (CDP)*. This gives your CRL a central location that all the certificate servers can share and use.

Remember to change the URL distribution point for the Authority Information Access (AIA) for any new root CA. You need to make this location accessible to all users in your organization's network. The offline root CA's default AIA points are not accessible to users on the network. If you do not change the location of the AIA, certificate chain verification fails.

Online Responder   The Online Responder is the server component of a certificate validation method called *Online Certificate Status Protocol (OCSP)*. When certificates get revoked, your certificate server needs to make sure that these certificates don't get used again. You can perform this validation in many ways. The most common validation methods are CRLs, delta CRLs, and OCSP responses. Previous versions of Windows Server supported only CRLs. Windows Vista, Windows 7, Windows 8, Windows 2008, Windows Server 2008 R2, and the Windows Server 2012 operating system support both CRL and OCSP as methods for determining certificate status. The OCSP support applies to both the client component and the server component (called the *Online Responder*).

Authority Information Access   When you build a certificate server, one of the jobs of the server is to issue certificates. When you build or purchase certificates, you place the certificates on the server so that they can be issued. The *Authority Information Access (AIA) extension* specifies where to find these up-to-date certificates.

In Exercise 7.3, you will examine how to change the Authority Information Access extension path.

EXERCISE 7.3

Modifying the AIA

1. Open the Certification Authority snap-in.

2. In the console tree, right-click the server name and then click Properties.

3. Click the Extensions tab.

4. In Select Extension, click Authority Information Access.

5. If the Specify Locations list does not include a valid location for the CA certificate, click Add to open the Add Location dialog box and type a valid location. Click OK.

6. In the Specify Locations list, click a location and then select the Include In The Authority Information Access Extension Of Issued Certificates check box.

7. Click OK.

8. Close the Certification Authority snap-in.

Once you have completed Exercise 7.3, you must restart Active Directory Certificate Services for the changes to take effect.

Exercise 7.4 walks you through the process of revoking a certificate using the Certification Authority MMC snap-in. (This MMC is installed automatically after the installation of your certificate server.) You must first have completed Exercise 7.1 and Exercise 7.2 to complete this exercise.

EXERCISE 7.4

Revoking a Certificate

1. Open the Certification Authority MMC.

2. On the left pane, expand the server name. Click the Issued Certificates folder. Right-click a certificate (right pane) and, in the menu, choose All Tasks ➢ Revoke Certificate.

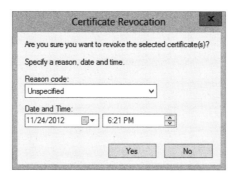

3. In the Certificate Revocation dialog box, you can choose the reason for the revocation and the effective date. Choose Unspecified, and enter today's date. Click Yes. Close the Certification Authority.

Configuring Additional CA Server Settings

You need to complete some important tasks while you are working on a certificate server. At this point, you have learned how to install an enterprise root CA, configure automatic certificate requests, set up web enrollment, and revoke a certificate. I will finish by covering the following tasks:

Key Archival   *Key archival* allows a key to be stored for later recoverability if necessary. In a Windows Server 2012 CA, key archival is automatic. The private key portion of a public-private key pair is archived and can be recovered when needed.

Note that when a private key is recovered, the data or messages with which it was associated are not recovered. Key recovery only allows an individual to recover lost or damaged keys, and it allows an administrator to assume the role of an account for data access or recovery.

Key Recovery Agent   The *key recovery agent* is a role (a set of rights) that you can give an individual so that they have the permission to recover a lost or damaged key.

Assigning Administrative Roles   Using the Certification Authority MMC, you can assign users or administrators rights to help manage the certificate server.

To assign an individual a role, right-click the name of the server in the Certification Authority MMC and choose Properties. Click the Security tab. Add the individual, and choose their roles.

Rights and permissions are discussed in detail in Chapter 13, "Understanding Security."

Auditing   One of the security features in a CA is auditing. You have the ability to audit many different events of a CA server in the security log of the Event Viewer. You can audit the following events:

- Back up and restore the CA database
- Change CA configurations
- Change CA security settings
- Issue and manage certificate requests
- Revoke certificates and publish the CRL
- Store and retrieve archived keys
- Start and stop Active Directory Certificate Services

Database Backup and Restore   One task that all administrators need to perform is backing up and restoring the certificates and keys. To back up and restore certificates, you use the Certification Authority MMC. Exercise 7.5 walks you through backing up your Certificate Authority server.

EXERCISE 7.5

Backing Up the Certification Authority Server

1. Open the Certification Authority MMC.

2. In the left pane, right-click the name of the server; then choose All Tasks ➢ Back Up CA.

3. When the Certification Authority Backup Wizard appears, click Next.

4. At the Items To Back Up screen, click the Private Key And CA Certificate check box. Next to the Back Up To This Location field, click the Browse button. Choose a location for your backup and click OK. Click Next.

5. At the Select A Password screen, enter and confirm a password. For this exercise, use **P@ssw0rd**. Click Next.

6. At the Completing The Certification Authority Backup Wizard screen, click Finish.

7. Close the Certification Authority MMC.

What's New in Windows Server 2012?

Microsoft CA servers are not new to the Windows Server family of products, but every new edition of Windows Server brings with it improvements to the CA server. Windows Server 2012 is no different.

Renew with the Same Key   One advantage of using the same certificate key is that your system already has the key associated with many of your applications. By enabling the Windows Server 2012 machine to allow users to use the same key, this can benefit them by not having to change applications or data to the new certificate. Renewing with the same key allows users to have the guarantee level of the original key maintained throughout its life cycle.

Support for CSPs, KSPs, and Provider Ordering   One new feature of Windows Server 2012 is the ability to set up the order of the cryptographic service providers (CSPs) or key storage providers (KSPs) on the Cryptography tab. One of the advantages of this feature is that the Windows Server 2012 certificate administrator can chose between CSPs and KSPs.

This allows the certificate administrator to select which providers to make available to the clients and to consolidate those providers in order of preference.

Allow Key-Based Renewal   Another new feature in Windows Server 2012 certificates is called *key-based renewals*. These allow an existing valid certificate to renew its own authentication. This gives computers that are not directly connected to the internal network the ability to renew an existing certificate automatically. To use the benefits of this feature, the client computers must be either Windows 8 or Windows Server 2012 based.

Deployment and Management Capabilities from Windows PowerShell   Microsoft has designed Windows Server 2012 with PowerShell capabilities in mind. All role services for AD CS can be configured and removed by using the Windows PowerShell cmdlets.

Understanding Active Directory Domain Services

With *Active Directory Domain Services (AD DS)*, you manage objects (users, computers, printers, and so forth) on a network. Active Directory is the database that stores all of your domain objects. In a Windows Server 2000, 2003, 2008/2008 R2, or 2012 network, you cannot have a domain without Active Directory.

Security Features Available for Domain Services

Two important security features are available for domain services in Windows Server 2012—RODCs and BitLocker Drive Encryption.

Read-Only Domain Controllers

As stated earlier, RODCs allow you to have a noneditable copy of Active Directory in an area that may be a security risk. RODCs hold an entire copy of Active Directory, and the replication traffic is unidirectional. *Unidirectional replication* means that other domain controllers can update an RODC but an RODC cannot update other domain controllers.

One advantage to having an RODC is that you can give a normal user the administrator role for the RODC and that user can do any type of maintenance on it. The user does not need to be a domain administrator; they are allowed to have the maintenance role for just the one RODC. This concept is known as *administrator role separation.*

You can also load DNS on an RODC. This makes a read-only copy of the DNS database. The downside to a read-only DNS server is that it does not allow dynamic updates (see Chapter 2, "Domain Name System"). The benefit is that you do not have to worry about hackers or unauthorized domain users changing the DNS database.

RODCs allow for authentication through credential caching, but not all accounts have to be cached. You can decide which accounts to cache on an RODC by using a *password replication policy.* This policy allows an administrator to determine which user groups will be allowed to use the RODC credential caching.

To install an RODC, use Server Core and do a normal installation just as you did in Chapter 3. In the Active Directory Domain Services Installation Wizard, on the Additional Domain Controller Options page, check the box labeled Read-Only Domain Controller (RODC)

Read-Only SYSVOL

When you create a read-only domain controller (RODC), the SYSVOL share becomes read-only. File Replication Service (FRS) and Distribute File System (DFS) Replication updates to the SYSVOL are performed on a writable domain controller and then replicated to the RODC. If you are using Windows Server 2003 domain function levels, FRS is used to replicate the SYSVOL share. If you are using the Windows Server 2008 or Windows Server 2012 domain functional level, DFS Replication (DFSR) can be used to replicate the SYSVOL share. If you are running Windows Server 2012, DFSR for the SYSVOL share on an RODC is absolutely read-only. If you are running Windows Server 2012, a delegated administrator could still write changes to SYSVOL on an RODC.

Staged Install of the RODC and RODC Administrative Role Separation

One way you can install an RODC is by doing it in a two-stage process. The advantage of installing an RODC in two stages is that two different individuals can complete part of the install.

The first stage of the RODC installation requires an individual with domain admin rights. The domain admin creates an account in Active Directory for the RODC. Also during the first stage, the Active Directory Installation Wizard records all data (that is, the domain controller account name and the site in which it will be placed) about the RODC. This data will then be stored in the distributed Active Directory database.

The second stage is the actual installation of the machine at the remote location. A new feature called *RODC Administrative Role Separation* allows an administrator to give a normal user the rights to perform the second stage. The second stage does not require domain admin rights. Also during the second stage, the Active Directory Installation Wizard attaches the server to the domain account that was previously created by the domain admin.

Another advantage of using RODC Administrative Role Separation is that a normal user can also help an administrator maintain the RODC.

Using the System Key Utility

The system key utility (Syskey.exe) is used to secure account data on a hard disk. It also helps member servers and client operating systems (for example, Windows Vista, Windows 7, and Windows 8) encrypt the passwords in their Security Account Manager (SAM) database. The system key utility further encrypts the passwords in the Active Directory database, allowing for stronger encryption algorithms beyond the default algorithms.

BitLocker Drive Encryption

Another way to add security in a nonsecure location is through the use of *BitLocker Drive Encryption*. The BitLocker data-protection feature on Windows Server 2012 allows an IT administrator to encrypt both the operating system volume and additional data volumes within the same server. BitLocker will protect your data in the event of a lost or stolen hard disk. If your disk is lost or stolen, the encryption prevents unauthorized access to the data. However, BitLocker is not installed by default. To install the BitLocker security, use Server Manager.

Features of Windows Server 2012

Active Directory Domain Services provides many features and benefits to Windows Server 2012. Many of these features improve Active Directory manageability, supportability, and performance.

Active Directory Recycle Bin   Administrators now have the ability to undo an accidentally deleted Active Directory object using the *Active Directory Recycle Bin*. When a user is deleted, the user's SID number is deleted. Even if you re-create the user (using the same username and password), that user would get a new SID number. All rights and permissions are associated with the SID number and not the username. You recover the user through the use of a backup. This takes time. Using the Active Directory Recycle Bin helps solve this issue. This feature is enabled in AD DS at the Windows Server 2008 R2 and Windows Server 2012 forest functional level.

Active Directory Module for Windows PowerShell and Windows PowerShell Cmdlets   The *Active Directory module for Windows PowerShell* allows an administrator to perform command-line scripting for administrative, configuration, and diagnostic tasks. This is beneficial to administrators because PowerShell uses a consistent vocabulary and syntax. Administrators using PowerShell can easily pipe cmdlets to build complex operations that allow end-to-end manageability with Exchange Server, Group Policy, and other services.

Active Directory Administrative Center The *Active Directory Administrative Center* is an MMC snap-in that allows you to configure and manage many of the day-to-day Active Directory tasks. The Active Directory Administrative Center can help administrators perform certain activities, such as making backups, adding a user, or doing diagnostic tasks to correct system failures.

Active Directory Best Practices Analyzer The *Active Directory Best Practices Analyzer (BPA)* takes a look at your Active Directory deployments and then identifies deviations from Microsoft's best practices. This helps administrators properly manage their Active Directory deployments following Microsoft recommendations. The Active Directory Best Practices Analyzer uses Windows PowerShell cmdlets to gather runtime data. The BPA then analyzes the Active Directory settings that can cause unexpected behavior and reports back its recommendations in the context of your deployment. The Active Directory BPA is available in Server Manager.

Active Directory Web Services *Active Directory Web Services (ADWS)* allows an administrator to manage Active Directory domains and AD LDS instances using a web service interface.

Offline Domain Join *Offline domain join* gives administrators the ability to preprovision computer accounts in the domain to prepare operating systems for deployments. At startup, computers can then join the domain without the need to contact a domain controller. This helps reduce the time it takes to deploy computers in a datacenter.

Managed Service Accounts This Windows Server 2012 feature makes the management of service accounts even simpler. *Managed service accounts* allow for easier management of service principal names (SPNs), and it also helps by reducing service outages for manual password resets and related issues. Administrators have the ability, without any human intervention for password management, to run one managed service account for each service that is running on a server.

Active Directory Management Pack The *Active Directory Management Pack* gives administrators the ability to monitor the availability and performance of Active Directory proactively.

Windows Server 2012 Hyper-V Windows Server 2012 has a role-based utility called Hyper-V. *Hyper-V* is a hypervisor-based virtualization feature. (A hypervisor is a virtual machine monitor, also called *virtual machine manager*.) It includes all of the necessary features to support machine virtualization. By using machine virtualization, a company can reduce costs, improve server utilization, and create a more dynamic IT infrastructure.

Active Directory Federation Services

Active Directory Federation Services (AD FS v2.1) provides Internet-based clients with a secure identity access solution that works on both Windows and non-Windows operating systems.

Normally when a user from one network tries to access an application in another network, they must have a secondary username and password. AD FS allows organizations to set up trust relationships between networks and supports *single sign-on (SSO)*, which allows users to access applications on other networks without needing secondary passwords. Security is improved and administrators spend less time resetting passwords when users don't have to remember multiple passwords.

AD FS requires an AD FS server on both ends of the connection. For example, if company A is going to set up a trust relationship with company B, the AD FS server needs to be configured at both company A and company B.

Installing AD FS

Exercise 7.6 shows you the steps you need to perform to install the AD FS through the Server Manager MMC.

EXERCISE 7.6

Installing the AD FS

1. Open the Server Manager MMC.

2. In the center pane, click the number 2 link, Add Roles and Features.

3. At the Before You Begin screen, click the Skip This Page By Default check box. Click Next.

4. Choose the role-based or feature-based installation radio button. Click Next.

5. On the Select Destination screen, choose your local server name and click Next.

6. On the Select Server Roles screen, click the Active Directory Federation Services check box.

7. A dialog box appears stating that additional features need to be installed. Click the Add Features button. Then click Next.

8. At the Features screen, just click Next.

9. At the AD FS introduction screen, click Next.

10. On the Select Role Services screen, click the AD FS Web Agents check box beside the Federation Services check box (already checked). Click Next.

11. Click the Install button at the confirmation screen.

12. When the results are complete, click Close.

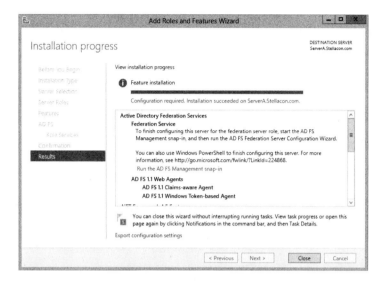

13. Restart the system, log in as the administrator, and open Server Manager.

14. In the left pane, click the AD FS link.

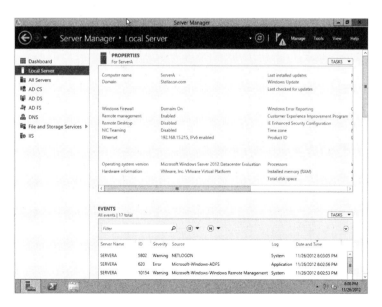

15. Click the More link on the top line next to Configuration Required For Federation Service.

EXERCISE 7.6 *(continued)*

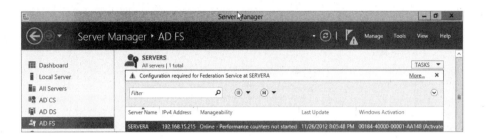

16. Under the Action section, click the link to run the AD FS management snap-in.

17. Click the AD FS Federation Server Configuration Wizard link.

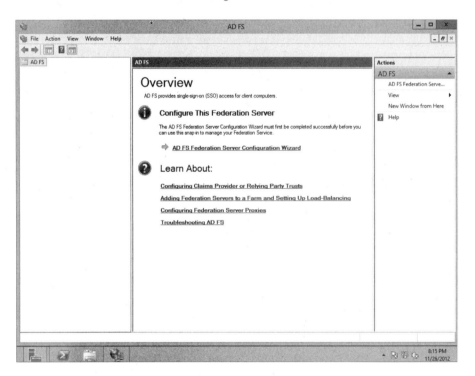

18. Click the Create A New Federation Service radio button and click Next.

19. Click the Stand Alone radio button and click Next.

20. At the Federation Service Name screen, accept the defaults and click Next.

21. At the Summary screen, click Next.

22. A screen appears showing you the installation status.

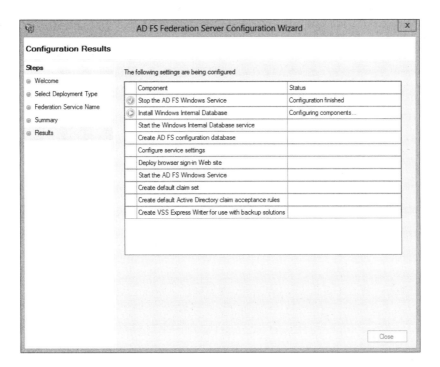

23. When the installation finishes, click Close.

Configuring AD FS

Now that AD FS is installed and running, you need to learn how to configure some of the important options. In AD FS, you can configure trust policies, AD FS agents, and user and group mapping.

AD FS Web Agents   Administrators have the ability to configure a Windows NT token-based Web Agent. To support this feature, Windows Server 2012 AD FS includes a user interface for the AD FS Web Agent role service. The Web Agent account is a service account that calls on other services.

Trust Policies   The *AD FS trust policy* is a file that outlines the set of rules that a Federation Service uses to recognize partners, certificates, account stores, claims, and the other numerous properties that are associated with it. AD FS administrators have the ability to create a federated trust between two organizations. There are two ways to create the federated trust:

- Importing and exporting policy files
- A manual process, which involves the mutual exchange of partner values

In Windows Server 2012, administrators using the export and import features can easily export their trust policy settings to an XML file. They can then send that file to the partner administrator so that the partner administrator can import it. This file provides all of the necessary information, including URIs, claim types, claim mappings, and other values and verification certificates, to create the federated trust between the two partner organizations.

One advantage of using AD FS is that you can integrate AD FS with companies that offer Cloud services. This gives your organization the ability to work with third party vendors in a cloud environment.

User and Group Claim Mapping   In basic terms, *claims* mean that each partnered location agrees and appropriately maps the AD FS trust policy for sharing between federation partner locations. A claim contains user information and helps users connect to a partner's resources. AD FS supports three types of claims:

Identity Claim   This claim type helps identify the user. The identity claim is included within a security token. A security token can contain up to three identity claims.

Group Claim   This claim type indicates membership in a group or role.

Custom Claim   This claim type provides any additional information that needs to be sent. An example might be DepartmentID. This is a custom field that in turn would be a custom claim. A custom claim can provide any attribute that is located in Active Directory.

Active Directory Lightweight Directory Services

Active Directory Lightweight Directory Services (AD LDS) is a Lightweight Directory Access Protocol (LDAP) directory service. *LDAP* is an application protocol used for querying and modifying directory services. This type of service allows directory-enabled applications to store and retrieve data without needing the dependencies AD DS requires.

You can understand LDAP by thinking of directory services as something similar to an address book—a set of names (your objects) that you organize in a logical and hierarchical manner (for example, alphabetically). Each name in the address book has an address and phone number (the attributes of your objects) associated with it. LDAP allows you to query or modify this address book.

Installing AD LDS

In Exercise 7.7, you will install AD LDS by using the Server Manager MMC.

EXERCISE 7.7

Installing AD LDS

1. Open the Server Manager MMC.

2. Click the number 2 link, Add Roles And Features link.

3. If the Before You Begin screen appears, click the Skip This Page By Default check box. Click Next.

4. Choose the role-based or feature-based installation radio button. Click Next.

5. On the Select Destination screen, choose your local server name and click Next.

6. On the Select Server Roles screen, click the Active Directory Lightweight Directory Services check box.

7. When the Add Features dialog box appears, click the Add Features button and then click Next.

8. Click Next at the Select Features screen.

9. Click Next at the AD LDS screen.

10. At the Confirmation screen, click Next.

11. After the installation is complete, click Close.

12. Close Server Manager and reboot.

Configuring AD LDS

Now that you have installed AD LDS, you have to configure it. You have the ability to configure the following:

An Authentication Store   Let's say that you have a web or data server and you want a way to save authorization information for it. Configuring an AD LDS authentication store can help you out in this type of situation. AD LDS works well as an authentication store because it can host user account objects even though they are not Windows security principals. You can authenticate non-Windows security principals by using LDAP simple binds.

The Data within AD LDS   Remember, earlier I said that AD LDS is like an address book, and you can edit who is in that address book by configuring the data within AD LDS. To configure the data within AD LDS, you can use the ADSI edit snap-in tool.

A Migration to AD LDS   What if your company is using an X.500-style directory service that is integrated into your company's legacy applications and you want to move to AD DS? You can use AD LDS to service the legacy applications while using Active Directory for the shared security infrastructure.

To configure AD LDS, you need to set up a service instance (or instance, for short), which is a single running copy of AD LDS. You can have multiple instances as part of a configuration set. The reason for having multiple instances is load balancing and fault tolerance. This way, if one instance becomes unavailable or overloaded, the other instances will pick up the slack.

In Exercise 7.8, you will use the Active Directory Lightweight Directory Services Wizard to set up your first AD LDS instance.

EXERCISE 7.8

Configuring an AD LDS Instance

1. Open the Active Directory Lightweight Directory Services Setup Wizard. You can do this by clicking the Windows key ➢ Administrative Tools ➢ Active Directory Lightweight Directory Services Setup.

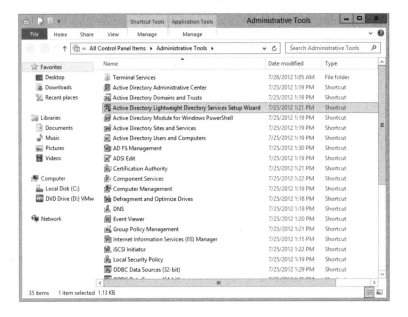

2. The Active Directory Lightweight Directory Services Setup Wizard appears. Click Next.

3. At the Setup Options screen, click the button labeled A Unique Instance. This option is for a new default instance. (If you choose the button labeled A Replica Of An Existing Instance, you will be getting a copy of an instance from another machine.) Click Next.

4. In the Instance Name screen, type the instance name you want to use and click Next.

5. The Ports screen shows the first available ports on the machine. Whatever ports you choose, make sure that any internal firewalls know these port numbers. After you choose ports (or leave the defaults), click Next.

6. On the Application Directory Partition screen, you need to decide whether you want to create a directory partition. For this exercise, choose No, Do Not Create An Application Directory Partition and then click Next.

7. In the File Locations screen, decide where you want to place your database files on your hard drive. For this exercise, leave the defaults and click Next.

8. On the Service Account Selection screen, you need to choose which service account AD LDS will use. This account has to have administrative rights. Choose Network Service Account and click Next.

9. At the AD LDS Administrators screen, choose which account will have the right to administer AD LDS. Choose Currently Logged On User and click Next.

10. On the Importing LDIF Files screen, choose which LDIF (Lightweight Directory Interchange Format) services you want to install. For this exercise, you will not install any services. Click Next.

11. On the Ready To Install screen, look over all your choices before continuing. Click Next.

12. Once the instance installation is complete, click Finish.

Installing AD LDS on Server Core

With Windows Server 2012, you can install Windows Server using a special minimum server installation called Server Core. *Server Core* allows an IT department to install Windows Server 2012 with a low-maintenance server environment that has limited functionality. One of the functions that Server Core can provide is AD LDS.

Because Server Core has limited functionality, it provides some strong benefits, including reduced servicing and management requirements, reduced attack surface, and reduced disk space usage.

Besides AD LDS, Server Core functionality includes the following:

- Active Directory Domain Services (AD DS)
- DNS
- DHCP server
- File server
- Hyper-V
- Media services
- Print server
- Web Services (IIS)

To install the AD LDS role on a Server Core installation, type in the following command at the command prompt:

```
Dism /online /enable-feature /featurename:DirectoryServices-ADAM-ServerCore
```

To uninstall the AD LDS role on a Server Core installation, type in the following command at the command prompt:

```
Dism /online /disable-feature /featurename:DirectoryServices-ADAM-ServerCore
```

Now that we have discussed Active Directory Lightweight Directory Services, let's take a look at the Active Directory Rights Management Services.

Active Directory Rights Management Services

Active Directory Rights Management Services (AD RMS), included with Microsoft Windows Server 2012, allows administrators or users to determine what access (open, read, modify, and so on) they give to other users in an organization. Access restrictions can improve security for email messages, internal websites, and documents.

 To secure documents, Microsoft Office 2003 Professional (Word, Excel, PowerPoint, and Outlook), Microsoft Office 2007 Enterprise, Professional Plus, Ultimate, Microsoft Office 2010 Professional, Professional Plus, or certain versions of Office 2013 is required.

You can apply AD RMS usage policy templates directly to confidential information.

You can install AD RMS easily using Server Manager, and you can administer it through the MMC snap-in. These three new administrative roles allow for delegation of AD RMS responsibilities:

- AD RMS Enterprise Administrators
- AD RMS Template Administrators
- AD RMS Auditors

AD RMS is integrated with AD FS, which means that two organizations can share information without needing AD RMS installed in both organizations. The following list includes some other advantages of using AD RMS:

Self-Enrollment   AD RMS server enrollment allows for the creation and signing of a *server licensor certificate (SLC)*. This SLC gives the AD RMS server the right to issue certificates and licenses whenever they are needed.

AD RMS Administrative Roles   When AD RMS is installed on your server, new administrative roles get created as local security groups. These new administrative roles allow an administrator to manage their AD RMS environment more efficiently. The new AD RMS administrative roles are as follows:

  AD RMS Service Group   When the AD RMS role is installed onto a server, an AD RMS service account is created and added to the AD RMS Service Group. The server uses the service account to start services at the system startup.

  AD RMS Enterprise Administrators   The AD RMS policies and settings are managed by members of the AD RMS Enterprise Administrators group. When AD RMS is installed onto the server, the user account installing the role is automatically added to the AD RMS Enterprise Administrators group. Only administrators who manage RMS should be added to this group.

AD RMS Template Administrators Users who belong to the AD RMS Templates Administrators group are allowed to manage rights policy templates. AD RMS Template Administrators have the rights to read cluster information, list rights policy templates, create new rights policy templates, modify existing rights policy templates, and export rights policy templates.

AD RMS Auditors The AD RMS Auditors role allows administrators who have this right to manage logs and reports. The AD RMS Auditors role is a read-only role that is restricted to running reports available on the AD RMS cluster, reading cluster information, and reading logging settings.

AD RMS Add-On for Internet Explorer If you would like the ability to view but not alter files with restricted permissions using Internet Explorer, you can download the Windows Rights Management Add-on for Internet Explorer. Because you can only view but not alter these restricted files, this prevents sensitive documents, web-based information, and email messages from being forwarded, edited, or copied by unauthorized individuals. In order for you to run the Rights Management Add-on (RMA) for Internet Explorer successfully, you must first install the Windows Rights Management (RM) client.

AD RMS Certificates For AD RMS to work properly, many components must work in conjunction with each other. These components have trusted connections that are implemented by a set of certificates. Making sure that these certificates are valid is a core function of AD RMS technology. The *Extensible rights Markup Language (XrML)* is the XML verbiage used by AD RMS to express usage rights for rights-protected content.

 AD RMS requires an AD RMS–enabled client. Windows Vista, Windows 7, and Windows 8 include the AD RMS client by default. If you are not using Windows Vista, Windows 7, Windows 8, Windows Server 2008, Windows Server 2008 R2, or Windows Server 2012, you can download the AD RMS client for previous versions of Windows from Microsoft's Download Center.

Now that you have a basic understanding of AD RMS, let's take the next step and install it. In Exercise 7.9, you will install AD RMS using the Server Manager MMC.

EXERCISE 7.9

Installing AD RMS

1. Open the Server Manager MMC.

2. Click the number 2 link, Add Roles And Features.

3. If the Before You Begin screen appears, select the Skip This Page By Default check box. Click Next.

4. Choose the role-based or feature-based installation radio button. Click Next.

5. On the Select Destination screen, choose your local server name and click Next.

6. On the Select Server Roles screen, click the Active Directory Rights Management Services check box. A dialog box appears stating that additional services need to be installed. Click the Add Required Role Services button, and then click Next.

7. At the Select Features screen, click Next.

8. At the AD RMS introduction screen, click Next.

9. On the Select Role Services screen, make sure both boxes are checked and click Next.

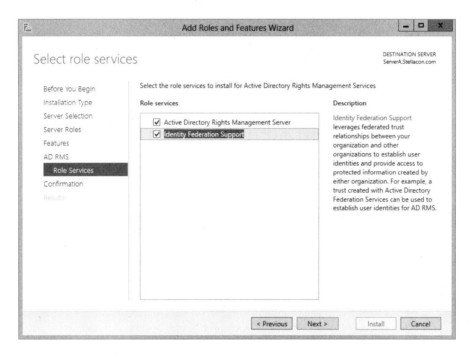

10. At the confirmation screen, click Install.

11. Once the installation is complete, click Close.

12. While still in Server Manager, click the AD RMS link on the left-hand side.

13. Click the More link next to Configuration Required For Active Directory Rights Management Service.

14. Under Action, click the Perform Additional Configuration link.

15. At the AD RMS introduction screen, click Next.

16. On the Create Or Join An AD RMS Cluster screen, choose Create A New AD RMS Cluster. (The other choice will not be available because you are installing the first AD RMS server and must start the cluster.) Click Next.

17. AD RMS uses a database to store configuration and policy information. At the Select Configuration Database screen, choose Use Windows Internal Database on this server. (The other option is to use a third-party database engine or MSSQL.) Click Next.

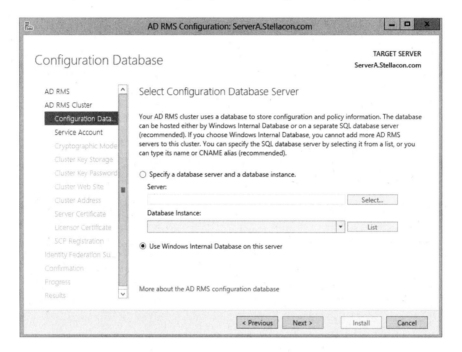

18. On the Specify Service Account screen, choose the service account the AD RMS will use. Click the Specify button, and type in an administrator account and password other than the ones with which you are currently logged in. Click Next.

19. At the Cryptographic Mode screen, choose Cryptographic Mode 2 and click Next.

20. At the Configure AD RMS Cluster Key Storage screen, choose Use AD RMS Centrally Managed Key Storage and click Next.

21. Next you will be asked to enter a password in the AD RMS Cluster Key Password field. The AD RMS cluster key password is used to encrypt the AD RMS cluster key that is stored in the AD RMS database. Type **P@ssw0rd**, confirm it, and then click Next.

22. On the Select Website screen, click default website and click Next. AD RMS needs to be hosted in IIS. This will set up a default website for AD RMS.

23. On the Specify Cluster Address screen, choose whether to use a secure or a non-secure website. Choose Use An SSL-Encrypted Connection (https://) check box. In the Internal Address box, type in the server name and click the Validate button. After the address is verified, click Next.

24. The Choose A Server Authentication Certificate For SSL Encryption screen appears. If you receive a message stating that the certificate for this server is already created, just click Next. If the message doesn't appear, choose one of your certificates and click Next.

25. The Name The Server Licensor Certificate screen appears. Accept the default server and click Next.

26. Next you have the option to register AD RMS now or later. If you register the server now, AD RMS will take effect immediately. If you register the server later, AD RMS will not work until you register. You will not register during this exercise. Choose Register Later and click Next.

27. At the Configure Identity Federation Support screen, specify the name of the web server that Identity Federation will use. Enter the friendly name from step 14, and click the Validate button. The Next button will become available once the server is validated. If an error appears during validation, it will not affect this exercise. Click Next.

28. At the Confirm Installation Selections screen, verify all your settings and click Install.

29. The install progress screen appears. When the install is complete, click Close.

30. Close the Server Manager MMC.

AD RMS Templates

As explained earlier, a template is a mold that you can use over and over again. AD RMS templates are no different. Before you start creating AD RMS templates, you must first create a shared directory where the templates can be stored. An administrator can then create AD RMS rights policy templates on the AD RMS cluster and export those templates to the shared directory.

If your users are connected to the company intranet and they are using AD RMS–enabled applications, they can access the AD RMS templates right from the shared directory as long as they have read access to the shared folder. If your users are not going to be connected to the company intranet, just copy the template to their computers and this will allow AD RMS–enabled applications to continue to function properly.

Summary

In this chapter, I talked about the certificate authority (CA) and explained why you need to use certificates and how to configure them. I discussed how a computer or user gets a certificate through a GPO, auto enrollment, or web enrollment. I then reviewed the steps and reasons for revoking a certificate.

I went on to discuss the Active Directory Domain Services (AD DS) and the advantages of using a read-only domain controller (RODC). After that, I talked about the Active Directory Federation Services (AD FS), which provides Internet-based clients with a secure identity access solution that works on both Windows and non-Windows operating systems.

The chapter continued with a discussion of Active Directory Lightweight Directory Services (AD LDS), a Lightweight Directory Access Protocol (LDAP) directory service. You saw how this type of service allows directory-enabled applications to store and retrieve data without needing the dependencies that AD DS requires.

Finally, I talked about Active Directory Rights Management Services (AD RMS). I explained that the AD RMS is included with Microsoft Windows Server 2012 and how it allows administrators or users to determine what access to give other users in an organization.

Exam Essentials

Understand the concepts behind certificate authority Certificate Authority servers manage certificates. Make sure you that understand why companies use certificate servers and how they work.

Understand certificate enrollment. You need to understand the many different ways to issue certificates to users and computers. You also need to understand the differences between installing certificates using GPOs, auto enrollment, and web enrollment.

Be familiar with the uses of read-only domain controllers. Windows Server 2012 has a type of domain controller called a read-only domain controller (RODC). This gives an organization the ability to install a domain controller in an area or location (on site or off site) that has limited security.

Know when to implement fine-grained password policies. Understand that in Windows Server 2012, you have the ability to have multiple password and account lockout policies. In Microsoft Windows Server 2000 and 2003, when an organization implemented a domain-based password policy, it applied to all users in that domain. Fine-grained password policies allow an organization to have different password and account lockout policies for different sets of users in the same domain.

Understand Active Directory Federation Service. Active Directory Federation Service (AD FS) gives users the ability to do a single sign-on (SSO) and access applications on other networks without needing a secondary password. Organizations can set up trust relationships with other trusted organizations so that a user's digital identity and access rights can be accepted without a secondary password.

Know how to install Active Directory Rights Management Services. Active Directory Rights Management Services (AD RMS), included with Microsoft Windows Server 2012, allows administrators or users to determine what access (open, read, modify, and so on) they give to other users in an organization. This access can be used to secure email messages, internal websites, and documents.

Understand how to configure Active Directory Lightweight Directory Services. You need to know that Active Directory Lightweight Directory Services (AD LDS) is a Lightweight Directory Access Protocol (LDAP) directory service. This type of service allows directory-enabled applications to store and retrieve data without needing the dependencies that AD DS requires.

Review Questions

1. You are the network administrator for the ABC Company. The ABC Company has all Windows Server 2012 Active Directory domains, and it uses an enterprise root certificate server. You need to verify that revoked certificate data is highly available. How should this be accomplished?

   A. Implement a Group Policy object (GPO) that has the Certificate Verification Enabled option.

   B. Using Network Load Balancing, implement an Online Certificate Status Protocol (OCSP) responder.

   C. Implement a Group Policy object (GPO) that enables the Online Certificate Status Protocol (OCSP) responder.

   D. Using Network Load Balancing, implement the Certificate Verification Enabled option.

2. You are the network administrator for your organization. Your company uses a Windows Server 2012 enterprise root CA. The company has issued a new policy that prevents port 443 and port 80 from being opened on domain controllers and on issuing CAs. Your users need to request certificates from a web interface. You have already installed the AD CS role. What do you need to do next?

   A. Configure the Certificate Authority Web Enrollment Service on a member server.

   B. Configure the Certificate Authority Web Enrollment Service on a domain server.

   C. Configure AD FS on a member server to allow secure web-based access.

   D. Configure AD FS on a domain controller to allow secure web-based access.

3. You are the network administrator for your organization. Your company uses a Windows Server 2012 Enterprise certification authority to issue certificates. You need to start using key archival. What should you do?

   A. Implement a distribution CRL.

   B. Install the smart card key retrieval.

   C. Implement a Group Policy object (GPO) that enables the Online Certificate Status Protocol (OCSP) responder.

   D. Archive the private key on the server.

4. You are the administrator for your organization. You have decided to implement certificate authority servers. You have routers located on your network. What component allows systems to receive a certificate even though they do not have an Active Directory account?

   A. Hardware Device Enrollment Service

   B. Network Device Enrollment Service

   C. Router Enrollment Service

   D. Network Hardware Enrollment Service

5. You are the network administrator for your organization. Your organization has two Windows Server 2012 servers, named ServerA and ServerB. ServerA is configured as an enterprise root certificate authority and ServerB has the Online Responder role service installed. You need to configure ServerA to support the Online Responder. What do you do?

    A. Configure a distributed CRL.

    B. Configure the AD FS role on ServerA.

    C. Configure the Authority Information Access (AIA) extension.

    D. Import the root CA key.

6. You are the network administrator for an organization with one main office and one branch office. In the branch office, you deploy a Windows Server 2012 RODC. You need to ensure that users in the branch office can log onto the domain by using the RODC. What should you do?

    A. Configure a password replication policy on the RODC.

    B. Configure authentication replication on the RODC.

    C. Configure authentication replication on the main office domain controller.

    D. Create a new RODC site link to the main office.

7. The administrator for your organization has decided to implement certificates for all of your internal users. What type of root certificate authority (CA) would the administrator implement?

    A. Enterprise

    B. Subordinate

    C. Stand-alone

    D. Web CA

8. You have decided to implement certificate authority (CA) servers, and you want all of your users to receive their certificates automatically without any user intervention. What two ways can you accomplish this goal? Choose all that apply.

    A. Auto enrollment

    B. GPO enrollment

    C. Internet enrollment

    D. Web enrollment

9. Which of the following provides Internet-based clients with a secure identity access solution that works on both Windows and non-Windows operating systems?

    A. Active Directory Federation Services (AD FS)

    B. Active Directory Rights Management Services (AD RMS)

    C. Active Directory Lightweight Directory Services (AD LDS)

    D. Active Directory Domain Services (AD DS)

10. Which of the following allows administrators to configure services for issuing and managing public key certificates, which help organizations implement network security?

A. Active Directory Federation Services (AD FS)

B. Active Directory Rights Management Services (AD RMS)

C. Active Directory Certificate Services (AD CS)

D. Active Directory Domain Services (AD DS)

Chapter

8

Using Virtualization in Windows Server 2012

THE FOLLOWING 70-410 EXAM OBJECTIVES ARE COVERED IN THIS CHAPTER:

✓ **Create and configure virtual machine settings**

   ▪ This objective may include, but is not limited to: Configure dynamic memory; configure smart paging; configure Resource Metering; configure guest integration services.

✓ **Create and configure virtual machine storage**

   ▪ This objective may include, but is not limited to: Create VHDs and VHDX; configure differencing drives; modify VHDs; configure pass-through disks; manage snapshots; implement a virtual Fibre Channel adapter.

✓ **Create and configure virtual networks**

   ▪ This objective may include, but is not limited to: Implement Hyper-V Network Virtualization; configure Hyper-V virtual switches; optimize network performance; configure MAC addresses; configure network isolation; configure synthetic and legacy virtual network adapters.

THE FOLLOWING 70-412 EXAM OBJECTIVES ARE COVERED IN THIS CHAPTER:

✓ **Manage Virtual Machine (VM) movement**

   ▪ This objective may include, but is not limited to: Perform Live Migration; perform quick migration; perform storage migration; import, export, and copy VMs; migrate from other platforms (P2V and V2V).

✓ **Configure site-level fault tolerance**

- This objective may include but is not limited to: Configure Hyper-V Replica including Hyper-V Replica Broker and VMs.

Hyper-V is a new server role in Windows Server 2012 that allows you to virtualize your environment and therefore run multiple virtual operating system instances simultaneously on a physical server. This not only helps you to improve server utilization, it also helps you to create a more cost-effective and dynamic system.

In this chapter, you will learn the basic concepts and features of Hyper-V that a Windows Server 2012 technical specialist must know. You will also get a solid understanding of what is important in virtualization and in what areas of your work life you can use it.

Hyper-V Overview

In the following sections, I'll introduce you to Hyper-V. To begin, we'll take a look at virtualization and what types of virtualization exist. We will then discuss Hyper-V features and the Hyper-V architecture before finishing up with the Hyper-V requirements for software and hardware.

What Is Virtualization?

Virtualization is a method for abstracting physical resources from the way they interact with other resources. For example, if you abstract the physical hardware from the operating system, you get the benefit of being able to move the operating system between different physical systems.

This is called *server virtualization*. But there are also other forms of virtualization available, such as presentation virtualization, desktop virtualization, and application virtualization. I will now briefly explain the differences between these forms of virtualization:

Server Virtualization   This basically enables multiple servers to run on the same physical server. Hyper-V is a server virtualization tool that allows you to move physical machines to virtual machines and manage them on a few physical servers. Thus you will be able to consolidate physical servers.

Presentation Virtualization   When you use *presentation virtualization*, your applications run on a different computer and only the screen information is transferred to your computer. An example of presentation virtualization is Microsoft Remote Desktop Services in Windows Server 2012.

Desktop Virtualization   *Desktop Virtualization* provides you with a virtual machine on your desktop, comparable to server virtualization. You run your complete operating system and applications in a virtual machine so that your local physical machine just needs to run a very basic operating system. An example of this form of virtualization is Microsoft Virtual PC.

Application Virtualization   *Application virtualization* helps prevent conflicts between applications on the same PC. Thus it helps you to isolate the application running environment from the operating system installation requirements by creating application-specific copies of all shared resources, and it helps reduce application-to-application incompatibility and testing needs. An example of an application virtualization tool is Microsoft Application Virtualization (App-V).

Hyper-V Features

As a lead-in to the virtualization topic and Hyper-V, I will start with a list of key features, followed by a list of supported guest operating systems. This should provide you with a quick, high-level view of this feature before we dig deeper into the technology.

Key Features of Hyper-V

The following list provides the key features of Hyper-V:

New Architecture   The hypervisor-based architecture, which has a 64-bit micro-kernel, provides a new array of device support as well as performance and security improvements.

Operating System Support   Both 32-bit and 64-bit operating systems can run simultaneously in Hyper-V. Also, different platforms like Windows, Linux, and others are supported.

Support for Symmetric Multiprocessors   Support for up to four processors in a virtual machine environment provides you with the ability to run applications as well as multiple virtual machines faster.

Network Load Balancing   Hyper-V provides support for *Windows Network Load Balancing (NLB)* to balance the network load across virtual machines on different servers.

New Hardware Architecture   Hyper-V's new architecture provides improved utilization of resources like networking and disks.

Quick Migration   Hyper-V's *quick migration* feature provides you with the functionality to run virtual machines in a clustered environment with switchover capabilities when there is a failure. Thus you can reduce downtime and achieve higher availability of your virtual machines.

Virtual Machine Snapshot   You can take snapshots of running virtual machines, which provides you with the capability to recover to any previous virtual machine snapshot state quickly and easily.

Resource Metering   Hyper-V *resource metering* allows an organization to track usage within the businesses departments. It allows an organization to create a usage-based billing solution that adjusts to the provider's business model and strategy.

Scripting   Using the Windows Management Instrumentation (WMI) interfaces and APIs, you can easily build custom scripts to automate processes in your virtual machines.

Fibre Channel   The virtual Fibre Channel feature allows you to connect to the Fibre Channel storage unit from within the virtual machine. *Virtual Fibre Channel* allows an administrator to use their existing Fibre Channel to support virtualized workloads. Hyper-V users have the ability to use Fibre Channel storage area networks (SANs) to virtualize the workloads that require direct access to SAN logical unit numbers (LUNs).

Dynamic Memory   *Dynamic Memory* is a new feature of Hyper-V that allows it to balance memory automatically among running virtual machines. Dynamic Memory allows Hyper-V to adjust the amount of memory available to the virtual machines in response to the needs of the virtual machine. It is currently available for Hyper-V in Windows Server 2012.

Supported Guest Operating Systems

The following guest operating systems have been successfully tested on Hyper-V and are hypervisor-aware. Table 8.1 shows all of the guest server operating systems and the maximum number of virtual processors. Table 8.2 shows all of the guest client operating systems and the maximum number of virtual processors.

TABLE 8.1   Hyper-V guest server operating systems

Guest Operating System (Server)	Maximum Number of Virtual Processors
Windows Server 2012	64
Windows Server 2008 R2 with Service Pack 1 (SP 1)	64
Windows Server 2008 R2	64
Windows Server 2008 with Service Pack 2 (SP 2)	8
Windows Home Server 2011	4
Windows Small Business Server 2011	Essentials edition: 2 Standard edition: 4
Windows Server 2003 R2 with Service Pack 2 (SP2)	2
Windows Server 2003 with Service Pack 2 (SP 2)	2
Red Hat Enterprise Linux 5.7 and 5.8	64
Red Hat Enterprise Linux 6.0–6.3	64
SUSE Linux Enterprise Server 11 SP2	64

TABLE 8.1 Hyper-V guest server operating systems *(continued)*

Guest Operating System (Server)	Maximum Number of Virtual Processors
Open SUSE 12.1	64
Ubuntu 12.04	64

TABLE 8.2 Hyper-V guest client operating systems

Guest Operating System (Client)	Maximum Number of Virtual Processors
Windows 8	32
Windows 7 with Service Pack 1 (SP 1)	4
Windows 7	4
Windows Vista with Service Pack 2 (SP2)	2
Windows XP with Service Pack 3 (SP3)	2
Windows XP x64 Edition with Service Pack 2 (SP 2)	2
CentOS 5.7 and 5.8	64
CentOS 6.0–6.3	64
Red Hat Enterprise Linux 5.7 and 5.8	64
Red Hat Enterprise Linux 6.0–6.3	64
SUSE Linux Enterprise Server 11 SP2	64
Open SUSE 12.1	64
Ubuntu 12.04	64

The list of supported guest operating systems may always be extended. Please check the official Microsoft Hyper-V site to get a current list of supported operating systems: www.microsoft.com/virtualization.

Hyper-V Architecture

This section will provide you with an overview of the Hyper-V architecture (see Figure 8.1). I'll explain the differences between a hypervisor-aware and non-hypervisor-aware child partition.

FIGURE 8.1 Hyper-V architecture

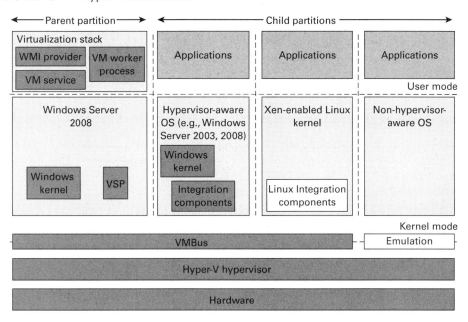

As you can see, Hyper-V is based on the new microkernel architecture. Hyper-V provides a virtualization layer called a *hypervisor* that runs directly on the system hardware. You can see that the hypervisor is similar to what the kernel is to Windows. It is a software layer responsible for the interaction with the core hardware and works in conjunction with an optimized instance of Windows Server 2012 that allows running multiple operating systems on a physical server simultaneously. The Hyper-V architecture consists of the hypervisor and parent and child partitions.

The Windows Server 2012 operating system runs in the parent partition and provides the WMI provider for scripting as well as the VM service.

Virtual machines each run in their own child partitions. Child partitions do not have direct access to hardware resources; instead, they have a virtual view of the resources, which are called *virtual devices*.

If you're running a hypervisor-aware operating system like Windows Server 2003, Windows Server 2008, Windows Server 2008 R2, or Windows Server 2012 in your virtual machine, any request to the virtual devices is redirected via the high-speed bus to the devices in the parent partition, which will manage the requests.

By default, only Windows Server 2008 R2 and 2012 are hypervisor-aware operating systems. Once you install the Hyper-V Integration Components on an operating system other than Windows Server 2008 R2 and above, it will be hypervisor aware. Microsoft provides a hypervisor adapter to make Linux hypervisor aware.

Non-hypervisor-aware operating systems (for example, Windows NT 4.0) use an emulator to communicate with the Windows hypervisor, which is slower than using the Imbues.

Hyper-V Requirements

The following sections will describe the hardware and software requirements for installing the Hyper-V server role. It is important to understand these requirements for obtaining your software license as well as for planning for server hardware. When you understand the requirements, you can design and configure a Hyper-V solution that will meet the needs of your applications.

Hardware Requirements

In addition to the basic hardware requirements for Windows Server 2012, there are requirements for running the Hyper-V server role on your Windows server. They are listed in Table 8.3.

TABLE 8.3   Hardware requirements for Hyper-V

Requirement Area	Definition
CPU	x64-compatible processor with Intel VT or AMD-V technology enabled. Hardware Data Execution Prevention (DEP), specifically Intel XD bit (execute disable bit) or AMD NX bit (no execute bit), must be available and enabled. Minimum: 1.4 GHz. Recommended: 2 GHz or faster.
Memory	Minimum: 1 GB RAM. Recommended: 2 GB RAM or greater. (Additional RAM is required for each running guest operating system.) Maximum: 1 TB
Hard disk	Minimum: 8 GB. Recommended: 20 GB or greater. (Additional disk space needed for each guest operating system.)

The Add Roles Wizard in Server Manager additionally verifies the hardware requirements. A good starting point is to check your hardware against the Microsoft hardware list to make sure Windows Server 2012 supports your hardware. If you try to install the Hyper-V server role on a computer that does not meet the CPU requirements, you'll get a warning window that looks like Figure 8.2.

FIGURE 8.2   Warning window that Hyper-V cannot be installed

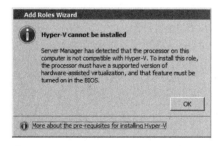

Software Requirements

To use virtualization in Windows Server 2012, you need to consider the basic software requirements for Hyper-V. Hyper-V runs only on the following editions of the Windows Server 2012 operating system:

- Windows Server 2012 Standard edition
- Windows Server 2012 Datacenter edition
- Microsoft Hyper-V Server 2012 edition

Hyper-V Installation and Configuration

The following sections explain how to install the Hyper-V role using Server Manager in Windows Server 2012 Full installation mode, or the command line mode in Windows Server 2012 Server Core. We will then take a look at Hyper-V as part of Server Manager before discussing how to use the Hyper-V Manager. Finally, we will look at the Hyper-V server settings and then cover two important areas for Hyper-V: virtual networks and virtual hard disks.

Install the Hyper-V Role

Now it's time to see how to install the Hyper-V server role on the two installation options of Windows Server 2012, namely a Full installation and Server Core installation.

Installing Hyper-V in Full Installation Mode

You can install the Hyper-V server role on any Windows Server 2012 installation for which the Full option was chosen. In addition, the server must meet both the hardware and software requirements. The installation process is simple, as Exercise 8.1 demonstrates.

EXERCISE 8.1

Installing Hyper-V in Full Installation Mode

1. Open Server Manager.

2. In Server Manager, choose number 2, Add Roles And Features.

3. At the Select Installation Type page, choose the role-based or feature-based installation. Click Next.

4. On the Select Destination Server screen, choose Select A Server From The Server Pool and choose the server to which you want to add this role. Click Next.

5. On the Select Server Roles screen, click the check box next to Hyper-V. When the Add Features dialog box appears, click the Add Features button. Then click Next.

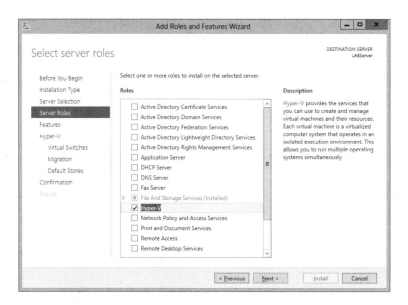

6. At the Select Features screen, just click Next.

7. At the Hyper-V introduction screen, just click Next.

8. At the Create Virtual Switches screen, choose your adapter and click Next.

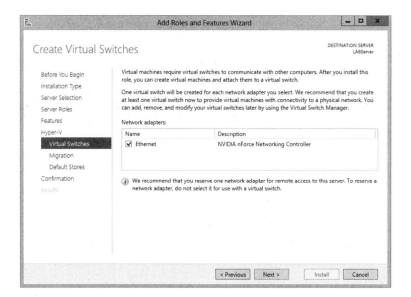

9. At the Virtual Machine Migration screen, just click Next. You want to use migration only if you have multiple Hyper-V servers. Since we will have only one for this exercise, just skip this screen.

10. At the Default Stores screen, accept the defaults and click Next.

11. At the Confirmation screen, click the Install button.

12. After the installation is complete, click the Close button.

13. Restart your server.

Installing Hyper-V in Server Core

The Server Core installation option is introduced in Windows Server 2012. It creates an operating system installation without a GUI shell. You can either manage the server remotely from another system or use the Server Core's command-line interface.

This installation option provides the following benefits:

- Reduces attack surface (because fewer applications are running on the server)
- Reduces maintenance and management (because only the required options are installed)
- Requires less disk space and produces less processor utilization
- Provides a minimal parent partition
- Reduces system resources required by the operating system as well as the attack surface

By using Hyper-V on a Server Core installation, you can fundamentally improve availability because the attack surface is reduced and downtime required for installing patches is optimized. It will thus be more secure and reliable with less management.

To install Hyper-V for a Windows Server 2012 installation, you must execute the following command in the command-line interface:

```
start /w ocsetup Microsoft-Hyper-V
```

Because the ocsetup command is case sensitive, make sure you write `Microsoft-Hyper-V` exactly as shown. Otherwise you will get an error message and Hyper-V won't be added as a server role.

To install Hyper-V on a Windows Server 2012 server, you can use the `DISM` command:

```
Dism /online /enable-feature /featurename:Microsoft-Hyper-V
```

Hyper-V in Server Manager

As with all of the other Windows Server 2012 roles, the Hyper-V role neatly integrates into Server Manager. Server Manager filters the information just for the specific role and thus displays only the required information. As you can see in Figure 8.3, the Hyper-V Summary page shows related event log entries, the state of the system services for Hyper-V, and useful resources and support.

FIGURE 8.3 Hyper-V in Server Manager

Using Hyper-V Manager

Hyper-V Manager is the central management console to configure your server and create and manage your virtual machines, virtual networks, and virtual hard disks. Unlike Virtual Server 2005, where you managed all virtual machines through a Web interface, Hyper-V Manager is managed through a Microsoft Management Console (MMC) snap-in. You can access it either in Server Manager or by using Administrative Tools ➢ Hyper-V Manager. Figure 8.4 shows how Hyper-V Manager looks once you start it.

FIGURE 8.4 Hyper-V Manager

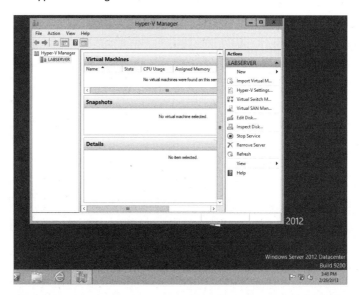

Hyper-V Manager is available for the following operating systems:

- Windows Server 2012
- Windows Server 2008 R2
- Windows Server 2008
- Windows 8
- Windows 7
- Windows Vista with Service Pack 1 (SP1)

Hyper-V Manager is installed on a Windows Server 2012 machine only when you install Hyper-V on it. On Windows Server 2008/2008 R2, Server 2003, Windows Vista, Windows 7, or Windows 8, you will need to install the Hyper-V Manager MMC.

You can use Hyper-V Manager to connect to any Full or Server Core installation remotely. Besides Hyper-V Manager, you can use the WMI interface for scripting Hyper-V.

Configure Hyper-V Settings

In this section, you will get an overview of the available Hyper-V settings for the server. You configure all server-side default configuration settings like default locations of your configuration files or the release key. You can open the Hyper-V Settings page (see Figure 8.5) in Hyper-V Manager by clicking Hyper-V Settings in the Actions pane.

FIGURE 8.5   Hyper-V Settings

The Hyper-V Settings page includes the following settings:

Virtual Hard Disks   Specifies the default location of your virtual hard disk files (.vhd).

Virtual Machines   Specifies the default location of your virtual machine configuration files. It includes the Virtual Machine XML configuration files (part of the Virtual Machines folder) as well as related snapshots (part of the Snapshot folder).

Physical GPUs   This feature allows for a Graphical Processing Unit (GPU) accelerated video within a virtual machine. The GPU will allow you to support 3D GPU accelerated graphics.

NUMA Spanning   An administrator can configure Hyper-V to allow virtual machines to span non-uniform memory architecture (NUMA) nodes. When the physical computer has NUMA nodes, this setting provides virtual machines with additional computing resources. Spanning NUMA nodes can help you run more virtual machines at the same time. However, using NUMA can decrease overall performance.

Live Migrations   *Live migration* allows a Hyper-V administrator to relocate running virtual machines easily from one node of the failover cluster to another node in the same cluster. Live Migration is explained in more detail later in this chapter.

Storage Migrations   *Storage Migration* allows an administrator to move their virtual machine storage from one location to another. This setting allows you to specify how many storage migrations can be performed at the same time on this system.

Replication Configuration   This setting allows you to configure this computer as a Replica Server to another Hyper-V server. Hyper-V Replica allows administrators to replicate their Hyper-V virtual machines from one Hyper-V host at a primary site to another Hyper-V host at the Replica site.

Each node of the failover cluster that is involved in Replica must have the Hyper-V server role installed. One of the servers in the Hyper-V replication needs to be set up as a Replica Broker to allow the replication to work properly.

Keyboard   Defines how to use Windows key combinations. Options are Physical Computer, Virtual Machine, and Virtual Machine Only When Running Full Screen.

Mouse Release Key   Specifies the key combination to release the mouse in your virtual machine. Options are Ctrl+Alt+left arrow, Ctrl+Alt+right arrow, Ctrl+Alt+space, and Ctrl+Alt+Shift.

Reset Check Boxes   Resets any check boxes that hide pages and messages when checked. This will bring any window up again on which you checked the Do Not Show This Window Again check box.

Manage Virtual Switches

A *virtual network* provides the virtual links between nodes in either a virtual or a physical network. Virtual networking in Hyper-V is provided in a secure and dynamic way because you can granularly define virtual network switches for their required usage. For example, you can define a private or internal virtual network if you don't want to allow your virtual machines to send packages to the physical network.

In order to allow your virtual machines to communicate with each other, you need virtual networks. Just like normal networks, virtual networks exist only on the host computer and allow you to configure how virtual machines communicate with each other, with the host, and with the network or the Internet. You manage virtual networks in Hyper-V using Virtual Switch Manager, shown in Figure 8.6.

FIGURE 8.6   Virtual Network Manager

Using *Virtual Switch Manager*, you can create, manage, and delete virtual switches. You can define the network type as external, internal only, or private:

External   Any virtual machine connected to this virtual switch can access the physical network. You would use this option if you want to allow your virtual machines to access, for example, other servers on the network or the Internet. This option is used in production environments where your clients connect directly to the virtual machines.

Internal   This option allows virtual machines to communicate with each other as well as the host system but not with the physical network. When you create an internal network, it also creates a local area connection in Network Connections that allows the host machine to communicate with the virtual machines. You can use this if you want to separate your host's network from your virtual networks.

Private   When you use this option, virtual machines can communicate with each other but not with the host system or the physical network; thus no network packets are hitting the wire. You can use this to define internal virtual networks for test environments or labs, for example.

On the external and internal-only virtual networks, you also can enable virtual LAN (VLAN) identification. You can use VLANs to partition your network into multiple subnets using a VLAN ID. When you enable virtual LAN identification, the NIC that is connected to the switch will never see packets tagged with VLAN IDs. Instead, all packets traveling from the NIC to the switch will be tagged with the access mode VLAN ID as they leave the switch port. All packets traveling from the switch port to the NIC will have their VLAN tags removed. You can use this if you are already logically segmenting your physical machines and also use it for your virtual ones.

Exercise 8.2 explains how to create an internal-only virtual switch.

EXERCISE 8.2

Creating an Internal Virtual Network

1.   Click the Windows Key ➢ Administrative Tools ➢ Hyper-V Manager.

2.   In Hyper-V Manager, in the Actions pane, choose Virtual Switch Manager.

3.   On the Virtual Switch page, select Private and click the Create Virtual Switch button.

4.   On the New Virtual Switch page, enter `Private Virtual Network` in the Name field.

5.   Click OK.

When you create the internal virtual switch, a network device is created in Network Connections, as shown in Figure 8.7.

This is also the case when you create an external virtual network, because it will replace the physical network card of the host machine to give the parent partition a virtual network card that is also used in the child partitions.

Unlike with Virtual Server 2005, Hyper-V binds the virtual network service to a physical network adapter only when an external virtual network is created. The benefit of this is that the performance is better if you do not use the external virtual network option. The downside, however, is that there will be a network disruption when you create or delete an external virtual network.

FIGURE 8.7   Virtual network card

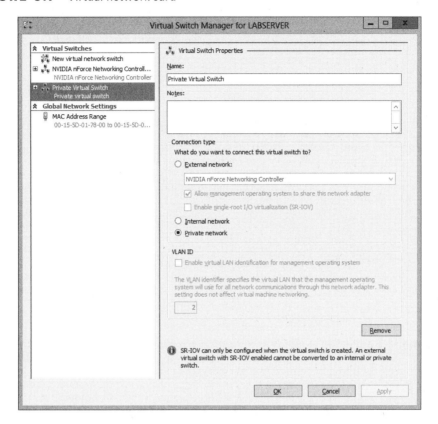

Communication between the virtual machine and the local host computer is not configured automatically. Once you install a virtual machine, you need to make sure that the TCP/IP settings are in agreement with the settings you define in the virtual network card. Start with a ping from your host machine to the virtual machines to verify that communication is working.

Managing Virtual Hard Disks

In addition to virtual networks, you need to manage virtual hard disks that you attach to your virtual machines. A virtual hard disk in Hyper-V, apart from a pass-through disk, is a VHD file that basically simulates a hard drive to your virtual machine.

The following sections will first show you what types of virtual hard disks are available and then show you how to create them. You will also learn about what options are available to manage virtual hard disks.

Types of Hard Disks

Depending on how you want to use the disk, Hyper-V offers various types, as described in Table 8.4.

TABLE 8.4 Virtual hard disks in Hyper-V

Type of Disk	Description	When to Use It
Dynamically expanding	This disk starts with a small VHD file and expands it on demand once an installation takes place. It can grow to the maximum size you defined during creation. You can use this type of disk to clone a local hard drive during creation.	This option is effective when you don't know the exact space needed on the disk and when you want to preserve hard disk space on the host machine. Unfortunately, it is the slowest disk type.
Fixed size	The size of the VHD file is fixed to the size specified when the disk is created. This option is faster than a dynamically expanding disk. However, a fixed-size disk uses up the maximum defined space immediately. This type is ideal for cloning a local hard drive.	A fixed-size disk provides faster access than dynamically expanding or differencing disks, but it is slower than a physical disk.
Differencing	This type of disk is associated in a parent-child relationship with another disk. The differencing disk is the child and the associated virtual disk is the parent. Differencing disks include only the differences to the parent disk. By using this type, you can save a lot of disk space in similar virtual machines. This option is suitable if you have multiple virtual machines with similar operating systems.	Differencing disks are most commonly found in test environments and should not be used in production environments.
Physical (or pass-through disk)	The virtual machine receives direct pass-through access to the physical disk for exclusive use. This type provides the highest performance of all disk types and thus should be used for production servers where performance is the top priority. The drive is not available for other guest systems.	This type is used in high-end datacenters to provide optimum performance for VMs. It's also used in failover cluster environments.

Creating Virtual Hard Disks

To help you gain practice in creating virtual hard disks, the following three exercises will teach you how to create a differencing hard disk, how to clone an existing disk by creating a new disk, and how to configure a physical or pass-through disk to your virtual machine. First, in Exercise 8.3, you will learn how to create a differencing virtual hard disk.

EXERCISE 8.3

Creating a Differencing Hard Disk

1. Open Hyper-V Manager.

2. In Hyper-V Manager, on the Actions pane, choose New ➢ Hard Disk.

3. In the New Virtual Hard Disk Wizard, click Next on the Before You Begin page.

4. At the Choose Disk Format screen, VHDX and click Next. The size of your VHDs, depends on which format you choose. If you're going to have a VHD larger than 2,040 GB, use VHDX. If your VHD is less than 2,040 GB, then you should use VHD.

5. On the Choose Disk Type page, select Fixed size and click Next.

6. On the Specify Name And Location page, enter the new name of the child disk (for example, newvirtualharddisk.vhd). You can also modify the default location of the new VHD file if you want. Click Next to continue.

7. Next, on the Configure Disk page, you need to specify the size of the VHD file. Choose a size based on your hard disk, and then click Next to continue. I used 60GB as our test size.

8. On the Completing The New Virtual Hard Disk Wizard page, verify that all settings are correct and click Finish to create the hard disk.

The process to add a physical or pass-through disk to a virtual machine is quite different. For this, first you need to create the virtual machine, and then you open the virtual machine settings to configure the physical disk. If you want to add a physical disk to a virtual machine, the physical disk must be set as Offline in Disk Management, as shown in Figure 8.8.

FIGURE 8.8 In Disk Management, you can set disks as Offline.

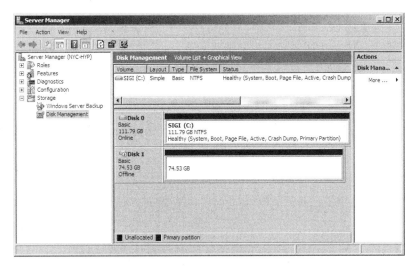

To access Disk Management, click the Windows key and choose Administrative Tools ➤ Computer Management, and then expand Storage in the left pane and click Disk Management.

 You cannot share a physical disk among multiple virtual machines or with the host system.

Physical or pass-through disks might not be that important if your use of virtualization is based on test environments, but they become crucial when you need to plan for highly available virtual datacenters. This is especially true if you consider using failover clusters to provide the Quick Migration feature, which is when you should consider matching one logical unit number (LUN) from your enterprise storage system or storage area network (SAN) as one physical disk. This provides you with the optimum performance you need in such an environment.

Managing Virtual Hard Disks

Hyper-V also provides two tools to manage virtual hard disks: Inspect Disk and Edit Disk. These tools are available on the Actions pane in Hyper-V Manager:

Inspect Disk   This provides you with information about the virtual hard disk. It shows you not only the type of the disk but also information like the maximum size for dynamically expanding disks and the parent VHD for differencing disks.

Edit Disk   This provides you with the Edit Virtual Hard Disk Wizard, which you can use to compact, convert, expand, merge, or reconnect hard disks. Figure 8.9 shows you the wizard's options when you select a dynamically expanding disk.

FIGURE 8.9   The Edit Virtual Hard Disk Wizard

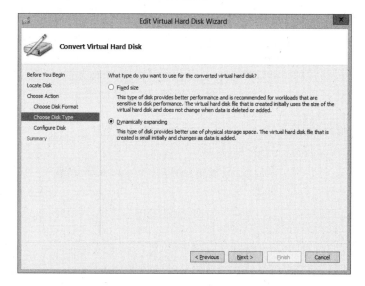

Table 8.5 provides you with an overview of what you can do with the wizard.

TABLE 8.5 Edit Disk overview

Action	Description
Compact	Reduces the size of a dynamically expanding or differencing disk by removing blank space from deleted files.
Convert	Converts a dynamically expanding disk to a fixed disk or vice versa.
Expand	Increases the storage capacity of a dynamically expanding disk or a fixed virtual hard disk.
Merge	Merges the changes from a differencing disk into either the parent disk or another disk (applies to differencing disks only!).
Reconnect	If a differencing disk no longer finds its referring parent disk, this option can reconnect the parent to the disk.

Configuring Virtual Machines

The following sections cover the topics of creating and managing virtual machines as well as how to back up and restore virtual machines using features like Import and Export and Snapshot. We'll also briefly look at Hyper-V's Live Migration feature.

Creating and Managing Virtual Machines

It is important to learn how to create a virtual machine, how to change its configuration, and how to delete it. We will take a look at the Virtual Machine Connection tool and install the Hyper-V Integration Components onto a virtual machine.

Virtual Machines

Virtual machines define the child partitions in which you run operating system instances. Each virtual machine is separate and can communicate with the others only by using a virtual network. You can assign hard drive(s), virtual network(s), DVD drives, and other system components to it. A virtual machine is similar to an existing physical server, but it no longer runs on dedicated hardware—it shares the hardware of the host system with the other virtual machines that run on the host.

Exercise 8.4 shows you how to create a new virtual machine.

EXERCISE 8.4

Creating a New Virtual Machine

1. Open Hyper-V Manager.

2. In Hyper-V Manager, on the Actions pane, choose New ➤ Virtual Machine.

3. In the New Virtual Machine Wizard, click Next on the Before You Begin page.

4. On the Specify Name And Location page, give your virtual machine a name and change the default location of the virtual machine configuration files. Click Next to continue.

5. On the Assign Memory page, define how much of your host computer's memory you want to assign to this virtual machine. Remember that once your virtual machine uses up all of your physical memory, it will start swapping to disk, thus reducing the performance of all virtual machines. Click Next to continue.

6. On the Configure Networking page, select the virtual network that you previously configured using Virtual Network Manager. Click Next to continue.

7. On the next page, you configure your virtual hard disk. You can create a new virtual hard disk, select an existing disk, or choose to attach the hard disk later. Be aware that you can create only a dynamically expanding virtual disk on this page; you cannot create a differencing, physical, or fixed virtual hard disk there. However, if you created the virtual hard disk already, you can, of course, select it. Click Next to continue.

8. On the Installation Options page, you can select how you want to install your operating system. You have the option to install an operating system later, install the operating system from a boot CD/DVD-ROM where you can select a physical device or an image file (ISO file), install an operating system from a floppy disk image (VFD file, or a virtual boot floppy disk), or install an operating system from a network-based installation server. The last option will install a legacy network adapter to your virtual machine so that you can boot from the network adapter. Select Install An Operating System Later and then click Next.

9. On the Completing The New Virtual Machine Wizard summary page, verify that all settings are correct. You also have the option to start the virtual machine immediately after creation. Click Next to create the virtual machine.

10. Repeat this process and create a few more virtual machines.

11. If you want to install an operating system on one of the VMs, start the VM, load a Windows Server 2012 installation disk into the DVD drive, and then, under the Media menu, choose DVD and Capture. Then just do a normal install.

After completing Exercise 8.4, you will have a virtual machine available in Hyper-V Manager. Initially, the state of the virtual machine will be Off. Virtual machines can have the following states: Off, Starting, Running, Paused, and Saved. You can change the state of a virtual machine in the Virtual Machines pane by right-clicking the virtual machine's name, as shown in Figure 8.10, or by using the Virtual Machine Connection window.

FIGURE 8.10   Options available when right-clicking a virtual machine

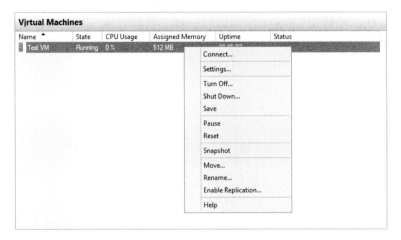

Here is a list of some of the state options (when the VM is running) available for a virtual machine:

Start   Turn on the virtual machine. This is similar to pressing the power button when the machine is turned off. This option is available when your virtual machine is Off or in Saved state.

Turn Off   Turn off the virtual machine. This is similar to pressing the power off button on the computer. This option is available when your virtual machine is in Running, Saved, or Paused state.

Shut Down   This option shuts down your operating system. You need to have the Hyper-V Integration Components installed on the operating system; otherwise, Hyper-V will not be able to shut down the system.

Save   The virtual machine is saved to disk in its current state. This option is available when your virtual machine is Running or in Paused state.

Pause   Pause the current virtual machine, but do not save the state to disk. You can use this option to release processor utilization quickly from this virtual machine to the host system.

Reset   Reset the virtual machine. This is like pressing the reset button on your computer. You will lose the current state and any unsaved data in the virtual machine. This option is available when your virtual machine is Running or in Paused state.

Resume   When your virtual machine is paused, you can resume it and bring it online again.

Changing Configuration on an Existing Virtual Machine

To change the configuration settings on an existing virtual machine, you right-click your virtual machine's name in the Virtual Machines pane in Hyper-V Manager and choose Settings. You can change settings like memory allocation and hard drive configuration. All items that you can configure are described in the following list:

Add Hardware   Add devices to your virtual machine, namely a SCSI controller, a network adapter, or a legacy network adapter. A legacy network adapter is required if you want to perform a network-based installation of an operating system.

BIOS   This is the replacement of the virtual machine's BIOS. Because you can no longer enter the BIOS during startup, you need to configure it with this setting. You can turn Num Lock on or off and change the basic startup order of the devices.

Memory   Change the amount of random access memory (RAM) allocated to the virtual machine.

Processor   Change the number of logical processors this virtual machine can use and define resource control to balance resources among virtual machines by using a relative weight.

IDE Controller   Add/change and remove devices from the IDE controller. You can have hard drives or DVD drives as devices. Every IDE controller can have up to two devices attached, and by default, you have two IDE controllers available.

Hard Drive   Select a controller to attach to this device as well as specify the media to use with your virtual hard disk. The available options are Virtual Hard Disk (.vhd), File (with additional buttons labeled New, Edit, Inspect, and Browse that are explained in the virtual hard disk section), and Physical Hard Disk. You can also remove the device here.

DVD Drive   Select a controller to attach to this device and specify the media to use with your virtual CD/DVD drive. The available options are None, Image File (ISO Image), and Physical CD/DVD Drive Connected To The Host Computer. You also can remove the device here.

SCSI Controller   Configure all hard drives that are connected to the SCSI controller. You can add up to 63 hard drives to each SCSI controller, and you can have multiple SCSI controllers available.

Network Adapter   Specify the configuration of the network adapter or remove it. You can also configure the virtual network and MAC address for each adapter and enable virtual LAN identification.

COM 1 and Com 2   Configure the virtual COM port to communicate with the physical computer through a named pipe. You have COM1 and COM2 available.

Diskette   Specify a virtual floppy disk file to use.

Name   Edit the name of the virtual machine and provide some notes about it.

Integration Services   Define what integration services are available to your virtual machine. Options are Operating System Shutdown, Time Synchronization, Data Exchange, Heartbeat, and Backup (Volume Snapshot).

Snapshot File Location   Define the default file location of your snapshot files.

Smart Paging File Location   This area allows you to set up a paging file for your virtual machine.

Windows Server 2012 has introduced a new Hyper-V feature called *Smart Paging*. If you have a virtual machine that has a smaller amount of memory than what it needs for startup memory, when the virtual machine gets restarted, Hyper-V then needs additional memory to restart the virtual machine. Smart Paging is used to bridge the memory gap between minimum memory and startup memory. This allows your virtual machines to restart properly.

Automatic Start   Define what this virtual machine will do when the physical computer starts. Options are Nothing, Automatically Start If The Service Was Running, and Always Start This Virtual Machine. You also can define a start delay here.

Automatic Stop   Define what this virtual machine will do when the physical computer shuts down. Options are Save State, Turn Off, and Shut Down.

 Please be aware that only some settings can be changed when the virtual machine's state is Running. It is best practice to shut down the virtual machine before you modify any setting.

Deleting Virtual Machines

You can also delete virtual machines using Hyper-V Manager. This deletes all of the configuration files, as shown in Figure 8.11.

FIGURE 8.11   Delete Virtual Machine warning window

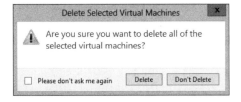

Make sure you manually delete any virtual disks that were part of the virtual machines to free up disk space. Virtual disks are *not* deleted when you delete a virtual machine.

Virtual Machine Connection

Similar to the Virtual Machine Remote Control (VMRC) client that was available with Virtual Server 2005 R2 and previous versions, Hyper-V comes with Virtual Machine Connection to connect to virtual machines that run on a local or remote server.

You can use it to log onto the virtual machine and use your computer's mouse and keyboard to interact with the virtual machine. You can open Virtual Machine Connection in Hyper-V Manager by double-clicking a virtual machine or right-clicking a virtual machine and selecting Connect. If your virtual machine is turned off, you might see a window similar to the one in Figure 8.12.

FIGURE 8.12   Virtual Machine Connection window when the machine is turned off

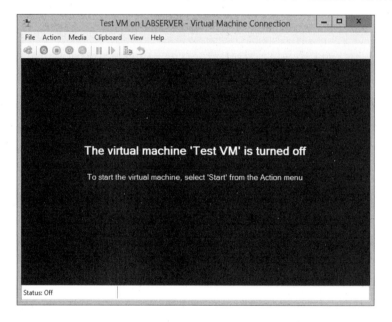

Virtual Machine Connection provides you with functionality similar to that of Hyper-V Manager, such as being able to change the state of a virtual machine, but it also provides you with additional features that are especially useful when you want to work with a virtual machine:

File Access Settings or Exit Virtual Machine Connection   Change the state of a virtual machine and create or revert a snapshot. Additionally, you have the options to send Ctrl+Alt+Delete to your virtual machine and Insert Integration Services Setup Disk.

Context-Sensitive Buttons Provide Quick Access to Key Features   These buttons are available under the menu bar to provide you with fast access to the most important features, as you can see in Figure 8.13. It shows the connection of a running VM, but the VM has not had an operating system installed yet and the figure shows the Windows Setup screen.

FIGURE 8.13 Virtual Machine Connection window showing a running Windows Server 2012 virtual machine

Installing Hyper-V Integration Components

Hyper-V *Integration Components*, also called *Integration Services*, are required to make your guest operating system "hypervisor aware." Similar to the VM Additions that were part of Microsoft Virtual Server 2005, these components improve the performance of the guest operating system once they are installed. From the architectural perspective, virtual devices are redirected directly via the VMBus, thus quicker access to resources and devices is provided.

If you do not install the Hyper-V Integration Components, the guest operating system uses emulation to communicate with the host's devices, which of course makes the guest operating system slower.

Exercise 8.5 shows you how to install Hyper-V Integration Components on one of your virtual machines running Windows Server 2012.

EXERCISE 8.5

Installing Hyper-V Integration Components

1. Open Hyper-V Manager.

2. In Hyper-V Manager, in the Virtual Machines pane, right-click the virtual machine on which you want to install Hyper-V Integration Components and click Start.

3. Right-click the virtual machine again and click Connect. Meanwhile, your virtual machine should already be booting.

4. If you need to log into the operating system of your virtual machine, you should do so.

5. Once the Windows Desktop appears, you need to select Insert Integration Services Setup Disk from the Actions menu of your Virtual Machine Connection window.

6. Once the Hyper-V Integration Components are installed, you are asked to perform a reboot.

After the reboot, Hyper-V Integration Components are installed on your operating system, and you will be able to use them.

Back Up and Restore Virtual Machines

The following sections cover exporting and importing virtual machines between host machines as well as taking a snapshot to back up a certain state of your virtual machine. I will also briefly discuss Quick Migration and Live Migration and how Hyper-V uses them.

Exporting and Importing Virtual Machines

This section explains how to move virtual machines between host computers or move them to a different drive. This is quite different from previous versions of Microsoft's virtualization software. To move a virtual machine in Virtual Server 2005, you stopped the machine and moved its configuration file (VMC) as well as its virtual hard disk file (VHD) to the target location, and then you changed the VMC file to point to the VHD file.

Using Hyper-V, you can no longer move the configuration files. You need to use the Export feature to export the virtual machine and then use Import on the target machine to import the virtual machine to Hyper-V.

To export a virtual machine, it must be either in the Off or Saved state. Open Hyper-V Manager, select the virtual machine that you want to export, and either right-click the virtual machine and select Export or click Export on the virtual machine name's pane.

In this window, you can set the export path for the virtual machine and choose whether to export your virtual machine state data or not.

Because Hyper-V will use the exported files after importing them, you should store the export directly on the target machine's disks and not on a file share.

Once you check Don't Export Virtual Machine State Data, only the virtual machine's configuration files will be exported. The virtual hard disk and snapshots will not be exported.

In the export path, a folder with the name of the virtual machine is created along with the following subfolders:

Virtual Machines   This includes the virtual machine configuration files as well as the virtual machine state if the machine is saved.

Virtual Hard Disks   If you exported the state data, this folder will include your virtual hard disks VHD file(s).

Snapshots   If you exported the state data, this folder will include all snapshot files.

Once the virtual machine finishes exporting, you can move the export folder to the target machine if you did not store it directly on the server's disks. Open Hyper-V Manager, and click Import Virtual Machine, which is located in the Actions pane.

The Import Virtual Machine dialog box asks you for the path to the exported virtual machine, and it allows you to decide if you want to reuse the old virtual machine ID.

You want to reuse old virtual machine IDs if you're moving all virtual machines from a host to a new target machine. The virtual machines are practically the same as on the source system. However, you do not want to reuse old virtual machine IDs if you used Export to clone a virtual machine.

When you import a virtual machine with state data, Hyper-V will use the import path for the virtual hard disks as well as snapshots in its virtual machine configuration XML. Thus you're able to import an exported machine only once. For that reason, the import folder should already be on the host's target disk.

If you import only the virtual machine configuration, without the state data or hard disks, you will receive a warning message. You receive this warning because the virtual machine has probably one or more hard drives configured that now point to no VHD file. You need to correct these settings before starting the virtual machine to have this work.

Managing Snapshots

With virtual machine snapshots, you can save a copy of the virtual machine at any point in time, including while the virtual machine is running. You can take multiple snapshots of a virtual machine and then revert it to any previous state by applying a snapshot.

Using snapshots makes it easier to diagnose the cause of errors by reducing the number of times you need to repeat a task or sequence within a virtual machine. The benefit is obvious; if you use snapshots to revert to a previous virtual machine configuration, you do not need to copy virtual machines to keep a state. Thus it is a quick and easy way to back up a certain state of your virtual machine.

You can create a snapshot when a virtual machine is in a running, saved, or turned-off state. It's only from a Paused state that you cannot perform a snapshot.

Snapshots

Snapshots are extremely useful in training classes or testing environments. When your company tests new software, you can make snapshots at every single step so that you can immediately go back if some problems or issues arise. In training classes, you can prepare each virtual machine for your students according to your special requirements, and once the course is finished, you just revert all virtual machines to their initial configuration. You'll no longer have hassles with experienced users who change your configuration without letting you know.

In Exercise 8.6, you'll create and rename a snapshot.

EXERCISE 8.6

Creating a Snapshot of a Virtual Machine

1. Open Hyper-V Manager.

2. In Hyper-V Manager, in the Virtual Machines pane, right-click the virtual machine.

3. Select Snapshot.

4. Once the snapshot is taken, it should appear in the Snapshots pane in Hyper-V Manager (as shown in the following screen shot). Right-click the snapshot and select Settings.

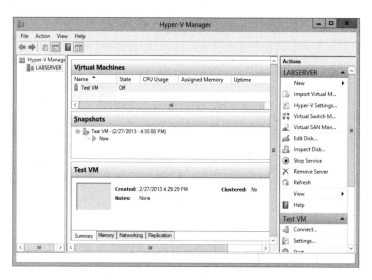

5. In the Settings window, on the Management pane, click Name and type **First Snapshot** as the name. You can also add some notes to make it easy to identify.

6. Click OK to apply the changes. You will now see that the snapshot has a new name.

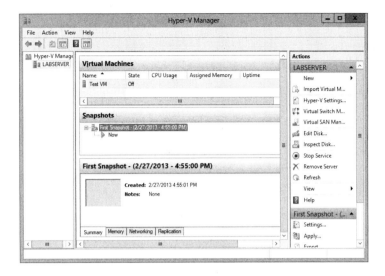

Technically speaking, when you make a snapshot, the following files will be created in the virtual machine's snapshot folder:

- A virtual machine configuration file
- Virtual machine saved state files
- Snapshot differencing disks (AVHDs)

Once you create a snapshot for a virtual machine, you will also have the Revert option available in the virtual machine name's pane in Hyper-V Manager. Reverting basically means that you restore the last snapshot made. You'll also see the last snapshot taken marked with a green arrow in the Snapshots pane.

However, you will also have options available directly on the snapshot level that let you perform certain actions (see Figure 8.14):

FIGURE 8.14   Snapshot properties

Settings   This opens the Settings window of the virtual machine. The only settings you can change are the Name and the Notes field. All others are read-only.

Apply   Applying a snapshot to a virtual machine technically means that you copy the virtual machine state from the snapshot to the active virtual machine. You can look at this as a "restore this snapshot" option. Because you would lose all unsaved data and settings from the active virtual machine, you will be asked if you want to create another snapshot before you apply this snapshot. If you just click Apply, the active machine will be overwritten and reverted to the state it was in when the snapshot was made. This snapshot will not be removed.

Export   Allows you to export the snapshot to another location.

Rename   You can change the name of the snapshot without the need to open the settings.

Delete Snapshot   Deleting a snapshot is like deleting a backup file. You will no longer be able to restore to that point in time. Deleting a single snapshot does not affect any other snapshots that you made for this virtual machine. You will delete only the selected snapshot. However, sometimes when you do delete a snapshot, the system needs to merge the differencing disks. This occurs in the background when the virtual machine is not running. The user does not see when it happens.

Delete Snapshot Subtree   This will delete the selected snapshot and all snapshots that are hierarchically underneath it. If you delete a snapshot with only one sub-snapshot, the configuration and saved state files for the snapshot will be deleted and the snapshot's differencing disks will be merged. If you have more sub-snapshots, merging will not take place.

In Exercise 8.7, you will apply a snapshot and thus revert to a previous virtual machine state.

EXERCISE 8.7

Applying a Snapshot

1. Click Start ➢ Administrative Tools ➢ Hyper-V Manager.

2. In Hyper-V Manager, in the Virtual Machines pane, click the virtual machine for which you created a snapshot.

3. In the Snapshots pane, select First Snapshot.

4. In the First Snapshot pane, under Actions, click Apply.

5. In the Apply Snapshot window, click Apply.

Live Migration

Another option for working with Hyper-V and clustering is live migration. As explained earlier, *live migration* allows a Hyper-V administrator to relocate running virtual machines easily from one node of the failover cluster to another node in the same cluster. This move can be done without a dropped network connection or perceived downtime of the virtual machine.

The failover clustering role must be installed and configured on the server running Hyper-V in order to use the live migration feature. Shared storage is also a requirement for failover clustering and live migration. The virtual machines need to be stored in a shared storage area, and one of the nodes will run the virtual machine state.

Only one live migration can be in progress at any given time on a server running Hyper-V. This means that an administrator does not have the ability to use live migration to move multiple virtual machines simultaneously.

Microsoft recommends using the Windows Server 2012 failover clustering feature called *Cluster Shared Volumes (CSV)* with live migration. While the backup process is in progress, the CSV will remain in redirected access. The advantage of using CSV is increased reliability when used with live migration and virtual machines. CSV also provides a single, consistent file namespace so that all servers running Windows Server 2012 see the same storage.

Quick Migration

In combination with Windows Server 2012's clustering support in Enterprise and Datacenter editions, *quick migration* enables high availability features for virtual machines. Thus if one server fails, its workload can be picked up by another node member with minimal interruption in user access.

Basically, each virtual machine is defined as a virtual machine application on a cluster node. Once the cluster node goes down, another cluster node can take over the virtual machine. Unfortunately, this means that in the event of failure, the system state of the virtual machine is lost because it does a normal bootup with the virtual machine. Planned failover saves the current state, moves it, and then restores it on the target side correctly.

Using Physical-to-Virtual (P2V) Conversion

Let's talk about ways to migrate machines into Hyper-V virtual machines. Converting physical machines to virtual machines is done through a process known as *physical-to-virtual (P2V) conversion*.

This gives an administrator the ability to convert servers that are already built and running on their network. One advantage of using the P2V is that you can use the Windows PowerShell command line to convert multiple servers using the P2V conversion.

To use the Windows PowerShell command-line utility, you must script the commands that will allow the conversion to function properly. When you are deciding which machines you want to convert using the P2V utility, you need to be aware of which operating systems can be converted using this utility. The P2V utility can convert the following operating systems into virtual machines:

- Windows 2000 Server SP4 or later (offline P2V only)
- Windows 2000 Advanced Server SP4 or later (offline P2V only)
- Windows Server 2003 (32-bit or 64-bit) SP1 or later
- Windows XP Professional (32-bit or 64-bit) SP2 or later
- Windows Vista (32-bit or 64-bit) SP1 or later
- Windows Server 2008 (32-bit or 64-bit)
- Windows Server 2008 R2
- Windows Server 2012

You may have noticed that some of the operating systems states are indicated as offline only in the preceding list. An *offline conversion* means that the machine's operating system, which you are migrating, must be taken offline before the conversion occurs. *Online conversions* mean that the system that you are converting can continue to operate normally during the conversion.

There are some other issues that you need to consider when choosing which machines you want to convert using the P2V utility. Windows servers that are underutilized are an excellent choice for converting over to virtual machines.

Using Virtual-to-Virtual (V2V) Conversion

There may be times when it is necessary for you to convert a virtual machine from another virtual environment over to Microsoft Hyper-V. Administrators have the ability to perform a *virtual-to-virtual machine (V2V) conversion*. A V2V conversion allows you to convert a VMware ESX server virtual machine to a Microsoft Hyper-V or Virtual Server virtual machine.

There are only certain situations where a V2V conversion is necessary. In many situations, a virtual machine migration may be all you need to do to accomplish your transfer. Table 8.6 shows you when to just migrate a virtual machine from another system or when to use the V2V conversion.

TABLE 8.6   V2V conversions

Current Virtualization Environment	Future Virtualization Environment	Use the Following Method
Hyper-V	Hyper-V	Migration
Virtual Server	Hyper-V	Migration
Virtual Server	Virtual Server	Migration
VMware ESX Server	Hyper-V	V2V conversion
VMware ESX Server	Virtual Server	V2V conversion

For the virtual-to-virtual (V2V) conversion, the operating system that is on the machine from which you are getting the virtual machine (the source machine) must be one of the following operating systems:

- Windows Server 2012
- Windows Server 2008 R2 (64-bit)
- Windows Server 2008 (32-bit or 64-bit)
- Windows 7 (32-bit and 64-bit)
- Windows 8 (32-bit and 64-bit)
- Windows 2000 Server or Advanced Server with SP4 minimum
- Windows XP Professional (32-bit or 64-bit) with SP2 minimum
- Windows Vista (32-bit or 64-bit) with SP1 minimum

Summary

Virtualization is quickly becoming a hot topic. The potential for consolidation is tremendous, and thus it will become more and more important.

After reading this chapter, you should have a good understanding of the Hyper-V architecture and what is required to install Hyper-V.

The section about installation and configuration covered various basic aspects of configuring the virtualization environment. You learned about the different types of virtual networks that are available, the options for installing the Hyper-V role, and the various types of virtual hard disks that you can use to optimize virtualization for your specific scenario.

You also learned how to configure virtual machines using the Hyper-V environment and how to create your own virtual datacenter on top of your Hyper-V machines. I showed you how to create and manage virtual machines, how to use Virtual Machine Connection to control a virtual machine remotely, and how to install Hyper-V Integration Components. You also learned how to export and import virtual machines as well as how to do snapshots of your virtual machine.

If you have never worked with virtualization software before, the information in this chapter may have been completely new to you. You should now be well prepared to try out Hyper-V in your own environment.

Exam Essentials

Understand Hyper-V's architecture.   When you have a good understanding of Hyper-V's architecture, especially when an operating system in a virtual machine is hypervisor aware versus non-hypervisor aware, you have a solid understanding of what is important from an architectural perspective.

You should know about the Hyper-V Integration Components and how they change the behavior of a virtual machine. Also know for which operating systems the integration components are available.

Know Hyper-V's requirements and how to install it.   Know the hardware and software requirements as well as how to install Hyper-V. Hyper-V requires an x64-based processor and Data Execution Protection (DEP). Hardware-assisted virtualization must be enabled—don't forget this! Also remember that you can install Hyper-V two ways: using Server Manager or using the command line in Server Core.

Understand virtual networks and virtual hard disks.   Virtual networks and hard disks are the two most tested topics. You definitely should know the types of virtual networks available (that is, external, internal only, and private virtual network) as well as all types of virtual hard disks (namely, dynamically expanding, fixed size, differential, and physical or pass-through). You should be able to apply the correct one when needed. Don't forget the Edit Virtual Hard Disk Wizard, which is also a good source for questions in the exam.

Know how to create and manage virtual machines.   You should be able to explain how to create a virtual machine, what options you have available to install an operating system in a virtual machine, and how to install the Hyper-V Integration Components on a virtual machine. Don't forget about the virtual machine states and the virtual machine settings!

Understand how to back up and restore virtual machines.   Have a good understanding of the concept of exporting and importing virtual machines, how snapshots work, and what lies behind a quick migration. Understand how you can export a virtual machine, what you should consider when moving it to a new host machine, and what happens after importing it to the import folder. The same applies to snapshots: You need to know what options you have available and what each option will do. Especially recognize the difference between applying and reverting a snapshot.

Review Questions

1. On which of the following x64 editions of Windows Server 2012 does Hyper-V run? (Choose all that apply.)

    A. Windows Server 2012 Web Edition

    B. Windows Server 2012 Standard Edition

    C. Windows Server 2012 Enterprise Edition

    D. Windows Server 2012 Datacenter Edition

2. You want to build a test environment based on virtual machines on a single Windows Server 2012 machine, but you also want to make sure the virtual machines communicate with only each other. What type of virtual network do you need to configure?

    A. External

    B. Internal only

    C. Private virtual machine network

    D. Public virtual machine network

3. Andy wants to change the memory of a virtual machine that is currently powered up. What does he need to do?

    A. Shut down the virtual machine, use the virtual machine's settings to change the memory, and start it again.

    B. Use the virtual machine's settings to change the memory.

    C. Pause the virtual machine, use the virtual machine's settings to change the memory, and resume it.

    D. Save the virtual machine, use the virtual machine's settings to change the memory, and resume it.

4. You want to make sure the hard disk space for your virtual machines is occupied only when needed. What type of virtual hard disk would you recommend?

    A. Dynamically expanding disk

    B. Fixed-size disk

    C. Differencing disk

    D. Physical or pass-through disk

5. How do you add a physical disk to a virtual machine?

    A. Use the Virtual Hard Disk Wizard.

    B. Use the Edit Virtual Hard Disk Wizard.

    C. Use the virtual machine's settings.

    D. Use the New Virtual Machine Wizard.

6. Rich bought a new server with an Itanium IA-64 processor, 4 GB RAM, and a SAN that provides 1 TB hard disk space. After installing Windows Server 2012 for Itanium-based systems, he wants to install Hyper-V on this server. Can Hyper-V be installed on this system?

    A. Yes

    B. No

7. What are the minimum CPU requirements for running Hyper-V on a machine? (Choose all that apply.)

    A. An x64-based processor (Intel or AMD).

    B. Hardware Data Execution Protection (DEP) must be enabled.

    C. Hardware-assisted virtualization must be enabled.

    D. The processor must at least have a dual core.

8. What is the command to install Hyper-V on a Windows Server 2008 machine that was installed in Server Core?

    A. `start /w ocsetup Hyper-V`

    B. `start /w ocsetup microsoft-hyper-v`

    C. `start /w ocsetup Microsoft-Hyper-V`

    D. `start /w ocsetup hyper-v`

9. On what operating systems can you install the Hyper-V Manager MMC? (Choose all that apply.)

    A. Windows Server 2008 R2

    B. Windows Server 2003

    C. Windows XP SP3

    D. Windows 7, Windows 8

10. What statement is correct for an external virtual network?

    A. The virtual machines can communicate with each other and with the host machine.

    B. The virtual machines can communicate with each other only.

    C. The virtual machines can communicate with each other, with the host machine, and with an external network.

    D. The virtual machines cannot communicate with each other.

Chapter

9

Configuring TCP/IP

THE FOLLOWING 70-410 EXAM OBJECTIVES ARE COVERED IN THIS CHAPTER:

✓ **Configure IPv4 and IPv6 addressing**

- This objective may include, but is not limited to: Configure IP address options; configure subnetting; configure supernetting; configure interoperability between IPv4 and IPv6; configure ISATAP; configure Teredo.

THE FOLLOWING 70-412 EXAM OBJECTIVES ARE COVERED IN THIS CHAPTER:

✓ **Deploy and manage IPAM**

- This objective may include, but is not limited to: Configure IPAM manually or by using Group Policy; configure server discovery; create and manage IP blocks and ranges; monitor utilization of IP address space; migrate to IPAM; delegate IPAM administration; manage IPAM collections.

In this chapter, I will discuss the most important protocol used in a Microsoft Windows Server 2012 network: *Transmission Control Protocol/Internet Protocol (TCP/IP)*.

TCP/IP is actually two sets of protocols bundled together: the Transmission Control Protocol (TCP) and the Internet Protocol (IP). TCP/IP is a suite of protocols developed by the US Department of Defense's Advanced Research Projects Agency in 1969.

This chapter is divided into two main topics: I'll talk first about TCP/IP version 4 and then discuss TCP/IP version 6. TCP/IP version 4 is still used in Windows Server 2012, and it was the primary version of TCP/IP in all previous versions of Windows. However, TCP/IP version 6 is the new release of TCP/IP, and it has been incorporated into Windows Server 2012.

Understanding TCP/IP

I mentioned that TCP/IP is actually two sets of protocols bundled together: TCP and IP. These protocols sit on a four-layer TCP/IP model.

Details of the TCP/IP Model

The four layers of the TCP/IP model are as follows (see Figure 9.1):

Application Layer   The *Application layer* is where the applications that use the protocol stack reside. These applications include File Transfer Protocol (FTP), Trivial File Transfer Protocol (TFTP), Simple Mail Transfer Protocol (SMTP), and Hypertext Transfer Protocol (HTTP).

Transport Layer   The *Transport layer* is where the two Transport layer protocols reside. These are TCP and the User Datagram Protocol (UDP). TCP is a connection-oriented protocol, and delivery is guaranteed. UDP is a connectionless protocol. This means UDP does its best job to deliver the message, but there is no guarantee.

Internet Layer   The *Internet layer* is where IP resides. *IP* is a connectionless protocol that relies on the upper layer (Transport layer) for guaranteeing delivery. *Address Resolution Protocol (ARP)* also resides on this layer. ARP turns an IP address into a Media Access Control (MAC) address. All upper and lower layers travel through the IP protocol.

Link Layer   The data link protocols like Ethernet and Token Ring reside in the *Link layer*. This layer is also referred to as the *Network Access layer*.

FIGURE 9.1   TCP/IP model

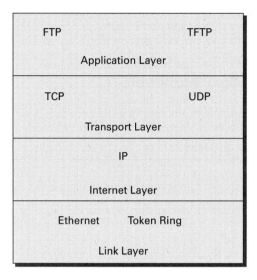

How TCP/IP Layers Communicate

When an application like FTP is called upon, the application moves down the layers and TCP is retrieved. TCP then connects itself to the IP protocol and gets released onto the network through the Link Layer (see Figure 9.2). This is a connection-oriented protocol because TCP is the protocol that guarantees delivery.

FIGURE 9.2   TCP/IP process

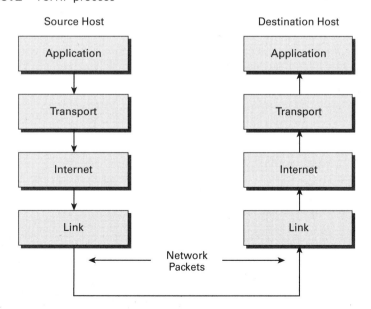

When an application like TFTP gets called, the application moves down the layers and UDP is retrieved. UDP then connects itself to the IP protocol and gets released onto the network through the Link layer. This is a connectionless protocol because UDP does not have guaranteed delivery.

Understanding Port Numbers

TCP and UDP rely on port numbers assigned by the *Internet Assigned Numbers Authority (IANA)* to forward packets to the appropriate application process. Port numbers are 16-bit integers that are part of a message header. They identify the application software process with which the packet should be associated. For example, let's say that a client has a copy of Internet Explorer and a copy of Mail open at the same time. Both applications are sending TCP requests across the Internet to retrieve web pages and email, respectively. How does the computer know which return packets to forward to Internet Explorer and which packets to forward to Mail?

When making a connection, the client chooses a source port for the communication that is usually in the range 1024–65535 (or sometimes in the range 1–65535). This source port then communicates with a destination port of 80 or 110 on the server side. Every packet destined for Internet Explorer has a source port number of 80 in the header, and every packet destined for Mail has a source port number of 110 in the header.

Table 9.1 lists the most common port numbers (you might need to know these for the exam). You can visit www.iana.org to get the most current and complete list of port numbers. It's good to become familiar with specific port numbers because it's a benefit to be able to determine from memory the ports that, for example, allow or block specific protocols in a firewall. Allowing only port 80, for instance, does not ensure that all web traffic will be allowed. You must also allow port 443 for certain secure web traffic.

 Simply because a port is "well known" doesn't mean that a given service must run on it. It's technically valid to run any service on any port, but doing so is usually a bad idea. For example, if you chose to run your web server on TCP port 25, clients would need to type www.example.com:25 to reach your website from most browsers.

TABLE 9.1   Common port numbers

Port Number	Description
20	FTP data
21	FTP control
23	Telnet

Port Number	Description
25	Simple Mail Transfer Protocol (SMTP)
53	Domain Name System (DNS)
80	Hypertext Transfer Protocol (HTTP), Web
88	Kerberos
110	Post Office Protocol v3 (POP3)
443	Secure HTTP (HTTPS)

Understanding IP Addressing

Understanding IP addressing is critical to understanding how IP works. An IP address is a numeric identifier assigned to each device on an IP network. This type of address is a logical software address that designates the device's location on the network. It isn't the physical hardware address hard-coded in the device's network interface card.

In the following sections, you will see how IP addresses are used to identify uniquely every machine on the network (MAC address).

 I'll assume you're comfortable with binary notation and math for the remainder of this discussion.

The Hierarchical IP Addressing Scheme

An IP address consists of 32 bits of information. These bits are divided into four sections (sometimes called *octets* or *quads*) containing 1 byte (8 bits) each. There are three common methods for specifying an IP address:

- Dotted-decimal, as in 130.57.30.56
- Binary, as in 10000010.00111001.00011110.00111000
- Hexadecimal, as in 82 39 1E 38

All of these examples represent the same IP address.

The 32-bit IP address is a structured, or hierarchical, address as opposed to a flat, or nonhierarchical, address. Although IP could have used either *flat addressing* or *hierarchical addressing*, its designers elected to use the latter for a very good reason, as you will now see.

Real World Scenario

Why Hierarchical Addressing Is Used

What's the difference between flat and hierarchical addressing? A good example of a flat addressing scheme is a US state driver's license number. There's no partitioning to it; the range of legal numbers isn't broken up in any meaningful way (say, by county of residence or date of issue). If this method had been used for IP addressing, every machine on the Internet would have needed a totally unique address, just as each driver's license number in a particular state is unique.

The good news about flat addressing is that it can handle a large number of addresses in 32 bits of data, namely, 4.3 billion. A 32-bit address space with two possible values for each position—either 0 (zero) or 1 (one)—gives you 2^{32} values, which equals approximately 4.3 billion.

The bad news—and the reason flat addressing isn't used in IP—relates to routing. If every address were totally unique, every router on the Internet would need to store the address of every other machine on the Internet. It would be fair to say that this would make efficient routing impossible, even if only a fraction of the possible addresses were used.

The solution to this dilemma is to use a hierarchical addressing scheme that breaks the address space into ordered chunks. Telephone numbers are a great example of this type of addressing. The first section of a US telephone number, the area code, designates a very large area. The area code is followed by the prefix, which narrows the scope to a local calling area. The final segment, the customer number, zooms in on the specific connection. By looking at a number such as 603-766-xxxx, you can quickly determine that the number is located in the southern part of New Hampshire (area code 603) in the Portsmouth area (the 766 exchange).

IP Address Structure

IP addressing works the same way. Instead of the entire 32 bits being treated as a unique identifier, one part of the IP address is designated as the network address (or network ID) and the other part as a node address (or host ID), giving it a layered, hierarchical structure. Together, the IP address, the network address, and the node address uniquely identify a device within an IP network.

The network address—the first two sets of numbers in an IP address—uniquely identifies each network. Every machine on the same network shares that network address as part of its IP address, just as the address of every house on a street shares the same street name. In the IP address 130.57.30.56, for example, 130.57 is the network address.

The node address—the second two sets of numbers—is assigned to, and uniquely identifies, each machine in a network, just as each house on the same street has a different house number. This part of the address must be unique because it identifies a particular machine—an individual, as opposed to a network. This number can also be referred to as a *host address*. In the sample IP address 130.57.30.56, the node address is .30.56.

Understanding Network Classes

The designers of the Internet decided to create classes of networks based on network size. For the small number of networks possessing a very large number of nodes, they created the Class A network. At the other extreme is the Class C network, reserved for the numerous networks with small numbers of nodes. The class of networks in between the very large and very small ones is predictably called the Class B network.

TABLE 9.2 Network address classes

Class	Mask Bits	Leading Bit Pattern	Decimal Range of First Octet of IP Address	Assignable Networks	Maximum Nodes per Network
A	8	0	1–126	126	16,777,214
B	16	10	128–191	16,384	65,534
C	24	110	192–223	2,097,152	254

The default subdivision of an IP address into a network and node address is determined by the class designation of your network. Table 9.2 summarizes the three classes of network, which will be described in more detail in the following sections.

 Classless Inter-Domain Routing (CIDR), explained in detail later in this chapter, has effectively done away with these class designations. You will still hear and should still know the meaning behind the class designations of addresses because they are important to understanding IP addressing. However, when you're working with IP addressing in practice, CIDR is more important to know.

To ensure efficient routing, Internet designers defined a mandate for the leading bits section of the address for each different network class. For example, because a router knows that a Class A network address always starts with a 0, it can quickly apply the default mask, if necessary, after reading only the first bit of the address. Table 9.2 illustrates how the leading bits of a network address are defined. When considering the subnet masking between network and host addresses, the number of bits to mask is important. For example, in a Class A network, 8 bits are masked, making the default subnet mask 255.0.0.0; in a Class C, 24 bits are masked, making the default subnet mask 255.255.255.0.

Some IP addresses are reserved for special purposes and shouldn't be assigned to nodes. Table 9.3 lists some of the reserved IP addresses. See RFC 3330 for others.

TABLE 9.3 Special network addresses

Address	Function
Entire IP address set to all 0s	Depending on the mask, this network (that is, the network or subnet of which you are currently a part) or this host on this network.
A routing table entry of all 0s with a mask of all 0s	Used as the default gateway entry. Any destination address masked by all 0s produces a match for the all 0s reference address. Because the mask has no 1s, this is the least desirable entry, but it will be used when no other match exists.
Network address 127	Reserved for loopback tests. Designates the local node, and it allows that node to send a test packet to itself without generating network traffic.
Node address of all 0s	Used when referencing a network without referring to any specific nodes on that network. Usually used in routing tables.
Node address of all 1s	Broadcast address for all nodes on the specified network, also known as a *directed broadcast*. For example, 128.2.255.255 means all nodes on the Class B network 128.2. Routing this broadcast is configurable on certain routers.
169.254.0.0 with a mask of 255.255.0.0	The "link-local" block used for autoconfiguration and communication between devices on a single link. Communication cannot occur across routers. Microsoft uses this block for Automatic Private IP Addressing (APIPA).
Entire IP address set to all 1s (same as 255.255.255.255) 10.0.0.0/8 172.16.0.0 to 172.31.255.255	Broadcast to all nodes on the current network; sometimes called a *limited broadcast* or an *all-1s broadcast*. This broadcast is not routable.
192.168.0.0/16	The private-use blocks for Classes A, B, and C. As noted in RFC 1918, the addresses in these blocks must never be allowed into the Internet, making them acceptable for simultaneous use behind NAT servers and non-Internet-connected IP networks.

In the following sections, we will look at the three network types.

Class A Networks

In a Class A network, the first byte is the network address and the three remaining bytes are used for the node addresses. The Class A format is Network.Node.Node.Node.

For example, in the IP address 49.22.102.70, the 49 is the network address, and the 22.102.70 is the node address. Every machine on this particular network would have the distinctive network address of 49. Within that network, however, you could have a large number of machines.

There are 126 possible Class A network addresses. Why? The length of a Class A network address is 1 byte, and the first bit of that byte is reserved, so 7 bits in the first byte remain available for manipulation. This means that the maximum number of Class A networks is 128. (Each of the 7 bit positions that can be manipulated can be either a 0 or a 1, and this gives you a total of 2^7 positions, or 128.) But to complicate things further, it was also decided that the network address of all 0s (0000 0000) would be reserved. This means that the actual number of usable Class A network addresses is 128 minus 1, or 127. Also, 127 is a reserved number (a network address of 0 followed by all 1s (0111 1111), so you actually start with 128 addresses minus the 2 reserved, and you're left with 126 possible Class A network addresses.

Each Class A network has 3 bytes (24 bit positions) for the node address of a machine, which means that there are 2^{24}, or 16,777,216, unique combinations. Because addresses with the two patterns of all 0s and all 1s in the node bits are reserved, the actual maximum usable number of nodes for a Class A network is 2^{24} minus 2, which equals 16,777,214.

Class B Networks

In a Class B network, the first 2 bytes are assigned to the network address and the remaining 2 bytes are used for node addresses. The format is Network.Network.Node.Node.

For example, in the IP address 130.57.30.56, the network address is 130.57 and the node address is 30.56.

The network address is 2 bytes, so there would be 2^{16} unique combinations. But the Internet designers decided that all Class B networks should start with the binary digits 10. This leaves 14 bit positions to manipulate; therefore, there are 16,384 (or 2^{14}) unique Class B networks.

This gives you an easy way to recognize Class B addresses. If the first 2 bits of the first byte can be only 10, that gives you a decimal range from 128 up to 191 in the first octet of the IP address. Remember that you can always easily recognize a Class B network by looking at its first byte, even though there are 16,384 different Class B networks. If the first octet in the address falls between 128 and 191, it is a Class B network, regardless of the value of the second octet.

A Class B network has 2 bytes to use for node addresses. This is 2^{16} minus the two patterns in the reserved-exclusive club (all 0s and all 1s in the node bits) for a total of 65,534 possible node addresses for each Class B network.

Class C Networks

The first 3 bytes of a Class C network are dedicated to the network portion of the address, with only 1 byte remaining for the node address. The format is Network.Network.Network.Node.

In the example IP address 198.21.74.102, the network address is 198.21.74 and the node address is 102.

In a Class C network, the first three bit positions are always binary 110. Three bytes, or 24 bits, minus 3 reserved positions leaves 21 positions. There are therefore 2^{21} (or 2,097,152) possible Class C networks.

The lead bit pattern of 110 equates to decimal 192 and runs through 223. Remembering our handy easy-recognition method, this means you can always spot a Class C address if the first byte is in the range 192–223, regardless of the values of the second and third bytes of the IP address.

Each unique Class C network has 1 byte to use for node addresses. This leads to 2^{8}, or 256, minus the two special patterns of all 0s and all 1s, for a total of 254 node addresses for each Class C network.

Class D networks, used for multicasting only, use the address range 224.0.0.0 to 239.255.255.255 and are used, as in broadcasting, as destination addresses only. Class E networks (reserved for future use at this point) cover 240.0.0.0 to 255.255.255.255. Addresses in the Class E range are considered within the experimental range.

Subnetting a Network

If an organization is large and has lots of computers, or if its computers are geographically dispersed, it makes good sense to divide its colossal network into smaller ones connected by routers. These smaller networks are called *subnets*. The benefits of using subnets are as follows:

Reduced Network Traffic   We all appreciate less traffic of any kind, and so do networks. Without routers, packet traffic could choke the entire network. Most traffic will stay on the local network—only packets destined for other networks will pass through the router and over to another subnet. This traffic reduction also improves overall performance.

Simplified Management   It's easier to identify and isolate network problems in a group of smaller networks connected together than within one gigantic one.

Understanding the Benefits of Subnetting

To understand one benefit of subnetting, consider a hotel or office building. Say a hotel has 1,000 rooms with 75 rooms to a floor. You could start at the first room on the first floor and number it 1; then when you get to the first room on the second floor, you could number it 76 and keep going until you reach room 1,000. But someone looking for room 521 would have to guess on which floor that room is located. If you were to "subnet" the hotel, you would identify the first room on the first floor with the number 101 (1 = Floor 1 and 01 = Room 1), the first room on the second floor with 201, and so on. The guest looking for room 521 would go to the fifth floor and look for room 21.

An organization with a single network address (comparable to the hotel building mentioned in the sidebar "Understanding the Benefits of Subnetting") can have a subnet address for each individual physical network (comparable to a floor in the hotel building). Each subnet is still part of the shared network address, but it also has an additional identifier denoting its individual subnetwork number. This identifier is called a *subnet address*.

Subnetting solves several addressing problems:

- If an organization has several physical networks but only one IP network address, it can handle the situation by creating subnets.

- Because subnetting allows many physical networks to be grouped together, fewer entries in a routing table are required, notably reducing network overhead.

- These things combine collectively to yield greatly enhanced network efficiency.

The original designers of the Internet Protocol envisioned a small Internet with only tens of networks and hundreds of hosts. Their addressing scheme used a network address for each physical network. As you can imagine, this scheme and the unforeseen growth of the Internet created a few problems. The following are two examples:

Not Enough Addresses   A single network address can be used to refer to multiple physical networks, but an organization can request individual network addresses for each one of its physical networks. If all of these requests were granted, there wouldn't be enough addresses to go around.

Gigantic Routing Tables   If each router on the Internet needed to know about every physical network, routing tables would be impossibly huge. There would be an overwhelming amount of administrative overhead to maintain those tables, and the resulting physical overhead on the routers would be massive (CPU cycles, memory, disk space, and so on). Because routers exchange routing information with each other, an additional, related consequence is that a terrific overabundance of network traffic would result.

Although there's more than one way to approach these problems, the principal solution is the one that I'll cover in this book—subnetting. As you might guess, *subnetting* is the process of carving a single IP network into smaller logical subnetworks. This trick is achieved by subdividing the host portion of an IP address to create a subnet address. The actual subdivision is accomplished through the use of a subnet mask (covered later in the chapter).

In the following sections, you will see exactly how to calculate and apply subnetting.

Implementing Subnetting

Before you can implement subnetting, you need to determine your current requirements and plan on how best to implement your subnet scheme.

How to Determine Your Subnetting Requirements

Follow these guidelines to calculate the requirements of your subnet:

1. Determine the number of required network IDs: one for each subnet and one for each wide area network (WAN) connection.

2. Determine the number of required host IDs per subnet: one for each TCP/IP device, including, for example, computers, network printers, and router interfaces.

3. Based on these two data points, create the following:

   ▪ One subnet mask for your entire network

   ▪ A unique subnet ID for each physical segment

   ▪ A range of host IDs for each unique subnet

How to Implement Subnetting

Subnetting is implemented by assigning a subnet address to each machine on a given physical network. For cxamplc, in Figure 9.3, each machine on subnet 1 has a subnet address of 1.

FIGURE 9.3 A sample subnet

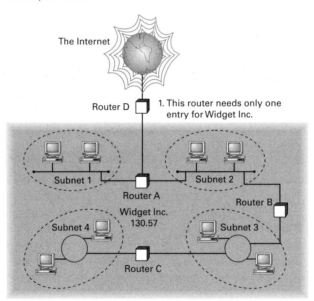

The default network portion of an IP address can't be altered without encroaching on another administrative domain's address space, unless you are assigned multiple consecutive classful addresses. In order to maximize the efficient use of the assigned address space, machines on a particular network share the same network address. In Figure 9.3, you can see that all of the Widget Inc. machines have a network address of 130.57. That principle is constant. In subnetting, it's the host address that's manipulated—the network address doesn't change. The subnet address scheme takes a part of the host address and recycles it as a subnet address. Bit positions are stolen from the host address to be used for the subnet identifier. Figure 9.4 shows how an IP address can be given a subnet address.

FIGURE 9.4 Network vs. host addresses

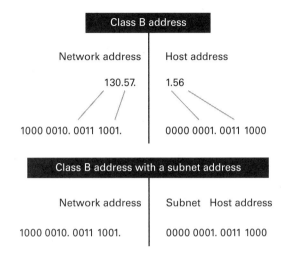

FIGURE 9.5 The network address and its subnet

Because the Widget Inc. network is a Class B network, the first two bytes specify the network address and are shared by all machines on the network, regardless of their particular subnet. Here every machine's address on the subnet must have its third byte read 0000 0001. The fourth byte, the host address, is the unique number that identifies the actual host within that subnet. Figure 9.5 illustrates how a network address and a subnet address can be used together.

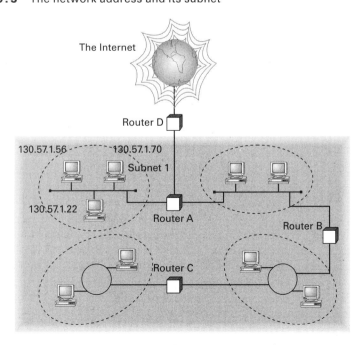

When implementing subnetting, you need some type of hardware installed onto the network. Most of us will just use a router. But if you do not want to purchase an expensive router, there is another way.

One way that you can implement subnetting is by using a Windows Server 2012 machine with multiple NIC adapters configured with routing enabled on the server. This type of router is called a *multihomed router*. This is an inexpensive way to set up a router using a Microsoft server, but it may not be the best way. Many companies specialize in routers, and these routers offer many more features and more flexibility than a multihomed router.

How to Use Subnet Masks

For the subnet address scheme to work, every machine on the network must know which part of the host address will be used as the network address. This is accomplished by assigning each machine a subnet mask.

The network administrator creates a 32-bit subnet mask comprising 1s and 0s. The 1s in the subnet mask represent the positions in the IP address that refer to the network and subnet addresses. The 0s represent the positions that refer to the host part of the address. Figure 9.6 illustrates this combination.

FIGURE 9.6   The subnet mask revealed

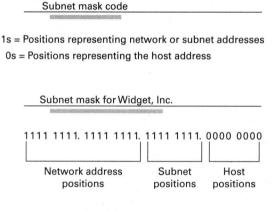

In the Widget Inc. example, the first two bytes of the subnet mask are 1s because Widget's network address is a Class B address, formatted as Network.Network.Node.Node. The third byte, normally assigned as part of the host address, is now used to represent the subnet address. Hence those bit positions are represented with 1s in the subnet mask. The fourth byte is the only part of the example that represents the host address.

The subnet mask can also be expressed using the decimal equivalents of the binary patterns. The binary pattern of 1111 1111 is the same as decimal 255. Consequently, the subnet mask in the example can be denoted in two ways, as shown in Figure 9.7.

FIGURE 9.7   Different ways to represent the same mask

Subnet mask in binary: 1111 1111. 1111 1111. 1111 1111. 0000 0000

Subnet mask in decimal: 255   .   255   .   255   .   0

(The spaces in the above example are only for illustrative purposes.
The subnet mask in decimal would actually appear as 255.255.255.0.)

Not all networks need to have subnets, and therefore they don't need to use custom subnet masks. In this case, they are said to have a *default* subnet mask. This is basically the same as saying they don't have any subnets except the one main subnet on which the network is running. Table 9.4 shows the default subnet masks for the different classes of networks.

TABLE 9.4   Default subnet masks

Class	Format	Default Subnet Mask
A	Network.Node.Node.Node	255.0.0.0
B	Network.Network.Node.Node	255.255.0.0
C	Network.Network.Network.Node	255.255.255.0

Once the network administrator has created the subnet mask and has assigned it to each machine, the IP software applies the subnet mask to the IP address to determine its subnet address. The word *mask* carries the implied meaning of "lens" in this case; that is, the IP software looks at its IP address through the lens of its subnet mask to see its subnet address. Figure 9.8 illustrates an IP address being viewed through a subnet mask.

FIGURE 9.8   Applying the subnet mask

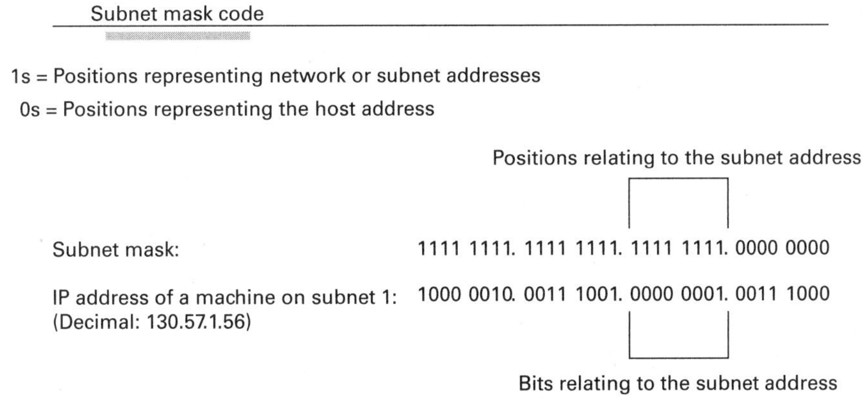

Subnet mask code

1s = Positions representing network or subnet addresses
0s = Positions representing the host address

Positions relating to the subnet address

Subnet mask: 1111 1111. 1111 1111. 1111 1111. 0000 0000

IP address of a machine on subnet 1:   1000 0010. 0011 1001. 0000 0001. 0011 1000
(Decimal: 130.57.1.56)

Bits relating to the subnet address

In this example, the IP software learns through the subnet mask that, instead of being part of the host address, the third byte of its IP address is now going to be used as a subnet address. The IP software then looks in its IP address at the bit positions that correspond to the mask, which are 0000 0001.

The final step is for the subnet bit values to be matched up with the binary numbering convention and converted to decimal. In the Widget Inc. example, the binary-to-decimal conversion is simple, as illustrated in Figure 9.9.

FIGURE 9.9   Converting the subnet mask to decimal

Binary numbering convention

Position/value: ◄——(continued)   128 64 32 16 8 4 2 1

Widget third byte: 0 0 0 0 0 0 0 1

Decimal equivalent: 0 + 1 = 1

Subnet address: 1

By using the entire third byte of a Class B address as the subnet address, it is easy to set and determine the subnet address. For example, if Widget Inc. wants to have a subnet 6, the third byte of all machines on that subnet will be 0000 0110 (decimal 6 in binary).

Using the entire third byte of a Class B network address for the subnet allows for a fair number of available subnet addresses. One byte dedicated to the subnet provides eight bit positions. Each position can be either a 1 or a 0, so the calculation is 2^8, or 256. Thus, Widget Inc. can have up to 256 total subnetworks, each with up to 254 hosts.

Although RFC 950 prohibits the use of binary all 0s and all 1s as subnet addresses, today almost all products actually permit this usage. Microsoft's TCP/IP stack allows it, as does the software in most routers (provided you enable this feature, which sometimes is not the case by default). This gives you two additional subnets. However, you should not use a subnet of 0 (all 0s) unless all the software on your network recognizes this convention.

How to Calculate the Number of Subnets

The formulas for calculating the maximum number of subnets and the maximum number of hosts per subnet are as follows:

2 × number of masked bits in subnet mask = maximum number of subnets

2 × number of unmasked bits in subnet mask – 2 = maximum number of hosts per subnet

In the formulas, *masked* refers to bit positions of 1, and *unmasked* refers to bit positions of 0. The downside to using an entire byte of a node address as your subnet address is that you reduce the possible number of node addresses on each subnet. As explained earlier, without a subnet, a Class B address has 65,534 unique combinations of 1s and 0s that can be used for node addresses. The question then is why would you ever want 65,534 hosts on a single physical network?

The trade-off is acceptable to most who ask themselves this question. If you use an entire byte of the node address for a subnet, you then have only 1 byte for the host addresses, leaving only 254 possible host addresses. If any of your subnets are populated with more than 254 machines, you'll have a problem. To solve it, you would then need to shorten the subnet mask, thereby lengthening the number of host bits and increasing the number of host addresses. This gives you more available host addresses on each subnet. A side effect of this solution is that it shrinks the number of possible subnets.

Figure 9.10 shows an example of using a smaller subnet address. A company called Acme Inc. expects to need a maximum of 14 subnets. In this case, Acme does not need to take an entire byte from the host address for the subnet address. To get its 14 different subnet addresses, it needs to snatch only 4 bits from the host address ($2^4 = 16$). The host portion of the address has 12 usable bits remaining ($2^{12} - 2 = 4094$). Each of Acme's 16 subnets could then potentially have a total of 4,094 host addresses, and 4,094 machines on each subnet should be plenty.

FIGURE 9.10   An example of a smaller subnet address

Acme, Inc.

Network address: 132.8 (Class B; net.net.host.host)

Example IP address: 1000 0100. 0000 1000. 0001 0010. 0011 1100

Decimal: 132 . 8 . 18 . 60

Subnet Mask Code

1s = Positions representing network or subnet addresses
0s = Positions representing the host address

Subnet mask:
Binary: 1111 1111. 1111 1111. 1111 0000. 0000 0000
Decimal: 255 . 255 . 240 . 0
(The decimal 240 is equal to the binary 1111 0000.)

Positions relating to the subnet address

Subnet mask: 1111 1111. 1111 1111. 1111 0000. 0000 0000
IP address of a Acme machine: 1000 0100. 0000 1000. 0001 0010. 0011 1100
(Decimal: 132.8.18.60)

Bits relating to the subnet address

Binary-to-Decimal Conversions for Subnet Address

Subnet mask positions:	1	1	1	1	0	0	0	0
Position/value: ←(continue)	128	64	32	16	8	4	2	1
Third byte of IP address:	0	0	0	1	0	0	1	0
Decimal equivalent:				0 + 16 = 16				
Subnet address for this IP address:				16				

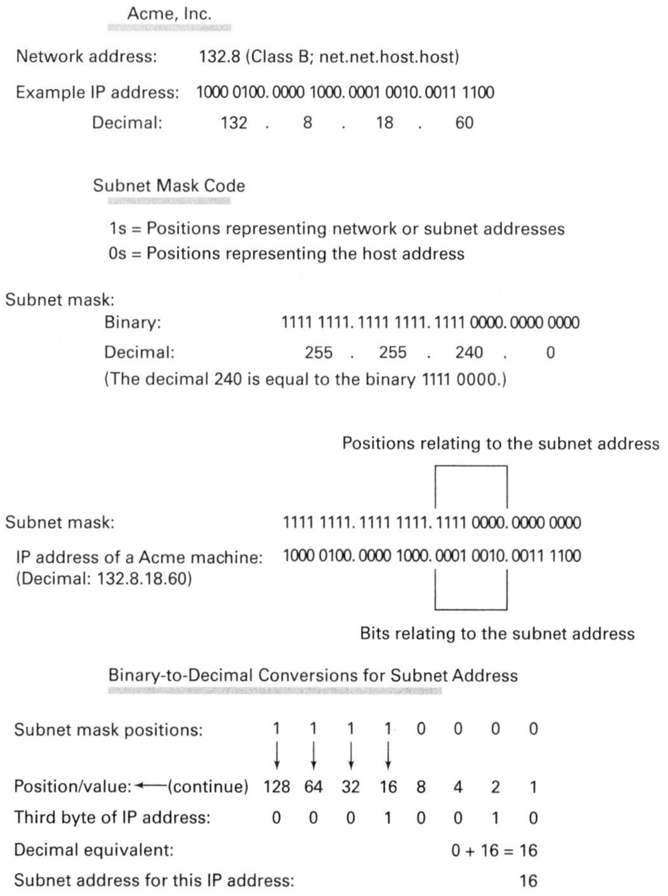

An Easier Way to Apply Subnetting

Now that you have the basics of how to subnet down, we'll show you an easier way.
If you have learned a different way and it works for you, stick with it. It does not matter
how you get to the finish line, just as long as you get there. But if you are new to subnetting,
Figure 9.11 will make it easier for you.

FIGURE 9.11   TCP/IP v4 subnetting chart

$2^{(X)}-2=Y$	128	64	32	16	8	4	2	1
255	1	1	1	1	1	1	1	1
254	1	1	1	1	1	1	1	0
252	1	1	1	1	1	1	0	0
248	1	1	1	1	1	0	0	0
240	1	1	1	1	0	0	0	0
224	1	1	1	0	0	0	0	0
192	1	1	0	0	0	0	0	0
128	1	0	0	0	0	0	0	0
0	0	0	0	0	0	0	0	0

0 = Hosts, 1 = Subnets

X (POWER)			X		Y
2^x	3	=	8	−2	6
2^x	4	=	16	−2	14
2^x	5	=	32	−2	30
2^x	6	=	64	−2	62
2^x	7	=	128	−2	126
2^x	8	=	256	−2	254
2^x	9	=	512	−2	510
2^x	10	=	1024	−2	1022
2^x	11	=	2048	−2	2046
2^x	12	=	4096	−2	4094
2^x	13	=	8192	−2	8190
2^x	14	=	16384	−2	16382
2^x	15	=	32768	−2	32766
2^x	16	=	65536	−2	65534
2^x	17	=	131072	−2	131070

This chart may look intimidating, but it's really simple to use once you have done it a
few times.

Remember that on this chart, 1s equal subnets and 0s equal hosts. If you
get this confused, you will get wrong answers in the following exercises.

Watch the Y column on the lower end of the chart. This represents the number of
addresses available to you after the two reserved addresses have been removed. The following exercises provide some examples.

SUBNET MASK EXERCISE 1

Class C, 10 Hosts per Subnet

You have a Class C address, and you require 10 hosts per subnet.

1. Write down **255.255.255.** _____ . The blank area is the number you need to fill in.

2. Look under the Y column and choose the first number that is larger than 10 (the number of hosts per subnet you need). You should have come up with 14.

3. Move across the page and look at number in the X (Power) column. The power number is 4.

4. Go to the top of the chart, and look for the row with exactly four 0s (hosts). Find the number at the beginning of the row.

The number at the beginning of the row is 240. That's your answer. The subnet mask should be 255.255.255.240.

SUBNET MASK EXERCISE 2

Class C, 20 Hosts per Subnet

You have a Class C address, and you need 20 hosts per subnet.

1. Write down 255.255.255. _____ .

2. Look under the Y column, and find the first number that covers 20. (This should be 30.)

3. Go across to the power number (5).

4. Go to the top part of the chart, and find the row with exactly five 0s from right to left.

The number at the beginning of the row is 224. Your answer should be 255.255.255.224.

SUBNET MASK EXERCISE 3

Class C, Five Subnets

Now you have a Class C address, and you need five subnets. Remember that subnets are represented by 1s in the chart.

1. First write down 255.255.255. _____ .

2. Look under the Y column, and find the first number that covers 5. (This should be 6.)

3. Go across to the power number. (This should be 3.)

4. Go to the top part of the chart, and find which row has exactly three 1s (remember, 1s are for subnets) from left to right.

Your answer should be 255.255.255.224.

SUBNET MASK EXERCISE 4

Class B, 1,500 Hosts per Subnet

This one is a bit harder. You have a Class B address, and you need 1,500 hosts per subnet. Because you have a Class B address, you need to fill in the third octet of numbers. The fourth octet contains eight 0s.

1. Write down 255.255. _____ .0.

2. Look at the Y column, and find the first number that covers 1,500. (This should be 2,046.)

3. Go across, and find the power number. (This should be 11.)

4. Remember, you already have eight 0s in the last octet. So you need only three more. Find the row with three 0s.

You should come up with an answer of 255.255.248.0. This actually breaks down to 11111111 .11111111.11111000.00000000, and that's how you got the 11 zeros.

SUBNET MASK EXERCISE 5

Class B, 3,500 Hosts per Subnet

You have a Class B address, and you need 3,500 hosts per subnet.

1. Write down 255.255. _____ .0.

2. Look at the Y column, and find the first number that covers 3,500. (This should be 4,094.)

3. Go across, and find the power number. (This should be 12.)

4. Remember, you already have eight 0s in the last octet, so you need only four more. Count for four zeros from right to left.

You should come up with an answer of 255.255.240.0. Again, this actually breaks down to 11111111.11111111.11110000.00000000, and that's how you got the 12 zeros.

If you get a question that gives you both the hosts and the subnets, always figure out the larger number first. Then, depending on the mask you have decided to use, make sure the lower number is also correct with that mask.

Now try some more subnet mask exercises using the data that follows:

Class B address	Class B address
1,000 hosts per subnet	25 subnets
Class C address	Class B address
45 hosts per subnet	4,000 hosts per subnet
192.168.0.0	Class B address
10 subnets	2,000 hosts per subnet
	25 subnets

Here are the answers. If any of your answers are wrong, follow the previous examples, and try to work through them again:

Class B address	Class B address
1,000 hosts per subnet 255.255.252.0	25 subnets 255.255.248.0
Class C address	Class B address
45 hosts per subnet 255.255.255.192	4,000 hosts per subnet 255.255.240.0
192.168.0.0	Class B address
10 subnets 255.255.255.240	2,000 hosts per subnet
	25 subnets 255.255.248.0

Applying Subnetting the Traditional Way

Sometimes subnetting can be confusing. After all, it can be quite difficult to remember all those numbers. You can step back a minute and take a look at the primary classes of networks and how to subnet each one. Let's start with Class C because it uses only 8 bits for the node address, so it's the easiest to calculate. In the following sections, I will explain how to subnet the various types of networks.

Subnetting Class C

If you recall, a Class C network uses the first 3 bytes (24 bits) to define the network address. This leaves you 1 byte (8 bits) with which to address hosts. So if you want to create subnets, your options are limited because of the small number of bits available.

If you break down your subnets into chunks smaller than the default Class C, then figuring out the subnet mask, network number, broadcast address, and router address can be confusing. To build a sturdy base for subnetting, study the following techniques for determining these special values for each subnet, but also learn and use the more efficient technique presented in the later section "Quickly Identifying Subnet Characteristics Using CIDR" and the earlier section "An Easier Way to Apply Subnetting." Table 9.5 summarizes how you can break down a Class C network into one, two, four, or eight smaller subnets, and it gives you the subnet masks, network numbers, broadcast addresses, and router addresses. The first three bytes have simply been designated x.y.z. (Note that the table assumes you can use the all-0s and all-1s subnets too.)

TABLE 9.5 Setting up Class C subnets

Number of Desired Subnets	Subnet Mask	*Network Number*	*Router Address*	*Broadcast Address*	Remaining Number of IP Addresses
1	255.255.255.0	x.y.z.0	x.y.z.1	x.y.z.255	253
2	255.255.255.128	x.y.z.0	x.y.z.1	x.y.z.127	125
	255.255.255.128	x.y.z.128	x.y.z.129	x.y.z.255	125
4	255.255.255.192	x.y.z.0	x.y.z.1	x.y.z.63	61
	255.255.255.192	x.y.z.64	x.y.z.65	x.y.z.127	61
	255.255.255.192	x.y.z.128	x.y.z.129	x.y.z.191	61
	255.255.255.192	x.y.z.192	x.y.z.193	x.y.z.255	61
8	255.255.255.224	x.y.z.0	x.y.z.1	x.y.z.31	29
	255.255.255.224	x.y.z.32	x.y.z.33	x.y.z.63	29
	255.255.255.224	x.y.z.64	x.y.z.65	x.y.z.95	29
	255.255.255.224	x.y.z.96	x.y.z.97	x.y.z.127	29
	255.255.255.224	x.y.z.128	x.y.z.129	x.y.z.159	29
	255.255.255.224	x.y.z.160	x.y.z.161	x.y.z.191	29
	255.255.255.224	x.y.z.192	x.y.z.193	x.y.z.223	29
	255.255.255.224	x.y.z.224	x.y.z.225	x.y.z.255	29

For example, suppose you want to chop up a Class C network, 200.211.192.*x*, into two subnets. As you can see in the table, you'd use a subnet mask of 255.255.255.128 for each subnet. The first subnet would have the network number 200.211.192.0, router address 200.211.192.1, and broadcast address 200.211.192.127. You could assign IP addresses 200.211.192.2 through 200.211.192.126—that's 125 additional different IP addresses.

Heavily subnetting a network results in the loss of a progressively greater percentage of addresses to the network number, broadcast address, and router address.

The second subnet would have the network number 200.211.192.128, router address 200.211.192.129, and broadcast address 200.211.192.255.

Why It's Best to Use Routers That Support Subnet 0

When subnetting a Class C network using the method in Table 9.5, if you use the $2^x - 2$ calculation, the subnet 128 in the table doesn't make sense. It turns out that there's a legitimate and popular reason to do it this way, however:

- Remember that using subnet 0 is not allowed according to the RFC standards, but by using it you can subnet your Class C network with a subnet mask of 128. This uses only 1 bit, and according to your calculator $2^1 - 2 = 0$, giving you zero subnets.

- By using routers that support subnet 0, you can assign 1–126 for hosts and 129–254 for hosts, as stated in the table. This saves a bunch of addresses! If you were to stick to the method defined by the RFC standards, the best you could gain is a subnet mask of 192 (2 bits), which allows you only two subnets ($2^2 - 2 = 2$).

Determining the Subnet Numbers for a Class C Subnet

The first subnet always has a 0 in the interesting octet. In the example, it would be 200.211.192.0, the same as the original nonsubnetted network address. To determine the subnet numbers for the additional subnets, first you have to determine the incremental value:

1. Begin with the octet that has an interesting value (other than 0 or 255) in the subnet mask. Then subtract the interesting value from 256. The result is the incremental value.

   If again you use the network 200.211.192.x and a mask of 255.255.255.192, the example yields the following equation: 256 – 192 = 64. Thus 64 is your incremental value in the interesting octet—the fourth octet in this case. Why the fourth octet? That's the octet with the interesting value, 192, in the mask.

2. To determine the second subnet number, add the incremental value to the 0 in the fourth octet of the first subnet.

    In the example, it would be 200.211.192.64.

3. To determine the third subnet number, add the incremental value to the interesting octet of the second subnet number.

    In the example, it would be 200.211.192.128.

4. Keep adding the incremental value in this fashion until you reach the actual subnet mask number.

    For example, 0 + 64 = 64, so your second subnet is 64. And 64 + 64 is 128, so your third subnet is 128. And 128 + 64 is 192, so your fourth subnet is 192. Because 192 is the subnet mask, this is your last subnet. If you tried to add 64 again, you'd come up with 256, an unusable octet value, which is always where you end up when you've gone too far. This means your valid subnets are 0, 64, 128, and 192.

The numbers between the subnets are your valid host and broadcast addresses. For example, the following are valid hosts for two of the subnets in a Class C network with a subnet mask of 192:

▪   The valid hosts for subnet 64 are in the range 65–126, which gives you 62 hosts per subnet.

    (You can't use 127 as a host because that would mean your host bits would be all 1s. The all-1s format is reserved as the broadcast address for that subnet.)

▪   The valid hosts for subnet 128 are in the range 129–190, with a broadcast address of 191.

As you can see, this solution wastes a few addresses—six more than not subnetting at all, to be exact. In a Class C network, this should not be hard to justify. The 255.255.255.128 subnet mask is an even better solution if you need only two subnets and expect to need close to 126 host addresses per subnet.

Calculating Values for an Eight-Subnet Class C Network

What happens if you need eight subnets in your Class C network?

By using the calculation of $2x$, where x is the number of subnet bits, you would need 3 subnet bits to get eight subnets ($2^3 = 8$). What are the valid subnets, and what are the valid hosts of each subnet? Let's figure it out.

11100000 is 224 in binary, and it would be the interesting value in the fourth octet of the subnet mask. This must be the same on all workstations.

You're likely to see test questions that ask you to identify the problem with a given configuration. If a workstation has the wrong subnet mask, the router could "think" that the workstation is on a different subnet than it actually is. When that happens, the misguided router won't forward packets to the workstation in question. Similarly, if the mask is incorrectly specified in the workstation's configuration, that workstation will observe the mask and send packets to the default gateway when it shouldn't.

To figure out the valid subnets, subtract the interesting octet value from 256 (256 – 224 = 32), so 32 is your incremental value for the fourth octet. Of course, the 0 subnet is your first subnet, as always. The other subnets would be 32, 64, 96, 128, 160, 192, and 224. The valid hosts are the numbers between the subnet numbers, except the numbers that equal all 1s in the host bits. These numbers would be 31, 63, 95, 127, 159, 191, 223, and 255. Remember that using all 1s in the host bits is reserved for the broadcast address of each subnet.

The valid subnets, hosts, and broadcasts are as follows:

Subnet	Hosts	Broadcast
0	1–30	31
32	33–62	63
64	65–94	95
96	97–126	127
128	129–158	159
160	161–190	191
192	193–222	223
224	225–254	255

You can add one more bit to the subnet mask just for fun. You were using 3 bits, which gave you 224. By adding the next bit, the mask now becomes 240 (11110000).

By using 4 bits for the subnet mask, you get 14 subnets because $2^4 = 16$. This subnet mask also gives you only 4 bits for the host addresses, or $2^4 - 2 = 14$ hosts per subnet. As you can see, the number of hosts per subnet gets reduced rather quickly for each host bit that gets reallocated for subnet use.

The first valid subnet for subnet 240 is 0, as always. Because 256 – 240 = 16, your remaining subnets are then 16, 32, 48, 64, 80, 96, 112, 128, 144, 160, 176, 192, 208, 224, and 240. Remember that the actual interesting octet value also represents the last valid subnet, so 240 is the last valid subnet number. The valid hosts are the numbers between the subnets, except for the numbers that are all 1s—the broadcast address for the subnet.

Table 9.6 shows the numbers in the interesting (fourth) octet for a Class C network with eight subnets.

TABLE 9.6   Fourth octet addresses for a Class C network with eight subnets

Subnet	Hosts	Broadcast
0	1–14	15
16	17–30	31
32	33–46	47
48	49–62	63
64	65–78	79
80	81–94	95
96	97–110	111
112	113–126	127
128	129–142	143
144	145–158	159
160	161–174	175
176	177–190	191
192	193–206	207
208	209–222	223
224	225–238	239
240	241–254	255

Subnetting Class B

Because a Class B network has 16 bits for host addresses, you have plenty of available bits to play with when figuring out a subnet mask. Remember that you have to start with the leftmost bit and work toward the right. For example, a Class B network would look like x.y.0.0, with the default mask of 255.255.0.0. Using the default mask would give you one network with 65,534 hosts.

The default mask in binary is 11111111.11111111.00000000.00000000. The 1s represent the corresponding network bits in the IP address, and the 0s represent the host bits. When you're creating a subnet mask, the leftmost bit(s) will be borrowed from the host bits

(0s will be turned into 1s) to become the subnet mask. You then use the remaining bits that are still set to 0 for host addresses.

If you use only 1 bit to create a subnet mask, you have a mask of 255.255.128.0. If you use 2 bits, you have a mask of 255.255.192.0, or 11111111.11111111.11000000.00000000.

As with subnetting a Class C address, you now have three parts of the IP address: the network address, the subnet address, and the host address. You figure out the subnet mask numbers the same way you did with a Class C network (see the previous section, "Calculating Values for an Eight-Subnet Class C Network"), but you'll end up with a lot more hosts per subnet.

There are four subnets, because $2^2 = 4$. The valid third-octet values for the subnets are 0, 64, 128, and 192 (256 − 192 = 64, so the incremental value of the third octet is 64). However, there are 14 bits (0s) left over for host addressing. This gives you 16,382 hosts per subnet ($2^{14} - 2 = 16,382$).

The valid subnets and hosts are as follows:

Subnet	Hosts	Broadcast
x.y.0.0	x.y.0.1 through x.y. 63.254	x.y.63.255
x.y.64.0	x.y.64.1 through x.y.127.254	x.y.127.255
x.y.128.0	x.y.128.1 through x.y.191.254	x.y.191.255
x.y.192.0	x.y.192.1 through x.y.255.254	x.y.255.255

You can add another bit to the subnet mask, making it 11111111.11111111.11100000 .00000000, or 255.255.224.0. This gives you eight subnets ($2^3 = 8$) and 8,190 hosts. The valid subnets are 0, 32, 64, 96, 128, 160, 192, and 224 (256 − 224 = 32). The subnets, valid hosts, and broadcasts are listed here:

Subnet	Hosts	Broadcast
x.y.0.0	x.y.0.1 through x.y.31.254	x.y.31.255
x.y.32.0	x.y.32.1 through x.y.63.254	x.y.63.255
x.y.64.0	x.y.64.1 through x.y.95.254	x.y.95.255
x.y.96.0	x.y.96.1 through x.y.127.254	x.y.127.255
x.y.128.0	x.y.128.1 through x.y.159.254	x.y.159.255
x.y.160.0	x.y.160.1 through x.y.191.254	x.y.191.255
x.y.192.0	x.y.192.1 through x.y.223.254	x.y.223.255
x.y.224.0	x.y.224.1 through x.y.255.254	x.y.255.255

The following are the breakdowns for a 9-bit mask and a 14-bit mask:

- If you use 9 bits for the mask, it gives you 512 subnets (2^9). With only 7 bits for hosts, you still have 126 hosts per subnet ($2^7 - 2 = 126$). The mask looks like this:

    11111111.11111111.11111111.10000000, or 255.255.255.128

- If you use 14 bits for the subnet mask, you get 16,384 subnets (2^{14}) but only two hosts per subnet ($2^2 - 2 = 2$). The subnet mask would look like this:

    11111111.11111111.11111111.11111100, or 255.255.255.252

 Real World Scenario

Subnet Mask Use in an ISP

You may be wondering why you would use a 14-bit subnet mask with a Class B address. This approach is actually very common. Let's say you have a Class B network and use a subnet mask of 255.255.255.0. You'd have 256 subnets and 254 hosts per subnet. Imagine also that you are an Internet service provider (ISP) and have a network with many WAN links, a different one between you and each customer. Typically, you'd have a direct connection between each site. Each of these links must be on its own subnet or network. There will be two hosts on these subnets—one address for each router port. If you used the mask described earlier (255.255.255.0), you would waste 252 host addresses per subnet. But by using the 255.255.255.252 subnet mask, you have more subnets available, which means more customers—each subnet with only two hosts, which is the maximum allowed on a point-to-point circuit.

You can use the 255.255.255.252 subnet mask only if you are running a routing algorithm such as Enhanced Interior Gateway Routing Protocol (EIGRP) or Open Shortest Path First (OSPF). These routing protocols allow what is called *Variable Length Subnet Masking (VLSM)*. VLSM allows you to run the 255.255.255.252 subnet mask on your interfaces to the WANs and run 255.255.255.0 on your router interfaces in your local area network (LAN) using the same classful network address for all subnets. It works because these routing protocols transmit the subnet mask information in the update packets that they send to the other routers. Classful routing protocols, such as RIP version 1, don't transmit the subnet mask and therefore cannot employ VLSM.

Subnetting Class A

Class A networks have even more bits available than Class B and Class C networks. A default Class A network subnet mask is only 8 bits, or 255.0.0.0, giving you a whopping 24 bits for hosts to play with. Knowing which hosts and subnets are valid is a lot more complicated than it was for either Class B or Class C networks.

If you use a mask of 11111111.1111111.00000000.00000000, or 255.255.0.0, you'll have 8 bits for subnets, or 256 subnets (2^8). This leaves 16 bits for hosts, or 65,534 hosts per subnet ($2^{16} - 2 = 65534$).

If you split the 24 bits evenly between subnets and hosts, you would give each one 12 bits. The mask would look like this: 11111111.11111111.11110000.00000000, or 255.255.240.0. How many valid subnets and hosts would you have? The answer is 4,096 subnets each with 4,094 hosts ($2^{12} - 2 = 4094$).

The second octet will be somewhere between 0 and 255. However, you will need to figure out the third octet. Because the third octet has a 240 mask, you get 16 (256 – 240 = 16) as your incremental value in the third octet. The third octet must start with 0 for the first subnet, the second subnet will have 16 in the third octet, and so on. This means that some of your valid subnets are as follows (not in order):

Subnet	Hosts	Broadcast
x.0-255.0.0	x.0-255.0.1 through x.0-255.15.254	x.0-255.15.255
x.0-255.16.0	x.0-255.16.1 through x.0-255.31.254	x.0-255.31.255
x.0-255.32.0	x.0-255.32.1 through x.0-255.47.254	x.0-255.47.255
x.0-255.48.0	x.0-255.48.1 through x.0-255.63.254	x.0-255.63.255

They go on in this way for the remaining third-octet values through 224 in the subnet column.

Working with Classless Inter-Domain Routing

Microsoft uses an alternate way to write address ranges, called *Classless Inter-Domain Routing* (*CIDR*; pronounced "cider"). CIDR is a shorthand version of the subnet mask. For example, an address of 131.107.2.0 with a subnet mask of 255.255.255.0 is listed in CIDR as 131.107.2.0/24 because the subnet mask contains 24 1s. An address listed as 141.10.32.0/19 would have a subnet mask of 255.255.224.0, or 19 1s (the default subnet mask for Class B plus 3 bits). This is the nomenclature used in all Microsoft exams (see Figure 9.12).

FIGURE 9.12 Subnet mask represented by 1s

Subnet mask in binary: 1111 1111. 1111 1111. 1111 1111. 0000 0000

Subnet mask in decimal: 255   .   255   .   255   .   0

(The spaces in the above example are only for illustrative purposes.
The subnet mask in decimal would actually appear as 255.255.255.0.)

Let's say an Internet company has assigned you the following Class C address and CIDR number: 192.168.10.0/24. This represents the Class C address of 192.168.10.0 and a subnet mask of 255.255.255.0.

Again, CIDR represents the number of 1s turned on in a subnet mask. For example, a CIDR number of /16 stands for 255.255.0.0 (11111111.11111111.00000000.00000000).

The following is a list of all the CIDR numbers (starting with a Class A default subnet mask) and their corresponding subnet masks.

CIDR	Mask	CIDR	Mask	CIDR	Mask
/8	255.0.0.0	/17	255.255.128.0	/25	255.255.255.128
/9	255.128.0.0	/18	255.255.192.0	/26	255.255.255.192
/10	255.192.0.0	/19	255.255.224.0	/27	255.255.255.224
/11	255.224.0.0	/20	255.255.240.0	/28	255.255.255.240
/12	255.240.0.0	/21	255.255.248.0	/29	255.255.255.248
/13	255.248.0.0	/22	255.255.252.0	/30	255.255.255.252
/14	255.252.0.0	/23	255.255.254.0	/31	255.255.255.254
/15	255.254.0.0	/24	255.255.255.0	/32	255.255.255.255
/16	255.255.0.0				

Quickly Identifying Subnet Characteristics Using CIDR

Given the limited time you have to dispatch questions in the structured environment of a Microsoft certification exam, every shortcut to coming up with the correct answer is a plus. The following method, using CIDR notation, can shave minutes off the time it takes you to complete a single question. Since you already understand the underlying binary technology at the heart of subnetting, you can use the following shortcuts, one for each address class, to come up with the correct answer without working in binary.

Identifying Class C Subnet Characteristics

Consider the host address 192.168.10.50/27. The following steps flesh out the details of the subnet of which this address is a member:

1. Obtain the CIDR-notation prefix length for the address by converting the dotted-decimal mask to CIDR notation.

   In this case, /27 corresponds to a mask of 255.255.255.224. Practice converting between these notations until it becomes second nature.

2. Using the closest multiple of 8 that is greater than or equal to the prefix length, compute the interesting octet (the octet that increases from one subnet to the next in increments other than 1 or 0). Divide this multiple by 8. The result is a number corresponding to the octet that is interesting.

    In this case, the next multiple of 8 greater than 27 is 32. Dividing 32 by 8 produces the number 4, pointing to the fourth octet as the interesting one.

3. To compute the incremental value in the interesting octet, subtract the prefix length from the next higher multiple of 8, which in this case is 32. The result (32 − 27) is 5. Raise 2 to the computed value (2^5 = 32). The result is the incremental value of the interesting octet.

4. Recall the value of the interesting octet from the original address (50 in this case). Starting with 0, increment by the incremental value until the value is exceeded. The values then are 0, 32, 64, and so on.

5. The subnet in question extends from the increment that is immediately less than or equal to the address's interesting octet value to the address immediately before the next increment. In this example, 192.168.10.50/27 belongs to the subnet 192.168.10.32, and this subnet extends to the address immediately preceding 192.168.10.64, which is its broadcast address, 192.168.10.63.

    Note that if the interesting octet is not the fourth octet, all octets after the interesting octet must be set to 0 for the subnet address.

6. The usable range of addresses for the subnet in question extends from one higher than the subnet address to one less than the broadcast address, making the range for the subnet in question 192.168.10.33 through 192.168.10.62. As you can see, 192.168.10.50/27 definitely falls within the subnet 192.168.10.32/27.

Identifying Class B Subnet Characteristics

Using the steps in the previous section, find the subnet in which the address 172.16.76.12 with a mask of 255.255.240.0 belongs:

1. The corresponding CIDR notation prefix length is /20.

2. The next multiple of 8 that is greater than 20 is 24. 24 × 8 = 3. Octet 3 is interesting.

3. 24 − 20 = 4, so the incremental value is 2^4 = 16.

4. The increments in the third octet are 0, 16, 32, 48, 64, 80, and so on.

5. The increments of 64 and 80 bracket the address's third-octet value of 76, making the subnet in question 172.16.64.0, after setting all octets after the interesting octet to 0. This subnet's broadcast address is 172.16.79.255, which comes right before the next subnet address of 172.16.80.0.

6. The usable address range then extends from 172.16.64.1 through 172.16.79.254.

Identifying Class A Subnet Characteristics

Try it one more time with 10.6.127.255/14. Combine some of the related steps if possible:

1. The prefix length is 14. The next multiple of 8 that is greater than or equal to 14 is 16. $16 \times 8 = 2$, so the second octet is interesting.

2. $16 - 14 = 2$, so the incremental value in the second octet is $2^2 = 4$.

3. The corresponding second-octet value of 6 in the address falls between the 4 and 8 increments. This means that the subnet in question is 10.4.0.0 (setting octets after the second one to 0) and its broadcast address is 10.7.255.255.

4. The usable address range is from 10.4.0.1 through 10.7.255.254.

Determining Quantities of Subnets and Hosts

The general technique described in the previous section is also useful when trying to determine the total number of subnets and hosts produced by a given mask with respect to the default mask of the class of address in question.

For example, consider the Class B address 172.16.0.0 with a subnet mask of 255.255.254.0.

This is a prefix length of 23 bits. When you subtract the default prefix length for a Class B address of 16 from 23, you get the value 7. Raising 2 to the 7th power results in the value 128, which is the number of subnets you get when you subnet a Class B address with the 255.255.254.0 mask.

Determining the number of hosts available in each of these 128 subnets is simple because you always subtract the prefix length that the subnet mask produces, 23 in this example, from the value 32, which represents the total number of bits in any IP address. The difference, 9, represents the remaining number of 0s, or host bits, in the subnet mask. Raising 2 to this value produces the total possible number of host IDs per subnet that this subnet mask allows. Remember to subtract 2 from this result to account for the subnet and broadcast addresses for each subnet. This gives you the actual number of usable host IDs per subnet. In this case, this value is $2^9 - 2 = 510$.

Repeated practice with this technique will reduce your time to obtain the desired answer to mere seconds, leaving time for the more challenging tasks in each question. You have a wealth of examples and scenarios in this chapter, as well as in the review questions, on which to try your technique and build your trust in this faster method.

Understanding IPv6

Internet Protocol version 6 (IPv6) is the first major revamping of IP since RFC 791 was accepted in 1981. Yes the operation of IP has improved, and there have been a few bells and whistles added (such as NAT, for example), but the basic structure is still being used as it was originally intended. IPv6 has actually been available to use in Microsoft operating systems since NT 4.0, but it always had to be manually enabled. Windows Vista was the first

Microsoft operating system to have it enabled by default. It is also enabled by default in Windows 7, Windows 8, Windows Server 2008, Windows Server 2008 R2, and Windows Server 2012, and it probably will be in all Microsoft operating systems from this point on.

TCP and UDP—as well as the IP applications, such as HTTP, FTP, SNMP, and the rest—are still being used in IPv4. So you might ask, why change to the new version? What does IPv6 bring to your networking infrastructure? What is the structure of an IPv6 address? How is it implemented and used within Windows Server 2012? I'll answer all those questions and more in the following sections.

IPv6 History and Need

In the late 1970s, as the IP specifications were being put together, the vision of the interconnected devices was limited compared to what we actually have today. To get an idea of the growth of the Internet, take a look at Hobbes' Internet Timeline in RFC 2235 (www.faqs .org/rfcs/rfc2235.html). As you can see, in 1984, the number of hosts finally surpassed 1,000—two years after TCP and IP were introduced. With 32 bits of addressing available in IPv4, it handled the 1,000+ hosts just fine. And even with the number of hosts breaking the 10,000 mark in 1987 and then 100,000 in 1989, there were still plenty of IP addresses to go around. But when the number of hosts exceeded 2 million in 1992 and 3 million in 1994, concern in the industry started to build. So in 1994, a working group was formed to come up with a solution to the quickly dwindling usable address availability in the IPv4 space. Internet Protocol next generation (IPng) was started.

Have you heard of IP address depletion being a problem today? Probably not as much. When the working group realized it could not have IPv6 standardized before the available addresses might run out, they developed and standardized *Network Address Translation (NAT)* as an interim solution. NAT, or more specifically an implementation of NAT called *Port Address Translation (PAT)*, took care of a big portion of the problem.

NAT works very well, but it does have some limitations, including issues of peer-to-peer applications with their IPv4 addresses embedded in the data, issues of end-to-end traceability, and issues of overlapping addresses when two networks merge. Because all devices in an IPv6 network will have a unique address and no network address translation will take place, the global addressing concept of IPv4 will be brought back (the address put on by the source device will stay all the way to the destination). Thus with the new-and-improved functionality of IPv6, the drawbacks of NAT and the limitations of IPv4 will be eliminated.

New and Improved IPv6 Concepts

Several elements of the IPv4 protocol could use some enhancements. Fortunately, IPv6 incorporates enhancements as well as new features directly into the protocol specification to provide better and additional functionality.

The following list includes new concepts and new implementations of old concepts in IPv6:

- Larger address space (128-bit vs. 32-bit).

- Autoconfiguration of Internet-accessible addresses with or without DHCP. (Without DHCP, it's called *stateless autoconfiguration*.)

- More efficient IP header (fewer fields and no checksum).

- Fixed-length IP header (the IPv4 header is variable length) with extension headers beyond the standard fixed length to provide enhancements.

- Built-in IP mobility and security. (Although available in IPv4, the IPv6 implementation is a much better implementation.)

- Built-in transition schemes to allow integration of the IPv4 and IPv6 spaces.

- ARP broadcast messages replaced with multicast request.

Here are more details about these features:

128-Bit Address Space   The new 128-bit address space will provide unique addresses for the foreseeable future. Although I would like to say that we will never use up all the addresses, history may prove me wrong. The number of unique addresses in the IPv6 space is 2^{128}, or 3.4×10^{38}, addresses. How big is that number? It's enough for toasters and refrigerators (and maybe even cars) to all have their own addresses.

As a point of reference, the nearest black hole to Earth is 1,600 light years away. If you were to stack 4mm BB pellets from here to the nearest black hole and back, you would need 1.51×10^{22} BBs. This means that you could uniquely address each BB from Earth to the black hole and back and still have quite a few addresses left over.

Another way to look at it is that the IPv6 address space is big enough to provide more than 1 million addresses per square inch of the surface area of the earth (oceans included).

Autoconfiguration and Stateless Autoconfiguration   Autoconfiguration is another added/ improved feature of IPv6. We've used DHCP for a while to assign IP addresses to client machines. You should even remember that APIPA can be used to assign addresses automatically to Microsoft DHCP client machines in the absence of a DHCP server. The problem with APIPA is that it confines communication between machines to a local LAN (no default gateway). What if a client machine could ask whether there was a router on the LAN and what network it was on? If the client machine knew that, it could not only assign itself an address, it could also choose the appropriate network and default gateway. The stateless autoconfiguration functionality of IPv6 allows the clients to do this.

Improved IPv6 Header   The IPv6 header is more efficient than the IPv4 header because it is fixed length (with extensions possible) and has only a few fields. The IPv6 header consists of a total of 40 bytes:

32 bytes   Source and destination IPv6 addresses

8 bytes   Version field, traffic class field, flow label field, payload length field, next header field, and hop limit field

You don't have to waste your time with a checksum validation anymore, and you don't have to include the length of the IP header (it's fixed in IPv6; the IP header is variable length in IPv4, so the length must be included as a field).

IPv6 Mobility   IPv6 is only a replacement of the OSI layer 3 component, so you'll continue to use the TCP (and UDP) components as they currently exist. IPv6 addresses a TCP issue, though. Specifically, TCP is connection oriented, meaning you establish an end-to-end communication path with sequencing and acknowledgments before you ever send any data, and then you have to acknowledge all of the pieces of data sent. You do this through a combination of an IP address, port number, and port type (socket).

If the source IP address changes, the TCP connection may be disrupted. But then how often does this happen? Well it happens more and more often, as more people are walking around with a wireless laptop or a wireless Voice over IP (VoIP) telephone. IPv6 mobility establishes a TCP connection with a home address and, when changing networks, it continues to communicate with the original endpoint from a care-of address as it changes LANs, which sends all traffic back through the home address. The handing off of network addresses does not disrupt the TCP connection state (the original TCP port number and address remain intact).

Improved Security   Unlike IPv4, IPv6 has security built in. *Internet Protocol Security (IPsec)* is a component used today to authenticate and encrypt secure tunnels from a source to a destination. This can be from the client to the server or between gateways. IPv4 lets you do this by enhancing IP header functionality (basically adding a second IP header while encrypting everything behind it). In IPv6, you add this as standard functionality by using extension headers. Extension headers are inserted into the packet only if they are needed. Each header has a "next header" field, which identifies the next piece of information. The extension headers currently identified for IPv6 are Hop-By-Hop Options, Routing, Fragment, Destination Options, Authentication, and Encapsulating Security Payload. The Authentication header and the Encapsulating Security Payload header are the IPsec-specific control headers.

IPv4 to IPv6 Interoperability   Several mechanisms in IPv6 make the IPv4-to-IPv6 transition easy:

- A simple dual-stack implementation where both IPv4 and IPv6 are installed and used is certainly an option. In most situations (so far), this doesn't work so well because most of us aren't connected to an IPv6 network and our Internet connection is not IPv6 even if we're using IPv6 internally. Therefore, Microsoft includes other mechanisms that can be used in several different circumstances.

- *Intra-Site Automatic Tunnel Addressing Protocol (ISATAP)* is an automatic tunneling mechanism used to connect an IPv6 network to an IPv4 address space (not using NAT). ISATAP treats the IPv4 space as one big logical link connection space.

- *6to4* is a mechanism used to transition to IPv4. This method, like ISATAP, treats the IPv4 address space as a logical link layer with each IPv6 space in transition using a 6to4 router to create endpoints using the IPv4 space as a point-to-point connection (kind of like a WAN, eh?). 6to4 implementations still do not work well through a NAT, although a 6to4 implementation using an Application layer gateway (ALG) is certainly doable.

- *Teredo* is a mechanism that allows users behind a NAT to access the IPv6 space by tunneling IPv6 packets in UDP.

Pseudo-interfaces are used in these mechanisms to create a usable interface for the operating system. Another interesting feature of IPv6 is that addresses are assigned to interfaces (or pseudo-interfaces), not simply to the end node. Your Windows Server 2012 will have several unique IPv6 addresses assigned.

New Broadcast Methods IPv6 has moved away from using broadcasting. The three types of packets used in IPv6 are unicast, multicast, and anycast. IPv6 clients then must use one of these types to get the MAC address of the next Ethernet hop (default gateway). IPv6 makes use of multicasting for this along with the new functionality called *neighbor discovery*. Not only does ARP utilize new functionality, but ICMP (also a layer 3 protocol) has been redone and is now known as ICMP6. *ICMP6* is used for messaging (packet too large, time exceeded, and so on) as it was in IPv4, but now it's also used for the messaging of IPv6 mobility. ICMP6 echo request and ICMP6 echo reply are still used for ping.

IPv6 Addressing Concepts

You need to consider several concepts when using IPv6 addressing. For starters, the format of the address has changed. Three types of addresses are used in IPv6 with some predefined values within the address space. You need to get used to seeing these addresses and be able to identify their uses.

IPv6 Address Format

For the design of IPv4 addresses, you present addresses as octets or the decimal (base 10) representation of 8 bits. Four octets add up to the 32 bits required. IPv6 expands the address space to 128 bits, and the representation is for the most part shown in hexadecimal (a notation used to represent 8 bits using the values 0–9 and A–F). Figure 9.13 compares IPv4 to IPv6.

A full IPv6 address looks like this example:

2001:0DB8:0000:0000:1234:0000:A9FE:133E

FIGURE 9.13 IPv4/IPv6 comparison

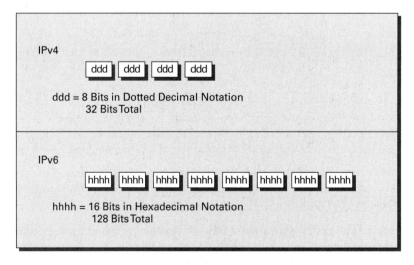

You can tell the implementation of DNS will make life a lot easier even for those who like to ping the address in lieu of the name. Fortunately, DNS already has the ability to handle IPv6 addresses with the use of an AAAA record. (*A* is short for *alias*.) An A record in IPv4's addressing space is 32 bits, so an AAAA record, or four *A*s, is 128 bits. The Windows Server 2012 DNS server handles the AAAA and the reverse pointer (PTR) records for IPv6.

IPv6 Address Shortcuts

There are several shortcuts for writing an IPv6 address. These are described in the following list:

- :0: stands for :0000:.

- You can omit preceding 0s in any 16-bit word. For example, :DB8: and :0DB8: are equivalent.

- :: is a variable standing for enough zeros to round out the address to 128 bits. :: can be used only once in an address.

You can use these shortcuts to represent the example address 2001:0DB8:0000:0000:1234:0000:A9FE:133E, as shown here:

- Compress :0000: into :0::

    2001:0DB8:0000:0000:1234:0:A9FE:133E

- Eliminate preceding zeros:

    2001:DB8:0000:0000:1234:0:A9FE:133E

- Use the special variable shortcut for multiple 0s:

    2001:DB8::1234:0:A9FE:133E

You now also use prefix notation or slash notation when discussing IPv6 networks. For example, the network of the previous address can be represented as: 2001:DB8:0000:0000:0000:0000:0000:0000. This can also be expressed as 2001:DB8:: /32. The /32 indicates 32 bits of network, and 2001:DB8: is 32 bits of network.

IPv6 Address Assignment

So, do you subnet IPv6? The answer depends on your definition of subnetting. If you are given 32 bits of network from your ISP, you have 96 bits with which to work. If you use some of the 96 bits to route within your network infrastructure, then you are subnetting. In this context, you do subnet IPv6. However, given the huge number of bits you have available, you will no longer need to implement VLSM. For example, Microsoft has a network space of 2001:4898:: /32. That gives the administrators a space of 96 bits (2^{96} = 79,228, 162,514,264,337,593,543,950,336 unique addresses using all 96 bits) with which to work.

You can let Windows Server 2012 dynamically/automatically assign its IPv6 address, or you can still assign it manually (see Figure 9.14). With dynamic/automatic assignment, the IPv6 address is assigned either by a DHCPv6 server or by the Windows Server 2012 machine. If no DHCPv6 server is configured, the Windows Server 2012 machine can query the local LAN segment to find a router with a configured IPv6 interface. If so, the server will assign itself an address on the same IPv6 network as the router interface and set its default gateway to the router interface's IPv6 address. Figure 9.14 shows that you have the same dynamic and manual choices as you do in IPv4; however, the input values for IPv6 must conform to the new format.

FIGURE 9.14 TCP/IPv6 Properties window

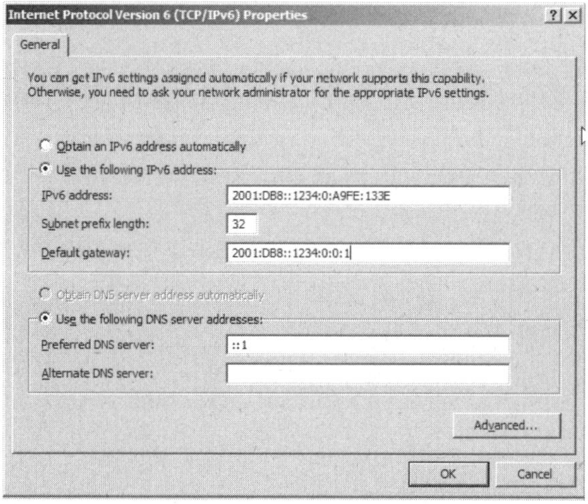

To see your configured IP addresses (IPv4 and IPv6), you can still use the ipconfig command. For example, I have configured a static IPv4 address and an IPv6 address on my server. The IPv6 address is the same as used in the earlier IPv6 example address. Figure 9.15 shows the result of this command on Windows Server 2012 for my server.

FIGURE 9.15 IPv6 configuration as seen from the command prompt

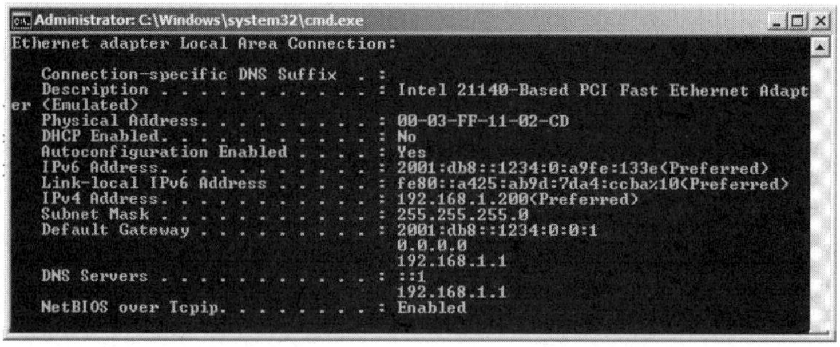

IPv6 Address Types

As stated earlier, there are three types of addresses in IPv6: anycast, unicast, and multicast. A description of each of these types of IPv6 addresses follows.

Note the absence of the broadcast type, which is included in IPv4. You can't use broadcasts in IPv6; they've been replaced with multicasts.

Anycast Addresses   Anycast addresses are not really new. The concept of anycast existed in IPv4 but was not widely used. An *anycast address* is an IPv6 address assigned to multiple devices (usually different devices). When an anycast packet is sent, it is delivered to one of the devices, usually the closest one.

Unicast Addresses   A *unicast packet* uniquely identifies an interface of an IPv6 device. The interface can be a virtual or pseudo-interface or a real (physical) interface.

Unicast addresses come in several types, as described in the following list:

Global Unicast Address   As of this writing, the global unicast address space is defined as 2000:: /3. The 2001::/32 networks are the IPv6 addresses currently being issued to business entities. As mentioned, Microsoft has been allocated 2001:4898:: /32. A Microsoft DHCPv6 server would be set up with scopes (ranges of addresses to be assigned) within this address space. There are some special addresses and address formats you will see in use as well. You'll find most example addresses listed as 2001:DB8:: /32; this space has been reserved for documentation. Do you remember the loopback address in IPv4, 127.0.0.1? In IPv6 the loopback address is ::1 (or 0:0:0:0:0:0:0:0001). You may also see an address with dotted-decimal used. A dual-stack Windows Server 2012 machine may also show you FE80::5EFE:192.168.1.200. This address form is used in an integration/migration model of IPv6 (or if you just can't leave the dotted-decimal era, I suppose).

Link-Local Address   Link-local addresses are defined as FE80:: /10. If you refer to Figure 9.15 showing the `ipconfig` command, you will see the link-local IPv6 address as fe80::a425:ab9d:7da4:ccba. The last 8 bytes (64 bits) are random to ensure a high probability of randomness for the link-local address. The link-local address is to be used on a single link (network segment) and should never be routed.

There is another form of the local-link IPv6 address called the *Extended User Interface 64-bit (EUI-64)* format. This is derived by using the MAC address of the physical interface and inserting an FFFE between the third and fourth bytes of the MAC. The first byte is also made 02 (this sets the universal/local or U/L bit to 1 as defined in IEEE 802 frame specification). Again looking at Figure 9.15, the EUI-64 address would take the physical (MAC) address 00-03-FF-11-02-CD and make the link-local IPv6 address FE80::0203:FFFF:FE11:02CD. (I've left the preceding zeros in the link-local IPv6 address to make it easier for you to pick out the MAC address with the FFFE inserted.)

AnonymousAddress   Microsoft Server 2012 uses the random address by default instead of EUI-64. The random value is called the *AnonymousAddress* in Microsoft Server 2012. It can be modified to allow the use of EUI-64.

Unique Local Address   The *unique local address* can be Fc00 or FD00, and it is used like the private address space of IPv4. RFC 4193 describes unique local addresses. They are not expected to be routable on the global Internet. They are used for private routing within an organization.

Multicast Address   *Multicast addresses* are one-to-many communication packets. Multicast packets are identifiable by their first byte (most significant byte, leftmost byte, leftmost 2 nibbles, leftmost 8 bits, and so on). A multicast address is defined as FF00::/8.

In the second byte shown (the 00 of FF00), the second 0 is what's called the *scope*. Interface-local is 01, and link-local is 02. FF01:: is an interface-local multicast.

There are several well-known (already defined) multicast addresses. For example, if you want to send a packet to all nodes in the link-local scope, you send the packet to FF02::1 (also shown as FF02:0:0:0:0:0:0:1). The all-routers multicast address is FF02::2.

You can also use multicasting to get the logical link layer address (MAC address) of a device with which you are trying to communicate. Instead of using the ARP mechanism of IPv4, IPv6 uses the ICMPv6 neighbor solicitation (NS) and neighbor advertisement (NA) messages. The NS and NA ICMPv6 messages are all part of the new *Neighbor Discovery Protocol (NDP)*. This new ICMPv6 functionality also includes router solicitation and router advertisements as well as redirect messages (similar to the IPv4 redirect functionality).

Unicast vs. Anycast

Unicast and anycast addresses look the same and may be indistinguishable from each other; it just depends on how many devices have the same address. If only one device has a globally unique IPv6 address, it's a unicast address. If more than one device has the same address, it's an anycast address. Both unicast and anycast are considered one-to-one communication, although you could say that anycast is one-to-"one of many."

Table 9.7 outlines the IPv6 address space known prefixes and some well-known addresses.

TABLE 9.7   Pv6 address space known prefixes and addresses

Address Prefix	Scope of Use
2000:: /3	Global unicast space prefix
FE80:: /10	Link-local address prefix
FC00:: /7	Unique local unicast prefix
FD00:: /8	Unique local unicast prefix
FF00:: /8	Multicast prefix
2001:DB8:: /32	Global unicast prefix used for documentation
::1	Reserved local loopback address
2001:0000: /32	Teredo prefix (discussed later in this chapter)
2002:: /16	6to4 prefix

IPv6 Integration/Migration

It's time to get into the mindset of integrating IPv6 into your existing infrastructure with the longer goal of migrating to IPv6. In other words, this is not going to be an "OK, Friday the Internet is changing over" rollout. You have to bring about the change as a controlled implementation. It could easily take three to five years before a solid migration occurs and probably longer. I think the migration will take slightly less time than getting the world to migrate to the metric system on the overall timeline. The process of integration/migration consists of several mechanisms:

Dual Stack   Simply running both IPv4 and IPv6 on the same network, utilizing the IPv4 address space for devices using only IPv4 addresses and utilizing the IPv6 address space for devices using IPv6 addresses

Tunneling   Using an encapsulation scheme for transporting one address space inside another

Address Translation   Using a higher-level application to change one address type (IPv4 or IPv6) to the other transparently so that end devices are unaware one address space is talking to another

I elaborate on these three mechanisms in the following sections.

IPv6 Dual Stack

The default implementation in Windows Server 2012 is an enabled IPv6 configuration along with IPv4; this is dual stack. The implementation can be dual IP layer or dual TCP/IP stack. Windows Server 2012 uses the dual IP layer implementation (see Figure 9.16). When an application queries a DNS server to resolve a hostname to an IP address, the DNS server may respond with an IPv4 address or an IPv6 address. If the DNS server responds with both, Windows Server 2012 will prefer the IPv6 address. Windows Server 2012 can use both IPv4 and IPv6 addresses as necessary for network communication. When looking at the output of the `ipconfig` command, you will see both address spaces displayed.

FIGURE 9.16   IPv6 dual IP layer diagram

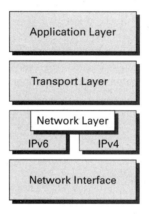

IPv6 Tunneling

Windows Server 2012 includes several tunneling mechanisms for tunneling IPv6 through the IPv4 address space. They include the following:

- Intra-Site Automatic Tunnel Addressing Protocol (ISATAP), which is used for unicast IPv6 communication across an IPv4 infrastructure. ISATAP is enabled by default in Windows Server 2012.

- 6to4, which is used for unicast IPv6 communication across an IPv4 infrastructure.

- Teredo, which is used for unicast IPv6 communication with an IPv4 NAT implementation across an IPv4 infrastructure.

   With multiple tunneling protocols available and enabled by default, you might ask, what's the difference and why is one used over the others? They all allow you to tunnel IPv6 packets through the IPv4 address space (a really cool thing if you're trying to integrate/migrate). Here are the details of these tunneling mechanisms:

ISATAP   *Intra-Site Automatic Tunnel Addressing Protocol (ISATAP)* is the automatic tunnel addressing protocol providing IPv6 addresses based on the IPv4 address of the end interface (node). The IPv6 address is automatically configured on the local device, and the dual stack machine can use either its IPv4 or IPv6 address to communicate on the local network (within the local network infrastructure). ISATAP can use the neighbor discovery mechanism to determine the router ID and network prefix where the device is located, thus making intrasite communication possible even in a routed infrastructure.

The format of an ISATAP address is as follows:

[64bits of prefix] [32bits indicating ISATAP] [32bits IPv4 Address]

The center 32 bits indicating ISATAP are actually 0000:5EFE (when using private IPv4 addresses). The ISATAP address of the example Windows Server 2012 machine using the link-local IPv6 address is FE80::5EFE:192.168.1.200. Each node participating in the ISATAP infrastructure must support ISATAP. If you're routing through an IPv4 cloud, a border router (a router transitioning from an IPv6 to IPv4 space) must support ISATAP. Windows Server 2012 can be configured as a border router, and it will forward ISATAP packets. ISATAP is experimental and is defined in RFC 4214.

6to4   *6to4* specifies a procedure for IPv6 networks to communicate with each other through an IPv4 space without the IPv6 nodes having to know what's happening. The IPv6 nodes do not need to be dual stacked to make this happen. The border router is the device responsible for knowing about the IPv6-to-IPv4 transition. The IPv6 packets are encapsulated at the border router (and decapsulated at the other end or on the way back). There is an assigned prefix for the 6to4 implementation: 2002:: /16. 6to4 is defined in RFC 3056.

Teredo   *Teredo* (named after a kind of shipworm that drills holes in the wood of ships) is a protocol designed to allow IPv6 addresses to be available to hosts through one or more layers of NAT. Teredo uses a process of tunneling packets through the IPv4 space using UDP. The Teredo service encapsulates the IPv6 data within a UDP segment (packet) and uses IPv4 addressing to get through the IPv4 cloud. Having a layer 4 (Transport layer) available to use as translation functionality is what gives you the ability to be behind a NAT. Teredo provides host-to-host communication and dynamic addressing for IPv6 nodes (dual stack), allowing the nodes to have access to resources in an IPv6 network and the IPv6 devices to have access to the IPv6 devices that have only connectivity to the IPv4 space (like home users who have an IPv6-enabled operating system connecting to IPv6 resources while their home ISP has only IPv4 capabilities). Teredo is defined in RFC 4380.

In Windows Server 2012, an IPv4 Teredo server is identified and configured (using the `netsh` command interface). The Teredo server provides connectivity resources (address) to the Teredo client (the node that has access to the IPv4 Internet and needs access to an IPv6 network/Internet. A Teredo relay is a component used by the IPv6 router to receive traffic destined for Teredo clients and forward the traffic appropriately. The defined prefix for Teredo address is 2001:0000:: /32. Teredo does add overhead like all the other implementations discussed. It is generally accepted that you should use the simplest model available. However, in the process of integration/migration for most of us behind a NAT, Teredo will be the process to choose.

From Windows Server 2012, use the `ipconfig /all` command to view the default configurations including IPv4 and IPv6. You may notice a notation that I didn't discuss, the percent sign at the end of the IPv6 address (see Figure 9.17). The number after the percent sign is the virtual interface identifier used by Windows Server 2012.

FIGURE 9.17   IPv6 interface identifier for `ipconfig` display

```
Link-local IPv6 Address . . . . . : fe80::a425:ab9d:7da4:ccba%10
```

Useful IPv6 Information Commands

You can use numerous commands to view, verify, and configure the network parameters of Windows Server 2012. Specifically, you can use the `netsh` command set and the `route` command set as well as the standard `ping` and `tracert` functions.

Use the `netsh` command interface (as well as the provided dialog boxes, if you wish) to examine and configure IPv6 functionality. The `netsh` command issued from the command interpreter changes into a network shell (`netsh`) where you can configure and view both IPv4 and IPv6 components.

Don't forget to use the ever-popular `route print` command to see the Windows Server 2012 routing tables (IPv4 and IPv6). The other diagnostic commands are still available for IPv4 as well as IPv6. In previous versions of Microsoft operating systems, `ping` was the IPv4 command, and `ping6` was the IPv6 command. This has changed in Windows Server 2012; `ping` works for both IPv4 and IPv6 to test layer 3 connectivity to remote devices. The IPv4 `tracert` command was `tracert6` for IPv6. The command is now `tracert` for both IPv4 and IPv6, and it will show you every layer 3 (IP) hop from source to destination. (This assumes that all of the administrators from here to there want you to see the hops and are not blocking ICMP. It also assumes that there are no IP tunnels, which your packets are traversing; you won't see the router hops in the tunnel either.)

Overall, the consortium of people developing the Internet and the Internet Protocol have tried to make all of the changes to communication infrastructures easy to implement. (This is a daunting task with the many vendors and various infrastructures currently in place.) The goal is not to daze and confuse administrators; it's designed to provide maximum flexibility with the greatest functionality. IPv6 is going to provide the needed layer 3 (Network layer, global addressing layer, logical addressing layer … call it what you like) functionality for the foreseeable future.

Subnetting with IPv6

Subnetting with IPv6 is a lot like subnetting with IPv4. You need to know how many bits you are going to use for the network mask to subnet it correctly.

For example, let's say you have an IPv6 prefix of 2001:DB8:BBCC:0000::/53 and you need to set up your network so that your IPv6 addressing scheme can handle 1,500 more subnets. How would you figure this out?

When determining any number of hosts or subnets, the calculation is 2 to the power (2^x). The first power number that is greater than or equal to the number you need is the power number that you add to the current network mask. Thus in the previous question, to get to 1,500 subnets, you would need to determine which 2^x is the first one that is greater than or equal to 1,500. If you calculate your powers correctly, 2^{11} ($2^{11} = 2,048$) is the first one that is greater than or equal to 1,500. So you would add the power of 11 to the /53 in the above address, and you would now use /64 as your network mask. Table 9.8 shows you some of the power numbers for the power of 2.

TABLE 9.8 Powers of 2

Power	Equals
2^2	4
2^3	8
2^4	16
2^5	32
2^6	64
2^7	128
2^8	256
2^9	512
2^{10}	1024
2^{11}	2048
2^{12}	4096

Understanding IP Address Management (IPAM)

A new advantage of Windows Server 2012 is the *IP Address Management (IPAM)* utility. IPAM is a built-in utility that allows an administrator to discover, monitor, audit, and manage the TCP/IP schema used on your network. IPAM provides an administrator with the ability to observe and administer the servers that are running Dynamic Host

Configuration Protocol (DHCP) and Domain Name Service (DNS). IPAM includes some of the following advantages:

Automatic IP Address Infrastructure Discovery   IPAM has the ability to discover automatically the domain's DHCP servers, DNS servers, and domain controllers. IPAM can do the discovery for any of the domains that you specify. Administrators also have the ability to enable or disable management of these servers using the IPAM utility.

Management of DHCP and DNS Services   IPAM gives administrators the capability to monitor and manage Microsoft DHCP and DNS servers across an entire network using the IPAM console.

Custom IP Address Management   Administrators now have the ability to customize the display of IP addresses and tracking and utilization data. IPAM allows the IP address space to be organized into IP address blocks, IP address ranges, and individual IP addresses. To help you organize the IP address space further, built-in or user-defined fields are also assigned to the IP addresses.

Auditing and Tracking of IP Address   IPAM allows administrators to track and audit IP addresses through the use of the IPAM console. IPAM allows IP addresses to be tracked using DHCP lease events and user logon events. These events are collected from the Network Policy Server (NPS), domain controllers, and DHCP servers. Administrators can track IP data by following the IP address, client ID, hostname, or user name.

As an administrator, there are a few things that you should understand before installing the IPAM feature. When setting up an IPAM server, you must NOT install IPAM on a domain controller. There are three main methods to deploy an IPAM server:

Distributed   This method allows an IPAM server deployment at every site in an enterprise network.

Centralized   This method allows only one IPAM server in an enterprise network.

Hybrid   This method uses a central IPAM server deployment along with dedicated IPAM servers at each site in the enterprise network.

> Remember, when installing IPAM in any of the scenarios mentioned, you cannot install the IPAM feature on an Active Directory domain controller.

If configured, IPAM automatically communicates on your domain. IPAM will try to locate your DNS servers, DHCP servers, and domain controllers as long as those servers are within the searching scope that you have configured. An administrator can configure whether the servers (DNS, DHCP, and domain controllers) are managed by IPAM or unmanaged.

If you want your servers to be managed by IPAM, you must make sure that you set up the network and the servers properly. For example, you will need to configure the security settings and firewall ports properly on the servers (DNS, DHCP, and domain controllers) in order to allow IPAM to access these servers and perform its configuration and monitoring. You can configure these server settings in one of two ways: manually or automatically through the use of a Group Policy object (GPO).

Exercise 9.1 will show you how to install the IPAM feature. You will install and configure the IPAM feature using Server Manager. This exercise has to be done on a member server.

EXERCISE 9.1

Installing the IPAM feature

1. Open Server Manager.

2. Click the number 2 link, Add Roles And Features.

3. Choose role-based or feature-based and click Next.

4. Choose your server and click Next.

5. On the Roles screen, just click Next.

6. On the Features screen, click the box for the IP Address Management (IPAM) server. Click the Add Features button when the box appears. Click Next.

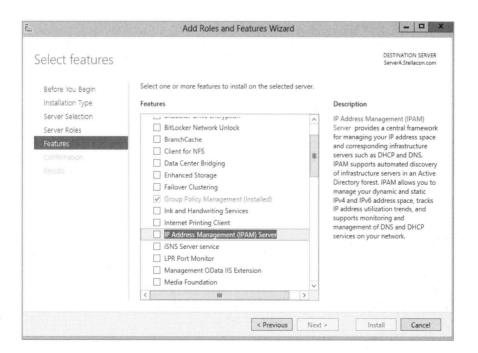

7. At the Confirmation screen, click the Install button.

8. Once the installation is complete, click the Close button.

9. While in Server Manager, click the IPAM link on the left side. This opens the IPAM Overview page.

10. Click number 2, Provision The IPAM Server.

11. Click Next at the Before You Begin screen.

12. At the Select Provisioning Method screen, choose GPO and put in a GPO suffix name. I used IPAM1 for the GPO suffix name. This is a unique name to help identify the IPAM.

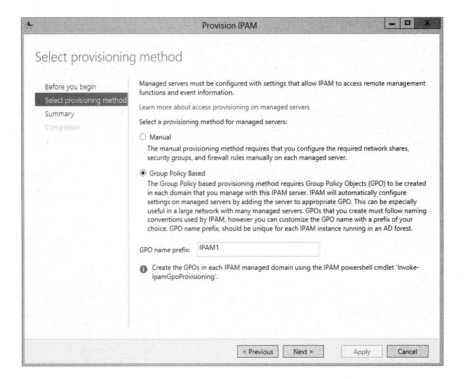

13. At the Summary screen, click the Apply button.

14. Once the process is completed, click the Close button.

15. In IPAM overview screen, under Manage, choose Add Servers.

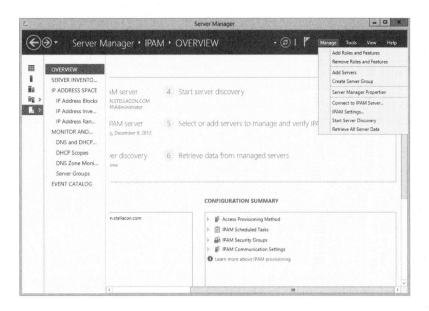

16. In the Add Servers box, click the DNS tab. In the search box, type the name of your DNS server and click the magnifying glass.

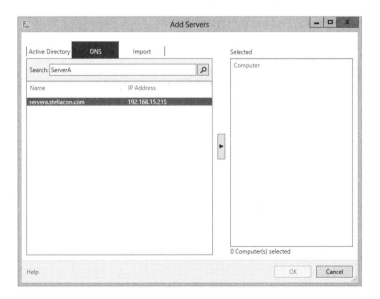

17. Under Name, double-click the server name. The server will be added to the right-side box. Click OK. Close Server Manager.

Summary

How TCP/IP is the primary protocol in use today was one of the important topics covered in this chapter. You also learned that the 32-bit IPv4 address is a structured and hierarchical one that is used to identify uniquely every machine on a network. You learned how to determine available IP addresses and implement subnetting. In addition, you learned how the new layer 3 IPv6 protocol is implemented, including the structure of the IPv6 address. Finally, I discussed the new functionality included in IPv6 addressing as well as several Windows Server 2012 integration/migration implementations.

Exam Essentials

Understand what subnetting is and when to use it. If an organization is large and has many computers, or if its computers are geographically dispersed, it's sensible to divide its large network into smaller ones connected by routers. These smaller networks are called *subnets*. Subnetting is the process of carving a single IP network into smaller, logical subnetworks.

Understand subnet masks. For the subnet address scheme to work, every machine on the network must know which part of the host address will be used as the subnet address. The network administrator creates a 32-bit subnet mask consisting of 1s and 0s. The 1s in the subnet mask represent the positions that refer to the network or subnet addresses. The 0s represent the positions that refer to the host portion of the address.

Understand IPv6. Understand the structure of an IPv6 address and how it's displayed. Know the shortcuts and rules (such as for displaying 0s) for writing IPv6 addresses. Know the integration/migration components for IPv6 included in Windows Server 2012, including tunneling and dual stack.

Review Questions

1. You are the network administrator for ABC Company. You have an IPv6 prefix of 2001:DB8:BBCC:0000::/53, and you need to set up your network so that your IPv6 addressing scheme can handle 1,000 more subnets. Which network mask would you use?

    A. /60

    B. /61

    C. /62

    D. /63

    E. /64

2. You are the network administrator for Stellacon Corporation. Stellacon has a Windows Server 2012 machine that needs to be able to communicate with all computers on the internal network. Stellacon has decided to add 15 new segments to its IPv6 network. How would you configure the IPv6 so that the server can communicate with all the segments?

    A. Configure the IPv6 address as fd00::2b0:e0ff:dee9:4143/8.

    B. Configure the IPv6 address as fe80::2b0:e0ff:dee9:4143/32.

    C. Configure the IPv6 address as ff80::2b0:e0ff:dee9:4143/64.

    D. Configure the IPv6 address as fe80::2b0:e0ff:dee9:4143/64.

3. You are the network administrator for a midsize organization that has installed Windows Server 2012 onto the network. You are thinking of moving all machines to Windows 7 and IPv6. You decide to set up a test environment with four subnets. What type of IPv6 addresses do you need set up?

    A. Global addresses

    B. Link-local addresses

    C. Unique local addresses

    D. Site-local addresses

4. You have a large IP-routed network using the address 137.25.0.0; it is composed of 20 subnets, with a maximum of 300 hosts on each subnet. Your company continues on a merger-and-acquisitions spree, and your manager has told you to prepare for an increase to 50 subnets with some containing more than 600 hosts. Using the existing network address, which of the following subnet masks would work for the requirement set by your manager?

    A. 255.255.252.0

    B. 255.255.254.0

    C. 255.255.248.0

    D. 255.255.240.0

5. Your company is growing dramatically via acquisitions of other companies. As the network administrator, you need to keep up with the changes because they affect the workstations, and you need to support them. When you started, there were 15 locations connected via routers, and now there are 25. As new companies are acquired, they are migrated to Windows Server 2012 and brought into the same domain as another site. Management says that they are going to acquire at least 10 more companies in the next two years. The engineers have also told you that they are redesigning the company's Class B address into an IP addressing scheme that will support these requirements and that there will never be more than 1,000 network devices on any subnet. What is the appropriate subnet mask to support this network when the changes are completed?

   A. 255.255.252.0

   B. 255.255.248.0

   C. 255.255.255.0

   D. 255.255.255.128

6. You work for a small printing company that has 75 workstations. Most of them run standard office applications such as word processing, spreadsheet, and accounting programs. Fifteen of the workstations are constantly processing huge graphics files and then sending print jobs to industrial-sized laser printers. The performance of the network has always been an issue, but you have never addressed it. You have now migrated your network to Windows 8 and Windows Server 2012 and have decided to take advantage of the routing capability built into Windows Server 2012. You choose the appropriate server and place two NICs in the machine, but you realize that you have only one network address, 201.102.34.0, which you obtained years ago. How should you subnet this address to segment the bandwidth hogs from the rest of the network while giving everyone access to the entire network?

   A. 255.255.255.192

   B. 255.255.255.224

   C. 255.255.255.252

   D. 255.255.255.240

7. You work for Carpathian Worldwide Enterprises, which has more than 50 administrative and manufacturing locations around the world. The size of these organizations varies greatly, with the number of computers per location ranging from 15 to slightly fewer than 1,000. The sales operations use more than 1,000 facilities, each of which contains 2 to 5 computers. Carpathian is also in merger talks with another large organization. If the merger materializes as planned, you will have to accommodate another 100 manufacturing and administrative locations, each with a maximum of 600 computers, as well as 2,000 additional sales facilities. You don't have any numbers for the future growth of the company, but you are told to keep growth in mind. You decide to implement a private addressing plan for the entire organization. More than half of your routers don't support Variable Length Subnet Masking. Which subnet masks would work for this situation? (Choose all that apply.)

A. 255.255.224.0

B. 255.255.240.0

C. 255.255.248.0

D. 255.255.252.0

E. 255.255.254.0

8. Which of the following subnet masks are represented with the CIDR of /27?

A. 255.255.255.254

B. 255.255.255.248

C. 255.255.255.224

D. 255.255.255.240

9. You are the administrator for a Windows Server 2012 network that uses DHCP. You notice that your DHCP database is getting too large, and you want to reduce the size of the database. What should you do?

A. From the folder containing the DHCP database, run `jetpack.exe dhcp.mdb temp.mdb`.

B. From the folder containing the DHCP database, run `shrinkpack.exe dhcp.mdb temp.mdb`.

C. From the folder containing the DHCP database, run `jetshrink.exe dhcp.mdb temp.mdb`.

D. From the folder containing the DHCP database, run `shrinkjet.exe dhcp.mdb temp.mdb`.

10. You ask one of your technicians to get the IPv6 address of a new Windows Server 2012 machine, and she hands you a note with FE80::0203:FFFF:FE11:2CD on it. What can you tell from this address? (Choose two.)

A. This is a globally unique IPv6 address.

B. This is a link-local IPv6 address.

C. This is a multicast IPv6 address.

D. In EUI-64 format, you can see the MAC address of the node.

E. In EUI-64 format, you can see the IPv4 address of the node.

Chapter

10

Managing DHCP

THE FOLLOWING 70-410 EXAM OBJECTIVES ARE COVERED IN THIS CHAPTER:

✓ **Deploy and configure Dynamic Host Configuration Protocol (DHCP) service**

- This objective may include, but is not limited to: Create and configure scopes; configure a DHCP reservation; configure DHCP options; configure client and server for PXE boot; configure DHCP relay agent; authorize DHCP server.

THE FOLLOWING 70-412 EXAM OBJECTIVES ARE COVERED IN THIS CHAPTER:

✓ **Implement an advanced Dynamic Host Configuration Protocol (DHCP) solution.**

- This objective may include, but is not limited to: Create and configure superscopes and multicast scopes; implement DHCPv6; configure high availability for DHCP including DHCP failover and split scopes; configure DHCP Name Protection.

In Chapter 9, "Configuring TCP/IP," I briefly discussed the Dynamic Host Configuration Protocol (DHCP) and how to configure DHCP clients. Planning for and using DHCP in Windows Server 2012 is relatively straightforward, but there's a lot you need to know to make sure that your installation proceeds without trouble.

In this chapter, you'll learn how to install and manage DHCP, including how to set up plain DHCP scopes, superscopes, and multicast scopes. You'll also learn how to set up integration between Dynamic DNS and DHCP and how to authorize a DHCP server to integrate with Active Directory.

There are two versions of DHCP: DHCP v4 and DHCP v6. In this chapter, I will just say DHCP server when referring to the physical DHCP server. If I am referring to a specific version of DHCP, I will specify the version.

Overview of DHCP

As you saw in Chapter 9, TCP/IP is the priority protocol for Windows Server 2012. There are two ways to have clients and servers get TCP/IP addresses:

- You can manually assign the addresses.
- The addresses can be assigned automatically.

Manually assigning addresses is a fairly simple process. An administrator goes to each of the machines on the network and assigns TCP/IP addresses. The problem with this method arises when the network becomes midsized or larger. Think of an administrator trying to assign individually 4,000 TCP/IP addresses, subnet masks, default gateways, and all other configuration options needed to run the network.

DHCP's job is to centralize the process of IP address and option assignment. You can configure a DHCP server with a range of addresses (called a *pool*) and other configuration information and let it assign all the IP parameters—addresses, default gateways, DNS server addresses, and so on.

DHCP is defined by a series of Request for Comments (RFC) documents, notably 2131 and 2132.

Introducing the DORA Process

An easy way to remember how DHCP works is to learn the acronym DORA. *DORA* stands for *Discover, Offer, Request,* and *Acknowledge*. In brief, here is DHCP's DORA process:

1. *Discover*: When IP networking starts up on a DHCP-enabled client, a special message called a DHCPDISCOVER is broadcast within the local physical subnet.

2. *Offer*: Any DHCP server that hears the request checks its internal database and replies with a message called a DHCPOFFER, which contains an available IP address.

    The contents of this message depend on how the DHCP server is configured—there are numerous options aside from an IP address that you can specify to pass to the client on a Windows Server 2008 R2 DHCP server.

3. *Request*: The client receives one or more DHCPOFFERs (depending on how many DHCP servers exist on the local subnet), chooses an address from one of the offers, and sends a DHCPREQUEST message to the server to signal acceptance of the DHCPOFFER.

    This message might also request additional configuration parameters.

    Other DHCP servers that sent offers take the request message as an acknowledgment that the client didn't accept their offer.

4. *Acknowledge*: When the DHCP server receives the DHCPREQUEST, it marks the IP address as being in use (that is, usually, though it's not required). Then it sends a DHC-PACK to the client.

    The acknowledgment message might contain requested configuration parameters.

    If the server is unable to accept the DHCPREQUEST for any reason, it sends a DHCPNAK message. If a client receives a DHCPNAK, it begins the configuration process over again.

5. When the client accepts the IP offer, the address is assigned to the client for a specified period of time, called a *lease*. After receiving the DHCPACK message, the client performs a final check on the parameters (sometimes it sends an ARP request for the offered IP address) and makes note of the duration of the lease. The client is now configured.

    If the client detects that the address is already in use, it sends a DHCPDECLINE.

    If the DHCP server has given out all the IP addresses in its pool, it won't make an offer. If no other servers make an offer, the client's IP network initialization will fail and the client will use Automatic Private IP Addressing (APIPA).

DHCP Lease Renewal

No matter how long the lease period, the client sends a new lease request message directly to the DHCP server when the lease period is half over (give or take some randomness required by RFC 2131). This period goes by the name *T1* (not to be confused with the T1 type of network connection). If the server hears the request message and there's no reason to reject it, it sends a DHCPACK to the client. This resets the lease period.

If the DHCP server isn't available, the client realizes that the lease can't be renewed. The client continues to use the address, and once 87.5 percent of the lease period has elapsed (again, give or take some randomness), the client sends out another renewal request. This interval is also known as *T2*. At that point, any DHCP server that hears the renewal can respond to this *DHCP request message* (which is a request for a lease renewal) with a DHCPACK and renew the lease. If at any time during this process the client gets a negative DHCPNACK message, it must stop using its IP address immediately and start the leasing process over from the beginning by requesting a new lease.

When a client initializes its IP networking, it always attempts to renew its old address. If the client has time left on the lease, it continues to use the lease until its end. If the client is unable to get a new lease by that time, all IP functions stop until a new, valid address can be obtained.

DHCP Lease Release

Although leases can be renewed repeatedly, at some point they might run out. Furthermore, the lease process is "at will," that is, the client or server can cancel the lease before it ends. In addition, if the client doesn't succeed in renewing the lease before it expires, the client loses its lease and reverts to APIPA. This release process is important for reclaiming extinct IP addresses used by systems that have moved or switched to a non-DHCP address.

Advantages and Disadvantages of DHCP

DHCP was designed from the start to simplify network management. It has some significant advantages, but it also has some drawbacks.

Advantages of DHCP

The following are advantages of DHCP:

- Configuration of large and even midsized networks is much simpler. If a DNS server address or some other change is necessary to the client, the administrator doesn't have to touch each device in the network physically to reconfigure it with the new settings.

- Once you enter the IP configuration information in one place—the server—it's automatically propagated to clients, eliminating the risk that a user will misconfigure some parameters and require you to fix them.

- IP addresses are conserved because DHCP assigns them only when requested.

- IP configuration becomes almost completely automatic. In most cases, you can plug in a new system (or move one) and then watch as it receives a configuration from the server. For example, when you install new network changes such as a gateway or DNS server, the client configuration is done at only one location—the DHCP server.

- It allows a preboot execution environment (PXE) client to get a TCP/IP address from DHCP. PXE clients (also called Microsoft Windows Deployment Services [WDS] clients) can get an IP address without needing to have an operating system installed. This allows WDS clients to connect to a WDS server through the TCP/IP protocol and download an operating system remotely.

Disadvantages of DHCP

Unfortunately, there are a few drawbacks with DHCP:

- DHCP can become a single point of failure for your network. If you have only one DHCP server and it's not available, clients can't request or renew leases.

- If the DHCP server contains incorrect information, the misinformation will automatically be delivered to all of your DHCP clients.

- If you want to use DHCP on a multisegment network, you must put either a DHCP server or a relay agent on each segment, or you must ensure that your router can forward Bootstrap Protocol (BOOTP) broadcasts.

Ipconfig Lease Options

The ipconfig command-line tool is useful for working with network settings. Its /renew and /release switches make it particularly handy for DHCP clients. These switches allow you to request renewal of, or give up, your machine's existing address lease. You can do the same thing by toggling the Obtain An IP Address Automatically button in the Internet Protocol (TCP/IP) Properties dialog box, but the command-line option is useful especially when you're setting up a new network.

For example, I spend about a third of my time teaching MCITP classes, usually in temporary classrooms set up at conferences, hotels, and so on. Laptops are used in these classes, with one brawny one set up as a DNS/DHCP/DC server. Occasionally, a client will lose its DHCP lease (or not get one, perhaps because a cable has come loose). The quickest way to fix it is to pop open a command-line window and type ipconfig/renew.

You can configure DHCP to assign options only to certain classes. *Classes*, defined by an administrator, are groups of computers that require identical DHCP options. The /setclassid*classID* switch of ipconfig is the only way to assign a machine to a class.

More specifically, the switches do the following:

ipconfig /renew Instructs the DHCP client to request a lease renewal. If the client already has a lease, it requests a renewal from the server that issued the current lease. This is equivalent to what happens when the client reaches the half-life of its lease. Alternatively, if the client doesn't currently have a lease, it is equivalent to what happens when you boot a DHCP client for the first time. It initiates the DHCP mating dance, listens for lease offers, and chooses one it likes.

ipconfig/release Forces the client to give up its lease immediately by sending the server a DHCP release notification. The server updates its status information and marks the client's old IP address as "available," leaving the client with no address bound to its network interface. When you use this command, most of the time it will be immediately followed by `ipconfig/renew`. The combination releases the existing lease and gets a new one, probably with a different address. (It's also a handy way to force your client to get a new set of settings from the server before the lease expiration time.)

`ipconfig /setclassid`_`classID`_   Sets a new class ID for the client. You will see how to configure class options later in the section "Setting Scope Options for IPv4." For now, you should know that the only way to add a client machine to a class is to use this command. Note that you need to renew the client lease for the class assignment to take effect.

If you have multiple network adapters in a single machine, you can provide the name of the adapter (or adapters) upon which you want the command to work, including an asterisk (*) as a wildcard. For example, one of my servers has two network cards: an Intel EtherExpress (ELNK1) and a generic 100 Mbps card. If you want to renew DHCP settings for both adapters, you can type **`ipconfig /renew *`**. If you just want to renew the Intel EtherExpress card, you can type **`ipconfig /renew ELNK1`**.

Understanding Scope Details

By now you should have a good grasp of what a lease is and how it works. To learn how to configure your servers to hand out those leases, however, you need to have a complete understanding of some additional topics: scopes, superscopes, exclusions, reservations, address pool, and relay agents.

Scope

Let's start with the concept of a *scope*, which is a contiguous range of addresses. There's usually one scope per physical subnet, and a scope can cover a Class A, Class B, or Class C network address or a TCP/IP v6 address. DHCP uses scopes as the basis for managing and assigning IP addressing information.

Each scope has a set of parameters, or scope options, that you can configure. *Scope options* control what data is delivered to DHCP clients when they're completing the DHCP negotiation process with a particular server. For example, the DNS server name, default gateway, and default network time server are all separate options that can be assigned. These settings are called *option types*. You can use any of the types provided with Windows Server 2012, or you can specify your own.

Superscope

A *superscope* enables the DHCP server to provide addresses from more than one scope to clients on the same physical subnet. This is helpful when clients within the same subnet have more than one IP network and thus need IPs from more than one address pool. Microsoft's DHCP snap-in allows you to manage IP address assignment in the superscope, though you must still configure other scope options individually for each child scope.

Exclusions and Reservations

The scope defines what IP addresses could potentially be assigned, but you can influence the assignment process in two additional ways by specifying exclusions and reservations:

Exclusions These are IP addresses within the range that you never want automatically assigned. These excluded addresses are off-limits to DHCP. You'll typically use exclusions to tag any addresses that you never want the DHCP server to assign at all. You might use exclusions to set aside addresses that you want to assign permanently to servers that play a vital role in your organization.

Reservations These are IP addresses within the range for which you want a permanent DHCP lease. They essentially reserve a particular IP address for a particular device. The device still goes through the DHCP process (that is, its lease expires, and it asks for a new one), but it always obtains the same addressing information from the DHCP server.

Exclusions are useful for addresses that you don't want to participate in DHCP at all. *Reservations* are helpful for situations in which you want a client to get the same settings each time they obtain an address.

An address cannot be simultaneously reserved and excluded. Be aware of this fact for the exam, possibly relating to a troubleshooting question.

 Real World Scenario

Using Reservations and Exclusions

Deciding when to assign a reservation or exclusion can sometimes be confusing. In practice, you'll find that certain computers in the network greatly benefit by having static IP network information. Servers such as DNS servers, the DHCP server itself, SMTP servers, and other low-level infrastructure servers are good candidates for static assignment. There are usually so few of these servers that the administrator is not overburdened if a change in network settings requires going out to reconfigure each individually. Chances are that the administrator would still need to reconfigure these servers manually (by using ipconfig /release and then ipconfig /renew), even if they did not have IP addresses reserved. Even in large installations, I find it preferable to manage these vital servers by hand than to rely on DHCP.

Reservations are also appropriate for application servers and other special but nonvital infrastructure servers. With a reservation in DHCP, the client device will still go through the DHCP process but will always obtain the same addressing information from the DHCP server. The premise behind this strategy is that these nonvital servers can withstand a short outage if DHCP settings change or if the DHCP server fails.

Address Pool

The range of IP addresses that the DHCP server can assign is called its *address pool*. For example, let's say you set up a new DHCP scope covering the 192.168.1 subnet. That gives you 255 IP addresses in the pool. After adding an exclusion from 192.168.1.240 to 192.168.1.254, you're left with 241 (255 – 14) IP addresses in the pool. That means (in theory, at least) that you can service 241 unique clients at a time before you run out of IP addresses.

DHCP Relay Agent

By design, DHCP is intended to work only with clients and servers on a single IP network to communicate. But RFC 1542 sets out how BOOTP (on which DHCP is based) should work in circumstances in which the client and server are on different IP networks. If no DHCP server is available on the client's network, you can use a DHCP relay agent to forward DHCP broadcasts from the client's network to the DHCP server. The relay agent acts like a radio repeater, listening for DHCP client requests and retransmitting them through the router to the server.

Installing and Authorizing DHCP

Installing DHCP is easy using the Windows Server 2012 installation mechanism. Unlike some other services discussed in this book, the installation process installs just the service and its associated snap-in, starting it when the installation is complete. At that point, it's not delivering any DHCP service, but you don't have to reboot.

Installing DHCP

Exercise 10.1 shows you how to install DHCP Server using Server Manager.

EXERCISE 10.1

Installing the DHCP Service

1. Choose Server Manager by clicking the Server Manager icon on the Taskbar.

2. Click number 2, Add Roles And Features.

3. Choose role-based or feature-based installation and click Next.

4. Choose your server and click Next.

5. Choose DHCP and click Next.

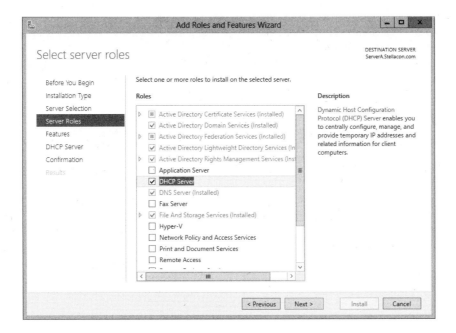

6. At the Features screen, click Next.

7. Click Next at the DHCP screen.

8. At the DHCP confirmation screen, click the Install button.

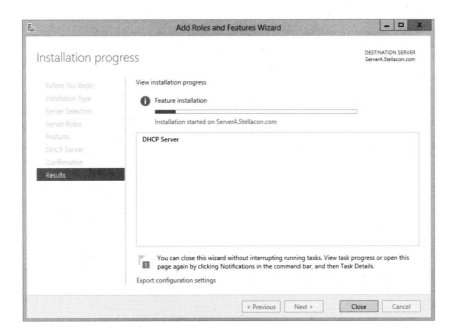

9. When the installation is complete, click the Close button.

10. On the left side, click the DHCP link.

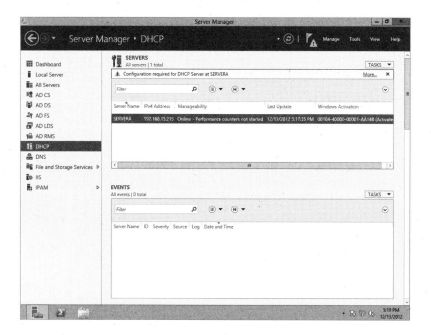

11. Click the More link next to Configuration Required For DHCP Server.

12. Under Action, click Complete DHCP Configuration.

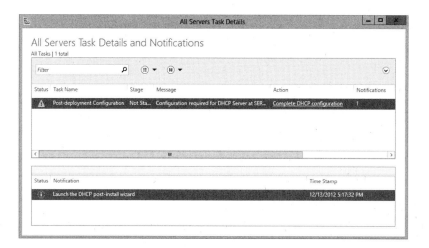

13. At the DHCP Description page, click Next.

14. At the Authorization screen, you must enter the administrator account for Active Directory authentication. After this information is entered, click Commit.

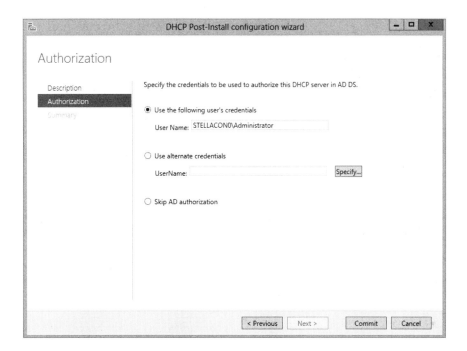

15. Click Close at the Summary screen.

16. Close Server Manager.

Introducing the DHCP Snap-In

When you install the DHCP server, the DHCP snap-in is also installed. You can open it by selecting Administrative Tools ➢ DHCP. Figure 10.1 shows the snap-in.

As you can see, the snap-in follows the standard MMC model. The left pane displays IPv4 and IPv6 sections and which servers are available; you can connect to servers other than the one to which you're already connected. A Server Options folder contains options that are specific to a particular DHCP server. Each server contains subordinate items grouped into folders. Each scope has a folder named after the scope's IP address range. Within each scope, four subordinate views show you interesting things about the scope, such as the following:

- The Address Pool view shows you what the address pool looks like.

- The Address Leases view shows one entry for each current lease. Each lease shows the computer name to which the lease was issued, the corresponding IP address, and the current lease expiration time.

- The Reservations view shows you the IP addresses that are reserved and which devices hold them.

- The Scope Options view lists the set of options you've defined for this scope.

FIGURE 10.1 DHCP snap-in

Authorizing DHCP for Active Directory

Authorization creates an Active Directory object representing the new server. It helps keep unauthorized servers off your network. Unauthorized servers can cause two kinds of problems. They may hand out bogus leases, or they may fraudulently deny renewal requests from legitimate clients.

When you install a DHCP server using Windows Server 2012 and Active Directory is present on your network, the server won't be allowed to provide DHCP services to clients until it has been authorized. If you install DHCP on a member server in an Active Directory domain or on a stand-alone server, you'll have to authorize the server manually. When you authorize a server, you're adding its IP address to the Active Directory object that contains the IP addresses of all authorized DHCP servers.

 You also have the ability to authorize a DHCP server during the installation of DHCP. (This is what you did in Exercise 10.1.)

At start time, each DHCP server queries the directory, looking for its IP address on the "authorized" list. If it can't find the list or if it can't find its IP address on the list, the DHCP service fails to start. Instead, it adds a message to the event log, indicating that it couldn't service client requests because the server wasn't authorized.

Exercise 10.2 shows you how to unauthorize a DHCP server in an Active Directory domain.

EXERCISE 10.2

Unauthorizing a DHCP Server

1. From Administrative Tools, choose DHCP to open the DHCP snap-in.

2. Right-click the server you want to unauthorize, and choose the Unauthorize command.

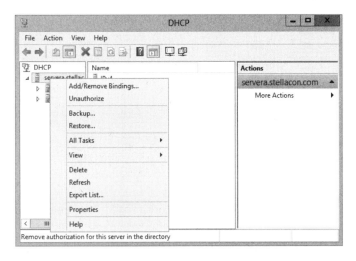

3. Click Yes on the dialog box asking if you are sure you want to complete this action.

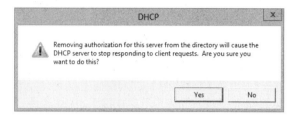

Exercise 10.3 shows you how to authorize a DHCP server in an Active Directory domain. Exercise 10.2 must be completed before you do Exercise 10.3.

EXERCISE 10.3

Authorizing a DHCP Server

1. From Administrative Tools, choose DHCP to open the DHCP snap-in.

2. Right-click the server you want to authorize, and choose the Authorize command.

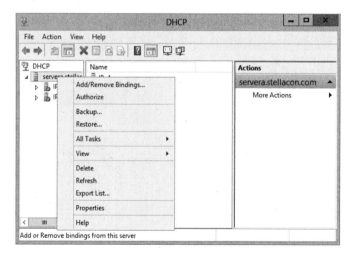

3. Wait a short time (30 to 45 seconds) to allow the authorization to take place.

4. Right-click the server again. Verify that the Unauthorize command appears in the pop-up menu. This indicates that the server is now authorized.

Creating and Managing DHCP Scopes

You can use any number of DHCP servers on a single physical network if you divide the range of addresses that you want assigned into multiple scopes. Each scope contains a number of useful pieces of data, but before you can understand them, you need to know some additional terminology.

You can perform the following management tasks on DHCP scopes:

- Create a scope.

- Configure scope properties.

- Configure reservations and exclusions.

- Set scope options.

- Activate and deactivate scopes.

- Create a superscope.

- Create a multicast scope.

- Integrate Dynamic DNS and DHCP.

I will cover each task in the following sections.

Creating a New Scope in IPv4

Like many other things in Windows Server 2012, the process of creating a new scope is driven by a wizard. You will most likely create a scope while installing DHCP, but you may need to create more than one. The overall process is simple, as long as you know beforehand what the wizard is going to ask. If you think about what defines a scope, you'll be well prepared. You need to know the following:

- The IP address range for the scope you want to create.

- Which IP addresses, if any, you want to exclude from the address pool.

- Which IP addresses, if any, you want to reserve.

- Values for the DHCP options you want to set, if any. This item isn't strictly necessary for creating a scope. However, to create a useful scope, you'll need to have some options to specify for the clients.

To create a scope, under the server name, right-click the IPv4 option in the DHCP snap-in and use the Action ➤ New Scope command. This starts the New Scope Wizard (see Figure 10.2). We will look at each page of the wizard in the following sections.

FIGURE 10.2   Welcome page of the New Scope Wizard

Setting the Screen Name

The Scope Name page allows you to enter a name and description for your scope. These will be displayed by the DHCP snap-in.

 It's a good idea to pick sensible names for your scopes so that other administrators will be able to figure out the purpose of the scope. For example, the name DHCP is likely not very helpful, whereas a name like 1st Floor Subnet is more descriptive and can help in troubleshooting.

Defining the IP Address Range

The IP Address Range page (see Figure 10.3) is where you enter the start and end IP addresses for your range. The wizard does minimal checking on the addresses you enter, and it automatically calculates the appropriate subnet mask for the range. You can modify the subnet mask if you know what you're doing.

FIGURE 10.3 IP Address Range page of the New Scope Wizard

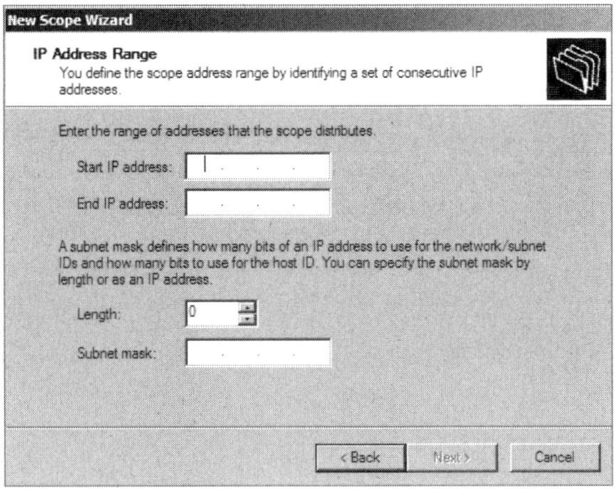

Adding Exclusions and Delay

The Add Exclusions And Delay page (see Figure 10.4) allows you to create exclusion ranges. Exclusions are TCP/IP numbers that are in the pool, but they do not get issued to clients. To exclude one address, put it in the Start IP Address field. To exclude a range, also fill in the End IP Address field. The delay setting is a time duration by which the server will delay the transmission of a DHCPOFFER message.

FIGURE 10.4 Add Exclusions And Delay page of the New Scope Wizard

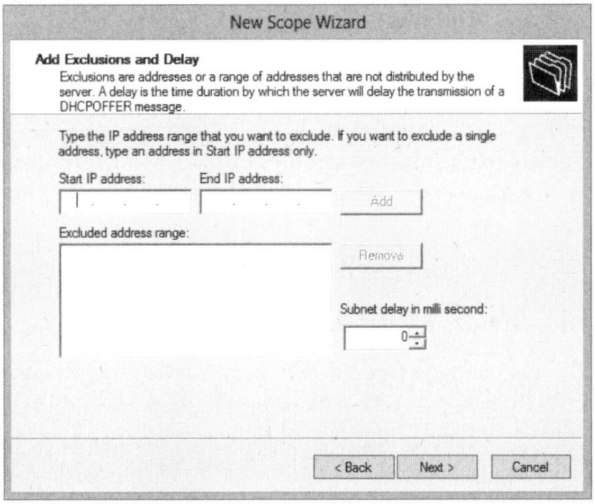

Although you can always add exclusions later, it's best to include them when you create the scope so that no excluded addresses are ever passed out to clients.

Setting a Lease Duration

The Lease Duration page (see Figure 10.5) allows you to set how long a device gets to use an assigned IP address before it has to renew its lease. The default lease duration is eight days. You may find that a shorter or longer duration makes sense for your network. If your network is highly dynamic, with lots of arrivals, departures, and moving computers, set a shorter lease duration; if it's less active, make it longer.

FIGURE 10.5   Lease Duration page of the New Scope Wizard

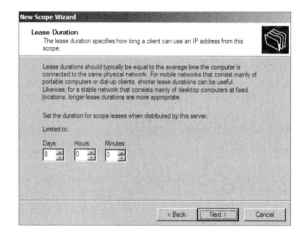

 Remember that renewal attempts begin when approximately half of the lease period is over (give or take a random interval), so don't set them too short.

Configuring Basic DHCP Options

The Configure DHCP Options page (see Figure 10.6) allows you to choose whether you want to set up basic DHCP options such as default gateway and DNS settings. The options are described in the following sections. If you choose not to configure options, you can always do so later. However, you should not activate the scope until you've configured the options you want assigned.

FIGURE 10.6   Configure DHCP Options page of the New Scope Wizard

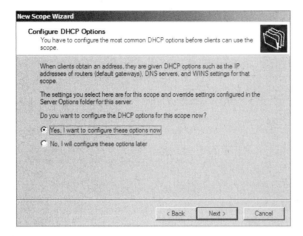

Configuring a Router

The first option configuration page is the Router (Default Gateway) page (see Figure 10.7), in which you enter the IP addresses of one or more routers (more commonly referred to as *default gateways*) that you want to use for outbound traffic. After entering the IP addresses of the routers, use the Up and Down buttons to order the addresses. Clients will use the routers in the order specified when attempting to send outgoing packets.

FIGURE 10.7   Router (Default Gateway) page of the New Scope Wizard

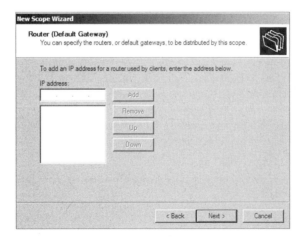

Providing DNS Settings

On the Domain Name And DNS Servers page (see Figure 10.8), you specify the set of DNS servers and the parent domain you want passed down to DHCP clients. Normally, you'll want to specify at least one DNS server by filling in its DNS name or IP address. You can also specify the domain suffix that you want clients to use as the base domain for all connections that aren't fully qualified. For example, if your clients are used to navigating based on server name alone rather than the fully qualified domain name (FQDN) of server .willpanek.com, then you'll want to place your domain here.

FIGURE 10.8 Domain Name And DNS Servers page of the New Scope Wizard

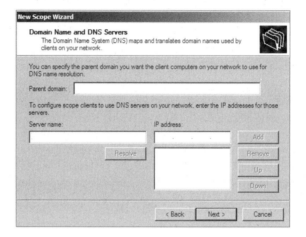

Providing WINS Settings

If you're still using Windows Internet Name Service (WINS) on your network, you can configure DHCP so that it passes WINS server addresses to your Windows clients. (If you want the Windows clients to honor it, you'll also need to define the WINS/NBT Node Type option for the scope.) As on the DNS server page, on the WINS Servers page (see Figure 10.9) you can enter the addresses of several servers and move them into the order in which you want clients to try them. You can enter the DNS or NetBIOS name of each server, or you can enter an IP address.

FIGURE 10.9   WINS Servers page of the New Scope Wizard

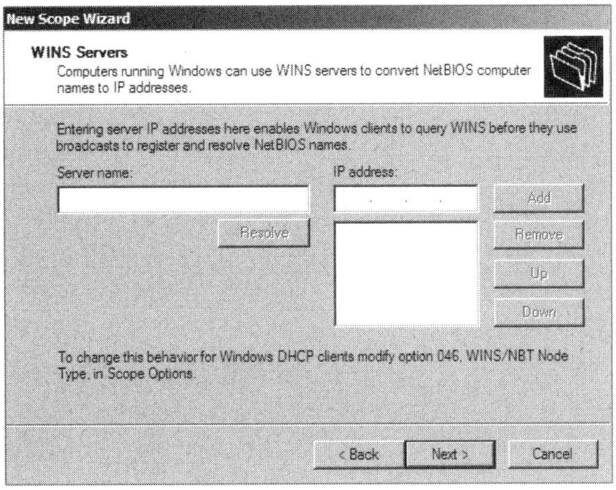

Here are some of the more common options you can set on a DHCP server:

003 Router   Used to provide a list of available routers or default gateways on the same subnet.

006 DNS Servers   Used to provide a list of DNS servers.

015 DNS Domain Name   Used to provide the DNS suffix.

028 Broadcast Address   Used to configure the broadcast address, if different than the default, based on the subnet mask.

44 WINS/NBNS Servers   Used to configure the IP addresses of WINS servers.

46 WINS/NBT Node Type   Used to configure the preferred NetBIOS name resolution method. There are four settings for node type:

    B node (0x1)   Broadcast for NetBIOS resolution

    P node (0x2)   Peer-to-peer (WINS) server for NetBIOS resolution

    M node (0x4)   Mixed node (does a B node and then a P node)

    H node (0x8)   Hybrid node (does a P node and then a B node)

051 Lease   Used to configure a special lease duration.

Activating the Scope

The Activate Scope page (see Figure 10.10) gives you the option to activate the scope immediately after creating it. By default, the wizard assumes that you want the scope activated unless you select the No, I Will Activate This Scope Later radio button, in which case the scope will remain dormant until you activate it manually.

FIGURE 10.10   Activate Scope page of the New Scope Wizard

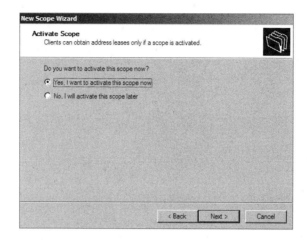

    Be sure to verify that there are no other DHCP servers assigned to the address range you choose!

In Exercise 10.4, you will create a new scope for the 192.168.0 private Class C network. First you need to complete Exercise 10.1 before beginning this exercise.

EXERCISE 10.4

Creating a New Scope

1. Open the DHCP snap-in by selecting Administrative Tools ➢ DHCP.

2. Right-click the IPv4 folder, and choose New Scope. The New Scope Wizard appears.

3. Click the Next button on the welcome page.

4. Enter a name and a description for your new scope, and click the Next button.

5. On the IP Address Range page, enter **192.168.0.2** as the start IP address for the scope and **192.168.0.250** as the end IP address. Leave the subnet mask controls alone (though when creating a scope on a production network, you might need to change them). Click the Next button.

6. On the Add Exclusions And Delay page, click Next without adding any excluded addresses or delays.

7. On the Lease Duration page, set the lease duration to 3 days, and click the Next button.

8. On the Configure DHCP Options page, click the Next button to indicate that you want to configure default options for this scope.

9. On the Router (Default Gateway) page, enter **192.168.0.1** for the router IP address, and then click the Add button. Once the address is added, click the Next button.

10. On the Domain Name And DNS Servers page, enter the IP address of a DNS server on your network in the IP Address field (for example, you might enter **192.168.0.251**), and click the Add button. Click the Next button.

11. On the WINS Servers page, click the Next button to leave the WINS options unset.

12. On the Activate Scope page, if your network is currently using the 192.168.0.*x* range, select Yes, I Want To Activate This Scope Now. Click the Next button.

13. When the wizard's summary page appears, click the Finish button to create the scope.

Creating a New Scope in IPv6

Now that you have seen how to create a new scope in IPv4, we'll go through the steps to create a new scope in IPv6.

To create a scope, right-click the IPv6 option in the DHCP snap-in under the server name and select the Action ➤ New Scope command. This starts the New Scope Wizard. Just as with creating a scope in IPv4, the welcome page of the wizard tells you that you've launched the New Scope Wizard. We will look at each page of the wizard in the following sections.

Setting the Screen Name

The Scope Name page (see Figure 10.11) allows you to enter a name and description for your scope. These will be displayed by the DHCP snap-in.

FIGURE 10.11   IPv6 Scope Name page of the New Scope Wizard

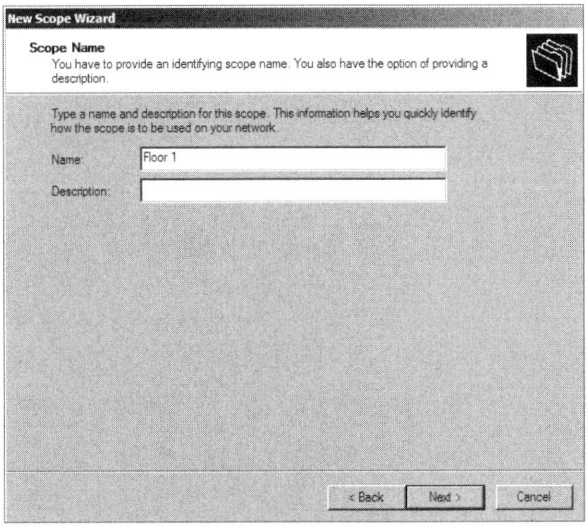

It's a good idea to pick a sensible name for your scopes so that other administrators will be able to figure out what the scope is for.

FIGURE 10.12   Scope Prefix page of the New Scope Wizard

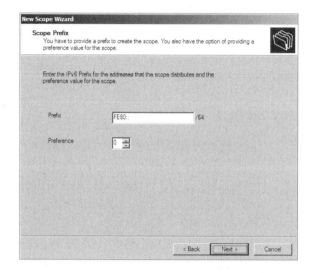

Scope Prefix

The Scope Prefix page (see Figure 10.12) gets you started creating the IPv6 scope. IPv6 has three types of addresses, which can be categorized by type and scope:

Unicast Addresses   *One-to-one.* A packet from one host is delivered to another host. The following are some examples of IPv6 unicast:

- The unicast prefix for site-local addresses is FEC0::/48.
- The unicast prefix for link-local addresses is FE80::/64.

Figure 10.12 shows the link-local prefix filled in.

The 6to4 address allows communication between two hosts running both IPv4 and IPv6. The way to calculate the 6to4 address is by combining the global prefix 2002::/16 with the 32 bits of a public IPv4 address of the host. This gives you a 48-bit prefix. 6to4 is described in RFC 3056.

Multicast addresses *One-to-many.* A packet from one host is delivered to multiple hosts (but not everyone). The prefix for multicast addresses is FF00::/8.

Anycast addresses A packet from one host is delivered to the nearest of multiple hosts (in terms of routing distance).

Adding Exclusions

As with the IPv4 New Scope Wizard, the Add Exclusions page (see Figure 10.13) allows you to create exclusion ranges. Exclusions are TCP/IP numbers that are in the pool but do not get issued to clients. To exclude one address, put it in the Start IPv6 Address field. To exclude a range, also fill in the End IPv6 Address field.

FIGURE 10.13 Add Exclusions page of the New Scope Wizard

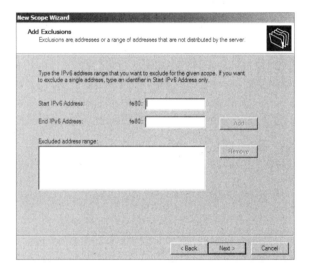

Setting a Lease Duration

The Scope Lease page (see Figure 10.14) allows you to set how long a device gets to use an assigned IP address before it has to renew its lease. You can set two different lease durations. The section labeled Non Temporary Address (IANA) is the lease time for your more permanent hosts (such as printers and server towers). The one labeled Temporary Address (IATA) is for hosts that might disconnect at any time, such as laptops.

FIGURE 10.14 Scope Lease page of the New Scope Wizard

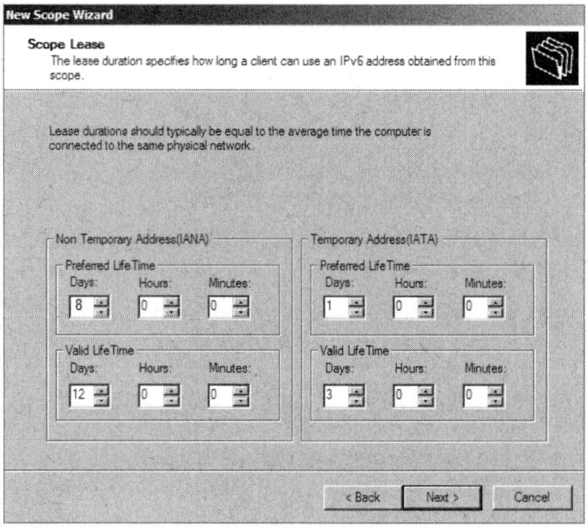

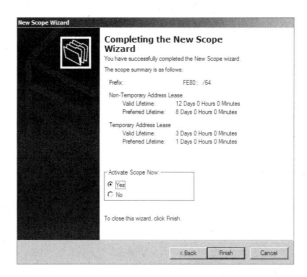

Activating the Scope

The Completing The New Scope Wizard page (see Figure 10.15) gives you the option to activate the scope immediately after creating it. By default, the wizard will assume that you want the scope activated. If you want to wait to activate the scope, choose No in the Activate Scope Now box.

FIGURE 10.15 Completing The New Scope Wizard page of the New Scope Wizard

Changing Scope Properties (IPv4 and IPv6)

Each scope has a set of properties associated with it. Except for the set of options assigned by the scope, you can find these properties on the General tab of the scope's Properties dialog box (see Figure 10.16). Some of these properties, such as the scope name and description, are self-explanatory. Others require a little more explanation:

- The Start IP Address and End IP Address fields allow you to set the range of the scope.
- For IPv4 scopes, the settings in the section Lease Duration For DHCP Clients control how long leases in this scope are valid.

FIGURE 10.16   General tab of the scope's Properties dialog box for an IPv4 scope

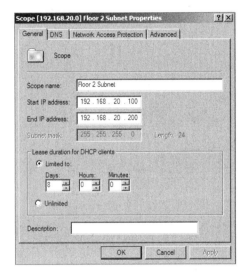

The IPv6 scope dialog box includes a Lease tab where you set the lease properties.

When you make changes to these properties, they have no effect on existing leases. For example, say that you create a scope from 172.30.1.1 to 172.30.1.199. You use that scope for a while and then edit its properties to reduce the range from 172.30.1.1 to 172.30.1.150. If a client has been assigned the address 172.30.1.180, which was part of the scope before you changed it, the client will retain that address until the lease expires but will not be able to renew it.

Changing Server Properties

Just as each scope has its own set of properties, so too does the server itself. You access the server properties by right-clicking the IPv4 or IPv6 object within the DHCP management console and selecting Properties.

IPv4 Server Properties

Figure 10.17 shows the IPv4 Properties dialog box.

FIGURE 10.17   General tab of the IPv4 Properties dialog box for the server

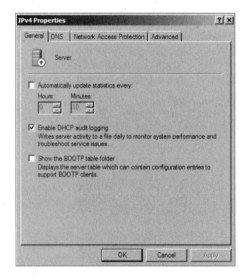

The IPv4 Properties dialog box has four tabs: General, DNS, Network Access Protection, and Advanced.

The Advanced tab, shown in Figure 10.18, contains the following configuration parameters:

- Audit Log File Path is where you enter the location for log files.

- Conflict Detection Attempts specifies how many ICMP echo requests (pings) the server sends for an address it is about to offer. The default is 0. Conflict detection is a way to verify that the DHCP server is not issuing IP addresses that are already being used on the network.

FIGURE 10.18   The Advanced tab of the IPv4 Properties dialog box for the server

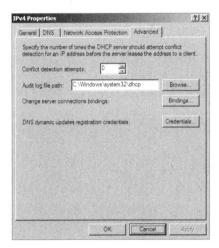

The Network Access Protection tab (see Figure 10.19) allows you to set up *Network Access Protection (NAP)*. With NAP, which is a new Windows Server 2012 service, an administrator can perform the following tasks:

- Carry out computer health policy validation.

- Ensure ongoing compliance with health policies.

- Optionally restrict the access of computers that do not meet with the computer health requirements.

FIGURE 10.19 The Network Access Protection tab of the IPv4 Properties dialog box for the server

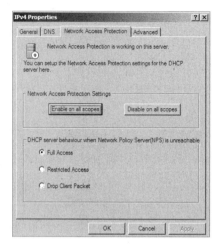

IPv6 Server Properties

The IPv6 Properties dialog box for the server has two tabs: General and Advanced. On the General tab (see Figure 10.20), you can configure the following settings:

- Frequency with which statistics are updated
- DHCP auditing

FIGURE 10.20 Server's IPv6 Properties, General tab

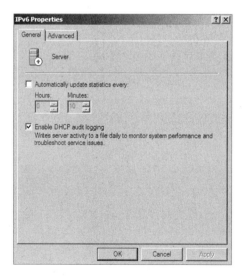

The Advanced tab (see Figure 10.21) allows you to configure the following settings:

- Database path for the audit log file path.
- Connection bindings.
- Registration credentials for dynamic DNS. The registration credential is the user account that DHCP will use to register clients with Active Directory.

FIGURE 10.21   Server's IPv6 Properties, Advanced tab

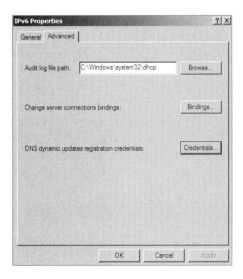

Managing Reservations and Exclusions

After defining the address pool for your scope, the next step is to create reservations and exclusions, which reduce the size of the pool. In the following sections, you will learn how to add and remove exclusions and reservations.

Adding and Removing Exclusions

When you want to exclude an entire range of IP addresses, you need to add that range as an *exclusion*. Ordinarily, you'll want to do this before you enable a scope because that prevents any of the IP addresses you want excluded from being leased before you have a chance to exclude them. In fact, you can't create an exclusion that includes a leased address—you have to get rid of the lease first.

Adding an Exclusion Range

Here's how to add an exclusion range:

1. Open the DHCP snap-in and find the scope to which you want to add an exclusion (either IPv4 or IPv6).

2. Expand the scope so that you can see its Address Pool item for IPv4 or the Exclusion section for IPv6.

3. Right-click the Address Pool or Exclusion section, and choose the New Exclusion Range command.

4. When the Add Exclusion dialog box appears (see Figure 10.22), enter the IP addresses you want to exclude. To exclude a single address, type it in the Start IP Address field. To exclude a range of addresses, also fill in the End IP Address field.

FIGURE 10.22   Add Exclusion dialog boxes for IPv4 and IPv6

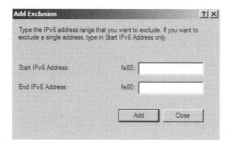

IPv4 Add Exclusion dialog box   IPv6 Add Exclusion dialog box

5. Click the Add button to add the exclusion.

When you add exclusions, they appear in the Address Pool node, which is under the Scope section for IPv4 and under the Exclusion section of IPv6.

Removing an Exclusion Range

To remove an exclusion, just right-click it and choose the Delete command. After confirming your command, the snap-in removes the excluded range and the addresses become immediately available for issuance.

Adding and Removing Reservations

Adding a reservation is simple as long as you have the MAC address of the device for which you want to create a reservation. Because reservations belong to a single scope, you create and remove them within the Reservations node beneath each scope.

Adding a Reservation

To add a reservation, perform the following tasks:

1. Right-click the scope, and select New Reservation.

   This displays the New Reservation dialog box, shown in Figure 10.23.

FIGURE 10.23   New Reservation dialog boxes for IPv4 and IPv6

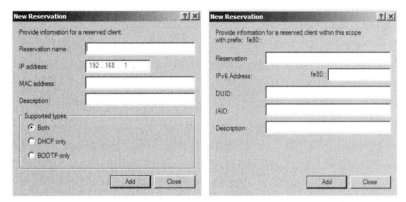

IPv4 New Reservation dialog box   IPv6 New Reservation dialog box

2. Enter the IP address and MAC address or ID for the reservation.

 To find the MAC address of the local computer, use the `ipconfig` command. To find the MAC address of a remote machine, use the `nbtstat-a`*computername* command.

3. If you want, you can also enter a name and description.
4. For IPv4, in the Supported Types section, choose whether the reservation will be made by DHCP only, BOOTP only (useful for remote-access devices), or both.

Removing a Reservation

To remove a reservation, right-click it and select Delete. This removes the reservation but does nothing to the client device.

 There's no way to change a reservation once it has been created. If you want to change any of the associated settings, you'll have to delete and re-create the reservation.

Setting Scope Options for IPv4

Once you've installed a server, authorized it in Active Directory, and fixed up the address pool, the next step is to set scope options that you want sent out to clients, such as router (that is, default gateway) and DNS server addresses. You must configure the options you want sent out before you activate a scope. If you don't, clients may register in the scope without getting any options, rendering them virtually useless. Thus configure the scope options, along with the IP address and subnet mask that you configured earlier in this chapter.

In the following sections, you will learn how to configure and assign scope options on the DHCP server.

Understanding Option Assignment

You can control which DHCP options are doled out to clients in five (slightly overlapping) ways:

Predefined Options   *Predefined options* are templates that are available in the Server, Scope, or Client Options dialog box.

Server Options   *Server options* are assigned to all scopes and clients of a particular server. That means that if there's some setting that you want all clients of a DHCP server to have, no matter what scope they're in, this is where you assign it. Specific options (those that are set at the class, scope, or client level) will override server-level options. That gives you an escape valve; it's a better idea, though, to be careful about which options you assign if your server manages multiple scopes.

Scope Options   If you want a particular option value assigned only to those clients in a certain subnet, you should assign it as a *scope option*. For example, it's common to specify different routers for different physical subnets; if you have two scopes corresponding to different subnets, each scope would probably have a separate value for the router option.

Class Options   You can assign different options to clients of different types; that is, *class options*. For example, Windows 2000, XP, Vista, Windows 7, Windows 8, Server 2003, Server 2003 R2, Server 2008, Server 2008 R2, and Server 2012 machines recognize a number of DHCP options that Windows 98, Windows NT, and Mac OS machines ignore and vice versa. By defining a Windows 2000 or newer class (using the `ipconfig /setclassid` command you saw earlier), you could assign those options only to machines that report themselves as being in that class.

Client Options   If a client is using DHCP reservations, you can assign certain options to that specific client. You attach *client options* to a particular reservation. Client options override scope, server, and class options. The only way to override a client option is to configure the client manually. The DHCP server manages client options.

   Client options override class options, class options override scope options, and scope options override server options.

Assigning Options

You can use the DHCP snap-in to assign options at the scope, server, reserved address, or class level. The mechanism you use to assign these options is the same for each; the only difference is where you set the options.

When you create an option assignment, remember that it applies to all of the clients in the server or the scope from that point forward. Option assignments aren't retroactive, and they don't migrate from one scope to another.

Creating and Assigning a New Option

To create a new option and have it assigned, follow these steps:

1. Select the scope or server where you want the option assigned.

2. Select the corresponding Options node, and choose Action ➢ Configure Options.

   To set options for a reserved client, right-click its entry in the Reservations node and select Configure Options.

   Then you'll see the Scope Options dialog box (see Figure 10.24), which lists all of the options that you might want to configure.

FIGURE 10.24   The Scope Options dialog box

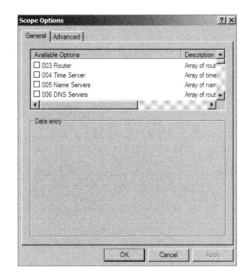

3. To select an individual option, check the box next to it and then use the controls in the Data Entry control group to enter the value you want associated with the option.

4. Continue to add options until you've specified all the ones that you want attached to the server or scope. Then click OK.

Configuring the DHCP Server for Classes

You saw how to assign classes to individual machines earlier in the chapter. Now you will learn how to configure the DHCP server to recognize your customized classes and configure options for them. In Exercise 10.5, you will create a new user class and configure options for the new class. Before you begin, make sure the computers you want to use in the class have been configured with the `ipconfig /setclassid` command as described in the section "Ipconfig Lease Options" earlier in this chapter.

EXERCISE 10.5

Configuring User Class Options

1. Open the DHCP snap-in by selecting Administrative Tools ➢ DHCP.

2. Right-click the IPv4 item, and select Define User Classes.

3. Click the Add button in the DHCP User Classes dialog box.

4. In the New Class dialog box, enter a descriptive name for the class in the Display Name field. Enter a class ID in the ID field. (Typically, you will enter the class ID in the ASCII portion of the ID field.) When you have finished, click OK.

5. The new class appears in the DHCP User Classes dialog box. Click the Close button to return to the DHCP snap-in.

6. Right-click the Scope Options node, and select Configure Options.

7. Click the Advanced tab. Select the class you defined in step 4 from the User Class pop-up menu.

8. Configure the options you want to set for the class. Click OK when you have finished. Notice that the options you configured (and the class with which they are associated) appear in the right pane of the DHCP window.

About the Default Routing and Remote Access Predefined User Class

Windows Server 2012 includes a predefined user class called the *Default Routing and Remote Access class*. This class includes options important to clients connecting to Routing and Remote Access, notably the 051 Lease option.

Be sure to know that the 051 Lease option is included within this class and that it can be used to assign a shorter lease duration for clients connecting to Routing and Remote Access.

Activating and Deactivating Scopes

When you've completed the steps in Exercise 10.5, and you're ready to unleash your new scope so that it can be used to make client assignments, the final required step is activating the scope. When you activate a scope, you're just telling the server that it's OK to start handing out addresses from that scope's address pool. As soon as you activate a scope, addresses from its pool may be assigned to clients. Of course, this is a necessary precondition to getting any use out of your scope.

If you later want to stop using a scope, you can, but be aware that it's a permanent change. When you deactivate a scope, DHCP tells all clients registered with the scope that they need to release their leases immediately and renew them someplace else—the equivalent of a landlord who evicts tenants when the building is condemned!

> **WARNING**   Don't deactivate a scope unless you want clients to stop using it immediately.

Creating a Superscope for IPv4

A superscope allows the DHCP server to provide multiple logical subnet addresses to DHCP clients on a single physical network. You create superscopes with the New Superscope command, which triggers the New Superscope Wizard.

> **NOTE**   You can have only one superscope per server.

The steps in Exercise 10.6 take you through the process of creating a superscope.

EXERCISE 10.6

Creating a Superscope

1. Open the DHCP snap-in by selecting Administrative Tools ➢ DHCP.

2. Follow the instructions in Exercise 10.4 to create two scopes: one for 192.168.0.2 through 192.168.0.127 and one for 192.168.1.12 through 192.168.1.127.

3. Right-click IPv4, and choose the New Superscope command. The New Superscope Wizard appears. Click the Next button.

4. On the Superscope Name page, name your superscope and click the Next button.

5. The Select Scopes page appears, listing all scopes on the current server. Select the two scopes you created in step 2, and then click the Next button.

6. The wizard's summary page appears. Click the Finish button to create your scope.

7. Verify that your new superscope appears in the DHCP snap-in.

Deleting a Superscope

You can delete a superscope by right-clicking it and choosing the Delete command. A superscope is just an administrative convenience, so you can safely delete one at any time—it doesn't affect the "real" scopes that make up the superscope.

Adding a Scope to a Superscope

To add a scope to an existing superscope, find the scope you want to add, right-click it, and choose Action ➢ Add To Superscope. A dialog box appears, listing all of the superscopes known to this server. Pick the one to which you want the current scope appended, and click the OK button.

Removing a Scope from a Superscope

To remove a scope from a superscope, open the superscope and right-click the target scope. The pop-up menu provides a Remove From Superscope command that will do the deed.

Activating and Deactivating Superscopes

Just as with regular scopes, you can activate and deactivate superscopes. The same restrictions and guidelines apply. You must activate a superscope before it can be used, and you must not deactivate it until you want all of your clients to lose their existing leases and be forced to request new ones.

To activate or deactivate a superscope, right-click the superscope name, and select Activate or Deactivate, respectively, from the pop-up menu.

Creating IPv4 Multicast Scopes

Multicasting occurs when one machine communicates to a network of subscribed computers rather than specifically addressing each computer on the destination network. It's much more efficient to *multicast* a video or audio stream to multiple destinations than it is to unicast it to the same number of clients, and the increased demand for multicast-friendly network hardware has resulted in some head scratching about how to automate the multicast configuration.

In the following sections, you will learn about MADCAP, the protocol that controls multicasting, and about how to build and configure a multicast scope.

Understanding the Multicast Address Dynamic Client Allocation Protocol

DHCP is usually used to assign IP configuration information for *unicast* (or one-to-one) network communications. With multicast, there's a separate type of address space assigned from 224.0.0.0 through 239.255.255.255. Addresses in this space are known as *Class D addresses*, or simply *multicast addresses*. Clients can participate in a multicast just by knowing (and using) the multicast address for the content they want to receive. However, multicast clients also need to have an ordinary IP address.

How do clients know what address to use? Ordinary DHCP won't help because it's designed to assign IP addresses and option information to one client at a time. Realizing this, the Internet Engineering Task Force (IETF) defined a new protocol: *Multicast Address Dynamic Client Allocation Protocol (MADCAP)*. MADCAP provides an analog to DHCP but for multicast use. A MADCAP server issues leases for multicast addresses only. MADCAP clients can request a multicast lease when they want to participate in a multicast.

DHCP and MADCAP have some important differences. First you have to realize that the two are totally separate. A single server can be a DHCP server, a MADCAP server, or both; no implied or actual relation exists between the two. Likewise, clients can use DHCP and/or MADCAP at the same time—the only requirement is that every MADCAP client has to get a unicast IP address from somewhere.

Remember that DHCP can assign options as part of the lease process but MADCAP cannot. The only thing MADCAP does is dynamically assign multicast addresses.

Building Multicast Scopes

Most of the steps you go through when creating a multicast scope are identical to those required for an ordinary unicast scope. Exercise 10.7 highlights the differences.

EXERCISE 10.7

Creating a New Multicast Scope

1. Open the DHCP snap-in by selecting Administrative Tools ➢ DHCP.

2. Right-click IPv4, and choose New Multicast Scope. The New Multicast Scope Wizard appears. Click the Next button on the welcome page.

3. In the Multicast Scope Name page, name your multicast scope (and add a description if you'd like). Click the Next button.

4. The IP Address Range page appears. Enter a start IP address of **224.0.0.0** and an end IP address of **224.255.0.0**. Adjust the TTL to 1 to make sure no multicast packets escape your local network segment. Click the Next button when you're finished.

5. The Add Exclusions page appears; click its Next button.

6. The Lease Duration page appears. Since multicast addresses are used for video and audio, you'd ordinarily leave multicast scope assignments in place somewhat longer than you would with a regular unicast scope, so the default lease length is 30 days (instead of 8 days for a unicast scope). Click the Next button.

7. The wizard asks you if you want to activate the scope now. Click the No radio button and then the Next button.

8. The wizard's summary page appears; click the Finish button to create your scope.

9. Verify that your new multicast scope appears in the DHCP snap-in.

Setting Multicast Scope Properties

Once you create a multicast scope, you can adjust its properties by right-clicking the scope name and selecting Properties.

The Multicast Scope Properties dialog box has two tabs. The General tab (see Figure 10.25) allows you to change the scope's name, its start and end addresses, its Time To Live (TTL) value, its lease duration, and its description—in essence, all of the settings you provided when you created it in the first place.

FIGURE 10.25   General tab of the Multicast Scope Properties dialog box

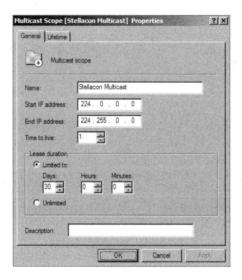

The Lifetime tab (see Figure 10.26) allows you to limit how long your multicast scope will be active. By default, a newly created multicast scope will live forever, but if you're creating a scope to provide MADCAP assignments for a single event (or a set of events of limited duration), you can specify an expiration time for the scope. When that time is reached, the scope disappears from the server but not before making all of its clients give up their multicast address leases. This is a nice way to make sure the lease cleans up after itself when you're finished with it.

FIGURE 10.26   Lifetime tab of the Multicast Scope Properties dialog box

Integrating Dynamic DNS and IPv4 DHCP

DHCP integration with Dynamic DNS is a simple concept but powerful in action. By setting up this integration, you can pass addresses to DHCP clients while still maintaining the integrity of your DNS services.

The DNS server can be updated in two ways. One way is for the DHCP client to tell the DNS server its address. Another way is for the DHCP server to tell the DNS server when it registers a new client.

Neither of these updates will take place, however, unless you configure the DNS server to use Dynamic DNS. You can make this change in two ways:

- If you change it at the scope level, it will apply only to the scope.

- If you change it at the server level, it will apply to all scopes and superscopes served by the server.

Which of these options you choose depends on how widely you want to support Dynamic DNS; most of the sites I visit have enabled DNS updates at the server level.

You also have to instruct the DNS server to accept Dynamic DNS updates. For more on how to do so, see Chapter 2, "Domain Name System."

FIGURE 10.27   DNS tab of the scope's IPv4 Properties dialog box

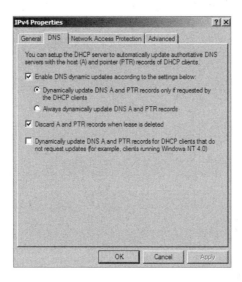

To update the settings at either the server or scope level, you need to open the scope or server properties by right-clicking the appropriate object and choosing Properties. The DNS tab of the Properties dialog box (see Figure 10.27) includes the following options:

Enable DNS Dynamic Updates According To The Settings Below   This check box controls whether this DHCP server will attempt to register lease information with a DNS server. It must be checked to enable Dynamic DNS.

Dynamically Update DNS A And PTR Records Only If Requested By The DHCP Clients   This radio button (which is on by default) tells the DHCP server to register the update only if the DHCP client asks for DNS registration. When this button is active, DHCP clients that aren't hip to DDNS won't have their DNS records updated. However, Windows 2000, XP, Vista, Windows 7, Windows 8, Server 2003, Server 2008 / 2008 R2, and Server 2012 DHCP clients are smart enough to ask for the updates.

Always Dynamically Update DNS A And PTR Records   This radio button forces the DHCP server to register any client to which it issues a lease. This setting may add DNS registrations for DHCP-enabled devices that don't really need them, such as print servers. However, it allows other clients (such as Mac OS, Windows NT, and Linux machines) to have their DNS information automatically updated.

Discard A And PTR Records When Lease Is Deleted   This check box has a long name but a simple function. When a DHCP lease expires, what should happen to the DNS registration? Obviously, it would be nice if the DNS record associated with a lease vanished when the lease expired. When this check box is checked (as it is by default), that's exactly what happens. If you uncheck this box, your DNS will contain entries for expired leases that are no longer valid. When a particular IP address is reissued on a new lease, the DNS will be updated, but in between leases you'll have incorrect data in your DNS—something that's always best to avoid.

Dynamically Update DNS A And PTR Records For DHCP Clients That Do Not Request Updates This check box lets you handle these older clients graciously by making the updates using a separate mechanism.

In Exercise 10.8, you will enable a scope to participate in Dynamic DNS updates.

Enabling DHCP-DNS Integration

1. Open the DHCP snap-in by selecting Administrative Tools ➢ DHCP.

2. Right-click the IPv4 item, and select Properties.

3. The Server Properties dialog box appears. Click the DNS tab.

4. Verify that the check box labeled Enable DNS Dynamic Updates According To The Settings Below is checked, and verify that the radio button labeled Dynamically Update DNS A And PTR Records Only If Requested By The DHCP Clients is selected.

5. Verify that the check box labeled Discard A And PTR Records When Lease Is Deleted is checked. If not, then check it.

6. Click the OK button to apply your changes and close the Server Properties dialog box.

Using Multiple DHCP Servers

DHCP can become a single point of failure within a network if there is only one DHCP server. If that server becomes unavailable, clients will not be able to obtain new leases or renew existing leases. For this reason, it is recommended that you have more than one DHCP server in the network. However, more than one DHCP server can create problems if they both are configured to use the same scope or set of addresses. Microsoft recommends the 80/20 rule for redundancy of DHCP services in a network.

Implementing the 80/20 rule calls for one DHCP server to make approximately 80 percent of the addresses for a given subnet available through DHCP while another server makes the remaining 20 percent of the addresses available. For example, with a /24 network of 254 addresses, say 192.168.1.1 to 192.168.1.254, you might have Server 1 offer 192.168.1.10 to 192.168.1.210 while Server 2 offers 192.168.1.211 to 192.168.254.

Working with the DHCP Database Files

DHCP uses a set of database files to maintain its knowledge of scopes, superscopes, and client leases. These files, which live in the *systemroot*\System32\DHCP folder, are always open when the DHCP service is running. DHCP servers use Joint Engine Technology (JET) databases to maintain their records.

> **WARNING** You shouldn't modify or alter the DHCP database files when the service is running.

The primary database file is dhcp.mdb—it has all the scope data in it.

The following files are also part of the DHCP database:

Dhcp.tmp This is a backup copy of the database file created during reindexing of the database. You normally won't see this file, but if the service fails during reindexing, it may not remove the file when it should.

J50.log This file (plus a number of files named J50*xxxxx*.log, where *xxxxx* stands for 00001, 00002, 00003, and so on) is a log file that stores changes before they're written to the database. The DHCP database engine can recover some changes from these files when it restarts.

J50.chk This is a checkpoint file that tells the DHCP engine which log files it still needs to recover.

In the following sections, you will see how to manipulate the DHCP database files.

Removing the Database Files

If you're convinced that your database is corrupt because the lease information that you see doesn't match what's on the network, the easiest repair mechanism is to remove the database files and start over with an empty database.

> **TIP** If you think the database is corrupt because the DHCP service fails at startup, you should check the event log.

To start over, follow these steps:

1. Stop the DHCP service by typing **netstopdhcpserver** at the command prompt.
2. Remove all the files from the *systemroot*\system32\DHCP folder.
3. Restart the service.
4. Reconcile the scope.

Changing the Database Backup Interval

By default, the DHCP service backs up its databases every 60 minutes. You can adjust this setting by editing the Backup Interval value under `HKEY_LOCAL_MACHINE\SYSTEM\Current-ControlSet\Services\DHCPServer\Parameters`. This allows you to make backups either more frequently (if your database changes a lot or if you seem to have ongoing corruption problems) or less often (if everything seems to be on an even keel).

Moving the DHCP Database Files

You may find that you need to dismantle or change the role of your DHCP server and offload the DHCP functions to another computer. Rather than spend the time re-creating the DHCP database on the new machine by hand, you can copy the database files and use them directly. This is especially helpful if you have a complicated DHCP database with lots of reservations and option assignments.

By copying the files, you also minimize the amount of human error that could be introduced by reentering the information by hand.

Compacting the DHCP Database Files

There may be a time when you need to compact the DHCP database. Microsoft has a utility called `jetpack.exe` that allows you to compact the JET database. Microsoft JET databases are used for WINS and DHCP databases. If you wanted to use the `jetpack` command, the proper syntax is

```
JETPACK.EXE <database name><temp database name>
```

After you compact the database, you rename the temp database to `dhcp.mdb`.

Summary

This chapter covered the DHCP lease process as it relates to TCP/IP configuration information for clients. The following stages were covered: IP discovery, IP lease offer, IP lease selection, and IP lease acknowledgment. You learned how to install and configure the DHCP server on Windows Server 2012 and how to create and manage DHCP scopes and scope options. I also discussed the authorization of DHCP servers within Active Directory and scopes for IPv4 and IPv6 and showed how to create them. And I covered superscopes as well as managing client leases with the options therein.

Exam Essentials

Know how to install and authorize a DHCP server. You install the DHCP service using the Add/Remove Windows Components Wizard. You authorize the DHCP server using the DHCP snap-in. When you authorize a server, you're actually adding its IP address to the Active Directory object that contains a list of the IP addresses of all authorized DHCP servers.

Know how to create a DHCP scope. You use the New Scope Wizard to create a new scope for both IPv4 and IPv6. Before you start, you'll need to know the IP address range for the scope you want to create; which IP addresses, if any, you want to exclude from the address pool; which IP addresses, if any, you want to reserve; and the values for the DHCP options you want to set, if any.

Understand how relay agents help with multiple physical network segments. A question about relay agents on the exam may appear to be a DHCP-related question. Relay agents assist DHCP message propagation across network or router boundaries where such messages ordinarily wouldn't pass.

Understand the difference between exclusions and reservations. When you want to exclude an entire range of IP addresses, you need to add that range as an exclusion. Any IP addresses within the range for which you want a permanent DHCP lease are known as reservations. Remember that exclusions are TCP/IP numbers in a pool that do not get issued and reservations are numbers in a TCP/IP pool that get issued only to the same client each time.

Review Questions

1. You are the network administrator for your Windows Server 2012 network. You have a DHCP server that fails. You restore the DHCP server from backup. You need to prevent the DHCP server from issuing any IP addresses that are already being used on the network. What can you do?

   A. On the DHCP scope, set the Duplicate Address option.

   B. On the DHCP server, set the Duplicate Address option.

   C. Set the Conflict Detection value to 0.

   D. Set the Conflict Detection value to 2.

2. You are the administrator for a Windows Server 2012 network that uses DHCP. You notice that your DHCP database is getting too large and you want to reduce the size of the database. What should you do?

   A. From the folder containing the DHCP database, run `jetpack.exe dhcp.mdb temp.mdb`.

   B. From the folder containing the DHCP database, run `shrinkpack.exe dhcp.mdb temp.mdb`.

   C. From the folder containing the DHCP database, run `jetshrink.exe dhcp.mdb temp.mdb`.

   D. From the folder containing the DHCP database, run `shrinkjet.exe dhcp.mdb temp.mdb`.

3. You administer a network that assigns IP addresses via DHCP. You want to make sure that one of the clients always receives the same IP address from the DHCP server. You create an exclusion for that address, but you find that the computer isn't being properly configured at bootup. What's the problem?

   A. You excluded the wrong IP address.

   B. You need to make a reservation for the client that ties the IP address to the computer's MAC address. Delete the exclusion.

   C. You need to create a superscope for the address.

   D. You must configure the client manually. You cannot assign the address via the DHCP server.

4. Your DHCP server crashed in the middle of the day. You rebooted the server, got it running within 5 minutes, and nobody but you seemed to notice that it had gone down at all. What additional steps must you take?

   A. None. If there were no lease-renewal requests during the 5-minute period in which the DHCP server was down, none of the clients will ever know that it went down.

   B. You need to renew all the leases manually.

   C. None. The DHCP server automatically assigned new addresses to all the clients on the network transparently.

   D. You must reboot all the client machines.

5. Your employer, the Stellacon Corporation, has used networking for years, starting with LAN Manager in the early 1990s. You migrated to Windows NT as an early adopter, and you recently also migrated to Windows 8 and Windows 2012 Server. You are using DHCP on your newly upgraded network, and you still have 100 Windows NT workstations to migrate before you're finished. You have added a new DNS server to the network and modified the scope on the DHCP server to reflect the new addition. You know the command for the Windows NT machines, but what command would you use to verify the IP configuration on the Windows 8 machines?

   A. `w2kipcfg /all`

   B. `ipconfig /all`

   C. `dhcpcfg /all`

   D. `tcpcfg /all`

   E. `winipcfg /all`

6. You have just finished migrating your workstations to Windows 8. Along with this migration, you changed all your static IP addresses to DHCP. A single router that supports BOOTP connects four subnets. The DHCP server has been installed on subnet 1, and it's functioning properly in delivering addresses. When you bring up the clients on subnet 3, the clients boot properly and can communicate with each other, but they cannot communicate with devices on the other subnets. When you run `ipconfig /all`, you discover that the computers on subnets 2, 3, and 4 are in the 169.254.*x.y* address block, which is not the correct network address for any of the subnets. What is the likely cause of this outcome?

   A. The DHCP server evaluated the scope for subnet 3, found it invalid, and substituted the default subnet information for the machines in that subnet.

   B. The DHCP discover request isn't reaching the DHCP server on subnet 1, and the clients are configuring themselves with APIPA addresses.

   C. DHCP servers can support only three subnets, and an additional DHCP server needs to be added to the network.

   D. One of the users has brought another DHCP server online, and it's conflicting with the administrator's DHCP server.

7. You are going to modify the IP configuration on your network to take advantage of DHCP. This will be new to your staff, and you need to explain how DHCP works so that they'll be able to troubleshoot problems if they arise. You particularly want your staff to understand how a client obtains an address from the DHCP server. What steps that occur in the initial DHCP lease process do you need to explain to your staff? (Choose all that apply.)

   A. DHCP lease search

   B. DHCP lease offer

   C. DHCP lease acknowledgment

   D. DHCP lease announce

   E. DHCP lease request

   F. DHCP discovery

   G. DHCP lease selection

   H. DHCP selection

8. You assign two DNS server addresses as part of the options for a scope. Later you find a client workstation that isn't using those addresses. What's the most likely cause?

    A. The client didn't get the option information as part of its lease.

    B. The client has been manually configured with a different set of DNS servers.

    C. The client has a reserved IP address in the address pool.

    D. There's a bug in the DHCP server service.

9. You are working on a client machine that gets its IP configuration via DHCP. You notice that the client received different configuration information the last few times its lease was renewed. Which of the following would cause this to occur?

    A. The DHCP server is not working properly.

    B. Another computer on the network has taken over your machine's configuration information since the last renewal.

    C. The client is receiving only the information that has changed since the last renewal. An administrator is changing the configuration information between lease renewals.

    D. When clients renew their leases, they receive all of their configuration information. An administrator is changing the configuration information between lease renewals.

10. The Spring Flowers Florist Company in Las Vegas has been migrated to Windows 8 and Server 2012 using Active Directory to manage the users and desktops with group policies. The company is in one location, and all the machines are on the same subnet. More recently, you decided to use DHCP to manage the address space more efficiently, so you installed the DHCP server on one of the Windows Server 2012 computers. The scope was created and activated for use. You also configured all of the Windows 8 workstations to use DHCP. However, when you reboot the Windows 8 workstations, they cannot obtain an IP address from the DHCP server. What is the most likely reason for the problem on this network?

    A. The DHCP relay agent has not been enabled for this subnet.

    B. The DHCP server has not been authorized to provide addresses in Active Directory.

    C. The DHCP relay agent needs to be installed on the DHCP server to pass the requests to the DHCP service.

    D. The Windows Server 2012 computer that hosts the DHCP server needs to be rebooted before the DHCP service will start.

Chapter

11

Managing and Maintaining Servers

THE FOLLOWING 70-411 EXAM OBJECTIVES ARE COVERED IN THIS CHAPTER:

✓ **Implement patch management**

- ▪ This objective may include, but is not limited to: Install and configure the Windows Server Update Services (WSUS) role; configure group policies for updates; configure client-side targeting; configure WSUS synchronization; configure WSUS groups.

✓ **Monitor servers**

- ▪ This objective may include, but is not limited to: Configure Data Collector Sets (DCS); configure alerts; monitor real-time performance; monitor virtual machines (VMs); monitor events; configure event subscriptions; configure network monitoring.

In this book, I have discussed how to set up clients on a network and how to keep their systems running on the network. In this chapter, I will discuss how to keep their systems updated using Windows Server Update Services (WSUS).

Another important task of an IT team is to keep the network up and running quickly and efficiently. Keeping your network running at its peak performance is one way to make sure your end users continue to use the network and its resources without problems or interruptions. Remember, everyone has clients—salespeople have theirs, accountants have theirs, and so do we as system administrators. Our clients are the end users. And it's our job to make sure our clients can do their jobs.

When you are working with servers, it is important that you make sure your system's information is safely backed up. Backups become useful when you lose data because of system failures, file corruptions, or accidental modifications of information. As a consultant, I can tell you from experience that backups are among the most important tasks that an IT person performs daily. In this chapter, I'll cover the many different types of backup strategies.

Sometimes, performance optimization can feel like a luxury, especially if you can't get your domain controllers to the point where they are actually performing the services you intend them to do, such as servicing printers or allowing users to share and work on files. The Windows Server 2012 operating system has been specifically designed to provide high-availability services solely intended to keep your mission-critical applications and data accessible even in times of disaster. Occasionally, however, you might experience intermittent server crashes on one or more of the domain controllers or other computers in your environment.

The most common cause of such problems is a hardware configuration issue. Poorly written device drivers and unsupported hardware can cause problems with system stability. Failed hardware components (such as system memory) may do so as well. Memory chips can be faulty, electrostatic discharge can ruin them, and other hardware issues can occur. No matter what, a problem with your memory chip spells disaster for your server.

Usually, third-party hardware vendors provide utility programs with their computers that can be used for performing hardware diagnostics on machines to help you find problems. These utilities are a good first step to resolving intermittent server crashes. When these utility programs are used in combination with the troubleshooting tips provided in this and other chapters of this book, you should be able to pinpoint most network-related problems that might occur.

In this chapter, I'll cover the tools and methods used for measuring performance and troubleshooting failures in Windows Server 2012. Before you dive into the technical details, however, you should thoroughly understand what you're trying to accomplish and how you'll meet this goal.

Knowing How to Locate and Isolate Problems

In a book such as this, it would be almost impossible to cover everything that could go wrong with your Windows Server 2012 system. This book covers many of the most common issues that you might come across—but almost anything is possible. Make sure that you focus on the methodology used and the steps required to locate and isolate a problem—even if you are not 100 percent sure about the cause of the problem. Use online resources to help you locate and troubleshoot the problem, but don't believe everything you read (some things that are posted online can be wrong or misleading). Test your changes in a lab environment, and try to read multiple sources. Always use Microsoft Support (http://support.microsoft.com/) as one of your sources because this site is most likely the right source for information. You won't be able to find and fix everything, but knowing where to find critical information that will help you in your efforts never hurts. One of the tools that many of us in the industry use is *Microsoft TechNet*. The full version of TechNet (a paid subscription) is a resource that will help you find and fix many real-world issues.

Configuring Windows Server Update Services

To keep your Windows operating systems up-to-date and secure, you can use Windows Update, Automatic Updates, WSUS, and the Microsoft Baseline Security Analyzer:

Windows Update   This utility attaches to the Microsoft website through a user-initiated process and allows Windows users to update their operating systems by downloading updated files (critical and noncritical software updates).

Automatic Updates   This utility extends the functionality of Windows Update by automating the process of updating critical files. With Automatic Updates, you can specify whether you want updates to be downloaded and installed automatically or whether you just want to be notified when updates are available.

Windows Server Update Services (WSUS)   This utility is used to deploy a limited version of Windows Update to a corporate server, which in turn provides the Windows updates to client computers within the corporate network. This allows clients that are limited to what they can access through a firewall to be able to keep their Windows operating systems up-to-date.

Microsoft Baseline Security Analyzer (MBSA)   You can download this utility from the Microsoft website to ensure that you have the most current security updates.

In the following sections, you will learn how to use these tools.

Windows Update

Windows Update is available through the Microsoft website and is used to provide the most current files for Windows operating systems. Examples of updates include security fixes, critical updates, updated help files, and updated drivers.

You can download Windows Update through the Help And Support page on the Microsoft website. Once it's installed, click the Scan For Updates link on the Welcome To Windows Update screen to search for new updates.

The results of the Windows Update search will be displayed on the left side of the Windows Update screen. You will see the following options:

Pick Updates To Install   This lists what updates are available for your computer and includes the following categories:

- Critical Updates And Service Packs
- Windows Server 2012 Family
- Driver Updates

Review And Install Updates   This allows you to view all updates that you have selected to install and installs the updates.

View Installation History   This allows you to track all the updates that you have applied to your server.

Personalize Windows Update   This customizes what you see when you use Windows Update.

Get Help And Support   This displays help and support information about Windows Update.

Sometimes the updates that are installed require that the computer be restarted before they can take effect. In this event, Windows Update uses a technology called *chained installation*. With chained installation, all updates that require a computer restart are applied before the computer is restarted. This eliminates the need to restart the computer more than once.

 The information that is collected by Windows Update includes the operating system and version number, the Internet Explorer version, the software version information for any software that can be updated through Windows Update, the Plug and Play ID numbers for installed hardware, and the region and language settings. Windows Update will also collect the product ID and product key to confirm that you are running a licensed copy of Windows, but this information is retained only during the Windows Update session and is not stored. No personal information that can be used to identify users of the Windows Update service is collected.

Windows Automatic Updates

The *Automatic Updates* application extends the functionality of Windows Update by automating the update process. With Automatic Updates, Windows Server 2012 recognizes when you have an Internet connection and will automatically search for any updates for your computer from the Windows Update website.

If any updates are identified, they will be downloaded using *Background Intelligent Transfer Services (BITS)*. BITS is a bandwidth-throttling technology that allows downloads to occur using idle bandwidth only. This means that downloading automatic updates will not interfere with any other Internet traffic.

If Automatic Updates detects any updates for your computer, you will see an update icon in the notification area of the Taskbar.

To configure Automatic Updates, you must have local administrative rights to the computer on which Automatic Updates is being configured. Requiring administrative rights prevents users from specifying that critical security updates not be installed. In addition, Microsoft must digitally sign any updates that are downloaded.

You configure Automatic Updates by selecting Start ➢ Control Panel ➢ Windows Update. You will see the Check For Updates button shown in Figure 11.1.

FIGURE 11.1 Windows Update control panel

You enable Automatic Updates by clicking the Change Settings link. With this setting enabled, Windows Update software may be automatically updated prior to applying any other updates (see Figure 11.2).

FIGURE 11.2 Change Settings window of the Windows Update control panel

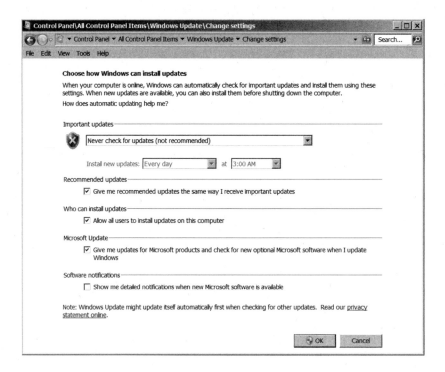

Using Windows Server Update Services

Windows Server Update Services (WSUS), formerly known as Software Update Services (SUS), is used to leverage the features of Windows Update within a corporate environment. WSUS downloads Windows updates to a corporate server, which in turn provides the updates to the internal corporate clients. This allows administrators to test and have full control over what updates are deployed within the corporate environment. WSUS is designed to work in medium-sized corporate networks that are not using System Center Essentials 2012.

Advantages of Using WSUS

Using WSUS has many advantages:

- It allows an internal server within a private intranet to act as a virtual Windows Update server.

- Administrators have selective control over what updates are posted and deployed from the public Windows Update site. No updates are deployed to client computers unless an administrator first approves them.

- Administrators can control the synchronization of updates from the public Windows Update site to the WSUS server either manually or automatically.

- Administrators can configure Automatic Updates on client computers to access the local WSUS server as opposed to the public Windows Update site.

- WSUS checks each update to verify that Microsoft has digitally signed it. Any updates that are not digitally signed are discarded.

- Administrators can selectively specify whether clients can access updated files from the intranet or from Microsoft's public Windows Update site, which is used to support remote clients.

- Administrators can deploy updates to clients in multiple languages.

- Administrators can configure a WSUS statistics server to log update access, which allows them to track which clients have installed updates. The WSUS server and the WSUS statistics server can coexist on the same computer.

- Administrators can manage WSUS servers remotely using HTTP or HTTPS if their web browser is Internet Explorer 6.0 or newer.

WSUS Server Requirements

To act as a WSUS server, the server must meet the following requirements:

- It must be running Windows 2000 Server with Service Pack 4 or newer, Windows Server 2003 SP1 or greater, Windows Vista, Windows 7, Windows 8, Windows Server 2008, Windows Server 2008 R2, or Windows Server 2012.

- It must have all of the most current security patches applied.

- It must be running Internet Information Services (IIS) 6.0 or greater.

- It must be connected to the network.

- It must have an NTFS partition with 100 MB free disk space to install the WSUS server software, and it must have 6 GB of free space to store all the update files.

- It must use BITS version 2.0.

- It must use Microsoft Management Console 3.0.

- It must use Microsoft Report Viewer Redistributable 2008.

If your WSUS server meets the following system requirements, it can support up to 15,000 WSUS clients:

- Pentium III 700 MHz processor

- 512 MB of RAM

Installing the WSUS Server

WSUS should run on a dedicated server, meaning that the server will not run any other applications except IIS, which is required. Microsoft recommends that you install a clean or new version of Windows Server 2003 SP1 or greater, Windows Server 2008, Windows Server 2008 R2, or Windows Server 2012 and apply any service packs or security-related patches.

Exercise 11.1 walks you through the installation process for WSUS.

EXERCISE 11.1

Installing a WSUS Server

1. Choose Server Manager by clicking the Server Manager icon on the Taskbar.

2. Click option number 2, Add Roles And Features.

3. Choose role-based or featured-based installation and click Next.

4. Choose your server and click Next.

5. Choose Windows Server Update Service. Click the Add Features button when the dialog box appears. Then click Next.

6. At the Select features screen, just click Next.

7. At the Windows Server Update Services screen, click Next.

8. At the Select Role Services screen, make sure that WID Database and WSUS Services are both checked. Click Next.

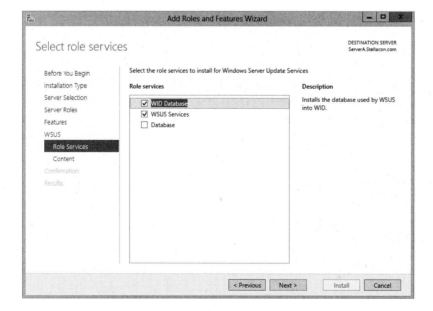

9. At the Content Location Selection screen, uncheck the box Store Updates In The Following Location and click Next. When you uncheck this box, updates are not stored locally. They are only downloaded from Microsoft once they are approved. This will help save hard drive space.

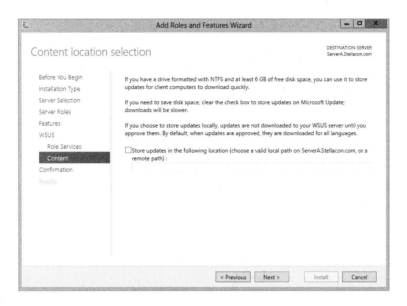

10. At the Confirmation screen, click the Install button.

11. The installation will begin, and you will see the progress. Once the installation is complete, click Close.

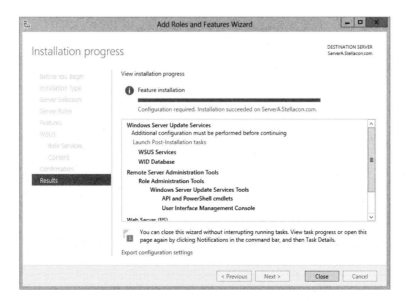

12. In Server Manager, click the WSUS link on the left-hand side. Then click the More link next to Configuration Required For Windows Server Update Services.

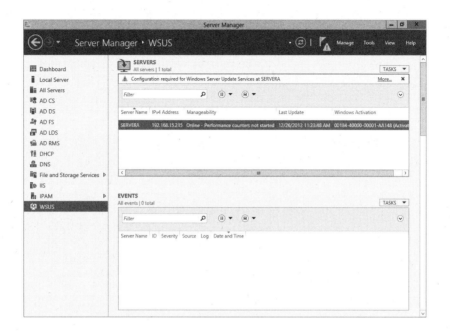

13. At the All Servers Task Details And Notifications screen, click the link for Launch Post-Installation Tasks.

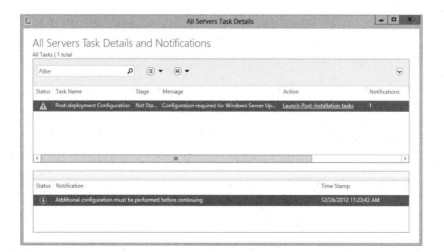

14. The installation process will automatically continue. Once it is finished, you will see Complete under Stage. Close the All Servers Task Details And Notifications screen.

15. Close Server Manager.

16. If a WSUS Configure Options box appears, just close it. You will set options in the next exercise.

Configuring a WSUS Server

Configuring a WSUS machine is a very straightforward process. The easiest way to do it is to use the WSUS Server Configuration Wizard. This wizard walks you through the WSUS setup process, and it makes it very easy to configure WSUS. When in the WSUS snap-in, you can configure different options.

Update Source And Proxy Server   This option allows you to configure whether this WSUS server synchronizes either from Microsoft Update or from another WSUS server on your network.

Products And Classifications   This option allows you to select the products for which you want to get updates and the type of updates that you want to receive.

Update Files And Languages   This option allows you to choose whether to download update files and where to store these update files. This option also allows you to choose which update languages you want downloaded.

Automatic Approvals   This option allows you to specify how to approve installation of updates automatically for selected groups and how to approve revisions to existing updates.

Synchronization Schedule   This option allows you to configure how and when you synchronize your updates. Administrators can choose to synchronize manually or to set up a schedule for daily automatic synchronization.

Computers   This option allows you to set computers to groups or use Group Policy or Registry settings on the computer to receive updates.

Server Cleanup Wizard   This option allows you to clean out old computers, updates, and update files from your server.

Reporting Rollup   This option allows you to choose whether to have replica downstream servers roll up computer and updates status to this WSUS server.

E-Mail Notifications   This option allows you to set up email notifications for WSUS. You can be notified when new updates are synchronized, or you can get email status reports. This option also allows you to set up the email server's information on your WSUS server.

Microsoft Update Improvement Program   This option allows you to choose whether or not you want to participate in the Microsoft Update Improvement program. When you choose to participate in this program, your WSUS server will automatically send information to Microsoft about the quality of your updates. This following information is included:

- How many computers are in the organization
- How many computers successfully installed each update
- How many computers failed to install each update

Personalization This option allows you to personalize the way that information is displayed for this server. This option also allows you to set up a To Do list for WSUS.

WSUS Server Configuration Wizard This option allows you to set up many of the preceding options by just using this one setup wizard.

In Exercise 11.2, you will learn how to set up some of the WSUS server options. To complete this exercise, you need to have an Internet connection that can communicate with Microsoft.

EXERCISE 11.2

Setting WSUS Server Options

1. Open the Windows Server Update Services snap-in from Administrative Tools by pressing the Windows key on the keyboard and then choosing Administrative Tools. The Windows Server Update Services snap-in will be at the bottom of the list alphabetically.

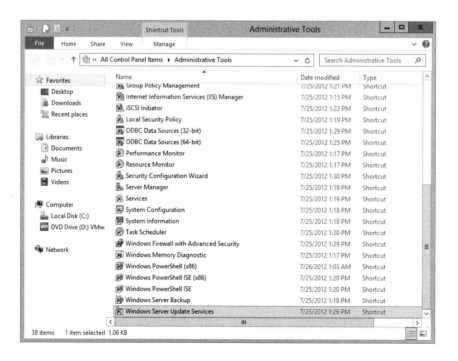

2. On the left-hand side, click the name of your server. Then, in the middle section under To Do, click the Options link.

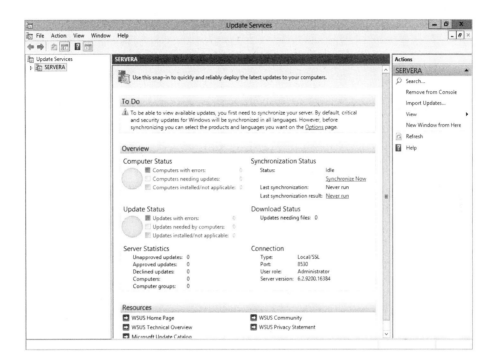

3. A WSUS Server Configuration Wizard appears at the bottom of the options list. Click this link.

4. Click Next at the Before You Begin screen.

5. At the Join Microsoft Update Improvement Program screen, uncheck the Yes box and click Next.

6. At the Choose Upstream Server screen, choose Synchronize From Microsoft Update and click Next.

7. Fill in the information at the Specify Proxy Server screen if you need to use a proxy server. If you do not need a proxy server, just click Next.

8. At the Connect To Upstream Server screen, click the Start Connecting button. This step can take a few minutes depending on your connection speed. Once it's finished connecting, click Next.

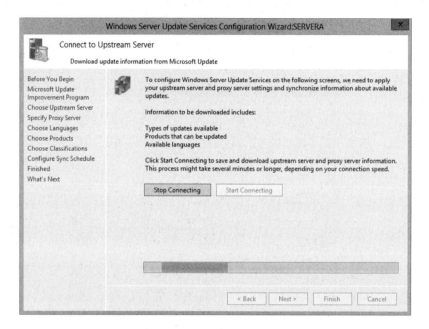

9. At the Choose Products screen, scroll down and choose the products for which you want to receive updates. Then click Next.

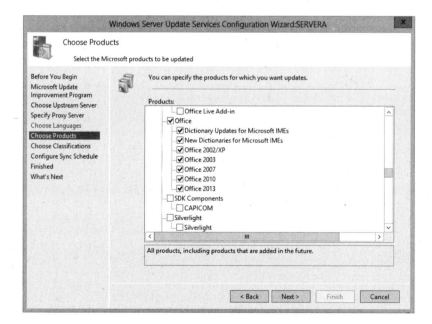

10. At the Choose Classifications screen, choose the classifications of updates you would like and click Next.

11. The Set Sync Schedule screen will appear next. At this screen, you can choose whether you want manual or automatic synchronizations. For this exercise, choose Synchronize Manually and click Next.

12. At the Finish screen, you can click Begin Initial Synchronization and click Finish. Be advised, this initial sync can take some time to finish. So if you don't have time to complete it now, you can always synchronize later.

13. Close WSUS.

Testing and Approving Updates

The administrator should test and approve updates before they get deployed to WSUS clients. The testing should be done on a test machine that is not used for daily tasks.

To approve updates, from the welcome screen, click Updates on the site's toolbar. Make your settings on the Updates page that appears.

Viewing the Synchronization Log

To view the synchronization log, click the Reports button on the site's toolbar from the welcome screen. The Reports page will appear. Click Synchronization Results to view the results.

Configuring a Disconnected Network

You have the ability to use WSUS on a disconnected network. To do so, you download the updates to the Internet-connected WSUS server. After the download is complete, you can export the updates and then import the updates to the disconnected network.

WSUS Client Requirements

WSUS clients run a special version of Automatic Updates that is designed to support WSUS. The following enhancements to Automatic Updates are included:

- Clients can receive updates from a WSUS server as opposed to the public Microsoft Windows Update site.
- The administrator can schedule when the downloading of updated files will occur.
- Clients can be configured via Group Policy or through editing the Registry.
- Updates can occur when an administrative account or nonadministrative account is logged on.

The following client platforms are the only ones that WSUS currently supports:

- Windows XP Home Edition (with Service Pack 3)
- Windows XP Professional (with Service Pack 3)
- Windows Server 2003 (SP1 or newer)

- Windows Vista (all platforms)
- Windows 7 (all platforms)
- Windows 8 (all platforms)
- Windows Server 2008 and 2008 R2 (all platforms)
- Windows Server 2012 (all platforms)

Configuring the WSUS Clients

You can configure WSUS clients in two ways. The method you use depends on whether you use Active Directory in your network.

In a nonenterprise network (not running Active Directory), you would configure Automatic Updates through the Control Panel using the same process that was defined in the section "Windows Automatic Updates" earlier in this chapter. Each client's Registry would then be edited to reflect the location of the server providing the automatic updates.

Within an enterprise network, using Active Directory, you would typically see Automatic Updates configured through Group Policy. Group policies are used to manage configuration and security settings via Active Directory. Group Policy is also used to specify what server a client will use for Automatic Updates. If Automatic Updates is configured through Group Policy, the user will not be able to change Automatic Updates settings by choosing Control Panel ➢ System (for XP) or Windows Update (for Windows 8, Windows 7, Windows Vista, Windows Server 2008, Windows Server 2008 R2, and Windows Server 2012).

Configuring a Client in a Non–Active Directory Network

The easiest way to configure the client to use Automatic Updates is through the Control Panel. However, you can also configure Automatic Updates through the Registry. The Registry is a database of all your server settings. You can access it by choosing Start ➢ Run and typing **regedit** in the Run dialog box. Automatic Updates settings are defined through HKEY_LOCAL_MACHINE\Software\Policies\Microsoft\Windows\WindowsUpdate\AU.

Table 11.1 lists some of the Registry options that you can configure for Automatic Updates.

TABLE 11.1   Selected Registry keys and values for Automatic Updates

Registry Key	Options for Values
NoAutoUpdate	0: Automatic Updates are enabled (default).
	1: Automatic Updates are disabled.
	2: Notify of download and installation.

Registry Key	Options for Values
	3: Autodownload and notify of installation.
	4: Autodownload and schedule installation.
	5: Automatic Updates is required but end users can configure.
ScheduledInstallDay	1: Sunday.
	2: Monday.
	3: Tuesday.
	4: Wednesday.
	5: Thursday.
	6: Friday.
	7: Saturday.
UseWUServer	0: Use public Microsoft Windows Update site.
	1: Use server specified in WUServer entry.

To specify what server will be used as the Windows Update server, you edit two Registry keys, which are found at

`HKEY_LOCAL_MACHINE\Software\Policies\Microsoft\Windows\WindowsUpdate`

- The WUServer key sets the Windows Update server using the server's HTTP name—for example, `http://intranetSUS`.
- The WUStatusServer key sets the Windows Update intranet WSUS statistics server by using the server's HTTP name—for example, `http://intranetSUS`.

Configuring a Client in an Active Directory Network

If the WSUS client is part of an enterprise network using Active Directory, you would configure the client via Group Policy. In Exercise 11.3, we will walk through the steps needed to configure the Group Policy object (GPO) for WSUS clients. The *Group Policy Management Console (GPMC)* needs to be installed to complete this exercise. If you don't have the GPMC installed, you can install it using the Server Manager utility.

EXERCISE 11.3

Configuring a GPO for WSUS

1. Open the GPMC by clicking the Windows key ➢ Administrative Tools ➢ Group Policy Management.

2. Expand the forest, domains, and your domain name. Under your domain name, click Default Domain Policy. Right-click and choose Edit.

3. Under the Computer Configuration section, expand Policies ➢ Administrative Templates ➢ Windows Components ➢ Windows Update.

4. In the right pane, double-click the Configure Automatic Updates option. The Configure Automatic Updates Properties dialog box appears. Click the Enabled button. Then, in the drop-down list, choose Auto Download And Notify For Install. Click OK.

5. Double-click Specify Intranet Microsoft Update Service Location Properties. This setting allows you to specify the server from which the clients will get the updates. Click Enabled. In the two server name boxes, enter **//servername** (the name of the server you installed WSUS on in Exercise 11.1). Click OK.

6. To configure the rescheduling of automatic updates, double-click Reschedule Automatic Updates Scheduled Installations. You can enable and schedule the amount of time that Automatic Updates waits after system startup before it attempts to proceed with a scheduled installation that was previously missed. Click Enabled. Enter **10** in the Startup (Minutes) box. Click OK.

7. To configure auto-restart for scheduled Automatic Updates installations, double-click No Auto-Restart For Scheduled Automatic Updates Installations. When you enable this option, the computer is not required to restart after an update. Enable this option and click OK.

8. Close the GPMC.

Overview of Windows Server 2012 Performance Monitoring

The first step in any performance optimization strategy is to measure performance accurately and consistently. The insight that you'll gain from monitoring factors such as network and system utilization will be extremely useful when you measure the effects of any changes.

The overall performance monitoring process usually involves the following steps:

1. Establish a baseline of current performance.
2. Identify the bottleneck(s).
3. Plan for and implement changes.
4. Measure the effects of the changes.
5. Repeat the process based on business needs.

Note that the performance optimization process is never really finished because you can always try to gain more performance from your system by modifying settings and applying other well-known tweaks. Before you get discouraged, realize that you'll reach some level of performance that you and your network and system users consider acceptable and that it's not worth the additional effort it will take to optimize performance any further. Also note that, as your network and system load increases (more users or users doing more), so too will the need to reiterate this process. By continuing to monitor, measure, and optimize, you will keep ahead of the pack and keep your end users happy.

Now that you have an idea of the overall process, let's focus on how changes should be made. It's important to keep in mind the following ideas when monitoring performance:

Plan Changes Carefully   Here's a rule of thumb you should always try to follow: *An hour of planning can save a week of work.* When you are working in an easy-to-use GUI-based operating system like Windows Server 2012, it's tempting to remove a check mark here or there and then retest the performance. You should resist the urge to do this because some changes can cause large decreases in performance or can impact functionality. Before you make haphazard changes (especially on production servers), take the time to learn about, plan for, and test your changes. Plan for outages and testing accordingly.

Utilize a Test Environment   *Test in a test lab that simulates a production environment.* Do not make changes on production environments without first giving warning. Ideally, change production environments in off-hours when fewer network and system users will be affected. Making haphazard changes in a production environment can cause serious problems. These problems will likely outweigh any benefits you may receive from making performance tweaks.

Make Only One Change at a Time   The golden rule of scientific experiments is that you should *always keep track of as many variables as possible.* When the topic is server optimization, this roughly translates into *making only one change at a time.*

One of the problems with making multiple system changes is that, although you may have improved overall performance, it's hard to determine exactly *which* change created the positive effects. It's also possible, for example, that changing one parameter increased performance greatly while changing another decreased it only slightly. Although the overall result was an increase in performance, you should identify the second, performance-reducing option so that the same mistake is not made again. To reduce the chance of obtaining misleading results, always try to make only one change at a time.

The main reason to make one change at a time, however, is that if you do make a mistake or create an unexpected issue, you can easily "back out" of the change. If you make two or three changes at the same time and are not sure which one created the problem, you will have to undo all the changes and then make one alteration at a time to find the problem. If you make only one change at a time and follow that methodology every time, you won't find yourself in this situation.

> It's important to remember that many changes (such as Registry changes) take place immediately; they do not need to be applied explicitly. Once the change is made, it's live. Be careful to plan your changes wisely.

Ensure Consistency in Measurements   When you are monitoring performance, consistency is extremely important. You should strive to have repeatable and accurate measurements. Controlling variables, such as system load at various times during the day, can help.

Assume, for instance, that you want to measure the number of transactions that you can simulate on the accounting database server within an hour. The results would be widely different if you ran the test during the month-end accounting close than if you ran the test on a Sunday morning. By running the same tests when the server is under a relatively static load, you will be able to get more accurate measurements.

Maintain a Performance History   In the introduction to this chapter, I mentioned that the performance optimization cycle is a continuous improvement process. Because many changes may be made over time, it is important to keep track of the changes that have been made and the results you experienced. Documenting this knowledge will help solve similar problems if they arise. I understand that many IT professionals do not like to document, but documentation can make life much easier in the long run.

As you can see, you need to keep a lot of factors in mind when optimizing performance. Although this might seem like a lot to digest and remember, do not fear; as a system administrator, you will learn some of the rules you need to know to keep your system running optimally. Fortunately, the tools included with Windows Server 2012 can help you organize the process and take measurements. Now that you have a good overview of the process, let's move on to look at the tools that can be used to set it in motion.

Using Windows Server 2012 Performance Tools

Because performance monitoring and optimization are vital functions in network environments of any size, Windows Server 2012 includes several performance-related tools.

Introducing Performance Monitor

The first and most useful tool is the Windows Server 2012 *Performance Monitor*, which was designed to allow users and system administrators to monitor performance statistics for various operating system parameters. Specifically, you can collect, store, and analyze information about CPU, memory, disk, and network resources using this tool, and these are only a handful of the things you can monitor. By collecting and analyzing performance values, system administrators can identify many potential problems.

You can use the Performance Monitor in the following ways:

Performance Monitor ActiveX Control The Windows Server 2012 Performance Monitor is an ActiveX control that you can place within other applications. Examples of applications that can host the Performance Monitor control include Web browsers and client programs such as Microsoft Word or Microsoft Excel. This functionality can make it easy for application developers and system administrators to incorporate the Performance Monitor into their own tools and applications.

Performance Monitor MMC For more common performance monitoring functions, you'll want to use the built-in Microsoft Management Console (MMC) version of the Performance Monitor.

System Stability Index The *System Stability Index* is a numerical value from 1 (least stable) to 10 (most stable) that represents the stability of your network. Performance Monitor calculates and creates the System Stability Index. You can view a graph of this index value. The graph can help a network administrator identify when the network started encountering problems. The System Stability Index also offers side-by-side comparisons. An administrator can view when system changes occurred (installing applications, devices, or drivers) and when system problems started to occur. This way you can determine whether any system changes caused the problems that you are encountering.

Data Collector Sets Windows Server 2012 Performance Monitor includes the Data Collector Set. This tool works with performance logs, telling Performance Monitor where the logs are stored and when the log needs to run. The Data Collector Sets also define the credentials used to run the set.

To access the Performance Monitor MMC, you open Administrative Tools and then choose Performance Monitor. This launches the Performance MMC and loads and initializes Performance Monitor with a handful of default counters.

You can choose from many different methods of monitoring performance when you are using Performance Monitor. A couple of examples are listed here:

- You can look at a snapshot of current activity for a few of the most important counters. This allows you to find areas of potential bottlenecks and monitor the load on your servers at a certain point in time.

- You can save information to a log file for historical reporting and later analysis. This type of information is useful, for example, if you want to compare the load on your servers from three months ago to the current load.

You'll get to take a closer look at this method and many others as you examine Performance Monitor in more detail.

In the following sections, you'll learn about the basics of working with the Windows Server 2012 Performance Monitor and other performance tools. Then you'll apply these tools and techniques when you monitor the performance of your network.

 Your Performance Monitor grows as your system grows, and whenever you add services to Windows Server 2012 (such as installing Exchange Server 2010), you also add to what you can monitor. You should make sure that, as you install services, you take a look at what it is you can monitor.

Deciding What to Monitor

The first step in monitoring performance is to decide *what* you want to monitor. In Windows Server 2012, the operating system and related services include hundreds of performance statistics that you can track easily. For example, you may want to monitor IPSec by monitoring Connection Security Rules. This is just one of many items that can be monitored. All performance statistics fall into three main categories that you can choose to measure:

Performance Objects   A *performance object* within Performance Monitor is a collection of various performance statistics that you can monitor. Performance objects are based on various areas of system resources. For example, there are performance objects for the processor and memory as well as for specific services such as Web services.

Counters   *Counters* are the actual parameters measured by Performance Monitor. They are specific items that are grouped within performance objects. For example, within the Processor performance object, there is a counter for % Processor Time. This counter displays one type of detailed information about the Processor performance object (specifically, the amount of total CPU time all of the processes on the system are using). Another set of counters you can use will allow you to monitor print servers.

Instances   Some counters will have *instances*. An instance further identifies which performance parameter the counter is measuring. A simple example is a server with two CPUs. If you decide you want to monitor processor usage (using the Processor performance object)—specifically, utilization (the % Total Utilization counter)—you must still specify *which* CPU(s) you want to measure. In this example, you would have the choice of monitoring either of the two CPUs or a total value for both (using the Total instance).

To specify which performance objects, counters, and instances you want to monitor, you add them to Performance Monitor using the Add Counters dialog box. Figure 11.3 shows the various options that are available when you add new counters to monitor using Performance Monitor.

FIGURE 11.3 Adding a new Performance Monitor counter

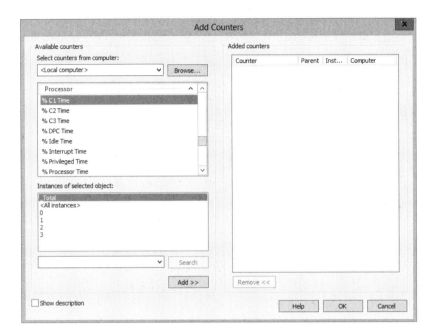

The items that you will be able to monitor will be based on your hardware and software configuration. For example, if you have not installed and configured the IIS, the options available within the Web Server performance object will not be available. Or, if you have multiple network adapters or CPUs in the server, you will have the option of viewing each instance separately or as part of the total value.

Viewing Performance Information

The Windows Server 2012 Performance Monitor was designed to show information in a clear and easy-to-understand format. Performance objects, counters, and instances may be displayed in each of three views. This flexibility allows system administrators to quickly and easily define the information they want to see once and then choose how it will be displayed based on specific needs. Most likely, you will use only one view, but it's helpful to know what other views are available depending on what it is you are trying to assess.

You can use the following main views to review statistics and information on performance:

Graph View The *Graph view* is the default display that is presented when you first access the Windows Server 2012 Performance Monitor. The chart displays values using the vertical axis and time using the horizontal axis. This view is useful if you want to display values over a period of time or see the changes in these values over that time period. Each point that is plotted on the graph is based on an average value calculated during the sample interval for the measurement being made. For example, you may notice overall CPU utilization starting at a low value at the beginning of the chart and then becoming much higher during later measurements. This indicates that the server has become busier (specifically, with CPU-intensive processes). Figure 11.4 provides an example of the Graph view.

FIGURE 11.4   Viewing information in Performance Monitor Graph view

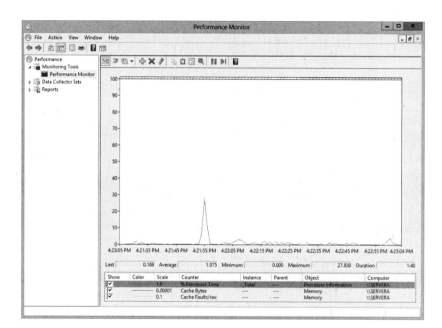

Histogram View   The *Histogram view* shows performance statistics and information using a set of relative bar charts. This view is useful if you want to see a snapshot of the latest value for a given counter. For example, if you were interested in viewing a snapshot of current system performance statistics during each refresh interval, the length of each of the bars in the display would give you a visual representation of each value. It would also allow you to compare measurements visually relative to each other. You can set the histogram to display an average measurement as well as minimum and maximum thresholds. Figure 11.5 shows a typical Histogram view.

Report View   Like the Histogram view, the *Report view* shows performance statistics based on the latest measurement. You can see an average measurement as well as minimum and maximum thresholds. This view is most useful for determining exact values because it provides information in numeric terms, whereas the Chart and Histogram views provide information graphically. Figure 11.6 provides an example of the type of information you'll see in the Report view.

FIGURE 11.5   Viewing information in Performance Monitor Histogram view

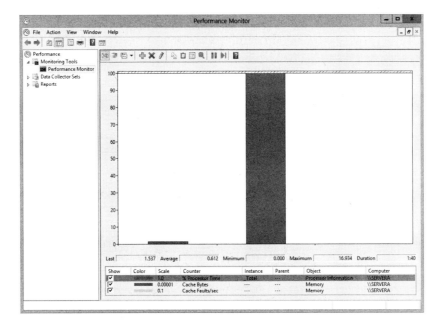

FIGURE 11.6   Viewing information in Performance Monitor Report view

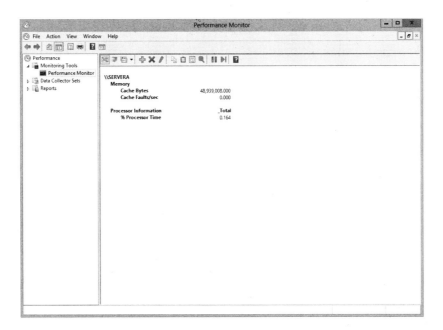

Managing Performance Monitor Properties

You can specify additional settings for viewing performance information within the properties of Performance Monitor. You can access these options by clicking the Properties button in the Taskbar or by right-clicking the Performance Monitor display and selecting Properties. You can change these additional settings by using the following tabs:

General Tab On the General tab (shown in Figure 11.7), you can specify several options that relate to Performance Monitor views:

FIGURE 11.7 General tab of the Performance Monitor Properties dialog box

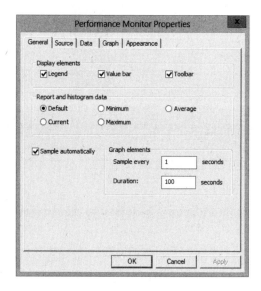

- You can enable or disable legends (which display information about the various counters), the value bar, and the toolbar.
- For the Report and Histogram views, you can choose which type of information is displayed. The options are Default, Current, Minimum, Maximum, and Average. What you see with each of these options depends on the type of data being collected. These options are not available for the Graph view because the Graph view displays an average value over a period of time (the sample interval).
- You can also choose the graph elements. By default, the display will be set to update every second. If you want to update less often, you should increase the number of seconds between updates.

Source Tab On the Source tab (shown in Figure 11.8), you can specify the source for the performance information you want to view. Options include current activity (the default setting) or data from a log file. If you choose to analyze information from a log file, you can also specify the time range for which you want to view statistics. We'll cover these selections in the next section.

FIGURE 11.8 Source tab of the Performance Monitor Properties dialog box

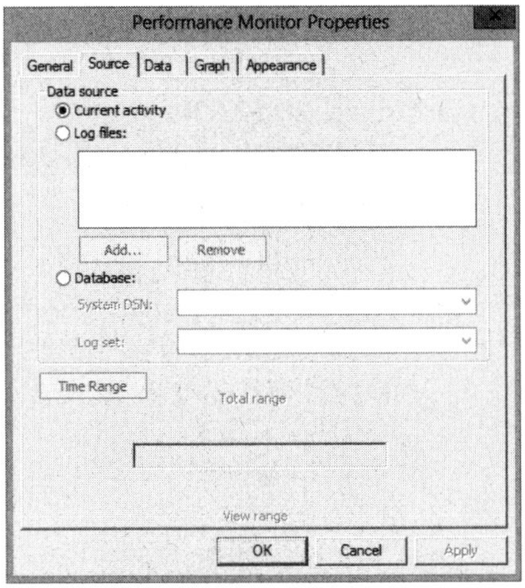

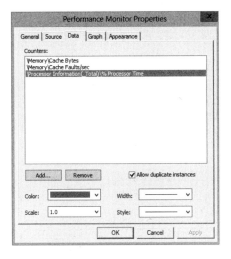

Data Tab   The Data tab (shown in Figure 11.9) lists the counters that have been added to the Performance Monitor display. These counters apply to the Chart, Histogram, and Report views. Using this interface, you can also add or remove any of the counters and change the properties, such as the width, style, and color of the line and the scale used for display.

FIGURE 11.9 The Data tab of the Performance Monitor Properties dialog box

Graph Tab   On the Graph tab (shown in Figure 11.10), you can specify certain options that will allow you to customize the display of Performance Monitor views. First you can specify what type of view you want to see (Line, Histogram, or Report). Then you can add a title for the graph, specify a label for the vertical axis, choose to display grids, and specify the vertical scale range.

FIGURE 11.10 The Graph tab of the Performance Monitor Properties dialog box

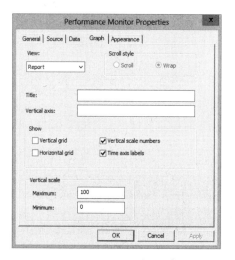

Appearance Tab Using the Appearance tab (see Figure 11.11), you can specify the colors for the areas of the display, such as the background and foreground. You can also specify the fonts that are used to display counter values in Performance Monitor views. You can change settings to find a suitable balance between readability and the amount of information shown on one screen. Finally, you can set up the properties for a border.

FIGURE 11.11 The Appearance tab of the Performance Monitor Properties dialog box

Now that you have an idea of the types of information Performance Monitor tracks and how this data is displayed, we'll take a look at another feature—saving and analyzing performance data.

Saving and Analyzing Data with Performance Logs and Alerts

One of the most important aspects of monitoring performance is that it should be done over a given period of time (referred to as a *baseline*). So far, I have shown you how you can use Performance Monitor to view statistics in real time. I have, however, also alluded to using Performance Monitor to save data for later analysis. Now let's take a look at how you can do this.

When viewing information in Performance Monitor, you have two main options with respect to the data on display:

View Current Activity   When you first open the Performance icon from the Administrative Tools folder, the default option is to view data obtained from current system information. This method of viewing measures and displays various real-time statistics on the system's performance.

View Log File Data   This option allows you to view information that was previously saved to a log file. Although the performance objects, counters, and instances may appear to be the same as those viewed using the View Current Activity option, the information itself was actually captured at a previous point in time and stored into a log file.

Log files for the View Log File Data option are created in the Performance Logs And Alerts section of the Windows Server 2012 Performance tool.

Three items allow you to customize how the data is collected in the log files:

Counter Logs   *Counter logs* record performance statistics based on the various performance objects, counters, and instances available in Performance Monitor. The values are updated based on a time interval setting and are saved to a file for later analysis.

Circular Logging   In *circular logging*, the data that is stored within a file is overwritten as new data is entered into the log. This is a useful method of logging if you want to record information only for a certain time frame (for example, the past four hours). Circular logging also conserves disk space by ensuring that the performance log file will not continue to grow over certain limits.

Linear Logging   In *linear logging*, data is never deleted from the log files, and new information is added to the end of the log file. The result is a log file that continually grows. The benefit is that all historical information is retained.

Now that you have an idea of the types of functions that are supported by the Windows Server 2012 Performance tools, you can learn how you can apply this information to the task at hand—monitoring and troubleshooting your Windows network.

🌐 **Real World Scenario**

Real-World Performance Monitoring

In our daily jobs as system engineers and administrators, we come across systems that are in need of our help...and may even ask for it. You, of course, check your Event Viewer and Performance Monitor and perform other tasks that help you troubleshoot. But what is really the most common problem that occurs? From my experience, I'd say that you suffer performance problems many times if your Windows Server 2012 operating system is installed on a subpar system. Either the server hardware isn't enterprise class or the minimum hardware requirements weren't addressed. Most production servers suffer from slow response times, lagging, and so on because money wasn't spent where it should have been in the first place—on the server's hardware requirements.

Using Other Performance-Monitoring Tools

Performance Monitor allows you to monitor different parameters of the Windows Server 2012 operating system and associated services and applications. However, you can also use three other tools to monitor performance in Windows Server 2012. They are Network Monitor, Task Manager, and Event Viewer. All three of these tools are useful for monitoring different areas of overall system performance and for examining details related to specific system events. In the following sections, you'll take a quick look at these tools and how you can best use them.

The Network Monitor

Although Performance Monitor is a great tool for viewing overall network performance statistics, it isn't equipped for packet-level analysis and doesn't give you much insight into what types of network traffic are traveling on the wire. That's where the Network Monitor tool comes in. *Network Monitor* has two main components: the Network Monitor Agent and the Network Monitor tool.

The Network Monitor Agent is available for use with Windows XP, Windows Server 2003, Windows Vista, Windows 7, Windows 8, Windows Server 2008, Windows Server 2008 R2, and Windows Server 2012. The agent allows you to track network packets. When you install the Network Monitor Agent, you will also be able to access the Network Segment System Monitor counter.

On Windows Server 2012 computers, you'll see the Network Monitor icon appear in the Administrative Tools program group. You can use the Network Monitor tool to capture data as it travels on your network.

A version of Network Monitor is available for free with Windows Server 2012. The full version of Network Monitor is available at Microsoft's download server. For more information, see www.microsoft.com/downloads/.

Once you have captured the data of interest, you can save it to a capture file or further analyze it using Network Monitor. Experienced network and system administrators can use this information to determine how applications are communicating and the types of data that are being passed via the network.

For the exam, you don't need to understand the detailed information that Network Monitor displays, but you should be aware of the types of information that you can view and when you should use Network Monitor.

Task Manager

Performance Monitor is designed to allow you to keep track of specific aspects of system performance over time. But what do you do if you want to get a quick snapshot of what the local system is doing? Creating a System Monitor chart, adding counters, and choosing a view is overkill. Fortunately, the Windows Server 2012 Task Manager has been designed to provide a quick overview of important system performance statistics without requiring any configuration. Better yet, it's always readily available.

You can easily access Task Manager in several ways:

- Right-click the Windows Taskbar, and then click Task Manager.

- Press Ctrl+Alt+Del, and then select Task Manager.

- Press Ctrl+Shift+Esc.

Each of these methods allows you to access a snapshot of the current system performance quickly.

Once you access Task Manager, you will see the following five tabs:

These tabs can be different on Windows Client machines. For example, Windows 7 has 6 tabs, not 5, and Windows 8 has 7 tabs now.

Processes Tab   The Processes tab shows you all the processes that are currently running on the local computer. By default, you'll be able to view how much CPU time and memory a particular process is using. By clicking any of the columns, you can quickly sort by the data values in that particular column. This is useful, for example, if you want to find out which processes are using the most memory on your server.

By accessing the performance objects in the View menu, you can add columns to the Processes tab. Figure 11.12 shows a list of the current processes running on a Windows Server 2012 computer.

FIGURE 11.12   Viewing process statistics and information using Task Manager

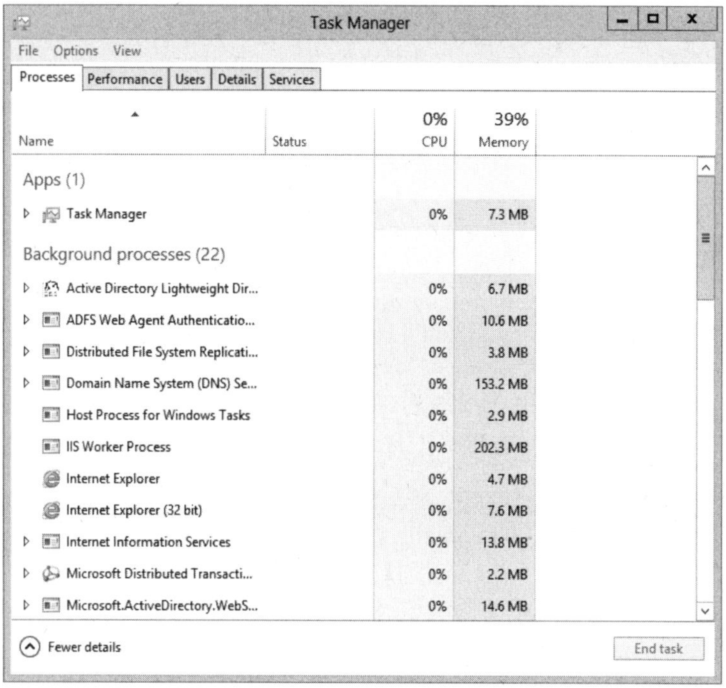

Performance Tab   One of the problems with using Performance Monitor to get a quick snapshot of system performance is that you have to add counters to a chart. Most system administrators are too busy to take the time to do this when all they need is basic CPU and memory information. That's where the Performance tab of Task Manager comes in. Using the Performance tab, you can view details about how memory is allocated on the computer and how much of the CPU is utilized (see Figure 11.13).

Users Tab   The Users tab (see Figure 11.14) lists the currently active user accounts. This is particularly helpful if you want to see who is online and quickly log off or disconnect users. You can also send a console message to any remote user in the list by clicking the Send Message button. (The button is grayed out in Figure 11.15 because you cannot send a message to yourself. If you select a different user, the button will be available.)

FIGURE 11.13   Viewing CPU and memory performance information using Task Manager

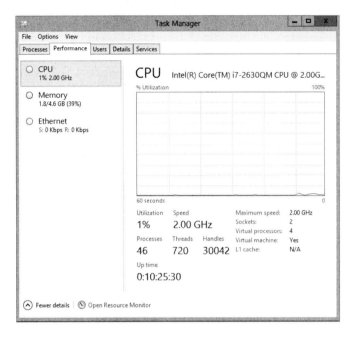

FIGURE 11.14   Viewing user information using Task Manager

Details Tab The Details tab (see Figure 11.15) shows you what applications are currently running on the system. From this location, you can stop an application from running by right-clicking the application and choosing Stop. You also have the ability to set your affinity level here. By setting the affinity, you can choose which applications will use which processors on your system.

FIGURE 11.15 Viewing user information using Task Manager

Name ▲	PID	Status	User name	CPU	Memory (p...	Description
certsrv.exe	1600	Running	SYSTEM	00	4,940 K	Microsoft® Certifica...
csrss.exe	340	Running	SYSTEM	00	968 K	Client Server Runtim...
csrss.exe	396	Running	SYSTEM	00	1,172 K	Client Server Runtim...
dfsrs.exe	1668	Running	SYSTEM	00	3,924 K	Distributed File Syste...
dfssvc.exe	1176	Running	SYSTEM	00	1,264 K	Windows NT Distrib...
dns.exe	1704	Running	SYSTEM	00	156,836 K	Domain Name Syste...
dsamain.exe	1412	Running	NETWORK...	00	6,880 K	Active Directory Lig...
dwm.exe	852	Running	DWM-1	00	20,300 K	Desktop Window M...
explorer.exe	3188	Running	Administra...	00	21,032 K	Windows Explorer
iexplore.exe	1348	Running	Administra...	00	4,836 K	Internet Explorer
iexplore.exe	3564	Running	Administra...	00	7,744 K	Internet Explorer
ifssvc.exe	2460	Running	SYSTEM	00	10,828 K	ADFS Web Agent Au...
inetinfo.exe	2340	Running	SYSTEM	00	14,160 K	Internet Information...
ismserv.exe	1776	Running	SYSTEM	00	1,040 K	Windows NT Intersit...
lsass.exe	500	Running	SYSTEM	00	15,936 K	Local Security Autho...
Microsoft.ActiveDire...	1456	Running	SYSTEM	00	14,936 K	Microsoft.ActiveDire...
Microsoft.IdentitySer...	3636	Running	NETWORK...	00	251,332 K	Microsoft.IdentitySe...
msdtc.exe	3824	Running	NETWORK...	00	2,292 K	Microsoft Distribute...
services.exe	492	Running	SYSTEM	00	3,816 K	Services and Control...
smss.exe	228	Running	SYSTEM	00	288 K	Windows Session M...
SMSvcHost.exe	1820	Running	LOCAL SE...	00	5,980 K	SMSvcHost.exe
spoolsv.exe	1384	Running	SYSTEM	00	3,784 K	Spooler SubSystem ...
sqlservr.exe	2128	Running	MSSQL$MI...	00	256,052 K	SQL Server Windows...

Services Tab The Services tab (see Figure 11.16) shows you what services are currently running on the system. From this location, you can stop a service from running by right-clicking the service and choosing Stop. The Open Services link launches the Services MMC.

FIGURE 11.16   Viewing services information using Task Manager

Name	PID	Description	Status	Group ▲
WSusCertServer		WSUS Certificate Server	Stopped	
WsusService	4048	WSUS Service	Running	
wmiApSrv		WMI Performance Adapter	Stopped	
WLMS	816	Windows Licensing Monitoring S...	Running	
WIDWriter	1960	Windows Internal Database VSS ...	Running	
VSS		Volume Shadow Copy	Stopped	
vds	2868	Virtual Disk	Running	
VaultSvc	500	Credential Manager	Running	
UI0Detect		Interactive Services Detection	Stopped	
TrustedInstaller		Windows Modules Installer	Stopped	
sppsvc		Software Protection	Stopped	
Spooler	1384	Print Spooler	Running	
SNMPTRAP		SNMP Trap	Stopped	
SamSs	500	Security Accounts Manager	Running	
RSoPProv		Resultant Set of Policy Provider	Stopped	
RpcLocator		Remote Procedure Call (RPC) Lo...	Stopped	
PerfHost		Performance Counter DLL Host	Stopped	
NtFrs		File Replication	Stopped	
NTDS	500	Active Directory Domain Services	Running	
NetTcpPortSharing	1820	Net.Tcp Port Sharing Service	Running	
NetTcpActivator	1820	Net.Tcp Listener Adapter	Running	
Netlogon	500	Netlogon	Running	
MSSQL$MICROSOFT##WID	2128	Windows Internal Database	Running	

Task Manager — File Options View
Tabs: Processes | Performance | Users | Details | **Services**

⌃ Fewer details   Open Services

As you can see, Task Manager is useful for providing important information about the
system quickly. Once you get used to using Task Manager, you won't be able to get by
without it!

Make sure that you use Task Manager and familiarize yourself with all that
it can do; you can end processes that have become intermittent, kill applications that may hang the system, view NIC performance, and so on. In
addition, you can access this tool quickly to get an idea of what could be
causing you problems. Event Viewer, Network Monitor, and Performance
Monitor are all great tools for getting granular information on potential
problems.

Event Viewer

Event Viewer is also useful for monitoring network information. Specifically, you can use
the logs to view any information, warnings, or alerts related to the proper functioning
of the network. You can access Event Viewer by selecting Administrative Tools ➢ Event

Viewer. Clicking any of the items in the left pane displays the various events that have been logged for each item. Figure 11.17 shows the contents of the Directory Service log.

FIGURE 11.17 Event Viewer

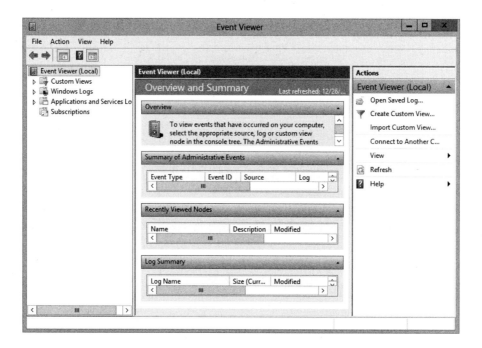

Each event is preceded by a blue "i" icon. That icon designates that these events are informational and do not indicate problems with the network. Rather, they record benign events such as Active Directory startup or a domain controller finding a global catalog server.

Problematic or potentially problematic events are indicated by a yellow warning icon or a red error icon, both of which are shown in Figure 11.18. Warnings usually indicate a problem that wouldn't prevent a service from running but might cause undesired effects with the service in question. For example, I was configuring a site with some fictional domain controllers and IP addresses. My local domain controller's IP address wasn't associated with any of the sites, and Event Viewer generated a warning. In this case, the local domain controller could still function as a domain controller, but the site configuration could produce undesirable results.

Error events almost always indicate a failed service, application, or function. For instance, if the dynamic registration of a DNS client fails, Event Viewer will generate an error. As you can see, errors are more severe than warnings because, in this case, the DNS client cannot participate in DNS at all.

FIGURE 11.18   Information, errors, and warnings in Event Viewer

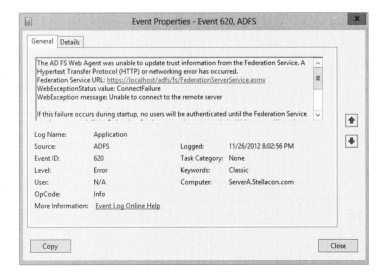

Double-clicking any event opens the Event Properties dialog box, as shown in Figure 11.19, which displays a detailed description of the event.

FIGURE 11.19   An Event Properties dialog box

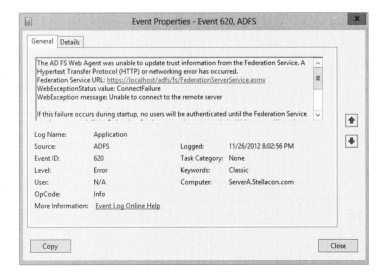

Event Viewer can display thousands of different events, so it would be impossible to list them all here. The important points of which you should be aware are the following:

- Information events are always benign.

- Warnings indicate noncritical problems.

- Errors indicate show-stopping events.

Let's discuss some of the logs and the ways that you can view data:

Applications and Services   The *applications and services logs* are part of Event Viewer where applications (for example, Exchange) and services (DNS) log their events. DFS events would be logged in this part of Event Viewer. An important log in this section is the DNS Server log (see Figure 11.20). This is where all of your DNS events get stored.

FIGURE 11.20   The applications and services DNS Server log

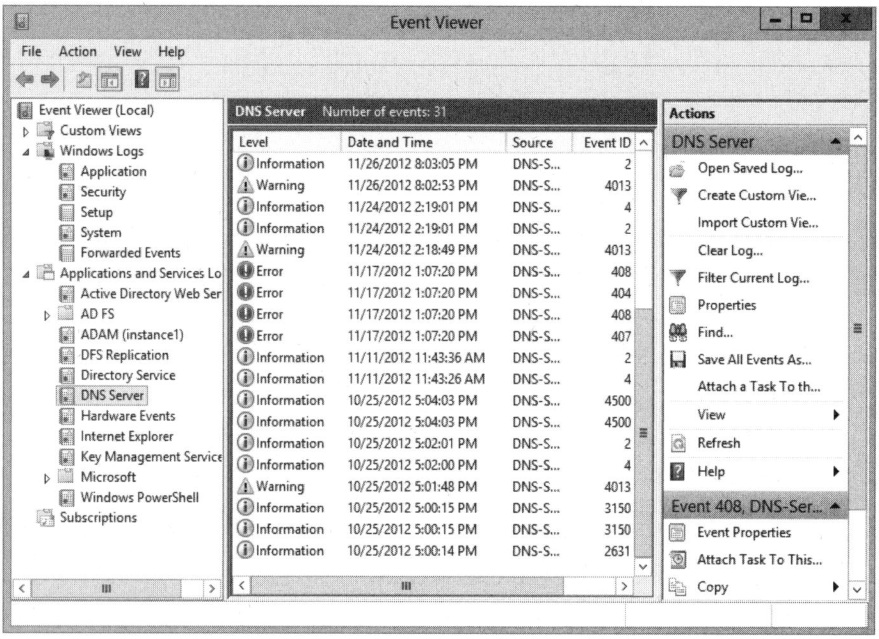

Custom Views   *Custom views* allow you to filter events (see Figure 11.21) to create your own customized look. You can filter events by event level (critical, error, warning, and so on), by logs, and by source. You also have the ability to view events occurring within a specific timeframe. This allows you to look only at the events that are important to you.

FIGURE 11.21 Create Custom View dialog box

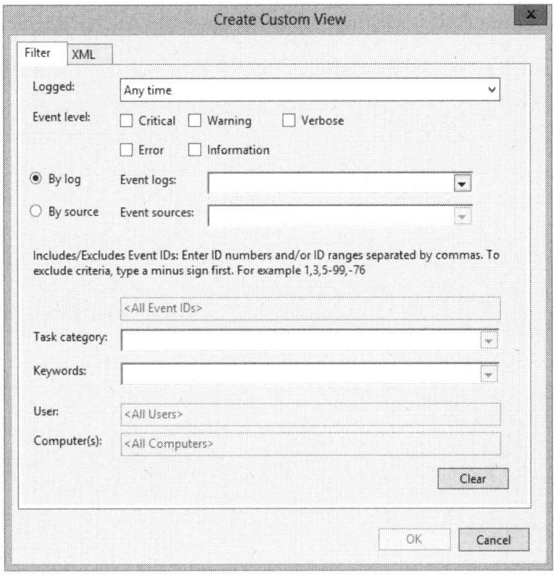

Subscriptions *Subscriptions* allow a user to receive alerts about events that you predefine. In the Subscription Properties dialog box (see Figure 11.22), you can define what type of events you want notifications about and the notification method. The Subscriptions section is an advanced alerting service to help you watch for events.

FIGURE 11.22 Subscription Properties dialog box

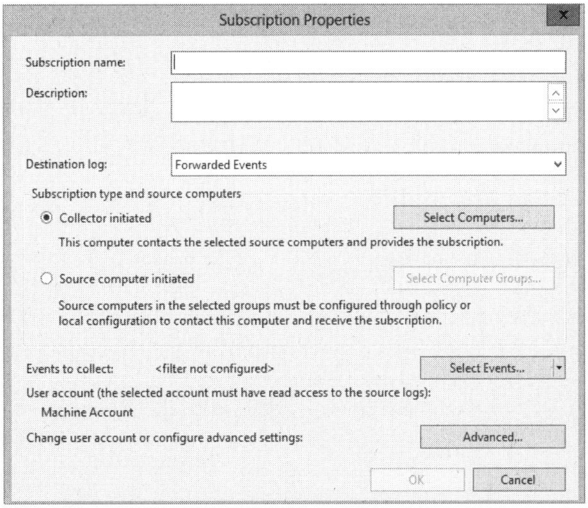

Microsoft Baseline Security Analyzer

The *Microsoft Baseline Security Analyzer (MBSA)* is a security assessment utility that you can download from the Microsoft website at the following location:

    http://www.microsoft.com/en-us/download/details.aspx?id=19892

The filename of the download is `mbsasetup.msi`. It verifies whether your computer has the latest security updates and whether any common security violation configurations have been applied to your computer. MBSA can scan the following programs and operating systems:

- Windows 2000
- Windows XP
- Windows Vista
- Windows 7
- Windows 8
- Windows Server 2003
- Windows Server 2008
- Windows Server 2008 R2
- Windows Server 2012
- IIS 5 or newer
- Internet Explorer, versions 6.0 and newer
- SQL Server 7 or newer
- Microsoft Office 2000 or newer
- Windows Media Player, versions 6.4 and newer

    To use MBSA, the computer must meet the following requirements:

- It must be running Windows XP, Windows Vista, Windows 7, Windows 8, Windows Server 2003, Windows Server 2008, or Windows Server 2008 R2.
- It must be running Internet Explorer 5.01 or newer.
- It must have an XML parser installed for full functionality.
- It must have the Workstation and the Server service enabled.
- It must have Client for Microsoft Networks installed.

Using the GUI Version of MBSA

Once you have installed MBSA, you can access it by using the Windows key and choosing Microsoft Baseline Security Analyzer or by opening the command prompt and executing `mbsa.exe`. This opens the Baseline Security Analyzer utility. You can select from Scan A Computer, Scan More Than One Computer, and View Existing Security Reports.

When you click Scan A Computer, the Pick A Computer To Scan dialog box appears. You can specify that you want to scan a computer based on a computer name or IP address. You can also specify the name of the security report that will be generated.

The following are options for the security scan:

- Check For Windows Vulnerabilities
- Check For Weak Passwords
- Check For IIS Vulnerabilities
- Check For SQL Vulnerabilities
- Check For Security Updates

If you use the Check For Security Updates option and are using WSUS, you can specify the name of the WSUS server that should be checked for the security updates.

Once you have made your selections, click Start Scan. When the scan is complete, the security report will be automatically displayed. If you have scanned multiple computers, you can sort the security reports based on issue name or score (worst first or best first).

Using the MBSA Command-Line Utility *mbsacli.exe*

After Microsoft Baseline Security Analyzer has been installed, you can use the command-line utility mbsacli.exe. Enter **mbsacli.exe/hf**, and then customize the command execution with any of the options defined in Table 11.2.

TABLE 11.2 mbsacli.exe /hf command-line options

Option	Description
-h *host name[, host name, . . .]*	Scans the specified host. You can specify that you want to scan multiple host computers by separating the hostnames with commas.
-fh *filename*	Scans the NetBIOS name of each computer that is to be scanned, and it saves the information as text within a file specified by *filename*.
-i *xxxx.xxxx.xxxx.xxxx [, xxxx.xxxx.xxxx.xxxx, . . .]*	Scans a computer based on the specified IP address. You can scan multiple computers by IP address by separating the IP addresses with commas.
-fip *filename*	Looks in the text file specified by *filename* for IP addresses and scans the computers with those IP addresses. The file can have up to a maximum of 256 IP addresses.
-d *domainname*	Scans the specified domain.
-n	Scans all of the computers on the local network.

Simple Network Management Protocol

The *Simple Network Management Protocol (SNMP)* is a TCP/IP protocol monitor. The SNMP service creates trap messages that are then sent to a trap destination. One way you might use SNMP is to trap messages that don't contain an appropriate hostname for a particular service.

When you set up SNMP, you set up communities. *Communities* are groupings of computers that help monitor each other.

Windows Server 2012 includes SNMP with the operating system. To install the service, you must use Server Manager. In Exercise 11.4, you will walk through the process of installing the SNMP service.

EXERCISE 11.4

Installing SNMP

1. Open Server Manager by clicking the Server Manager icon on the Taskbar.

2. Click option number 2, Add Roles And Features.

3. Choose role-based or feature-based installation and click Next.

4. Choose your server and click Next.

5. Click Next at the Select Server Roles screen.

6. When the Select Features window appears, click the SNMP Services check box. If an ADD Features dialog box appears, click the Add Features button. Click Next.

7. The Confirm Installation page appears. Click Install.

8. Click Close. Exit the Server Manager application.

Now that you have installed the SNMP service, you have to set up your community so that you can start trapping messages. As stated earlier, communities are a grouping of computers to help monitor each other. After you have created the initial community, you can add other computer systems to the community.

In Exercise 11.5, you will walk through the steps to set up the SNMP service and also set up your first community name. To complete this exercise, you must have completed Exercise 11.4.

EXERCISE 11.5

Configuring SNMP

1. Open Computer Management by pressing the keyboard's Windows Key ➢ Administrative Tools ➢ Computer Management.

2. Expand Services And Applications. Click Services. In the right pane, double-click SNMP Service.

3. The SNMP Service Properties window will open. Click the Traps tab. In the Community Name box, enter **Community1**. Click the Add To List button.

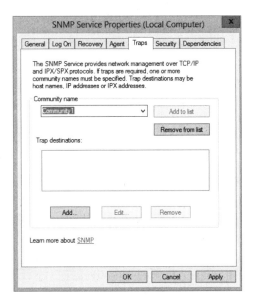

4. Click the General tab. Click the Start button to start the service. Click OK.

5. Close Computer Management.

Summary

This chapter began with a discussion on WSUS and what Windows Update can do for your network. You learned why you would want to use a WSUS server instead of having clients manually connect to the Internet to receive their updates.

The chapter also covered file server and print server optimization and reliability, including many tools that can help you monitor and manage your systems and the basics of troubleshooting the network in times of disaster.

Monitoring performance on servers is imperative to rooting out any issues that may affect your network. If your systems are not running at their best, your end users may experience issues such as latency, or worse, you may experience corruption in your network data. Either way, it's important to know how to monitor the performance of your servers. We also looked at ways system administrators can optimize the operations of servers to ensure that end users experience adequate performance.

We also examined how to use the various performance-related tools that are included with Windows Server 2012. Tools such as Performance Monitor, Task Manager, Network Monitor, and Event Viewer can help you diagnose and troubleshoot system performance issues. These tools will help you find typical problems related to memory, disk space, and any other hardware-related issues you may experience. Knowing how to use tools to troubleshoot and test your systems is imperative, not only to passing the exam, but also to performing your duties at work. To have a smoothly running network environment, it is vital that you understand the issues related to the reliability and performance of your network servers and domain controllers.

Exam Essentials

Understand WSUS.   Windows Server Update Services is one way to have your end users receive important updates from Microsoft. WSUS gives administrators the ability to download, test, and approve updates before they get released onto the network.

Understand the methodology behind troubleshooting performance.   By following a set of steps that involves making measurements and finding bottlenecks, you can systematically troubleshoot performance problems.

Be familiar with the features and capabilities of the Windows Server 2012 Performance Monitor tool for troubleshooting performance problems.   The Performance Monitor administrative tool is a very powerful method for collecting data about all areas of system performance. Through the use of performance objects, counters, and instances, you can choose to collect and record only the data of interest and use this information for pinpointing performance problems.

Know the importance of common performance counters.   Several important performance-related counters deal with general system performance. Know the importance of monitoring memory, print server, CPU, and network usage on a busy server.

Understand the role of other troubleshooting tools.   Windows Task Manager, Network Monitor, SNMP, Baseline Security Analyzer, and Event Viewer can all be used to diagnose and troubleshoot configuration- and performance-related issues.

Understand how to troubleshoot common sources of server reliability problems.   Windows Server 2012 has been designed to be a stable, robust, and reliable operating system. Should you experience intermittent failures, you should know how to troubleshoot device drivers and buggy system-level software.

Review Questions

1. You need to stop an application from running in Task Manager. Which tab would you use to stop an application from running?

    A. Performance

    B. Users

    C. Options

    D. Details

2. You are the network administrator for a Fortune 500 company. You are responsible for all client computers at the central campus. You want to make sure that all of the client computers are secure. You decide to use MBSA to scan your client computers for possible security violations. You want to use the command-line version of MBSA to scan your computers based on IP address. Which of the following commands should you use?

    A. `mdsacli.exe /hf -i xxxx.xxxx.xxxx.xxxx`

    B. `mdsacli.exe /ip xxxx.xxxx.xxxx.xxxx`

    C. `mbsa.exe /hf -ip xxxx.xxxx.xxxx.xxxx`

    D. `mbsa.exe /ip xxxx.xxxx.xxxx.xxxx`

3. You are the network administrator for a Fortune 500 company. You are responsible for all client computers at the central campus. You want to make sure that all of the client computers have the most current software installed for their operating systems, including software in the categories Critical Updates and Service Packs, Windows Server 2012 Family, and Driver Updates. You want to automate the process as much as possible, and you want the client computers to download the updates from a central server that you are managing. You decide to use Windows Server Update Services. The WSUS server software has been installed on a server called WSUSServer. You want to test the WSUS server before you set up group policies within the domain. You install Windows 8. Which of the following Registry entries needs to be made for the client to specify that the client should use WSUSServer for Windows Update? (Choose all that apply.)

    A. Use `HKEY_LOCAL_MACHINE\Software\Policies\Microsoft\Windows\Windows Update\AU\UseWUServer`, and specify 0 data.

    B. Use `HKEY_LOCAL_MACHINE\Software\Policies\Microsoft\Windows\Windows Update\AU\UseWUServer`, and specify 1 for data.

    C. Use `HKEY_LOCAL_MACHINE\Software\Policies\Microsoft\Windows\Windows Update\AU\WUServer`, and specify `http://WSUSServer`.

    D. Use `HKEY_LOCAL_MACHINE\Software\Policies\Microsoft\Windows\Windows Update\AU\WUServer`, and specify `WSUSServer`.

    E. Use `HKEY_LOCAL_MACHINE\Software\Policies\Microsoft\Windows\Windows Update\WUServer`, and specify `http://WSUSServer`.

    F. Use `HKEY_LOCAL_MACHINE\Software\Policies\Microsoft\Windows\Windows Update\WUServer`, and specify `WSUSServer`.

4. You are the administrator of a new Windows Server 2012 machine. You need to install WSUS. From where do you install WSUS?

   A. Add/Remove Programs

   B. Programs

   C. Server Manager

   D. Administrative Tools

5. You are a network administrator for your company. The network consists of a single Active Directory domain. All servers run Windows Server 2012. Windows Server Update Services (WSUS) is installed on two servers, SERVERA and SERVERB. SERVERA receives software updates from Microsoft Windows Update servers. You manually synchronized SERVERB with the Windows Update servers, and now you need to complete the WSUS configuration on SERVERB. Which of the following is *not* a step you might take to complete the configuration of WSUS on SERVERB?

   A. Approve the current updates.

   B. Set SERVERB to receive updates from SERVERA and automatically synchronize with approved updates on SERVERA.

   C. Set SERVERB to draw updates automatically from whichever sources SERVERA is set to draw from.

   D. Set SERVERB to receive daily updates automatically at a given time.

6. You are the network administrator for your company. The network consists of a single Active Directory domain. All servers run Windows Server 2012. All client computers run Windows 7. The company has 16 mobile sales representatives who are all members of the Power Users local group on their computers. From 6 p.m. until 7 a.m., the sales representatives' laptops are usually turned off and disconnected from the corporate network. The mobile sales representatives' computers must receive software updates every day with minimal user interaction. While verifying the recent updates on one of the laptops, you notice that the updates from the Windows Update servers were not applied. On the Automatic Updates tab of the System Properties dialog box of the mobile computer, what should you do to make sure that software updates are applied to the computer? (Choose three.)

   A. Set the scheduled time to every day at 12 a.m.

   B. Select the option Automatically Download The Updates, And Install Them On The Schedule That I Specify.

   C. Select the option Notify Me Before Downloading Any Updates And Notify Me Again Before Installing Them On My Computer.

   D. Select the Keep My Computer Up To Date check box.

   E. Select the option Download The Updates Automatically And Notify Me When They Are Ready To Be Installed.

   F. Set the scheduled time to every day at 12 p.m.

7. You are responsible for managing several Windows Server 2012 domain controller computers in your environment. Recently, a single hard disk on one of these machines failed, and the Active Directory database was lost. You want to perform the following tasks:

- Determine which partitions on the server are still accessible.

- Restore as much of the system configuration (including the Active Directory database) as possible.

Which of the following could be used to help meet these requirements?

A. Event Viewer

B. Performance Monitor

C. A hard disk from another server that is not configured as a domain controller

D. A valid system state backup from the server

8. You have been hired as a consultant to research a network-related problem at a small organization. The environment supports many custom-developed applications that are not well documented. A manager suspects that some computers on the network are generating excessive traffic and bogging down the network. You want to do the following:

- Determine which computers are causing the problems.

- Record and examine network packets that are coming to/from specific machines.

- View data related only to specific types of network packets.

What tool should you use to accomplish all of the requirements?

A. Task Manager

B. Performance Monitor

C. Event Viewer

D. Network Monitor

9. You need to install Microsoft Baseline Security Analyzer. How do you need to do the install?

A. Download MBSA from Microsoft's website.

B. Install from Server Manager.

C. Use Add/Remove Programs.

D. Programs

10. While setting up WSUS, you need to configure the server from which you will be getting your Microsoft updates. Under which option would you set this up?

A. Products And Classifications

B. Update Files and Languages

C. Update Source And Proxy Server

D. Synchronization Schedule

Chapter

12

Configuring Network Access

THE FOLLOWING 70-411 EXAM OBJECTIVES ARE COVERED IN THIS CHAPTER:

✓ **Configure VPN and routing**

- This objective may include, but is not limited to: Install and configure the Remote Access role; implement Network Address Translation (NAT); configure VPN settings; configure remote dial-in settings for users; configure routing.

As the use of TCP/IP internetworking has grown, so has the demand for easy-to-install and easy-to-configure routers. Not every small business that wants to connect to the Internet or connect two remote offices can afford an expensive router and a certified professional to administer it. Microsoft's first attempt to solve this problem was the version of the Routing and Remote Access Services (RRAS) included in the Windows NT 4.0 Option Pack, which is the direct ancestor of the RRAS components included in Windows Server 2012.

The Windows Server 2012 version of RRAS is a fully functional, multiprotocol router. Third parties can also extend it to add network protocols or routing methods. The idea behind using RRAS for routing is that you can enable RRAS on a Windows Server 2012 machine and use it as a router in addition to whatever else you have it doing. For example, you could use a Windows Server 2012 computer with RRAS for routing, Internet Information Services (IIS) for Simple Mail Transfer Protocol (SMTP) mail and Web Services, and two network interface cards (NICs) to serve as a combination firewall/router/Internet server.

This chapter will begin with a discussion of how routing works and the ways routing is integrated into Windows Server 2012.

Understanding Routing

Routing is the process of delivering traffic to the correct destination. IP routing is simple to understand at the most basic level. Packets have addresses, and the process of routing involves getting a packet from its source to its destination. The mechanics of how that happens are a little more complicated, though. In the following sections, you will see exactly what routing does, how routing works, and how Windows Server 2012 handles routing.

What Routing Does

An *internetwork* is just a network of networks. A sample internetwork might contain five distinct networks, which might be named after the cities they are based in, such as, for example, Atlanta, Boston, Orlando, Portland, and San Diego. The internetwork is the collection of all these networks, any of which could ordinarily stand alone.

> An internetwork is not the same as the Internet. Actually, it's the other way around. The Internet we all use is just a really large, really complex internetwork.

Complex internetworks like the Internet require routing. Consider what happens when you try to send a file over the Internet. Suppose you're on the East Coast and the destination is in California. If you look at a map of the physical topology of the Internet, you'll see that there are a large number of potential routes to get from here to there. Some may be better than others, however. For example, one route would carry packets east, across the Atlantic, through Europe, and across Russia and the Pacific Ocean to the West Coast of the United States. That's a legal route, but it would be inefficient.

Routing associates the routes a message might take with costs. Routing systems allow administrators to attach a metric, or cost, to each leg of a route. Shortly, you'll see how routing systems use this metric information to calculate the most efficient route for packets to take.

> The actual way in which the metric information is used in calculations varies depending on which routing protocol is being used. Some of the routing protocols are Routing Information Protocol (RIP) version 1, RIP version 2, and Open Shortest Path First (OSPF). This last routing protocol is not supported in Windows Server 2012 Routing and Remote Access. The important point to remember is that all three routing protocols (discussed in more detail throughout this chapter) use metrics to figure out the "best" route in any situation.

How Routing Works

The basic underlying idea in the routing process is that each packet on a network has a source address and a destination address, which means that any device that receives the packet can inspect its headers to determine where it came from and where it's going. If such a device also has some information about the network's design and implementation, such as how long it takes packets to travel over a particular link, it can intelligently change the routing to minimize the total cost.

Figure 12.1 shows an imaginary network consisting of six interconnected local networks. These networks, named A through F, are connected by links of varying speeds and costs. This accurately mirrors what happens in the real world, where it's common for internal networks (or Internet service providers) to have multiple ways to establish a link between two points.

FIGURE 12.1   An example network

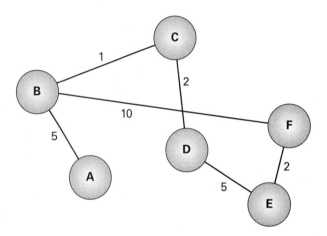

Imagine that a client machine on network B wants to send traffic to a machine on network E. The most obvious route would probably be B to F to E, but you could also use B to C to D to E. Notice the costs: B-F-E has a total cost of 12, while the seemingly longer B-C-D-E actually has a lower cost of 8. That doesn't appear to make sense because the latter route has a longer path. When you consider what cost really means, though, you'll understand why this makes sense.

Assigning link costs is entirely up to you. Usually, you assign costs that reflect your preference for how you want traffic to flow. An expensive or slow link would probably deserve a higher cost than a cheaper or faster link; if you assign a high cost to your most financially expensive links (for example, metered ISDN connections), they would not be used if there were more cost-efficient links available.

Now revisit Figure 12.1 with the assumption that each circle is really a router. You can hide all of the complexity of the network behind a router, because only the router is in charge of moving packets. Call your client machine X and your server Y. When X wants to send traffic to Y, it already knows the destination IP address of its target. X will build a packet, including its IP address as the source and Y's address as the destination. X will then use its default gateway setting to send that packet to router B.

 According to the Open Systems Interconnection (OSI) model, a gateway and a router are two different things. However, Microsoft uses the terms interchangeably, and so too will we.

Router B receives the packet and has both source and destination address information. By examining the IP addresses, it can determine that it doesn't "know" a direct route to the network where Y is located. However, two intermediate nodes claim to know how to reach Y: C and F. Because C has the lowest link cost, the router at B will send the packet to C in a simple routing algorithm. When C receives it, it will go through the same process, forwarding the packet on to D, and so on. Eventually the packet arrives at its destination.

Let's take a look at some of the specific ways in which RRAS actually performs the steps in the preceding example.

Routing Tables

A *routing table* is a database that stores route information. Think of it as a road map for the internetwork—the routing table lists the routes that exist between networks so that the router or host can look up the necessary information when it encounters a packet bound for a foreign network. Each entry in the routing table contains the following five pieces of information:

- The network address of the remote host or network
- The netmask associated with the entry
- The forwarding address to which traffic for the remote network should be sent
- The network interface that should be used to send the packet to the forwarding address
- A cost, or metric, that indicates what relative priority should be assigned to this route

For example, you could write the San Diego–Atlanta route as 10.1.1.0:255.255.255.12 8:10.10.1.254:ATL:1, assuming that the interface name is ATL and that you want to use a metric of 1. The actual format in which these entries are stored isn't important (in fact, it's not visible in RRAS); what's important for you to know is that every routing table entry contains that information.

Routing tables actually can contain these three different kinds of routes:

- *Network routes* provide a route to an entire network. For example, the route from San Diego to Atlanta is a network route because it can be used to route traffic from any host in San Diego to any host in Atlanta.

- *Host routes* provide a route to a single system or to a broadcast address. Think of them as shortcuts—they provide a slightly more efficient way for a router to "know" how to get traffic to a remote machine, so they're usually used when you want to direct traffic to remote networks through a particular machine.

- *Default routes* are where packets go when there's no explicit route for them. They are similar to the default gateway you're used to configuring for IP clients. Any time a router encounters a packet bound for some remote network, it will first search the routing table; if it can't find a network or host route, it will use the default route instead. This saves you from having to configure a network or host route for every network to which you might ever want to talk.

Static Routing

Static routing provides predefined routes in a table called, predictably, a *static routing table*. Static routing systems don't make any attempt to discover other routers or systems on their networks. Instead, you manually tell the routing engine how to get data to other networks; specifically, you tell it what other networks are reachable from your network by specifying the network addresses, subnet masks, and a metric for each network. This information goes into the system's routing table. When an outgoing packet arrives at the routing engine, the engine can examine the routing table to select the lowest-cost route to the destination. If there's no explicit entry in the routing table for that network, the packet goes to the default gateway, which is then entrusted with getting the packet to where it needs to go.

Static routing is faster and more efficient than dynamic routing. Static routing works well with a small network that doesn't change much. You can identify the remote networks to which you want to route and then add static routes to them to reflect the costs and topology of your network. In Windows Server 2012, you maintain static routes with the route command, which allows you to either see the contents of the routing table or modify it by adding and removing static routes to individual networks.

Dynamic Routing

Unlike static routing, *dynamic routing* doesn't depend on your adding fixed, unchangeable routes to remote networks. Instead, a dynamic routing engine can discover its surroundings by finding and communicating with other nearby routers in an internetwork.

This process, usually called *router discovery*, enables a newly added (or rebooted) router to configure itself. This is roughly equivalent to the process that happens when you move into a new neighborhood. Within a short time of your arrival, you'll probably meet most of the people who live nearby, either because they come to you or because you go to them. At that point, you have useful information about the surrounding environment that could come only from people who were already there.

The dynamic routing protocol in Windows Server 2012 is the Routing Information Protocol. In previous versions, the Open Shortest Path First protocol was also used, but in Windows Server 2012, OSPF has been discontinued. RIP has its advantages and disadvantages. Each router (whether a hardware device, a Windows Server 2012 machine, or otherwise) is connected to at least two separate physical networks. When the router starts, the only information it has comes from its internal routing table. Usually, that means it knows about all the attached networks plus whatever static routes have been previously defined. The router then receives configuration information that tells it about the state and topology of the network.

As time goes on, the network's physical topology can change. For example, take a look at the network in Figure 12.2. If network G suddenly lost its connection, the routers in sites A, D, and E would need to readjust their routing tables because they could no longer route traffic directly to G. The process by which this adjustment happens is what makes the routing dynamic, and it's also the largest area of difference between the two dynamic routing protocols for IP.

FIGURE 12.2 A more complex, dynamically routed network

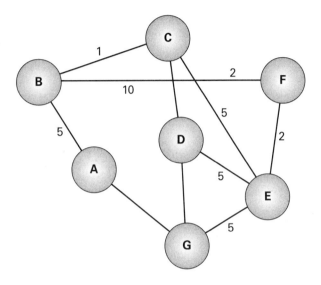

In the following sections, we will look at both RIP and OSPF more closely.

The Routing Information Protocol

Routing Information Protocol (RIP) is a distance-vector routing protocol that is generally simple and easy to configure, but it has performance limitations that restrict its usefulness on medium and large networks. RIP routers begin with a basically empty routing table, but they immediately begin sending out announcements that they know will reach the networks to which they're connected.

 RIP uses UDP as a transport protocol and port 520 by default.

RIP announcements may be broadcast or multicast. Routers on other networks that hear these announcements can add the advertised routes to their own routing tables. The process works both ways, of course; your router will hear announcements from other routers and add the advertised routes to its list of places it knows how to reach. Unfortunately, RIP supports a maximum of only 15 hop counts (the number of routers through which a packet can pass).

Microsoft's RIP implementation in Server 2012 supports RIPv2. You should be aware of these important differences between RIPv1 and RIPv2:

- The primary, or most important, difference between version 1 and version 2 of RIP is that RIPv2 supports *Variable Length Subnet Masking (VLSM)*. VLSM helps preserve IP address space by enabling networks to be subdivided into smaller blocks based on need.

- RIPv2 supports simple (that is, plain text) username/password authentication, which is handy to prevent unwanted changes from cluttering your routing tables.

- RIPv2 routers add the ability to receive triggered updates. When you know that your network topology is changing (perhaps because you've added connectivity to another network), you can send out a trigger that contains information about the changes. This trigger forces all the RIP routers you own to assimilate the changes immediately. Triggered updates are also useful because routers that detect a link or router failure can update their routing tables and announce the change, making their neighbors aware of it sooner rather than later.

You can use the Routing And Remote Access snap-in to set up two kinds of filters that screen out some types of RIP updates:

- Route filters allow you to pick and choose the networks that you want to admit knowing about and for which you want to accept announcements.

- Peer filters give you control over the neighboring routers to which your router will listen.

RIP also incorporates features that attempt to prevent route loops. In Figure 12.2 (shown earlier in the chapter), the network topology has the potential to cause a route loop. For instance, say that someone in E wants to send a packet to a machine in A, but the G-A and D-C links are down. E sends the packet to G, which recognizes that it can't reach A. Also, G knows that the route D-C-B-A will work, so it sends the packet to D. When the packet reaches D, D knows it can't talk to C, so it sends the packet to E because E-G-A is usually a valid route. You can see that the packet will never reach its destination and will loop continually. This might seem like a contrived example, but in real life, where internetwork links are often concentrated among a small number of physical links, it's a real problem. RIP offers several methods for resolving and preventing loops, including the split-horizon and poison-reverse algorithms.

RIP has two operation modes:

- In *periodic update mode*, a RIP router sends out its list of known routes at periodic intervals (which you define). The router marks any routes it learns about from other routers as RIP routes, which means they remain active only while the router is running.

If the router is stopped, the routes vanish. This mode is the default for RIP on LAN interfaces, but it's not suitable for demand-dial connections because you don't want your router bringing up a connection just to announce its presence.

- In *autostatic update mode*, the RRAS router broadcasts the contents of its routing table only when a remote router asks for it. Better still, the routes that the RRAS router learns about from its RIP neighbors are marked as static routes in the routing table, and they persist until you manually delete them—even if the router is stopped and restarted or if RIP is disabled for that interface. Autostatic mode is the default for demand-dial interfaces.

One drawback to RIP in either version is that it causes the router to send its entire routing table with every update. This can generate a large amount of traffic and makes RIP inappropriate for many of today's networks. Another routing protocol, Open Shortest Path First, solves this problem by sending updates for only routes that have changed.

The Open Shortest Path First Protocol

RIP is designed for fairly small networks; it can handle only 15 router-to-router hops. If you have a network that spans more than 16 routers at any point, RIP won't be able to cache routes for it, and some parts of the network will appear to be (or in fact will be) unreachable. The OSPF routing protocol is a link-state protocol designed for use on medium, large, and very large networks. It's much more efficient than RIP, but it also requires more knowledge and experience to set up and administer. Also, as stated earlier in the chapter, OSPF is no longer supported by Windows Server 2012 RRAS.

RIP routers continually exchange routing data with one another, which allows incorrect route entries to propagate. Instead of exchanging routing data, each OSPF router maintains a map of the state of the internetwork. This map, called a *link-state map*, provides a continually updated reference to the state of each internetwork link. Neighboring routers group into an *adjacency* (similar to a neighborhood). Within an adjacency, routers synchronize any changes to the link-state map. When the network topology changes, whichever router notices it first floods the internetwork with change notifications. Each router that receives the notification updates its copy of the link map and then recalculates its internal routing table.

The "shortest path first" in OSPF refers to the algorithm that OSPF systems use to calculate routes. Routes are calculated so that the shortest path (the one with the lowest cost) is used first. SPF-calculated routes are always free of loops, which is another nice advantage over RIP.

OSPF networks are broken down into subparts called *areas*; an area is a collection of interconnected networks. Think of an area as a subsection of an internetwork. Areas are interconnected by backbones. Each OSPF router keeps a link-state database only for the areas to which it's connected. Special OSPF routers called *area border routers* interlink areas. Figure 12.3 shows how this looks.

FIGURE 12.3   A simple OSPF network

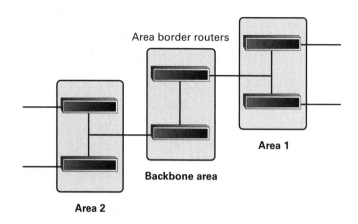

Border routing

Internal routing refers to routing that occurs within your internetwork. By contrast, *border routing* is what happens when packets leave your internetwork and go to another router someplace else. Consider what happens when you use your home computer to browse a website. TCP/IP packets from your machine go to your ISP (probably via PPP, over an analog, cable, DSL, or ISDN connection). The ISP examines the destination address of the packets and determines that they should go to some other network, usually a network for which the ISP doesn't maintain a direct connection.

For example, when you want to fetch a web page from Microsoft's website, you essentially lease an Internet connection from a local ISP that likely leases lines from another, larger provider, which maintains peering connections at *national access points (NAPs)*. These peering connections maintain routing tables for various networks on the Internet. They forward your packet to the next-nearest hop, and then on to the next-nearest hop, until the packet reaches its destination.

Figure 12.4 shows an example of the Internet service provider: Core Digital Communication Services (later ExecPC/Voyager). The local router represents a home user or business connected to the ISP. From there, the Panek Point router forwarded packets over a DS3 to Stellacon; from there they traveled to Milwaukee and on to the NAP in Chicago. The thick black lines between borders indicate backbone links that join border areas together. Even though this network was all owned by ExecPC/Voyager, it utilized different OSPF areas up to the NAP where Border Gateway Protocol (BGP) was used. The true border of this network was at the NAP.

In a border routing network, some routers are responsible for handling packets inside the area while others manage network communication with other areas. These border routers are responsible for storing routes to other borders that they can reach over the backbone.

FIGURE 12.4   Networks are divided into areas linked by backbones.

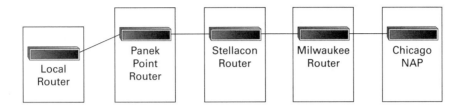

Multicast Routing

IP multicasting works by sending a packet that is read by many hosts to a single IP address. The hosts all have individual IP addresses, but they belong to a multicast group that shares a single, separate IP address. Multicast group membership is dynamic, and groups can contain unlimited hosts on separate IP networks provided that routers between the networks support multicast traffic. In fact, even computers that aren't part of a multicast group can send multicast packets.

Multicasting uses a special range of IP addresses, called the *Class D address space*, which is reserved exclusively for multicasting. The multicast address range contains the IP addresses 224.0.0.0 through 239.255.255.255. Each multicast group uses a single address in the Class D address space. In addition, just as with regular IP addresses, the multicast address range reserves a few special addresses that are used for specific purposes. Table 12.1 contains a partial list of these special multicast addresses.

TABLE 12.1   Special multicast addresses

Address	Description
224.0.0.0	Base address (reserved)
224.0.0.1	All hosts, all systems on the same network segment
224.0.0.2	All routers, all routers on the same network segment
224.0.0.5	All OSPF routers, used to send routing information to all OSPF routers on the network
224.0.0.6	All designated OSPF routers, used to send routing information to all designated OSPF routers
224.0.0.9	All RIP 2 routers, used to send routing information to all RIPv2 routers on the network
224.0.1.24	Used to support replication for WINS servers

⊕ Real World Scenario

Is a Multihomed Computer a Router?

For several years, your company has been growing steadily, from a small network of 50 Windows Server 2003 servers to a medium-sized network of more than 200 Windows 7 and Windows 8 workstations and more than 10 Windows Server 2008 R2 servers. Everything functions properly, but performance is beginning to suffer. After analyzing the network traffic, you realize that you need to segment the network into subnets to control the traffic and improve the performance. You are considering using multihomed computers to save money when purchasing dedicated routers.

Windows Server 2012 has expanded support with RIP. Before you leap at the cost savings of using a multihomed Windows Server 2012 computer, however, you want to take a closer look.

Despite some added cost, there is a lot to be said for using specialized routing computers for the connection points in networks. When there is a significant utilization of bandwidth across your network, it's questionable whether the multihomed host will be able to provide the level of service you need. General-purpose operating systems such as Windows Server 2012 will always pale in comparison to a computer that's designed to perform singular tasks. In addition, with the basic routing protocols, you can use many tools and services to guarantee levels of service and to set up filters and access control lists.

Windows Server 2012 doesn't really make sense as a router for small offices either, with the cost of basic routers being so low. Make sure you are applying these Windows Server 2012 routing services in the areas that are appropriate for the particular load and scale of your situation.

Internet Group Management Protocol (IGMP) is used to exchange multicast group membership information between multicast-capable routers. You can configure RRAS in two modes:

- *IGMP router mode* listens for IGMP membership report packets and tracks group membership. IGMP router mode must be attached to any interfaces that connect to multicast-configured hosts.

- *IGMP proxy mode* essentially acts like a multicast host, except that it forwards IGMP membership report packets to an IGMP router. This provides a list of multicast-enabled hosts to an upstream router that normally wouldn't be aware of the hosts. Typically, IGMP proxy is used on single-router networks connected to the Internet. The IGMP proxy sends the list of multicast hosts to the multicast-capable portion of the Internet known as the *Internet multicast backbone*, or MBone, so that the hosts can receive multicast packets.

You may need to send multicast traffic across non-multicast-compatible routers. This is made possible through the use of *IP-in-IP interfaces* (or *IP-in-IP tunnels*). An IP-in-IP interface actually encapsulates packets with an additional IP header. The encapsulated packets can be sent across any router because they appear to be ordinary IP packets. You create and manage IP-in-IP interfaces in RRAS the same way you configure other interfaces.

Routing in Windows Server 2012

RRAS provides a multiprotocol router. In other words, the RRAS routing engine can handle multiple network protocols and multiple routing methods on multiple NICs. RRAS provides some specific features of interest when the conversation turns to network routing:

- *Demand-dial routing* can open connections to specific networks when the router receives packets addressed to those networks. This feature allows you to use on-demand links instead of permanent connections. It's especially nice for Integrated Services Digital Network (ISDN), which combines per-minute fees in most places with really fast call setup times. Point-to-Point Tunneling Protocol (PPTP) connections can be demand-dialed too, or you can use demand-dial interfaces to make long-distance connections only when they're needed.

- You can establish static routes that specify where packets bound for certain networks should go. The most common use of this feature is to link a remote network with your LAN. The remote network gets one static route that basically says, "Any traffic leaving my subnet should be sent to the router." RRAS handles it from there.

- Dynamic routing using RIPv1 and RIPv2 protocols provides ways for your router to share routing information with other routers "near" it in network space.

- Packet filtering screens out undesirable packets in both directions. For example, you can create a packet filter to keep out FTP traffic, or you can add a filter to a demand-dial interface so that it will be opened only for web or mail traffic. Other traffic types will pass if the link is up, but they won't cause RRAS to open the link if it's not already open. (See the section "Configuring TCP/IP Packet Filters" later in the chapter for more details.)

- In unicast routing, one machine sends directly to one destination address. In multicast routing, one machine sends to an entire network. RRAS supports both methods.

- *Network Address Translation (NAT)* is a service that allows multiple LAN clients to share a single public IP address and Internet connection. Let's say that you have 200 users and you decide to use a private IP address like 10.10.0.0. If these users want to access the Internet, you need some type of mechanism to allow them to access the Internet. This is where NAT comes in handy. NAT allows a user to swap their private IP address and use an Internet-acceptable IP address.

About NAT

NAT provides an advantage with routing. NAT (also referred to as *network masquerading*) allows a router to translate one IP address to another.

For example, let's say you have two networks (10.10.0.0 and 192.168.1.0), and they are configured with two separate sets of TCP/IP addresses. The router can use NAT so that a user from the 10.10.0.0 network goes to the 192.168.1.0 network and gets a valid IP address for that network. Basically, the NAT swaps its 10.10.0.0 address for a 192.168.1.0 address.

NAT is also commonly used for Internet connections. For example, let's say that you have an Internet service provider that issues you only six valid Internet TCP/IP addresses for you to use on your network. You can set up NAT and program it to use those six valid addresses. Then, when a user from the network wants to access the Internet, NAT swaps the user's internal IP address for one of the valid IP addresses.

Installing RRAS

To use RRAS, you need to install the RRAS components on computers running Windows Server 2012 because they're not installed by default. You can do this through the Server Manager MMC's Add Roles Wizard. Exercise 12.1 leads you through the process of installing RRAS as a router. To complete this exercise, you must have two NIC adapters available.

EXERCISE 12.1

Installing RRAS for IP Routing

1. Open Server Manager.

2. Click number 2, Add Roles And Features.

3. Choose role-based or feature-based installation and click next.

4. Choose your server and click Next.

5. Choose Remote Access. Click the Add Features button when the dialog box appears. Then click Next.

6. At the Select Features screen, click Next.

7. At the Remote Access screen, click Next.

8. At the Select Roles screen, make sure that both boxes (Direct Access and VPN (RAS) and Routing) are checked. Click Next.

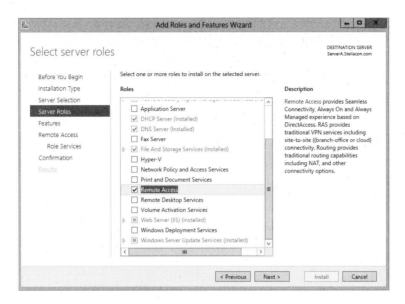

9. At the Confirmation screen, click the Install button.

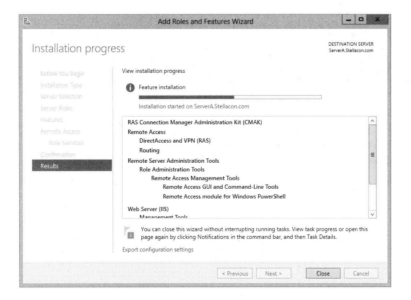

10. On the left side, choose Remote Access.

EXERCISE 12.1 *(continued)*

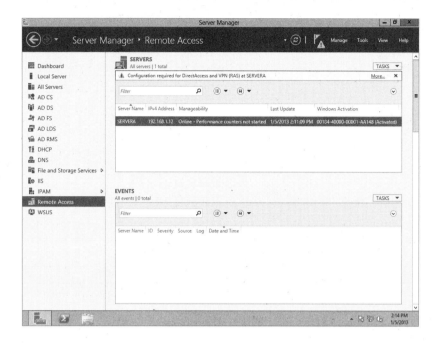

11. To the right of Configuration Required For DirectAccess And VPN, click the More link.

12. Under Action, click the link that states Open The Getting Started Wizard.

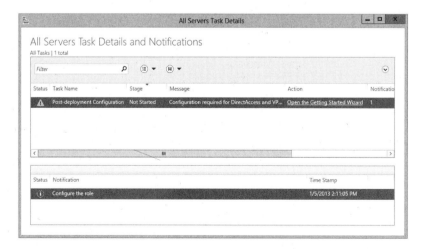

13. A dialog box will appear. (It may appear behind Server Manager.) Click Deploy VPN Only.

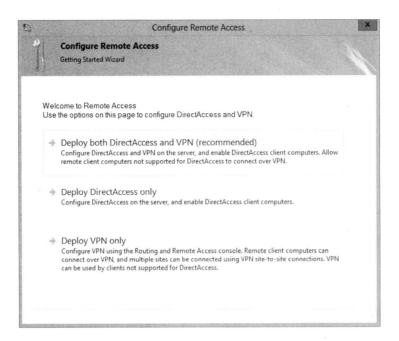

14. You will see a red down arrow next to your server name. Click the server, and then right-click and choose Configure And Enable Routing And Remote Access.

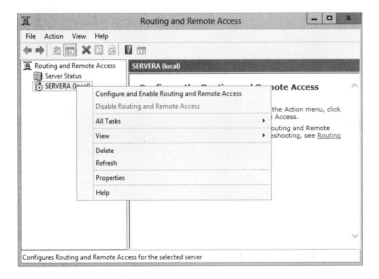

15. The Routing And Remote Access Wizard starts. Click next.

16. Choose Custom Configuration and click Next.

EXERCISE 12.1 *(continued)*

17. Choose LAN Routing and click Next.

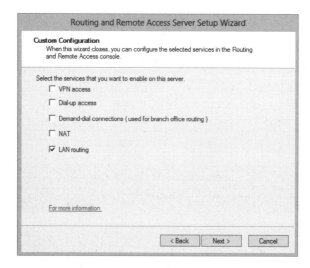

18. Click the Finish button at the completion screen.

19. If a dialog box appears, click the Start Service button.

20. Next to your server's name, you should now have a green up arrow. Close Routing And Remote Access.

Configuring IP Routing

Continuing from the previous exercise, when the summary page of the Routing And Remote Access Server Setup Wizard appears, it's going to remind you to do the following things, depending on whether you chose to use demand-dial connections:

- Add demand-dial interfaces if you want to support demand dialing.

- Give each routable interface a network address for each protocol it carries. For example, if you're using IP on a computer with three NICs, each NIC that participates in routing needs to have distinct IP and IPX addresses.

- Install and configure the routing protocols (for example, RIP for IP in this case) on the interfaces that should support them.

These three actions form the core of what you must do to make your RRAS server into an IP router. In the following sections, I'll cover how RRAS treats LAN, demand-dial, and RIP interfaces. Next, I'll show how to configure properties that affect RRAS in general, such as error logging and route preferences. You'll also learn how to install and configure RIP. Finally, you'll see how to manage static routes with the route command.

Creating and Managing Interfaces

The Network Interfaces node in the Routing And Remote Access snap-in (shown in Figure 12.5) summarizes the routable interfaces available on your machine for *all* protocols. It lists all of the LAN and demand-dial interfaces, plus two special interfaces maintained by RRAS: loopback and internal. Each of the interfaces displayed has a type, a status (either Enabled or Disabled), and a connection status associated with it. For example, a Windows Server 2012 machine in the default configuration with a single NIC displays the local area connection interface. Each of those interfaces represents a potential destination for routed packets.

FIGURE 12.5   The Network Interfaces node

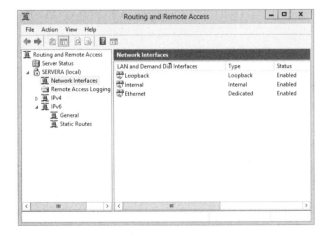

What "Unreachable" Really Means

A demand-dial interface can be in any of several different states:

- First, the Enabled and Disabled states that appear in the Status column indicate whether the link is administratively available—that is, whether you're allowing people to use it.

- The Connection State column shows you whether the connection is working. The default state for a demand-dial connection is Disconnected, which is perfectly reasonable. When RRAS tries to establish a connection, the state changes to Connected—also eminently logical. In both the Connected and Disconnected states, any static routes tied to the demand-dial interface are available.

- When RRAS tries to dial a number and fails to connect, it will continue to try until it reaches the redial limit set on the Dialing tab of the interface's Properties dialog box (the default redial limit is 10 minutes). If the redial limit is reached, the interface will be marked as Unreachable for a time-out period.

As long as the interface is unreachable, any static routes pointing to it will be unavailable—they'll actually disappear from the routing table. After the time-out period, RRAS will try again to dial; if it fails again, it tacks another 10 minutes onto the time-out and tries again. If the time-out period reaches the maximum (6 hours by default), the counter will stop incrementing so RRAS will try again to connect every 6 hours until a successful connection is made or until you restart the RRAS service.

You can adjust both the minimum and maximum values for this time-out from their defaults (10 minutes and 6 hours, respectively). You make this change in the Registry by adding two REG_DWORD values to HKLM\System\CurrentControlSet\Services\Router\Interfaces*InterfaceName* (where *InterfaceName* matches the name of the interface you want to change). The MinUnreachabilityInterval value controls both the minimum retry interval and how much the retry interval is incremented after each failure; the MaxUnreachabilityInterval sets the upper limit. Both of these values must be expressed in seconds.

You can right-click each interface to get a pop-up menu with some useful commands, including Disable, Enable, and Unreachability Reason (which tells you why an interface is marked as Unreachable). The menu also contains some commands specific to demand-dial interfaces, which will be covered in the following sections.

Managing LAN Interfaces

LAN interface options appear when you select the General node under the IPv4 node in the Routing And Remote Access snap-in. These options correspond to the LAN interfaces you've defined in RRAS. You can set general properties for the LAN interfaces. After you add specific routing protocols to the interfaces, you can configure those protocols individually (as you'll see later in this chapter).

To see the properties for an interface, select the General node in the console, click the interface in the pane on the right, and select Action ➢ Properties, which opens the local area connection Properties dialog box (Figure 12.6).

FIGURE 12.6   The General tab of the local area connection Properties dialog box

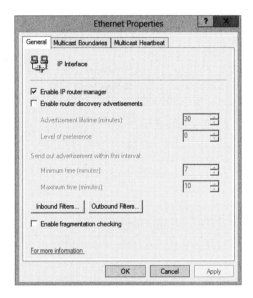

The General tab allows you to set some useful parameters for the entire interface, including whether this interface will send out router discovery advertisements so that other routers on your network can find it.

The controls on the General tab do the following:

- The Enable IP Router Manager check box controls whether this interface allows IP routing at all. When it's checked, the administrative status of this interface will appear as Up, indicating that it's available for routing traffic. When it's unchecked, the interface will be marked as Down; it won't route any packets, and other routers won't be able to communicate with it.

- The Enable Router Discovery Advertisements check box controls whether this router will broadcast router discovery messages. These messages allow clients to find a "nearby" (in network terms) router without any manual configuration on your part. When this check box is enabled, the controls below it become active so that you can set the following properties:

- The Advertisement Lifetime (Minutes) field determines how long advertisements are valid. Clients will ignore any advertisement they receive after its lifetime has expired.

- The Level Of Preference field determines how clients use this router in comparison with other routers on your network. Clients use routers with higher preferences first; if there are routers with equal preference levels, the client can randomly select one.

- RRAS will send out advertisements at a randomly chosen interval that falls between the minimum and maximum time intervals for sending advertisements. The default settings mean RRAS will send an advertisement every 7 to 10 minutes.

- The Inbound Filters and Outbound Filters buttons allow you to accept or reject packets selectively on the specified interface. You can accept all packets that don't trigger a filter or accept only those packets that match filter criteria. Each type of filter can use the source or destination IP address and netmask as filter criteria. For example, you can construct a filter that rejects all packets from 206.151.234.0 with a netmask of 255.255.255.0. This effectively screens out any traffic from that subnet.

- The Enable Fragmentation Checking check box tells your router to reject any fragmented IP packets instead of accepting them for processing. Because flooding a router with fragmented IP packets is a popular denial-of-service attack, you may want to check this box.

Setting Up Demand-Dial Interfaces

When you install RRAS, it will automatically create an interface for each LAN connection it can find. If you want to create new demand-dial interfaces, you'll have to do it yourself. Fortunately, there's an easy way to do this with the Demand-Dial Interface Wizard. To activate the wizard, right-click the Network Interfaces node in the Routing And Remote Access snap-in and choose the New Demand-Dial Interface command.

The following sections cover the steps involved in setting up demand-dial interfaces.

Naming the Interface

The first page of the wizard is the Interface Name page. This is where you specify the name of the new interface. This is the name you'll see in the Routing And Remote Access snap-in, so you should choose a name that identifies the source and destination of the connection (for example, HSV-ATL for a connection between Huntsville and Atlanta). This is particularly useful when you want to use one RRAS console somewhere on a network to manage many RRAS servers because having an easy way to see which link you're working with can be very valuable.

Choosing a Connection Type

The Connection Type page of the wizard allows you to specify which type of demand-dial interface you will create. Demand-dial interfaces can use a physical device (such as a modem or an ISDN adapter) or a virtual private network (VPN) connection. For example, you can have a demand-dial connection that opens a VPN tunnel to a remote network when it sees traffic destined for that network. Depending on which option you choose here, the remaining wizard pages will differ.

Assuming you choose to use a physical device as the basis for your network, the Select A Device page of the wizard prompts you to choose a device (such as a modem or ISDN terminal adapter) to use for this demand-dial interface. If the device you want to use isn't already set up, you'll need to add it; for that reason, you're probably better off adding and configuring modems before setting up RRAS.

If you specify that you want to use a VPN connection, you'll see the VPN Type page where you can specify what type of VPN connection to use. You have the following three choices:

- The Automatic radio button tells RRAS to figure out the connection type when negotiating with the remote server. This is the most flexible choice, so it's selected by default.

- The Point-To-Point Tunneling Protocol (PPTP) radio button tells RRAS that this connection will always use PPTP.

- Likewise, the Layer 2 Tunneling Protocol (L2TP) radio button indicates that you want this connection to always use L2TP.

Determining Who to Call

The next step is the same for both VPN and physical connections, even though the wizard page is labeled differently. For VPNs, you'll see the Network Address page. For ordinary dial-up connections, the page is labeled Phone Number. In either case, you should enter the phone number or IP address (whichever is appropriate) of the remote router.

Setting Routing and Security Options

The next page is the Protocols And Security page, which contains four configuration check boxes:

- The Route IP Packets On This Interface Or Route IPX Packets On This Interface box controls whether this interface will handle the specified packet types. By default, IP routing is enabled but IPX routing isn't.

- If you want to add a user account so that a remote router (running RRAS or not) can dial in, check the Add A User Account So A Remote Router Can Dial In box.

- Some routers can handle Password Authentication Protocol (PAP), Challenge Handshake Authentication Protocol (CHAP), or Microsoft Challenge Handshake Authentication Protocol (MS-CHAP) authentication, but others can handle only PAP. If your remote partner works only with PAP, make sure that the Send A Plain-Text Password If That Is The Only Way To Connect box is checked.

- If your RRAS server is calling a system that isn't running RRAS, the system may expect you to interact with it manually, perhaps through a terminal window. This is what the last check box, Use Scripting To Complete The Connection With The Remote Router, is for. Check it and you'll get a terminal window after the modem connects so that you can provide whatever commands or authenticators you need.

Setting Dial-In Credentials

If you choose to allow remote routers to dial in to the RRAS machine that you're setting up, you'll have to create a user account with appropriate permissions. The Demand-Dial Interface Wizard handles the account-creation process for you, assuming that you fill out the fields on the Dial-In Credentials page.

Setting Dial-Out Credentials

If you want your router to initiate calls to another router, you'll need to tell your local RRAS installation which credentials to use when it makes an outgoing call. Although RRAS uses the information you enter in the Dial-In Credentials page, it makes no attempt to do anything with the credentials that you provide on the Dial-Out Credentials page. The credentials that you provide here must match the credentials that the remote router expects to see. If they don't match, your router won't be able to authenticate itself to the remote end.

In Exercise 12.2, you will continue from Exercise 12.1 with configuring the Demand-Dial Interface Wizard. In this exercise, you'll create a simple demand-dial interface. This requires you to have the phone number, username, and password for the remote end as well as a demand-dial-capable device installed in the machine.

 The Demand-Dial Interface Wizard automatically appears after you complete Exercise 12.1.

EXERCISE 12.2

Creating a Demand-Dial Interface

1. Open Routing And Remote Access by clicking the Windows Key ➢ Administrative Tools ➢ Routing And Remote Access. If any wizards appear, just close them.

2. Right-click the server name, and choose Properties.

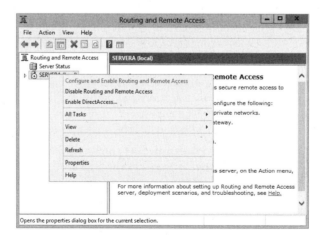

3. On the General tab, make sure that under IPv4 Routing section, LAN and demand-dial routing is selected. Also make sure that IPv4 Remote access server is selected. Click OK.

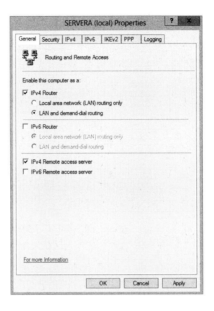

4. A dialog box will appear stating that the changes to the router require the router to be restarted. Click the Yes button to continue.

5. Under the server name, click Network Interfaces. Right-click, and choose New Demand-Dial Interface.

6. The Demand-dial Interface Wizard starts. Click Next at the Welcome screen.

7. On the Interface Name screen, name your interface. For this exercise, I used Test Router as the interface name. Click Next.

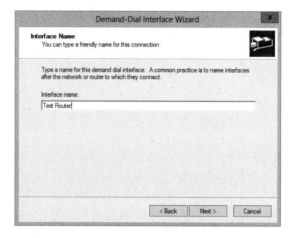

8. The Connection Type page appears. You can connect to the remote router via a VPN interface or through a Point-to-Point Protocol over Ethernet (PPPoE) connection. Make sure the Connect Using Virtual Private Networking (VPN) option is selected, and click Next.

9. On the VPN Type page, choose Automatic Selection. This page allows you to choose which VPN connection you want to use.

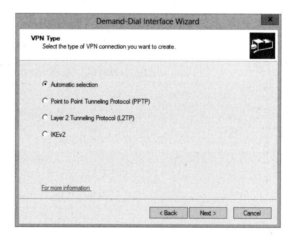

10. The Destination Address page appears next. Here is where you enter the IP address of the other router to which you are connecting. Type the IP address of one of your routers (if you are at home and have a small home router, type that IP address). For this example, I entered 192.168.1.1. Click Next after you've entered the IP address.

11. On the Protocols And Security page, make sure the Route IP Packets On This Interface box is the only one checked.

12. If you have not yet defined any static routes, you will be asked to do so before you can activate the demand-dial connection. On the Static Routes For Remote Networks page, click the Add button and enter the IP address, subnet mask, and metric of the remote router. Click OK when you've finished. You will notice the new static route in the list. Click Next.

13. On the Dial-Out Credentials page, fill in the username, domain (if any), and password needed to connect to the remote network. Click Next.

14. When the wizard's summary page appears, click the Finish button to create the interface.

15. Close Routing And Remote Access.

Creating and Removing RIP Interfaces

After you create the physical interfaces (using either demand-dial or LAN interfaces), the next step you must take is to create an interface for the routing protocol that you want to use. After you install the routing protocols (see the section "Managing Routing Protocols" later in this chapter), RIP nodes appear in the Routing And Remote Access snap-in. To create an interface, right-click the RIP node, and choose New Interface. That displays the New Interface dialog box, which lists all of the physical interfaces that are available for the selected protocol.

Once you select the interface you want to use, if RRAS can create the interface, the interface is added to the appropriate item in the console, and the corresponding Properties dialog box opens.

You can remove a RIP interface by selecting it in the appropriate folder and pressing the Delete key, by selecting Action ➢ Delete, or by choosing Delete from the pop-up menu.

Setting RIP Interface Properties

RIP interfaces have their own properties, all of which are specific to RIP. You adjust these settings by selecting the RIP node, clicking the appropriate RIP interface in the right pane, and selecting Properties from the pop-up or Action menu.

In the following sections, I'll cover the various options available in a RIP interface's Properties dialog box.

The General Tab

The General tab of the RIP interface's Properties dialog box (see Figure 12.7) lets you control the router's operational mode, which protocols it uses to send and accept packets, and a couple of other useful things.

FIGURE 12.7 The General tab of the RIP interface's Properties dialog box

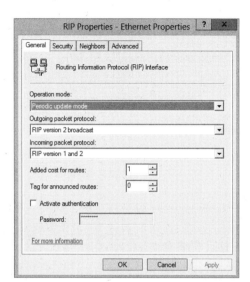

Here's what you can do with the General tab:

- The Operation Mode drop-down list controls the router's mode. By default, demand-dial interfaces will be set to Autostatic Update Mode, while LAN interfaces will be set to Periodic Update Mode.

- The Outgoing Packet Protocol drop-down list controls what kind of RIP packets this router sends:

  - If your network has all RIPv2 routers, choose RIP Version 2 Multicast to make RRAS send efficient RIP multicasts.

  - If you have a version 1 or a mix of version 1 and version 2, there are selections for those too.

  - The fourth choice, Silent RIP, is useful when you want your RRAS router to listen to other routers' routes but not advertise any of its own. Typically, you'll use Silent RIP when you're using RRAS to connect a small network (such as a branch office) that doesn't have any other routers to a larger network—the small network doesn't have any routes to advertise because it's connected to only one remote network.

- Use the Incoming Packet Protocol drop-down list to specify what kinds of RIP packets this interface will accept. You can choose to accept any of the following:

  - Only RIPv1 packets

  - Only RIPv2 packets

  - Both version 1 and version 2 packets

  - No packets at all

The default setting is to accept both version 1 and version 2 packets.

- The Added Cost For Routes field lets you control how much this router will increase the route cost. Usually, it's best to leave this set to 1 because setting it too high may increase the interface's cost so much that no one uses it.

- The Tag For Announced Routes field gives you a way to supply a tag included in all RIP packets sent by this router. RRAS doesn't use RIP tags, but other routers can use them.

- The Activate Authentication check box and Password field give you an identification tool for use with your routers. If you turn on authentication, all incoming and outgoing RIP packets must contain the specified password. Therefore, all of this router's neighbors need to use the same password. The password is transmitted as cleartext, so this option doesn't provide you with any security.

The Security Tab

The Security tab (see Figure 12.8) helps you regulate which routes your RIP interface will accept from and broadcast to its peers. There are good reasons to be careful about which routes you accept into your routing table because a malicious attacker could simply flood your router with bogus routes and watch, laughing, as your routers send traffic off on a wild goose chase. Likewise, you may not want to advertise every route in your routing table, particularly if the same routers handle both Internet and intranet traffic. You can use the controls on this tab to discard routes that fall within a particular range of addresses, or you can accept only those routes that fall within a particular range.

FIGURE 12.8   The Security tab of the RIP interface's Properties dialog box

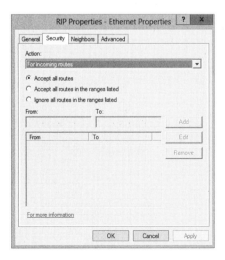

The default setting is to accept all routes, but you can change it using these controls:

- The Action drop-down list lets you choose whether you want to impose settings on incoming routes that your router hears from its peers or on outgoing routes that it announces. Depending upon which of these options you choose, the wording of the three radio buttons below the drop-down will change.

- The restriction radio buttons in the center of the dialog box control the action applied to incoming or outgoing routes:

  - The default setting, Announce All Routes (for outgoing routes) or Accept All Routes (for incoming routes), does just that—all routes are accepted or announced, no matter the source.

  - Announce All Routes In The Ranges Listed (outgoing) or Accept All Routes In The Ranges Listed (incoming) causes RRAS silently to ignore any routes that fall outside the specified ranges. You'd usually use this option when you wanted to limit the scope of routes over which your router can exchange traffic.

  - Do Not Announce All Routes In The Ranges Listed (outgoing) or Ignore All Routes In The Ranges Listed (incoming) tells RRAS to ignore silently any routes that fall within the specified ranges. This is useful for filtering out routes that you don't want to make available or those that you don't want to use to reach remote systems.

- The From and To fields; the Add, Edit, and Remove buttons; and the address range list are all used to specify which set of addresses you want to use with the restriction radio buttons.

The Neighbors Tab

The Neighbors tab (see Figure 12.9) gives you a finer degree of control over how this particular interface interacts with its peer RIP routers. By specifying a list of trusted neighbor routers, you can choose to use neighboring routers' routes in addition to, or instead of, broadcast and multicast RIP announcements.

FIGURE 12.9   The Neighbors tab of the RIP interface's Properties dialog box

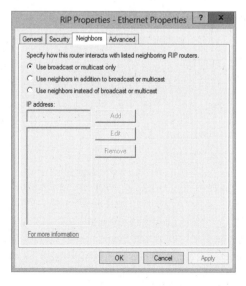

You will see the following radio buttons on the Neighbors tab:

- The Use Broadcast Or Multicast Only radio button tells RRAS to ignore any RIP neighbors. This is the default setting. It means that any router that can successfully broadcast or multicast routes to you can load its routes into your routing table.

- The Use Neighbors In Addition To Broadcast Or Multicast radio button tells RRAS to accept routes from RIP peers as well as from the neighbors you've specified.

- The Use Neighbors Instead Of Broadcast Or Multicast radio button indicates that you don't trust RIP announcements that your router picks up from the network; instead, you're telling RRAS to trust only those neighbors that are defined in the neighbor list.

You manage the list of trusted neighbor routers using the IP Address field; the Add, Edit, and Remove buttons; and the list itself. These controls are enabled when you specify that you want to use neighbor-supplied routing information; once the controls are activated, you can add router IP addresses to the neighbor list.

The Advanced Tab

The Advanced tab (see Figure 12.10) contains 12 controls that govern some fairly esoteric RIP behavior.

FIGURE 12.10   The Advanced tab of the RIP interface's Properties dialog box

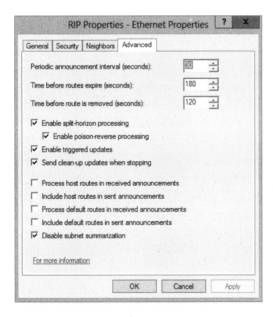

The first three controls are active only when you turn on Periodic Update Mode on the General tab:

- The Periodic Announcement Interval (Seconds) field controls the interval at which periodic router announcements are made.

- The Time Before Routes Expire (Seconds) field controls how long the route may stay in the routing table before it's considered to be expired. The arrival of a new RIP announcement for the route resets the timer—it will be marked as invalid only if it reaches the expiration timer without being renewed through a new announcement.

- The Time Before Route Is Removed (Seconds) field controls the interval that may pass between the time a route expires and the time it's removed.

The next group of check boxes updates processing and loop detection:

- The Enable Split-Horizon Processing check box turns on split-horizon processing, in which a route learned by an RIP router on a network is not rebroadcast to that network. Split-horizon processing helps prevent routing loops, so it's on by default.

  - The Enable Poison-Reverse Processing check box is active only when the Enable Split-Horizon Processing check box is on. This option modifies the way split-horizon processing works. When poison-reverse processing is turned on, routes learned from a network are rebroadcast to the network with a metric of 16, a special value that tells other routers that the route is unreachable. This option prevents routing loops while still keeping the routing tables up-to-date.

- The Enable Triggered Updates check box indicates whether you want routing table changes to be sent out immediately when they're noticed (the default). Triggered updates help keep the routing table up-to-date with minimum latency.

- The Send Clean-Up Updates When Stopping check box controls whether RRAS will send announcements that mark the routes it was handling as unavailable. This immediately lets its RIP peers know that the routes it was servicing are no longer usable.

The last set of controls governs what happens with host and default routes:

- By default, RRAS ignores any host routes it sees in RIP announcements. Check the Process Host Routes In Received Announcements box if you want it to honor those routes instead of ignoring them.

- The Include Host Routes In Sent Announcements check box directs RRAS to send host route information as part of its RIP announcements. Normally, it won't do this.

- The Process Default Routes In Received Announcements and Include Default Routes In Sent Announcements check boxes have the same function as their host route check boxes described earlier.

- The Disable Subnet Summarization check box is active only if you have RIPv2 specified as the outbound packet type for the router. When subnet summarization is turned off, RIP won't advertise subnets to routers that are on other subnets.

Setting IP Routing Properties

The IPv4 and IPv6 nodes in the Routing And Remote Access snap-in have several sub-nodes, including the General node. When you click the General node and select Properties from the Action menu, you'll find settings that apply to all installed IP routing protocols on the server. These settings give you some additional control over how routing works.

In the following sections, we'll look at the options in the General Properties dialog box. These options are available for configuring settings that apply to IP routing in general.

 The Multicast Scopes tab of the General Properties dialog box is for setting and managing multicast scopes.

The Logging Tab

The Logging tab (see Figure 12.11) contains four radio buttons that you use to control what information the IP routing components of RRAS log:

- The Log Errors Only radio button instructs the server to log IP routing–related errors and nothing else. This gives you an adequate indication of problems after they happen, but it doesn't point out potential problems noted by warning messages.

- The Log Errors And Warnings radio button is the default choice. It instructs RRAS to log error and warning messages to the event log without adding any informational messages. If you get in the habit of carefully reviewing your event logs, these warning messages may give you welcome forewarning of incipient problems.

FIGURE 12.11   The Logging tab of the General Properties dialog box

- The Log The Maximum Amount Of Information radio button causes the IP routing stack to log messages about almost everything it does. This gives you a lot of useful fodder when you're troubleshooting, but it can flood your logs with minutiae if you're not careful—don't turn it on unless you're trying to isolate and fix a problem.

- The Disable Event Logging radio button turns off all IP routing event logging.

 WARNING Don't use the Disable Event Logging option because it will keep you from being able to review the service's logs in case of a problem.

The Preference Levels Tab

The Preference Levels tab (see Figure 12.12) gives you a way to change the router's behavior by telling it what class of routes to prefer. In the earlier discussion of routing, you read that the router selects routes based on cost metric information. The other factor that comes into play is the preference level of the routing source. The default configuration for RRAS causes it to prefer local and static routes to dynamically discovered routes.

For example, say that there are two routing table entries indicating routes to 216.80.*—one that you've entered as a static route and one that your router has discovered via an RIP peer. In the example shown in Figure 12.12, the router will always try to use the static route first; if it can't, it will try to use the RIP-generated route. You can change the router's class preference by selecting the class you want to change and using the Move Up and Move Down buttons.

FIGURE 12.12   The Preference Levels tab

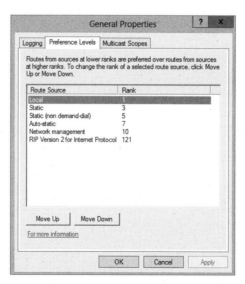

Managing Routing Protocols

Routing protocols typically don't take a lot of management. Once you install RIP, the protocol engine takes care of exchanging routes with remote routers. You can't directly edit the contents of the routing table generated by dynamic routing protocols. (This feature is available only with dedicated routers using a router operating system, such as Cisco's IOS.) That means your management of these protocols is pretty much limited to installing them, configuring them to meet your needs, and watching them as they run.

In the following sections, you will learn how to install routing protocols and set routing protocol properties.

Installing RIP

You add routing protocols from the General section of the IPv4 node in the Routing And Remote Access snap-in. Exercise 12.3 explains how to install RIP. You'll need the protocol installed to complete the exercises later in the chapter.

EXERCISE 12.3

Installing the RIP Protocols

1. Open the Routing And Remote Access snap-in.

2. Select the server you want to configure in the left pane of the MMC. Expand it until you see General beneath IPv4.

3. Right-click General, and select New Routing Protocol.

4. Select the routing protocol you want to install. In this case, choose RIP Version 2 for Internet Protocol, and click the OK button.

5. The RRAS console refreshes its display, revealing a new node labeled RIP under the IP Routing node.

Managing Static Routes

Static routes are simple to manage and configure because they don't participate in any kind of automatic discovery process. Static routes are conceptually very simple—they combine a destination network address with a subnet mask to provide a list of potential destinations. The destination addresses are reached through a particular interface on your router, and they're sent to a specified gateway (normally another router). Finally, there's a metric associated with the static route. The metric value is like a cost that you can set to determine which route is preferred. The lower the metric, the more the route gets used.

You create new static routes in two ways: by using the route add command from the command line or by right-clicking the Static Routes node in the Routing And Remote Access snap-in and selecting New Static Route.

In the following sections, I'll show you how those methods work.

Using *route add* to Create a Static Route

With the route add command, you can add new static routes and choose whether these routes remain in the routing table after the system reboots. Routes that stick around in this manner are called *persistent routes*. To make a route persistent, you need to add the -p switch to the route add command. The command syntax itself is simple:

```
route add -p destination Mask netMask gateWay metric interfaceID
```

The following two examples would be setting the router to see the 131.107.16.0 subnet on a 255.255.240.0 subnet mask using 131.107.32.1 as the gateway to get there:

```
route add -p 131.107.16.0 mask 255.255.240.0 131.107.32.1
route add -p 131.107.16.0/20 131.107.32.1
```

You specify the destination, netmask, gateway, metric, and interface ID on the command line. These parameters are all required. The route add command does some basic checking to make sure that the netmask and destination match and that you haven't omitted anything. You have to specify the interface as a number, not as a name. However, the route print command (which will be covered a little later in this chapter) lists its interfaces and the associated numbers.

Using RRAS to Create a Static Route

To create a new static route using the RRAS console, right-click the Static Routes node in the Routing And Remote Access snap-in, and select New Static Route. This opens the IPv4 Static Route dialog box (see Figure 12.13).

You have to provide the same parameters as with the route add command—the interface you want to use to connect, the destination and network mask, the gateway for the outbound packets, and a metric.

If you're creating a route that's not bound to a LAN interface, you can use the Use This Route To Initiate Demand-Dial Connections check box to specify that the route should open a new demand-dial connection on the specified interface.

FIGURE 12.13   Use the IPv4 Static Route dialog box to create new static routes.

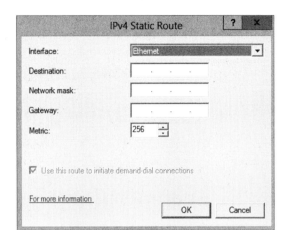

Exercise 12.4 shows you how to add and remove static routes. To complete Exercise 12.4, first you must have completed Exercise 12.1.

EXERCISE 12.4

Adding and Removing Static Routes

1.   Open the Routing And Remote Access snap-in.

2.   Select the server you want to configure in the left pane of the MMC. Expand IPv4 until you see Static Routes.

3.   Right-click the Static Routes node, and select New Static Route. The Static Route dialog box appears.

4.   Select the interface you want to use from the Interface drop-down list. Choose Ethernet for this exercise.

5.   Enter the destination address (try **10.10.10.0**), and enter a netmask of **255.255.255.0**.

6.   For the gateway address, enter **10.10.10.1** (if you used 10.10.10.0).

7.   Click the OK button. The Routing And Remote Access snap-in reappears.

8.   Right-click Static Routes in the left pane, and choose Show IP Routing Table. The IP Routing Table window appears. Verify that your newly added static route is present in the table.

EXERCISE 12.4 *(continued)*

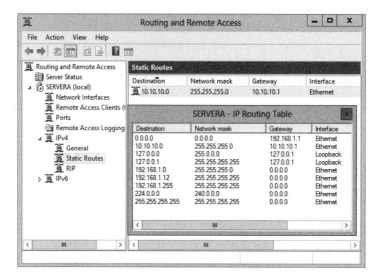

9. Close the IP Routing Table window.

10. Right-click the static route you added, and use the Delete command to remove it.

Configuring TCP/IP Packet Filters

One of the most useful features in RRAS is its ability to filter TCP/IP packets selectively in both directions.

Filters are usually used to block out undesirable traffic. In general, the idea is to keep out packets that your machine doesn't need to see. You can construct filters that allow traffic into or deny traffic out of your network based on rules that specify source and destination addresses and ports.

The basic idea behind packet filtering is simple:

1. You specify filter rules.

2. Incoming packets are measured against those rules.

    There are two types of filter rules:

-   Accept all packets except those prohibited by a rule.

-   Drop all packets except those permitted by a rule.

Filters are associated with a particular interface; the filters assigned to one interface are totally independent of those on all other interfaces. Inbound and outbound filters are likewise separate.

The following are some examples of filters:

- Block all packets to a web server except those on TCP ports 80 and 443.

- Block all outgoing packets on the ports used by the Yahoo! and AOL instant messaging tools.

- Filters on a PPTP or L2TP server can screen out everything except VPN traffic. This allows you to expose a Windows Server 2012 VPN server without fear of compromise.

You create and remove filters by using the Input Packet Filters and Output Packet Filters buttons on the General tab of the local area network Properties dialog box. The mechanics of working with incoming and outbound filters are identical; just remember the following guidelines:

- You create inbound filters to screen traffic coming to the interface.

- You create outbound filters to screen traffic going back out through that interface.

To create a filter, find the interface on which you want the filter and then open its Properties dialog box. Click the appropriate packet filter button, and you'll see the Inbound Filters dialog box (see Figure 12.14).

FIGURE 12.14   The Inbound Filters dialog box

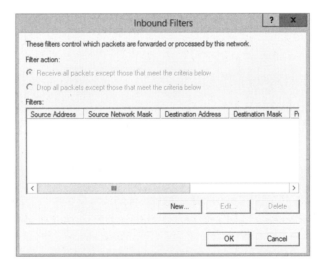

This dialog box has the following six parts:

- Receive All Packets Except Those That Meet The Criteria Below excludes the packets you specify and accepts everything else.

    This option is inactive until you create a filter rule.

- Drop All Packets Except Those That Meet The Criteria Below accepts only those packets you specify and excludes everything else.

This option is inactive until you create a filter rule.

- The Filters list, which is initially empty, shows you which filters are defined on this interface. Each entry in the list shows the following:
  - Source address and mask
  - Destination address and mask
  - Protocol, port, and traffic type specified in the rule
- The New, Edit, and Delete buttons allow you to add, edit, and remove filters.

To create a filter, click the New button and you'll see the Add IP Filter dialog box (see Figure 12.15). The conditions you specify here must all be true to trigger the rule. For example, if you specify both the source and destination addresses, only traffic from the defined source to the defined destination will be filtered.

FIGURE 12.15 The Add IP Filter dialog box

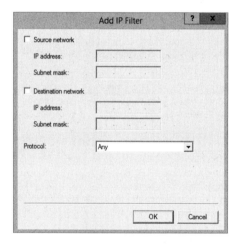

Use these tips to fill out the Add IP Filter dialog box:

- To create a filter that blocks packets by their origin or source address, check the Source Network box and supply the IP address and subnet mask for the source you want to block.
- To create a filter that blocks packets according to their destination address, check the Destination Network box and fill in the appropriate address and subnet mask.
- To filter by protocol, choose the protocol you want to block:
  - Any, which blocks everything
  - TCP

- TCP (Established), which means that the TCP/IP has an established connection already
- IP
- UDP
- ICMP
- Other, with a fill-in field for a protocol number

For each of these protocols, you'll have to enter some additional information. For example, if you select TCP, you have to specify the source or destination port numbers (or both).

Once you've specified the filter you want, click the OK button and you'll see it in the filter list. Filters go into effect as soon as you close the interface's Properties dialog box. You can go back and add, edit, or remove filters at any time.

Configuring VPN Packet Filters

Packet filters provide a useful security mechanism for blocking unwanted traffic on particular machines. It's a good idea to use packet filters to keep non-VPN traffic out of your VPN servers. The rules for doing this are fairly straightforward, as you will see in the following sections.

PPTP Packet Filters

You need at least two filters to screen out non-PPTP traffic adequately:

- The first filter allows traffic with a protocol ID of 47—the Generic Routing Encapsulation (GRE) protocol—to pass to the destination address of the PPTP interface.
- The second filter allows inbound traffic bound for TCP port 1723 (the PPTP port) to come to the PPTP interface.

You can add a third filter if the PPTP server also works as a PPTP client. In that case, the third filter needs the interface's destination address, a protocol type of TCP (established), and a source port of 1723.

Once you've created these filters, you open the Inbound Filters dialog box and select the radio button labeled Drop All Packets Except Those That Meet The Criteria Below.

Then you repeat the process on the outbound side, creating two or three corresponding output filters that screen out any traffic not originating from the VPN interface and using the correct protocols.

In Exercise 12.5, you'll set up RRAS IP packet filters that block everything except PPTP traffic on the specified interface.

WARNING Don't attempt this exercise on your production VPN server until you've been successful trying it on another, less-critical machine.

EXERCISE 12.5

Configuring PPTP Packet Filters

1. Open the Routing And Remote Access snap-in. Expand the server and IPv4 nodes to expose the General node of the server on which you're working. Select the General node.

2. Right-click the Ethernet interface, and choose Properties.

3. In the General tab of the interface's Properties dialog box, click the Inbound Filters button. The Inbound Filters dialog box appears.

4. Click the New button, and the Add IP Filter dialog box appears.

5. Fill out the Add IP Filter dialog box as follows:

   Check the Destination Network check box.

   Fill in the destination IP Address field with the IP address of the remote VPN interface. (For this exercise, I entered **192.168.1.254**. You can use the same.)

   Enter a destination subnet mask of **255.255.255.255**.

   Select a protocol type of TCP, and then specify a source port of **0** and a destination port of **1723**.

   Click the OK button.

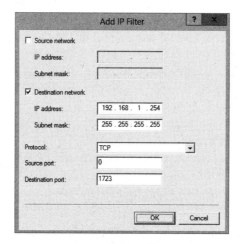

6. The Inbound Filters dialog box reappears, listing the new filter you created in step 5. Add another new filter using the same IP address and subnet mask, but this time specify Other in the Protocol field and fill in a protocol number of **47**.

   When you've finished, click the OK button to return to the Inbound Filters dialog box.

7. In the Inbound Filters dialog box, click the Drop All Packets Except Those That Meet The Criteria Below radio button, and click the OK button.

8. Close the interface's Properties dialog box.

L2TP Packet Filters

To use L2TP packet filters, you have to go through the same basic process as you do with PPTP packet filters (see the previous section), but the filters you need are slightly different. Four filters are required—two input filters and two output filters:

- Two input filters with a destination of the VPN interface address and a netmask of 255.255.255.255, filtering UDP:
  - One with a source and destination port of 500
  - The second with a source and destination port of 1701
- Two output filters with a source of the VPN interface address and a netmask of 255.255.255.255, filtering UDP:
  - One with a source and destination port of 500
  - The second with a source and destination port of 1701

Managing IP Routing

Managing IP routing is fairly simple. If you understand how the options described earlier in this chapter work, you know most of what you need to know to keep IP routing working smoothly. All of the remaining skills you'll need center on monitoring your routers to make sure that traffic is flowing smoothly and troubleshooting the occasional problem.

A number of status displays are built into the Routing And Remote Access snap-in. Knowing that they exist and what they display makes it much easier to see all the various health and status data that RRAS maintains. Each of these commands shows you something different:

The General ➢ Show TCP/IP Information Command   As you would expect, this display shows a broad general selection of IP routing data, including the number of routes in the route table, the number of IP and UDP datagrams received and forwarded, and the number of connection attempts. To customize the view, you can right-click the TCP/IP Information window and choose the Select Columns command.

The Static Routes ➢ Show IP Routing Table Command   This command shows you the entire contents of the routing table, including the destination, netmask, and gateway for each route. This version of the routing table doesn't show you where the route came from (for example, whether it was learned by RIP).

The RIP ≻ Show Neighbors Command   This command shows you which RIP neighbors exist. For each router, you can see how many bad packets and bad routes that neighbor has tried to foist off on your router.

Exercise 12.6 shows you how to monitor IP routing.

EXERCISE 12.6

Monitoring Routing Status

1.   Open the Routing And Remote Access snap-in.

2.   Select the server whose status you want to monitor in the left pane of the MMC.

3.   Select the Network Interfaces node. Notice that the right pane of the MMC now lists all known interfaces along with their status and connection state.

4.   Select the General node beneath IPv4. Notice that the right pane of the MMC updates to show the IP interfaces, their IP addresses, their administrative and operational states, and whether IP filtering is enabled on each interface.

5.   Right-click the General node, and choose the Show TCP/IP Information command. Check the number of IP routes shown.

6.   Right-click the Static Routes node, and choose the Show IP Routing Table command. Note that the number of routes listed corresponds to the route count in the TCP/IP Information window and that some of the routes listed are automatically generated.

Now let's revisit the route command you saw earlier but in the context of route monitoring.

Using the *routeprint* Command

You already learned how to use the route add command to add a new static route from the command line. The route print command can show you all or part of the routing table from the command line. Just entering **route print** into a command window gives you a complete dump of the entire routing table. Adding a wildcard IP address displays only routes that match the address you specify. For example, route print 206.151.* displays only routes that match 206.151.

Troubleshooting IP Routing

A comprehensive overview of IP routing troubleshooting is beyond the scope of this book. Microsoft's online help is pretty good at suggesting probable causes and solutions for most routing problems. If you understand the topics presented in this chapter, then you shouldn't have many troubleshooting problems in RRAS, as long as you verify the following points:

- The RRAS service is running and configured to act as an IP router.
- The router's TCP/IP configuration is correct (including a static IP address).
- You have IP routing protocols attached to each interface on which you need them.

Next you need to verify the following routing-specific settings and behaviors:

- Check to be sure that your router is receiving routes from its peers. Do this by opening the routing table and looking at the Protocol column. Seeing entries marked as RIP tells you that at least some peers are getting routing information through. If you don't see any RIP routes, that's a bad sign.
- You need to have a static default route enabled if your router hasn't received any default routes. To do this, add a new static route with a destination of **0.0.0.0**, a netmask of **0.0.0.0**, and either a demand-dial or a LAN interface appropriate for your network setup.

Troubleshooting Example

In Exercise 12.7, you will perform some troubleshooting. The exercise assumes the following:

- Your Windows 2012 Server R2 server doesn't have any packet filters or firewall running.
- Your server uses the IP address of 192.168.1.64 as its main interface address.

The goal is to allow only necessary traffic to this server using an IP packet filter. It was your understanding that another network administrator was going to enable a firewall outside the Windows Server 2012 server. However, after performing a scan of the server using nmap from a nearby Linux server, you find these ports open:

```
PORT     STATE SERVICE
53/tcpopen  domain
135/tcp  openmsrpc
139/tcp  opennetbios-ssn
445/tcp  openmicrosoft-ds
1025/tcpopen  NFS-or-IIS
1723/tcpopen  pptp
```

Obviously, the other firewall is not yet in place. The server acts as a PPTP VPN server for a Windows network and therefore needs only port 1723/TCP open for inbound connections. Your job is to enable some type of filtering as soon as possible in order to protect this Windows Server 2012 server.

EXERCISE 12.7

Troubleshooting Your Server

1. Open the Routing And Remote Access snap-in.

2. Expand IPv4 or IPv6, and click the General node.

   If you don't have an IPv4 or IPv6 node, open the server's Properties dialog box, and make sure the Router box is checked. If it's not, select it.

3. In the General window of the IPv4 node in the Routing And Remote Access snap-in, right-click the main network interface for the server, Ethernet, and then select Properties.

4. Click the Inbound Filters button. This opens the Inbound Filters dialog box.

5. In the Inbound Filters dialog box, click New. This opens the Add IP Filter dialog box.

6. The first order of business is to allow established TCP connections into the server. These are necessary for any connection that originates from the computer. Within the Add IP Filter dialog box, use the Protocol drop-down, and select TCP (Established). Leave the Source Port and Destination Port text boxes empty. Click OK to return to the Inbound Filters dialog box.

7. In the Inbound Filters dialog box, which now has one filter in it, change the filter action to Drop All Packets Except Those That Meet The Criteria Below. This is an important step because it changes the policy from "accept everything by default" to "deny everything by default," which is a better filtering policy.

8. Add another filter by clicking New in the Inbound Filters dialog box. For this filter, change the protocol to UDP, and set the source port at **53**. This allows the server to receive responses from DNS queries that it sends. Click OK to return to the Inbound Filters dialog box.

9. Back at the Inbound Filters dialog box, click New once again. This time add a filter for PPTP traffic, which runs on 1723/TCP. To do this, select TCP from the Protocol drop-down box, and type **1723** in the Destination Port text box. Then click OK.

10. Check the final group of filters in the Inbound Filters dialog box. Click OK at the Inbound Filters dialog box and OK again at the local area connection Properties dialog box.

Scanning the server again reveals that the only port open from a remote location is 1723/TCP:

```
PORT      STATE SERVICE
1723/tcpopen  pptp
```

You've now effectively blocked access to this server except for traffic on the PPTP port of TCP/1723. Outbound traffic has not been filtered.

As extra credit, you could enable ICMP echo requests and replies by adding inbound filters. You could also add outbound filters to ensure that only authorized traffic is being sent from the server. For example, only PPTP traffic and HTTPS traffic to Windows Update might be allowed from this server.

In Exercise 12.7, you worked with RRAS to create packet filters for inbound traffic. These were created through the IP Routing section of the Routing And Remote Access snap-in. You added filters for established TCP connections, for responses to outgoing DNS requests, and finally for the PPTP traffic itself. The policy for the filter was set to "deny by default."

Summary

In this chapter, you learned how IP routing connects networks by intelligently delivering network traffic to the correct destination in the internetwork, how to create and manage demand-dial and the RIP interface for IP routing, how to install RIP and set routing parameters, how to manage static routes with the route add command and the Routing And Remote Access snap-in, how to configure TCP/IP packet filters for blocking undesirable traffic, and finally, how to manage demand-dial routing. I also discussed the OSPF routing protocol and how OSPF is no longer supported by Windows Server 2012 RRAS.

I then discussed VPN connections and protocols. I talked about the inbound and outbound filters that you can set up on your VPN connection. I also discussed NAT and how it can help minimize TCP/IP numbers needed for Internet and remote network connections.

Exam Essentials

Know the difference between static routing and dynamic routing.   Static routing systems don't make any attempt to discover other routers or systems on their networks. Instead, you tell the routing engine how to get data to other networks. Dynamic routing doesn't depend on you adding fixed, unchangeable routes to remote networks. Instead, a dynamic routing engine can discover its surroundings by finding and communicating with other nearby routers in an internetwork.

Understand RRAS.   RRAS provides Windows Server 2012 computers with routing capabilities. You can establish static routes that specify where packets bound for certain networks should go. RRAS provides dynamic routing using versions 1 and 2 of the Routing Information Protocol (RIP). It also provides packet filtering to screen out undesirable packets in both directions.

Understand the difference between RIP and OSPF.   A RIP-capable router periodically sends out announcements while simultaneously receiving announcements from its peers. This exchange of routing information enables each router to learn what routers exist on the network and which destination networks each router knows how to reach. OSPF networks are broken down into areas. An area is a collection of interconnected networks. Think of an area as a subsection of an internetwork. Areas are interconnected by backbones. Each OSPF router keeps a link-state database only for the areas to which it's connected.

Know how to install RRAS and configure IP routing. The RRAS components are not installed by default on computers running Windows Server 2012. To enable your server to route IP packets, you have to install, activate, and configure RRAS using the Routing and Remote Access Server Setup Wizard in the Routing And Remote Access snap-in. You then need to add demand-dial interfaces if you want to support demand-dialing, give each routable interface a network address for each protocol it carries, and install and configure the routing protocols on the interfaces that should support them.

Know how to configure TCP/IP packet filters. You can construct filters that allow or deny traffic into or out of your network based on rules that specify source and destination addresses and ports. To create a filter, find the interface on which you want the filter, open its Properties dialog box, and click the appropriate packet filter button.

Review Questions

1. You work on a network with four subnets whose addresses are 208.45.231.0, 208.45.232.0, 208.45.233.0, and 208.45.234.0. Your routers are configured with these IP addresses:

   Router 1: 208.45.231.1 and 208.45.232.1

   Router 2: 208.45.231.2 and 208.45.233.1

   Router 3: 208.45.232.2 and 208.45.234.1

   Router 4: 208.45.233.2 and 208.45.234.2

   Router 2 is connected to the Internet. The connection between Router 2 and Router 4 is a very slow 56K dial-up line. Your computer's IP address is 208.45.231.25. Your default gateway is 208.45.231.2, because that's the address of the router that's connected to the Internet. You want to make sure your computer always routes information to 208.45.234.0 through Router 1 (unless Router 1 becomes unavailable) because the 56K line is so slow. Which command should you use to accomplish this?

   A. `route add 208.45.231.1 mask 255.255.255.0 208.45.234.0 metric 1 route add 208.45.231.2 mask 255.255.255.0 208.45.234.0 metric 2`

   B. `route add 208.45.234.0 mask 255.255.255.0 208.45.231.1 metric 2 route add 208.45.234.0 mask 255.255.255.0 208.45.231.2 metric 1`

   C. `route add 208.45.234.0 mask 255.255.255.0 208.45.231.1 metric 1 route add 208.45.234.0 mask 255.255.255.0 208.45.231.2 metric 2`

   D. `route add 208.45.234.0 mask 255.255.255.0 208.45.232.1 metric 1 route add 208.45.234.0 mask 255.255.255.0 208.45.233.1 metric 2`

2. You administer a network that consists of four subnets. Your manager wants to reduce costs as much as possible. You decide to configure at least one Windows Server 2012 computer on each subnet with RRAS and a nonpersistent demand-dial connection. You want to have the routers dynamically update themselves. Which of the following should you use to accomplish these goals?

   A. RIPv2

   B. OSPF

   C. EIGRP

   D. Area border routers

3. Leigh is setting up an RRAS router at a remote site so that it can connect to the corporate LAN. Which of the following interfaces will Leigh need?

   A. A demand-dial interface for connecting the remote and LAN routers

   B. RIP for routing discovery

   C. A demand-dial interface as well as RIP or OSPF

   D. None of the above

4. You upgraded all of your locations to Windows Server 2012 and implemented the routing capability built into the servers. You chose to implement RIP. After implementing the routers, you discover that routes that you don't want your network to consider are updating your RIP routing tables. What can you do to control which networks the RIP routing protocol will communicate with on your network?

    A. Configure TCP/IP filtering.

    B. Configure RIP route filtering.

    C. Configure IP packet filtering.

    D. Configure RIP peer filtering.

    E. There is no way to control this behavior.

5. You are the network administrator for your organization. You need to see the routing table from the command line. What command-line utility can you use?

    A. `route add`

    B. `route view`

    C. `route print`

    D. `route monitor`

6. Joe set up a new RRAS router that seems to be functioning properly, but it isn't routing traffic. He has already verified that RRAS is running and properly configured. Which of the following are possible causes of the problem? (Choose all that apply.)

    A. No routes are being learned from peer routers.

    B. There is no static default route.

    C. No RIP neighbors are defined.

    D. The router's authentication credentials are wrong.

7. Your company has six locations that have been connected in a hub-and-spoke design with your location as the center. The network is designed that way because it grew over time and you simply added another connection to your Windows Server 2003 server each time one was needed. You are concerned that if your connection goes down, the entire network will go down with it and all of your users across the country will lose connectivity. You have now migrated all of your servers to Windows Server 2012, and you are well on your way to migrating Windows XP to Windows 8. You decide that each RRAS server will have at least three separate connections to other RRAS servers in the network so that you will always have a way to find a path through the network. You want to accomplish this with the least amount of administrative effort. How should you configure the RRAS computers to ensure these objectives?

    A. Configure RIPv2 on all routing interfaces.

    B. Configure OSPF on all routing interfaces.

    C. Configure RIPv1 and OSPF on all routing interfaces.

    D. Configure static routes.

    E. Configure RIP version 2 and OSPF on all routing interfaces.

8. You work for a very large accounting company that has more than 1,000 workstations in three locations over a routed network. You have upgraded all of the servers to Windows Server 2012 and are well under way in bringing all the workstations to Windows 7 and Windows 8. Two of the locations are connected to the central office, which has a T1 connection to the Internet. All of the users on all three networks are funneled through this RRAS server for Internet access. Your company has a policy that personal Internet browsing from company equipment is not acceptable. The main purposes of Internet access within the company are email connectivity and VPN traffic to your business partners. Also, some staff members occasionally download new regulations and forms from a few government websites. How can you implement this policy using the tools and services on your Windows Server 2012 network?

 A. Configure TCP/IP filters to control access to the Internet.

 B. Configure IP packet filters to control access to the Internet.

 C. Configure the Internet browsers through global policies to control the websites users can and cannot visit.

 D. Create static routing tables to control the websites, based on address, the users can reach.

9. You notice that packets sent to your RRAS router aren't being routed. You determine that the packets are indeed reaching the router. What should you check in order to troubleshoot the problem?

 A. The RRAS service status

 B. The RRAS routing configuration

 C. The RRAS server's TCP/IP configuration

 D. All of the above

10. You are the administrator of a network consisting of six subnets that are routed together through an ISP that doesn't support multicasting. You are connected to the ISP at all locations with Windows Server 2012 RRAS servers. The Marketing department is interested in providing audio and video presentations between the corporate office and one of the other locations; these presentations will be a test of how audio and video presentations could be used throughout the company. Your company is growing rapidly, and you plan to build a private network to support more flexibility in your routing capability. However, that isn't going to happen in time for the test. What can you do on your side of the network to allow the multicasting traffic to reach the intended destinations?

 A. Configure multicast boundaries on each of the appropriate RRAS routers.

 B. Install RIPv2 to carry the multicast traffic.

 C. Configure an IP-in-IP tunnel interface on the appropriate RRAS routers.

 D. Configure the multicast heartbeat on the appropriate RRAS routers.

Chapter

13

Understanding Security

THE FOLLOWING 70-410 EXAM OBJECTIVES ARE COVERED IN THIS CHAPTER:

✓ **Configure security policies**

- This objective may include, but is not limited to: Configure User Rights Assignment; configure Security Options settings; configure Security templates; configure Audit Policy; configure Local Users and Groups; configure User Account Control (UAC).

THE FOLLOWING 70-411 EXAM OBJECTIVES ARE COVERED IN THIS CHAPTER:

✓ **Configure account policies**

- This objective may include, but is not limited to: Configure domain user password policy; configure and apply Password Settings Objects (PSOs); delegate password settings management; configure local user password policy; configure account lockout settings.

✓ **Configure advanced audit policies**

- Implement auditing using Group Policy and AuditPol.exe; create expression-based audit policies; create removable device audit policies.

THE FOLLOWING 70-412 EXAM OBJECTIVES ARE COVERED IN THIS CHAPTER:

✓ **Implement Dynamic Access Control (DAC)**

- This objective may include but is not limited to: Configure user and device claim types; implement policy changes and staging; perform access-denied remediation; configure file classification.

So far in this book, I have covered many important aspects of Active Directory. The most important aspect of any network, including Active Directory, is security. If your network is not secure, then hackers (internal or external) can make your life as a member of IT a living nightmare.

All network operating systems (NOSs) offer some way to grant or deny access to resources, such as files and printers. Active Directory is no exception. You can define fundamental security objects through the use of the users, groups, and computers security principals. Then you can allow or disallow access to resources by granting specific permissions to each of these objects.

In this chapter, you'll learn how to implement security within Active Directory. By using Active Directory tools, you can quickly and easily configure the settings that you require in order to protect information.

Proper planning for security permissions is an important prerequisite of setting up Active Directory. Security is always one of the greatest concerns for an IT administrator.

If your security settings are too restrictive, users may not be able to perform their job functions. Worse yet, they may try to circumvent security measures. They may even complain to their management teams, and eventually you will be confronted with these complaints. On the other end of the spectrum, if security permissions are too lax, users may be able to access and modify sensitive company resources.

You may continuously try to seek a balance—to have enough security and, at the same time, be somewhat transparent to the end users, who simply want to do their jobs and not be bothered by what's between the lines.

You should have a security policy that states what is expected of every computer user in your company. Fine-tuning Active Directory to comply with your security policy and allowing end users to function without an issue should be your goals.

You should know how to use Active Directory to apply permissions to resources on the network. An administrator should pay particular attention to the evaluation of permissions when applied to different groups and the flow of permissions through the organizational units (OUs) via group policies. With all of this in mind, let's start looking at how you can manage security within Active Directory.

In order to complete the exercises in this chapter, you should understand the basics of working with Active Directory objects. If you are not familiar with creating and managing users, groups, computers, and OUs, you should review the information in Chapter 4, "Administering Active Directory," before you continue.

Active Directory Security Overview

One of the fundamental design goals for Active Directory is to define a single, centralized repository of users and information resources. Active Directory records information about all of the users, computers, and resources on your network. Each domain acts as a logical boundary, and members of the domain (including workstations, servers, and domain controllers) share information about the objects within them.

The information stored within Active Directory determines which resources are accessible to which users. Through the use of *permissions* that are assigned to Active Directory objects, you can control all aspects of network security.

Throughout this chapter, you'll learn the details of security as it pertains to Active Directory. Note, however, that Active Directory security is only one aspect of overall network security. You should also be sure that you have implemented appropriate access control settings for the file system, network devices, and other resources. Let's start by looking at the various components of network security, which include working with security principals and managing security and permissions, access control lists (ACLs), and access control entries (ACEs).

NOTE   When you are setting up a network, you should always keep in mind that 90 percent of all hacks on a network are internal. This means that internal permissions and security (as well as external security) need to be as strong as possible while still allowing users to do their jobs.

Understanding Security Principals

Security principals are Active Directory objects that are assigned *security identifiers (SIDs)*. An SID is a unique identifier that is used to manage any object to which permissions can be assigned. Security principals are assigned permissions to perform certain actions and access certain network resources.

The following basic types of Active Directory objects serve as security principals:

User Accounts   User accounts identify individual users on your network by including information such as the user's name and their password. User accounts are the fundamental unit of security administration.

Groups   There are two main types of groups: *security groups* and *distribution groups*. Both types can contain user accounts. System administrators use security groups to ease the management of security permissions. They use distribution groups, on the other hand, solely to send email. Distribution groups are not security principals. You'll see the details of groups in the next section.

Computer Accounts *Computer accounts* identify which client computers are members of particular domains. Because these computers participate in the Active Directory database, system administrators can manage security settings that affect the computer. They use computer accounts to determine whether a computer can join a domain and for authentication purposes. As you'll see later in this chapter, system administrators can also place restrictions on certain computer settings to increase security. These settings apply to the computer and, therefore, also apply to any user who is using it (regardless of the permissions granted to the user account).

Note that other objects—such as OUs—do not function as security principals. What this means is that you can apply certain settings (such as Group Policy) on all of the objects within an OU; however, you cannot specifically set permissions with respect to the OU itself. The purpose of OUs is to organize other Active Directory objects logically based on business needs, add a needed level of control for security, and create an easier way to delegate.

You can manage security by performing the following actions with security principals:

- You can assign them permissions to access various network resources.

- You can give them user rights.

- You can track their actions through auditing (covered later in this chapter).

The major types of security principals—user accounts, groups, and computer accounts—form the basis of the Active Directory security architecture. As a system administrator, you will likely spend a portion of your time managing permissions for these objects.

 It is important to understand that, since a unique SID defines each security principal, deleting a security principal is an irreversible process. For example, if you delete a user account and then later re-create one with the same name, you'll need to reassign permissions and group membership settings for the new account. Once a user account is deleted, its SID is deleted.

Users and groups are two types of fundamental security principals employed for security administration. In the following sections, you'll learn how users and groups interact and about the different types of groups that you can create.

Types of Groups

When dealing with groups, you should make the distinction between local security principals and domain security principals:

Local Users and Groups You use *local users and groups* to assign the permissions necessary to access the local machine. For example, you may assign the permissions you need to reboot a domain controller to a specific domain local group.

Domain Users and Groups *Domain users and groups*, on the other hand, are used throughout the domain. These objects are available on any of the computers within the Active Directory domain and between domains that have a trust relationship.

Here are the two main types of groups used in Active Directory:

Security Groups   *Security groups* are considered security principals. They can contain user accounts, computers, or groups. To make administration simpler, system administrators usually grant permissions to groups. This allows you to change permissions easily at the Active Directory level (instead of at the level of the resource on which the permissions are assigned).

You can also place Active Directory Contact objects within security groups, but security permissions will not apply to them.

Distribution Groups   Distribution groups are not considered security principals because they do not have SIDs. As mentioned earlier, they are used only for the purpose of sending email messages. You can add users to distribution groups just as you would add them to security groups. You can also place distribution groups within OUs so that they are easier to manage. You will find them useful, for example, if you need to send email messages to an entire department or business unit within Active Directory.

Understanding the differences between security and distribution groups is important in an Active Directory environment. For the most part, system administrators use security groups for daily administration of permissions. On the other hand, system administrators who are responsible for maintaining email distribution lists generally use distribution groups to group members of departments and business units logically. (A system administrator can also email all of the users within a security group, but to do so, they would have to specify the email addresses for the accounts.)

When you are working in Windows Server 2003, Server 2008, Server 2008 R2, or Server 2012 functional-level domains, you can convert security groups to or from distribution groups. When group types are running in a Windows 2000 mixed domain functional level, you cannot change them.

It is vital that you understand group types when you are getting ready to take the Microsoft exams. Microsoft likes to include trick questions about putting permissions on distribution groups. Remember, only security groups can have permissions assigned to them.

Group Scope

In addition to being classified by type, each group is given a specific scope. The scope of a group defines two characteristics. First, it determines the level of security that applies to a group. Second, it determines which users can be added to the group. *Group scope* is an important concept in network environments because it ultimately defines which resources users are able to access.

The three types of group scope are as follows:

Domain Local   The scope of *domain local groups* extends as far as the local domain. When you're using the Active Directory Users and Computers tool, domain local accounts apply to the computer for which you are viewing information. Domain local groups are used to assign permissions to local resources, such as files and printers. They can contain domain locals, global groups, universal groups, and user accounts.

Global   The scope of *global groups* is limited to a single domain. Global groups may contain any of the users that are a part of the Active Directory domain in which the global groups reside or other global groups. Global groups are often used for managing domain security permissions based on job functions. For example, if you need to specify permissions for the Engineering department, you could create one or more global groups (such as EngineeringManagers and EngineeringDevelopers). You could then assign security permissions to each group.

Universal   *Universal groups* can contain accounts or other universal groups from any domains within an Active Directory forest. Therefore, system administrators use them to manage security across domains. When you are managing multiple domains, it often helps to group global groups within universal groups. For instance, if you have an Engineering global group in the `research.stellacon.com` domain and an Engineering global group in the `asia.stellacon.com` domain, you can create a universal AllEngineers group that contains both of the global groups. Now whenever you must assign security permissions to all engineers within the organization, you need only assign permissions to the AllEngineers universal group.

For domain controllers to process authentication between domains, information about the membership of universal groups is stored in the global catalog (GC). Keep this in mind if you ever plan to place users directly into universal groups and bypass global groups because all of the users will be enumerated in the GC, which will impact size and performance.

Fortunately, universal group credentials are cached on domain controllers that universal group members use to log on. This process is called *universal group membership caching*. The domain controller obtains the cached data whenever universal group members log on, and then it is retained on the domain controller for 8 hours by default. This is especially useful for smaller locations, such as branch offices, that run less-expensive domain controllers. Most domain controllers at these locations cannot store a copy of the entire GC, and frequent calls to the nearest GC would require an inordinate amount of network traffic.

When you create a new group using the Active Directory Users and Computers tool, you must specify the scope of the group. Figure 13.1 shows the New Object – Group dialog box and the available options for the group scope.

FIGURE 13.1   The New Object – Group dialog box

However, changing group scope can be helpful when your security administration or business needs change. You can change group scope easily using the Active Directory Users and Computers tool. To do so, access the properties of the group. As shown in Figure 13.2, you can make a group scope change by clicking one of the options.

FIGURE 13.2   The Domain Admins Security Group's Properties dialog box

Built-in Domain Local Groups

System administrators use built-in domain local groups to perform administrative functions on the local server. Because these have pre-assigned permissions and privileges, they allow system administrators to assign common management functions easily. Figure 13.3 shows the default built-in groups that are available on a Windows Server 2012 domain controller.

FIGURE 13.3   Default built-in local groups

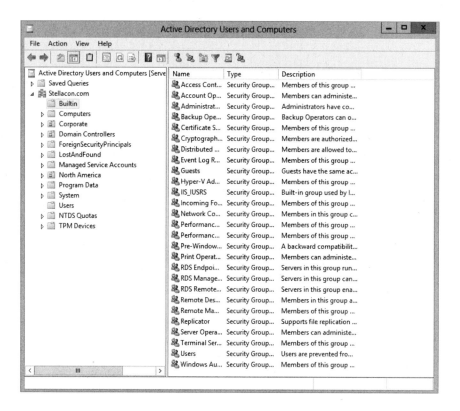

The list of built-in local groups includes some of the following:

Account Operators   These users can create and modify domain user and group accounts. Members of this group are generally responsible for the daily administration of Active Directory.

Administrators   By default, members of the Administrators group are given full permissions to perform any functions within the Active Directory domain and on the local computer. This means that they can access all files and resources that reside on any server within the domain. As you can see, this is a very powerful account.

In general, you should restrict the number of users who are included in this group because most common administration functions do not require this level of access.

Backup Operators   One of the problems associated with backing up data in a secure network environment is that you need to provide a way to bypass standard file system security so that you can copy files. Although you could place users in the Administrators group, doing so usually provides more permissions than necessary. Members of the Backup Operators group can bypass standard file system security for the purpose of backup and recovery only. They cannot, however, directly access or open files within the file system.

Generally, backup software applications and data use the permissions assigned to the Backup Operators group.

Certificate Service DCOM Access   Members of the Certificate Service DCOM Access group can connect to certificate authority servers in the enterprise.

Cryptographic Operators   Members of the Cryptographic Operators group are authorized to perform cryptographic operations. *Cryptography* allows the use of codes to convert data, which then allows a specific recipient to read it using a key.

Guests   Typically, you use the Guests group to provide access to resources that generally do not require security. For example, if you have a network share that provides files that should be made available to all network users, you can assign permissions to allow members of the Guests group to access those files.

Print Operators   By default, members of the Print Operators group are given permissions to administer all of the printers within a domain. This includes common functions such as changing the priority of print jobs and deleting items from the print queue.

Replicator   The Replicator group allows files to be replicated among the computers in a domain. You can add accounts used for replication-related tasks to this group to provide those accounts with the permissions they need to keep files synchronized across multiple computers.

Server Operators   A common administrative task is managing server configuration. Members of the Server Operators group are granted the permissions they need to manage services, shares, and other system settings.

Users   The Users built-in domain local group is used to administer security for most network accounts. Usually, you don't give this group many permissions, and you use it to apply security settings for most employees within an organization.

Windows Server 2012 also includes many different default groups, which you can find in the Users folder. As shown in Figure 13.4, these groups are of varying scopes, including domain local, global, and universal groups. You'll see the details of these groups in the next section.

FIGURE 13.4   Contents of the default Users folder

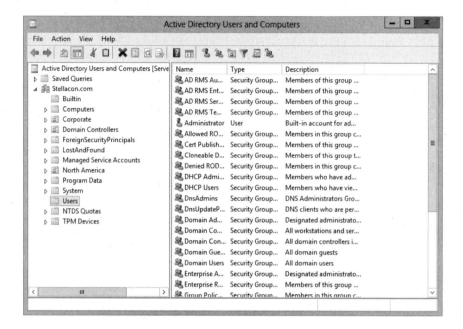

Three important user accounts are created during the promotion of a domain controller:

- The *Administrator account* is assigned the password a system administrator provides during the promotion process, and it has full permissions to perform all actions within the domain.

- The Guest account is disabled by default. The purpose of the *Guest account* is to provide anonymous access to users who do not have an individual logon and password to use within the domain. Although the Guest account might be useful in some situations, it is generally recommended that this account be disabled to increase security.

- Only the operating system uses the *krbtgt*, or *Key Distribution Center Service, account* for Kerberos authentication while it is using DCPromo.exe. This account is disabled by default. Unlike other user accounts, the krbtgt account cannot be used to log on to the domain and therefore it does not need to be enabled. Since only the operating system uses this account, you do not need to worry about hackers gaining access by using this account.

Predefined Global Groups

As mentioned earlier in this chapter, you use global groups to manage permissions at the domain level. Members of each of these groups can perform specific tasks related to managing Active Directory.

The following predefined global groups are installed in the Users folder:

Cert Publishers   Certificates are used to increase security by allowing for strong authentication methods. User accounts are placed within the *Cert Publishers group* if they must publish security certificates. Generally, Active Directory security services use these accounts.

Domain Computers   All of the computers that are members of the domain are generally members of the *Domain Computers group*. This includes any workstations or servers that have joined the domain, but it does not include the domain controllers.

Domain Admins   Members of the *Domain Admins group* have full permissions to manage all of the Active Directory objects for this domain. This is a powerful account; therefore, you should restrict its membership only to those users who require full permissions.

Domain Controllers   All of the domain controllers for a given domain are generally included within the *Domain Controllers group*.

Domain Guests   Generally, by default, members of the *Domain Guests group* are given minimal permissions with respect to resources. System administrators may place user accounts in this group if they require only basic access or temporary permissions within the domain.

Domain Users   The *Domain Users group* usually contains all of the user accounts for the given domain. This group is generally given basic permissions to resources that do not require higher levels of security. A common example is a public file share.

Enterprise Admins   Members of the *Enterprise Admins group* are given full permissions to perform actions within the entire forest. This includes functions such as managing trust relationships and adding new domains to trees and forests.

Group Policy Creator Owners   Members of the *Group Policy Creator Owners group* are able to create and modify Group Policy settings for objects within the domain. This allows them to enable security settings on OUs (and the objects that they contain).

Schema Admins   Members of the *Schema Admins group* are given permissions to modify the Active Directory schema. As a member of Schema Admins, you can create additional fields of information for user accounts. This is a very powerful function because any changes to the schema will be propagated to all of the domains and domain controllers within an Active Directory forest. Furthermore, you cannot undo changes to the schema (although you can disable some).

In addition to these groups, you can create new ones for specific services and applications that are installed on the server. (You'll notice that the list in Figure 13.4 includes more than just the ones in the preceding list.) Specifically, services that run on domain controllers and servers will be created as security groups with domain local scope. For example, if a domain controller is running the DNS service, the DnsAdmins and DnsUpdateProxy groups become available. In addition, there are two read-only domain controller (RODC) local groups: the Allowed RODC Password Replication and the Denied RODC Password Replication groups. Similarly, if you install the DHCP service, it automatically creates the DHCP Users and DHCP Administrators groups. The purpose of these groups depends on the functionality of the applications being installed.

Foreign Security Principals

In environments that have more than one domain, you may need to grant permissions to users who reside in multiple domains. Generally, you manage this using Active Directory trees and forests. However, in some cases, you may want to provide resources to users who belong to domains that are not part of the forest.

Active Directory uses the concept of *foreign security principals* to allow permissions to be assigned to users who are not part of an Active Directory forest. This process is automatic and does not require the intervention of system administrators. You can then add the foreign security principals to domain local groups for which, in turn, you can grant permissions for resources within the domain. You can view a list of foreign security principals by using the Active Directory Users and Computers tool. Figure 13.5 shows the contents of the ForeignSecurityPrincipals folder.

FIGURE 13.5 The ForeignSecurityPrincipals folder

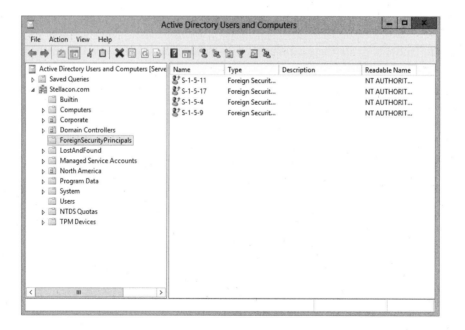

Managing Security and Permissions

Now that you understand the basic issues, terms, and Active Directory objects that pertain to security, it's time to look at how you can apply this information to secure your network resources. The general practice for managing security is to assign users to groups and then grant permissions and logon parameters to the groups so that they can access certain resources.

For management ease and to implement a hierarchical structure, you can place groups within OUs. You can also assign Group Policy settings to all of the objects contained within an OU. By using this method, you can combine the benefits of a hierarchical structure (through OUs) with the use of security principals. Figure 13.6 provides a diagram of this process.

FIGURE 13.6   An overview of security management

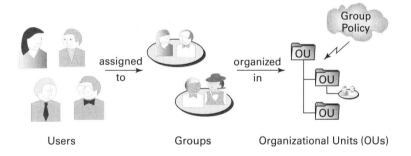

| Users | Groups | Organizational Units (OUs) |

The primary tool you use to manage security permissions for users, groups, and computers is the Active Directory Users and Computers tool. Using this tool, you can create and manage Active Directory objects and organize them based on your business needs. Common tasks for many system administrators might include the following:

- Resetting a user's password (for example, in cases where they forget their password)
- Creating new user accounts (when, for instance, a new employee joins the company)
- Modifying group memberships based on changes in job requirements and functions
- Disabling user accounts (when, for example, users will be out of the office for long periods of time and will not require network resource access)

Once you've properly grouped your users, you need to set the actual permissions that affect the objects within Active Directory. The actual permissions available vary based on the type of object. Table 13.1 provides an example of some of the permissions that you can apply to various Active Directory objects and an explanation of what each permission does.

TABLE 13.1   Permissions of Active Directory objects

Permission	Explanation
Control Access	Changes security permissions on the object
Create Child	Creates objects within an OU (such as other OUs)
Delete Child	Deletes child objects within an OU
Delete Tree	Deletes an OU and the objects within it
List Contents	Views objects within an OU
List Object	Views a list of the objects within an OU
Read	Views properties of an object (such as a username)
Write	Modifies properties of an object

Using ACLs and ACEs

Each object in Active Directory has an *access control list (ACL)*. The ACL is a list of user accounts and groups that are allowed to access the resource. For each ACL, there is an access control entry (ACE) that defines what a user or a group can actually do with the resource. Deny permissions are always listed first. This means that if users have Deny permissions through user or group membership, they will not be allowed to access the object, even if they have explicit Allow permissions through other user or group permissions. Figure 13.7 shows an ACL for the Sales OU.

FIGURE 13.7   The ACL for an OU named Sales

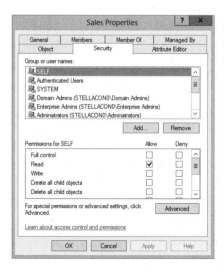

The Security tab is enabled only if you selected the Advanced Features option from the View menu in the Active Directory Users and Computers tool.

 Real World Scenario

Using Groups Effectively

You are a new system administrator for a medium-sized organization, and your network spans a single campus environment. The previous administrator had migrated the network from Windows 2003 to Windows Server 2012, and everyone seems fine with the network and new workstations. As you familiarize yourself with the network, you realize that the previous administrator applied a very ad hoc approach. Many of the permissions to resources had been given to individual accounts on request. It seems there was no particular strategy with regard to administration.

Management tells you that the company has acquired another company, hopefully the first of several acquisitions. They tell you about these plans because they do not want any hiccups in the information system as necessary changes ensue.

You immediately realize that management practices of the past must be replaced with the best practices that have been developed for networks over the years. One of the fundamental practices that you need to establish for this environment is the use of groups to apply permissions and give privileges to users throughout the network.

It is quite simple to give permissions individually, and in some cases, it seems like overkill to create a group, give permissions to the group, and then add a user to the group. Using group-based permissions really pays off in the long run, however, regardless of how small your network is today.

One constant in the networking world is that networks grow. When they grow, it is much easier to add users to a well-thought-out system of groups and consistently applied policies and permissions than it is to patch these elements together for each individual user.

Don't get caught up in the "easy" way of dealing with each request as it comes down the pike. Take the time to figure out how the system will benefit from a more structured approach. Visualize your network as already large with numerous accounts, even if it is still small; this way, when it grows, you will be well positioned to manage the network as smoothly as possible.

Implementing Active Directory Security

So far, you have looked at many different concepts that are related to security within Active Directory. You began by exploring security principals and how they form the basis for administering Active Directory security. Then you considered the purpose and function of groups, how group scopes can affect how these groups work, and how to create a list of the predefined users and groups for new domains and domain controllers. Based on all of this information, it's time to see how you can implement Active Directory security.

In this section, you'll take a look at how you can create and manage users and groups. The most commonly used tool for working with these objects is the Active Directory Users and Computers tool. Using this tool, you can create new user and group objects within the relevant OUs of your domain, and you can modify group membership and group scope.

In addition to these basic operations, you can use some additional techniques to simplify the administration of users and groups. One method involves using user templates. Additionally, you'll want to be able to specify who can make changes to user and group objects. That's the purpose of delegation. Both of these topics are covered later in this section.

Let's start with the basics. In Exercise 13.1, you learn how to create and manage users and groups.

WARNING
This exercise involves creating new OUs and user accounts within an Active Directory domain. Be sure that you are working in a test environment to avoid any problems that might occur because of the changes that you make.

EXERCISE 13.1

Creating and Managing Users and Groups

1. Open the Active Directory Users and Computers MMC snap-in by clicking the Windows Key (on the keyboard), choosing Administrative tools ➢ Active Directory Users and Computers.

2. Create the following top-level OUs:

    Sales

    Marketing

    Engineering

    HR

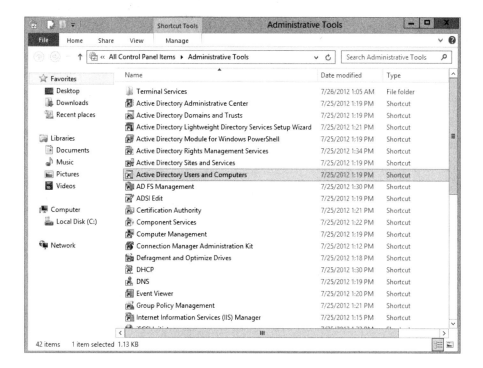

3. Create the following User objects within the Sales container (use the defaults for all fields not listed):

   a. First Name: **John**

   Last Name: **Sales**

   User Logon Name: **JSales**

   b. First Name: **Linda**

   Last Name: **Manager**

   User Logon Name: **LManager**

4. Create the following User objects within the Marketing container (use the defaults for all fields not listed):

   a. First Name: **Jane**

   Last Name: **Marketing**

   User Logon Name: **JMarketing**

   b. First Name: **Monica**

   Last Name: **Manager**

   User Logon Name: **MManager**

5. Create the following User object within the Engineering container (use the defaults for all fields not listed):

    First Name: **Bob**

    Last Name: **Engineer**

    User Logon Name: **BEngineer**

6. Right-click the HR container, and select New ➤ Group. Use the name Managers for the group, and specify Global for the group scope and Security for the group type. Click OK to create the group.

7. To assign users to the Managers group, right-click the Group object and select Properties. Change to the Members tab, and click Add. Enter **Linda Manager** and **Monica Manager**, and then click OK. You will see the group membership list. Click OK to finish adding the users to the group.

8. When you have finished creating users and groups, close the Active Directory Users and Computers tool.

Notice that you can add users to groups regardless of the OU in which they're contained. In Exercise 13.1, for example, you added two user accounts from different OUs into a group that was created in a third OU. This type of flexibility allows you to manage user and group accounts easily based on your business organization.

The Active Directory Users and Computers tool also allows you to perform common functions simply by right-clicking an object and selecting actions from the context menu. For example, you could right-click a user account and select Add Members To Group to change group membership quickly. You even have the ability in Active Directory Users and Computers to drag users from one OU and drop them into another.

You may have noticed that creating multiple users can be a fairly laborious and a potentially error-prone process. As a result, you are probably ready to take a look at a better way to create multiple users—by using user templates, discussed in the next section.

Using User Templates

Sometimes you will need to add several users with the same security settings. Rather than creating each user from scratch and making configuration changes to each one manually, you can create one user template, configure it, and copy it as many times as necessary. Each copy retains the configuration, group membership, and permissions of the original, but you must specify a new username, password, and full name to make the new user unique.

In Exercise 13.2, you create a user template, make configuration changes, and create a new user based on the template. This exercise shows you that the new user you create will belong to the same group as the user template that you copied it from. You must have completed Exercise 13.1 first before you begin this one.

EXERCISE 13.2

Creating and Using User Templates

1. Open the Active Directory Users and Computers tool.

2. Create the following User object within the Sales container (use the defaults for all fields not listed):

   First Name: **Sales User**

   Last Name: **Template**

   User Logon Name: **SalesUserTemplate**

3. Create a new global security group called Sales Users, and add SalesUserTemplate to the group membership.

4. Right-click the SalesUserTemplate User object, and select Copy from the context menu.

5. Enter the username, first name, and last name for the new user.

6. Click the Next button to move on to the password screen, and enter the new user's password information. Close the Copy Object – User dialog box when you've finished.

7. Right-click the user you created in step 5, select Properties, and click the Member Of tab.

8. Verify that the new user is a member of the Sales Users group.

Delegating Control of Users and Groups

A common administrative function related to the use of Active Directory involves managing users and groups. You can use OUs to group objects logically so that you can easily manage them. Once you have placed the appropriate Active Directory objects within OUs, you are ready to delegate control of these objects.

Delegation is the process by which a higher-level security administrator assigns permissions to other users. For example, if Admin A is a member of the Domain Admins group, they are able to delegate control of any OU within the domain to Admin B. You can access the Delegation of Control Wizard through the Active Directory Users and Computers tool. You can use it to perform common delegation tasks quickly and easily. The wizard walks you through the steps of selecting the object(s) for which you want to perform delegation, what permission you want to allow, and which users will have those permissions.

Exercise 13.3 walks through the steps required to delegate control of OUs. To complete the steps in this exercise, you must first have completed Exercise 13.1.

EXERCISE 13.3

Delegating Control of Active Directory Objects

1.   Open the Active Directory Users and Computers tool.

2.   Create a new user within the Engineering OU using the following information (use the default settings for any fields not specified):

     First Name: **Robert**

     Last Name: **Admin**

     User Logon Name: **radmin**

     Password: **P@ssw0rd**

3.   Right-click the Sales OU, and select Delegate Control. This starts the Delegation of Control Wizard. Click Next.

4.   To add users and groups to which you want to delegate control, click the Add button. In the Add dialog box, enter **Robert Admin** for the name of the user to add. Note that you can specify multiple users or groups using this option.

5.   Click OK to add the account to the delegation list, which is shown in the Users Or Groups page. Click Next to continue.

6.   On the Tasks To Delegate page, you must specify which actions you want to allow the selected user to perform within this OU. Select the Delegate The Following Common Tasks option, and place a check mark next to the following options:

     Create, Delete, And Manage User Accounts

     Reset User Passwords And Force Password Change At Next Logon

     Read All User Information

     Create, Delete And Manage Groups

     Modify The Membership Of A Group

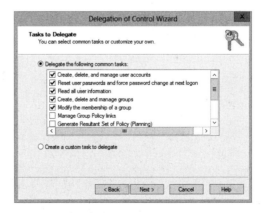

7. Click Next to continue. The wizard provides you with a summary of the selections that you have made on the Completing The Delegation Of Control Wizard page. To complete the process, click Finish to have the wizard commit the changes.

    Now when the user Robert Admin logs on (using *radmin* as his logon name), he will be able to perform common administrative functions for all of the objects contained within the Sales OU.

8. When you have finished, close the Active Directory Users and Computers tool.

Understanding Dynamic Access Control

One of the advantages of Windows Server 2012 is the ability to apply data governance to your file server. This will help control who has access to information and auditing. We get these advantages through the use of Dynamic Access Control (DAC). Dynamic Access Control allows you to identify data by using data classifications (both automatic and manual) and then control access to these files based on these classifications.

DAC also gives administrators the ability to control file access by using a central access policy. This central access policy will also allow an administrator to setup audit access to files for reporting and forensic investigation.

DAC allows an administrator to setup Active Directory Rights Management Service (AD RMS) encryption for Microsoft Office documents. For example, you can setup encryption for any documents that contain financial information.

Dynamic Access Control gives an administrator the flexibility to configure file access and auditing to domain based file servers. To do this, DAC controls claims in the authentication token, resource properties, and conditional expressions within permission and auditing entries.

Administrators have the ability to give users access to files and folders based on Active Directory attributes. For example; a user named Dana is given access to the file server share because in the user's Active Directory (department attribute) properties, the value contains the value Sales.

 For DAC to function properly, an administrator must enable Windows 8 computers and Windows Server 2012 file servers to support claims and compound authentication.

Using Group Policy for Security

As discussed in Chapter 5, "Managing Group Policy Objects," a very useful and powerful feature of Active Directory is a technology known as a *Group Policy*. Through the use of Group Policy settings, system administrators can assign literally thousands of different settings and options for users, groups, and OUs. Specifically, in relation to security, you can use many different options to control how important features such as password policies, user rights, and account lockout settings can be configured.

The general process for making these settings is to create a *Group Policy object (GPO)* with the settings that you want and then link it to an OU or other Active Directory object.

Table 13.2 lists many Group Policy settings, which are relevant to creating a secure Active Directory environment. Note that this list is not comprehensive—many other options are available through Windows Server 2012's administrative tools.

TABLE 13.2   Group Policy settings used for security purposes

Setting Section	Setting Name	Purpose
Account Policies ➢ Password Policy	Enforce Password History	Specifies how many passwords will be remembered. This option prevents users from reusing the same passwords whenever they're changed.
Account Policies ➢ Password Policy	Minimum Password Length	Prevents users from using short, weak passwords by specifying the minimum number of characters that the password must include.
Account Policies ➢ Account Lockout Policy	Account Lockout Threshold	Specifies how many bad password attempts can be entered before the account gets locked out.
Account Policies ➢ Account Lockout Policy	Account Lockout Duration	Specifies how long an account will remain locked out after too many bad password attempts have been entered. By setting this option to a reasonable value (such as 30 minutes), you can reduce administrative overhead while still maintaining fairly strong security.
Account Policies ➢ Account Lockout Policy	Reset Account Lockout Counter After	Specifies how long the Account Lockout Threshold counter will hold failed logon attempts before resetting to 0.
Local Policies ➢ Security Options	Accounts: Rename Administrator Account	Often, when trying to gain unauthorized access to a computer, individuals attempt to guess the administrator password. One method for increasing security is to rename this account so that no password allows entry using this logon.
Local Policies ➢ Security Options	Domain Controller: Allow Server Operators To Schedule Tasks	This option specifies whether members of the built-in Server Operators group are allowed to schedule tasks on the server.

Setting Section	Setting Name	Purpose
Local Policies ➤ Security Options	Interactive Logon: Do Not Display Last User Name	Increases security by not displaying the name of the last user who logged onto the system.
Local Policies ➤ Security Options	Shutdown: Allow System To Be Shut Down Without Having To Log On	Allows system administrators to perform remote shutdown operations without logging on to the server.

You can use several different methods to configure Group Policy settings using the tools included with Windows Server 2012. Exercise 13.4 walks through the steps required to create a basic group policy for the purpose of enforcing security settings. To complete the steps of this exercise, you must have completed Exercise 13.1.

Applying Security Policies by Using Group Policy

1. Open the Group Policy Management Console tool.

2. Expand Domains, and then click the domain name.

3. In the right pane, right-click the Default Domain Policy and choose Edit.

4. In the Group Policy Management Editor window, expand Computer Configuration ➤ Policies ➤ Windows Settings ➤ Security Settings ➤ Account Policies ➤ Password Policy.

5. In the right pane, double-click the Minimum Password Length setting.

6. In the Security Policy Setting dialog box, make sure the box labeled Define This Policy Setting Option is checked. Increase the Password Must Be At Least value to 8 characters.

7. Click OK to return to the Group Policy Management Editor window.

8. Expand the User Configuration ➢ Policies ➢ Administrative Templates ➢ Control Panel. Double-click Prohibit Access To The Control Panel And PC settings, select Enabled, and then click OK.

9. Close the Group Policy window.

Fine-Grained Password Policies

The Windows 2012 operating systems allow an organization to have different password and account lockout policies for different sets of users in a domain. In versions of Active Directory before 2008, an administrator could set up only one password policy and account lockout policy per domain.

The Default Domain Policy for the domain is where these policy settings were configured. Because domains could have only one password and account lockout policy, organizations that wanted multiple password and account lockout settings had to either create a password filter or deploy multiple domains.

Fine-grained password policies allow you to specify multiple password policies within a single domain. Let's say that you want administrators not to have to change their password as frequently as salespeople. Fine-grained password policies allow you to do just that.

In Exercise 13.5, we will walk through the creation of a custom password policy using the ADSI Edit tool, and then we will link that policy to a group using Active Directory Users and Computers. Before completing this exercise, create a new global group named Passgroup in Active Directory Users and Computers.

EXERCISE 13.5

Fine-Grained Password Policy

1. Open ADSI Edit by clicking the Windows key and choosing ADSI Edit.

2. Right-click ADSI Edit, and then choose Connect To.

3. When the Connection Settings dialog box appears, click OK.

4. In the left-hand window, expand Default Naming Context ➢ DC=yourdomainname,DC=com ➢ CN=System ➢ CN=Password Settings Container.

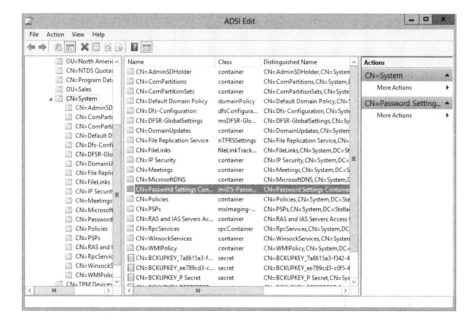

5. Right-click CN=Password Settings Container, and choose New ➢ Object.

6. In the Select A Class box, choose msDS-PasswordSettings and click Next.

7. At the Common Name screen, type **CustomPolicy** and click Next.

8. At the Password Settings Precedence screen, enter **10** as the value. This works as a cost value. The lowest priority takes precedence.

9. At the Password Reversible Encryption Status For Users Accounts screen, set the value to False (recommended by Microsoft).

10. The Password History Length screen shows how many passwords are remembered before a password can be used again. You can set this for up to 1,024 remembered passwords. Set the value to **12**. Click Next.

11. At the Password Complexity screen, set the value to True.

12. The next screen will be the Minimum Password Length screen. Set the value to **8**, and click Next.

13. At the Minimum Password Age screen, you must enter a value for the amount of time you want the password to be used at a minimum. Time is done in the I8 format, thus:

    -600000000 = 1 minute

    -36000000000 = 1 hour

    -864000000000 = 1 day

    So if you want the minimum to be 10 days, you must calculate -864000000000 x 10 (equaling -8640000000000).

    Enter **-8640000000000** (10 zeros) as your value for 10 days and click Next. You must put the - (minus) sign in the front of the value.

14. At the Maximum Password Age screen, set the value as **-51840000000000** (10 zeros). This value equals 60 days. Click Next.

15. At the Lockout Threshold screen, enter **3** and click Next.

16. At the Observation Window screen, enter **-3000000000** (5 minutes) and click Next.

17. At the Lockout Duration screen, enter **-18000000000** (30 minutes) and click Next.

18. Click Finished. If you received any errors, check all your times to be sure the - (minus) sign appears in front of the number.

19. Close ADSI Edit.

20. Open the Active Directory Users and Computers snap-in.

21. On the View menu along the top, make sure Advanced Features is checked.

22. In the left-hand window, expand Active Directory Users and Computers ➢ *yourdomain* ➢ System ➢ Password Settings Container.

23. In the details pane on the right side, right-click CustomPolicy, and choose Properties.

24. Click the Attribute Editor tab.

25. Scroll down and select the msDS-PsoAppliesTo attribute. Click Edit.

26. In the Multi-valued Distinguished Name dialog box, click Add Windows Account.

27. Type in **Passgroup** (this is the group you created before the exercise), and click the Check Name button. Click OK.

28. Click OK twice more and then you are finished. Close the Active Directory Users and Computers snap-in.

Understanding Smart Card Authentication

In the previous section, I discussed password policies and account lockout policies that increase security for Windows Server 2012. However, the standard account logon process is still fairly insecure due to the fact that a malicious attacker needs only a single piece of information—a password—to log on to the network. This problem is compounded by the fact that users or administrators probably would not detect a stolen password until after it had been used by a hacker to break into the system. Smart cards, which are similar in appearance to credit cards, solve both of these problems.

Smart cards store user certificate information in a magnetic strip (barcode) or on a gold chip on a plastic card. As an alternative to the standard username and password logon process, users can insert a smart card into a special smart card reader attached to the computer and enter a unique PIN on the keyboard. This provides the system with a double-verification (two-factor authentication) secure logon (the smart card and the PIN) and reduces the likelihood that a user's authentication method will be stolen without detection.

To deploy a smart card solution in the enterprise, you must have a certificate authority (CA) and a public key infrastructure (PKI) on your intranet. In each domain, you must configure the security permissions of the Smart Card User, Smart Card Logon, and Enrollment Agent certificate templates to allow smart card users to enroll for certificates. You must also set up the CA to issue smart card certificates and Enrollment Agent certificates.

After you've configured your certificate server to meet the requirements for smart card authentication, you can set up a smart card enrollment station and begin issuing smart cards to users. Most organizations that use smart card authentication don't allow standard authentication at all, so Microsoft provides a Group Policy setting that requires the use of smart cards.

Preparing a Smart Card Certificate Enrollment Station

To begin issuing smart cards, you must prepare a smart card certificate enrollment station where you physically transfer the authentication information to smart cards. You need to install a smart card reader on the enrollment station, which in this case doubles as a smart card writer.

TIP

Smart card readers are available from a variety of manufacturers, so you should always make sure that any smart card reader your company purchases is listed on the Windows Server 2012 hardware compatibility list (HCL).

After you've properly installed the smart card reader, you need to install an Enrollment Agent certificate on the enrollment station, which you obtain from your CA.

Configuring Group Policy Settings for Smart Cards

Now that you've seen how to configure a smart card enrollment station and set up smart cards for user logon, you should begin to think about Group Policy settings for enforcing smart card logon. One of the most common mistakes that administrators make when administering a smart card policy is not to require smart card logon at all. This means that users with smart cards can log on with either their smart cards or through the standard username and password procedure, which defeats the point of issuing smart cards in the first place! Exercise 13.6 shows you how to configure Group Policy to require smart card authentication.

EXERCISE 13.6

Configuring Group Policy to Require Smart Card Logon

1. Open the Active Directory Users and Computers tool.

2. Create a new top-level OU called Smart Card Test.

3. Close the Active Directory Users and Computers tool, and open the Group Policy Management Console.

4. Right-click the Smart Card Test OU, and select Create A GPO In This Domain And Link It Here.

5. In the New GPO dialog box, enter Smart Card GPO Test in the Name box and click OK. Right-click the new GPO, and then click the Edit button.

6. In the Group Policy Object Editor window, expand Computer Configuration ➢ Policies ➢ Windows Settings ➢ Security Settings ➢ Local Policies ➢ Security Options.

7. Double-click the Interactive Logon: Require Smart Card policy.

8. Check the box labeled Define This Policy Setting, and then select Enabled and click OK.

9. Close the Group Policy Management Console.

Understanding Security Configuration and Analysis Tools

The power and flexibility of Windows-based operating systems are both benefits and liabilities. On the plus side, the many configuration options available allow users and system administrators to modify and customize settings. On the negative side, however, when system administrators allow all users full functionality, problems can arise. For example, novice users might attempt to delete critical system files or incorrectly uninstall programs to free up disk space.

So how can you prevent these types of problems? One method is to control the types of actions that users can perform. Because you can configure most settings for the Windows Server 2012 interface in the Registry, you could edit the appropriate settings using the RegEdit command. However, this process can become quite tedious. Furthermore, manually modifying the Registry is a dangerous process and one that is bound to cause problems due to human error. To make creating and applying security settings easier, Microsoft has included the Security Configuration and Analysis utility with Windows Server 2012. It has also built this utility's functionality into a command-line utility called secedit.exe.

Using the Security Configuration and Analysis Utility

You can use the *Security Configuration and Analysis utility* together with security template files to create, modify, and apply security settings in the Registry. *Security templates* allow system administrators to define security settings once and then store this information in a file that can be applied to other computers.

These template files offer a user-friendly way to configure common settings for Windows Server 2012 operating systems. For example, instead of searching through the Registry (which is largely undocumented) for specific keys, a system administrator can choose from a list of common options. The template file provides a description of the settings, along with information about the Registry key(s) to which the modifications must be made. Templates can be stored and applied to users and computers. For example, you could create three configurations named Level 1, Level 2, and Level 3. You may use the Level 3 template for high-level managers and engineers and the Level 1 and Level 2 templates for all other users who need only basic functionality.

The overall process for working with the Security Configuration and Analysis utility is as follows:

1. Open or create a security database file.
2. Import an existing template file.
3. Analyze the local computer.
4. Make any setting changes.
5. Save any template changes.
6. Export the new template (optional).

7.   Apply the changes to the local computer (optional).

The Security Configuration and Analysis utility has no default icon. In order to access it, you must manually choose this snap-in from within the MMC.

Understanding the *secedit.exe* Command

All of the functionality of the Security Configuration and Analysis utility has also been built into a command-line utility called secedit.exe. One advantage of using secedit.exe is that you can perform a batch analysis without having to use the graphical tools.

Just like the Security Configuration and Analysis utility, the command-line utility is database driven, meaning that you can use switches to access database and configuration files. The secedit.exe command performs the following high-level functions: analysis, configuration, export function, and validation. These are the same functions carried out by the Security Configuration and Analysis graphical utility (described in the previous section and exercise).

Table 13.3 lists the secedit.exe switches and their functions.

If any errors occur during the security configuration and analysis process, the results will be stored in the log file that is created. Be sure to examine this file for any errors that might be present in your configuration.

TABLE 13.3   secedit.exe switches

Switch	Valid with Switch	Function
/analyze	Independent function	Analyzes system security.
/configure	Independent function	Configures system security by applying a stored template.
/refreshpolicy	Independent function	Reapplies security settings to the GPO.
/export	Independent function	Exports a template from the database to the template file.
/validate	Independent function	Validates the syntax of a security template.
[/DB *filename*]	/analyze, /configure, /export	Required with the /analyze and /configure commands. Optional with others. Specifies the path to the database file.
[/CFG *filename*]	/analyze, /configure, /export	Required if a new database file is specified. Specifies the path to a security template to import into the database.
[/log *logpath*]	/analyze, /configure, /export	Specifies the path to the log file generated during the operation.

Switch	Valid with Switch	Function
[/verbose]	/analyze, /configure, /export	Specifies more detailed progress information.
[/quiet]	/analyze, /configure, /export	Suppresses screen output during the operation.
[/overwrite]	/configure	Optional only if [/CFG *filename*] is used. Completely overwrites the database rather than appending the database.
[/areas *area1 area2*]	/configure, /export	Specifies security areas to be applied to the system. Default is all areas. Options are SECURITYPOLICY, GROUP_MGMT, USER_RIGHTS, REGKEYS, FILESTORE, and SERVICES.
Machine_policy	/refreshpolicy	Refreshes security settings for the local computer.
User_policy	/refreshpolicy	Refreshes security settings for the current local user account.
/enforce	/refreshpolicy	Refreshes security settings even if no changes have been made to the GPO.
/MergedPolicy	/export	Merges local and domain policy in the export file.
Filename	/validate	Indicates the filename of the template to validate.

Implementing an Audit Policy

One of the most important aspects of controlling security in networked environments is ensuring that only authorized users are able to access specific resources. Although system administrators often spend much time managing security permissions, it is almost always possible for a security problem to occur.

Sometimes, the best way to find possible security breaches is actually to record the actions that specific users take. Then, in the case of a security breach (the unauthorized shutdown of a server, for example), system administrators can examine the log to find the cause of the problem.

The Windows Server 2012 operating system and Active Directory offer you the ability to audit a wide range of actions. In the following sections, you'll see how to implement auditing for Active Directory.

Overview of Auditing

The act of *auditing* relates to recording specific actions. From a security standpoint, auditing is used to detect any possible misuse of network resources. Although auditing does not necessarily prevent resources from being misused, it does help determine when security violations have occurred (or were attempted). Furthermore, just the fact that others know that you have implemented auditing may prevent them from attempting to circumvent security.

You need to complete several steps in order to implement auditing using Windows Server 2012:

1. Configure the size and storage settings for the audit logs.

2. Enable categories of events to audit.

3. Specify which objects and actions should be recorded in the audit log.

Note that there are trade-offs to implementing auditing. First and foremost, recording auditing information can consume system resources. This can decrease overall system performance and use up valuable disk space. Second, auditing many events can make the audit log impractical to view. If too much detail is provided, system administrators are unlikely to scrutinize all of the recorded events. For these reasons, you should always be sure to find a balance between the level of auditing details provided and the performance-management implications of these settings.

Implementing Auditing

Auditing is not an all-or-none type of process. As is the case with security in general, system administrators must choose specifically which objects and actions they want to audit.

The main categories for auditing include the following:

- Audit account logon events
- Audit account management
- Audit directory service access
- Audit logon events
- Audit object access
- Audit policy change
- Audit privilege use
- Audit process tracking
- Audit system events

In this list of categories, four of the categories are related to Active Directory. Let's discuss these auditing categories in a bit more detail.

Audit Account Logon Events You enable this auditing event if you want to audit when a user authenticates with a domain controller and logs onto the domain. This event is logged in the security log on the domain controller.

Audit Account Management   This auditing event is used when you want to watch what changes are being made to Active Directory accounts. For example, when another administrator creates or deletes a user account, it would be an audited event.

Audit Directory Service Access   This auditing event occurs whenever a user or administrator accesses Active Directory objects. Let's say an administrator opens Active Directory and clicks a user account; even if nothing is changed on that account, an event is logged.

Audit Logon Events   Account logon events are created for domain account activity. For example, you have a user who logs on to a server so that they can access files; the act of logging onto the server creates this audit event.

Audit Object Access   Audit object access allows you to audit objects within your network such as folders, files, and printers. If you suspect someone is trying to hack into an object (for example, the finance folder), this is the type of auditing that you would use. You still would need to enable auditing on the actual object (for example, the finance folder).

Audit Policy Change   Audit policy change allows you to audit changes to user rights assignment policies, audit policies, or trust policies. This auditing allows you to see if anyone changes any of the other audit policies.

Audit Privilege Use   Setting the audit privilege use allows an administrator to audit each instance of a user exercising a user right. For example, if a user changes the system time on a machine, this is a user right. Log on locally is another common user right.

In order to audit access to objects stored within Active Directory, you must enable the Audit Directory Service Access option. Then you must specify which objects and actions should be tracked.

Exercise 13.7 walks through the steps you must take to implement auditing of Active Directory objects on domain controllers. In order to complete the steps in this exercise, you must first have completed Exercise 13.1.

EXERCISE 13.7

Enabling Auditing of Active Directory Objects

1. Open the Local Security Policy tool (located in the Administrative Tools program group).

2. Expand Local Policies ➢ Audit Policy.

3. Double-click the setting for Audit Directory Service Access.

4. In the Audit Directory Service Access Properties dialog box, place check marks next to Success and Failure. Click OK to save the settings.

5. Close the Local Security Policy tool.

Viewing Auditing Information

One of the most important aspects of auditing is regularly monitoring the audit logs. If this step is ignored, as it often is in poorly managed environments, the act of auditing is useless. Fortunately, Windows Server 2012 includes the *Event Viewer* tool, which allows system administrators to view audited events quickly and easily. Using the filtering capabilities of Event Viewer, they can find specific events of interest.

Exercise 13.8 walks you through the steps that you must take to generate some auditing events and to examine the data collected for these actions. In this exercise, you will perform some actions that will be audited, and then you will view the information recorded within the audit logs. In order to complete this exercise, you must first have completed the steps in Exercise 13.1 and Exercise 13.7.

EXERCISE 13.8

Generating and Viewing Audit Logs

1. Open the Active Directory Users and Computers tool.

2. Within the Engineering OU, right-click the Bob Engineer user account and select Properties.

3. On the Bob Properties dialog box, add the middle initial **A** for this user account, and specify **Software Developer** in the Description box. Click OK to save the changes.

4. Within the Engineering OU, right-click the Robert Admin user account, and select Properties.

5. On the Robert Properties dialog box, add the description **Engineering IT Admin** and click OK.

6. Close the Active Directory Users and Computers tool.

7. Open the Event Viewer tool from the Administrative Tools program group. Select the Security item under Windows Logs. You will see a list of audited events categorized under Directory Service Access. Note that you can obtain more details about a specific item by double-clicking it.

8. When you have finished viewing the security log, close the Event Viewer tool.

Using the *Auditpol.exe* Command

There may be a time when you need to look at your actual auditing policies set on a user or a system. This is where an administrator can use the Auditpol.exe command. Auditpol allows administrators the ability to not only view an audit policy but Auditpol also allows an administrator to set, configure, modify, restore, and even remove an audit policy. Auditpol is a command line utility and there are multiple switches that can be used with

Auditpol. The following is the syntax used with Auditpol along with a table (table 13.4) showing some of the switches.

```
Auditpol command [<sub-command><options>]
```
Example:

```
Auditpol /get /user:wpanek /category:"Detailed Tracking" /r
```

TABLE 13.4 Auditpol Commands

Command	Description
/backup	Allows an administrator to save the audit policy to a file.
/clear	Allows an administrator to clear an audit policy.
/get	Gives administrators the ability to view the current audit policy.
/list	Allows you to view selectable policy elements.
/remove	Removes all per-user audit policy settings and disables all system audit policy settings.
/restore	Allows an administrator to restore an audit policy from a file that was previously created by using auditpol /backup.
/set	Gives an administrator the ability to set an audit policy.
/?	Displays help.

What's New in Windows Server 2012 Auditing

Auditing in Windows Server 2012 and Windows 8 has been enhanced in many ways. Microsoft has increased the level of details in the security auditing logs. Microsoft has also simplified the deployment and management of auditing policies. The following list includes some of the major enhancements:

Global Object Access Auditing Administrators using Windows Server 2012 and Windows 8 now have the ability to define computer-wide system access control lists (SACLs). Administrators can define SACLs for either the file system or the Registry. After the specified SACL is defined, the SACL is then applied automatically to every single object of that type. This can be very helpful to administrators for verifying that all critical files, folders, and Registry settings on a computer are protected. This is also helpful for identifying when an issue occurs with a system resource.

"Reason For Access" Reporting When an administrator is performing auditing in Windows Server 2012 and Windows 8, they can now see the reason why an operation was successful or unsuccessful. Previously, they lacked the ability to see the reason why an operation succeeded or failed.

Advanced Audit Policy Settings   In Windows Server 2012, there are 53 new Advanced Audit Policy settings that can be used in place of the 9 basic auditing settings. These advanced audit settings also help eliminate the unnecessary auditing activities that can make audit logs difficult to manage and decipher.

Expression-based Audit Policies   Administrators have the ability, due to Dynamic Access Control, to create targeted audit policies by using expressions based on user, computer, and resource claims. For example, an administrator has the ability to create an audit policy that tracks all Read and Write operations for files that are considered high-business impact. Expression-based audit policies can be directly created on a file or folder or created through the use of a Group Policy.

Removable Storage Device Auditing   Administrators have the ability to monitor attempts to use a removable storage device on your network. If an administrator decides to implement this policy, an audit event is created every time one of your users attempts to copy, move, or save a network resource onto a removable storage device.

Summary

In this chapter, we talked about planning for and implementing security with Active Directory. You cannot overlook security; it's always important to consider how security may affect your deployment or how the lack of it will ultimately affect your system if it is hacked.

We also looked at the differences between security and distribution groups. Distribution groups are used for only one thing: email distribution lists. These groups are used with email applications (such as Microsoft Exchange Server 2013) to send email to the members of the group you create. They do not allow you to assign permissions, and you cannot use them to filter Group Policy settings. In the Windows Server 2012 operating system, security groups are used to manage user account and computer account access to shared resources and to filter Group Policy settings.

We also explained other important items that pertain to security, such as which default groups are available after a base install of the operating system and how to secure the most vulnerable accounts.

We then examined how permissions are managed. You can change permissions with Group Policy or simply by altering them right on the object. We also covered how delegation of control can be used to distribute administrative responsibilities. We wrapped up this chapter by discussing auditing—why it's important and how to get it done.

Thoroughly understanding each of these topics is important when you're implementing Active Directory in a business environment (as well as when you're preparing for the exam). In the next chapter, we focus on Active Directory reliability and how to optimize it.

Exam Essentials

Understand the purpose of security principals. Security principals are Active Directory objects that can be assigned permissions. Understanding how they work is vital to creating a secure Active Directory environment. Security principals include users, groups, and computers.

Understand group types and group scope. The two major types of groups are security and distribution groups, and they have different purposes. Groups can be local, global, or universal. Domain local groups are used to assign permissions to local resources, such as files and printers. The scope of global groups is limited to a single domain. Universal groups can contain users from any domains within an Active Directory forest.

Understand the purpose and permissions of built-in groups. The Active Directory environment includes several built-in local and global groups that are designed to simplify common system administration tasks. For instance, members of the Administrators group are given full permissions to perform any functions within the Active Directory domain and on the local computer.

Understand how to use Group Policy to manage password and other security-related policies. Through the use of Group Policy settings, you can configure password and account-related options. You can also specify to which users, groups, and OUs many of the settings apply.

Understand how to configure smart card authentication. Smart card authentication requires a CA for issuing smart card certificates. To enroll a smart card certificate, you must first prepare a smart card enrollment station and then write certificate information to the smart cards using a smart card reader. Finally, to make smart cards useful, you should enable the Interactive Logon: Require Smart Card policy in the Group Policy Object Editor.

Understand how to use the Delegation of Control Wizard to allow distributed administration. Delegation is the process by which a higher-level security administrator assigns permissions to other users. The Delegation of Control Wizard walks you through the steps of selecting the object(s) for which you want to perform delegation, what permissions you want to allow, and which users will have those permissions.

Learn how the Security Configuration and Analysis utility can simplify the implementation of security policies. You can use the Security Configuration and Analysis utility together with security template files to create, modify, and apply security settings in the Registry. Security templates allow system administrators to define security settings once and then store this information in a file that can be applied to other computers.

Understand the purpose and function of auditing. Auditing helps determine the cause of security violations and helps troubleshoot permissions-related problems.

Review Questions

1. You want to create multiple password policies for the users in your domain. What utility do you use to complete this task?

   A. MMC

   B. Schema editor

   C. ADSI Edit

   D. Secedit.exe

2. You are the system administrator for a medium-sized Active Directory domain. Currently, the environment supports many different domain controllers, some of which are running Windows 2003 and Server 2012. When you are running domain controllers in this type of environment, which of the following types of groups can you not use? (Choose all that apply.)

   A. Universal security groups.

   B. Global groups.

   C. Domain local groups.

   D. None. You can use all group types.

3. Isabel is a system administrator for an Active Directory environment that is running in Native mode. Recently, several managers have reported suspicions about user activities and have asked her to increase security in the environment. Specifically, the requirements are as follows:

   - The accessing of certain sensitive files must be logged.

   - Modifications to certain sensitive files must be logged.

   - System administrators must be able to provide information about which users accessed sensitive files and when they were accessed.

   - All logon attempts for specific shared machines must be recorded.

   Which of the following steps should Isabel take to meet these requirements? (Choose all that apply.)

   A. Enable auditing with the Computer Management tool.

   B. Enable auditing with the Active Directory Users and Computers tool.

   C. Enable auditing with the Active Directory Domains and Trusts tool.

   D. Enable auditing with the Event Viewer tool.

   E. View the audit log using the Event Viewer tool.

   F. View auditing information using the Computer Management tool.

   G. Enable failure and success auditing settings for specific files stored on NTFS volumes.

   H. Enable failure and success auditing settings for logon events on specific computer accounts.

4. A system administrator wants to allow another user the ability to change user account information for all users within a specific OU. Which of the following tools would allow them to do this most easily?

   A. Domain Security Policy

   B. Domain Controller Security Policy

   C. Computer Management

   D. Delegation of Control Wizard

5. Will, an IT manager, has full permissions over several OUs within a small Active Directory domain. Recently, Will has hired a junior system administrator named Crystal to take over some of the responsibilities of administering the objects within these OUs. Will gives Crystal access to modify user accounts within two OUs. This process is known as what?

   A. Inheritance

   B. Transfer of control

   C. Delegation

   D. Transfer of ownership

6. You are the network administrator for your organization. A new company policy has been released wherein if a user enters their password incorrectly three times within 5 minutes, they are locked out for 30 minutes. What three actions do you need to set to comply with this policy? (Choose all that apply.)

   A. Set Account Lockout Duration to 5 minutes.

   B. Set Account Lockout Duration to 30 minutes.

   C. Set the Account Lockout Threshold setting to 3 invalid logon attempts.

   D. Set the Account Lockout Threshold setting to 30 minutes.

   E. Set the Reset Account Lockout Counter setting to 5 minutes.

   F. Set the Reset Account Lockout Counter setting to 3 times.

7. You have almost finished helping with the migration of a Windows Server 2003 network to a Windows Server 2012 network. The current domain functional level is Windows 2003 mode. There are three locations, and the engineers are creating a single domain for now. Many rumors are surfacing that a merger with one of your competitors is going to happen, and the designers are considering adding a new domain to bring those users into the network. One of your jobs is to help come up with the administrative plans for the designers to manage the users. To outline your task, you are going to build a best-practices approach to giving permissions to resources on your mixed network. Which of the following approaches best suits your situation?

   A. Apply permissions to the domain local group, and add the accounts to this group.

   B. Apply permissions to the domain local groups, add users to global groups, and add the global groups to the domain local groups.

C. Apply permissions to global groups, add users to universal groups, and place these universal groups into global groups.

D. Apply permissions to domain local groups, add the users to global groups, add the global groups to universal groups, and add the universal groups to the domain local groups.

8. Which of the following folders in the Active Directory Users and Computers tool is used when users from outside the forest are granted access to resources within a domain?

   A. Users

   B. Computers

   C. Domain Controllers

   D. Foreign Security Principals

9. You create a GPO and link it to the Sales OU. You want to monitor users in the Sales OU who connect to the file server. What type of auditing do you enable?

   A. Audit Object Access

   B. Audit Logon Events

   C. Audit System Events

   D. Audit Process Tracking

10. Alexis is a system administrator for an Active Directory environment that contains four domains. Recently, several managers have reported suspicions about user activities and have asked her to increase security in the environment. Specifically, the requirements are as follows:

   ▪ Audit changes to User objects that are contained within a specific OU.

   ▪ Allow a special user account called Audit to view and modify all security-related information about objects in that OU.

   Which of the following steps should Alexis take to meet these requirements? (Choose all that apply.)

   A. Convert all volumes on which Active Directory information resides to NTFS.

   B. Enable auditing with the Active Directory Users and Computers tool.

   C. Create a new Active Directory domain, and create restrictive permissions for the suspected users within this domain.

   D. Reconfigure trust settings using the Active Directory Domains and Trusts tool.

   E. Specify auditing options for the OU using the Active Directory Users and Computers tool.

   F. Use the Delegation of Control Wizard to grant appropriate permissions to view and modify objects within the OU to the Audit user account.

Managing File and Print Services

THE FOLLOWING 70-410 EXAM OBJECTIVES ARE COVERED IN THIS CHAPTER:

✓ **Configure file and share access**

 ▪ This objective may include, but is not limited to: Create and configure shares; configure share permissions; configure offline files; configure NTFS permissions; configure access-based enumeration (ABE); configure Volume Shadow Copy Service (VSS); configure NTFS quotas.

✓ **Configure print and document services**

 ▪ This objective may include, but is not limited to: Configure the Easy Print print driver; configure Enterprise Print Management; configure drivers; configure printer pooling; configure print priorities; configure printer permissions.

THE FOLLOWING 70-411 EXAM OBJECTIVES ARE COVERED IN THIS CHAPTER:

✓ **Configure Distributed File System (DFS)**

 ▪ This objective may include, but is not limited to: Install and configure DFS namespaces; configure DFS Replication Targets; configure Replication Scheduling; configure Remote Differential Compression settings; configure staging; configure fault tolerance.

✓ **Configure File Server Resource Manager (FSRM)**

 ▪ This objective may include but is not limited to: Install the FSRM role; configure quotas; configure file screens; configure reports.

✓ **Configure file and disk encryption**

> This objective may include, but is not limited to:
> Configure BitLocker encryption; configure the
> Network Unlock feature; configure BitLocker
> policies; configure the EFS recovery agent; manage
> EFS and BitLocker certificates including backup
> and restore.

THE FOLLOWING 70-412 EXAM OBJECTIVES ARE COVERED IN THIS CHAPTER:

✓ **Configure advanced file services**

> ▪ This objective may include but is not limited to:
> Configure NFS data store; configure BranchCache;
> configure File Classification Infrastructure (FCI)
> using File Server Resource Manager (FSRM);
> configure file access auditing.

✓ **Configure DirectAccess**

> ▪ This objective may include, but is not limited to:
> Implement server requirements; implement client
> configuration; configure DNS for Direct Access;
> configure certificates for Direct Access.

Now that I have covered remote access and security, I'll explain how to set up your servers so your network users have something to access. Before you can set up a server, you have to determine the purpose of the server. Is it going to be a print server, a file storage server, a remote access server, or a domain controller?

After you have decided how the machine is going to help your network, you must implement your decision. In this chapter, I'll show you how to set up a print server and a file server. In addition, I will discuss how to set up permissions and security for these servers and how you can limit the amount of space your users can have on a server.

 Microsoft Windows Server 2012 is used for all the server types in this chapter. Although other operating systems can be used, this chapter refers only to Windows Server 2012.

Understanding File Servers

Before you configure a file server, you must understand what a file server actually does. *File servers* are machines on your network that store data files to share among network clients. The same machine can be a file server and another type of server. For example, a machine can both host network files and run Exchange Server 2010. Such a machine would have both file server and application server functions. (*Application servers* are machines that host applications used by network clients.)

 Real World Scenario

Multiple Server Types on One Machine

In today's world, most IT departments have to worry about budgets. The problem is that often the IT department has the smallest budget in a company. You are typically stuck between a rock and a hard place because if your network is running well, people (including executives) forget about you. This makes it hard when you ask for anything that may have an impact on your budget.

Because of the lack of money, many times you must leverage one machine to perform many server tasks. I have seen IT managers in many companies where the IT department had to have the same machine running both as an application server and as a file server.

> You must consider many factors before allowing a machine to run multiple server types. How many processors do you have? What are the processor speeds? How much RAM does the machine have? What is the hard drive speed? What type of applications will be hosted on the machine?
>
> After you have gathered all of your information about the machine, then you can decide whether the machine can host multiple server types. Keep this one fact in mind, however—because of the requirements and demands on the computer system, it's always a good idea to host SQL Server on a dedicated machine.

I have been doing consulting for many years, and one thing I stress to all of my clients is to perform regular backups. After all, most organizations would not be able to recover after losing all of their data. Usually, companies back up only their servers, and this is why home folders are so important. *Home folders* are one of the most common file types on a file server; they are folders set up on the server for users to store information. Users have a location on the server to store their important data, and therefore that data will be backed up when the company does its regular backups.

Home folders are just one example of how to use a file server. I will be discussing other examples throughout this chapter.

Configuring File Servers

Now that you have an understanding of what a file server does, it's time to discuss how to configure these servers. Setting up a file server properly encompasses many steps. As always, one major concern is security. In the following sections, I will first describe how to share and publish online and offline files and folders. Then I will discuss the two types of security—shared permissions and NTFS security—that an administrator can set when sharing files or folders.

Sharing Folders

A file server is for sharing and storing data. To use one, you need to know how to set up a share, or a shared folder, on your server. A *shared folder* is exactly what it says; it's a folder that is shared on your network so that users can access the data within that folder. As an administrator, you have the ability to determine which users can access which files within a shared folder.

One of the main goals of Active Directory is to make resources easy to find. Active Directory also makes it easy to determine which files are available to users. That said, I will explain how Active Directory manages to publish shared folders.

Making Active Directory Objects Available to Users

With Active Directory, a system administrator can control which objects users can see. The act of making an Active Directory object available is known as *publishing*. The two main publishable objects are Printer objects and Shared Folder objects.

The general process for creating server shares and shared printers has remained unchanged from previous versions of Windows. You create the various objects (printers or file system folders) and then enable them for sharing.

To make these resources available via Active Directory, however, there's an additional step: You must publish the resources. Once an object has been published in Active Directory, clients will be able to find it.

When you publish objects in Active Directory, you should know the server name and share name of the resource. This information, however, doesn't matter to your users. A system administrator can change the resource to which an object points without having to reconfigure or even notify clients. For example, if you move a share from one server to another, all you need to do is update the Shared Folder's object's properties to point to the new location. Active Directory clients still refer to the resource with the same path and name as they used before.

Exercise 14.1 will walk you through the steps for sharing and publishing a folder for use on your network.

Creating and Publishing a Shared Network Folder

1. Create a new folder in the root directory of your C: partition, and name it **Test Share**.

2. Right-click the Test Share folder, and choose Share With ➢ Specific People.

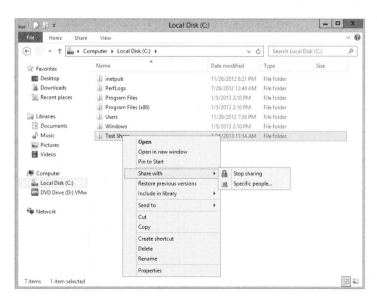

3. In the File Sharing dialog box, enter the names of users with whom you want to share this folder. In the upper box, enter **Everyone**, and then click Add. Note that Everyone appears in the lower box. Click in the Permission Level column next to Everyone, and choose Read/Write from the drop-down menu. Then click Share.

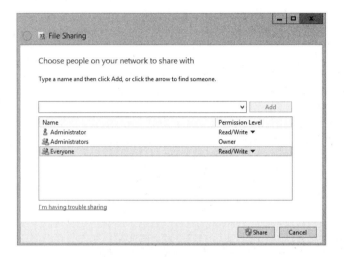

4. You see a message that your folder has been shared. Click Done.

5. Open the Active Directory Users and Computers tool. Expand the current domain, and right-click RD OU. Select New ➢ Shared Folder.

6. In the New Object – Shared Folder dialog box, type `Shared Folder Test` for the name of the folder. Then type the UNC path to the share (for example, `\\serverA\Test Share`). Click OK to create the share.

One of the main benefits of having all your resource information in Active Directory is that you can easily find the information you're seeking using the Find dialog box. When setting up objects in Active Directory, I recommend that you always enter as much information as possible for the objects you're creating. The extra effort will pay off when your users start doing searches for these objects. The more information you enter, the more that users can search to find the appropriate resource they need.

Configuring Offline Folders

If you have been in this industry long enough, you have seen a major change in end user computers. Years ago, only a few select users had laptops. They were big and bulky, and they weighed almost as much as today's desktop computers.

The pendulum has swung in the opposite direction. It probably seems like every one of your end users now has a laptop. As an IT administrator, this gives you a whole new set of challenges and problems to address.

One challenge that you have to address is how users can work on files while outside of the office. If you have a user who wants to work at home, how do you give them the files they need to get their work done?

The answer is *offline folders*. These folders contain data that can be worked on by users while outside the office. An IT administrator can set up offline folders through the use of *Group Policy objects (GPOs)*.

When you decide to make folders available for offline use, these folders need to synchronize with the laptops so that all of the data matches between both systems. As an administrator, one decision that you will need to make is when the offline folders will be synchronized. There are three synchronization options that you can set in the GPO (see Figure 14.1).

You can set up any combination of these options:

FIGURE 14.1   Synchronization options in a GPO

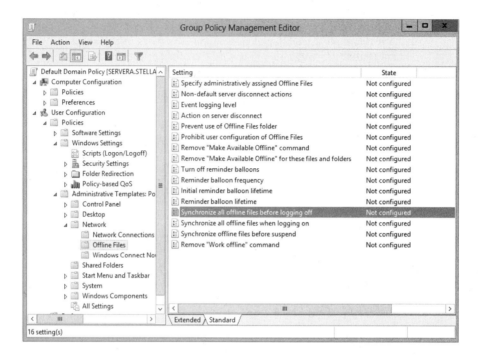

- When you select Synchronize All Offline Files Before Logging Off, offline folders are synchronized when the user logs off the network.

- When you select Synchronize All Offline Files When Logging On, offline folders are synchronized when the user logs on to the network.

- When you select Synchronize Offline Files Before Suspend, offline folders are synchronized before the user does a system suspend.

In Exercise 14.2, I will show you the steps necessary to configure offline folder options by using a GPO. This exercise uses the Group Policy Management Console (GPMC). If your GPMC is not installed, use the Server Manager MMC (under Features) to install it.

EXERCISE 14.2

Configuring Offline Folder Options

1. Open the Group Policy Management Console.

2. In the left pane, expand your forest and then your domain. Under your domain name, there should be a default domain policy.

3. Right-click the default domain policy, and choose Edit.

4. In the User Configuration section, expand Policies ➢ Administrative Templates ➢ Network and then click Offline Files.

5. Right-click Synchronize All Offline Files Before Logging Off, and choose Edit. The GPO setting dialog box appears. Choose the Enabled option, and click OK.

6. Right-click Synchronize All Offline Files When Logging On, and choose Edit. The GPO setting dialog box appears. Choose the Enabled option, and click OK.

7. Right-click Synchronize Offline Files Before Suspend, and choose Edit. The GPO setting dialog box appears. Choose the Enabled option. In the Action drop-down box, make sure Quick is selected. Click OK.

8. Close the GPMC.

Now that you have set up a GPO for synchronization, it's time to share a folder for offline usage. In Exercise 14.3, you will set up a folder for offline access. You must complete Exercise 14.1 before doing this exercise.

EXERCISE 14.3

Configuring a Shared Network Folder for Offline Access

1. Right-click the Test Share folder you created in Exercise 14.1, and choose Properties.

2. Click the Sharing tab, and then click the Advanced Sharing button.

3. When the Advanced Sharing dialog box appears, click the Caching button.

4. When the Offline Settings dialog box appears, choose the All Files And Programs That Users Open From The Shares Will Be Automatically Available Offline option. Click OK.

5. Click OK twice more to close the Properties dialog box.

Volume Shadow Copy Services (VSS)

Windows includes a feature that allows you to create a point in time image of one or more volumes. The *Volume Shadow Copy Service (VSS)* is the feature within Windows that allows an administrator take an image (shadow copy) of one or more volumes. Shadow copies have the ability to provide both file system and application.

Understanding Permissions

You have gone through the steps necessary to set up a shared folder, publish it to Active Directory, and set it up for offline access. Now you will see how you can protect these files and folders by using permissions.

You can secure folders using permissions in two ways, and you can secure files in one way. You can set up permissions and security through NTFS or through sharing.

Understanding NTFS

NTFS is an option that you have when you are formatting a hard drive. You can format a hard drive for a Microsoft operating system in three ways:

- File Allocation Table (FAT) is supported on older operating systems only (Server 2003, Server 2000, XP, and so on).
- FAT32 is supported on Windows Server 2012.
- NTFS is supported on Windows Server 2012.

NTFS has many advantages over FAT and FAT32. They include the following:

Compression   Compression helps compact files or folders to allow for more efficient use of hard drive space. For example, a file that usually takes up 20 MB of space might use only 13 MB after compression. To enable compression, just open the Advanced Attributes dialog box for a folder and check the Compress Contents To Save Disk Space box (see Figure 14.2).

FIGURE 14.2   Setting up compression on a folder

Quotas   *Quotas* allow you to limit how much hard drive space users can have on a server. Quotas are discussed in greater detail later in the section "Configuring Disk Quotas."

Encryption   *Encrypting File System (EFS)* allows a user or administrator to secure files or folders by using encryption. Encryption employs the user's security identification (SID) number to secure the file or folder. To implement encryption, open the Advanced Attributes dialog box for a folder, and check the Encrypt Contents To Secure Data box (see Figure 14.3).

If files are encrypted using EFS and an administrator has to unencrypt the files, there are two ways to do this. First, you can log in using the user's account (the account that encrypted the files) and unencrypt the files. Second, you can become a recovery agent and manually unencrypt the files.

FIGURE 14.3 Setting up encryption on a folder

 If you use EFS, it's best not to delete users immediately when they leave a company. Administrators have the ability to recover encrypted files, but it is much easier to gain access to the user's encrypted files by logging in as the user who left the company and unchecking the encryption box.

Security One of the biggest advantages of NTFS is security. As stated in previous chapters, security is one of the most important aspects of an IT administrator's job. An advantage of NTFS security is that the security can be placed on individual files and folders. It does not matter whether you are local to the share (in front of the machine where the data is stored) or remote to the share (coming across the network to access the data); the security is always in place with NTFS.

The default security permission is Users = Read on new folders or shares.

NTFS security is *additive*. In other words, if you are a member of three groups (Marketing, Sales, and R&D) and these three groups have different security settings, you get the highest level of permissions. For example, let's say you have a user by the name of wpanek who belongs to all three groups (Marketing, Sales, and R&D). Figure 14.4 shows this user's permissions. The Marketing group has Read and Execute permissions to the Stellacon Documents folder. The Sales group has Read and Write, and the R&D group has Full Control. Since wpanek is a member of all three groups, wpanek would get Full Control (the highest level).

FIGURE 14.4 Security settings on the Stellacon Documents folder

Stellacon Documents

Marketing	Sales	R&D
RX	RW	FC

The only time that this does not apply is with the Deny permission. Deny overrides any other group setting. Taking the same example, if Sales has Deny permission for the Stellacon Documents folder, the user wpanek would be denied access to that folder. The only way around this Deny is if you added wpanek directly to the folder and gave him individual permissions (see Figure 14.5). Individual permissions override a group Deny. In this example, the individual right of wpanek would override the Sales group's Deny. The user's security permission for the Stellacon Documents folder would be Full Control.

FIGURE 14.5 Security settings with individual settings

Stellacon Documents

Marketing	Sales	R&D	wpanek
RX	Deny	FC	FC

WARNING   Give users only the permissions necessary to do their jobs. Do not give them higher levels than necessary.

Understanding Shared Permissions

When you set up a folder to be shared, you have the ability to assign that folder's permissions. *Shared permissions* can be placed only on the folder and not on individual files. Files have the ability to inherit their permissions from the parent folder.

Shared folder permissions are in effect only when users are remote to the shared data. In other words, if computer A shares a folder called Downloads and assigns that folder shared permissions, those permissions would apply only if you connected to that share from a machine other than computer A. If you were sitting in front of computer A, the shared permissions would not apply.

Like NTFS permissions (discussed in the previous section), shared permissions are additive, so users receive the highest level of permissions granted by the groups of which they are members.

Also as with NTFS permissions, the Deny permission (see Figure 14.6) overrides any group permission, and an individual permission overrides a group Deny.

FIGURE 14.6   Setting up permissions on a shared folder

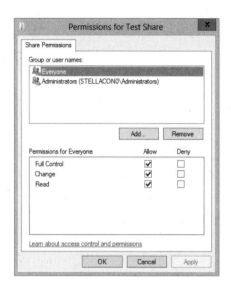

The default shared permission is Administrators = Full Control. The shared permissions going from lowest to highest are Read, Change, Full Control, and Deny. Table 14.1 compares the two different types of permissions and security.

TABLE 14.1   NTFS security vs. shared permissions

Description	NTFS	Shared
Folder-level security.	Yes	Yes
File-level security.	Yes	No
In effect when local to the data.	Yes	No
In effect when remote to the data.	Yes	Yes
Permissions are additive.	Yes	Yes
Group Deny overrides all other group settings.	Yes	Yes
Individual settings override group settings.	Yes	Yes

How NTFS Security and Shared Permissions Work Together

When you set up a shared folder, you need to set up shared permissions on that folder. If you're using NTFS, you will also need to set up NTFS security on the folder. Since both shared permissions and NTFS security are in effect when the user is remote, what happens when the two conflict?

There are two basic rules of thumb:

- The local permission is the NTFS permission.

- The remote permission is the more restrictive set of permissions between NTFS and shared.

This is easy to do as long as you do it in steps. Let's look at Figure 14.7 and walk through the process of figuring out what wpanek has for rights.

FIGURE 14.7 NTFS security and shared permissions example

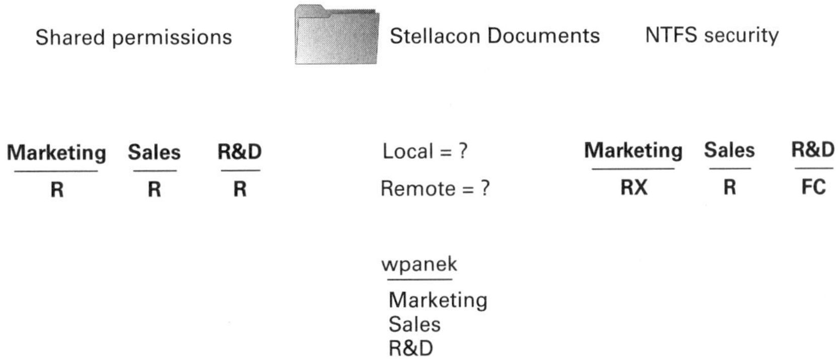

Shared permissions				Stellacon Documents	NTFS security		
Marketing	**Sales**	**R&D**		Local = ?	**Marketing**	**Sales**	**R&D**
R	R	R		Remote = ?	RX	R	FC

wpanek

Marketing
Sales
R&D

As you can see, wpanek belongs to three groups (Marketing, Sales, and R&D), and all three groups have settings for the Stellacon Documents folder. In the figure, you will notice that there are two questions: Remote = ? and Local = ? That's what you need to figure out—what are wpanek's effective permissions when he is sitting at the computer that shares the folder, and what are his effective permissions when he connects to the folder from another computer (remotely)? To figure this out, follow these steps:

1. Add up the permissions on each side separately.

   Remember, permissions and security are *additive*. You get the highest permission. So if you look at each side, the highest shared permission is the Read permission. The NTFS security side should add up to equal Full Control. Thus now you have Read permission on shared and Full Control on NTFS.

2. Determine the local permissions.

   Shared permissions do not apply when you are local to the data. Only NTFS would apply. Thus the local permission would be Full Control.

3. Determine the remote permissions.

Remember, the remote permission is the most restrictive set of permissions between NTFS and shared. Since Read is more restrictive than Full Control, the remote permission would be Read.

Let's try another. Look at Figure 14.8, and see whether you can come up with wpanek's local and remote permissions.

FIGURE 14.8 NTFS security and shared permissions

Shared permissions				Stellacon Documents	NTFS security		

Marketing	Sales	R&D		Local = ?	Marketing	Sales	R&D
R	R	FC		Remote = ?	R	R	R

wpanek

Marketing
Sales
R&D

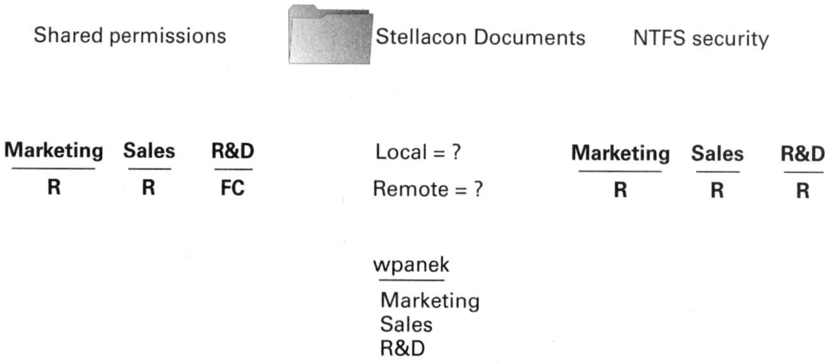

Your answer should match the following:

Local = Read

Remote = Read

Remember, first you add up each side to get the highest level of rights. NTFS would be Read, and shared would be Full Control. The local permission is always just NTFS (shared does not apply to local permissions), and remote permission is whichever permission (NTFS or shared) is the most restrictive (which would be Read on the NTFS side).

Exercise 14.4 walks you through the process of setting both NTFS and shared permissions. You must complete Exercise 14.1 before doing this exercise.

EXERCISE 14.4

Configuring Shared and NTFS Settings

1. Right-click the Test Share folder you created in Exercise 14.1, and choose Properties.

2. Click the Sharing tab, and then click the Advanced Sharing button. (You will set the shared permissions first.)

3. Click the Permissions button. Click the Add button. When the Select User page appears, choose a group from Active Directory. (I used the Sales group.) Once you find your group, click OK.

4. The Permissions dialog box appears. With your group highlighted, click the Allow check box next to Full Control and click OK. (All of the other Allow check boxes will automatically become checked.)

5. On the Advanced Sharing page, click OK. Now click the Security tab. (This allows you to set the NTFS security settings.)

6. Click the Edit button. That takes you to the Permissions page. Now click the Add button. When the Select User page appears, choose a group from Active Directory. (I used the Sales group.) Once you find your group, choose OK.

7. The Permissions dialog box appears. With your group highlighted, click the Allow check box next to Modify, and click OK. (All of the check boxes below Modify will automatically become checked.)

8. Click Close.

Share and Storage Management Console

Microsoft gives you the ability to manage storage area networks (SANs) and shared folders using the Share and Storage Management console. Using a Shared Folder Wizard in the Share and Storage Management console, administrators have the ability to share the contents of folders and volumes on their servers. This Shared Folder Wizard walks you through the process to share a folder or volume and assign all appropriate properties to it. As an administrator, you will have the ability to perform the following tasks:

- Specify which folder or volume to share or create a new folder to share.
- Specify which network sharing protocol will be used to access the shared resource.
- Change the local NTFS permissions for the folder or volume you will be sharing.
- Specify which share access permissions, along with user limits and offline access to files, are assigned to the shared resource.
- Publish any or all shared resources to the Distributed File System (DFS).
- If Services for Network File System (NFS) has been installed, specify which NFS-based access permissions are assigned to the shared resource. The NFS Protocol allows you to transfer files between computers running Windows Server 2012 and non-Windows operating systems such as UNIX. Windows Server 2012 gives you the ability to set up a NFS Data Store by using the NFS MMC snap-in.
- Apply storage quotas to the new shared resource, and create file screens to limit the type of files that can be stored in it, if File Server Resource Manager (FSRM) is installed on the server.

Using the Share and Storage Management console allows an administrator to configure storage on disks that are available on the server. The Shared and Storage Management tool also allows an administrator to configure the storage subsystems that support Virtual Disk Service (VDS).

The Provision Storage Wizard walks administrators through the steps needed for creating a volume on an existing disk or on a storage subsystem attached to your server. If the volume is going to be created on a storage subsystem, the wizard will also walk administrators through the process of creating a logical unit number (LUN) to host that volume. An administrator also has the option of creating only the LUN and using Disk Management to create the volume.

The Share and Storage Management console also allows you to monitor and manage the volumes that you have created as well as any other volumes that are available on your server. Using Share and Storage Management you can do the following:

- Extend the size of a volume.

- Format a volume.

- Delete a volume.

- Change volume properties like compression, security, offline availability, and indexing.

- Access disk tools for error checking, defragmentation, and backup.

Understanding File Server Resource Manager (FSRM)

When an administrator needs to control and manage the amount and type of data stored on their servers, Microsoft has created tools to help us do just that. The File Server Resource Manager (FSRM) is a suite of tools that allows an administrator to place quotas on folders or volumes, filter file types, and create detailed storage reports. These tools allow an administrator to properly plan and implement policies on data as needed.

One of the advantages of using FSRM is all of the included features that allow an administrator to manage the data that is stored on your file servers. Some of the features included with FSRM:

File Management Tasks FSRM allows an administrator to apply a policy or action to data files. Some of the actions that can be performed is the ability to encrypt files or run a custom command.

Quota Management Quotas give an administrator the ability to limit how much disk space a user can use on a file server. Administrators have the ability to limit space to an entire volume or specific folders.

File Classification Infrastructure Administrators can set file classifications and then manage the data more effectively by using these classifications. By classifying files and then setting policies to those classifications allows an administrator to set policies on those classifications. These policies include restricting file access, file encryption, and file expirations.

File Screening Management Administrators can set file screening on the server and limit what types of files that are being stored on that server. For example, an administrator can set a file screen on the server so that any file ending in BMP gets rejected.

Storage Reports   Administrators can create reports that show them how data is classified and accessed. You also have the ability to see what users are trying to save unauthorized file extensions.

Installing FSRM is easy when using either Server Manager or PowerShell. To install using Server Manager, you go into Add Features and choose File And Storage Services ➢ File Services ➢ File Server Resource Manager. To install FSRM using PowerShell, you would use the following command;

      Install-WindowsFeature -Name FS-Resource-Manager -IncludeManagementTools

      When configuring FSRM using the Windows GUI version is straight forward but setting up FSRM using PowerShell is a bit more challenging. Table 14.2 shows you some of the PowerShell commands for FSRM.

TABLE 14.2   PowerShell commands for FSRM

PowerShell Cmdlet	Description
Get-FsrmAutoQuota	Gets auto apply quotas on a server.
Get-FsrmClassification	Gets the status of the running file classification.
Get-FsrmClassificationRule	Gets classification rules.
Get-FsrmFileGroup	Gets file groups.
Get-FsrmFileScreen	Gets file screens.
Get-FsrmFileScreenException	Gets file screen exceptions.
Get-FsrmQuota	Gets quotas on the server.
Get-FsrmSetting	Gets the current FSRM settings.
Get-FsrmStorageReport	Gets storage reports.
New-FsrmAutoQuota	Creates an auto apply quota.
New-FsrmFileGroup	Creates a file group.
New-FsrmFileScreen	Creates a file screen.
New-FsrmQuota	Creates a FSRM quota.
New-FsrmQuotaTemplate	Creates a quota template.
Remove-FsrmClassificationRule	Removes classification rules.
Remove-FsrmFileScreen	Removes a file screen.
Remove-FsrmQuota	Removes a FSRM quota from the server.
Set-FsrmFileScreen	Changes configuration settings of a file screen.
Set-FsrmQuota	Changes configuration settings for a FSRM quota.

Using BitLocker Drive Encryption

To prevent individuals from stealing your computer and viewing personal and sensitive data found on your hard disk, some editions of Windows come with a new feature called *Bit-Locker Drive Encryption*. BitLocker encrypts the entire system drive. New files added to this drive are encrypted automatically, and files moved from this drive to another drive or computers are decrypted automatically.

Only Windows 7 Enterprise, Windows 7 Ultimate, Windows 8 Pro, Windows 8 Enterprise, Windows Server 2008, Windows Server 2008 R2, and Windows Server 2012 include BitLocker Drive Encryption, and only the operating system drive (usually C:) or internal hard drives can be encrypted with BitLocker. Files on other types of drives must be encrypted using BitLocker To Go. BitLocker To Go allows you to put BitLocker on removable media such as external hard disks or USB drives.

BitLocker uses a Trusted Platform Module (TPM) version 1.2 or higher to store the security key. A TPM is a chip that is found in newer computers. If you do not have a computer with a TPM, you can store the key on a removable USB drive. The USB drive will be required each time you start the computer so that the system drive can be decrypted.

If the TPM discovers a potential security risk, such as a disk error or changes made to BIOS, hardware, system files, or startup components, the system drive will not be unlocked until you enter the 48-digit BitLocker recovery password or use a USB drive with a recovery key as a recovery agent.

BitLocker must be set up within either the Local Group Policy editor or through the BitLocker icon in Control Panel. One advantage of using BitLocker is that you can prevent any unencrypted data from being copied onto a removable disk, thus protecting the computer.

BitLocker Recovery Password

The BitLocker recovery password is very important. Do not lose it or you may not be able to unlock the drive. Even if you do not have a TPM, be sure to keep your recovery password in case your USB drive becomes lost or corrupted.

BitLocker requires that you have a hard disk with at least two partitions, both formatted with NTFS. One partition will be the system partition that will be encrypted. The other partition will be the active partition that is used to start the computer. This partition will remain unencrypted.

What's New in BitLocker?

As with any new version of Windows, Microsoft continues to improve on technologies for Windows Server 2012 and Windows 8. The following sections cover the new or improved features of BitLocker.

BitLocker Provisioning

In previous versions of BitLocker (Windows Vista and Windows 7), the BitLocker provisioning (system and data volumes) was completed during the post installation of the BitLocker utility. The BitLocker provisioning was done either through the command line interface (CLI) or the Control Panel. In the Windows 8/Windows Server 2012 version of BitLocker, an administrator can choose to provision BitLocker before the operating system is even installed.

Administrators have the ability to enable BitLocker, prior to the operating system deployment, from the Windows Preinstallation Environment (WinPE). BitLocker is applied to the formatted volume and BitLocker encrypts the volume prior to running the Windows setup process.

If an administrator wants to check the status of BitLocker on a particular volume, the administrator can view the status of the drive in either the BitLocker control panel applet or Windows Explorer.

Used Disk Space Only Encryption

Windows 7 BitLocker has a requirement that all data and free space on the drive has to be encrypted. Because of this, the encryption process can take a very long time on larger volumes. In Windows 8 BitLocker, administrators have the ability to encrypt either the entire volume or just the space being used. When you choose to encrypt the Used Disk Space Only option, only the section of the drive that has data will be encrypted. Because of this, encryption is completed much faster.

Standard User PIN and Password Change

One issue that BitLocker has had is that you need to be an administrator to configure Bit-Locker on operating system drives. This can be an issue in a large organization due to the fact deploying the Trusted Platform Module (TPM) + PIN to a large number of computers can be very challenging.

Even with the new operating system changes, administrative privileges are still needed to configure BitLocker, but now your users have the ability to change the BitLocker PIN for the operating system or change the password on the data volumes.

When a user gets to choose their own PIN and password, they normally choose something that has meaning and something easy for them to remember. That is a good thing and a bad thing. It's good because when your users choose their own PIN and password, normally they don't need to write it down—they just know it. It's bad because if anyone knows the user well, they can have an easier time figuring out the person's PIN and password. Even when you allow your users to choose their own PIN and password, make sure you set a GPO to require password complexity.

Network Unlock

One of the new features of BitLocker is called Network Unlock. *Network Unlock* allows administrators to easily manage desktop and servers that are configured to use BitLocker. Network Unlock allows an administrator to configure BitLocker to unlock automatically an encrypted hard drive during a system reboot when that hard drive is connected to their trusted corporate environment. For this to function properly on a machine, there has to be a DHCP driver implementation in the system's firmware.

If your operating system volume is also protected by the TPM + PIN protection, the administrator has to be sure to enter the PIN at the time of the reboot. This protection can actually make using Network Unlock more difficult to use, but they can be used in combination.

Support for Encrypted Hard Drives for Windows

One of the new advantages of using BitLocker is *Full Volume Encryption (FVE)*. BitLocker provides built-in encryption for Windows data files and Windows operating system files. The advantage of this type of encryption is that encrypted hard drives that use *Full Disk Encryption (FDE)* get each block of the physical disk space encrypted. Because each physical block gets encrypted, it offers much better encryption. The only down side to this is because each physical block is encrypted, it adds some degradation to the hard drive speed. So, as an administrator, you have to decide if you want better speeds or better security on your hard disk.

Windows 7 & 2008 R2 vs. Windows 8 & 2012

The real question is what's the difference between Windows 7 and Windows 2008 R2 versus Windows 8 and Windows Server 2012. Table 14.3 shows you many of the common features and how they worked then and now.

TABLE 14.3   BitLocker then and now

Feature	Windows 7/Server 2008 R2	Windows 8/Server 2012
Reset the BitLocker PIN or password	The user's privileges must be set to an administrator if you want to reset the BitLocker PIN on an operating system drive and the password on a fixed or removable data drive.	Standard users now have the ability to reset the BitLocker PIN and password on operating system drives, fixed data drives, and removable data drives.
Disk encryption	When BitLocker is enabled, the entire disk is encrypted.	When BitLocker is enabled, users have the ability to choose whether to encrypt the entire disk or only the used space on the disk.
Hardware Encrypted Drive support	Not supported.	If the Windows logo hard drive comes pre-encrypted from the manufacturer, BitLocker is supported.
Unlocking using a network-based key to provide dual-factor authentication	Not available.	If a computer is rebooted on a trusted corporate wired network, key protector then allows a key to unlock and skip the PIN entry.
Protection for clusters	Not available.	Windows Server 2012 BitLocker includes the ability to support cluster shared volumes and failover clusters as long as they are running in a domain that was established by a Windows Server 2012 domain controller with the Kerberos Key Distribution Center Service enabled.
Linking a BitLocker key protector to an Active Directory account	Not available.	BitLocker allows a user, group, or computer account in Active Directory to be tied to a key protector. This key protector allows a protected data volumes to be unlocked.

In Exercise 14.5, you will enable BitLocker on the Windows Server 2012 system.

EXERCISE 14.5

Enabling BitLocker in Windows Server 2012

1. Open Server Manager by selecting the Server Manager icon or running servermanager.exe.

2. Select Add Roles and features.

3. Select Next at the Before You Begin pane (if shown).

4. Select Role-Based or Feature-Based installation, and select Next to continue.

5. Select the Select A Server From The Server Pool option and click Next.

6. At the Select Server Roles screen, click Next.

7. At the Select Features screen, click the check box for BitLocker Drive Encryption. When the Add Roles And Features dialog box appears, click the Add Features button. Then click Next.

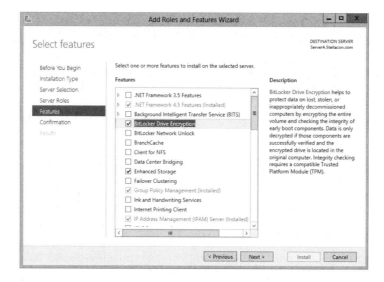

8. Select the Install button on the Confirmation pane of the Add Roles and Features Wizard to begin BitLocker feature installation. The BitLocker feature requires a restart to complete. Selecting the Restart The Destination Server Automatically If Required option in the Confirmation pane will force a restart of the computer after installation is complete.

9. If the Restart The Destination Server Automatically If Required check box is not selected, the Results pane of the Add Roles and Features Wizard will display the success or failure of the BitLocker feature installation. If required, a notification of additional action necessary to complete the feature installation, such as the restart of the computer, will be displayed in the results text.

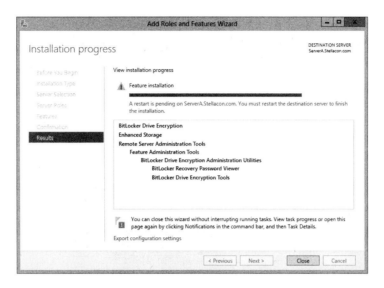

You also can install BitLocker by using the Windows PowerShell utility. To install Bit-Locker, use the following PowerShell commands:

```
Install-WindowsFeature BitLocker -IncludeAllSubFeature -IncludeManagementTools
-Restart
```

Understanding BranchCache

BranchCache is a technology that was introduced with Windows Server 2008 R2 and Windows 7. BranchCache allows an organization with slower links between offices to cache data so that downloads between offices do not have to occur each time a file is accessed.

For example, John comes into work and logs into the network. John accesses the corporate website and downloads a media file that takes four minutes to download. With BranchCache enabled, when Judy comes into work and connects to the corporate website and tries to download the same media file, the file will be cached from the previous download and Judy will have immediate access to the file.

There are two types of BranchCache configurations that you can set up, distributed cache mode and hosted mode:

Distributed Cache Mode   In the distributed cache mode configuration, all Windows 7 and Windows 8 client machines cache the files locally on the client machines. So in the previous example, after John downloaded the media file, Judy would receive the cached media file from John's Windows 7 or Windows 8 machine.

Hosted Mode   In the hosted mode configuration, the cache files are cached on a local (within the site) Windows Server 2012 machine. So in the previous example, after John downloaded the media file, the cached file would be placed on a Windows Server 2012 machine by default and all other users (Judy) would download the media file from the Windows Server 2012 machine.

Distributed Cache Mode Requirements

If you decide to install BranchCache in the distributed cache mode configuration, a hosted cache server running Windows Server 2012 is not required at the branch office. To set up distributed cache mode, the client machines must be running Windows 7 Enterprise, Windows 7 Ultimate, Windows 8 Pro, or Windows 8 Enterprise.

The Windows 7 or Windows 8 machines would then download the data files from the content servers at the main branch office, and then these Windows 7 machines become the local cache servers. To set up distributed cache mode, you must install a Windows Server 2012 content server at the main office first. After the content server is installed, physical connections (WAN or VPN connections) between the sites and branch offices must be established.

Client computers running Windows 7 and Windows 8 have BranchCache installed by default. However, you must enable and configure BranchCache and configure firewall exceptions. Complete Exercise 14.6 to configure BranchCache firewall rule exceptions.

EXERCISE 14.6

Configuring BranchCache Firewall Exceptions

1. On a domain controller, open the Group Policy Management Console.

2. In the Group Policy Management Console, expand the following path: Forest ➤ Domains ➤ Group Policy Objects. Make sure the domain you choose contains the BranchCache Windows 7/Windows 8 client computer accounts that you want to configure.

3. In the Group Policy Management Console, right-click Group Policy Objects and select New. Name the policy **BranchCache Client** and click OK. Right-click BranchCache Client, and click Edit. The Group Policy Management Editor console opens.

4. In the Group Policy Management Editor console, expand the following path: Computer Configuration ➤ Policies ➤ Windows Settings ➤ Security Settings ➤ Windows Firewall With Advanced Security ➤ Windows Firewall With Advanced Security – LDAP ➤ Inbound Rules.

5. Right-click Inbound Rules, and then click New Rule. The New Inbound Rule Wizard opens.

6. On the Rule Type screen, click Predefined, expand the list of choices, and then click BranchCache – Content Retrieval (Uses HTTP). Click Next.

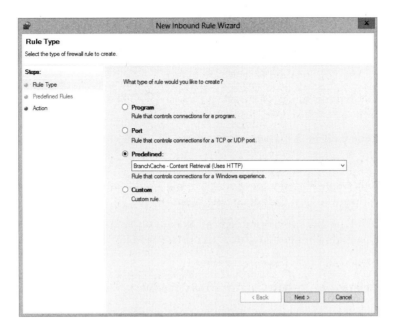

7. On the Predefined Rules screen, click Next.

8. On the Action screen, ensure that Allow The Connection is selected, and then click Finish. You must select Allow The Connection for the BranchCache client to be able to receive traffic on this port.

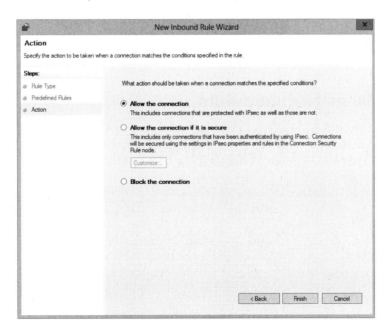

9.   Now, to create the WS-Discovery firewall exception, right-click Inbound Rules and click New Rule. The New Inbound Rule Wizard opens.

10. On the Rule Type screen, click Predefined, expand the list of choices, and then click BranchCache – Peer Discovery (Uses WSD). Click Next.

11. On the Predefined Rules screen, click Next.

12. On the Action screen, ensure that Allow The Connection is selected, and then click Finish.

13. In the Group Policy Management Editor console, right-click Outbound Rules and then click New Rule. The New Outbound Rule Wizard opens.

14. On the Rule Type screen, click Predefined, expand the list of choices, and then click BranchCache – Content Retrieval (Uses HTTP). Click Next.

15. On the Predefined Rules screen, click Next.

16. On the Action screen, ensure that Allow The Connection is selected and then click Finish.

17. Create the WS-Discovery firewall exception by right-clicking Outbound Rules, and then click New Rule. The New Outbound Rule Wizard opens.

18. On the Rule Type screen, click Predefined, expand the list of choices, and then click BranchCache – Peer Discovery (Uses WSD). Click Next.

19. On the Predefined Rules screen, click Next.

20. On the Action screen, ensure that Allow The Connection is selected and then click Finish.

Now that we have looked at the distributed cache mode configuration, let's take a look at the hosted mode configuration.

Hosted Mode Requirements

To set up a hosted mode BranchCache configuration, you must first set up a Windows Server 2012 hosted cache server at the main and branch offices. You also need Windows 7 Enterprise, Windows 7 Ultimate, Windows 8 Pro, or Windows 8 Enterprise computers at the branch offices.

The Windows 7 or Windows 8 machines download the data from the main cache server, and then the hosted cache servers at the branch offices obtain a copy of the downloaded data for other users to access.

Your network infrastructure must also allow for physical connections between the main office and the branch offices. These connections can be VPNs or some type of WAN links. After these requirements are met, your cache server must obtain a server certificate so that the client computers in the branch offices can positively identify the cache servers.

Exercise 14.7 walks you through the process of installing the BranchCache feature on a Windows Server 2012 machine. To begin this exercise, you must be logged into the Windows Server 2012 machine as an administrator.

EXERCISE 14.7

Installing BranchCache on Windows Server 2012

1. Open Server Manager by selecting the Server Manager icon or running `server manager.exe`.

2. Select Add Roles And Features.

3. Select Next at the Before You Begin pane (if shown).

4. Select Role-Based or Feature-Based installation, and select Next to continue.

5. Select the Select A Server From The Server Pool option and click Next.

6. At the Select Server Roles screen, click Next.

7. At the Select Features screen, click the check box for BranchCache. Then click Next.

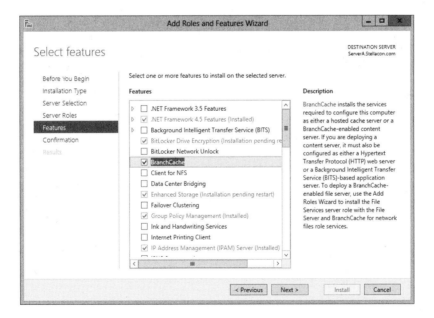

8. Check the box to Restart The Destination Server If Required, and then click the Install button. If a dialog box appears about a restart, click the Yes button. The system should restart.

9. After the system restarts, log in as the administrator.

Make sure to repeat this exercise on all branch office cache servers. One of the requirements for BranchCache is a physical connection between the main office and the branch offices.

BranchCache and PowerShell

As stated throughout this book, PowerShell is a command-line shell and scripting tool. BranchCache has many different PowerShell cmdlets that allow you to configure and maintain the BranchCache feature. Table 14.4 shows just some of the different PowerShell cmdlets for BranchCache.

TABLE 14.4   PowerShell cmdlets for BranchCache

Cmdlet	Description
Add-BCDataCacheExtension	Increases the amount of cache storage space that is available on a hosted cache server by adding a new cache file.
Clear-BCCache	Deletes all data in all data and hash files.
Disable-BC	Disables the BranchCache service.
Disable-BCDowngrading	Disables downgrading so that client computers that are running Windows 8 Consumer Preview do not request Windows 7–specific versions of content information from content servers.
Enable-BCDistributed	Enables BranchCache, and configures a computer to operate in distributed cache mode.
Enable-BCHostedClient	Configures BranchCache to operate in hosted cache client mode.
Enable-BCHostedServer	Configures BranchCache to operate in hosted cache server mode.
Enable-BCLocal	Enables the BranchCache service in local caching mode.
Export-BCCachePackage	Exports a cache package.
Export-BCSecretKey	Exports a secret key to a file.
Get-BCClientConfiguration	Gets the current BranchCache client computer settings.
Get-BCContentServer-Configuration	Gets the current BranchCache content server settings.
Get-BCDataCache	Gets the BranchCache data cache.

Cmdlet	Description
Get-BCStatus	Gets a set of objects that provide BranchCache status and configuration information.
Import-BCCachePackage	Imports a cache package into BranchCache.
Import-BCSecretKey	Imports the cryptographic key that BranchCache uses for the generation of segment secrets
Set-BCAuthentication	Specifies the BranchCache computer authentication mode.
Set-BCCache	Modifies the cache file configuration.
Set-BCSecretKey	Sets the cryptographic key used in the generation of segment secrets.

What's New in Windows Server 2012 BranchCache?

Microsoft continues to improve on many of the features of Windows Server, and Branch-Cache is no different. Microsoft has improved BranchCache in Windows Server 2012 and Windows 8. The following list includes some of the changes:

Office sizes and the number of branch offices are not limited.   Windows Server 2012 BranchCache now allows any number of offices along with any number of users once an administrator deploys hosted cache mode with multiple hosted cache servers.

No requirements for a Group Policy object (GPO) for each office location, streamlining deployment.   All that is required to deploy BranchCache is a single GPO that contains a small number of settings.

Client computer configuration is automatic.   Administrators have the ability to configure their clients through the use of a Group Policy object. If this is done, client configuration will automatically be configured through the GPO, and if a client can't find a hosted cache server, the client will automatically self-configure as a hosted cache mode client.

BranchCache is deeply integrated with the Windows file server.   BranchCache is automatically integrated with Windows file server technology. Because of this, the process of finding duplicate pieces in independent files is greatly improved.

Duplicate content is only stored and downloaded once   BranchCache only stores one instance of the content on a hosted cache server or content server and, because of this, you get greater disk storage savings. Since client computers at the remote offices only download one instance of any content, your network saves on additional WAN bandwidth.

Small changes to large files produce bandwidth savings   One new advantage of Branch-Cache is the file server chunking system that helps divide files and Web pages into smaller parts. Now when a file is changed, only the part of that file that has been changed gets replicated. This allows BranchCache to use lower bandwidth requirements.

Offline content creation   When BranchCache is deployed as content or file servers, the data is calculated offline before a client even has the chance to request it. Because of this, the systems get faster performance and bandwidth.

Cache Encryption   BranchCache now stores its cached data as encrypted data. This guarantees data security without the need to encrypt the entire drive.

Deployment of multiple hosted cache servers   In Windows 7 and Windows Server 2008 R2, BranchCache was only able to deploy one hosted cache server per office location. Windows Server 2012 allows you to deploy as many hosted cache servers as are needed at a location.

Configuring DirectAccess

DirectAccess was also introduced in the Windows Server 2008 R2 and Windows 7 operating systems, and it is also now available in Windows 8 and Windows Server 2012. *DirectAccess* allows a remote user to work on their corporate network when they are away from the office without the need for a VPN. As long as the remote user is connected to the Internet, DirectAccess will automatically connect the remote user to the corporate network without the need for any user intervention.

When a user's DirectAccess-enabled laptop is connected to the Internet, a bidirectional connection is automatically established with the user's corporate network. Because the connection is bidirectional, the IT administrator can also remotely manage the Windows 7 or Windows 8 machine while the machine is away from the network.

DirectAccess vs. VPNs

There are a few problems with using VPNs to connect to a network. One issue is that when a user gets disconnected from their VPN connection, they must reestablish the VPN connection.

Another issue with VPNs is that many organizations filter VPN connection traffic. It may not be possible for an organization to open a firewall to allow VPN traffic. Also, if your intranet and your Internet connections are the same as your VPN connections, this can cause your Internet to be slower.

DirectAccess does not face the same limitations of a VPN. DirectAccess allows a laptop or desktop that is configured properly to connect automatically using a bidirectional connection between the client and the server.

To establish this connection, DirectAccess uses Internet Protocol Security (IPsec) and IPv6. IPsec provides a high level of security between the client and the server, and IPv6 is the protocol that the machines use.

Understanding How DirectAccess Works

To understand DirectAccess better, it helps to understand the process involved with how DirectAccess operates. The following steps, taken from the Microsoft white papers, show how DirectAccess operates.

1. The Windows 8 DirectAccess client determines if the machine is connected to a network or the Internet.

2. The Windows 8 DirectAccess computer tries to connect to the web server specified during the DirectAccess setup configuration.

3. The Windows 8 DirectAccess client computer connects to the Windows Server 2012 DirectAccess server using IPv6 and IPsec. Because most users connect to the Internet using IPv4, the client establishes an IPv6-over-IPv4 tunnel using 6to4 or Teredo.

4. If an organization has a firewall that prevents the DirectAccess client computer using 6to4 or Teredo from connecting to the DirectAccess server, the Windows 8 client automatically attempts to connect using the IP-HTTPS protocol.

5. As part of establishing the IPsec session, the Windows 8 DirectAccess client and server authenticate each other using computer certificates for authentication.

6. The DirectAccess server uses Active Directory membership, and the DirectAccess server verifies that the computer and user are authorized to connect using DirectAccess.

7. The DirectAccess server begins forwarding traffic from the DirectAccess client to the intranet resources to which the user has been granted access.

Now that you understand how DirectAccess works, let's look at the requirements for setting up DirectAccess on your network.

Knowing the DirectAccess Infrastructure Requirements

To set up DirectAccess, you must make sure your network infrastructure meets some minimum requirements. The following are the requirements for setting up DirectAccess:

- Windows Server 2012 configured to use DirectAccess. The Windows Server 2012 machine will be set up as a multihomed system. This means that your server will need two network adapters so that one adapter is connected directly to the Internet and a second adapter is connected to the intranet. Each network adapter will be configured with its own TCP/IP address.

- Windows 7 or Windows 8 client machines configured to use DirectAccess.

- Minimum of one domain controller and one Domain Name System (DNS) server running Windows Server 2008 SP2, Windows Server 2008 R2, or Windows Server 2012.

- Certificate authority (CA) server that will issue computer certificates, smart card certificates, or health certificates.

- IPsec policies to specify protection for traffic.

- IPv6 on the DirectAccess server that uses ISATAP, Teredo, or 6to4.

Complete Exercise 14.8 to install the DirectAccess feature onto a Windows Server 2012 machine. Remember that the DirectAccess feature needs to be installed on Windows Server 2012.

Installing the DirectAccess Feature

1. Open Server Manager by selecting the Server Manager icon or running servermanager .exe.

2. Select Add Roles And Features.

3. Select Next at the Before you begin pane (if shown).

4. Select Role-Based or Feature-Based installation, and select Next to continue.

5. Select the Select A Server From The Server Pool option and click Next.

6. At the Select Server Roles screen, click the Remote Access checkbox. DirectAccess is part of Remote Access. Click Next. If a dialog box appears asking to add features, click the Add Features button.

7. At the Select Features screen, click Next.

8. At the confirmation screen, click the Install Button.

9. Reboot the system if the server does not reboot automatically.

After the DirectAccess feature is installed, the DirectAccess Manager will appear in the Administrative Tools section. When you start the DirectAccess Manager, click Setup and the DirectAccess Setup Wizard will start.

The setup wizard walks you through a four-stage process (setting up the remote clients, DirectAccess server, infrastructure servers, and application servers), and it will allow you to choose which Windows 8 computers can use DirectAccess. Follow the wizard to complete the installation. To complete the setup and allow this to function properly, you also need to set up a certificate server, domain controller, and DNS.

Configuring Disk Quotas

In this chapter so far, you have seen how to set up a share and publish it to Active Directory. You've also learned how to set up permissions and security and how NTFS and shared permissions work with each other. It's time to learn how to limit users' hard drive space on the servers.

Disk quotas give administrators the ability to limit how much storage space a user can have on a hard drive. As mentioned earlier in this chapter, disk quotas are an advantage of using NTFS over FAT32. If you decide to use FAT32 on a volume or partition, quotas will not be available.

You have a few options available to you when you set up disk quotas. You can set up disk quotas based on volume or on users.

 A good rule of thumb is to set up an umbrella quota policy that covers the entire volume and then let individual users exceed the umbrella as needed.

Setting Quotas by Volume   One way to set up disk quotas is by setting the quota by volume, on a per-volume basis. This means that if you have a hard drive with C:, D:, and E: volumes, you would have to set up three individual quotas (one for each volume). This is your umbrella. This is where you set up an entire disk quota based on the volume for all users.

Setting Quotas by User   You have the ability to set up quotas on volumes by user. Here is where you would individually let users have independent quotas that exceed your umbrella quota.

Specifying Quota Entries   You use quota entries to configure the volume and user quotas. You do this on the Quotas tab of the volume's Properties dialog box. (See Exercise 14.9.)

Creating Quota Templates   Quota templates are predefined ways to set up quotas. Templates allow you to set up disk quotas without needing to create a disk quota from scratch. One advantage of using a template is that when you want to set up disk quotas on multiple volumes (C:, D:, and E:) on the same hard drive, you do not need to re-create the quota on each volume.

Exercise 14.9 will show you how to set up an umbrella quota for all users and then have an individual account in your Active Directory exceed this quota.

EXERCISE 14.9

Configuring Disk Quotas

1. Open Windows Explorer.

2. Right-click the local disk (C:), and choose Properties.

3. Click the Quotas tab.

4. Check the Enable Quota Management check box. Also check the Deny Disk Space To Users Exceeding Quota Limit box.

5. Click the Limit Disk Space To option, and enter **1000MB** in the box.

6. Enter **750MB** in the Set Warning Level To boxes.

7. Click the Apply button. If a warning box appears, click OK. This warning is just informing you that the disk may need to be rescanned for the quota.

8. Now that you have set up an umbrella quota to cover everyone, you'll set up a quota that exceeds the umbrella. Click the Quota Entries button.

9. The Quotas Entries for (C:) window appears. You will see some users already listed. These are users who are already using space on the volume. Click the Quota menu at the top, and choose New Quota Entry.

    Notice the N/A entry in the Percent Used column. This belongs to the administrator account, which by default has no limit.

10. On the Select User page, choose a user that you want to allow to exceed the quota (for this example, I used the wpanek account). Click OK.

11. This opens the Add New Quota Entry dialog box. Click the Do Not Limit Disk Usage option, and click OK.

12. You will notice that the new user has no limit. Close the disk quota tool.

Configuring Distributed File System

One problem that network administrators have is deciding how to share folders and communicating to the end users how to find the shares. For example, if you share a folder called Stellacon Documents on server A, how do you make sure that your users will find the folder and the files within it? The users have to know the server name and the share name. This can be a huge problem if you have hundreds of shares on multiple servers. If you want to have multiple copies of the folder called Stellacon Documents for fault tolerance and load balancing, the problem becomes even more complicated.

Distributed File System (DFS) in Windows Server 2012 offers a simplified way for users to access geographically dispersed files. DFS allows you to set up a tree structure of virtual directories that allow users to connect to shared folders throughout the entire network.

Administrators have the ability to take shared folders that are located on different servers and transparently connect them to one or more DFS namespaces—virtual trees of shared folders throughout an organization. The advantage of using DFS is that if one of the folders becomes unavailable, DFS has failover capability that will allow your users to connect to the data on a different server.

Administrators can use the DFS tools to choose which shared folders will appear in the namespace and also to decide how the names of these shared folders will show up in the virtual tree listing.

Advantages of DFS

One of the advantages of DFS is that when a user views this virtual tree, the shared folders appear to be located on a single machine. The following list includes some other advantages of DFS:

Simplified Data Migration   DFS gives you the ability to move data from one location to another without the user needing to know the physical location of the data. Because the users do not need to know the physical location of the shared data, administrators can simply move data from one location to another.

Security Integration   Administrators do not need to configure additional security for the DFS shared folders. The shared folders use the NTFS and shared folder permissions that an administrator has already assigned when the share was set up.

Access-Based Enumeration (ABE)   This DFS feature (disabled by default) displays only the files and folders that a user has permissions to access. If a user does not have access to a folder, Windows hides the folder from the user's DFS view. This feature is not active if the user is viewing the files and folders locally.

Types of DFS

The following are types of DFS:

DFS Replication   Administrators have the ability to manage replication scheduling and bandwidth throttling using the DFS management console. Replication is the process of sharing data between multiple machines. As explained earlier in the section, replicated shared folders allow you to balance the load and have fault tolerance. DFS also has read-only replication folders.

DFS Namespaces   The DFS Namespace service is the virtual tree listing in the DFS server. An administrator can set up multiple namespaces on the DFS, allowing for multiple virtual trees within DFS. DFS Namespaces was once known as Distributed File System in Windows 2000 Server and Windows Server 2003 (in case you still use Server 2003).

In Exercise 14.10, you will install the DFS Namespace service on the file server. You need to start the installation using the Server Manager MMC.

EXERCISE 14.10

Installing the DFS Namespace Service

1. Open Server Manager by selecting the Server Manager icon or running servermanager.exe.

2. Select Add Roles And Features.

3. Select Next at the Before You Begin pane (if shown).

4. Select Role-Based or Feature-Based installation, and select Next to continue.

5. Select the Select A Server From The Server Pool option and click Next.

6. At the Select Server Roles screen, expand File and Storage Services and check the DFS Namespace and DFS Replication check boxes. Then click Next. If a dialog box appears, click the Add Features button.

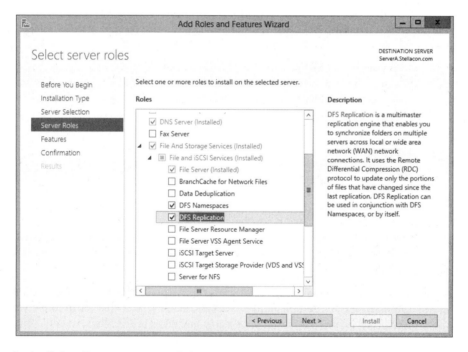

7. At the Select Features screen, click Next.

8. At the Confirmation screen, click the Install button.

9. After the installation is complete, click the Close button.

10. Close Server Manager.

Once you have installed DFS, it's time to learn how to manage DFS with the DFS Management MMC. The DFS Management console (see Figure 14.9) gives you one place to do all of your DFS configurations. The DFS Management console allows you to set up DFS Replication and DFS Namespace. Another task you can do in the DFS Management console is to add a folder target—a folder that you add to the DFS Namespace (the virtual tree) for all your users to share.

FIGURE 14.9   DFS Management console

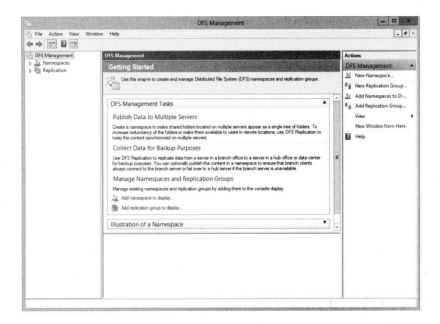

Remote Differential Compression (RDC)

One issue that can arise occurs when files are changed. There has to be some mechanism that helps files stay accurate. That's where The *Remote Differential Compression (RDC)* feature comes into play. RDC is a group of application programming interfaces (APIs) that programs can use to determine if files have changed. Once RDC determines that there has been a change, RDC then helps to detect which portions of the files contain the changes. RDC has the ability to detect insertions, removals, and rearrangements of data in files. This feature becomes very helpful with limited-bandwidth networks when they replicate changes.

To install the RDC feature, use Server Manager and then run the Add Features Wizard, or type the following command at an elevated command prompt:

```
Servermanagercmd -Install Rdc
```

Understanding Printing

One of the most important components on a network is the printer. Printers today are almost as important as the computers themselves. Think about your network. What would your network be like without a printer? Even small networks or home networks have a printer today.

How many printers do you want on your network? It is not feasible to put a printer on every user's desk. What if some users need black and white while others need color? Do you give each user two printers? What if they need laser printing for reports but ink-jets will work fine for every other type of print job? These are all questions that you must answer before buying any printers for your networks.

This is also where network printers and print servers come into play. *Network printers* are printers that can be directly connected to the network through some form of network interface card. These printers usually have settings that can be configured for your network needs. For example, if your network uses DHCP, you can set the printer to be a DHCP client.

Print servers are servers that have a connected printer, where the server handles all printing issues. This is an excellent solution for printers that cannot directly connect to the network. Once the printer is connected to the network (through the use of a NIC or a server), the end user just connects to the printer and prints. To the end user, there is no real difference between the two options.

Before an end user can print to a network printer, an administrator must connect, set up, share, and publish the printer for use. An administrator must also set the permissions on the printer to allow users to print to that printer. The following sections will discuss these items in detail.

Creating and Publishing Printers

Once your printer is installed, you must share the printer and then publish the printer to Active Directory before users can print to it. Printers can be published easily within Active Directory. This makes them available to users in your domain.

Exercise 14.11 walks you through the steps you need to take to share and publish a Printer object by having you create and share a printer. To complete the printer installation, you need access to the Windows Server 2012 installation media (via the hard disk, a network share, or the CD drive). If you do not have a printer for this exercise, just choose one from the list and continue the exercise.

EXERCISE 14.11

Creating and Publishing a Printer

1. Click the Windows key ➢ Control Panel ➢ Devices And Printers ➢ Add Printer. This starts the Add Printer Wizard.

2. On the Add Printer page, click the link The Printer That I Want Isn't Listed.

3. Choose Add A Local Printer and click Next.

4. On the Choose A Printer Port page, select Use An Existing Port. From the drop-down list beside that option, make sure LPT1: (Printer Port) is selected. Click Next.

5. On the Install The Printer Driver page, select Generic for the manufacturer, and for the printer, highlight Generic/Text Only. Click Next.

6. If a driver page appears, choose Use The Driver That Is Currently Installed and click Next.

7. On the Type A Printer Name page, type **Text Printer**. Uncheck the Set As The Default Printer box, and then click Next.

8. The Installing Printer page appears. After the system is finished, the Printer Sharing page appears. Make sure that the Share This Printer So That Others On Your Network Can Find And Use It box is selected, and accept the default share name of Text Printer.

9. In the Location section, type **Building 203**, and in the Comment section, add the following comment: **This is a text-only printer**. Click Next.

10. On the You've Successfully Added Text Printer page, click Finish.

11. Next you need to verify that the printer will be listed in Active Directory. Right-click the Text Printer icon, and select Text Printer Properties.

12. Next select the Sharing tab, and make sure that the List In The Directory box is checked. Click OK to accept the settings.

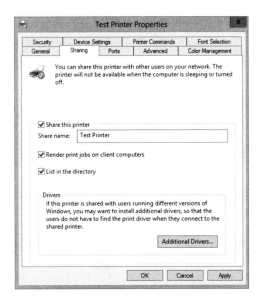

13. Close the printer Properties, and close Devices And Printers.

Note that when you create and share a printer this way, an Active Directory Printer object is not displayed within the Active Directory Users and Computers tool.

Configuring Printers

The printer has now been installed and published to Active Directory. It's time to set all of the different configuration options. To get to the options, right-click the Printer object and choose Properties. The following are just some of the tabs you can configure:

FIGURE 14.10   The General tab of the printer's Properties dialog box

The General Tab   The General tab (see Figure 14.10) allows you to set some basic printer attributes:

- The field at the top of the dialog box contains the display name of the Printer object.
- The Location field should contain text that helps users physically locate the printer. This allows users to search for printers based on location (location-aware printing).
- The Comment field allows an administrator to put in any additional information, such as the printer type.
- The Printing Preferences button takes you to controls that allow you to change the layout and paper type of the printer.

FIGURE 14.11   The Sharing tab of the printer's Properties dialog box

The Sharing Tab   The Sharing tab (see Figure 14.11) allows you to configure your printer for sharing on your network. This is what allows users to use a network printer (if they have the proper permissions on the printer).

- The Share This Printer check box allows you to share the printer on the network.

- Share Name is the name your users will see on the network.

- When Render Print Jobs On Client Computers is checked, the client computer caches the print job until the printer is ready to print. If unchecked, the print server will cache the entire job before it prints to the printer.

- When List In The Directory is checked, users can search the directory for the printer.

- The Additional Drivers button allows you to load additional drivers for your clients. It is especially useful for giving access to drivers for older client systems. One advantage of a print server is that the server will automatically download drivers to client computers.

FIGURE 14.12   The Ports tab of the printer's Properties dialog box

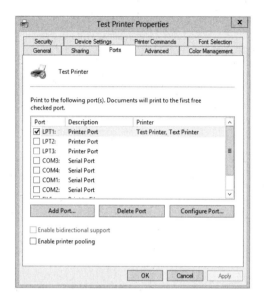

The Ports Tab   The Ports tab (see Figure 14.12) allows you to configure the port to which your printer is connected. You can add ports or configure existing ports.

- The Port check boxes allow you to choose to which port your printer is connected. Options are the printer port, serial port, local port, and print to file port.

- The Add Port button allows you to add a custom port (for example, a TCP/IP port).

- The Delete Port button allows you to remove a port from the Port list.

- The Configure Port button gives you settings to configure an existing port. For example, if you use TCP/IP, this button allows you to change the TCP/IP options.

- Enable Bidirectional Support allows your printer and computer to communicate back and forth. If this check box is disabled, your printer cannot support two-way communications.

- A *printer pool* allows two or more identical printers to share the print load. When a document is sent to the printer pool, the first available printer receives the print job and prints it. Enable Printer Pooling allows a large department or organization to get print jobs done faster. Users do not have to wait for one printer to get their print job. You should follow a couple of rules when setting up a printer pool:

    - All printers in the pool need to be the same model and type.

    - All printers in the pool should be in the same physical location. Print jobs will be printed to the first available printer. If these printers are located all over the company, it may take a user too long to find their print job.

FIGURE 14.13   Advanced tab of the printer's Properties dialog box

The Advanced Tab   The Advanced tab (see Figure 14.13) is where you can set availability, priority, and many other options:

- The availability controls let you set the hours when this printer can be used. You can set it to be always available or available only between the hours you set.

- If multiple print shares are set up to go to the same printer, you can specify a priority with the Priority field for each share. The higher the number, the faster a print job sent to that share will access the printer. The highest priority is 99, and the default (lowest) is 1. If two users send jobs to the same printer at the same time, one with a 99 priority and the other with a 1 priority, the 99 priority would print first.

- Driver is the default driver that the printer is using.

- The print spooling controls let you decide how the print job will spool. You can choose to have the entire job spool first before printing (this ensures that the entire job is received by the print queue before printing), to start printing immediately while the job is still spooling, or to print directly to the printer without spooling. (The last option requires a printer with a large amount of RAM on the motherboard.)

- Hold Mismatched Documents allows the spooler to hold any print jobs that don't match the setup for the print device.

- Print Spooled Documents First allows a completely spooled printer job to be printed first even if it has a lower priority number than a job that is still spooling.

- Usually, after a print job has been printed, the print queue deletes the print job. If you check the Keep Printed Documents box, the print queue will not delete the print job after it is printed.

- Enable Advanced Printing Features allows you to set some advanced features such as the Page Order and Pages Per Sheet settings.

The Color Management Tab   This tab allows you to adjust the color of your printing jobs.

FIGURE 14.14   Security tab of the printer's Properties dialog box

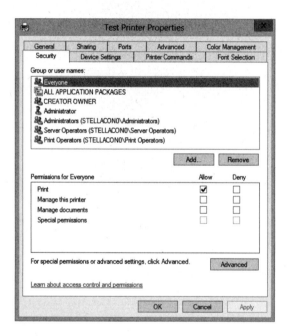

The Security Tab   The Security tab (see Figure 14.14) is where you can set the permissions for your printer. This allows users to print, manage printers, manage documents, and take advantage of special permissions:

- The Add button allows you to add users and groups to the printer.

- The Remove button allows you to remove users and groups from the printer.

- The following controls, available in the Permissions For Everyone box, apply to everyone on your network:

    - Print gives everyone the right to print to this printer.

- Manage Printers gives everyone the right to manage this printer, including deleting print jobs, setting priorities, setting availability, and so on.

- Manage Documents gives everyone the right to manage print jobs.

- Special Permissions allows you to set unique permissions such as Print, Manage Printers, Read permissions, Change permissions, and Take Ownership.

Migrating Print Servers

In a network environment, an administrator may find it necessary to replace older print servers or to consolidate multiple print servers into one. To do this print server migration or replacement, you can use the Printer Migration Wizard or the `Printbrm.exe` command-line tool. These two utilities allow you to export print queues, printer settings, printer ports, and language monitors. These utilities then allow you to import these settings on another print server running Windows Server 2012.

Easy Print Driver

One printer configuration that is a little different than normal is when you are setting up a printer for a Remote Desktop server. However, Microsoft has included a feature to help you out. That feature is called the *Easy Print Driver.*

Remote Desktop Services gives you the ability to do printer redirection. What this means is Remote Desktop can route printing jobs from a server to a printer that is attached to a client computer. On an RD Session Host server, an administrator has the ability to use the Remote Desktop Easy Print printer driver to help simplify printer configuration.

The RD Session Host server first tries to use the Remote Desktop Easy Print driver, and if the RD client computer does not support this driver, the server looks for a matching printer driver on the server.

Summary

In this chapter, I discussed file servers and how they can be effective on your network. I also discussed sharing folders for users to access and then I discussed how to publish those share folders to Active Directory.

You learned about NTFS security versus shared folder permissions and how to limit users' hard drive space by setting up disk quotas. The chapter also covered the Encrypting File System (EFS) and how users can encrypt and compress files.

The Distributed File System (DFS) allows you to set up a tree structure of virtual directories that allow users to connect to a shared folder anywhere throughout the entire network.

Finally, you learned about print servers and configuring printers. I talked about how to share and publish printers within Active Directory as well as print permissions, printer priorities, and print pooling.

Exam Essentials

Learn How Resources Can Be Published A design goal for Active Directory was to make network resources easier for users to find. With that in mind, you should understand how using published printers and shared folders can simplify network resource management.

Know How to Configure Offline Folders Offline folders give you the opportunity to set up folders so that users can work on the data while outside the office and later synchronize it with a master copy. You can set up GPOs to help with offline folder synchronization.

Know How to Configure NTFS Security One of the major advantages of using NTFS over FAT32 is access to additional security features. NTFS allows you to put security at the file and folder layers. NTFS security is in effect whether the user is remote or local to the computer with the data.

Know How to Configure Shared Permissions Shared permissions allow you to determine the access a user will receive when connecting to a shared folder. Shared permissions are allowed only at the folder layer and are in effect only when the user is remote to the computer with the shared data.

Understand How NTFS and Shared Permissions Work Together NTFS and shared permissions are individually additive—you get the highest level of security and permissions within each type. NTFS is always in effect, and it is the only security available locally. Shared permissions are in effect only when connecting remotely to access the shared data. When the two types of permissions meet, the most restrictive set of permissions applies.

Know How to Configure Disk Quotas Disk quotas allow an organization to determine the amount of disk space users can have on a volume of a server. An administrator can set up disk quotas based on volumes or by users. Each volume must have its own separate set of disk quotas.

Know How to Configure DFS Distributed File System in Windows Server 2012 offers a simplified way for users to access geographically dispersed files. The DFS Namespace service allows you to set up a tree structure of virtual directories that allow users to connect to shared folders throughout the entire network.

Know How to Configure Printing We discussed network printers versus print servers. Understand that when you create a printer, you want to publish the printer within Active Directory so that your users can find it throughout the domain. Understand the different printer permissions and how to install print drivers.

Review Questions

1. The company for which you work has a multilevel administrative team that is segmented by departments and locations. There are four major locations, and you are in the Northeast group. You have been assigned to the administrative group that is responsible for creating and maintaining network shares for files and printers in your region. The last place you worked was a large Windows Server 2003 network, where you had a much wider range of responsibilities. You are excited about the chance to learn more about Windows Server 2012.

   For your first task, you have been given a list of file and printer shares that need to be created for the users in your region. You ask how to create them in Windows Server 2012, and you are told that the process of creating a share is the same as with Windows Server 2003. You create the shares and use NETUSE to test them. Everything appears to work fine, so you send out a message that the shares are available. The next day, you start receiving calls from users who say they cannot see any of resources you created. What is the most likely reason for the calls from the users?

   A. You forgot to enable NetBIOS for the shares.

   B. You need to force replication for the shares to appear in the directory.

   C. You need to publish the shares in the directory.

   D. The shares will appear within the normal replication period.

2. You want to publish a printer to Active Directory. Where would you click in order to accomplish this task?

   A. The Sharing tab

   B. The Advanced tab

   C. The Device Settings tab

   D. The Printing Preferences button

3. A system administrator creates a local Printer object, but it doesn't show up in Active Directory when a user executes a search for all printers. Which of the following are possible reasons for this? (Choose all that apply.)

   A. The printer was not shared.

   B. The printer is offline.

   C. The client does not have permission to view the printer.

   D. The printer is malfunctioning.

4. You are the network administrator for a mid-size coffee bean distributor. Your company's network has four Windows 2012 servers, and all of the clients are running either Windows 8 or Windows 7. Most of your end users use laptops to do their work, and many of them work away from the office. What should you configure to help them work on documents when away from the office?

    A.   Online file access

    B.   Offline file access

    C.   Share permissions

    D.   NTFS permissions

5.   Your company has decided to implement a Windows 2012 server. The company IT manager before you always used FAT32 as the system partition. Your company wants to know whether it should move to NTFS. Which of the following are some advantages of NTFS? (Choose all that apply.)

    A.   Security

    B.   Quotas

    C.   Compression

    D.   Encryption

6.   Will, the IT manager for your company, has been asked to give Moe the rights to read and change documents in the `Stellacon Documents` folder. The following table shows the current permissions on the shared folder:

Group/User	NTFS	Shared
Sales	Read	Change
Marketing	Modify	Change
R&D	Deny	Full Control
Finance	Read	Read
Tylor	Read	Change

Moe is a member of the Sales and Finance groups. When Moe accesses the `Stellacon Documents` folder, he can read all the files, but the system won't let him change or delete files. What do you need to do to give Moe the minimum amount of rights to do his job?

    A.   Give Sales Full Control to shared permissions.

    B.   Give Moe Full Control to NTFS security.

    C.   Give Finance Change to shared permissions.

    D.   Give Finance Modify to NTFS security.

    E.   Give Moe Modify to NTFS security.

7. You are the administrator of your network, which consists of two Windows Server 2012 systems. One of the servers is a domain controller, and the other server is a file server for data storage. The hard drive of the file server is starting to fill up. You do not have the ability to install another hard drive, so you decide to limit the amount of space everyone gets on the hard drive. What do you need to implement to solve your problem?

    A. Disk spacing

    B. Disk quotas

    C. Disk hardening

    D. Disk limitations

8. You are the IT manager for your company. You have been asked to give the Admin group the rights to read, change, and assign permissions to documents in the Stellacon Documents folder. The following table shows the current permissions on the Stellacon Documents shared folder:

Group/User	NTFS	Shared
Sales	Read	Change
Marketing	Modify	Change
R&D	Deny	Full Control
Finance	Read	Read
Admin	Change	Change

    What do you need to do to give the Admin group the rights to do their job? (Choose all that apply.)

    A. Give Sales Full Control to shared permissions.

    B. Give Full Control to NTFS security.

    C. Give Admin Full Control to shared permissions.

    D. Give Finance Modify to NTFS security.

    E. Give Admin Full Control to NTFS security.

9. You are the administrator for a large organization. You have multiple Windows Server 2012 systems that all contain files that need to be shared for all users. The files and folders constantly move among servers, and users are having a hard time finding files they need. What can you implement to help your users out?

    A. Encrypting File System (EFS)

    B. Distributed File System (DFS)

    C. Shared File System (SFS)

    D. Published File System (PFS)

10. You have been hired by a small company to implement new Windows Server 2012 systems. The company wants you to set up a server for users' home folder locations. What type of server would you be setting up?

A. PDC server

B. Web server

C. Exchange server

D. File server

Chapter

15

Managing Remote Access Services

THE FOLLOWING 70-411 EXAM OBJECTIVES ARE COVERED IN THIS CHAPTER:

✓ **Configure VPN and routing**

  ▪ This objective may include, but is not limited to: Install and configure the Remote Access role; configure VPN settings; configure remote dial-in settings for users.

✓ **Configure Network Policy Server (NPS)**

  ▪ This objective may include but is not limited to: Configure multiple RADIUS server infrastructures; configure RADIUS clients; manage RADIUS templates; configure RADIUS accounting; configure certificates.

✓ **Configure NPS policies**

  ▪ This objective may include, but is not limited to: Configure connection request policies; configure network policies for VPN clients (multilink and bandwidth allocation, IP filters, encryption, IP addressing); manage NPS templates; import and export NPS policies.

✓ **Configure Network Access Protection (NAP)**

  ▪ This objective may include, but is not limited to: Configure System Health Validators (SHVs); configure health policies; configure NAP enforcement using DHCP and VPN; configure isolation and remediation of non-compliant computers using DHCP and VPN; configure NAP client settings.

Now that you understand how routing works, it's time to discuss how clients connect using remote access. *Routing and Remote Access Services (RRAS)* includes some security features necessary to provide remote access effectively. For example, you'll probably want the ability to restrict user dial-up access by group membership, time of day, or other factors. You'll also need a way to specify the various callback, authentication, and encryption options that the protocols support.

In this chapter, you'll learn about *virtual private networks (VPNs)*, which provide remote access to private networks across public connections. That is, using the Internet, clients can dial in to an Internet service provider (ISP) and connect to your private network. The main benefit of VPNs is reduced cost because it means that long-distance calls are unnecessary. VPNs are becoming more popular because of the increased popularity of high-speed Internet connections, such as cable and digital subscriber lines (DSL).

Many of the features included in Windows Server 2012 are simply carried over from Windows Server 2008, with a few minor additions. This is the case with the Routing and Remote Access console.

Before we can get into the details of what these features do and how to configure them to provide remote access for your network, you need to understand some of the terms and concepts specific to RRAS. That's where we'll begin in this chapter, and then we'll move on to reviewing the features and configuration settings that you need to understand to meet the exam objectives.

Overview of Dial-Up Networking

LANs provide relatively high-speed connectivity to attached machines, but where does that leave those of us who work from home, who travel, or who need to access data on a remote computer? Until wireless access is available worldwide, we have the option of using dial-up networking in which the client computer uses a modem to dial in and connect to a remote server. Once the connection is established, a variety of protocols and services make it possible for us to view web pages, transfer files and email, and do pretty much anything we could do with a hardwired LAN connection, albeit at a reduced speed.

In the following sections, you will learn more about what dial-up networking does and how it works by examining the specific technologies and protocols associated with remote access.

What DUN Does

At this point in the book, you should understand that Windows Server 2012 network protocols are actually implemented as drivers. These drivers normally work with hardware network interfaces to get data from point A to point B. How do dial-up connections fit in? Many people may read this and say, "Who still uses dial-up?" Well, as a person who lives in New Hampshire, I can tell you that we still have many areas that can't get broadband or even satellite access.

Think back to the OSI model. Each layer has a function, and each layer serves as an intermediary between the layer above it and the one below it. By substituting one driver for another at some level in the stack, you can dramatically change how things work. That's exactly what the Windows Server 2012's *Dial-Up Networking (DUN)* subsystem does. It makes the dial-up connection appear to be just another network adapter.

The DUN driver takes care of the work of making a slow asynchronous modem appear to work just like a fast LAN interface. Applications and services that use TCP/IP on your DUN connection never know the difference. In fact, you can configure Windows Server 2012 to use your primary connection first and then to pass traffic over a secondary connection (such as a dial-up link) if the primary connection is down. This does not affect the applications with which you're working (except that they might run more slowly).

On the server side, DUN allows you to host one or more network users who dial into your Windows Server 2012 machine. Windows XP Professional, Windows Vista, Windows 7, and Windows 8, allow up to 10 concurrent dial-up connections, and Windows Server 2012 allows up to 255. (Be aware that by the time you allow 255 concurrent connections, you'll probably be overloading your server.)

Depending on how you configure the DUN server, users who dial in can see the whole network or only specific resources on the server. You also get to control who can log on, when they can log on, and what they can do once they've logged on. As far as Windows Server 2012 is concerned, a user connected via DUN is no different from one using resources over your LAN, so all the access controls and permissions you apply remain in force for DUN users.

How DUN Works

A lot of pieces are required to complete a dial-up call successfully from your computer to a server at another physical location. Understanding what these pieces are, how they work, and what they do for you is important. The following sections will cover the DUN infrastructure, how the *Point-to-Point Protocol (PPP)* helps with this connection, the relationship between PPP and the network protocols, and how multilink can be used to increase the speed and efficiency of your remote connections.

The DUN Infrastructure

We'll start with a look at the physical layer that underlies voice and data calls. Most of the following material will be familiar to anyone who has ever used a modem, but you should still understand the details you may not have considered before.

Plain Old Telephone Service

Plain Old Telephone Service (POTS) connections offer a theoretical maximum speed of 56 Kbps; in practice, many users routinely get connections at 51 or 52 Kbps.

The word *modem* is actually short for *modulator-demodulator*. The original Bell System modems took digital data and modulated it into screechy analog audio tones suitable for use on regular phone lines. Because phone lines are purposely designed to pass only the low end of the audible frequency range that most can hear, the amount of data was limited. However, in the early 1990s, an engineer discovered that you could communicate much faster when the path between the sender and receiver was all digital.

An all-digital path doesn't have any analog components that induce signal loss, so it preserves the original signal quality faithfully. This in turn makes it possible to put more information into the original signal. As it happens, phone companies nationwide were in the process of making major upgrades to replace their analog equipment with newer and better digital equivalents. These upgrades made it possible for people in most areas to get almost 56 Kbps speeds without changing any of the wiring in their homes or offices. The connection between the house and the phone office was still analog, but the connections between phone offices were digital, ensuring high-quality connections.

Integrated Services Digital Network

In the mid-1970s, *Integrated Services Digital Network (ISDN)* was designed. At the time, no one had any idea that you'd be able to get 56 Kbps speeds out of an ordinary phone line. ISDN speeds of up to 128 Kbps over a single pair of copper wires seemed pretty revolutionary. In addition, ISDN had features such as call forwarding, caller ID, and multiple directory numbers (so you could have more than one number, perhaps with different ringing patterns, associated with a single line).

Unfortunately, ISDN requires an all-digital signal path. It also requires special equipment on both ends of the connection. The phone companies were slow to promote ISDN as a faster alternative to regular dial-up service, so customers avoided it.

ISDN still has some advantages, though. Because it's all digital, call setup times are much shorter than they are for analog modems—it takes only about half a second to establish a new ISDN call. Modern ISDN adapters and ISDN-capable routers can seamlessly stitch together multiple ISDN channels to deliver bandwidth in 64 Kbps increments. Because you can use ISDN lines for regular analog voice, data, and fax traffic, you can make a single ISDN act like two voice lines, a single 128 Kbps data line, or a 64 Kbps data line plus a voice line.

ISDN is quickly being replaced by faster broadband services such as DSL and cable modems. In fact, you should resort to ISDN only if these other solutions are not available in your area. Note that DSL (a misnomer because they are all digital) and cable modems do not use PPP (discussed later), so they are technically not considered dial-up connections.

Other Connection Methods

Any other on-demand connection that's established using the Point-to-Point Protocol can be thought of as a dial-up connection, and Windows Server 2012 doesn't make any distinction between POTS, ISDN, and other dial-ups—they're all treated identically.

Connecting with PPP

The Point-to-Point Protocol enables any two devices to establish a TCP/IP connection over a serial link. That usually means a dial-up modem connection, but it could just as easily be a direct serial cable connection, an infrared connection, or any other type of serial connection. When one machine dials another, the machine that initiates the connection is referred to as a *client* and the machine that receives the call is a *server*—even though PPP itself makes no such distinction.

PPP negotiation involves three phases that are required to establish a remote access connection. Actually, at least six distinct protocols run on top of PPP. Understanding what they do helps to make the actual PPP negotiation process clearer. These protocols are as follows:

The Link Control Protocol   The *Link Control Protocol (LCP)* handles the details of establishing and configuring the lowest-level PPP link. In that regard, you can think of LCP as if it were almost part of the Physical layer. When one PPP device calls another, the devices use LCP to agree that they want to establish a PPP connection.

The Challenge Handshake Authentication Protocol   The *Challenge Handshake Authentication Protocol (CHAP)*—as well as MS-CHAPv2 and PAP—allow the client to authenticate itself to the server. This authentication functions much like a regular network logon; once the client presents its logon credentials, the server can figure out what access to grant.

The Callback Control Protocol   The *Callback Control Protocol (CBCP)* is used to negotiate whether a callback is required, whether it's permitted, and when it happens. Once the client has authenticated itself, the server can decide whether it should hang up and call the client back. The client can also request a callback at a number it provides. Although this isn't as secure as having the server place a call to a predetermined number, it provides some additional flexibility. If a callback occurs, the connection is reestablished and reauthenticated, but the CBCP stage is skipped.

The Compression Control Protocol   The *Compression Control Protocol (CCP)* allows the two sides of the connection to determine what kind of compression, if any, they want to use on the network data. Because PPP traffic actually consists of wrapped-up IP datagrams and because IP datagram headers tend to be fairly compressible, negotiating effective compression can significantly improve overall PPP throughput.

The IP Control Protocol   At this point in the call, the two sides have agreed to authentication, compression, and a callback. They haven't yet agreed on what IP parameters to use for the connection. These parameters, which include the maximum packet size to be sent over the link (the *maximum transmission unit*, or *MTU*), have a great impact on the overall link performance, so the client and server use the *IP Control Protocol (IPCP)* to negotiate them based on the traffic they expect to be passed.

The Internet Protocol   Once the IPCP negotiation has been completed, each end has complete knowledge of how to communicate with its peer. That knowledge allows the two sides to begin exchanging Internet Protocol (IP) datagrams over the link, just as they would over a standard LAN connection.

The Relationship between PPP and Network Protocols

Usually, when you hear about network communication, you hear about using TCP/IP on a hardwired LAN. How does this protocol fit in with PPP? In the case of TCP/IP, that's an easy question to answer: The client routes all (or some) of its outgoing TCP/IP traffic to its PPP peer, which can then inspect the IP datagrams it gets back from the PPP stack to analyze and route them properly.

Windows Server 2012 supports only TCP/IP, so consider what has to happen when a client using AppleTalk needs to connect via dial-up. Because the server will not use those other protocols, it will drop the call or cause the client to warn its user (that's what Windows Server 2012 does). After the other PPP setup steps are finished, the client and server can wrap other types of network traffic inside an IP datagram. This process, called *encapsulation*, allows the client to take a packet with some kind of private content, wrap it inside an IP datagram, and send it to the server. The server, in turn, processes the IP datagram, routing real datagrams normally and handling any encapsulated packets with the appropriate protocol. At that point, the client can communicate with the server without knowing that its non-TCP/IP packets are being encapsulated in any way—that detail is hidden deep in the layers of the OSI model.

Understanding the Benefits of Multilink

Many parts of the world don't have high-speed broadband access yet. In fact, many places don't have ISDN or even phone lines that support 56 Kbps modems. The *multilink extensions* to the Point-to-Point Protocol provide a way to take several independent PPP connections and make them look like one line so that they act as a single connection.

For example, if you use two phone lines and modems to place a two-line multilink call to your ISP, instead of getting the usual 48 Kbps connection, you would end up with an apparent bandwidth of 96 Kbps. The multilink PPP software on your Windows Server 2012 machine and on the ISP's router takes care of stringing all the packets together to make this process seamless. Windows Server 2012's RRAS supports multilink PPP for inbound and outbound calls.

   The primary drawback to multilink calls is that they take up more than one phone line apiece.

Overview of Virtual Private Networks

Private networks offer superior security. You own the wires, so you have control over what they're used for, who can use them, and what kind of data passes over them. However, they're not very flexible because they require you to configure and manage costly leased lines between remote locations. To make things worse, most private networks face a dilemma: implementing enough capacity to handle peak loads almost guarantees that much of that capacity will remain idle much of the time, even though it still has to be paid for.

One way to work around this problem is to maintain private dial-up services. Such services allow, for example, a field rep in Chicago to dial the home office in Boston. But dial-ups are expensive, and they have the same excess capacity problem as truly private networks. As an added detriment, someone has to pay long-distance or toll-free number charges.

Virtual private networks (VPNs) offer a solution. You get the security of a true private network with the flexibility, ubiquity, and low cost of the Internet. In the following sections, I will cover VPNs, including what they are used for and how they work (in general and with Windows Server 2012).

What VPNs Do

At any time, two parties can create a connection over the Internet. The idea behind a VPN is that you can use these connections to let two parties establish an *encrypted tunnel* between them using the Internet as a transportation medium. The VPN software on each end takes care of encrypting the VPN packets as they go; when the packets leave one end of the tunnel, their payloads are encrypted and encapsulated inside regular IP packets that cause them to be delivered to the remote machine. Figure 15.1 shows one way to conceptualize this process.

FIGURE 15.1   Drilling a tunnel through the Internet

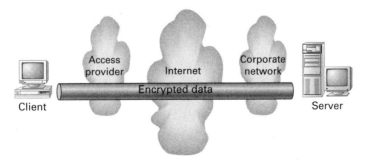

As an example, let's say you're in the field at a client site. As long as you're somewhere that your ISP serves, you can dial into the client's local point of presence and get connected to the Internet. At that point, you can open a VPN connection back to the servers at your office and do whatever you could do when sitting in front of a regular desktop machine.

VPNs and Windows Server 2012

Windows Server 2012 includes support for Microsoft's proprietary *Point-to-Point Tunneling Protocol* and Layer 2 Tunneling Protocol. *Layer 2 Tunneling Protocol (L2TP)* provides a more generic tunneling mechanism than PPTP; when combined with IPsec, L2TP also allows you to establish VPNs using a wide range of Microsoft or non-Microsoft hardware and software products, including routers and access devices from companies such as Cisco, Red Creek, and Nortel.

Windows Server 2012's VPN support includes the following worthwhile features:

- You can set up account lockout policies for dial-up and VPN users. This capacity has existed for network and console users for some time.

- The *Extensible Authentication Protocol (EAP)* allows Microsoft or third parties to write modules that implement new authentication methods and retrofit them to servers. One example is the EAP-TLS module, which implements access control based on smart cards and certificates for VPN and dial-up users.

How you enable VPN support on your Windows Server 2012 machine depends on whether you're using a server or a client (Windows XP, Windows Vista, Windows 7, Windows 8, and so on).

Client configuration is easy. Just install the Dial-Up Networking service, and then use the Make New Connection Wizard to create a new VPN connection. On the server side, you'll need to install and configure RRAS and then enable it to accept incoming VPN connections.

How VPNs Work

The VPN client assumes that the VPN server is already connected to the Internet in some way. Here's how the VPN connection process works:

1. The client establishes a connection to the Internet. Dial-up networking or any other connection method can be used for this connection. The client must be able to send packets to the Internet.

2. The client sends a VPN connection request to the server. The exact format of the request varies, depending on whether the VPN is using PPTP, L2TP, or SSTP.

3. The client authenticates itself to the server. Again, the exact process varies according to the VPN protocol in use. If the client can't provide valid credentials, the connection is terminated.

4. The client and server negotiate parameters for the VPN session. This negotiation allows the two ends to agree on an encryption algorithm and strength.

5. The client and server go through the PPP negotiation process because both L2TP and PPTP depend on the lower-level PPP.

Because the contents of data passed around in step 2 and step 3 vary according to the tunneling protocol in use, I'll explain the differences. First, though, you should understand encapsulation and how VPNs use it to wrap one kind of data inside another.

An Encapsulation Primer

Most of yesterday's networks could carry only one kind of data. Each network vendor had its own protocol, and most of the time there was no way to intermingle data using different protocols on the same line. Over time, vendors began to find ways to allow a single network to carry many different types of traffic, resulting in the current assortment of traffic types found on most large networks. However, the Internet works only with IP, which is why it's called Internet Protocol. If you need to send other types of traffic, such as AppleTalk, across the Internet, you can encapsulate it within IP.

How does encapsulation work? Software at each level of the OSI model has to see header information to figure out where a packet is coming from and where it's going. However, the payload contents aren't important to most of those components, and the payload is what's encapsulated. By fabricating the right kind of header and prepending it for whatever you want in the payload, you can route foreign traffic types through IP networks with no trouble.

VPNs depend on encapsulation because their security method depends on being able to keep the payload information encrypted. The following steps demonstrate what happens to a typical packet as it goes from being a regular IP datagram to a PPTP packet (see Figure 15.2):

1. An application creates a block of data bound for a remote host. In this case, it's a web browser.

2. The client-side IP stack takes the application's data and turns it into an IP packet; first by adding a TCP header and then by adding an IP header. This is called the *IP datagram* because it contains all of the necessary addressing information to be delivered by IP.

3. The client is connected via PPP, so it adds a PPP header to the IP datagram. This PPP+IP combination is called a *PPP frame*.

4. If you are using PPP instead of a VPN protocol, the packet goes across the PPP link without further modification. When you are using a VPN (as in this example), the next step is for the VPN to encrypt the PPP frame, turning it into unreadable information to be transported over the Internet.

5. A *Generic Routing Encapsulation (GRE) header* is combined with the encrypted payload. GRE really is generic; in this case, the protocol ID field in the GRE header says that this is an encapsulated PPTP packet.

FIGURE 15.2 The encapsulation process

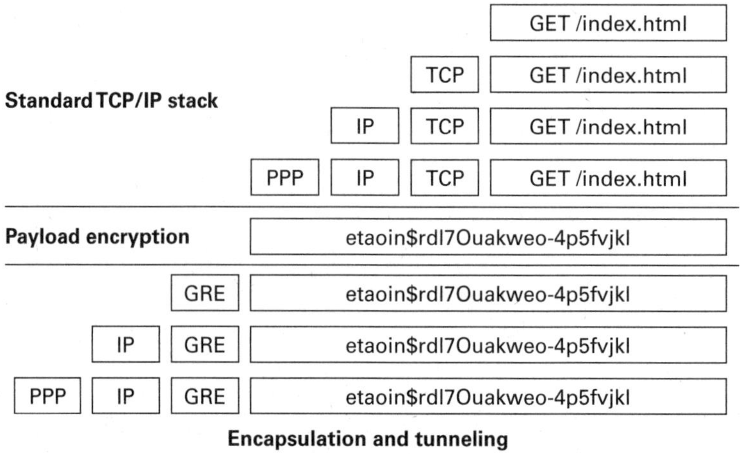

				GET /index.html
Standard TCP/IP stack			TCP	GET /index.html
		IP	TCP	GET /index.html
	PPP	IP	TCP	GET /index.html

Payload encryption	etaoin$rdl7Ouakweo-4p5fvjkl

			GRE	etaoin$rdl7Ouakweo-4p5fvjkl
		IP	GRE	etaoin$rdl7Ouakweo-4p5fvjkl
	PPP	IP	GRE	etaoin$rdl7Ouakweo-4p5fvjkl

Encapsulation and tunneling

6. Now that there is a tag to tell you what's in the payload, the PPTP stack can add an IP header (specifying the destination address of the VPN server) and a PPP header.

7. Now the packet can be sent out over your PPP connection. The IP header specifies that it should be routed to the VPN server.

8. When the packet arrives at the VPN server, the server reverses steps 1 through 6 to extract the payload.

Encapsulation allows the use of VPN data inside ordinary-looking IP datagrams, which is part of what makes VPNs so powerful—you don't have to change any of your applications, routers, or network components (unless they have to be configured to recognize and pass GRE packets).

PPTP Tunneling

PPTP is a pretty straightforward protocol. It works by encapsulating packets using the mechanism described in the previous section, "An Encapsulation Primer," and performs encryption (step 4) using the *Microsoft Point-to-Point Encryption (MPPE) algorithm*. The encryption keys used to encrypt the packets are generated dynamically for each connection; in fact, the keys can be changed periodically during the connection.

When the client and server have successfully established a PPTP tunnel, the authorization process begins. This process is an exchange of credentials that allows the server to decide whether the client is permitted to connect:

1. The server sends a challenge message to the client.

2. The client answers with an encrypted response.

3. The server checks the response to see whether the answer is right. The challenge-response process allows the server to determine which account is trying to make a connection.

4. The server determines whether the user account is authorized to make a connection.

5. If the account is authorized, the server accepts the inbound connection; any access controls or remote access restrictions still apply.

L2TP/IPsec Tunneling

L2TP is much more flexible than PPTP, but it's also more complicated. It was designed to be a general-purpose tunneling protocol not limited to VPN use.

L2TP itself doesn't offer any kind of security. When you use L2TP, you're setting up an unencrypted, unauthenticated tunnel. Using L2TP by itself over the Internet, therefore, would be dangerous because anyone who wanted to could read your traffic.

The overall flow of an L2TP/IPsec tunnel session looks a little different from that of a PPTP session because IPsec security is different. Here's how the L2TP/IPsec combination works:

1. The client and server establish an IPsec security association using the ISAKMP and Oakley protocols. At this point, the two machines have an encrypted channel between them.

2. The client builds a new L2TP tunnel to the server. Because this happens after the channel has been encrypted, there's no security risk.

3. The server sends an authentication challenge to the client.

4. The client encrypts its answer to the challenge and returns it to the server.

5. The server checks the challenge response to see whether it's valid; if so, the server can determine which account is connecting. At this point the server can accept the inbound connection, subject to whatever access policies you've put in place.

Note that steps 3 through 5 mirror the steps described for PPTP tunneling. This is because the authorization process is a function of the remote access server, not the VPN stack. All the VPN does is provide a secure communications channel, and something else has to decide who gets to use it.

SSTP Tunneling

The *Secure Sockets Tunneling Protocol (SSTS)* is a secure way to make a VPN connection using the Secure Sockets Layer v.3 (SSL) port 443. The following steps show how SSTP operates and functions:

1. The client connects to the server through the Internet using port 443.

2. During the TCP session, SSL negotiation takes place.

3. During the SSL authentication phase, the client machine receives the server certificate.

4. The client machine will send HTTPS requests on the top of the encrypted SSL session.

5. The client machine will then also send SSTP control packets on top of the HTTPS session.

6. PPP negotiation now takes place on both ends of the connection.

7. After PPP is finished, both ends are ready to send IP packets to each other.

Configuring Your Remote Access Server

Most of the configuration necessary for a remote access server happens at the server level. You use the server's Properties dialog box to control whether the server allows remote connections, what protocols and options it supports, and so forth. Because all of the protocols are carried via PPP, you can set some generic PPP options as well. I will cover these options in the following sections. You also have to configure settings for your users, which you'll read about in the next section.

Configuring PPP Options

You can use the PPP tab of the RRAS server's Properties dialog box (see Figure 15.3) to control the PPP layer options available to clients that call in. The settings you specify here control whether the related PPP options are available to clients; you can use remote access policies to control whether individual connections can use them.

FIGURE 15.3   The PPP tab of the RRAS server's Properties dialog box

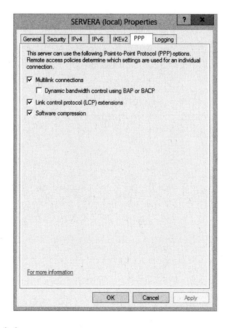

This tab has four check boxes:

- The Multilink Connections check box, which is selected by default, controls whether the server will allow clients to establish multilink connections when they call in.

- The Dynamic Bandwidth Control Using BAP Or BACP check box determines whether clients and servers are allowed to add or remove links dynamically during a multilink session. If you enable this feature, you can throttle the amount of available bandwidth up or down on demand. It's available only when the Multilink Connections check box is selected. (BAP stands for Bandwidth Allocation Protocol, and BACP stands for Bandwidth Allocation Control Protocol.)

- The Link Control Protocol (LCP) is used to establish a PPP link and negotiate its settings. A variety of LCP extensions are defined in various RFCs; these extensions allow a client and server to agree dynamically about which protocols are being passed back and forth, among other things. The Link Control Protocol (LCP) Extensions check box controls whether these extensions are available. Windows 9*x*, NT, 2000, Vista, XP, Windows 7, and Windows 8 clients depend on the LCP extensions, so you should leave this check box selected.

- The Software Compression check box controls whether RRAS will allow a remote client to use the Compression Control Protocol (CCP) to compress PPP traffic. In some cases, hardware compression at the modem level is more efficient, but not everyone has a compression-capable modem. You should leave this check box selected as well.

Configuring IP-Based Connections

TCP/IP is far and away the most commonly used remote access protocol; coincidentally, it's also the most configurable of the protocols that Windows Server 2012 supports. Both of these facts are reflected in the IPv4 and IPv6 tabs of the server's Properties dialog box. Figure 15.4 shows the IPv4 tab.

FIGURE 15.4   The IPv4 tab of the RRAS server's Properties dialog box

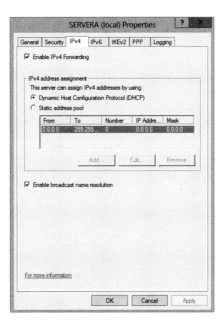

The controls on the IPv4 tab do the following:

- The Enable IPv4 Forwarding check box controls whether RRAS will route IPv4 packets between the remote client and other interfaces on your RRAS server. When this box is checked, as it is by default, remote clients' packets can go to the RRAS server or to any other host to which the RRAS server has a route. To allow clients to access resources on the RRAS server only, uncheck this box.

- The IP Address Assignment control group lets you specify how you want remote clients to get their IP addresses. The default settings here depend on what you told the RRAS Setup Wizard during setup:

  - If you want to use a DHCP server on your network as the source of IP addresses for remote clients, select the Dynamic Host Configuration Protocol (DHCP) radio button and make sure you have the DHCP relay agent installed and running.

  - If you'd rather use static address allocation, select the Static Address Pool radio button. Then, in the list below, specify which IP address ranges you want issued to clients.

  - The Enable Broadcast Name Resolution option allows remote clients to resolve TCP/IP names without the use of a WINS or DNS server. This feature is enabled by default, and it is new for Windows Server 2012.

Figure 15.5 shows the IPv6 tab of the RRAS server's Properties dialog box.

FIGURE 15.5 The IPv6 tab of the RRAS Server's Properties dialog box

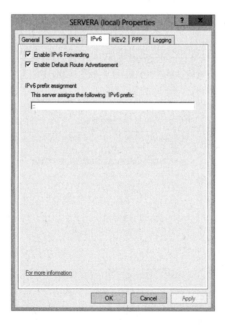

The controls on the IPv6 tab do the following:

- The Enable IPv6 Forwarding check box controls whether RRAS will route IPv6 packets between the remote client and other interfaces on your RRAS server. When this box is checked, as it is by default, remote clients' packets can go to the RRAS server or to any other host to which the RRAS server has a route. To allow clients to access resources on the RRAS server only, uncheck this box.

- The Enable Default Route Advertisement check box (enabled by default) makes the *Border Gateway Protocol (BGP)* routing protocol available. BGP can exchange routing information between Windows Server 2012 routers. When this box is checked, your Windows Server 2012 router can announce its route to other routers.

- On the IPv6 tab, you can also set up your IPv6 prefix assignment (assigning IPv6 prefixes were discussed in Chapter 9).

In Exercise 15.1, you'll configure your RRAS server so that it accepts only those inbound calls that use the Internet Protocol.

EXERCISE 15.1

Configuring Incoming Connections

1. Open the RRAS MMC console by pressing the Windows Key ➢ Administrative Tools ➢ Routing And Remote Access.

2. Right-click the server you want to configure in the left pane of the MMC, and choose the Properties command. The server's Properties dialog box appears.

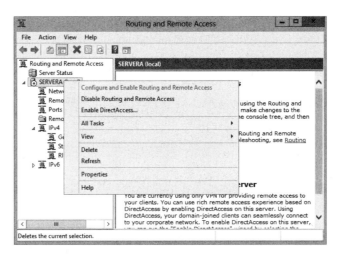

3. Click the IPv4 tab and verify that the Enable IPv4 Forwarding check box is selected.

4. Make sure the Dynamic Host Configuration Protocol (DHCP) radio button is selected.

5. Click the OK button.

Installing a VPN

Conventional dial-up access works well, but as you saw earlier, it can be expensive to implement, painful to manage, and extremely slow by today's standards. VPNs offer a way around these problems by providing low initial and ongoing costs, easy management, and excellent speeds (depending on your connection). Windows Server 2012's RRAS component includes two complete VPN implementations: one using Microsoft's PPTP and one using a combination of the Internet-standard IPsec protocol and L2TP or SSTP.

The basic process of setting up a VPN is simple, but you need to think some things through before plunging ahead. Getting the VPN installation right may require small hardware or networking changes plus proper configuration of the VPN service. We will look at this process in the following sections.

How VPN Works

A VPN sits between your internal network and the Internet, accepting connections from clients in the outside world. In Figure 15.6, clients 1 and 2 are using different ISPs (probably because they're at different physical locations). For example, a packet from client 1 goes from its computer to its ISP and then through some route, unknown to you, that eventually delivers it to the VPN server, which transforms it into a packet suitable for use on the internal network.

FIGURE 15.6 VPNs provide private connections between clients and servers across the Internet.

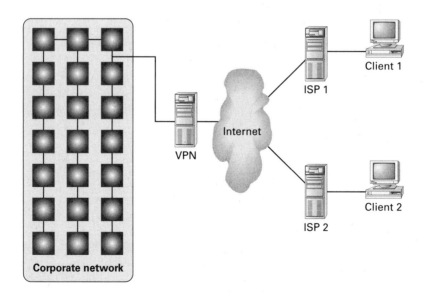

Imagine a line around the internal network, and think of it as a security boundary. In general, you'll want your VPN server to be outside any firewalls or network security measures you have in place. The most common configuration is to use two NICs: one connects to the Internet, and the other connects either to the private network or to an intermediate network that itself connects to the private network. Of course, you can use any type of Internet connection you want for the VPN server: cable modem, DSL, T1, satellite, or whatever.

The point behind giving the VPN its own network adapter is that your VPN clients need a public IP address to which they can connect, and you probably don't want them calling directly into your internal network. That also means that things will be easiest for your VPN users if the IP address for your VPN server's external interface is statically assigned so that it won't be changing on them when they least expect it.

Enabling RRAS as a VPN

If you're already using RRAS for IP routing or remote access, you can enable it as a VPN server without reinstalling.

The General tab of the server's Properties dialog box allows you to specify whether your RRAS server is a router, a remote access server, or both. The first step in converting your existing RRAS server to handle VPN traffic is to make sure the IPv4 Remote Access Server or IPv6 Remote Access Server check box is selected on this tab.

Making this change requires you to stop and restart the RRAS service, but that's OK because the snap-in will do it for you. Then you must configure VPN ports, as shown in the following sections.

Configuring a VPN

VPN configuration is extremely simple, at least for PPTP. Either a server can accept VPN calls or it can't. If it can, it will have a certain number of VPN ports, all of which are configured identically. You don't have to change or tweak much to get a VPN server set up, but you can adjust a few things as you like.

Configuring VPN Ports

The biggest opportunity to configure your VPN server is to adjust the number and kind of VPN ports available for clients to use. You can enable or disable either PPTP or L2TP, depending on what you want your remote users to be able to access. You accomplish this through the Ports Properties dialog box.

For conventional remote access servers, this dialog box shows you a list of hardware ports, but for servers that support VPN connections, there are two WAN Miniport device selections: one for PPTP and one for L2TP. (These aren't really devices; they're actually virtual ports maintained by RRAS for accepting VPN connections.) You configure these ports by selecting one and clicking the Configure button, which displays the Configure Device – WAN Miniport (PPTP) dialog box (see Figure 15.7).

FIGURE 15.7   The Configure Device – WAN Miniport (PPTP) dialog box

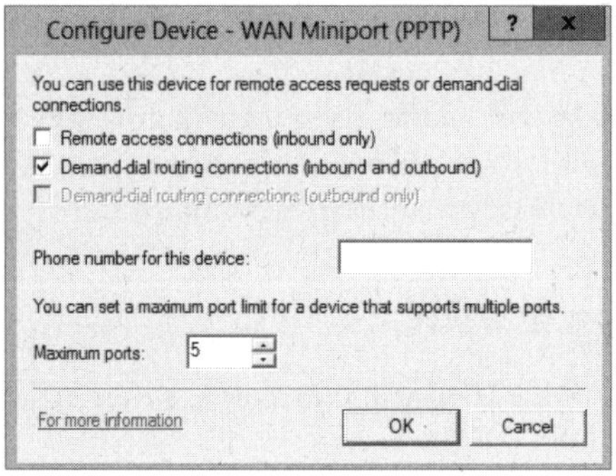

Three controls are pertinent to a VPN configuration:

- The Remote Access Connections (Inbound Only) check box must be activated in order to accept VPN connections with this port type. To disable a VPN type (for instance, if you want to turn off L2TP), uncheck this box.

- The Demand-Dial Routing Connections (Inbound And Outbound) check box controls whether this VPN type can be used for demand-dial connections. By default, this box is checked; you'll need to uncheck it if you don't want to use VPN connections to link your network with other networks.

- The Maximum Ports control lets you set the number of inbound connections that this port type will support. By default, you get 5 PPTP and 5 L2TP ports when you install RRAS; you can use from 0 to 250 ports of each type by adjusting the number here.

You can also use the Phone Number For This Device field to enter the IP address of the public interface to which VPN clients connect. You might want to do this if your remote access policies accept or reject connections based on the number called by the client. Because you can assign multiple IP addresses to a single adapter, you can control VPN traffic by throttling which clients can connect to which addresses through a policy.

Troubleshooting VPNs

The two primary problems you might encounter with VPN are as follows:

- Inability to establish a connection at all
- Inability to reach some needed resource once connected

There's a lot of common ground between the process of troubleshooting a VPN connection and the process of troubleshooting an ordinary remote access connection.

The following are some extremely simple—but sometimes overlooked—things to check when your VPN clients can't connect. First, make sure that your clients can make the underlying connection to their ISP, and then check the following:

- Is RRAS installed and configured on the server?

    - Is the server configured to allow remote access? Check the General tab of the server's Properties dialog box.

    - Is the server configured to allow VPN traffic? Check the Ports Properties dialog box to make sure that the appropriate VPN protocol is enabled and that the number of ports for that protocol is greater than 0.

    - Are there any available VPN ports? If you have 10 L2TP ports allocated, the 11th caller will not be able to connect.

- Do the client and server match?

    - Is the VPN protocol used by the client enabled on the server? Windows 2000 and newer clients will try L2TP first and switch to PPTP as a second choice. However, clients on other OSs (including Windows NT) can normally expect L2TP, PPTP, or SSTP.

- Are the client and server authenticated correctly?

    - Are the username and password correct?

    - Does the user account in question have remote access permissions, either directly on the account or through a policy?

    - Do the authentication settings in the server's policies (if any) match the supported set of authentication protocols?

If you check all of the simple stuff and find nothing wrong, it's time to move on to checking more complex issues. These tend to affect more than one user, as opposed to the simple (and generally user-specific) issues just outlined. The problems include the following:

Policy Problems   If you're using a native-mode Windows Server 2012 domain and you're using policies, those policies may cause some subtle problems that show up under some circumstances:

- Are there any policies whose Allow or Deny settings conflict with each other? Remember that all conditions of all policies must match to gain user access; if any condition of any policy fails or if there are any policies that deny access, the connection will be denied.

- Does the user match all of the necessary conditions that are in place, such as time and date?

Network Problems   If you're using dynamic IP addressing, are there any addresses left in the pool? If the VPN server can't assign an address, it won't accept the connection.

Domain Problems   Windows Server 2012 RRAS servers can coexist with Windows NT RRAS servers, and both of them can interoperate with RADIUS servers from Microsoft and other vendors. Sometimes, though, this interoperation doesn't work exactly as you'd expect. Here are some questions to ask:

- Is the RRAS server's domain membership correct? Your RRAS servers don't have to be domain members unless you want to use native-mode features such as remote access policies.

- If you're in a domain, are the server's group memberships correct? The server account must be a member of the RAS group and Internet Authentication Servers security group.

Managing Your Remote Access Server

RRAS server management is generally pretty easy because, in most cases, there's not much to manage. You set up the server, and it answers calls. You'll probably find it necessary to monitor the server's ongoing activity, however, and you may find it necessary to log activity for accounting or security purposes.

You can monitor your server's activity in a number of ways, including having the server keep local copies of its logs or having it send logging data to a remote RADIUS server. In addition, you can monitor the current status of any of the ports on your system.

Microsoft's documentation distinguishes between event logging, which records significant things that happen, such as the RRAS service starting up and shutting down, and authentication and accounting logging, which tracks things like when a user logged on and logged off. The settings for both types of logging are intermingled in the RRAS snap-in.

Managing Remote Users with a RADIUS Server

Remote Authentication Dial-In User Service (RADIUS) allows for maintaining and managing your remote users. A RADIUS server allows Remote Access Service (RAS) clients and dial-up routers to be authenticated.

Network Policy Server (NPS) is Microsoft's implementation of a RADIUS server in Windows Server 2012. NPS is replacing Windows Server 2003 Internet Authentication Service (IAS). NPS, working as a RADIUS server, allows for authentication, authorization, and accounting for wireless and VPN networks.

NPS allows a server to perform the duties of a RADIUS proxy. A RADIUS proxy allows the routing of RADIUS messages between RADIUS clients (RAS) and RADIUS servers. NPS also gives you the ability to record information about forwarded messages in an accounting log.

Monitoring Overall Activity

The Server Status node in the RRAS snap-in shows you a summary of all the RRAS servers known to the system. When you select the Server Status item, the right pane of the MMC will list each known RRAS server. Each entry in the list tells you whether the server is up, what kind of server it is, how many ports it has, how many ports are currently in use, and how long the server has been up. You can right-click any Windows Server 2012 RRAS server in this view to start, stop, restart, pause, or resume its RRAS service; disable RRAS on the server; or remove the server's advertisement from Active Directory (provided, of course, that you're using Active Directory).

Controlling Remote Access Logging

A standard RRAS installation will always log some data locally, but that's pretty useless unless you know what gets logged and where it goes. Each RRAS server on your network has its own set of logs, which you manage through the `Remote Access Logging` folder. Within that folder, you'll usually see a single item labeled *Local File*, which is the log file stored on that particular server.

 If you don't have Windows accounting or Windows authentication turned on, you won't have a local log file. Depending on whether you're using RADIUS accounting and logging, you may see additional entries.

Setting Server Logging Properties

You can control server logging at the server level. You use the Logging tab to control what level of detail you want in the server's event log.

 These controls regulate all logging by RRAS, not just remote access log entries.

You have four choices for the level of logged detail:

- The Log Errors Only radio button instructs the server to log errors and nothing else. This gives you an adequate indication of problems after they happen, but it doesn't point out potential problems noted by warning messages.

- The Log Errors And Warnings radio button is the default choice. This forces the server to log error and warning messages to the event log, giving you a nice balance between information content and log volume.

- The Log All Events radio button causes the RRAS service to log mass quantities of messages, literally covering everything the server does. Although this voluminous output is useful for troubleshooting (or even for getting a better understanding of how remote access works), it's overkill for everyday use.

- The Do Not Log Any Events radio button turns off all event logging for RRAS.

WARNING   Don't use the Do Not Log Any Events option. The service's logs are important in case of a problem.

The Log Additional Routing And Remote Access Information check box allows you to turn on the logging of all PPP negotiations and connections. This can provide valuable information when you're trying to figure out what's wrong, but it adds a lot of unnecessary bulk to your log files. Don't turn it on unless you're trying to pin down a problem.

Setting Log File Properties

By selecting an individual log file in the snap-in, you can change what events will be logged in that file. The Local Log File Properties dialog box has two tabs:

- The Settings tab controls what gets logged in the file:

  - Accounting Requests governs whether events related to the service will be logged (as well as accounting data). You should always leave this checked.

  - Authentication Requests adjusts whether successful and failed logon requests are logged. You should always leave this checked.

  - Periodic Status controls whether interim accounting packets are permanently stored on disk. You should usually leave this checked.

  - Periodic Authentication Requests adjusts whether successful and failed logon requests are periodically logged. You should always leave this checked.

- The Log File tab (see Figure 15.8) controls the format of the file, specifically, how the log file is written to disk. You use this tab to designate three things:

  - The Directory field shows where the log file is stored. By default, each server logs its data in *systemroot*\system32\LogFiles. You can change this location to wherever you want.

  - The Format controls determine the format of the log file. By default, Windows Server 2000, 2003, 2008/2008 R2, and 2012 use the database-compatible file format. This format makes it easy for you to take log data and store it in a database, enabling more sophisticated postprocessing for things such as billing and chargebacks.

  - The Create A New Log File controls determine how often new log files are created. For example, some administrators prefer to start a new log file each week or each month, whereas others are content to let the log file grow without end. You can choose to have RRAS start new log files every day, week, month, never, or when the log file reaches a certain size.

Having correct accounting and authorization data is critical to maintaining a good level of security. Exercise 15.2 walks you through configuring remote access logging.

FIGURE 15.8   The Log File tab of the Local File Properties dialog box

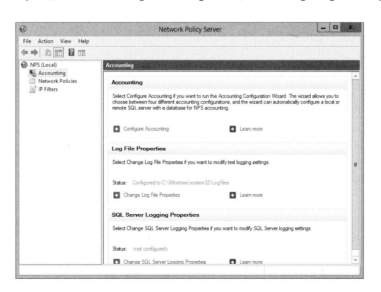

EXERCISE 15.2

Changing Remote Access Logging Settings

1. Open the RRAS MMC snap-in by pressing the Windows Key ➢ Administrative Tools ➢ Routing And Remote Access.

2. Navigate to the `Remote Access Logging and Policies` folder. Right-click the folder, and select Launch NPS.

3. On the left pane, click Accounting. On the right side, click Change Log File Properties.

4. The Local File Logging dialog box appears. On the Settings tab, make sure that all check boxes are marked.

5. Switch to the Log File tab, and in the Create A New Log File controls, select the When Log File Reaches This Size option, and enter **50** to set the maximum size of the log file to 50 MB.

6. Click the OK button. Close the Network Policy Server window.

Reviewing the Remote Access Event Log

You use the Log File tab to specify the format, size, and location of the log file. Once you have a log file, however, what do you do with the log information? Windows Server 2012 online help has an exhaustive list of all the fields logged for each connection attempt and accounting record. Because of the availability of online help, you don't need to have all of those fields memorized, and you don't have to remember exactly how to make sense of the log entries.

Why bother reviewing the logs? One nice feature is that each entry in the authentication log indicates which remote access policy was applied (either to accept or to reject the connection). This is a good way to identify problems with policies because sometimes multiple policies can combine to have an effect that you didn't expect.

Furthermore, if it's desirable in your environment, you can use the logged data to generate accounting reports to tell you things such as the average utilization of your dial-in ports, the top 10 users of dial-in connect time, or how much online time accounts or certain Windows groups use.

Monitoring Ports and Port Activity

You can monitor port status and activity from the RRAS snap-in. The Ports folder under the server contains one entry for each defined port. When you select the Ports folder, you'll see a list of the ports and their current status. The list indicates whether each port is a dial-in or VPN port and whether it's active, so you can get a quick summary of your server's workload at any time.

Double-clicking an individual port displays the Port Status dialog box (see Figure 15.9). This dialog box shows information such as a port's line speed (Line BPS), the amount of transmitted and received data (Bytes In and Bytes Out), and the network address for each protocol being carried on the port. This is a useful tool for verifying whether a port is in active use, and it gives you a count of the number of transmission and reception errors on the port.

FIGURE 15.9   The Port Status dialog box

Configuring a RAS or VPN Client

Dial-up RAS clients and VPN clients are similar. Almost all of the options that are available when you set up a RAS client are also available when you set up a VPN client. The main differences are as follows:

- VPN clients specify the server's IP address, whereas RAS clients specify the server's phone number.
- VPN clients require an underlying connection to the Internet.

Client configuration is not a focus of the exam, so in this chapter you will learn how to configure a VPN client but not a RAS client. Just remember that the RAS client configuration is extremely similar.

VPN connections are almost always created on client workstations, so this section describes the settings in Windows 7 and Windows 8.

When you establish a virtual private network connection, you're actually building an encrypted tunnel between you and some other machine. The tunneled data is carried over an insecure network, such as the Internet.

Once you've created a connection, you can change its properties at any time by opening its Properties dialog box. The Dial-Up Connection Properties dialog box has a total of five tabs you can use to adjust all of the pertinent settings for each connection.

Don't confuse these settings with the ones in the Local Area Connection Properties dialog box; they serve entirely different purposes.

The General Tab

The General tab of the Connection Properties dialog box (the box is called Dial-Up Connections or VPN Connections, depending on whether you're configuring dial-up RAS or VPN) is where you specify either the IP address of the VPN server or the modem and phone number to use with this particular connection. Some fields have been filled in already from when you used the Network Connection Wizard. Figure 15.10 shows the VPN settings.

FIGURE 15.10   General tab of the VPN Connection Properties dialog box

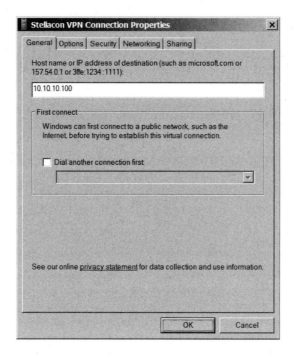

The General tab has a field where you enter the VPN server address or hostname. The First Connect group lets you specify which dial-up connection, if any, you want brought up before the VPN connection is established.

With the General tab, you can also do the following:

- Set VPN options:
  - Enter the VPN server address or hostname.
  - Specify whether to dial another connection automatically first, and then specify the connection to dial.
- Set RAS options:
  - Change the modem this connection uses, or the settings for the modem you already have, with the Configure button.

 When configuring dial-up, you can also use the Phone And Modem Options control panel to adjust a broader range of modem settings.

The Options Tab

The Options tab holds settings that control how DUN dials and redials the connection. The controls in this dialog box are segregated into two groups. The Dialing Options group holds controls that govern DUN's interface behavior while dialing, and the Redialing Options group controls whether and how DUN will redial if it doesn't immediately connect (see Figure 15.11).

FIGURE 15.11   Options tab of the VPN Connection Properties dialog box

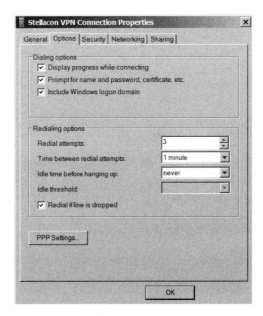

Dialing Options

Four dialing options are available in the Dialing Options group:

- The Display Progress While Connecting check box (selected by default) instructs DUN to keep you updated on its progress as it attempts to raise the connection.

- The Prompt For Name And Password, Certificate, Etc. check box is also selected by default. When it's on, Windows will prompt you for any credentials it needs to authenticate your connection to the remote server. This may be a username, a password, a public key certificate, or some combination of the three, depending on what the remote end requires.

- The Include Windows Logon Domain check box is unchecked by default. It forces DUN to include the domain name of the domain to which you're logged on as part of the authentication credential. Leave this unchecked unless you're dialing into a Windows NT/2000 network that has a trust relationship with your logon domain.

- For RAS connections, a Prompt For Phone Number check box tells DUN to display the phone number in the connection dialog box. This box is checked by default. This gives you a chance to edit the phone number before dialing; you may want to uncheck it if you (or your users) are prone to making accidental changes.

Redialing Options

The settings in the Redialing Options group control how DUN will attempt to redial the specified number if the remote end is busy or doesn't answer with a recognizable carrier tone. These settings are as follows:

- The Redial Attempts field controls how many attempts DUN will make to raise the other end before giving up. The default value is 3, but you can set any value from 0 (meaning that DUN won't attempt to redial) to 999,999,999.

- The Time Between Redial Attempts drop-down menu controls how long DUN will wait after each failed call before it tries again. Values in the drop-down menu range from 1 second all the way to 10 minutes, with various increments in between.

- The Idle Time Before Hanging Up drop-down menu lets you specify an inactivity timer. If your connection is idle for longer than the specified period, your client will terminate the call. Note that the remote end may drop the call sooner than your client, depending on how it's configured. By default, this drop-down menu is set to Never, meaning that your client will never drop a call. If you want an inactivity timer, you can pick values ranging from 1 minute to 24 hours.

- The Redial If Line Is Dropped check box automatically redials the number if you are disconnected.

The Security Tab

How useful you find the Security tab will depend on whom you're calling. The default settings it provides will work fine with most Internet service providers and corporate dial-up facilities, but Windows 7 and Windows 8 has a broad range of security settings that you can change if you require. The Security Options group contains controls that directly affect the security of your connection. The Advanced (Custom Settings) radio button controls settings such as encryption and authentication protocols.

Security Options

The controls in the Security Options group are pretty straightforward. The security settings in effect for this connection are governed by your choice between the Typical (Recommended Settings) and Advanced (Custom Settings) radio buttons (see Figure 15.12).

FIGURE 15.12   Security tab of the VPN Connection Properties dialog box

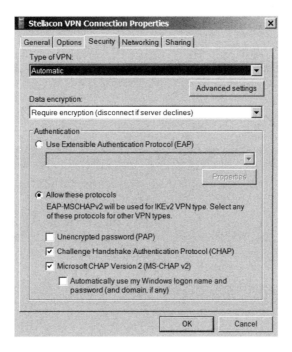

Typical (Recommended Settings)

Usually, it's best to stick with the Typical (Recommended Settings) option and use its subordinate controls to pick a canned setting that matches your needs. These subordinate controls are as follows:

- The Validate My Identity As Follows drop-down menu lets you choose among the following authentication methods:

  - Unsecured passwords (the default, and the only type of authentication that most networks support)

- Secured passwords
- Smart card authentication (useful only when calling another Windows 2000, 2003, 2008 /2008 R2, or 2012 network)

- If you choose to require a secured password, the Automatically Use My Windows Logon Name And Password (And Domain If Any) check box instructs DUN to offer to the remote end the logon credentials you used to log on to the computer or domain. This is useful only if you're dialing into a network that has access to your domain authentication information.

- If you require a secured password or smart card authentication, the Require Encryption (Disconnect If None) check box allows you to have either an encrypted connection or none at all. If you check this box, your client and the remote server will attempt to negotiate a common encryption method. If they can't (perhaps because the remote end doesn't offer encryption), your client will hang up.

Advanced (Custom Settings)

If you select the Advanced (Custom Settings) radio button and then click the Settings button, you'll see the Advanced Security Settings dialog box. Its controls are more complex than the ones on the Security tab.

The first field is the Data Encryption drop-down menu. Windows 8 offers you the opportunity to encrypt both sides of network connections using IPsec. This capability extends to dial-up connections too. The drop-down menu gives you the following four choices:

- No Encryption Allowed means that the server will drop your call if it requires encryption because you can't provide it.

- Optional Encryption tells the client to request encryption but to continue the call if it's not available.

- Require Encryption tells the client to request encryption and to refuse to communicate with servers that don't support it.

- Maximum Strength Encryption tells the client to communicate only with servers that offer the same strength encryption it does. For example, with this setting in force, a North American Windows Server 2008 R2 machine running 3DES won't communicate with a French Windows XP machine because the French machine uses the weaker exportable encryption routines.

The Authentication section controls which authentication protocols this client can use. The default setting, Use Extensible Authentication Protocol (EAP), is for standard Windows authentication (using the MD5-Challenge method) or certificate-based authentication (using the Smart Card Or Other Certificate choice in the drop-down menu).

The Allow These Protocols radio button is followed by a long list of authentication protocols. Although the specifics of how they work are different, the basic idea behind all of these protocols is the same. Each provides a secure way for a client to prove its identity to a server. By selecting the appropriate check boxes, you can make your client use the same protocols as the remote end.

The Networking Tab

You use the Networking tab (see Figure 15.13) to control which protocols your client will attempt to use when communicating with other servers.

The list box in the middle of the tab shows the network protocols installed on the client. Protocols marked with a check are available for use with this connection. Usually, when configuring RAS, you'll see TCP/IP and Client For Microsoft Networks marked, which indicates that those two protocols can be used over the connection.

The Install, Uninstall, and Properties buttons work just as they do in the Local Area Connection Properties dialog box. By using them, you can control which protocols are on your machine and their settings.

It's worth mentioning that selecting Internet Protocol (TCP/IP) in the protocols list and opening its Properties dialog box gives you access to a set of properties that are completely distinct from any TCP/IP settings that may apply to your LAN interfaces. Usually, the dial-up TCP/IP settings are configured to obtain an IP address and DNS information from the remote server, although if you need to, you can override these settings.

FIGURE 15.13   Networking tab of the VPN Connection Properties dialog box

The Sharing Tab

Internet Connection Sharing allows other users to connect to the Internet through this machine. The machine on which you enable this works like a gateway to the Internet (see Figure 15.14).

FIGURE 15.14   Sharing tab of the VPN Connection Properties dialog box

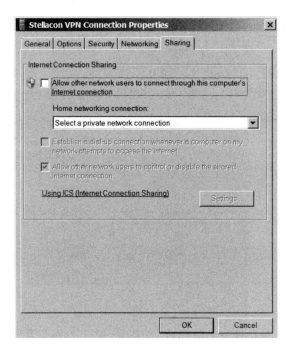

Overview of Wireless Access

In today's computer world, it seems like everyone has a laptop. We do a lot of traveling, and when you go to any airport, it seems like everyone is working on a laptop while they wait for their plane.

Because laptops have grown in popularity, IT professionals must account for them on their networks. Laptops offer IT administrators a unique set of challenges that must be dealt with on a day-to-day basis.

One major concern for IT administrators is security. Years ago we never had to worry about users copying documents to a desktop computer and then walking out with the computer. But today, users can copy company documents to laptop computers and then walk out the door with the computer and the documents. Next I will discuss wireless networks, protocols, and security.

Windows 8, Windows 7, Windows Vista, Windows 2008/2008 R2, and Windows Server 2012 have enhanced the IEEE 802.11 wireless support to include some of the following changes:

- Single sign-on
- 802.11 wireless diagnostics
- WPA2 support
- Native Wi-Fi architecture
- User interface improvements for wireless connections
- Wireless Group Policy enhancements
- Changes in Wireless Auto Configuration
- Integration with Network Access Protection when using 802.1X authentication
- EAP Host infrastructure
- Command-line support for configuring wireless settings
- Network Location Awareness and network profiles
- Next-generation TCP/IP stack enhancements for wireless environments

Configuring Wireless Access

Windows 8, Windows 7, Windows Vista, Windows XP, and Windows Server 2003, 2008/2008 R2, and 2012 provide built-in support for 802.11 wireless LAN networking. Inside the Network Connections folder, an installed 802.11 wireless LAN network adapter appears as a wireless network connection. The following are some of the items that you can configure:

Operating Modes   There are two types of operating modes:

Infrastructure Mode   This mode uses at least one wireless access point (WAP) and/or a device that bridges the wireless computers to each other.

Ad Hoc Mode   Using this mode, wireless network computers connect directly to each other without the use of an AP or bridge.

Wired Equivalent Privacy   All of us (on a laptop) have tried to find a wireless network at one time or another. *Wired Equivalent Privacy (WEP)* is a wireless encryption that was originally defined in 802.11. WEP helps prevent unauthorized wireless users from accessing your wireless network by the use of a shared secret key:

- If your wireless network is using the infrastructure mode, the WEP key must be configured on the wireless AP and all of the wireless clients.
- If your wireless network is using the ad hoc mode, the WEP key must be configured on all of the wireless clients.

The WEP key can be either 40-bit or 104-bit depending on what your hardware can accommodate.

Wi-Fi Protected Access An organization of wireless equipment vendors called the Wi-Fi Alliance created an interim standard called *Wi-Fi Protected Access (WPA)* while the IEEE 802.11i wireless LAN security standard was still being completed. WPA uses a strong encryption method called the *Temporal Key Integrity Protocol (TKIP)* to replace the weaker WEP standard. You have the ability to use the *Advanced Encryption Standard (AES)* for encryption that is provided by WPA.

WPA can be used in two different mode types:

WPA-Personal This is used for a home office or small company.

WPA-Enterprise This was designed for a mid-size to large organization.

Wi-Fi Protected Access 2 Wi-Fi Protected Access 2 (WPA2) was officially designed to replace the WEP standard. WPA2 certifies that equipment used in a wireless network is compatible with the IEEE 802.11i standard. This certification is used to help standardize the use of the additional security features of the IEEE 802.11i standard that are not already included in WPA.

WPA2 can be used in two different mode types:

WPA2-Personal This is used for a home office or small company.

WPA2-Enterprise This was designed for a mid-size to large organization.

Service Set Identifier To specify a wireless network by name, you specify the *service set identifier (SSID)*, also known as the *wireless network name*:

Infrastructure Mode The SSID is configured on the wireless access point.

Ad Hoc Mode The SSID is configured on the initial wireless client.

To help wireless clients discover and join the wireless network, the wireless AP or the initial wireless client periodically advertises the SSID (this can be disabled for security).

Group Policies for Wireless You have the ability to use Group Policy settings for Vista, Windows 7, Windows 8, Windows 2008/2008 R2, and Windows Server 2012 for WPA2. Group Policy settings allow you to configure WPA2 options at the server for all wireless clients.

Remote Access Security

In the past, remote access was seldom part of most companies' networks. It was too hard to implement, too hard to manage, and too hard to secure. It's reasonably easy to secure your networks from unauthorized physical access, but it was perceived to be much harder to do so for remote access. Recently, a number of security policies, protocols, and technologies have been developed to ease this problem. First I'll discuss the user authentication protocols.

User Authentication

One of the first steps in establishing a secure remote access connection involves allowing the user to present some credentials to the server. You can use any or all of the following authentication protocols that Windows Server 2012 supports:

Password Authentication Protocol   The *Password Authentication Protocol (PAP)* is the simplest authentication protocol. It transmits all authentication information in cleartext with no encryption, which makes it vulnerable to snooping if attackers can put themselves between the modem bank and the remote access server. However, this type of attack is unlikely in most networks. The security risk with PAP is largely overemphasized considering the difficulty of setting up a sniffer in between the modems and the remote access server. If an attacker has the ability to install a sniffer this deep in the network, you have larger problems to address. PAP is the most widely supported authentication protocol, and therefore you may find that you need to leave it enabled.

Microsoft CHAPv2   Microsoft created *Microsoft CHAPv2 (MS-CHAPv2)* as an extension of the CHAP protocol to allow the use of Windows authentication information. Version 2 is more secure than version 1, and version 1 is not supported by Windows Server 2008 and above. Some other operating systems (besides Microsoft) support MS-CHAP version 1.

Extensible Authentication Protocol   The *Extensible Authentication Protocol (EAP)* doesn't provide any authentication itself. Instead, it relies on external third-party authentication methods that you can retrofit to your existing servers. Instead of hardwiring any one authentication protocol, a client/server pair that understands EAP can negotiate an authentication method. The computer that asks for authentication (the *authenticator*) is free to ask for several pieces of information, making a separate query for each one. This allows the use of almost any authentication method, including smart cards, secure access tokens such as SecurID, one-time password systems such as S/Key, or ordinary username/password systems.

Each authentication scheme supported in EAP is called an *EAP type*. Each EAP type is implemented as a plug-in module. Windows Server 2012 can support any number of EAP types at once; the Routing and Remote Access Services (RRAS) server can use any EAP type to authenticate if you've allowed that module to be used and the client has the module in question.

Windows Server 2012 comes with *EAP-Transport Level Security (TLS)*. This EAP type allows you to use public key certificates as an authenticator. TLS is similar to the familiar Secure Sockets Layer (SSL) protocol used for web browsers. When EAP-TLS is turned on, the client and server send TLS-encrypted messages back and forth. EAP-TLS is the strongest authentication method you can use; as a bonus, it supports smart cards. However, EAP-TLS requires your RRAS server to be part of a Windows 2000, Windows Server 2003, Windows Server 2008/2008 R2, or Windows Server 2012 domain.

EAP-RADIUS is another authentication method included with Windows Server 2012. EAP-RADIUS is a fake EAP type that passes any incoming message to a Remote Authentication Dial-In User Service (RADIUS) server for authentication.

TLS/SSL (Schannel)   *TLS/SSL (Schannel)* implements both the Secure Sockets Layer (SSL) and Transport Layer Security (TLS) Internet standard authentication protocols. Administrators can use TLS/SSL to authenticate servers and client computers. Administrators also have the ability to use the protocol to encrypt messages between the authenticated parties (client and server).

The Transport Layer Security (TLS) protocol, Secure Sockets Layer (SSL) protocol, Datagram Transport Layer Security (DTLS), and Private Communications Transport (PCT) protocol are all based on the public key cryptography. The Security Channel (Schannel) authentication protocol suite provides these protocols, and this protocol is based on the client/server model.

NTLMv2   *NTLMv2* helps the authentication process for Windows NT 4 systems or earlier, and it allows for transactions between any two computers running these older systems. Networks that use NTLMv2 are referred to as *mixed mode*.

Kerberos   Active Directory domain authentication is done by using the *Kerberos authentication protocol*. By default, all computers joined to a Windows Server 2012 domain use the Kerberos authentication protocol. Kerberos allows for single sign-on to network resources on a domain or on a trusted domain. Administrators have the ability to control certain parameters through the Kerberos security settings of the account policies.

802.1X   The IEEE has a standard for wireless authentication called 802.1X. 802.1X allows wireless networks to authenticate onto wired Ethernet networks or wireless 802.11 networks. The IEEE 802.1X standard uses EAP for exchanging messages during the authentication process.

Connection Security

You can use some additional features to provide connection-level security for your remote access clients:

- The *Callback Control Protocol (CBCP)* allows your RRAS servers or clients to negotiate a callback with the other end. When CBCP is enabled, either the client or the server can ask the server at the other end to call the client back at a number supplied by the client or a prearranged number stored on the server.

- You can program the RRAS server to accept or reject calls based on the caller ID or automatic number identification (ANI) information transmitted by the phone company. For example, you can instruct your primary RRAS server to accept calls from only your home analog line. That means you can't call the server when you're on the road, and it also keeps the server from talking to strangers.

- You can specify various types and levels of encryption to protect your connection from interception or tampering.

Real World Scenario

The Limits of Caller ID

It's risky to rely on ANI information for any type of authentication or caller verification. First, caller ID information can be forged. Therefore, if an attacker knows the telephone numbers from which your network accepted calls, they could make their ANI report as one of those numbers and be authenticated onto the network.

Another problem with relying on ANI for authentication is that not all telephone companies pass ANI information with the call. Therefore, if your users are in remote locations (which is why they'd be dialing in anyway), they might not be able to authenticate. Even when ANI information is sent, some telephone companies pass different pieces of the information, which can also result in authentication failures.

Finally, not all incoming line types support ANI. If your site uses a network access server or modem bank that doesn't receive this information based on the type of T1 connection used for incoming calls, the ANI information might not be there at all.

Access Control

Apart from the connection-level measures that you can use to prohibit outside callers from talking to your servers, you can restrict which users can make remote connections in a number of ways:

- You can allow or disallow remote access from individual user accounts. This is the same limited control you have in Windows NT, but it's just the start for Windows Server 2012.

- You can use network access policies to control whether users can get access.

  Like group policies, network access policies give you an easy way to apply a consistent set of policies to groups of users. However, the policy mechanism is a little different: You create rules that include or exclude the users you want in the policy.

  Unlike group policies, network access policies are available only in Windows 2000 native, Windows Server 2003, Windows Server 2008, and Windows Server 2008 R2 domain functional level (that is, in domains in which there are no Windows NT domain controllers present). This means that you may not have the option to use network access policies until your Windows 2000, Windows Server 2003, Windows Server 2008/2008 R2, and Windows Server 2012 deployment is further along.

  In the next sections, you will learn how to configure user access control.

Configuring User Access

Now it's time to determine who can actually use the remote access services. You do this in two ways:

- By setting up remote access profiles on individual accounts
- By creating and managing network access policies that apply to groups of users

This distinction is subtle but important because you manage and apply profiles and policies in different places.

Setting Up User Profiles

Windows Server 2012 stores a lot of information for each user account. Collectively, this information is known as the account's *profile*, and it's normally stored in Active Directory. Some settings in the user's profile are available through one of the two user-management snap-ins:

- If your RRAS server is part of an Active Directory domain, the user profile settings are in the Active Directory Users and Computers snap-in.
- If your RRAS server is *not* part of an Active Directory domain, the user profile settings are in the Local Users and Groups snap-in.

In either case, the interesting part of the profile is the Dial-In tab of the user's Properties dialog box (see Figure 15.15). This tab has a number of controls that regulate how the user account can be used for dial-in access.

FIGURE 15.15 The Dial-In tab of the user's Properties dialog box

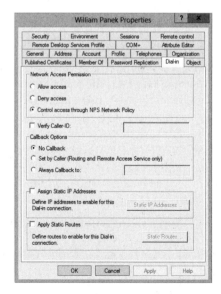

These controls include the following:

Network Access Permission Control Group   The first, and probably most familiar, controls on this tab are in the Network Access Permission control group. These options control whether the user has dial-in permission. Windows Server 2012 has a feature that, in addition to explicitly allowing or denying access, you can control access through *Network Access Protection (NAP)*.

Verify Caller-ID Check Box   RRAS can verify a user's caller ID information and use the results to allow or deny access. When you check the Verify Caller-ID check box and enter a phone number in the field, you're telling RRAS to reject a call from anyone who provides that username and password but whose caller ID information doesn't match what you enter. This means that the user can call in only from a single phone number.

Callback Options Control Group   The Callback Options control group gives you three choices for regulating callback:

> **No Callback**   This is the default setting. It means that the server will never honor callback requests from this account.

> **Set By Caller**   This setting allows the calling system to specify a number at which it wants to be called back. The RRAS server will call the client back at that number.

> **Always Callback To**   This setting allows you to enter a number that the server will call back no matter from where the client is actually calling. This option is less flexible but more secure than the Set By Caller option.

Assign Static IP Addresses Check Box   If you want this user always to get the same static IP address, you can arrange to do so by selecting the Assign Static IP Addresses check box and then entering the desired IP address. This allows you to set up nondynamic DNS records for individual users, guaranteeing that their machines will always have a valid DNS entry. On the other hand, this can be more prone to typographical errors on setup than the dynamic DNS-DHCP combination you could use instead.

Apply Static Routes Check Box   In an ordinary LAN, you don't have to do anything special to clients to enable them to route packets—just configure them with a default gateway, and the gateway handles the rest. For dial-up connections, though, you may want to define a list of static routes that will enable the remote client to reach hosts on your network, or elsewhere, without requiring that packets be sent to a gateway in between. Depending on the remote access server, though, the client may be able to use Address Resolution Protocol (ARP) for local devices too. If you want to define a set of static routes on the client, you'll have to do it manually. If you want to assign static routes on the server, select the Apply Static Routes check box and then use the Static Routes button to add and remove routes as necessary.

> Remember that these settings apply to individual users, so you can assign different routes, caller ID, or callback settings to each user.

Using Network Access Policies

Windows Server 2012 includes support for two additional configuration systems:

- Network access policies (which used to be called *remote access policy*)
- Remote access profiles (covered later in this chapter)

Policies determine who can and cannot connect; you define rules with conditions that the system evaluates to see whether a particular user can connect.

You can have any number of policies in a native Windows Server 2012 domain; each policy must have exactly one profile associated with it.

> Settings in an individual user's profile override settings in a network access policy.

You manage network access policies through the Remote Access Logging & Policies folder in the RRAS snap-in. Policies contain conditions that you pick from a list. When a caller connects, the policy's conditions are evaluated, one by one, to see whether the caller gets in. All of the conditions in the policy must match for the user to gain access. If there are multiple policies, they're evaluated according to an order you specify.

In the following sections, you will see how to create and configure network access policies.

Network Policy Attributes

To create a policy, right-click the Remote Access Logging & Policies folder and select Launch NPS (see Figure 15.16). Then right-click Network Policies, and choose New. This command starts the New Network Policy Wizard, which uses a series of steps to help you define the policy.

The Select Condition dialog box (see Figure 15.17) is part of the New Network Policy Wizard. It lists the attributes that you can evaluate in a policy. Table 15.1 lists the attributes that you can set. These attributes are drawn from the RADIUS standards, so you can (and in some cases, should) intermix your Windows Server 2012 RRAS servers with RADIUS servers.

FIGURE 15.16   The Launch NPS option in RRAS

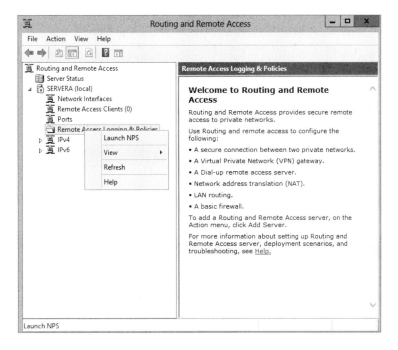

FIGURE 15.17   Select Condition Dialog Box of New Network Policy Wizard

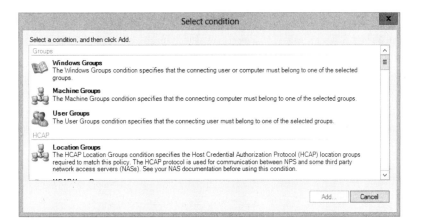

When setting up any policies, you must base your policy on company rules and standards. Remember, policies can allow or restrict users from remotely accessing your network. The needs of the organization determine the policy and when to use it.

Once you choose an attribute and click the Add button, its corresponding editor appears. You use the editor to set the value of the attribute. For example, if you select the Day And Time Restrictions attribute, you'll see the Time Of Day Constraints dialog box, which offers a calendar grid that lets you select which days and times are available for logging on.

TABLE 15.1 Network access policy attributes

Attribute Name	What It Specifies
Authentication Type	Specifies the authentication methods required to match this policy.
Allowed EAP Types	Specifies the EAP types required for the client computer authentication method configuration to match this policy.
Called Station Id	Specifies the phone number of the remote access port called by the caller.
Calling Station Id	Specifies the caller's phone number.
Client Friendly Name	Specifies the name of the RADIUS server that's attempting to validate the connection.
Client IP Address (IPv4 and IPv6)	Specifies the IP address of the RADIUS server that's attempting to validate the connection.
Client Vendor	Specifies the vendor of the remote access server that originally accepted the connection. This is used to set different policies for different hardware.
Day And Time Restrictions	Specifies the weekdays and times when connection attempts are accepted or rejected.
Framed Protocol	Specifies the protocol to be used for framing incoming packets (for example, PPP, SLIP, and so on).
HCAP (Host Credential Authorization Protocol) User Groups	Used for communications between NPS and some third-party network access servers (NASs).
Location Groups	Specifies the HCAP location groups required to match this policy. This is used for communications between HCAP and some third-party network access servers (NASs).

Attribute Name	What It Specifies
MS RAS Vendor	Specifies the vendor identification number of the network access server (NAS) that is requesting authentication.
NAS Identifier	Specifies the friendly name of the remote access server that originally accepted the connection.
NAS IP Address (IPv4 and IPv6)	Specifies the IP address of the remote access server that originally accepted the connection.
NAS Port Type	Specifies the physical connection (for example, ISDN, POTS) used by the caller.
Service Type	Specifies Framed or Async (for PPP) or login (Telnet).
Tunnel Type	Specifies which tunneling protocol should be used (L2TP or PPTP).
Windows Groups	Specifies which Windows groups are allowed access.

After you select an attribute and give it a value, you can add more attributes or move to the next page by clicking the Next button on the Select Condition page.

Once you're finished setting attributes, you arrive at the Specify Access Permission page of the wizard. This page has only two radio buttons: Grant Remote Access Permissions and Deny Remote Access Permissions. These buttons specify whether the policy you create *allows* users to connect or *prevents* users from connecting. The page also includes an Access Is Determined By User Dial-In Properties check box. If this box is checked and there is a conflict between the network policy and user dial-in properties, the user dial-in properties take precedence.

Creating a Network Access Policy

In Exercise 15.3, you'll create an adjunct policy that adds time and day restrictions to the default policy. (An *adjunct policy* is one used in conjunction with another policy.) This exercise requires that you have completed the previous exercises in this chapter.

EXERCISE 15.3

Creating a Network Access Policy

1. Open the RRAS MMC snap-in by pressing the Windows Key ➢ Administrative Tools ➢ Routing And Remote Access.

2. Expand the server you want to configure in the left pane of the MMC.

3. Right-click the Remote Access Logging And Policies folder.

4. Right-click, and then select Launch NPS.

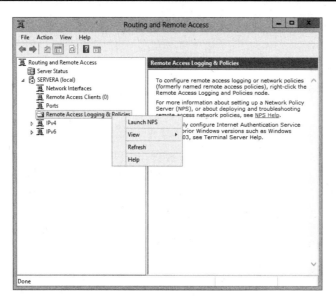

5. Once the Network Policy Server page appears, right-click Network Policies and then choose New.

6. The New Network Policy Wizard starts. In the Policy Name box, enter **Test Policy** and then click Next (leave the other settings as they are).

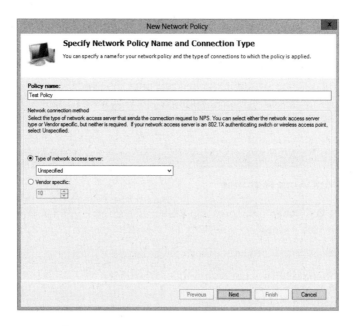

7. On the Specify Conditions page, click the Add button.

8. In the Select Condition dialog box, scroll down and click Day And Time Restrictions. Click Add.

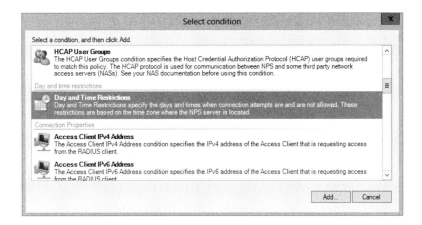

9. The Time Of Day Constraints dialog box appears. Use the calendar controls to allow remote access Monday through Saturday from 7 a.m. to 7 p.m., and then click the OK button.

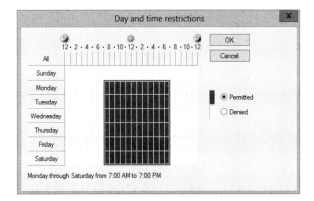

10. The Select Conditions dialog box reappears, this time with the new condition listed. Click the Next button.

11. The Specify Access Permission page appears. Select the Access Granted radio button, and click Next to continue.

12. The Configure Authentication Methods page appears next. This page is where you choose which authentication methods will be used for this connection. Make sure that MS-CHAP and MS-CHAPv2 are both checked, along with the check boxes associated with them. Click Next.

13. The Configure Constraints page appears. Under Constraints, click Session Timeout. On the right side, click the Disconnect After The Following Maximum Session Time box, and type **60** in the field (the value represents minutes). Click Next.

14. The Configure Settings page appears. This page allows you to configure any additional settings for this network policy. Click Next.

15. On the Completing New Network Policy page, click Finish.

Using Remote Access Profiles

Remote access profiles are an integral part of network access policies. Profiles determine what happens during call setup and completion. Each policy has a profile associated with it; the profile determines what settings will be applied to connections that meet the conditions stated in the policy.

For security reasons, it's usually a good idea to limit access to the administrative accounts on your network. In particular, as a consultant, I usually tell clients to restrict remote access for the administrator account; that way, the potential exposure from a dial-up compromise is reduced. In Exercise 15.4, you will learn how to configure the administrator account's user profile to restrict dial-up access.

EXERCISE 15.4

Restricting a User Profile for Dial-In Access

1. Log on to your computer using an account that has administrative privileges.

2. If you're using an RRAS server that's part of an Active Directory domain, open the Active Directory Users and Computers snap-in by pressing the Windows Key ➢ Administrative Tools ➢ Active Directory Users And Computers. If not, open the Local Users and Groups snap-in by selecting Windows Key ➢ Administrative Tools ➢ Computer Management ➢ Local Users And Groups.

3. Expand the tree to the Users folder. Right-click the Administrator account in the right pane, and choose Properties. The Administrator Properties dialog box appears.

4. Switch to the Dial-In tab. On machines that participate in Active Directory, make sure the Control Access Through NPS Network Policy option (in the Permissions group) is selected.

5. Click the Deny Access radio button to prevent the use of this account over a dial-in connection.

6. Click the OK button.

You can create one profile for each policy. The profile contains settings that fit into specific areas. Each area has its own link in the profile's Properties dialog box.

The Constraints Tab

The Constraints tab has most of the settings that you think of when you consider dial-in access controls. The controls here allow you to adjust how long the connection can be idle before it gets dropped, how long it can be up, the dates and times for establishing the connection, and what dial-in port and medium can be used to connect.

Authentication Link

In the Authentication Methods pane (see Figure 15.18), you can specify which authentication methods are allowed on this specific policy. Note that these settings, like the other policy settings, will be useful only if the server's settings match. For example, if you turn EAP authentication off in the server's Properties dialog box, turning it on in the Authentication Methods pane of the profile's Properties dialog box will have no effect.

FIGURE 15.18 Authentication Methods settings

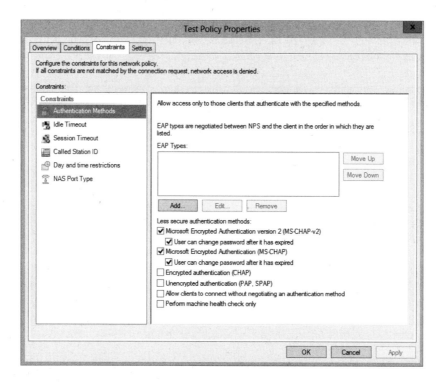

You'll notice that each authentication method has a check box. Check the appropriate boxes to control the protocols that you want this profile to use. If you enable EAP, you can also choose which specific EAP type you want the profile to support. You can also choose to allow totally unauthenticated access (which is unchecked by default).

Settings Tab   The Settings tab of the policy's Properties dialog box has several useful sections, which are described in the following list:

IP Settings Pane   The IP Settings pane (see Figure 15.19) gives you control over the IP-related settings associated with an incoming call. If you think back to the server-specific settings covered earlier, you'll remember that the server preferences include settings for protocols other than IP; this is not so in the network access profile. In this pane, you can specify where the client gets its IP address.

FIGURE 15.19   IP Settings pane of the Settings tab

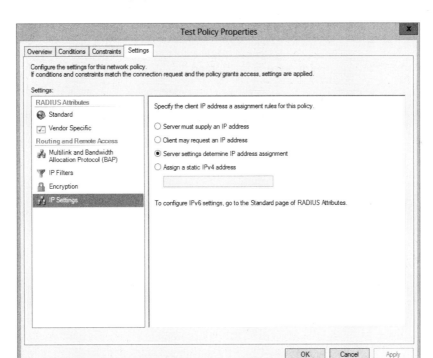

Multilink And Bandwidth Allocation Protocol (BAP) Pane   The profile mechanism gives you a degree of control over how the server handles multilink calls. You exert this control through the Multilink And Bandwidth Allocation Protocol (BAP) pane of the profile Properties dialog box. Your first choice is to decide whether to allow multilink calls at all and, if so, how many ports you want to let a single client use at once. Normally, this setting is configured so that the server-specific settings take precedence, but you can override them.

Bandwidth Allocation Protocol Group   The Bandwidth Allocation Protocol control group gives you a way to control what happens during a multilink call when the bandwidth usage drops below a certain threshold. For example, why tie up three analog lines to provide 168 Kbps of bandwidth when the connection is using only 56 Kbps? You can tweak the capacity and time thresholds. By default, a multilink call will drop one line every time the bandwidth usage falls to less than 50 percent of the available bandwidth and stays there for 2 minutes. The Require BAP For Dynamic Multilink Requests check box allows you to refuse calls from clients that don't support BAP. This is an easy way to make sure that no client can hog your multilink bandwidth.

Encryption Pane   The Encryption pane of the Settings tab (see Figure 15.20) controls which type of encryption you want your remote users to be able to access. The following radio buttons are on the Encryption pane:

FIGURE 15.20   Encryption pane of the Settings tab of the policy's Properties dialog box

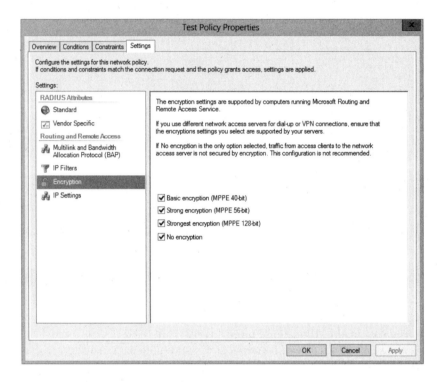

- Basic Encryption (MPPE 40-Bit) means single Data Encryption Standard (DES) for IPsec or 40-bit Microsoft Point-to-Point Encryption (MPPE) for Point-to-Point Tunneling Protocol (PPTP).

- Strong Encryption (MPPE 56-Bit) means 56-bit encryption (single DES for IPsec; 56-bit MPPE for PPTP).

- Strongest Encryption (MPPE 128-Bit) means triple DES for IPsec or 128-bit MPPE for PPTP connections.

- No Encryption allows users to connect using no encryption at all. Unless this button is selected, a remote connection must be encrypted, or it'll be rejected.

In Exercise 15.5, you'll force all connections to your server to use encryption. Any client that can't use encryption will be dropped. You must complete Exercise 15.3 before you do this exercise.

Don't do this exercise on your production RRAS server unless you're sure that all of your clients are encryption capable.

EXERCISE 15.5

Configuring Encryption

1. Open the RRAS MMC snap-in by pressing the Windows Key ➢ Administrative Tools ➢ Routing And Remote Access.

2. Expand the server you want to configure in the left pane of the MMC.

3. Right-click the Remote Access Logging & Policies folder.

4. Select Launch NPS.

5. Once the Network Policy Server page appears, click the hours policy you created in Exercise 15.3. (I named mine Test Policy.)

6. Select Action ➢ Properties. The policy's Properties dialog box appears.

7. Click the Settings tab. Select Encryption in the left pane.

8. In the right pane, uncheck the No Encryption check box. Make sure that the Basic, Strong, and Strongest check boxes are all selected.

9. Click the OK button. When the policy Properties dialog box reappears, click the OK button.

Setting Up a VPN Network Access Policy

Earlier in this chapter, you learned how to use the Network Access Policy mechanism on a Windows Server 2012 domain. Now it's time to apply what you've learned to a virtual private network (VPN). Recall that you have two ways to control which specific users can access a remote access server:

- You can grant and deny dial-up permission to individual users in each user's Properties dialog box.

- You can create a network access policy that embodies whatever restrictions you want to impose.

It turns out that you can do the same thing for VPN connections, but there are a few additional things to consider.

Granting and Denying Per-User Access

To grant or deny VPN access to individual users, all you have to do is make the appropriate change on the Dial-In tab of each user's Properties dialog box. Although this is the easiest method to understand, it gets tedious quickly if you need to change VPN permissions for more than a few users. Furthermore, this method offers you no way to distinguish between dial-in and VPN permissions.

Creating a Network Access Policy for VPNs

You may find it helpful to create network access policies that enforce the permissions you want end users to have. You can accomplish this result in a number of ways; which one you use will depend on your overall use of network access policies.

The simplest way is to create a policy that allows all of your users to use a VPN. Earlier in this chapter, you learned how to create network access policies and specify settings for them; one thing you may have noticed was that there's a NAS-Port-Type attribute that you can use in the policy's conditions. That attribute is the cornerstone of building a policy that allows or denies remote access via VPN because you use it to accept or reject connections arriving over a particular type of VPN connection. For best results, you'll use the Tunnel-Type attribute in conjunction with the NAS-Port-Type attribute, as described in Exercise 15.6.

EXERCISE 15.6

Creating a VPN Network Access Policy

1. Open the RRAS MMC snap-in by pressing the Windows Key ➤ Administrative Tools ➤ Routing And Remote Access.

2. Expand the server you want to configure in the left pane of the MMC.

3. Right-click the Remote Access Logging & Policies folder.

4. Select Launch NPS.

5. Once the Network Policy Server page appears, right-click Network Policies and choose New.

6. The New Network Policy Wizard starts. In the Policy Name box, enter **VPN Network Policy**, and click Next (leave the other settings as they are).

7. On the Specify Conditions page, click the Add button.

8. On the Select Condition page, scroll down, click NAS-Port-Type Attribute, and click Add. When the NAS Port Type page appears, click Virtual VPN in the Common Dial-Up And VPN Tunnel Types box. Click OK, and then click the Next button.

9. The Specify Conditions page reappears, this time with the new condition listed. Click the Next button.

10. The Specify Access Permission page appears. Select the Access Granted radio button, and click Next to continue.

11. Next the Configure Authentication Methods page will appear. This page is where you choose which authentication methods will be used for this connection. Make sure that

MS-CHAP and MS-CHAPv2 are both checked along with their associated check boxes. Click Next.

12. The Configure Constraints page appears. Under Constraints, click Session Timeout. On the right side, click the Disconnect After The Following Maximum Session Time box, and type **60** in the box (the value specifies minutes). Click Next.

13. The Configure Settings page appears. This page allows you to configure any additional settings for this network policy. Click Next.

14. At the Completing New Network Policy page, click Finish.

If you don't want to grant VPN access to everyone, you can make some changes to the process in Exercise 15.6 to fine-tune it. First you'll probably want to move the VPN policy to the top of the list. (When you first add the policy described in the exercise, it is placed at the end of the policy list. Unless you move it, the default policies will take effect before the VPN-specific policy does.)

Next you can create an Active Directory group and put your VPN users in it. You can then create a policy using the two conditions outlined in Exercise 15.6 plus a condition that uses the Windows-Groups attribute to specify the new group. You can also use this process to allow everyone dial-up access and reserve VPN capability for a smaller group.

Connection Manager

To help administrators create and manage remote access connections, Microsoft includes within Windows Server 2012 a suite of components called Connection Manager. Connection Manager is not installed by default. You can install the Connection Manager using Server Manager ➤ Add Roles ➤ Network Access Services.

Connection Manager allows an administrator to create remote access connections called *service profiles*. These profiles then appear on client machines as network connections. You can use these network connections to connect client machines to VPNs or remote networks.

Configuring Security

When configuring remote access security, you must consider several aspects, the most fundamental of which involves configuring the types of authentication and encryption the server will use when accepting client requests. We will look at each of these in the following sections.

Controlling Server Security

The Security tab of the server's Properties dialog box (see Figure 15.21) allows you to specify which authentication and accounting methods RRAS uses. You can choose one of two authentication providers by using the Authentication Provider drop-down list.

FIGURE 15.21   The Security tab of the RRAS server's Properties dialog box

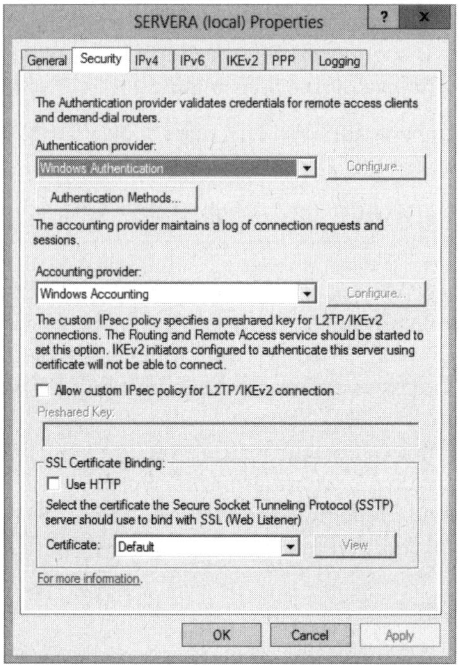

Your choices include the following:

Windows Authentication   This is a built-in authentication suite included with Windows Server 2012

RADIUS Authentication   This authentication allows you to send all authentication requests heard by your server to a RADIUS server for approval or denial.

You can also use the Accounting Provider drop-down list on the Security tab to choose between the following:

Microsoft-Developed Accounting   With this type of accounting, connection requests are maintained in the event log.

RADIUS Accounting   In this type of accounting, all accounting events, such as call start and call stop, are sent to a RADIUS server for action.

RADIUS Authentication Settings

When you select the RADIUS Authentication option from the Authentication Provider drop-down menu, you are enabling a RADIUS client that passes authentication duties to a RADIUS server. This communication is sent via UDP on port 1645 or 1812, depending on the version of RADIUS being used.

Click the Configure button to open the RADIUS Authentication dialog box. From here, you can set the following options:

- Click the Add button to add the name or address of a RADIUS server to which the RAS server will pass authentication duties.

- You must also enter the correct secret, which is initially set by the RADIUS server.

- The Time-Out option determines how long the RRAS server will attempt to authenticate the remote user before giving up.

- The Initial Score option is similar to the cost value used by routers. The RAS server will attempt to authenticate users on the RADIUS server with the highest score first. If that attempt fails, the RAS server will use the RADIUS server with the next highest score, and so on.

- Although the Port option can be changed, the default setting is part of RFC 2866, "RADIUS Accounting," and it should not be altered unless extraordinary circumstances call for it.

The Internet Assigned Numbers Authority (IANA) is the official source for port number assignment. You can view current port number assignments and other valuable information at www.iana.org/assignments/port-numbers.

Windows Authentication Settings

Select the Windows Authentication option from the Authentication Provider drop-down menu if you want the local machine to authenticate your remote access users. To configure the server by telling it which authentication methods you want it to use, click the Authentication Methods button, which displays the Authentication Methods dialog box. If you look at the list of authentication protocols earlier in the chapter, you'll find that each one has a corresponding check box here: EAP, MS-CHAPv2, CHAP, and PAP. You can also turn on unauthenticated access by checking the Allow Remote Systems To Connect Without Authentication box, but that is not recommended because it allows anyone to connect to, and use, your server (and thus by extension your network).

There's actually a special set of requirements for using CHAP because it requires access to each user's encrypted password. Windows Server 2012 normally doesn't store user passwords in a format that CHAP can use, so you have to take some additional steps if you want to use CHAP:

1. Enable CHAP at the server and policy levels.

2. Edit the default domain GPO's Password Policy object to turn on the Store Password Using Reversible Encryption policy setting.

3. Change or reset each user's password, which forces Windows Server 2012 to store the password using reversible encryption.

After these steps are completed for an account, that account can be used with CHAP.

> These steps aren't required for MS-CHAPv2; for that protocol, you just enable MS-CHAPv2 at the server and policy levels.

Configuring Network Access Protection

Another way you can have security is to allow users to access resources based on the identity of the client computer. This new security solution is called *Network Access Protection (NAP)*. Determined by the client needs, network administrators now have the ability to define granular levels of network access using NAP. NAP also allows administrators to determine client access based on compliancy with corporate governance policies. The following are some of the NAP features:

Network Layer Protection   *Network layer protection* is the ability to secure communications at the Network layer of the OSI model.

All communications travel through the seven layers of the OSI model. Starting at the top (layer 7), the seven layers are the Application, Presentation, Session, Transport, Network, Data-Link, and Physical layers.

DHCP Enforcement   If a computer wants to receive unlimited IPv4 network access, the computer must be compliant with corporate governance policies. *DHCP enforcement* verifies that a computer is compliant before granting unlimited access. If a computer is noncompliant, the computer receives an IPv4 address that has limited network access and a default user profile.

When a client computer attempts to receive an IP address from DHCP, the DHCP enforcement checks the health policy requirements of the system to make sure they meet the compliancy.

VPN Enforcement   *VPN enforcement* works a lot like DHCP enforcement, except that VPN enforcement verifies the compliancy of the system before the VPN connection is given full access to the network.

IPsec Enforcement   *IPsec enforcement* will allow a computer to communicate with other computers as long as the computers are IPsec compliant. You have the ability to configure the requirements for secure communications between the two compliant computer systems. You can configure the IPsec communications based on IP address or TCP/UDP port numbers.

802.1X Enforcement   For a computer system to have 802.1X unlimited access to network connections (Ethernet 802.11 or wireless access point), the computer system must be 802.1X compliant. *802.1X enforcement* verifies that the connecting system is 802.1X connection compliant. Noncompliant computers will obtain only limited access to network connections.

Flexible Host Isolation　*Flexible host isolation* allows a server and domain to isolate computers to help make it possible to design a layer of security between computers or networks. Even if a hacker gains access to your network using an authorized username and password, the server and domain isolation can stop the attack because the computer is not an authorized domain computer.

Multi-configuration System Health Validator　This feature allows you to specify multiple configurations of a *System Health Validator (SHV)*. When an administrator configures a network policy for health evaluation, the administrator will select a specific health policy. Using this feature allows you to specify different network policies for different sets of health requirements based on a specific configuration of the SHV. For example, an administrator can create a network policy that specifies that all internal computers must have antivirus software enabled and a different network policy that specifies that VPN-connected computers must have their antivirus software enabled and signature files up-to-date.

Summary

In this chapter, you learned how to install and configure Routing and Remote Access Services to handle dial-in connections, how to configure appropriate encryption and security settings so that communication between the client and server is encrypted and authenticated, how to install RRAS to provide VPN service using the PPTP and L2TP protocols, how to configure VPN services on the server and client, and finally, how to troubleshoot common problems with VPNs.

I also discussed using wireless networking and what types of security encryption you can use to help support your wireless network. You learned about the different components of wireless access and using group policies to configure wireless clients. Finally, I discussed Internet Connection Sharing and the benefits of using it.

Exam Essentials

Know how to install and configure RAS at the server level.　The RAS installation process is driven by the Routing and Remote Access Server Setup Wizard, which you use to set up a dial-up server. You can specify whether the server acts as a remote access server, specify what authentication providers and settings you want the server to use, control the settings applied to each protocol you have installed, specify which PPP protocols (including multilink) the clients on this server are allowed to use, and control what level of log detail is kept for incoming connections.

Know how to install and configure a VPN server.   If you don't have RRAS installed, you'll need to install it, activate it, and configure it as a VPN server. If you're already using RRAS for IP routing or remote access, you can enable it as a VPN server without reinstalling. VPN configuration is extremely simple, at least for PPTP. Either a server can accept VPN calls or it can't. If it can, it will have a certain number of VPN ports, all of which are configured identically.

Know how to configure an RRAS client.   Most client connections are made on Windows 8, Windows 7, Vista, or XP Professional workstations. Dial-in and VPN connections are configured very similarly, but when creating a VPN connection, you must substitute an IP address for a phone number.

Review Questions

1. You have a local DHCP server for your dial-in clients, but you also want to use the DHCP relay agent to forward requests to a remote DHCP server if the local server doesn't answer a request. To do this, you must do which of the following?

    A. Add a static route to the remote server.

    B. Adjust the boot threshold on the DHCP relay agent interface for the remote network so that the local server has enough time to respond.

    C. Adjust the DHCP Forwarding Time parameter in the Registry.

    D. Adjust the forwarding time in the DHCP Relay Agent Global Properties dialog box.

2. You are considering multilink PPP in order to increase bandwidth available for a dial-up client. Which of the following is not a benefit of multilink?

    A. Multilink can make the client experience faster by combining multiple phone lines and creating one logical PPP connection.

    B. Multilink enables the encryption of data between the client and the server.

    C. Multilink can be relatively low in cost and can utilize existing infrastructure.

    D. Multilink is easy to use and included in Windows Server 2012 for both inbound and outbound calls.

3. Your company has offices in five locations around the country. Most of the users' activity is local to their own network. Occasionally, some of the users in one location need to send confidential information to one of the other four locations or to retrieve information from one of them. The communication between the remote locations is sporadic and relatively infrequent, so you have configured RRAS to use demand-dial lines to set up the connections. Management's only requirement is that any communication between the office locations be appropriately secured. Which of the following steps should you take to ensure compliance with this requirement? (Choose all that apply.)

    A. Configure CHAP on all the RRAS servers.

    B. Configure PAP on all the RRAS servers.

    C. Configure MPPE on all the RRAS servers.

    D. Configure L2TP on all the RRAS servers.

    E. Configure MS-CHAPv2 on all the RRAS servers.

4. Your small financial consulting company has a stand-alone Windows 2012 server that provides a central location for your home-based consultants to upload and download spreadsheet files using Windows 8. A few of the consultants still use Windows XP Professional workstations. You want to set up VPN connections between the consultants and the RRAS server. The RRAS server is connected to a small peer-to-peer network of five Windows XP Professional workstations that use the network for storing files, including the files that the consultants are uploading and downloading. What authentication protocol should you use for the VPN?

    A. CHAP

    B. MS-CHAPv2

    C. EAP-TLS

    D. PAP

5. You recently migrated your company's Windows 2003 network to Windows Server 2012. This migration includes 300 Windows 7 and Windows 8 workstations and 8 Windows Server 2012 servers. Your company has just acquired another company with offices down the street. It has a Windows NT network that needs to be migrated to Windows Server 2012 as well, and you have already begun to move the servers to the new operating system and associated services. Because you have a tight cap on expenses for network additions, you presently can't afford leased lines between the buildings. Until you can get support for them, you are going to create a VPN that is both encrypted and authenticated between the two facilities over the Internet connections that already exist. What do you need to implement to achieve this goal? (Choose all that apply.)

    A. L2TP

    B. PPTP

    C. IPsec

    D. RADIUS

    E. MS-CHAPv2

6. You have implemented VPNs to connect the various locations of your organization. These locations include offices in New York, Sacramento, Memphis, and Omaha, with a significant LAN in each one. The RRAS server is set up such that the users aren't aware of the intricacies of the connections. You are beginning to have problems with the connections between the offices, and as a result, the number of support calls is growing dramatically. What configurations could you use to troubleshoot the communication problems?

    A. L2TP using MPPE

    B. L2TP unencrypted

    C. L2TP using IPsec in transport mode

    D. L2TP using IPsec in tunnel mode

7. Your company's 450 sales reps are finally going to receive laptops so that they can communicate with the corporate office whenever they need information stored on the corporate network. The corporate network is fully upgraded to Windows Server 2012, including the default configuration of the RRAS server for the remote connectivity over VPNs. You have installed Windows 8 with the default configuration on all of the laptops and have added the sales reps to a special group in Active Directory. After you test the laptops, everything appears to work fine. You ship them out, and as they reach the sales reps, you monitor their initial connections. During the next few days, you begin receiving support calls from people complaining they cannot connect to the network. What is the most likely cause of the problem?

A. The Windows 8 clients are not configured to support a VPN.

B. The default RRAS configuration does not support VPNs.

C. The default RRAS configuration does not support enough VPN connections.

D. The default RRAS configuration does not support L2TP.

E. The Windows 8 client default configuration does not support L2TP.

8. You are the network administrator for a company with two offices: one is located on the East Coast and the other is located on the West Coast. Sales information needs to be sent from the East Coast to the West Coast office on a regular basis, and some accounting reports and payroll information needs to be sent back to the East Coast. The owner of your company has been reading stories in the press about security problems on the Internet and refuses to allow any company information to travel through the Internet, regardless of how much you talk about securing those transmissions. The communications between the sites occur approximately once a week. What steps would you take to ensure secure authentication and secure transmission while not spending too much money? (Choose all that apply.)

A. Configure PAP as the authentication method between the servers.

B. Install RRAS on a server at each location, and keep the line open with an ISDN connection that will always be available for the communication.

C. Install RRAS on a server at each location, and configure demand-dial to open the connection each time the transmission occurs.

D. Configure CHAP as the authentication method between the servers.

E. Configure MS-CHAPv2 as the authentication method between the servers.

F. Configure IPsec as the encryption method between the servers.

G. Configure MPPE as the encryption method between the servers.

H. Configure L2TP as the encryption method between the servers.

9. You are using an RRAS server to manage remote access to your small Windows Server 2012 network that serves a single location. RRAS provides access to several remote users and to the people who have machines on the local network but occasionally want to access the network from home or from hotels when on the road. Regardless of the category of user, everyone is authenticated through Active Directory. You haven't spent much time reviewing the use of this remote connectivity since you configured the system, but now there is a concern about unauthorized users as well as intermittent problems that remote users are experiencing when connecting to the network. You've been asked to prepare a report for management describing the extent of these problems in the company. You recall that when you set up the system, you configured the logging to track all connection attempts using local Windows accounting. Where will you find the logging information that you need for preparing your report?

A. The Performance Monitor log

B. Active Directory

C. The *systemroot*\System32\LogFiles folder

D. The system event log

E. The RRAS authentication log

10. Your area of responsibility at the All-Terrain Vehicle Rentals Company is to build, deploy, and maintain the remote access system for the Windows Server 2012 network. The system consists of four RRAS servers that serve 200 users across the country. The users often travel from location to location, and they access different servers depending on where they call in. You put together a management station to monitor all of the RRAS servers so that you can keep an eye on this critical aspect of your network. What tool do you use to accomplish this?

A. The Server Monitor of the RRAS snap-in

B. The Server Status node of the RRAS snap-in

C. The System Monitor snap-in

D. The MMC

Chapter 16

Configuring High Availability in Windows Server 2012

THE FOLLOWING 70-412 EXAM OBJECTIVES ARE COVERED IN THIS CHAPTER:

✓ **Configure Network Load Balancing (NLB)**

- This objective may include, but is not limited to: Install NLB nodes; configure NLB prerequisites; configure affinity; configure port rules; configure cluster operation mode; upgrade an NLB cluster.

✓ **Configure servers**

- This objective may include, but is not limited to: configure NIC Teaming.

✓ **Configure failover clustering**

- This objective may include, but is not limited to: Configure Quorum; configure cluster networking; restore single node or cluster configuration; configure cluster storage; implement Cluster Aware Updating; upgrade a cluster.

✓ **Manage failover clustering roles**

- This objective may include, but is not limited to: Configure role-specific settings including continuously available shares; configure VM monitoring; configure failover and preference settings.

✓ **Configure site-level fault tolerance**

- This objective may include, but is not limited to: configure multi-site clustering including network settings, Quorum, and failover settings.

Windows Server 2012 has improved the options for high availability as well as the ease of configuring them. High availability can be better achieved with Windows Server 2012's superior software stability and improved failover and network load-balanced clustering. The exam will cover the basic configuration and operational functions for both a failover cluster and Network Load Balancing. This chapter will provide an introduction to achieving high availability with hardware and operational changes as well as using the high availability features of Windows Server 2012.

One of the Microsoft objectives listed at the beginning of this chapter is to "configure VM monitoring." Microsoft listed this under the section "Manage failover clustering roles." This was already covered in Chapter 8, "Using Virtualization in Windows Server 2012" and thus is not covered in this chapter.

Components of High Availability

High availability is a buzzword that many application and hardware vendors like to throw around to get you to purchase their product. Many different options are available to achieve high availability, and there also seem to be a number of different definitions and variations that help vendors sell their products as high-availability solutions.

When it comes right down to it, however, high availability is simply providing services with maximum uptime by avoiding unplanned downtime. Often, *disaster recovery (DR)* is also closely lumped into discussions of high availability, but DR encompasses the business and technical processes that are used to recover once a disaster has happened.

Defining a high availability plan usually starts with a *service-level agreement (SLA)*. At its most basic, an SLA defines the services and metrics that must be met for availability and performance of an application or service. Often, an SLA is created for an IT department or service provider to provide a specific level of service. An example of this might be an SLA for a Microsoft Exchange server. The SLA for an Exchange server might have uptime metrics on how much time during the month the mailboxes need to be available to end users, or it might define performance metrics for the amount of time it takes for email messages to be delivered.

When determining what goes into an SLA, two other factors need to be considered. However, you will often see them discussed only in the context of disaster recovery even though they are important for designing a highly available solution. These factors are *recovery point objective (RPO)* and *recovery time objective (RTO)*.

An RTO is the length of time an application can be unavailable before service must be restored to meet the SLA. For example, a single component failure would have an RTO of less than 5 minutes, and a full-site failure might have an RTO of 3 hours. An RPO is essentially the amount of data that must be restored for a failure. For example, in a single server or component failure, the RPO would be 0, but in a site failure, the RPO might allow for up to 20 minutes of lost data.

SLAs, on the other hand, are usually expressed in percentages of the time the application is available. These percentages are also often referred to by the number of nines the percentage includes, as shown in Table 16.1.

TABLE 16.1 Availability percentages

Availability Rating	Allowed Unplanned Downtime/Year
99%	3.7 days
99.9%	8.8 hours
99.99%	53 minutes
99.999%	5.3 minutes

Two important factors that affect an SLA are the *mean time between failure (MTBF)* and the *mean time to recover (MTTR)*. To be able to reduce the amount of unplanned downtime, the time between failures must be increased and the time it takes to recover must be reduced. Modifying these two factors will be covered in the next several sections of this chapter.

Achieving High Availability

As the information presented during installation states, Windows Server 2012 is the most secure and reliable Windows version to date. It also is the most stable, mature, and capable of any version of Windows. Although we have seen similar claims made for previous versions of Windows Server, you can rest assured that Windows Server 2012 is much better than previous versions for a variety of reasons.

An honest look at the feature set and real-world experience should prove that this latest version of Windows provides the most suitable foundation for creating a highly available solution. However, more than just good software is needed to be able to offer high availability for applications.

High Availability Foundation

Just as a house needs a good foundation, a highly available Windows server needs a stable and reliable hardware platform on which to run. Although Windows Server 2012 will technically run on desktop-class hardware, high availability is more easily achieved with server-class hardware. What differentiates desktop-class from server-class hardware? Server-class hardware has more management and monitoring features built into it so that the health of the hardware is capable of being monitored and maintained.

Another large difference is that server-class hardware has redundancy options. Server-class hardware often has options to protect from drive failures, such as RAID controllers, and to protect against power supply failures, such as multiple power supplies. And enterprise-class servers have even more.

More needs to be done than just installing Windows Server 2012 to ensure that the applications remain running with the best availability possible. Just as a house needs maintenance and upkeep to keep the structure in proper repair, so too does a server. In the case of a highly available server, this means *patch management*.

Installing Patches

Microsoft releases monthly updates to fix security problems with its software, both for operating system fixes and for applications. To ensure that you're highly available applications are immune to known vulnerabilities, these patches need to be applied in a timely manner during a scheduled maintenance window. Also, to address stability and performance issues, updates and service packs are released regularly for many applications, such as Microsoft SQL Server, Exchange Server, and SharePoint Portal Server. Many companies have a set schedule—daily, weekly, or monthly—to apply these patches and updates after they are tested and approved.

To continue even further with the house analogy, if you were planning to have crown molding installed, would you rather hire a college student on spring break looking to make some extra money to do the job or a seasoned artisan? Of course you would want someone with experience and a proven record of accomplishment to install your expensive crown molding.

Likewise, with any work that needs to be done on your highly available applications, it's best to hire only adequately qualified individuals. This is why obtaining a Microsoft certification is definitely an excellent start in becoming qualified to configure a server properly to be highly available. There is no substitute for real-life and hands-on experience. Working with highly available configurations in a lab and in production will help you to know not only what configurations are available but also how the changes should be made.

For example, it may be possible to use failover clustering for a WINS server, but in practice it may be easier to support and require less expensive hardware to use WINS replication to provide high availability. This is something you would know only if you had enough experience to make this decision.

As with your house, once you have a firm and stable foundation built by skilled artisans, and a maintenance plan has been put into place, you need to ascertain what more is needed. If you can't achieve enough uptime with proper server configuration and mature operational processes, a cluster may be needed.

Windows Server 2012 provides for two types of clustering: failover clustering and Network Load Balancing (NLB). Failover clustering is used for applications and services such as SQL Server and Exchange Server. Network Load Balancing is used for network-based services such as web and FTP servers. The remaining sections of the chapter will cover both of these clustering options in detail.

To Cluster or Not to Cluster

Clustering is often thrown into the mix when someone wants to achieve higher availability. This is often a good step toward improved availability, but the return on the investment of a cluster doesn't always add up. Although Windows Server 2012 greatly simplifies both the creation and management of a failover cluster, there is added complexity and cost in terms of hardware, software, and personnel.

How do you determine whether to cluster applications? Sometimes, even though it is possible to cluster applications, they perform worse when clustered. At other times, only a small improvement is made when a cluster is created. You have to balance the slight improvement over the increased hardware cost, increased complexity, and the increased level of training required for administrators.

Achieving High Availability with Failover Clustering

Taking high availability to the next level for enterprise services often means creating a failover cluster. In a failover cluster, all of the clustered application or service resources are assigned to one node or server in the cluster. Commonly clustered applications are SQL Server and Exchange Server; commonly clustered services are File and Print. Since the differences between a clustered application and a clustered service are primarily related to the number of functions or features, for simplicity's sake I will refer to both as *clustered applications*.

If there is a failure of the primary node, or if the primary node is taken offline for maintenance, the clustered application is started on another cluster node. The client requests are then automatically redirected to the new cluster node to minimize the impact of the failure.

How does failover clustering improve availability? By increasing the number of server nodes available on which the application can run, you can move the application to a healthy server if there is a problem, if maintenance needs to be completed on the hardware or the operating system, or if patches need to be applied. The clustered application can be moved from node to node without having to restart.

Usually, moving an application between nodes is transparent to the clients. Only severe node failures will require the application to be restarted before it is able to service clients. Figure 16.1 shows an example of SQL Server running on the first node of a Windows Server 2012 failover cluster.

FIGURE 16.1   Using failover clustering to cluster SQL Server

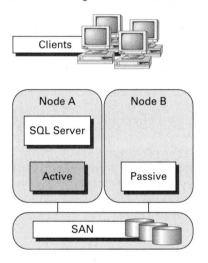

The clustered SQL Server in Figure 16.2 can be failed over to another node in the cluster and still service database requests.

FIGURE 16.2   Failing the SQL Server service to another node

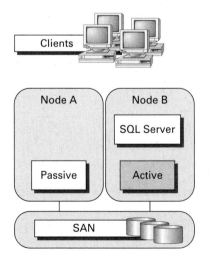

Failover clustering is notorious for being complicated and expensive. Windows Server 2012 makes strides in removing both of these concerns. Troubleshooting and other advanced concepts are outside the scope of the Microsoft MCSA exams and thus this book, so I will cover only the basic requirements and concepts needed to configure a failover cluster.

Failover Clustering Requirements

To be able to configure a failover cluster, you must have the required components. A single failover cluster can have up to 64 nodes when using Windows Server 2012; however, the clustered service or application must support that number of nodes.

To create a failover cluster, an administrator must ensure that all hardware meets cluster requirements. To be supported by Microsoft, all hardware must be certified for Windows Server 2012 and the complete failover cluster solution must pass all tests in the Validate a Configuration Wizard. Although the exact hardware will depend on the clustered application, a few requirements are standard:

- Server components must be marked with the "Certified for Windows Server 2012" logo.
- Server hardware should match and contain the same or similar components.
- All of the Validate a Configuration Wizard tests must pass.
- All servers in a cluster must run the same processor architecture, such as x64-based or Itanium-based architecture.

The requirements for failover clustering storage have changed from previous versions of Windows. For example, Parallel SCSI is no longer a supported storage technology for any of the clustered disks. There are, however, additional requirements that need to be met for the storage components:

- Disks available for the cluster must be Fibre Channel, iSCSI, or Serial Attached SCSI.
- Each cluster node must have a dedicated network interface card for iSCSI connectivity. The network interface card you use for iSCSI should not be used for network communication.
- Multipath software must be based on Microsoft's Multipath I/O (MPIO).
- Storage drivers must be based on `storport.sys`.
- Drivers and firmware for the storage controllers on each server node in the cluster should be identical.
- Storage components must be marked with the "Certified for Windows Server 2012" logo.

In addition, there are network requirements that must be met for failover clustering:

- Cluster nodes should be connected to multiple networks for communication redundancy.

- Network adapters should be the same make, use the same driver, and have the firmware version in each cluster node.
- Network components must be marked with the "Certified for Windows Server 2012" logo.

There are two types of network connections in a failover cluster. These should have adequate redundancy because total failure of either could cause loss of functionality of the cluster. The two types are as follows:

Public Network   This is the network through which clients are able to connect to the clustered service application.

Private Network   This is the network used by the nodes to communicate with each other.

To provide redundancy for these two network types, additional network adapters would need to be added to the node and configured to connect to the networks.

In previous versions of Windows Server, support was given only when the entire cluster configuration was tested and listed on the HCL. The tested configuration listed the server and storage configuration down to the firmware and driver versions. This proved to be very difficult and expensive from both a vendor and consumer perspective to deploy supported Windows clusters.

When problems did arise and Microsoft support was needed, it caused undue troubleshooting complexity as well. With Windows Server 2012 failover clustering, simplified requirements, including the "Certified for Windows Server 2012" logo program and the Validate a Configuration Wizard, all but eliminate the guesswork that was put into getting the cluster components configured in a way that will follow best practices and allow for Microsoft support to assist you easily in case it might be needed.

Cluster Quorum

When a group of people sets out to accomplish a single task or goal, a method for settling disagreements and for making decisions is required. In the case of a cluster, the goal is to provide a highly available service in spite of failures. When a problem occurs and a cluster node loses communication with the other nodes because of a network error, the functioning nodes are supposed to try to bring the redundant service back online.

How, though, is it determined which node should bring the clustered service back online? If all of the nodes are functional despite the network communications issue, each one might try. Just like a group of people with their own ideas, a method must be put in place to determine which idea, or node, to grant control of the cluster. Windows Server 2012 failover clustering, like other clustering technologies, requires that a quorum exist between the cluster nodes before a cluster becomes available.

A *quorum* is a consensus of the status of each of the nodes in the cluster. Quorum must be achieved in order for a clustered application to come online by obtaining a majority of the votes available (see Figure 16.3). Windows Server 2012 has four quorum models, or methods, for determining quorum and for adjusting the number and types of votes available:

- Node Majority (no witness)
- Node majority with witness (disk or file share)
- Node and File Share Majority
- No Majority (Disk witness only)

FIGURE 16.3   Majority needed

When a majority of the nodes are communicating, the cluster is functional.

When a majority of the nodes are not communicating, the cluster stops.

Witness Configuration

As an administrator, there are some basic rules that most of us follow. For example, when you configure a quorum, the voting components in the cluster should be an odd number. For example, if I set up a quorum for five elements and I lose one element, I continue to work. If I lose two elements, I continue to work. If I lose three elements, the cluster stops—as soon as it hits half plus 1, the cluster stops. This works well with an odd number.

If the cluster contains an even number of voting elements, an administrator should then configure a disk witness or a file share witness. The advantage to using a witness (disk or file share) is that the cluster will continue to run even if half of the cluster nodes simultaneously go down or are disconnected. The ability to configure a disk witness is only possible if the storage vendor supports read-write access from all sites to the replicated storage.

One of the advantages of Windows Server 2012 is the advanced quorum configuration option. This option allows you to assign or remove quorum votes on a per-node basis. Administrators now have the ability to remove votes from nodes in certain configurations. For example, if your organization uses a multisite cluster, you may choose to remove votes from the nodes in the backup site. This way, those backup nodes would not affect your quorum calculations.

Dynamic Quorum Management

Another new advantage in Windows Server 2012 is dynamic quorum management. *Dynamic quorum management* automatically manages the vote assignment to nodes. With this feature enabled, votes are automatically added or removed from nodes when that node either joins or leaves a cluster. In Windows Server 2012, dynamic quorum management is enabled by default.

Validating a Cluster Configuration

Configuring a failover cluster in Windows Server 2012 is much simpler than in previous versions of Windows Server. Before a cluster can be configured, the Validate a Configuration Wizard should be run to verify that the hardware is configured in a fashion that is supportable. Before you can run the Validate a Configuration Wizard, however, the Failover Clustering feature needs to be installed using Server Manager. The account that is used to create a cluster must have administrative rights on each of the cluster nodes and have permissions to create a cluster name object in Active Directory. Follow these steps:

1. Prepare the hardware and software perquisites.

2. Install the Failover Clustering feature on each server.

3. Log in with the appropriate user ID, and run the Validate a Configuration Wizard.

4. Create a cluster.

5. Install and cluster applications and services.

To install the Failover Clustering feature on a cluster node, follow the steps outlined in Exercise 16.1.

EXERCISE 16.1

Installing the Failover Cluster Feature

1. Press the Windows Key ➤ Administrative Tools ➤ Server Manager.

2. Select number 2, Add Roles And Features.

3. At the Select Installation Type screen, choose role-based or feature-based installation.

4. At the Select Destination Server screen, choose Select A Server From The Server Pool and click Next.

5. At the Select Server Roles screen, click Next.

6. At the Select Features screen, click the Failover Clustering check box. If the Add Features dialog box appears, click the Add Features button. Click Next.

7. At the Confirmation screen, click the Install button.

8. Once the installation is complete, click the close button.

9. Close Server Manager.

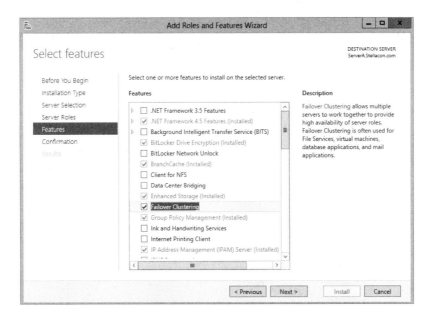

Using the Validate a Configuration Wizard before creating a cluster is highly recommended. This wizard validates that the hardware and software configuration for the potential cluster nodes are in a supported configuration. Even if the configuration passes the tests, take care to review all warnings and informational messages so that they can be addressed or documented before the cluster is created.

Running the Validate a Configuration Wizard does the following:

- Conducts four types of tests: Software and Hardware Inventory, Network, Storage, and System Configuration.

- Confirms that the hardware and software settings are supportable by Microsoft support staff.

You should run the Validate a Configuration Wizard before creating a cluster or after making any major hardware or software changes to the cluster. Doing this will help identify any misconfigurations that could cause problems with the failover cluster.

In the next section, I will cover the process for running the Validate a Configuration Wizard.

Running the Validate a Configuration Wizard

The Validate a Configuration Wizard, shown in Figure 16.4, is simple and straightforward to use, as its "wizard" name would suggest. It should be run after the Failover Clustering feature has been installed on each of the cluster nodes, and it can be run as many times as required.

FIGURE 16.4 The Validate a Configuration Wizard

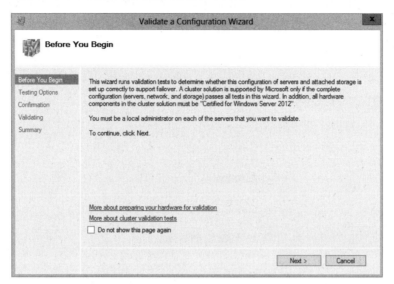

When you are troubleshooting cluster problems or have changed the configuration of the cluster hardware, it is a good idea to run the Validate a Configuration Wizard again to help pinpoint potential cluster configuration problems.

If you already have a cluster configured and want to run the Validate a Configuration Wizard, you can do so; however, you will not be able to run all of the storage tests without taking the clustered resources offline. You will be prompted either to skip the disruptive tests or take the clustered resources offline so that the tests can complete.

Exercise 16.2 shows the exact steps to follow to run the Validate a Configuration Wizard successfully on clusters named NODEA and NODEB, which are not yet clustered.

I am using NODEA and NODEB in the exercises. You need to replace these two nodes with your own two servers to complete these exercises.

EXERCISE 16.2

Running the Validate a Configuration Wizard

1. Press the Windows Key ➢ Administrative Tools ➢ Failover Cluster Management.

2. In the Actions pane (right hand side of screen), click Validate Configuration.

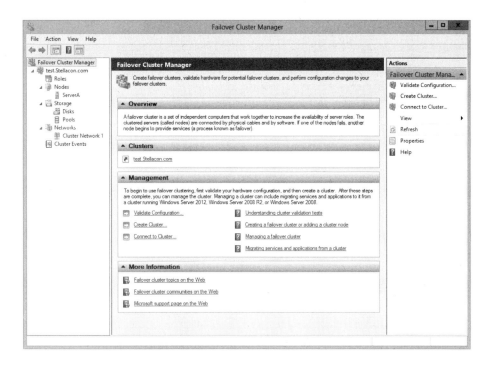

3. At the Before You Begin screen, click Next.

4. Type **NODEA** in the Enter Name field and click Add.

5. Type **NODEB** in the Enter Name field and click Add.

6. Click Next.

7. Leave Run All Tests (Recommended) selected and click Next.

8. Click Next at the Confirmation screen.

9. Let the test complete, review the report in the Summary window, and then click Finish.

Addressing Problems Reported by the Validate a Configuration Wizard

After the Validate a Configuration Wizard has been run, it will show the results, as shown in Figure 16.5. This report can also be viewed in detail later using a web browser. The report is named with the date and time the wizard was run, and it is stored in %windir%\ cluster\Reports.

FIGURE 16.5 Validate a Configuration Wizard results

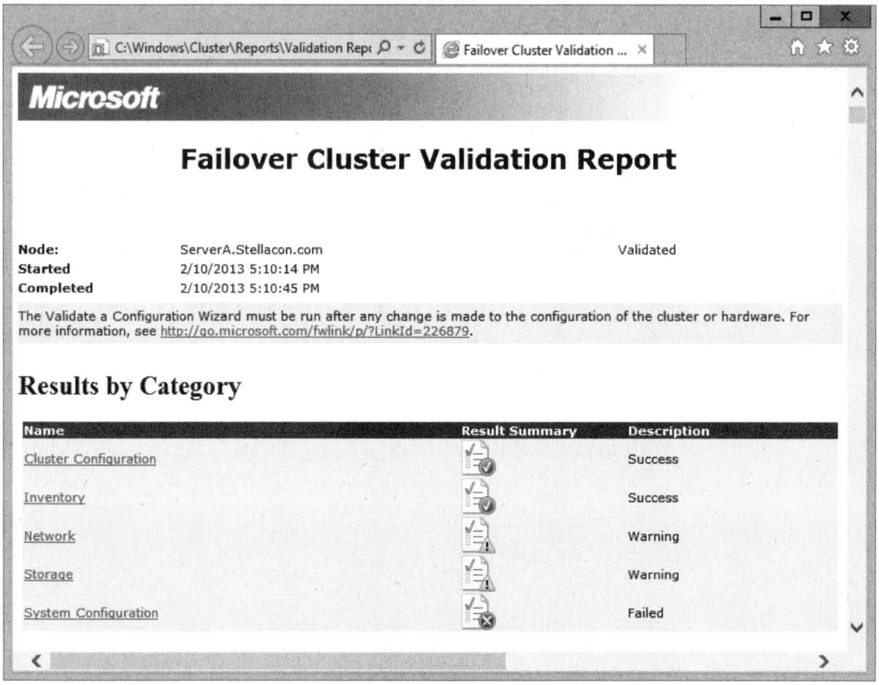

How should errors listed in the report be addressed? Often, the errors reported by the Validate a Configuration Wizard are self-explanatory; however, there are times when additional help is required. The following three guidelines should help troubleshoot the errors:

- Read all of the errors because multiple errors may be related.

- Use the checklists available in the Windows Server help files to ensure that all of the steps have been completed.

- Contact the hardware vendor for updated drivers, firmware, and guidance for using the hardware in a cluster.

Multisite or Geographically Dispersed Clusters (Geoclustering)

One issue that you can run into is if you have multiple sites or if the cluster is geographically dispersed. If the failover cluster does not have a shared common disk, data replication between nodes might not pass the cluster validation "storage" tests.

Setting up a cluster in a multisite or geocluster configuration is a common practice. As long as the cluster solution does not require external storage to fail over, it will not need to pass the storage test to function properly.

Creating a Cluster

After you have successfully validated a configuration and the cluster hardware is in a supportable state, you can create a cluster. The process for creating a cluster is straightforward and similar to the process of running the Validate a Configuration Wizard. To create a cluster with two servers, follow the instructions in Exercise 16.3.

EXERCISE 16.3

Creating a Cluster

1. Open the Failover Cluster Management MMC.

2. In the Management section of the center pane, select Create A Cluster.

3. Read the Before You Begin information and click Next.

4. In the Enter Server Name box, type **NODEA** and then click Add.

5. Again, in the Enter Server Name box, type **NODEB** and then click Add. Click Next.

6. At the Validation screen, choose No for this exercise and then click Next.

7. In the Access Point For Administering The Cluster section, enter **Cluster1** for the cluster name.

8. Type an IP address and then click Next. This IP address will be the IP address of the cluster.

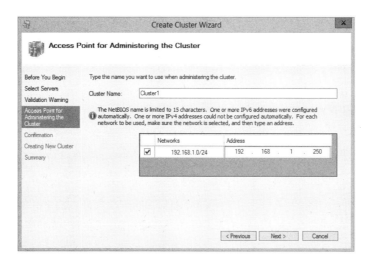

9. In the Confirmation dialog box, verify the information and then click Next.

10. On the Summary page, click Finish.

Working with Cluster Nodes

Once a cluster is created, a couple of actions are available. First you can add another node to the cluster by using the Add Node Wizard from the Failover Cluster Management Actions pane.

At this point, you also have the option to pause a node, which prevents resources from being failed over or moved to the node. You typically would pause a node when the node is involved in maintenance or troubleshooting. After a node is paused, it must be resumed to allow resources again to be run on it.

Another action available to perform on a node at this time is *evict*. Eviction is an irreversible process. Once you evict the node, it must be re-added to the cluster. You would evict a node when it is damaged beyond repair or is no longer needed in the cluster. If you evict a damaged node, you can repair or rebuild it and then add it back to the cluster using the Add Node Wizard.

Clustering Roles, Services, and Applications

Once the cluster is created, applications, services, and roles can be clustered. Windows Server 2012 includes a number of built-in roles and features that can be clustered.

The following roles and features can be clustered in Windows Server 2012 (see Figure 16.6):

- DFS Namespace Server
- DHCP Server
- Distributed Transaction Coordinator (DTC)
- File Server
- Generic Application
- Generic Script
- Generic Service
- Hyper-V Replica Broker
- iSCSI Target Server
- iSCSI Server
- Message Queuing
- Other Server
- Virtual Machine
- WINS Server

In addition, other common services and applications are clustered on Windows Server 2012 clusters:

- Enterprise database services, such as Microsoft SQL Server
- Enterprise messaging services, such as Microsoft Exchange Server

FIGURE 16.6   High-Availability Roles

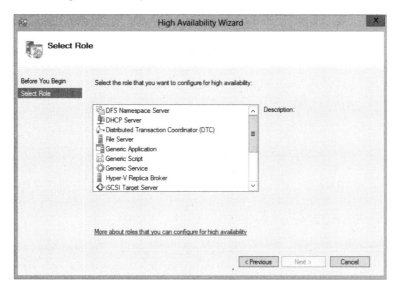

To cluster a role or feature such as Print Services, the first step is to install the role or feature on each node of the cluster. The next step is to use the Configure a Service or Application Wizard in the Failover Cluster Management tool. Exercise 16.4 shows you how to cluster the Print Services role once an appropriate disk has been presented to the cluster.

EXERCISE 16.4

Clustering the Print Services Role

1. Open the Failover Cluster Management MMC.

2. In the console tree, click the arrow next to the cluster name to expand the items underneath it.

3. Right click Roles, and choose Configure Role.

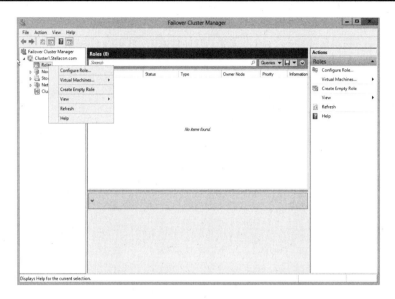

4. Click Next on the Before You Begin page.

5. Click Other Server on the Select Role screen and then click Next.

6. Type the name of the print server, such as **Print1**, and type in the IP address that will be used to access the print service, such as **192.168.1.108**. Then click Next.

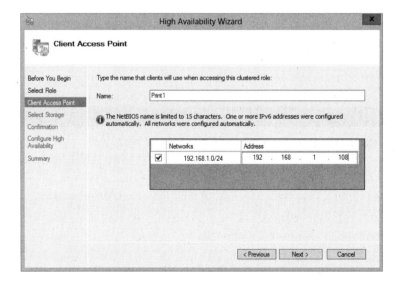

7. At the Select Storage page, just click Next.

8. Click Next at the Confirmation page.

9. After the wizard runs and the Summary page appears, you can view a report of the tasks the wizard performed by clicking View Report.

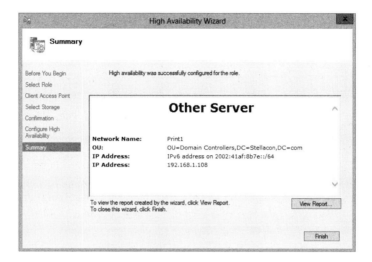

10. Close the report and click Finish.

The built-in roles and features all are configured in a similar fashion. Other applications, such as Microsoft Exchange Server 2013, have specialized cluster configuration routines that are outside the scope of this exam. Applications that are not developed to be clustered can also be clustered using the Generic Application, Generic Script, or Generic Service option in the Configure a Service or Application Wizard, as shown in Figure 16.7.

FIGURE 16.7 Configuring a generic application

Clustered Application Settings

Windows Server 2012 has options that allow an administrator to fine-tune the failover process to meet the needs of their business. In the next few sections, those options will be covered.

Failover occurs when a clustered application or service moves from one node to another. The process can be triggered automatically because of a failure or server maintenance or manually by an administrator. The failover process works as follows:

1. The cluster service takes all the resources in the application offline in the order set in the dependency hierarchy.

2. The cluster service transfers the application to the node that is listed next on the application's list of preferred host nodes.

3. The cluster service attempts to bring all of the application's resources online, starting at the bottom of the dependency hierarchy.

 These steps can change depending on the use of Live Migration.

In a cluster that is hosting multiple applications, it may be important to set specific nodes to be primarily responsible for each clustered application. This can be helpful from a troubleshooting perspective since a specific node is targeted for hosting service. To set a preferred node and an order of preference for failover, use the General tab on the Properties dialog box of the clustered application.

Also, the order of failover is set in this same dialog box by moving the order in which the nodes are listed. If NODEA should be the primary node and NODEC should be the server that the application fails to first, NODEA should be listed first and selected as the preferred owner. NODEC should be listed second, and the remaining cluster nodes should be listed after NODEC.

FIGURE 16.8 Clustered application failover settings

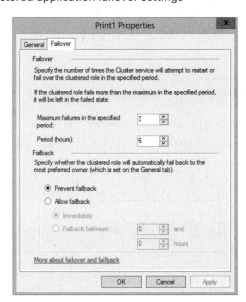

As shown in Figure 16.8, a number of failover settings can be configured for the clustered service. The failover settings control the number of times a clustered application can fail in a period of time before the cluster stops trying to restart it. Typically, if a clustered application fails a number of times, some sort of manual intervention will be required to return the application to a stable state.

Specifying the maximum number of failures will keep the application from trying to restart until it is manually brought back online after the problem has been resolved. This is beneficial because if the application continues to be brought online and then fails, it may show as being functional to the monitoring system even though it continues to fail. After the application is put in a failed state, the monitoring system will not be able to contact the application and should report it as being offline.

Figure 16.8 also shows the failback settings for Print1. Failback settings control whether or not and when a clustered application would fail back to the preferred cluster node once it becomes available. The default setting is Prevent Failback. If failback is allowed, two additional options are available, either to fail back immediately after the preferred node is available or to fail back within a specified time.

The time is specified in the 24-hour format. If you want to allow failback between 10:00 p.m. and 11:00 p.m., you would set the failback time to be between 22 and 23. Setting a failback time to off hours is an excellent way to ensure that your clustered applications are running on the designated nodes and automatically scheduling the failover process for a time when it will impact the fewest users.

One tool that is valuable in determining how resources affect other resources is the dependency viewer. The *dependency viewer* visualizes the dependency hierarchy created for an application or service. Using this tool can help when troubleshooting why specific resources are causing failures and allow an administrator to visualize the current configuration better and adjust it to meet business needs. Exercise 16.5 will show you how to run the dependency viewer.

EXERCISE 16.5

Using the Dependency Viewer

1. Open the Failover Cluster Management MMC.

2. In the console tree, click the arrow to expand the cluster.

3. Click Roles.

4. Under the Roles section in the center of the screen, click one of the roles (such as Print1).

5. Right click the role and under More Actions, click Show Dependency Report.

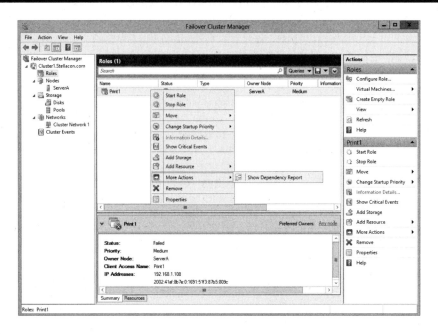

6. Review the dependency report.

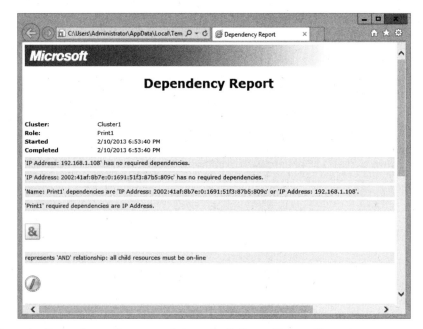

7. Close the Dependency Report, and close the Failover Cluster Manager.

Exercise 16.5 generated a dependency report that shows how the print service is dependent on a network name and a clustered disk resource. The network name is then dependent on an IP address.

Resource Properties

Resources are physical or logical objects, such as a file share or IP address, which the failover cluster manages. They may be a service or application available to clients, or they may be part of the cluster. Resources include physical hardware devices such as disks and logical items such as network names. They are the smallest configurable unit in a cluster and can run on only a single node in a cluster at a time.

Like clustered applications, resources have a number of properties available for meeting business requirements for high availability. This section covers resource dependencies and policies.

Dependencies can be set on individual resources and control how resources are brought online and offline. Simply put, a dependent resource is brought online after the resources that it depends on and is taken offline before those resources. As shown in Figure 16.9, dependencies can be set on a specific resource, such as the print spooler.

FIGURE 16.9   Resource dependencies

Resource policies are settings that control how resources respond when a failure occurs and how resources are monitored for failures. The Policies tab of a resource's Properties dialog box is shown in Figure 16.10.

FIGURE 16.10 Resource Policies

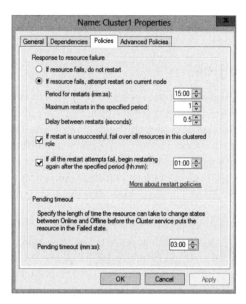

The Policies tab sets configuration options for how a resource should respond in the event of a failure. The options available are as follows:

If Resource Fails, Do Not Restart   This option, as it would lead you to believe, leaves the failed resource offline.

If Resource Fails, Attempt Restart On Current Node   With this option set, the resource tries to restart if it fails on the node on which it is currently running. There are two additional options if this is selected so that the number of restarts can be limited. They set the number of times the resource should restart on the current node in a specified length of time. For example, if you specify 5 for Maximum Restarts In The Specified Period and 10:00 (mm:ss) for the Period For Restarts, the cluster service will try to restart the resource five times during that 10-minute period. After the fifth restart, the cluster service will no longer attempt to restart the service on the active node.

If Restart Is Unsuccessful, Fail Over All Resources In This Service or Application   If this option is selected, when the cluster service is no longer trying to restart the resource on the active node, it will fail the entire service or application to another cluster node. If you wanted to leave the application or service with a failed resource on the current node, you would clear this check box.

If All The Restart Attempts Fail, Begin Restarting Again After The Specified Period (hh:mm)   If this option is selected, the cluster service will restart the resource at a specified interval if all previous attempts have failed.

Pending Timeout   This option is used to set the amount of time in minutes and seconds that the cluster service should wait for this resource to respond to a change in states. If a resource takes longer than the cluster expects to change states, the cluster will mark it as having failed. If a resource consistently takes longer than this timer, and the problem cannot be resolved, you may need to increase this value. The Advanced Policies tab is shown in Figure 16.11.

FIGURE 16.11   Resource Advanced Policies

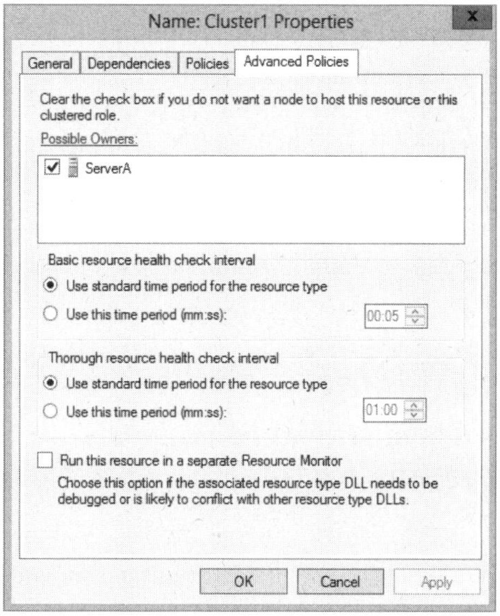

The options available on the Advanced Policies tab are as follows:

Possible Owners   This option allows an administrator to remove specific cluster nodes from running this resource. Using this option is valuable when there are issues with a resource on a particular node and the administrator wants to keep the applications from failing over to that node until the problem can be repaired.

Basic Resource Health Check Interval   This option allows an administrator to customize the health check interval for this resource.

Thorough Resource Health Check Interval   This option allows an administrator to customize the thorough heath check interval for this resource.

Run This Resource In A Separate Resource Monitor   If the resource needs to be debugged by a support engineer, or if the resource conflicts with other resources, this option may need to be used.

Windows Server 2012 Clustering Features

When Microsoft released Windows Server 2008 clustering, they made many improvements over previous Windows Server clustering. Microsoft has taken Windows Server 2012 clustering a step further. Now that you have an understanding of clustering, let's look at some of the improvements and new features.

Windows PowerShell Cmdlets for Failover Clusters   As I have explained throughout this book, Windows PowerShell is a command-line shell and scripting tool. Windows Server 2012 clustering has new cmdlets that provide powerful ways to script cluster configuration and management tasks. Windows PowerShell cmdlets will eventually replace the Cluster .exe command-line interface.

Cluster Shared Volumes   *Cluster Shared Volumes (CSV)* allows for the configuration of clustered virtual machines. Cluster Shared Volumes allows you to do the following:

- Reduce the number of LUNs (disks) required for your virtual machines.

- Make better use of disk space. The free space on a Cluster Shared Volume can be used by any VHD file on that LUN.

- More easily track the paths to VHD files and other files used by virtual machines.

- Use a few Cluster Shared Volumes to create a configuration that supports many clustered virtual machines.

Management of large-scale clusters   One new advantage of Windows Server 2012 clusters is the ability for Server Manager to discover and manage the nodes in a cluster. By starting the Failover Cluster Manager from Server Manager, you can do remote multiserver management and role and feature installation. An administrator now has the ability to manage a cluster from one convenient location.

Management and mobility of clustered virtual machines   As we have stated in previous chapters, Microsoft has built Windows Server 2012 "from the cloud up." Microsoft, as well as the industry as a whole, is moving toward the cloud and virtualization. With that in mind, administrators can now configure settings like prioritizing the starting or placing of virtual machines in the clustered workloads. This allows administrators to allocate resources efficiently to your cluster.

Cluster-Aware Updating   One issue that every administrator has dealt with is updating systems and applications while the application or system is running. For example, if you are running Microsoft Exchange and you want to do an Exchange update, when do you take the server offline to do the update? It always seems that someone is on the system 24 hours a day. Well Windows Server 2012 clustering has a solution.

Cluster-Aware Updating (CAU) is a new automated feature that allows system updates to be applied automatically while the cluster remains available during the entire update process.

Achieving High Availability with Network Load Balancing

Some applications that need to be highly available do not require failover clustering, such as applications based on web services. These applications typically are able to use *Network Load Balancing (NLB)* to balance connections across a number of server nodes. This is more easily done with applications that are sessionless or have a minimal amount of session data.

An NLB cluster load-balances client TCP/IP connections between cluster nodes and does not share any application data between nodes. If application data needs to be shared between cluster nodes, another facility such as replication will need to be used or the application will need to be able to retrieve this data. This can be accomplished by using data replication, accessing data from a centralized location, or using other methods.

NLB is used for both fault tolerance and scalability. When it's used for fault tolerance, a failed node can be removed from the cluster and another node will automatically start servicing requests that were handled by the failed node. In some cases, one server does not have enough resources to handle all of the requests; when this occurs, NLB can be used to spread the connection load across multiple nodes. When NLB is configured this way, it is configured for scalability.

How Does Network Load Balancing Work?

As the name suggests, an NLB cluster uses the network to provide load balancing and redundancy. It is able to accomplish this using a virtual IP address and a virtual Media Access Control (MAC) address that is shared among all of the nodes in the cluster. Client connections are all made to this virtual IP address. When an incoming packet is addressed to the virtual IP address, all of the NLB nodes receive it, but only the appropriate node responds.

When a client request arrives, all hosts simultaneously perform a calculation in order to determine which node should handle the request. The chosen node then accepts and responds to the client request, and the other cluster nodes discard it.

If all nodes are configured identically, the same percentage of client requests will be load-balanced to each node; however, this can be customized to match server capabilities. All nodes synchronize their data about which node should respond to each request and which nodes are active members of the cluster. A number of significant improvements were made to NLB in Windows Server 2012, as follows:

- Support for IPv6 addresses.
- Support of Network Driver Interface Specification (NDIS) 6.0 with compatibility with older versions.
- Network Load Balancing can detect and notify applications of excessive load or attack scenarios.
- Rolling upgrades can be done from Windows Server 2008 to Windows Server 2012.

Network Load Balancing Requirements

Failover clusters require that all of the cluster nodes run either the Standard or Datacenter edition of Windows Server 2012. Network Load Balancing is a feature that is available in all editions of Windows Server 2012.

What sort of hardware is required to leverage NLB? The recommended configuration uses two network adapters on each node in the cluster. The primary network adapter is used for client communication, and the second network adapter facilitates the communication between the cluster nodes. In some configurations, a single network adapter can be used, but the network hardware must support multicast traffic.

If multicast is chosen, additional network hardware requirements must be taken into consideration. For instance, upstream network hardware might need the multicast MAC address statically entered in the Address Resolution Protocol (ARP) table. This is because some network hardware does not accept an ARP response that resolves unicast IP addresses to multicast MAC addresses.

Also, using the Internet Group Management Protocol (IGMP) multicast option enables IGMP support for limiting switch flooding by limiting traffic to Network Load Balancing ports only. This ensures that traffic intended for an NLB cluster passes only through those network ports serving the cluster hosts and not all ports. If standard multicasting is used, switches might require additional configuration to set the ports that are used for the multicast traffic.

Creating an NLB Cluster

The first step in creating an NLB cluster is to prepare each cluster node. In this example, I am going to use two servers, each with two network adapters. The network adapter that will host the load-balanced virtual IP and that is used for client connections is renamed Client Network, and the network adapter that is used for cluster communications is renamed Cluster Network. Finally, the Network Load Balancing feature is installed on both servers to prepare for configuration. Exercise 16.6 walks you through installing the NLB Feature.

EXERCISE 16.6

Creating a Network Load Balancing Cluster

1. Open Server Manager.

2. Select number 2, Add Roles And Features.

3. At the Select Installation Type screen, choose role-based or feature-based installation.

4. At the Select Destination Server screen, choose Select A Server From The Server Pool and click Next.

5. At the Select Server Roles screens, click Next.

6. At the Select Features screen, click the Network Load Balancing check box. If the Add Features dialog box appears, click the Add Features button. Click Next.

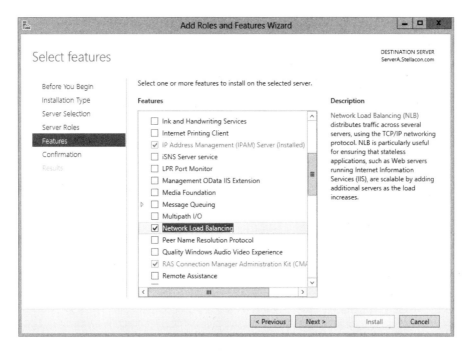

7. At the Confirmation screen, click the Install button.

8. Click the Close button when the installation is complete.

9. Close Server Manager.

Modifying Cluster Properties

As mentioned earlier, port rules modify how traffic is directed to NLB cluster nodes. The filtering mode in a port rule defines how requests are distributed among nodes in the NLB cluster. You have the following options for filtering modes:

Multiple Host   By default, this option is set. It configures all NLB nodes to respond based on the weight assigned to each node. This spreads the load across multiple cluster nodes to increase scalability. If this option is selected, one of the Affinity options also needs to be selected. The higher the weight setting, the more load the node will handle.

Single Host   When configured, this option makes it so that only the NLB node with the highest priority responds. If the highest-priority node fails, then the next-highest-priority node begins to respond. Sending requests to a single node increases availability but does not increase scalability.

Disable This Port Range This option blocks all packets for this port range. This option is used when the cluster does not run any applications on a specific port range.

The Affinity options, available when the Multiple Host option is selected in the filter, control how requests are distributed to the available cluster nodes. The options for Affinity are as follows:

None When this option is set, any available node can respond to any client request. This is suitable for applications such as static web pages that don't require state information to be saved. For example, the client may retrieve the first web page from Node A and the second web page from Node B.

Single When this option is set, a single node responds to all requests from a single client IP address. This is required for applications that you must authenticate or that require session state or encryption. This would be important for web applications that have user session variables, such as shopping carts.

Network When this option is set, a single node responds to all requests from a specific Class C network. This is useful when clients are accessing the NLB cluster from behind a group of proxy servers. This option ensures that a client connection can be maintained to a specific server, even when the source IP address varies within the same subnet.

When changing port rules for a specific node, make sure that the changes are reflected on the other nodes; otherwise, the cluster nodes may never complete convergence, which is needed for all of the available cluster nodes to work properly.

Managing NLB Clusters

The *Network Load Balancing Manager* is the graphical interface used to configure and manage NLB clusters, and nlb.exe is the command-line counterpart.

There are five main functions that can be performed on active NLB cluster nodes: Start, Stop, Drainstop, Suspend, and Resume. These actions are used when managing an NLB cluster. Each of the options has a slightly different function and reason for use:

Start This action starts a stopped NLB cluster node so that it can handle NLB traffic.

Stop This action temporarily stops the node from participating in the cluster and handling NLB traffic.

Drainstop This action stops the node from taking new sessions, and then it waits for active sessions to end before completely stopping participation in the cluster.

Suspend This action is different from Stop because suspending NLB stops NLB on the node and suspends all NLB cluster-control commands on the node, except for the resume and query commands.

Resume This action will start NLB on a node that has been suspended.

After the NLB cluster is created and configured, the application also needs to be installed and configured on each server. In the case of a website, it would need to be created on each server and then the content either copied or provided over a network connection to be served.

NIC Teaming

NIC Teaming, also known as load balancing and failover (LBFO), gives an administrator the ability to allow multiple network adapters on a system to be placed into a team. Independent hardware vendors (IHVs) have required NIC Teaming but until Windows Server 2012, NIC Teaming was NOT part of the Windows Server Operating System.

To be able to use NIC Teaming, the computer system must have at least one Ethernet adapter. If you want to provide fault protection, an administrator must have a minimum of two Ethernet adapters. One advantage of Windows Server 2012 is that an administrator can setup 32 network adapters in a NIC Team.

NIC Teaming is a very common practice when setting up virtualization. This is one way that you can have load balancing with Hyper-V.

NIC Teaming gives an administrator the ability to allow a virtual machine to use virtual network adapters in Hyper-V. The advantage of using NIC Teaming in Hyper-V is that the administrator can use NIC Teaming to connect to more than one Hyper-V switch. This allows Hyper-V to still have connectivity even if the network adapter under the Hyper-V switch gets disconnected.

An administrator can configure NIC Teaming in either Server Manager or PowerShell.

Summary

High availability is more than just clustering. It is achieved through improved hardware, software, and processes. This chapter focused on how to configure failover clustering and Network Load Balancing (NLB) to achieve high availability and scalability.

High availability should be approached through proper hardware configuration, training, and operational discipline. Failover clustering provides a highly available base for many applications, such as databases and mail servers.

These clusters require the Datacenter Edition of Windows Server 2012. Network load-balanced clusters are used to provide high availability and scalability for network-based applications, such as VPNs and Web servers. Network load-balanced clusters can be configured with any edition of Windows Server 2012.

Exam Essentials

Know how to modify failover and failback settings. These settings are set on the clustered service or application but can be modified by settings on the resources.

Know the hardware requirements for failover clustering and Network Load Balancing. Failover clustering and Network Load Balancing have distinct hardware requirements. Know the differences.

Review Questions

1. Which of the following editions of Windows Server 2012 can be configured in a failover cluster? (Choose all that apply.)

    A. Windows Server 2012 Web Edition

    B. Windows Server 2012 Standard Edition

    C. Windows Server 2012 Enterprise Edition

    D. Windows Server 2012 Datacenter Edition

2. Which of the following editions of Windows Server 2012 can be configured in a Network Load Balancing cluster? (Choose all that apply.)

    A. Windows Server 2012 Web Edition

    B. Windows Server 2012 Standard Edition

    C. Windows Server 2012 Enterprise Edition

    D. Windows Server 2012 Datacenter Edition

3. What is the maximum number of nodes that can participate in a Windows Server 2012 failover cluster?

    A. 2

    B. 4

    C. 16

    D. 64

4. Which of the following actions should be performed against an NLB cluster node if maintenance needs to be performed while not terminating current connections?

    A. Evict

    B. Drainstop

    C. Pause

    D. Stop

5. What is the maximum number of nodes that can participate in a Windows Server 2012 NLB cluster?

    A. 4

    B. 8

    C. 16

    D. 32

6. Which of the following applications would be better suited on a failover cluster instead of a network load-balanced cluster? (Choose all that apply.)

    A. SQL Server

    B. Website

    C. Exchange Mailbox Server

    D. VPN services

7. Which of the following applications would be better suited on a Network Load Balancing cluster instead of a failover cluster? (Choose all that apply.)

    A. SQL Server

    B. Website

    C. Database Servers

    D. Terminal Services

8. To configure an NLB cluster with unicast, what is the minimum number of network adapters required in each node?

    A. One

    B. Two

    C. Three

    D. Six

9. In a four-node cluster set to a Node and File Share Majority quorum model, how many votes can be lost before quorum is lost?

    A. One

    B. Two

    C. Three

    D. Four

10. In a three-node cluster set to a Node Majority quorum model, how many cluster nodes can be offline before quorum is lost?

    A. Zero

    B. One

    C. Two

    D. Three

Chapter

17

Configuring File and Storage Services

THE FOLLOWING 70-410 EXAM OBJECTIVES ARE COVERED IN THIS CHAPTER:

✓ **Configure local storage**

- This objective may include, but is not limited to: Design storage spaces; configure basic and dynamic disks; configure MBR and GPT disks; manage volumes; create and mount virtual hard disks (VHDs); configure storage pools and disk pools.

✓ **Configure Windows Firewall**

- This objective may include, but is not limited to: Configure rules for multiple profiles using Group Policy; configure connection security rules; configure Windows Firewall to allow or deny applications, scopes, ports, and users; configure authenticated firewall exceptions; import and export settings.

THE FOLLOWING 70-412 EXAM OBJECTIVES ARE COVERED IN THIS CHAPTER:

✓ **Configure and optimize storage**

- This objective may include, but is not limited to: Configure iSCSI Target and Initiator; configure Internet Storage Name server (iSNS); implement thin provisioning and trim; manage server free space using Features on Demand.

Disk storage is a requirement for just about every computer and application used in any corporate environment. Administrators have some familiarity with storage, whether it is internal storage, a locally attached set of disks, or network attached storage (NAS). In this chapter, we will examine the various aspects of Windows Server 2012 storage and firewall services. Though I'll discuss the various types of storage technologies, this chapter will primarily focus on iSCSI because of the native features in Windows Server 2012. We will also look at how to protect your disk and system by using Windows Firewall.

Storage in Windows Server 2012

As an IT administrator, you'll need to ask many questions before you start setting up a server. What type of disks should be used? What type of RAID sets should be made? What type of hardware platform should be purchased? These are all questions that must be asked when planning for storage in a Windows Server 2012 server. In the following sections, we will answer these questions so that you can make the best decisions for storage in your network's environment.

Initializing Disks

To begin, we must first discuss how to add disk drives to a server. Once a disk drive has been physically installed, it must be initialized by selecting the type of partition. Different types of partition styles are used to initialize disks: *Master Boot Record (MBR)* and *GUID Partition Table (GPT)*.

MBR has a partition table that indicates where the partitions are located on the disk drive, and with this particular partition style, only volumes up to 2 terabytes (2,048 gigabytes) are supported. An MBR drive can have up to four primary partitions or three primary partitions and one extended partition that can be divided into unlimited logical drives.

Windows Server 2012 can boot off only an MBR disk unless it is based on the Extensible Firmware Interface (EFI); then it can boot from GPT. An Itanium server is an example of EFI-based system. GPT is not constrained by the same limitations as MBR. In fact, a GPT disk drive can support volumes of up to 18 exabytes (18,874,368 million terabytes) and 128 partitions. As a result, GPT is recommended for disks larger than 2 TB or disks used on Itanium-based computers. Exercise 17.1 demonstrates the process of initializing additional disk drives to an active computer running Windows Server 2012. If you're not adding a new drive, then stop after step 4.

EXERCISE 17.1

Initializing Disk Drives

1. Open Computer Management under Administrative Tools.

2. Select Disk Management.

3. After disk drives have been installed, right-click Disk Management and select Rescan Disks.

4. A pop-up box appears indicating that the server is scanning for new disks. If you did not add a new disk, go to step 9.

5. After the server has completed the scan, the new disk appears as Unknown.

6. Right-click the Unknown disk and select Initialize Disk.

7. A pop-up box appears asking for the partition style. For this exercise, choose MBR.

8. Click OK.

9. Close Computer Management.

The disk will now appear online as a basic disk with unallocated space.

Working with Basic and Dynamic Disks

Windows Server 2012 supports two types of disk configurations: basic and dynamic. Basic disks are divided into partitions and can be used with previous versions of Windows. Dynamic disks are divided into volumes and can be used with Windows 2000 Server and later releases.

When a disk is initialized, it is automatically created as a basic disk, but when a new fault-tolerant (RAID) volume set is created, the disks in the set are converted to dynamic disks. Fault-tolerance features and the ability to modify disks without having to reboot the server are what distinguish dynamic disks from basic disks.

Fault Tolerance (RAID) is discussed in detail later in this chapter in the "Redundant Array of Independent Disks" section.

A basic disk can simply be converted to a dynamic disk without loss of data. When a basic disk is converted, the partitions are automatically changed to the appropriate volumes. However, converting a dynamic disk back to a basic disk is not as simple. First, all of the data on the dynamic disk must be backed up or moved. Then all of the volumes on the dynamic disk have to be deleted. The dynamic disk can then be converted to a basic disk. Partitions and logical drives can be created and the data restored.

The following are actions that can be performed on basic disks:

- Format partitions.
- Mark partitions as active.
- Create and delete primary and extended partitions.
- Create and delete logical drives.
- Convert from a basic disk to a dynamic disk.

The following are actions that can be performed on dynamic disks:

- Create and delete simple, striped, spanned, mirrored, or RAID-5 volumes.
- Remove or break a mirrored volume.
- Extend simple or spanned volumes.
- Repair mirrored or RAID-5 volumes.
- Convert from a dynamic disk to basic after deleting all volumes.

In Exercise 17.2, you'll convert a basic disk to a dynamic disk.

EXERCISE 17.2

Converting a Basic Disk to a Dynamic Disk

1. Open Computer Management under Administrative Tools.

2. Select Disk Management.

3. Right-click a basic disk that you want to convert, and select Convert To Dynamic Disk.

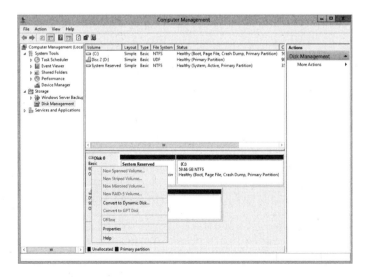

4. The Convert To Dynamic Disk dialog box appears. From here, select all of the disks that you want to convert to dynamic disks. In this exercise, only one disk will be converted.

5. Click OK.

6. The Convert To Dynamic Disk dialog box changes to the Disks To Convert dialog box and shows the disk/disks that will be converted to dynamic disks.

7. Click Convert.

8. Disk Management will warn that if you convert the disk to dynamic, you will not be able to start the installed operating system from any volume on the disk (except the current boot volume).

9. Click Yes.

10. Close Computer Management.

The converted disk will now show as dynamic in Disk Management.

Working with Volume Sets

A *volume set* is created from volumes that span multiple drives by using the free space from those drives to construct what will appear to be a single drive. The following list includes the various types of volume sets and their definitions:

- *Simple volume* uses only one disk or a portion of a disk.

- *Spanned volume* is a simple volume that spans multiple disks, with a maximum of 32. Use a spanned volume if the volume needs are too great for a single disk.

- *Striped volume* stores data in stripes across two or more disks. A striped volume gives you fast access to data but is not fault tolerant, nor can it be extended or mirrored. If one disk in the striped set fails, the entire volume fails.

- *Mirrored volume* duplicates data across two disks. This type of volume is fault tolerant because if one drive fails, the data on the other disk is unaffected.

- *RAID-5 volume* stores data in stripes across three or more disks. This type of volume is fault tolerant because if a drive fails, the data can be re-created from the parity off of the remaining disk drives. Operating system files and boot files cannot reside on the RAID-5 disks.

Exercise 17.3 illustrates the procedure for creating a volume set.

EXERCISE 17.3

Creating a Volume Set

1. Open Computer Management under Administrative Tools.

2. Select Disk Management.

3. Select and right-click a disk that has unallocated space. If there are no disk drives available for a particular volume set, that volume set will be grayed out as a selectable option. In this exercise, you'll choose a spanned volume set, but the process after the volume set selection is the same regardless of which kind you choose. The only thing that differs is the number of disk drives chosen.

4. The Welcome page of the New Spanned Volume Wizard appears and explains the type of volume set chosen. Click Next.

5. The Select Disks page appears. Select the disk that will be included with the volume set and click Add. Repeat this process until all of the desired disks have been added. Click Next.

6. The Assign Drive Letter Or Path page appears. From here you can select the desired drive letter for the volume, mount the volume in an empty NTFS folder, or choose not to assign a drive letter. The new volume is labeled as E. Click Next.

7. The Format Volume page appears. Choose to format the new volume. Click Next.

8. Click Finish.

9. If the disks have not been converted to dynamic, you will be asked to convert the disks. Click Yes.

The new volume will appear as a healthy spanned dynamic volume with the new available disk space of the new volume set.

Redundant Array of Independent Disks

The ability to support drive sets and arrays using Redundant Array of Independent Disks (RAID) technology is built into Windows Server 2012. RAID can be used to enhance data performance, or it can be used to provide fault tolerance to maintain data integrity in case of a hard disk failure. Windows Server 2012 supports three different types of RAID technologies: RAID-0, RAID-1, and RAID-5.

RAID-0 (Disk Striping)   *Disk striping* is using two or more volumes on independent disks created as a single striped set. There can be a maximum of 32 disks. In a striped set, data is divided into blocks that are distributed sequentially across all of the drives in the set. With RAID-0 disk striping, you get very fast read and write performance because multiple blocks of data can be accessed off of multiple drives simultaneously. However, RAID-0 does not offer the ability to maintain data integrity during a single disk failure. In other words, RAID-0 is not fault tolerant; a single disk event will cause the entire striped set to be lost, and it will have to be re-created through some type of recovery process, such as a tape backup.

RAID-1 (Disk Mirroring)　*Disk mirroring* is two logical volumes on two separate identical disks created as a duplicate disk set. Data is written on two disks at the same time; that way, in the event of a disk failure, data integrity is maintained and available. Although this fault tolerance gives administrators data redundancy, it comes with a price because it diminishes the amount of available storage space by half. For example, if an administrator wants to create a 300 GB mirrored set, they would have to install two 300 GB hard drives into the server, thus doubling the cost for the same available space.

RAID-5 Volume (Disk Striping with Parity)　With a Raid-5 volume, you have the ability to use a minimum of three disks and a maximum of 32 disks. Raid-5 volumes allow data to be striped across all of the disks with an additional block of error-correction called parity. *Parity* is used to reconstruct the data in the event of a disk failure. RAID-5 has slower write performance than the other RAID types because the OS must calculate the parity information for each stripe that is written but the read performance is equivalent to a stripe set, RAID-0, because the parity information is not read. Like RAID-1, RAID-5 comes with additional cost considerations. For every RAID-5 set, roughly an entire hard disk is consumed for storing the parity information. For example, a minimum RAID-5 set requires three hard disks, and if those disks are 300 GB each, approximately 600 GB of disk space is available to the OS and 300 GB is consumed by parity information, which equates to 33.3 percent of the available space. Similarly, in a five-disk RAID-5 set of 300 GB disks, approximately 1200 GB of disk space is available to the OS, which means that 20 percent of the total available space is consumed by the parity information. The words *roughly* and *approximately* are used when calculating disk space because a 300 GB disk will really be only about 279 GB of space. This is because vendors define a gigabyte as one billion bytes, but the OS defines it as 2^{30} (1,073,741,824) bytes. Also remember that file systems and volume managers have overhead as well.

Software RAID is a nice option for a small company, but hardware RAID is definitely a better option if the money is available.

Table 17.1 breaks down the various aspects of the supported RAID types in Window Server 2012.

TABLE 17.1 Supported RAID-level properties on Windows Server 2012

RAID Level	RAID Type	Fault Tolerant	Advantages	Minimum Number of Disks	Maximum Number of Disks
0	Disk striping	No	Fast reads and writes	2	32
1	Disk mirroring	Yes	Data redundancy and faster writes than RAID-5	2	2
5	Disk striping with parity	Yes	Data redundancy with less overhead and faster reads than RAID-1	3	32

Creating RAID Sets

Now that you understand the concepts of RAID and how to use it, we can look at the creation of RAID sets in Windows Server 2012. The process of creating a RAID set is the same as the process for creating a simple or spanned volume set except for the minimum disk requirements associated with each RAID type.

Creating a mirrored volume set is basically the same as creating a volume set, as shown in Exercise 17.3, except that you will select New Mirrored Volume. It is after the disk select wizard appears that you'll begin to see the difference. Since a new mirrored volume is being created, the volume requires two disks.

During the disk select process, if only one disk is selected, the Next button will be unavailable because the disk minimum has not been met. Refer to Figure 17.1 to view the Select Disks page of the New Mirrored Volume Wizard during the creation of a new mirrored volume, and notice that the Next button is not available.

FIGURE 17.1 Select Disks page of the New Mirrored Volume Wizard

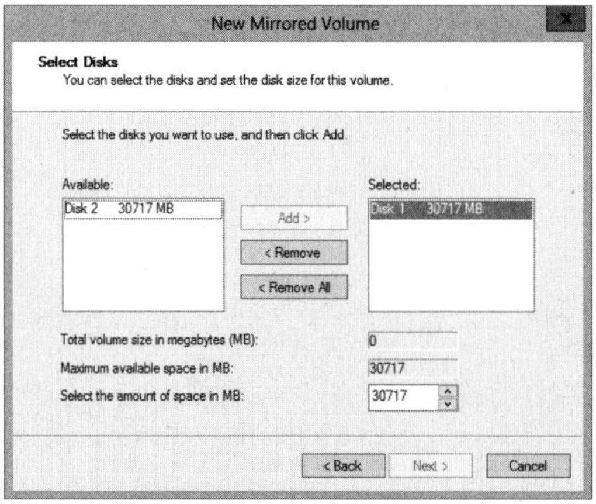

To complete the process, you must select a second disk by highlighting the appropriate disk and adding it to the volume set. Once the second disk has been added, the Add button becomes unavailable and the Next button is available to complete the mirrored volume set creation (see Figure 17.2).

FIGURE 17.2   Adding the second disk to complete a mirrored volume set

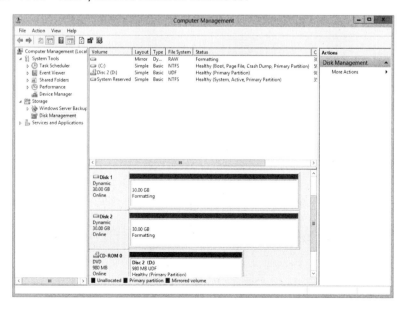

After you click Next, the creation of the mirrored volume set is again just like the rest of the steps in Exercise 17.3. A drive letter will have to be assigned, and the volume will need to be formatted. The new mirrored volume set will appear in Disk Management. In Figure 17.3, notice that the capacity of the volume equals one disk even though two have been selected.

FIGURE 17.3   Newly created mirrored volume set

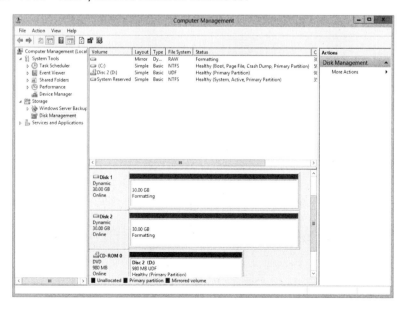

To create a RAID-5 volume set, you use the same process that you use to create a mirrored volume set. The only difference is that a RAID-5 volume set requires that a minimum of three disks be selected to complete the volume creation. The process is simple: Select New RAID-5 Volume, and then select the three disks that will be used in the volume set. Assign a drive letter, and format the volume. Figure 17.4 shows a newly created RAID-5 volume set in Disk Management.

FIGURE 17.4   Newly created RAID-5 volume set

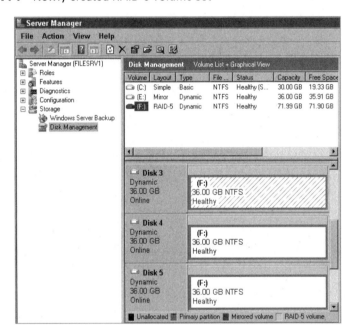

Mount Points

With the ever-increasing demands of storage, mount points are used to surpass the limitation of 26 drive letters and to join two volumes into a folder on a separate physical disk drive. A *mount point* allows you to configure a volume to be accessed from a folder on another existing disk.

Through Disk Management, a mount point folder can be assigned to a drive instead of using a drive letter, and it can be used on basic or dynamic volumes that are formatted with NTFS. However, mount point folders can be created only on empty folders within a volume. Additionally, mount point folder paths cannot be modified; they can only be removed once they have been created. Exercise 17.4 shows the steps to create a mount point.

EXERCISE 17.4

Creating Mount Points

1. Open Server Manager.

2. Click and then expand Storage.

3. Select Disk Management.

4. Right-click the volume where the mount point folder will be assigned and select Change Drive Letter And Paths.

5. Click Add.

6. Either type the path to an empty folder on an NTFS volume, or click Browse to select or make a new folder for the mount point.

When you explore the drive, you'll see the new folder created. Notice that the icon indicates that it is a mount point.

Microsoft MPIO

Multipath I/O (MPIO) is associated with high availability because a computer will be able to use a solution with redundant physical paths connected to a storage device. Thus, if one path fails, an application will continue to run because it can access the data across the other path.

The MPIO software provides the functionality needed for the computer to take advantage of the redundant storage paths. MPIO solutions can also load-balance data traffic across both paths to the storage device, virtually eliminating bandwidth bottlenecks to the computer. What allows MPIO to provide this functionality is the new native *Microsoft Device Specific Module (Microsoft DSM)*. The Microsoft DSM is a driver that communicates with storage devices—iSCSI, Fibre Channel, or SAS—and it provides the chosen load-balancing policies. Windows Server 2012 supports the following load-balancing policies:

Failover   In a failover configuration, there is no load balancing. There is a primary path that is established for all requests and subsequent standby paths. If the primary path fails, one of the standby paths will be used.

Failback   This is similar to failover in that it has primary and standby paths. However, with failback you designate a preferred path that will handle all process requests until it fails, after which the standby path will become active until the primary reestablishes a connection and automatically regains control.

Round Robin   In a round-robin configuration, all available paths will be active and will be used to distribute I/O in a balanced round-robin fashion.

Round Robin with a Subset of Paths   In this configuration, a specific set of paths will be designated as a primary set and another as standby paths. All I/O will use the primary set of paths in a round-robin fashion until all of the sets fail. Only at this time will the standby paths become active.

Dynamic Least Queue Depth   In a dynamic least queue depth configuration, I/O will route to the path with the least number of outstanding requests.

Weighted Path   In a weighted path configuration, paths are assigned a numbered weight. I/O requests will use the path with the least weight—the higher the number, the lower the priority.

Exercise 17.5 demonstrates the process of installing the Microsoft MPIO feature for Windows Server 2012.

EXERCISE 17.5

Installing Microsoft MPIO

1. Choose Server Manager by clicking the Server Manager icon on the Taskbar.

2. Click number 2, Add Roles And Features.

3. Choose role-based or feature-based installation and click next.

4. Choose your server and click Next.

5. Click Next at the Roles screen.

6. At the Select Features screen, choose the Multipath I/O checkbox. Click Next.

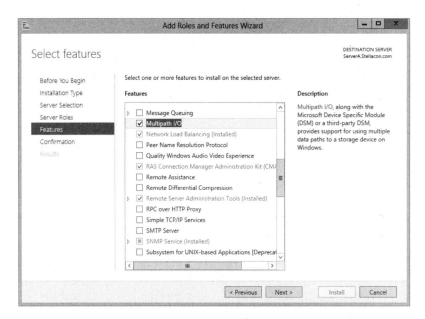

7. On the Confirm Installation Selections page, verify that Multipath I/O is the feature that will be installed. Click Install.

8. After the installation completes, the Installation Results page appears stating that the server must be rebooted to finish the installation process.

9. Click Close.

10. Restart the system.

Typically, most storage arrays work with the Microsoft DSM. However, some hardware vendors require DSM software that is specific to their products. Third-party DSM software is installed through the MPIO utility as follows:

1. Open Administrative Tools ➤ MPIO.

2. Select the DSM Install tab (see Figure 17.5).

FIGURE 17.5　　The DSM Install tab on the MPIO Properties dialog box

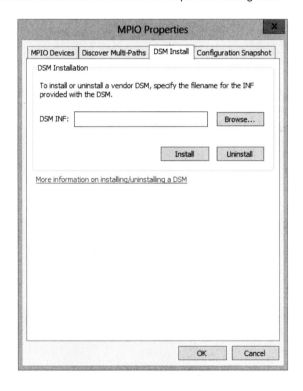

3. Add the path of the INF file and click Install.

iSCSI

Internet Small Computer System Interface (iSCSI) is an interconnect protocol used to establish and manage a connection between a computer (initiator) and a storage device (target). It does this by using a connection through TCP port 3260, which allows it to be used over a LAN, a WAN, or the Internet. Each initiator is identified by its iSCSI Qualified Name (iqn), and it is used to establish its connection to an iSCSI target.

iSCSI was developed to allow block-level access to a storage device over a network. This is different than using a network attached storage (NAS) device that connects through the use of Common Internet File System (CIFS) or Network File System (NFS).

Block-level access is important to many applications that require direct access to storage. MS-Exchange and MS-SQL are examples of applications that require direct access to storage.

By being able to leverage the existing network infrastructure, iSCSI was also developed as an alternative to Fibre Channel storage by alleviating the additional hardware costs associated with a Fibre Channel storage solution.

iSCSI also has another advantage over Fibre Channel in that it can provide security for the storage devices. iSCSI can use Challenge Handshake Authentication Protocol (CHAP or MS-CHAP) for authentication and Internet Protocol Security (IPsec) for encryption. Windows Server 2012 is able to connect an iSCSI storage device out of the box with no additional software needing to be installed. This is because the Microsoft iSCSI initiator is built into the operating system.

Windows Server 2012 supports two different ways to initiate an iSCSI session:

- Through the native Microsoft iSCSI software initiator that resides on Windows Server 2012

- Using a hardware iSCSI host bus adapter (HBA) that is installed in the computer

Both the Microsoft iSCSI software initiator and iSCSI HBA present an iSCSI Qualified Name that identifies the host initiator. When the Microsoft iSCSI software initiator is used, the CPU utilization may be as much as 30 percent higher than on a computer with a hardware iSCSI HBA. This is because all of the iSCSI process requests are handled within the operating system. Using a hardware iSCSI HBA, process requests can be offloaded to the adapter, thus freeing the CPU overhead associated with the Microsoft iSCSI software initiator. However, iSCSI HBAs can be expensive, whereas the Microsoft iSCSI software initiator is free.

It is worthwhile to install the Microsoft iSCSI software initiator and perform load testing to see how much overhead the computer will have prior to purchasing an iSCSI HBA or HBAs, depending on the redundancy level. Exercise 17.6 explains how to install and configure an iSCSI connection.

EXERCISE 17.6

Configuring iSCSI Storage Connection

1. Click the Windows Key ➢ Administrative Tools ➢ iSCSI Initiator.

2. If a dialog box appears, click Yes to start the service.

3. Click the Discovery tab.

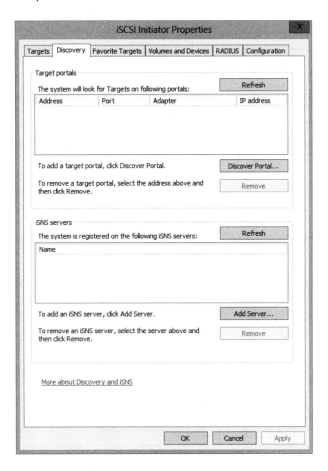

3. In the Target Portals portion of the page, click Discover Portal.

4. Enter the IP address of the target portal and click OK.

5. The IP address of the target portal appears in the Target Portals box.

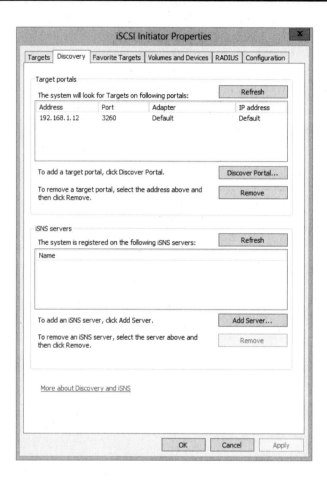

6. Click OK.

To use the storage that has now been presented to the server, you must create a volume on it and format the space. Refer to Exercise 17.3 to review this process.

Internet Storage Name Service

Internet Storage Name Service (iSNS) allows for central registration of an iSCSI environment because it automatically discovers available targets on the network. The purpose of iSNS is to help find available targets on a large iSCSI network.

The Microsoft iSCSI initiator includes an iSNS client that is used to register with the iSNS. The iSNS feature maintains a database of clients that it has registered either through DCHP discovery or through manual registration. iSNS DHCP is available after the installation of the service and is used to allow iSNS clients to discover the location of the iSNS. However, if iSNS DHCP is not configured, iSNS clients must be registered manually with the `iscsicli` command.

To execute the command, launch a command prompt on a computer hosting the Microsoft iSCSI and type the following: **`iscsicli addisnsserver <servername>`**, where **`<servername>`** is the name of the computer hosting iSNS. Exercise 17.7 walks you through the steps required to install the iSNS feature on Windows Server 2012, and then it explains the different tabs in iSNS.

EXERCISE 17.7

Installing the iSNS Feature on Windows Server 2012

1. Choose Server Manager by clicking the Server Manager icon on the Taskbar.

2. Click number 2, Add Roles And Features.

3. Choose role-based or featured-based installation and click Next.

4. Choose your server and click Next.

5. Click Next at the Roles screen.

6. At the Select Features screen, choose the iSNS Server Service check box. Click Next.

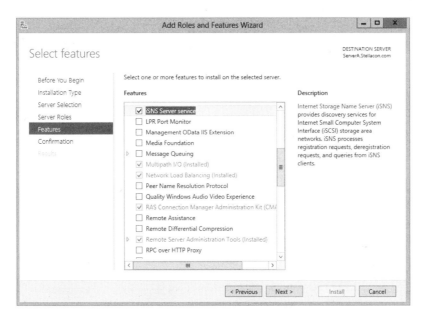

7. At the Confirmation screen, click the Install button.

8. Click the Close button. Close Server Manager and reboot.

9. Log in and open the iSNS server under Administrative Tools.

10. Click the General tab. This tab displays the list of registered initiators and targets. In addition to their iSCSI Qualified Name (iqn), it lists storage node type (Target or Initiator), alias string, and entity identifier (the Fully Qualified Domain Name (FQDN) of the machine hosting the iSNS client).

11. Click the Discovery Domains tab. The purpose of Discovery Domains is to provide a way to separate and group nodes. This is very similar to zoning in Fibre Channel. The following options are available on the Discovery Domains tab:

- Create is used to create a new discovery domain.

- Refresh is used to repopulate the Discovery Domain drop-down list.

- Delete is used to delete the currently selected discovery domain.

- Add is used to add nodes that are already registered in iSNS to the currently selected discovery domain.

- Add New is used to add nodes by entering the iSCSI Qualified Name (iqn) of the node. These nodes do not have to be currently registered.

- Remove Used to remove selected nodes from the discovery domain.

12. Click the Discovery Domain Sets tab. The purpose of discovery domain sets is to further separate discovery domains. Discovery domains can be enabled or disabled, giving administrators the ability to further restrict the visibility of all initiators and targets. The options on the Discovery Domain Sets tab are as follows:

- The Enable check box is used to indicate the status of the discovery domain sets and to turn them off and on.

- Create is used to create new discovery domain sets.

- Refresh is used to repopulate the Discovery Domain Sets drop-down list.

- Delete is used to delete the currently selected discovery domain set.

- Add is used to add discovery domains to the currently selected discovery domain set.

- Remove is used to remove selected nodes from the discovery domain sets.

13. Close the iSNS Server.

Fibre Channel

Fibre Channel storage devices are similar to iSCSI storage devices in that they both allow block-level access to their data sets and can provide MPIO policies with the proper hardware configurations. However, Fibre Channel requires a Fibre Channel HBA, fiber-optic cables, and Fibre Channel switches to connect to a storage device.

A *World Wide Name (WWN)* from the Fibre Channel HBA is used from the host and device so that they can communicate directly with each other, similar to using a NIC's MAC address. In other words, a logical unit number (LUN) is presented from a Fibre Channel storage device to the WWN of the host's HBA. Fibre Channel has been the preferred method of storage because of the available connection bandwidth between the storage and the host.

Fibre Channel devices supports 1 Gb/s, 2 Gb/s, and 4 Gb/s connections and soon will support 8 Gb/s connections, but now that 10 Gb/s Ethernet networks are becoming more prevalent in many datacenters, iSCSI can be a suitable alternative. It is important to consider that 10 Gb/s network switches can be more expensive than comparable Fibre Channel switches.

N-Port Identification Virtualization (NPIV) is a Fibre Channel facility allowing multiple N-Port IDs to share a single physical N-Port. This allows multiple Fibre Channel initiators to occupy a single physical port. By using a single port, this eases hardware requirements in Storage Area Network (SAN) design.

Network Attached Storage

The concept of a *network attached storage (NAS)* solution is that it is a low-cost device for storing data and serving files through the use of an Ethernet LAN connection. A NAS device accesses data at the file level via a communication protocol such as NFS, CIFS, or even HTTP, which is very different from iSCSI or FC Fibre Channel storage devices that access the data at the block level. NAS devices are best used in file-storing applications, and they do not require a storage expert to install and maintain the device. In most cases, the only setup that is required is an IP address and an Ethernet connection.

Virtual Disk Service

Virtual Disk Service (VDS) was created to ease the administrative efforts involved in managing all of the various types of storage devices. Many storage hardware providers used their own applications for installation and management, and this made administering all of these various devices very cumbersome.

VDS is a set of application programming interfaces (APIs) that provides a centralized interface for managing all of the various storage devices. The native VDS API enables the management of disks and volumes at an OS level, and hardware vendor-supplied APIs manage the storage devices at a RAID level. These are known as software and hardware providers.

A *software provider* is host based, and it interacts with Plug and Play Manager because each disk is discovered and operates on volumes, disks, and disk partitions. VDS includes two software providers: basic and dynamic. The basic software provider manages basic disks with no fault tolerance, whereas the dynamic software providers manage dynamic disks with fault management. A hardware provider translates the VDS APIs into instructions specific to the storage hardware. This is how storage management applications are able to communicate with the storage hardware to create LUNs or Fibre Channel HBAs to view the WWN. The following are Windows Server 2012 storage management applications that use VDS:

- The *Disk Management snap-in* is an application that allows you to configure and manage the disk drives on the host computer. You have already seen this application in use when you initialized disks and created volume sets.

- *DiskPart* is a command-line utility that configures and manages disks, volumes, and partitions on the host computer. It can also be used to script many of the storage management commands. DiskPart is a very robust tool that you should study on your own as it is beyond the scope of this book. Figure 17.6 shows the various commands and their function in the DiskPart utility.

FIGURE 17.6   DiskPart commands

- *DiskRAID* is also a scriptable command-line utility that configures and manages hardware RAID storage systems. However, at least one VDS hardware provider must be installed for DiskRAID to be functional. DiskRAID is another useful utility that you should study on your own because it's beyond the scope of this book.

Booting from a VHD

Once you have installed each operating system, you can choose the operating system that you will boot to during the boot process. You will see a boot selection screen that asks you to choose which operating system you want to boot.

The Boot Configuration Data (BCD) store contains boot information parameters that were previously found in boot.ini in older versions of Windows. To edit the boot options in the BCD store, use the bcdedit utility, which can only be launched from a command prompt. To open a command prompt window, do the following:

1. Launch \Windows\system32\cmd.exe.

2. Open the Run command by pressing the Windows key plus the R key and then entering **cmd.**

3. Type **cmd.exe** in the Search Programs And Files box and press Enter.

After the command prompt window is open, type **bcdedit** to launch the bcdedit utility. You can also type **bcdedit /?** to see all of the different bcdedit commands.

Virtualization is covered in greater detail in Chapter 8, "Using Virtualization In Windows Server 2012."

Configuring Windows Firewall Options

Now that we have talked about disks, let's discuss one way to protect those disks from illegal access. Before we can start talking about firewall options, you must first understand what a firewall does. A *firewall* is a software or hardware device that checks the information that is received from an outside (Internet) or external network and uses that information to determine whether the packet should be accepted or declined.

Depending on the firewall, you have the ability to check all potential remote users against Active Directory to verify that the remote user has an authorized domain account. This process is called *Active Directory account integration*.

Microsoft Windows Server 2012 has a built-in firewall. The following are some of the configuration options included in the Windows Firewall Settings dialog box:

Domain Profile Tab   On the Domain Profile tab, you have the ability to turn the firewall on or off by using the Firewall State drop-down menu. When setting the Firewall State in this tab, it's for turning the firewall on or off for the domain only. When turning the firewall on, you also have the ability to block inbound and outbound connections (see Figure 17.7). Administrators also have the ability to control the Windows Firewall behavior along with setting up logging.

FIGURE 17.7   Domain Profile tab of Windows Firewall Settings

Private Profile Tab   On the Private Profile tab, you have the ability to turn the firewall on or off by using the Firewall State drop-down menu. When setting the Firewall State in this tab, it's for turning the firewall on or off for the Private Profile only. When turning the firewall on, you also have the ability to block inbound and outbound connections (see Figure 17.8). Administrators also have the ability to control the Windows Firewall Private Profile behavior along with setting up logging.

FIGURE 17.8   Private Profile tab of Windows Firewall Settings

Public Profile   On the Public Profile tab, you have the ability to turn the firewall on or off by using the Firewall State drop-down menu. When setting the Firewall State in this tab, it's for turning the firewall on or off for the Public Profile only. When turning the firewall on, you also have the ability to block inbound and outbound connections (see Figure 17.9). Administrators also have the ability to control the Windows Firewall Public Profile behavior along with setting up logging.

FIGURE 17.9   Public Profile tab of Windows Firewall

IPsec Settings Tab   The IPsec Setting tab allows you to set up the IPsec defaults, IPsec exemptions, and IPsec tunnel authorization. The IPsec defaults button allows you to specify settings used by IPsec to establish secured connections. The IPsec exemptions allow you to set up ICMP exemptions from IPsec. Finally, you can set up IPsec tunnel authorization, which allows you to specify the users and computers that are authorized to establish an IPSec tunnel (see Figure 17.10).

Windows Server 2012 takes firewalls a step further than just the normal firewall settings in Control Panel. An MMC snap-in called *Windows Firewall with Advanced Security* (see Figure 17.11) can block all incoming and outgoing connections based on its configuration.

One of the major advantages to using the Windows Firewall with Advanced Security snap-in is the ability to set firewall configurations on remote computers using group policies. Another advantage to using this MMC is the ability to set up firewalls using IPsec security. The Windows Firewall with Advanced Security snap-in allows an administrator to set more in-depth rules for Microsoft Active Directory users and groups, source and destination Internet Protocol (IP) addresses, IP port numbers, ICMP settings, IPsec settings, specific types of interfaces, and services.

FIGURE 17.10 IPsec Settings tab of Windows Firewall Settings

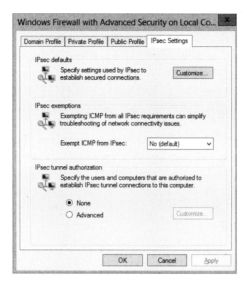

FIGURE 17.11 Windows Firewall with Advanced Security snap-in

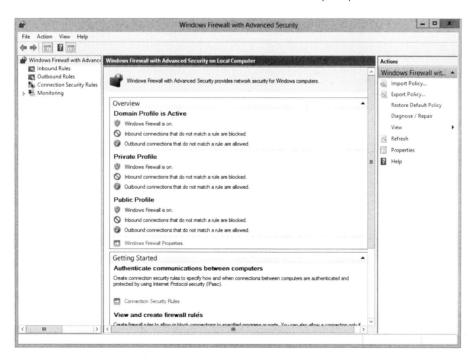

You can configure more advanced settings by configuring Windows Firewall with Advanced Security. To access Windows Firewall with Advanced Security, click the Windows key and choose Control Panel ➢ Large Icons View ➢ Windows Firewall, and then click the Advanced Settings link.

The scope pane to the left shows that you can set up specific inbound and outbound rules, connection security rules, and monitoring rules. The central area shows an overview of the firewall's status as well as the current profile settings. Let's take a look at these in more detail.

Inbound and Outbound Rules

Inbound and outbound rules consist of many preconfigured rules that can be enabled or disabled. Obviously, inbound rules (see Figure 17.12) monitor inbound traffic, and outbound rules monitor outbound traffic. By default, many are disabled. Double-clicking a rule will bring up its Properties dialog box, as shown in Figure 17.13.

FIGURE 17.12   Inbound rules

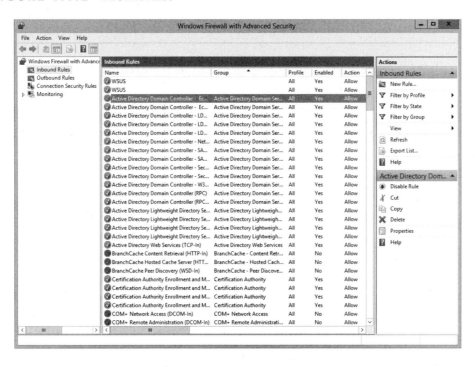

FIGURE 17.13   An inbound rule's Properties dialog box for WSUS

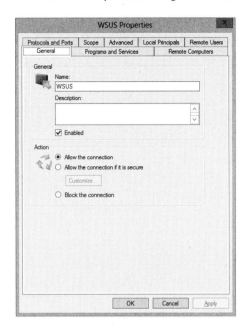

You can filter the rules to make them easier to view. Filtering can be performed based on the profile the rule affects or whether the rule is enabled or disabled or based on the rule group.

If you can't find a rule that is appropriate to your needs, you can create a new rule by right-clicking Inbound Rules or Outbound Rules in the scope pane and then selecting New Rule. The New Inbound (or Outbound) Rule Wizard will launch, and you will be asked whether you want to create a rule based on a particular program, protocol or port, pre-defined category, or custom settings.

Exercise 17.8 will walk you through the steps needed to create a new inbound rule that will allow only encrypted TCP traffic. In this exercise, you will have the ability to create a custom rule and then specify which authorized users and computers can connect using this rule.

EXERCISE 17.8

Configuring Windows Firewall

1. Press the Windows Key ➢ Control Panel ➢ Large Icon View ➢ Windows Firewall.

2. Click Advanced Settings on the left-hand side.

3. Right-click Inbound Rules and select New Rule.

4. Choose a rule type. For this exercise, choose Custom so that you can see all of the options available to you; then click Next.

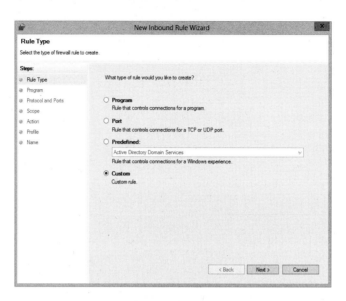

5. Choose the programs or services that are affected by this rule. For this exercise, choose All Programs; then click Next.

6. Choose the protocol type as well as the local and remote port numbers that are affected by this rule. For this exercise, choose TCP, and make sure that All Ports is selected for both Local Port and Remote Port. Click Next to continue.

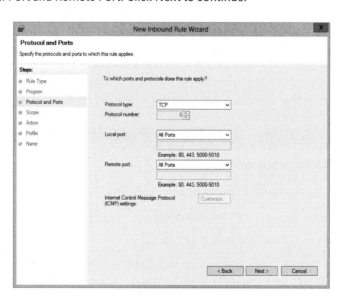

7. Choose the local and remote IP addresses that are affected by this rule. Choose Any IP Address for both local and remote; then click Next.

8. Specify whether this rule will allow the connection, allow the connection only if it is secure, or block the connection. Select the option Allow The Connection If It Is Secure; then click Next.

9. Specify whether connections should be allowed only from certain users. You can experiment with these options if you want. Then click Next to continue.

10. Specify whether connections should be allowed only from certain computers. Again you can experiment with these options if you want. Then click Next to continue.

11. Choose which profiles will be affected by this rule. Select one or more profiles, and click Next to continue.

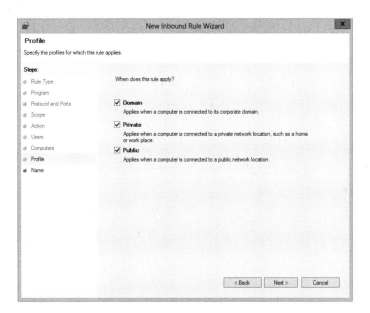

12. Give your profile a name and description; then click Finish. Your custom rule will appear in the list of Inbound Rules, and the rule will be enabled.

13. Double-click your newly created rule. Notice that you can change the options that you previously configured.

14. Disable the rule by right-clicking the rule and choosing Disable Rule.

15. Close Windows Firewall.

Now let's take a look at setting up Connection Security Rules through Windows Firewall with Advanced Security.

Configuring Windows Firewall with a GPO

If you wanted to configure Windows Firewall on all of your client machines, you have two options. You can either manually configure each machine or set up a GPO to configure your Windows Firewall. To set up a GPO for Windows Firewall, configure the Computer section ➢ Windows Settings ➢ Security ➢ Windows Firewall With Advanced Security.

Import/Export Policies

One advantage of configuring Windows Firewall is the ability to export and import policy settings. For example, I set up a policy for 35 machines; I created the policy on one of the 35 machines and then exported the policy. I then imported the policy to the other 34 machines, so I did not have to re-create the policy over and over again. To export a policy, right-click Windows Firewall With Advanced Security and choose Export Policy. Choose Import Policy on the other machines to import the policy.

IPsec Policy Settings in Windows Firewall

When configuring options for Windows Firewall with Advanced Security, you have the ability to configure some IPsec policies. The three options are:

IPsec Defaults   Specify settings used by IPsec to establish secure connections.

IPsec Exemptions   Exempting ICMP from all IPsec requirements can simplify trouble-shooting of network connectivity issues.

IPsec Tunnel Authorization   Specify the computers or users that are authorized to establish IPsec tunnel connections to this computer.

Monitoring

The Monitoring section shows detailed information about the firewall configurations for the Domain Profile, Private Profile, and Public Profile settings. These network location profiles determine which settings are enforced for private networks, public networks, and networks connected to a domain.

 Real World Scenario

Firewalls

When I'm doing consulting, it always make me laugh when I see small to mid-sized companies using Microsoft Windows Firewall and no other protection.

Microsoft Windows Firewall should be your *last* line of defense, not your only one. You need to make sure that you have good hardware firewalls that separate your network from the world.

Also watch Windows Firewall when it comes to printing. I have run into many situations where a printer that needs to talk to the operating system has issues when Windows Firewall is enabled. If this happens, make sure the printer is allowed in the Allowed Programs section.

Summary

In this chapter, we examined the various aspects of Windows Server 2012 Storage Services as well as the various types of storage technologies and native Windows Server 2012 storage management tools. We started the chapter by discussing initializing disks and choosing a partition type, MBR or GPT. We then discussed the types of disk configurations, dynamic and basic, that are supported in Windows Server 2012. You learned that various properties are associated with each type of configuration. Then we discussed the different types of RAID and the properties of each.

The next section explored storage technologies, namely iSCSI, Fibre Channel, and NAS. We primarily focused on iSCSI because of the native support in Window Server 2012. You learned how to configure an iSCSI initiator and a connection to an iSCSI target. After that, we looked at its iSNS server and how to configure it.

We concluded the chapter by looking at Storage Manager for SANs and Storage Explorer, which are built-in management tools in Windows Server 2012 for storage devices and firewall settings.

Exam Essentials

Know disk types.   Know how to initialize disks and the type of partitioning to choose. Also know the difference between dynamic and basic disks and when to use them.

Understand RAID.   Know the various RAID types, the requirements for each, and when it is appropriate to use each type.

Know storage technologies.   Understand how to use the storage technologies Fibre Channel, iSCSI, and NAS. Know how to configure an iSCSI initiator and how to establish a connection to a target. Know the various MPIO policies.

Understand how to manage storage.   Know what type of administrative features are available for Storage Manager for SANs and Storage Explorer.

Understand Windows Firewall.   A firewall helps protect your network from unauthorized access. Windows Server 2012 has two different ways to configure a firewall: the Windows Firewall Settings control panel and the Firewall With Advanced Security MMC.

Review Questions

1. What are the various supported RAID types in Windows Server 2012? (Choose three.)
   A. RAID-5
   B. RAID-1
   C. RAID-0
   D. RAID-1+0

2. What type of MPIO policy allows load balancing across multiple active paths?
   A. Failover
   B. Round robin
   C. Dynamic Least Queue Depth
   D. Weighted path

3. What is the minimum number of disks required in a RAID-5 set?
   A. One
   B. Two
   C. Three
   D. Four

4. What is the minimum number of disks required in a RAID-1 set?
   A. One
   B. Two
   C. Three
   D. Four

5. What is the default TCP port for iSCSI?
   A. 3389
   B. 1433
   C. 21
   D. 3260

6. What is the largest partition size available for MBR?
   A. 1 TB
   B. 2 TB
   C. 3 TB
   D. 4 TB

7. How many primary partitions can be made on a disk drive with MBR?

   A. One

   B. Two

   C. Three

   D. Four

8. Which of the following names/terms identifies a Fibre Channel HBA?

   A. WWN

   B. iqn

   C. UNC

   D. MAC

9. True or False: A basic disk can be configured in a RAID-5 volume set.

   A. True

   B. False

10. Five 100 GB disk drives are used in a RAID-5 set. Approximately how much disk space is available?

   A. 200 GB

   B. 100 GB

   C. 500 GB

   D. 400 GB

   E. 300 GB

Chapter

18

Implementing Disaster Recovery

THE FOLLOWING 70-411 EXAM OBJECTIVES ARE COVERED IN THIS CHAPTER:

✓ **Maintain Active Directory**

- This objective may include but is not limited to: Back up Active Directory and SYSVOL; manage Active Directory offline; optimize an Active Directory database; clean up metadata; configure Active Directory snapshots; perform object- and container-level recovery; perform Active Directory restore.

THE FOLLOWING 70-412 EXAM OBJECTIVES ARE COVERED IN THIS CHAPTER:

✓ **Configure and manage backups**

- This objective may include, but is not limited to: Configure Windows Server backups; configure Windows Online backups; configure role-specific backups; manage VSS settings using VSSAdmin; create System Restore snapshots.

✓ **Recover servers**

- This objective may include, but is not limited to: Restore from backups; perform a Bare Metal Restore (BMR); recover servers using Windows Recovery Environment (Win RE) and safe mode; apply System Restore snapshots; configure the Boot Configuration Data (BCD) store.

Throughout this book, I have stressed the importance of setting up your network properly. Once your network is set up and running properly, your users will get the most functionality out of the network. Your users will also become dependent on the network. Try taking a network offline for even 10 minutes, and your users will scream and complain.

Now that you have your users hooked, you must protect the network and the data. If your company loses their data, can they survive? Probably not. Most companies would go bankrupt if they lost all of their data and had no way to recover it. Data protection and recoverability is one of the most critical jobs that we have as administrators.

It is important to have multiple servers available to provide backup in case of a problem. The same goes for Active Directory itself—it too should be backed up. This way, if there is a massive disaster after which you need to restore your directory services, you will have that option available to you.

The process of reformatting a computer from scratch after a catastrophic system failure is known as a *bare metal restore*. This process usually involves reinstalling the operating system and all of the system software.

In this chapter, we will look at all of the different ways to protect and recover your system.

Protecting the System

One of the worst events you will experience is a computer that won't boot. An even worse experience is discovering that there is no recent backup for that computer.

The first step in preparing for disaster recovery is to expect that a disaster will happen at some point and to take proactive measures to plan for recovery before the failure occurs. Here are some of the preparations you can make:

- Keep your computer up-to-date with Windows Update.
- Perform regular system backups.
- Use current software to scan for malware (such as viruses, spyware, and adware) and make sure that you have the most recent updates.
- Perform regular administrative functions, such as monitoring the logs in the Event Viewer utility.

If you can't start Windows Server 2012, there are several options and utilities that can be used to identify and resolve Windows errors. The following is a broad list of troubleshooting options:

- If you have recently made a change to your computer's configuration by installing a new device driver or application and Windows Server 2012 will not load properly, you can use the Last Known Good Configuration, roll back the driver, or use System Restore to restore a previous system configuration.

- If you can boot your computer to Safe mode, and you suspect that you have a system conflict, you can temporarily disable an application or processes, troubleshoot services, or uninstall software.

- If your computer will not boot to Safe mode, you can use the Startup Repair tool to replace corrupted system files.

- If necessary, you can use the Windows Server Backup utility to restore files from backup media and to restore a complete image of your computer.

- You can also use Driver Rollback. If you install a driver that causes issues on your system, you can use the Driver Rollback utility to return the driver to its previous version.

To safeguard your server, one of the most important functions is to protect Active Directory. Active Directory is the heart and soul of a Microsoft Network, and losing your data would be a catastrophic event. So let's start by discussing how to protect Active Directory.

Backup and Recovery of Active Directory

If you have deployed Active Directory in your network environment, your users now depend on it to function properly in order to do their jobs. From network authentications to file access to print and web services, Active Directory has become a mission-critical component of your business. Therefore, the importance of backing up the Active Directory data store should be evident.

As I discussed in earlier chapters, it is important to have multiple domain controllers available to provide backup in case of a problem. The same goes for Active Directory itself—it too should be backed up by being saved. This way, if a massive disaster occurs in which you need to restore your directory services, you will have that option available to you.

Backups are just good common sense, but here are several specific reasons to back up data:

Protect against Hardware Failures   Computer hardware devices have finite lifetimes, and all hardware eventually fails. We discussed this when we mentioned MTBF earlier. *Mean Time Between Failures (MTBF)* is the average time a device will function before it actually fails. There is also a rating derived from benchmark testing of hard disk devices that tells you when you may be at risk for an unavoidable disaster. Some types of failures, such as corrupted hard disk drives, can result in significant data loss.

Protect against Accidental Deletion or Modification of Data Although the threat of hardware failures is very real, in most environments mistakes in modifying or deleting data are much more common. For example, suppose a systems administrator accidentally deletes all of the objects within a specific OU. Clearly, it's very important to be able to retrieve this information from a backup.

Keep Historical Information Users and systems administrators sometimes modify files and then later find out that they require access to an older version of the file. Or a file is accidentally deleted, and a user does not discover that fact until much later. By keeping multiple backups over time, you can recover information from prior backups when necessary.

Protect against Malicious Deletion or Modification of Data Even in the most secure environments, it is conceivable that unauthorized users (or authorized ones with malicious intent!) could delete or modify information. In such cases, the loss of data might require valid backups from which to restore critical information.

Windows Server 2012 includes a Backup utility that is designed to back up operating system files and the Active Directory data store. It allows for basic backup functionality, such as scheduling backup jobs and selecting which files to back up. Figure 18.1 shows the main screen of the Windows Server 2012 Backup utility.

FIGURE 18.1 The main screen of the Windows Server 2012 Backup utility

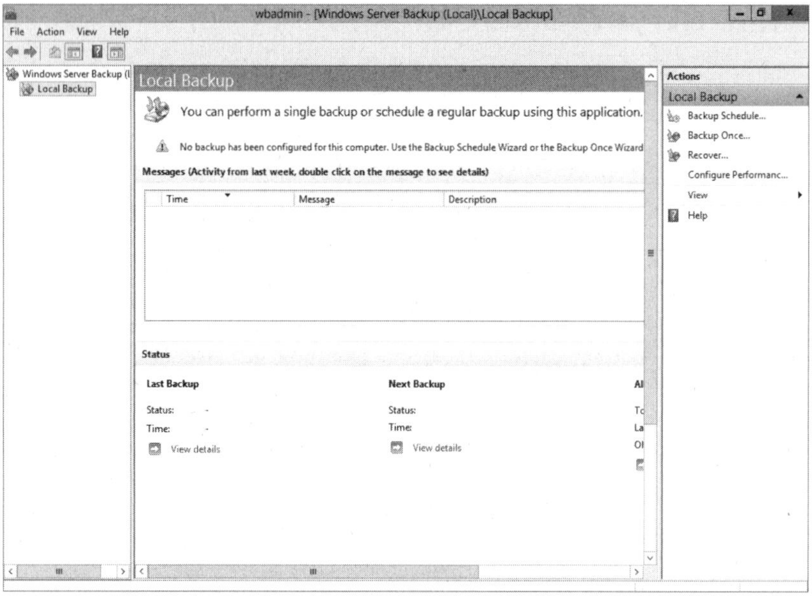

In the following sections, we'll look at the details of using the Windows Server 2012 Backup utility and how you can restore Active Directory when problems do occur.

Overview of the Windows Server 2012 Backup Utility

Although the general purpose behind performing backup operations—protecting information—is straightforward, system administrators must consider many options when determining the optimal backup-and-recovery scenario for their environment. Factors include what to back up, how often to back up, and when the backups should be performed.

In this section, you'll see how the Windows Server 2012 Backup utility makes it easy to implement a backup plan for many network environments.

Although the Windows Server 2012 Backup utility provides the basic functionality required to back up your files, you may want to investigate third-party products that provide additional functionality. These applications can provide options for specific types of backups (such as those for Exchange Server and SQL Server) as well as disaster recovery options, networking functionality, centralized management, and support for more advanced hardware.

Backup Types

One of the most important issues you will have to deal with when you are performing backups is keeping track of which files you have backed up and which files you need to back up. Whenever a backup of a file is made, the Archive bit for the file is set. You can view the attributes of system files by right-clicking them and selecting Properties. By clicking the Advanced button on the Properties dialog box, you will access the Advanced Attributes dialog box. Here you will see the option Folder Is Ready For Archiving. Figure 18.2 shows an example of the attributes for a folder.

FIGURE 18.2   Viewing the Archive attributes for a folder

Although it is possible to back up all of the files in the file system during each backup operation, it's sometimes more convenient to back up only selected files (such as those that have changed since the last backup operation). When performing backups, you can back up to removable media (DVD) or to a network location.

It is recommended by Microsoft to do a backup to a network location. The reason for this is that if your company suffers from a disaster (fire, hurricane, and so forth), your data can all still be lost—including the backup. If you back up to a removable media source, a copy of the backup can be taken off-site. This protects against a major disaster. Several types of backups can be performed:

 Although Windows Server 2012 does not support all of these backup types, it's very important that you understand the most common backup types. Most Administrators use third-party software for their backups. That's why it's important to know all of the different types.

Normal   Normal backups (also referred to as *system* or *full backups*) back up all of the selected files and then mark them as backed up. This option is usually used when a full system backup is made. This backup is supported by Windows Server 2012.

Copy   *Copy backups* back up all of the selected files but do not mark them as backed up. This is useful when you want to make additional backups of files for moving files offsite or you want to make multiple copies of the same data for archival purposes.

Incremental   *Incremental backups* copy any selected files that are marked as ready for backup (typically because they have not been backed up or they have been changed since the last backup) and then mark the files as backed up. When the next incremental backup is run, only the files that are not marked as having been backed up are stored. Incremental backups are used in conjunction with normal (full) backups.

The most common backup process is to make a full backup and then make subsequent incremental backups. The benefit to this method is that only files that have changed since the last full or incremental backup will be stored. This can reduce backup times and disk or tape storage space requirements.

When recovering information from this type of backup method, a system administrator must first restore the full backup and then restore each of the incremental backups.

Differential   *Differential backups* are similar in purpose to incremental backups with one important exception: Differential backups copy all files that are marked for backup but do not mark the files as backed up. When restoring files in a situation that uses normal and differential backups, you need only restore the normal backup and the latest differential backup.

Daily   *Daily backups* back up all of the files that have changed during a single day. This operation uses the file time/date stamps to determine which files should be backed up and does not mark the files as having been backed up.

Backing Up System State Data

When you are planning to back up and restore Active Directory, be aware that the most important component is known as the *System State data*. System State data includes the components upon which the Windows Server 2012 operating system relies for normal operations. The Windows Server 2012 Backup utility offers you the ability to back up the System State data to another type of media (such as a hard disk or network share). Specifically, it will back up the following components for a Windows Server 2012 domain controller:

Active Directory   The *Active Directory data store* is at the heart of Active Directory. It contains all of the information necessary to create and manage network resources, such as users and computers. In most environments that use Active Directory, users and system administrators rely on the proper functioning of these services in order to do their jobs.

Boot Files   *Boot files* are the files required for booting the Windows Server 2012 operating system and can be used in the case of boot file corruption.

COM+ Class Registration Database   The *COM+ Class Registration database* is a listing of all of the COM+ Class registrations stored on the computer. Applications that run on a Windows Server 2012 computer might require the registration of various share code components. As part of the System State backup process, Windows Server 2012 stores all of the information related to Component Object Model+ (COM+) components so that it can be quickly and easily restored.

Registry   The Windows Server 2012 *Registry* is a central repository of information related to the operating system configuration (such as desktop and network settings), user settings, and application settings. Therefore, the Registry is absolutely vital to the proper functioning of Windows Server 2012.

***Sysvol* Directory**   The *Sysvol directory* includes data and files that are shared between the domain controllers within an Active Directory domain. Many operating system services rely on this information in order to function properly.

Bare Metal Backups and Restores

One of the options you have in Windows Server 2012 is to do a *Bare Metal Restore (BMR)*. This is a restore of a machine after the machine has been completely wiped out and formatted. This type of restore is done usually after a catastrophic machine failure or crash.

Windows Server 2012 gives you the ability to backup all of the files needed for a Bare Metal Restore by choosing the Bare Metal Recovery checkbox (see Figure 18.3).

FIGURE 18.3 Bare Metal Option

When you choose the Bare Metal Restore option in Windows Server 2012, all of the sub-options (System State, System Reserved, and Local disk) automatically get checked.

When preparing your network for a Bare Metal Backup, you want to make sure that you have everything you need on hand to complete this type of restore. You may want to keep a copy of the server software, server drivers, and so forth on hand and ready to go, just in case you have to do a full restore.

Scheduling Backups

In addition to specifying which files to back up, you can schedule backup jobs to occur at specific times. Planning *when* to perform backups is just as important as deciding *what* to back up. Performing backup operations can reduce overall system performance; therefore, you should plan to back up information during times of minimal activity on your servers.

To add a backup operation to the schedule, you can simply click the Add button on the Specify Backup Time window.

Restoring System State Data

In some cases, the Active Directory data store or other System State data may become corrupt or unavailable. This could be due to many different reasons. A hard disk failure might, for example, result in the loss of data. Or the accidental deletion of an OU and all of its objects might require a restore operation to be performed.

The actual steps involved in restoring System State data are based on the details of what has caused the data loss and what effect this data loss has had on the system. In the best-case scenario, the System State data is corrupt or inaccurate but the operating system can still boot. If this is the case, all you must do is boot into a special *Directory Services Restore Mode (DSRM)* and then restore the System State data from a backup. This process will replace the current System State data with that from the backup. Therefore, any changes that have been made since the last backup will be completely lost and must be redone.

In a worst-case scenario, all of the information on a server has been lost or a hardware failure is preventing the machine from properly booting. If this is the case, here are several steps that you must take in order to recover System State data:

1. Fix any hardware problem that might prevent the computer from booting (for example, replace any failed hard disks).

2. Reinstall the Windows Server 2012 operating system. This should be performed like a regular installation on a new system.

3. Reinstall any device drivers that may be required by your backup device. If you backed up information to the file system, this will not apply.

4. Restore the System State data using the Windows Server 2012 Backup utility.

I'll cover the technical details of performing restores later in this section. For now, however, you should understand the importance of backing up information and, whenever possible, testing the validity of backups.

Backing Up and Restoring Group Policy Objects

Group Policy objects (GPOs) are a major part of Active Directory. When you back up Active Directory, GPOs can also get backed up. You also have the ability to back up GPOs through the Group Policy Management Console (GPMC). This gives you the ability to back up and restore individual GPOs.

To back up all GPOs, open the GPMC and right-click the Group Policy Objects container. You will see the option Back Up All. After you choose this option, a wizard will start asking you for the backup location. Choose a location and click Backup.

To back up an individual GPO, right-click the GPO (in the Group Policy Objects container) and choose Backup. Again, after you choose this option, a wizard will start asking you for the backup location. Choose a location and click Backup.

To restore a GPO, it's the same process as above except, instead of choosing Backup, you will either choose Manage Backups (to restore all GPOs) or Restore (for an individual GPO).

Setting Up an Active Directory Backup

The Windows Server 2012 Backup utility makes it easy to back up the System data (including Active Directory) as part of a normal backup operation. We've already covered the ideas behind the different backup types and why and when they are used.

Exercise 18.1 walks you through the process of backing up the domain controller. In order to complete this exercise, the local machine must be a domain controller, and you must have a DVD burner or network location to back up the System State.

The Windows Server 2012 Backup utility is not installed by default. If you have already installed the Windows Server 2012 Backup utility, skip to step 9.

EXERCISE 18.1

Backing Up Active Directory

1. To install the Windows Server 2012 Backup utility, click the Windows Key ➢ Administrative Tools ➢ Server Manager.

2. In the center console, click the link for Add Roles And Features.

3. At the Select Installation Type screen, choose role-based or feature-based installation and click Next.

4. The Select Destination Server screen appears. Choose Select A Server From The Server Pool, and choose your server under Server Pool. Click Next.

5. Click Next at the Select Server Roles screen.

6. At the Select Features screen, scroll down and check the box next to Windows Server Backup. Click Next.

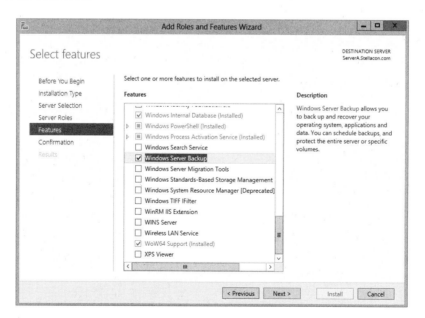

7. At the Confirmation screen, click the checkbox to Restart the destination server automatically. This will bring up a dialog box. Click Yes, and then click the Install button.

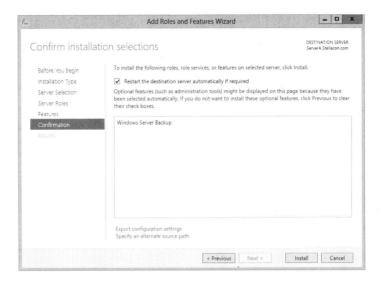

8. Click the Close button when finished. Close Server Manager.

9. Open Windows Backup by clicking the Windows Key ➢ Administrative Tools ➢ Windows Server Backup.

10. On the left-hand side, click Local Backup. Then, under Actions, click Backup Once.

11. When the Backup Once Wizard appears, click Different Options and click Next.

12. At the Select Backup Configuration screen, choose Custom and click Next.

13. Click the Add Items button. Choose System State and click OK. Click Next.

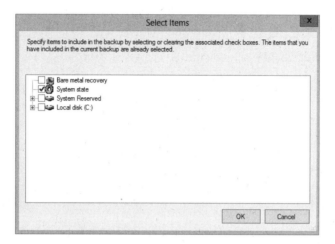

14. At the Specify Destination Type, choose Remote Shared Folder. Click Next.

15. Put in the shared path you want to use and click Next.

16. At the Confirmation screen, click the Backup button.

17. Once the backup is complete, close the Windows Server Backup utility.

Restoring Active Directory

Active Directory has been designed with fault tolerance in mind. For example, it is highly recommended by Microsoft that each domain have at least two domain controllers. Each of these domain controllers contains a copy of the Active Directory data store. Should one of the domain controllers fail, the available one can take over the failed server's functionality. When the failed server is repaired, it can then be promoted to a domain controller in the existing environment. This process effectively restores the failed domain controller without incurring any downtime for end users because all of the Active Directory data is replicated to the repaired server in the next scheduled replication.

In some cases, you might need to restore Active Directory from a backup. For example, suppose a system administrator accidentally deletes several hundred users from the domain and does not realize it until the change has been propagated to all of the other domain controllers. Manually re-creating the accounts is not an option because the objects' security identifiers will be different (and all permissions must be reset). Clearly, a method for restoring from backup is the best solution. You can elect to make the Active Directory restore authoritative or nonauthoritative, as described in the following sections.

Overview of Authoritative Restore

Restoring Active Directory and other System State data is an important process should system files or the Active Directory data store become corrupt or otherwise unavailable. Fortunately, the Windows Server 2012 Backup utility allows you to restore data easily from a backup, should the need arise.

I mentioned earlier that in the case of the accidental deletion of information from Active Directory, you might need to restore the Active Directory from a recent backup. But what happens if there is more than one domain controller in the environment? Even if you did perform a restore, the information on this domain controller would be seen as outdated and it would be overwritten by the data from another domain controller. This data from the older domain controller is exactly the information you want to replace. The domain controller that was reloaded using a backup would have an older time stamp, and the other domain controllers would re-delete the information from the backup.

Fortunately, Windows Server 2012 and Active Directory allow you to perform what is called an *authoritative restore*. The authoritative restore process specifies a domain controller as having the authoritative (or master) copy of the Active Directory data store. When other domain controllers communicate with this domain controller, their information will be overwritten with Active Directory data stored on the local machine.

Now that you have an idea of how an authoritative restore is supposed to work, let's move on to looking at the details of performing the process.

Performing an Authoritative Restore

When you are restoring Active Directory information on a Windows Server 2012 domain controller, make sure that Active Directory services are not running. This is because the restore of System State data requires full access to system files and the Active Directory data store. If you attempt to restore System State data while the domain controller is active, you will see an error message.

In general, restoring data and operating system files is a straightforward process. It is important to note that restoring a System State backup will replace the existing Registry, Sysvol, and Active Directory files, so that any changes you made since the last backup will be lost.

In addition to restoring the entire Active Directory database, you can also restore only specific subtrees within Active Directory using the restoresubtree command in the ntdsutil utility. This allows you to restore specific information and is useful in the case of an accidental deletion of isolated material.

Following the authoritative restore process, Active Directory should be updated to the time of the last backup. Furthermore, all other domain controllers for this domain will have their Active Directory information overwritten by the results of the restore operation. The result is an Active Directory environment that has been recovered from media.

Overview of Nonauthoritative Restore

Now that you understand why you would use an authoritative restore and how it is performed, it's an easy conceptual jump to understand a *nonauthoritative restore*. Remember that by making a restore authoritative, you are simply telling other domain controllers in the domain to recognize the restored machine as the newest copy of Active Directory for replication purposes. If you only have one domain controller, the authoritative restore process becomes moot; you can simply skip the steps required to make the restore authoritative and begin using the domain controller immediately after the normal restore is complete.

If you have more than one domain controller in the domain and you need to perform a nonauthoritative restore, simply allow the domain controller to receive Active Directory database information from other domain controllers in the domain using normal replication methods.

Active Directory Recycle Bin

The Active Directory Recycle Bin is a great feature that allows an administrator to restore an active directory object that has been deleted.

Let's say that you have a junior administrator who has been making changes to Active Directory for hours. The junior admin then deletes an OU from Active Directory. You would then have to reload the OU from a tape backup, or even worse, you may have to reload the entire Active Directory (depending on your backup software), thus losing the hours of work the junior admin has completed.

The problem here is that when you delete a security object from Active Directory, the object's Security ID (SID) gets removed. All users' rights and permissions are associated with the users' SID number and not their account name. This is where the AD Recycle Bin can help.

The *Active Directory Recycle Bin* allows you to preserve and restore accidentally deleted Active Directory objects without the need of using a backup.

The Active Directory Recycle Bin works for both the Active Directory Domain Services (AD DS) and the Active Directory Lightweight Directory Services (AD LDS) environments.

By enabling (disabled by default) the Active Directory Recycle Bin, any deleted Active Directory objects are preserved and Active Directory objects can be restored, in their entirety, to the same condition that they were in immediately before deletion. This means that all group memberships and access rights that the object had before deletion will remain intact.

To enable the Active Directory Recycle Bin, you must do the following (you must be a member of the Schema Admins group):

- Run the `adprep /forestprep` command to prepare the forest on the server that holds the schema master to update the schema.

- Run the `adprep /domainprep /gpprep` command to prepare the domain on the server that holds the infrastructure operations master role.

- If a read-only domain controller (RODC) is present in your environment, you must also run the `adprep /rodcprep` command.

- Make sure that all domain controllers in your Active Directory forest are running Windows Server 2012 or Windows Server 2008 R2.

- Make sure that the forest functional level is set to Windows Server 2012 or Windows Server 2008 R2.

Restartable Active Directory

Administrators have the ability to stop and restart Active Directory in the Windows Server 2012 operating system without the need to reboot the entire system. Administrators can perform these actions by using either the Microsoft Management Console (MMC) snap-ins or the command line.

With *Restartable Active Directory Services*, an administrator has the ability to stop Active Directory Services so that updates and other tasks can be applied to a domain controller. One task that an administrator can perform while Active Directory is stopped is an offline defragmentation of the database.

One of the advantages of a Restartable Active Directory is that other services running on the same server do not depend on Active Directory to continue to function properly while Active Directory is stopped. An administrator has the ability to stop and restart the Active Directory Domain Services in the Local Services MMC snap-in.

Offline Maintenance

As you learned in the preceding section, there are times when you have to be offline to do maintenance. For example, you need to perform authoritative and nonauthoritative restores while the domain controller is offline. The main utility we use for offline maintenance is `ntdsutil`.

Ntdsutil.exe

The primary method by which system administrators can do offline maintenance is through the ntdsutil command-line tool. You can launch this tool by simply entering **ntdsutil** at a command prompt. The ntdsutil command is both interactive and context sensitive. That is, once you launch the utility, you'll see an ntdsutil command prompt. At this prompt, you can enter various commands that set your context within the application. For example, if you enter **domain management**, you'll be able to enter domain-related commands. Several operations also require you to connect to a domain, a domain controller, or an Active Directory object before you perform a command.

Table 18.1 provides a list of the domain-management commands supported by the ntdsutil tool. You can access this functionality by typing the command at a command prompt.

TABLE 18.1   Ntdsutil offline maintenance commands

Ntdsutil Domain Management Command	Purpose
Help or ?	Displays information about the commands that are available within the Domain Management menu of the ntdsutil utility
compact to (at the file maintenance prompt)	Allows you to compact the Active Directory database (offline defragmentation)
metadata cleanup	Removes metadata from decommissioned domain controllers
Set DSRM Password	Resets the Directory Service Restore mode administrator account password

Active Directory Database Mounting Tool

One issue that an administrator may run into when trying to restore Active Directory is the need to restore several backups to compare the Active Directory data that each backup contains. Windows Server 2012 has a utility called the Active Directory database mounting tool (Dsamain.exe), which can resolve this issue.

The Dsamain.exe tool can help the recovery processes by giving you a way to compare data as it exists in snapshots (taken at different times) so that you have the ability to decide which Active Directory database to restore.

Creating snapshots on a regular basis will allow you to have enough data so that you can keep accurate records of how the Active Directory database changes over time. The ntdsutil utility allows you to take snapshots by using the ntdsutil snapshot operation.

You are not required to run the `ntdsutil snapshot` operation to use `Dsamain.exe`. You have the ability to use a backup of the Active Directory database.

You must be a member of the Domain Admins group or the Enterprise Admins group to view any snapshots taken due to the fact that these snapshots contain sensitive Active Directory data.

Compact the Directory Database File (Offline Defragmentation)

One task that all of us having been doing for years is the process of defragging the operating systems that we run. We have used the defragmentation utility since Windows NT. Defragging a system helps return free space from data to the hard drive.

You can also use the defragmentation process to compact the Active Directory database while it's offline. Offline defragmentation helps return free disk space and check Active Directory database integrity.

To perform an offline defragmentation, you would use the `ntdsutil` command. When you perform a defragmentation of the Active Directory database, a new compacted version of the database is created. This new database file can be created on the same machine (if space permits) or on a network location. After the new file is created, copy the compacted `Ntds.dit` file back to the original location.

It is a good practice, if space allows, to maintain a copy of the older, original database file. You can either rename the older database file and keep it in its current location or copy the older database file to an alternate location.

Monitoring Replication

At times you may need to keep an eye on how your replication traffic is working on your domain controllers. We are going to examine the replication utility that you can use to help determine if there are problems on your domain.

Repadmin Utility

The `Repadmin` utility is included when you install Windows Server 2012. This command-line tool helps administrators diagnose replication problems between Windows domain controllers.

`Repadmin` can allow administrators to view the replication topology of each domain controller as seen from the domain controller's perspective. Administrators can also use `Repadmin` to create the replication topology manually. By manually creating the replication topology, administrators can force replication events between domain controllers and view the replication metadata vectors.

To access the Repadmin utility, open a command prompt using an elevated privilege (Run ≻ CMD). At the command prompt, type **Repadmin.exe**, and all of the available options will appear.

Using the ADSI Editor

Another utility that allows you to manage objects and attributes in Active Directory is the Active Directory Service Interfaces Editor (ADSI Edit). In Chapter 13, "Understanding Security," we used ADSI Edit (Adsiedit.msc) to create multiple password policies to allow for fine-grained password policies. ADSI Edit allows you to view every object and attribute in an Active Directory forest.

One advantage to using the Adsiedit.msc MMC snap-in is that this tool allows you to query, view, create, and edit attributes that are not exposed through other Active Directory Microsoft Management Console (MMC) snap-ins.

ADSI Edit allows you to administer an AD LDS instance. To do this, you must first connect and bind to the instance. After you connect and bind to the instance, you can administer the containers and objects within the instance by browsing to the containers or objects and then right-clicking them. To complete this task, you must be a member of the Administrators group for the AD LDS instance.

Wbadmin Command Line Utility

The wbadmin command allows you to back up and restore your operating system, volumes, files, folders, and applications from a command prompt.

You must be a member of the Administrators group to configure a backup schedule. You must be a member of the Backup Operators or the Administrators group (or you must have been delegated the appropriate permissions) to perform all other tasks using the wbadmin command.

To use the wbadmin command, you must run wbadmin from an elevated command prompt (to open an elevated command prompt, click Start, right-click Command Prompt, and then click Run As Administrator). Table 18.2 shows some of the wbadmin commands.

TABLE 18.2   Wbadmin commands

Command	Description
Wbadmin enable backup	Configures and enables a daily backup schedule
Wbadmin disable backup	Disables your daily backups
Wbadmin start backup	Runs a one-time backup
Wbadmin stop job	Stops the currently running backup or recovery operation

Command	Description
Wbadmin get items	Lists the items included in a specific backup
Wbadmin start recovery	Runs a recovery of the volumes, applications, files, or folders specified
Wbadmin get status	Shows the status of the currently running backup or recovery operation
Wbadmin start systemstaterecovery	Runs a system state recovery
Wbadmin start systemstatebackup	Runs a system state backup
Wbadmin start sysrecovery	Runs a recovery of the full system state

Understanding Shadow Copies

An excellent way to protect your shared folders is by using *shadow copies* (Volume Snapshot Service [VSS]). Shadow copies allow an administrator to back up shared folders to a remote location. Shadow copies are designed to help recover files that were accidentally deleted, overwritten, or that have become corrupt. One major advantage to shadow copies is that open files can be backed up. This means that even if users are currently working on files in a shared folder that has shadow copies enabled, the shadow copies will continue to function.

Once administrators have configured and enabled shadow copies (using the Computer Management snap-in), network users can restore earlier versions of files. After the initial shadow copy of the shared folder is created, only changes are copied and not the entire file.

You can enable shadow copies of entire volumes.

Following are some of the settings that you can configure when setting up shadow copies:

Schedule   You have the ability to set the schedule of the shadow copies. You can set this schedule to run daily, weekly, monthly, once, at system startup, at logon, or when the system is idle. You can also set the time at which the shadow copy will run.

Storage Locations   An administrator needs to set the location of the shadow copy backup. If you are on a network, it is a good idea to place the shadow copy on a network drive.

Maximum Size   You can set a maximum size on your shadow copies, or you can specify that they have no size limit. One of the predetermined settings is 64 shadow copies per volume.

In Exercise 18.2, you'll set up a volume to make shadow copies every Monday at 7 a.m. To set up the shadow copies, you will use the Computer Management MMC snap-in.

EXERCISE 18.2

Configuring a Shadow Copy on a Volume

1. Open Computer Management by clicking the Windows Key ➢ Administrative Tools ➢ Computer Management.

2. Expand Storage, and then right-click Disk Management. Choose All Tasks ➢ Configure Shadow Copies.

3. When the Shadow Copies dialog box appears, click the Settings button.

4. When the Settings windows appears, click the Schedule button.

5. In the Schedule window, set the schedule task to weekly and the start time for 7 a.m. Uncheck all of the days-of-the-week boxes except Mon. Click OK.

6. When the Settings window reappears, click OK.

7. If the Enable button is enabled, click it. Then click OK.

8. Exit the Computer Management MMC.

To recover a previous version of a file from a shadow copy, you use the \\servername\ sharename path. The operating system determines how you will gain access to the shared folders and shadow copies. Shadow copies are built into Windows XP (SP1), Windows Vista, Windows 7, Windows 8, Windows Server 2003, Windows Server 2008/2008 R2, and Windows Server 2012. If you are using a different Microsoft operating system, you need to download the Shadow Copy Client Pack from the Microsoft download center.

VssAdmin Command

Another way to create, configure, and manage shadow copies is by using the vssadmin.exe command-line utility (see Figure 18.4). The vssadmin.exe command allows you to create, delete, list, and resize shadow copies and shadow storage.

FIGURE 18.4   vssadmin.exe command-line utility

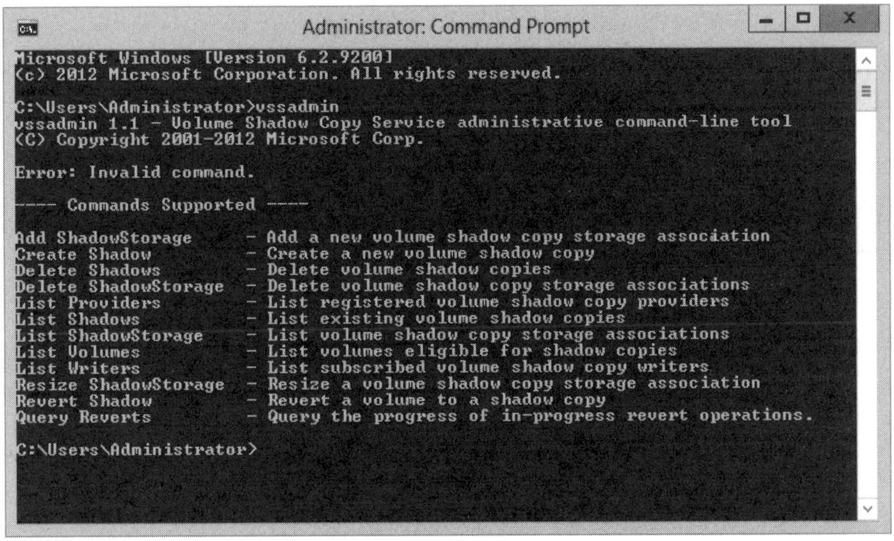

Table 18.3 shows the vssadmin.exe command and the different commands associated with the vssadmin utility.

TABLE 18.3 Vssadmin.exe commands

Command	Description
Add ShadowStorage	Add a new volume shadow copy storage association.
Create Shadow	Create a new volume shadow copy.
Delete Shadows	Delete volume shadow copies.
Delete ShadowStorage	Delete the volume shadow copy storage associations.
List Providers	List registered volume shadow copy providers.
List Shadows	List existing volume shadow copies.
List ShadowStorage	List volume shadow copy storage associations.
List Volumes	List volumes eligible for shadow copies.
List Writers	List subscribed volume shadow copy writers.
Resize ShadowStorage	Resize a volume shadow copy storage association.
Revert Shadow	Revert a volume to a shadow copy.
Query Reverts	Query the progress of in-progress revert operations.

Data Protection Manager

System Center 2012 *Data Protection Manager (DPM)* is an application that runs on the server and allows disk-based and tape-based data protection and recovery. This recovery is for all of the computers in the Active Directory domain. One of the nice features of DPM is that all replication, synchronization, and recovery point creation is done by DPM.

Because you are able to use DPM and setup recoverability for your computers, if a system needs to be recovered, DPM provides reliable protection and rapid recovery of the computer's data either by the system administrator and/or by end users.

DPM uses multiple features to help keep the computers in your network safe. These features include replication, the Volume Shadow Copy Service (VSS) infrastructure, and a policy-driven engine. DPM helps provide protection and fast data recovery for businesses of all sizes.

Using Advanced Boot Options

The Windows Server 2012 advanced startup options can be used to troubleshoot errors that keep Windows Server 2012 from successfully booting.

To access the Windows Server 2012 advanced startup options, start or reboot the computer and press the F8 key after the firmware POST process but before Windows Server 2012 is loaded. This will bring up the Advanced Boot Options menu, which offers numerous options for booting Windows Server 2012.

These advanced startup options are covered in the following three sections (see Figure 18.5).

FIGURE 18.5   Advanced Boot Options

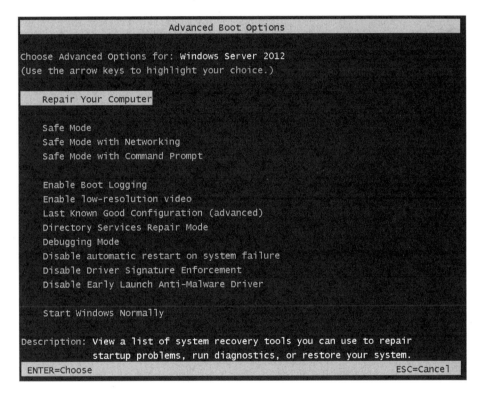

Starting in Safe Mode

When your computer will not start, one of the fundamental troubleshooting techniques is to simplify the configuration as much as possible. This is especially important when you do not know the cause of your problem and you have a complex configuration. After you have simplified the configuration, you can determine whether the problem is in the basic configuration or is a result of your complex configuration.

If the problem is in the basic configuration, you have a starting point for troubleshooting. If the problem is not in the basic configuration, you should proceed to restore each configuration option you removed, one at a time. This helps you to identify what is causing the error.

If Windows Server 2012 will not load, you can attempt to load the operating system through *Safe mode*. When you run Windows Server 2012 in Safe mode, you are simplifying your Windows configuration as much as possible. Safe mode loads only the drivers needed to get the computer up and running.

The drivers that are loaded with Safe mode include basic files and drivers for the mouse, monitor, keyboard, hard drive, standard video driver, and default system services. Safe mode is considered a diagnostic mode, so you do not have access to all of the features and devices in Windows Server 2012 to which you have access when you boot normally, including networking capabilities.

A computer booted to Safe mode will show Safe Mode in the four corners of your Desktop.

If you boot to Safe mode, check all of your computer's hardware and software settings in Device Manager and try to determine why Windows Server 2012 will not boot properly. After you take steps to fix the problem, try to boot to Windows Server 2012 as you normally would.

In Exercise 18.3, you will boot your computer to Safe mode.

EXERCISE 18.3

Booting Your Computer to Safe Mode

1. If your computer is currently running, restart the system.

2. During the boot process, press the F8 key to access the Advanced Boot Options menu.

3. Highlight Safe Mode, and press Enter.

4. When Windows Server 2012 starts, log in.

5. You will see a Help And Support dialog box letting you know what Safe mode is. Exit Help And Support.

6. You should see in the lower-right corner that a network connection is not available.

7. Don't restart your computer yet; you will do this as a part of the next exercise.

Enabling Boot Logging

Boot logging creates a log file that tracks the loading of drivers and services. When you choose the Enable Boot Logging option from the Advanced Boot Options menu, Windows Server 2012 loads normally, not in Safe mode. This allows you to log all of the processes that take place during a normal boot sequence.

This log file can be used to troubleshoot the boot process. When logging is enabled, the log file is written to \WINDOWS\Ntbtlog.txt (see Figure 18.6).

FIGURE 18.6   Ntbtlog.txt file

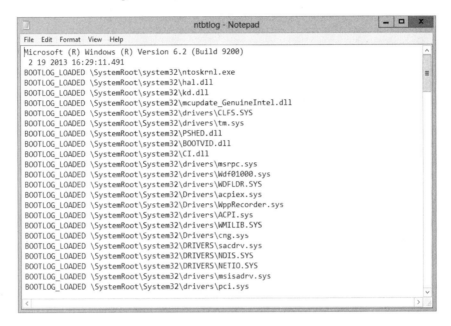

In Exercise 18.4, you will create and access a boot log file.

EXERCISE 18.4

Using Boot Logging

1. Restart your computer.

2. During the boot process, press the F8 key to access the Advanced Boot Options menu.

3. Highlight Enable Boot Logging and press Enter.

4. When Windows Server 2012 starts, log in.

5. Click the Folders icon on the bottom left of the desktop, and browse to C:\WINDOWS\ Ntbtlog.txt. Double-click this file.

6. Examine the contents of your boot log file.

7. Shut down your computer, and restart it without using Advanced Boot Options.

The boot log file is cumulative. Each time you boot to Safe mode, you are writing to this file. This enables you to make changes, reboot, and see whether you have fixed any problems. If you want to start from scratch, you should manually delete this file and reboot to an Advanced Boot Options menu selection that supports logging.

Using Other Advanced Boot Options Menu Modes

In this section, you will learn about additional Advanced Boot Options menu modes. These include the following:

Safe Mode With Networking   This is the same as the Safe Mode option, but it adds networking features. You might use this mode if you need networking capabilities to download drivers or service packs from a network location.

Safe Mode With Command Prompt   This starts the computer in Safe mode, but after you log in to Windows Server 2012, only a command prompt is displayed. This mode does not provide access to the desktop. Experienced troubleshooters use this mode.

Enable Low-Resolution Video (640×480)   This loads a standard VGA driver without starting the computer in Safe mode. You might use this mode if you changed your video driver, did not test it, and tried to boot to Windows Server 2012 with a bad driver that would not allow you to access video. The Enable VGA mode bails you out by loading a default driver, providing access to video so that you can properly install (and test!) the correct driver for your computer.

 Safe mode starts Windows Server 2012 at a resolution of 800×600.

Last Known Good Configuration (Advanced)   This boots Windows Server 2012 by using the Registry information that was saved the last time the computer was successfully booted. You would use this option to restore configuration information if you improperly configured the computer and did not successfully reboot it. When you use the *Last Known Good Configuration* option, you lose any system configuration changes that were made since the computer last successfully booted.

Directory Services Restore Mode   This option is used for domain controllers only, and it is not relevant to Windows Server 2012.

Debugging Mode   This runs the Kernel Debugger, if it is installed. The Kernel Debugger is an advanced troubleshooting utility.

Disable Automatic Restart On System Failure   This prevents Windows from restarting when a critical error causes Windows to fail. This option should be used only when Windows fails every time you restart so that you are not able to access the Desktop or any configuration options.

Disable Driver Signature Enforcement   This allows drivers to be installed even if they do not contain valid signatures.

Start Windows Normally   This boots to Windows Server 2012 in the default manner. This option is on the Advanced Boot Options menu in case you accidentally hit F8 during the boot process but really wanted to boot Windows Server 2012 normally.

Windows Recovery Environment

When your Windows Server 2012 machine fails to start, it will automatically enter into the *Windows Recovery Environment (Windows RE)*. This environment is an extensible recovery platform based on Windows Preinstallation Environment (Windows PE).

When your server starts in the Windows RE, the Startup Repair tool starts the diagnosis and it will begin to help you repair the system. The Windows RE is also an environment in which you can use various tools to help you do a manual system recovery. The boot options for the Windows RE are as follows:

- Start recovery, troubleshooting, or diagnostic tools
- Boot from a device
- Access the Firmware menu
- Choose which operating system to boot, if multiple operating systems are installed on the same computer

Administrators also have the ability to configure a hardware button to run an alternate boot path that includes the Windows RE. This gives administrators the ability to help their users get to the Windows RE menus more easily. This allows your users to recover their PCs easily in the event of a corrupted system.

There are certain instances where Windows RE will automatically try to repair the system:

- Two successive failed attempts to start Windows
- Two successive unexpected shutdowns that occur within two minutes of boot completion
- A Secure Boot error (except for issues related to `Bootmgr.efi`)
- A BitLocker error on touch-only devices

Using the Startup Repair Tool

If your Windows Server 2012 computer will not boot because of missing or corrupted system files, you can use the *Startup Repair tool* to correct these problems. Startup Repair cannot repair hardware failures. Additionally, Startup Repair cannot recover personal files that have been corrupted, damaged by viruses, or deleted. To ensure that you can recover your personal files, you should use the Backup and Restore utility discussed in the next section.

To use the Startup Repair tool, follow these steps:

1. Boot your computer using the Windows Server 2012 media.

2. When the Install Windows dialog box appears, select the language, time and currency format, and the keyboard or input method. Click Next to continue.

3. The Install Now button appears in the center of the screen. Click Repair Your Computer in the lower-left corner.

4. Select the operating system to recover and click Next. If you do not see your operating system, you might need to load your hard disk drivers by clicking the Load Drivers button.

5. The System Recovery Options dialog box appears. You can choose one of the following options:

   - Startup Repair
   - System Restore
   - Windows Complete PC Restore
   - Windows Memory Diagnostic Tool
   - Command Prompt

   Choose Startup Repair to continue.

6. Startup Repair checks your computer for problems and attempts to repair them. After Startup Repair has finished, click Shut Down or Restart.

 If you were not provided the Windows Server 2012 media when you purchased your computer, the computer manufacturer might have placed the files on a recovery partition—or they might have replaced the Startup Repair tool with one of their own. Check with the manufacturer for more information.

If Startup Repair is unable to correct the problem, you might have to reinstall Windows Server 2012. This should be done as a last resort. This is a reason why you should always back up your Windows Server 2012 machine.

Summary

In this chapter, you learned about the different ways to recover and protect your Windows Server 2012 machine from hardware and software issues. We discussed using the Advanced Boot Options such as Last Known Good, Safe mode, Debugging mode, and VGA mode. We also discussed the advantage of using the Driver Rollback utility.

Another important item that needs to be completed on a Windows Server 2012 machine is backups and restores. Backing up a Windows Server 2012 machine protects it in the event of a hardware or software failure.

Another way to protect data is by the use of shadow copies. Shadow copies (System Protection) allow you to keep previous versions of data and revert back to that previous version in the event of a problem.

Exam Essentials

Understand the various backup types available with the Windows Server 2012 Backup utility. The Windows Server 2012 Backup utility can perform full and incremental backup operations. Some third-party backup utilities also support differential and daily backups. You can use each of these operations as part of an efficient backup strategy.

Know how to back up Active Directory. The data within the Active Directory database on a domain controller is part of the System State data. You can back up the System State data to a file using the Windows Server 2012 Backup utility.

Know how to restore Active Directory. Restoring the Active Directory database is considerably different from other restore operations. In order to restore some or the entire Active Directory database, you must first boot the machine into Directory Services Restore mode.

Understand the importance of an authoritative restore process. You use an authoritative restore when you want to restore earlier information from an Active Directory backup and you want the older information to be propagated to other domain controllers in the environment.

Understand offline maintenance using `ntdsutil`. The ntdsutil command-line tool is a primary method by which system administrators perform offline maintenance. Understand how to launch this tool by entering **ntdsutil** at a command prompt.

Review Questions

1. You need to ensure that you can recover your Windows Server 2012 configuration and data if the computer's hard disk fails. What should you do?

   A. Create a complete PC Backup and Restore image.

   B. Create a backup of all file categories.

   C. Perform an Automated System Recovery (ASR) backup.

   D. Create a system restore point.

2. After you update multiple drivers on your Windows Server 2012 machine, the machine hangs at the logon screen and you can't log into the machine. You need to get this computer up and running as quickly as possible. Which of the following repair strategies should you try first to correct your problem?

   A. Restore your computer's configuration with your last backup.

   B. Boot your computer with the Safe Mode option.

   C. Boot your computer with the Last Known Good Configuration option.

   D. Boot your computer to the Recovery Console, and manually copy the old driver back to the computer.

3. You are the system administrator for a large organization that uses Windows Server 2012 and Windows 8. You have a Windows 8 machine and have enabled System Protection. You want the machine to retain only the last System Protection snapshot that was taken. What should you do?

   A. Run Disk Cleanup for System Restore and then run Shadow Copies.

   B. Disable Shadow Copies and run System Protection.

   C. Set the Keep Only Last Shadow Copy option in System Protection.

   D. Enable Shadow Copies and then set the Keep Only Last Shadow Copy option.

4. You are the network administrator for a small company. You manage the computers for the marketing department, all of which are running the Windows Server 2012 operating system. You are making several configuration changes to the manager's computer to enhance performance. Before you make any changes, you want to create a restore point that can be used if any problems arise. How do you manually create a restore point?

   A. By using the System Restore utility

   B. By using the Shadow Copies tab of the System Properties dialog box

   C. By using the System Configuration utility

   D. By using the Startup Repair tool

5. Your computer uses a SCSI adapter that supports a SCSI drive, which contains your Windows 8 system and boot partitions. After updating the SCSI driver, you restart your computer, but Windows 8 will not load. You need to get this computer up and running as quickly as possible. Which of the following repair strategies should you try first to correct your problem?

   A. Restore your computer's configuration with your last backup.

   B. Boot your computer with the Last Known Good Configuration.

   C. Boot your computer with the Safe Mode option.

   D. Boot your computer to the Recovery Console and manually copy the old driver back to the computer.

6. You enable the Boot Logging option on the Advanced Boot Options menu. Where can you find the log file that is created?

   A. `\Windows\netlog.txt`

   B. `\Windows\System32\netlog.txt`

   C. `\Windows\ntbtlog.txt`

   D. `\Windows\System32\netboot.log`

7. After you updated Will's computer, his system files became corrupted due to a virus and now need to be restored. Which of the following processes should you use to fix the problem?

   A. Restore a backup.

   B. Restore an image.

   C. Use the Startup Repair tool.

   D. Boot to Safe mode.

8. You are unable to boot your Windows Server 2012 computer, so you decide to boot the computer to Safe mode. Which of the following statements regarding Safe mode is false?

   A. When the computer is booted to Safe mode, there is no network access.

   B. Safe mode loads all of the drivers for the hardware that is installed on the computer.

   C. When you run Safe mode, boot logging is automatically enabled.

   D. When you run Safe mode, the screen resolution is set to 800×600.

9. You need to back up the existing data on a computer before you install a new application. You also need to ensure that you are able to recover individual user files that are replaced or deleted during the installation. What should you do?

   A. Create a System Restore point.

   B. Perform an Automated System Recovery (ASR) backup and restore.

   C. In the Windows Server Backup utility, click the Backup Once link.

   D. In the Backup And Restore Center window, click the Back Up Computer button.

10. Your data recovery strategy must meet the following requirements:

- Back up all data files and folders in C:\Data.
- Restore individual files and folders in C:\Data.
- Ensure that data is backed up to and restored from external media.

What should you do?

A. Use the Previous Versions feature to restore the files and folders.

B. Use the System Restore feature to perform backup and restore operations.

C. Use the NTBackup utility to back up and restore individual files and folders.

D. Use the Windows Server Backup to back up and restore files.

Appendix
A

Answers to Review Questions

Chapter 1: Installing and Configuring Windows Server 2012

1. B. Windows Server 2012 Server Core is a more secure, slimmed-down version of Windows Server. Web versions of Windows Server 2012 are not available. You would use Windows Server 2012 Standard as a Web server.

2. C. One of the new advantages of Windows Server 2012 is that you can convert Server Core and GUI versions without the need to reinstall the operating system files completely.

3. B. Microsoft recommends that you upgrade your Windows Server 2008 or Windows Server 2008 R2 Web server to Windows Server 2012 Standard.

4. A. Windows Server 2012 Datacenter was designed for organizations that are seeking to migrate to a highly virtualized, private cloud environment. Windows Server 2012 Datacenter has full Windows Server functionality with unlimited virtual instances.

5. D. Windows Server 2012 Foundation was designed for smaller companies that need a Windows Server experience for as few as 15 users. Windows Server 2012 Foundation is general-purpose server with basic server functionality and no virtualization rights.

6. C. Windows Server 2012 Essentials is ideal for small businesses that have as many as 25 users and 50 devices. It has a simple interface, preconfigured connectivity to cloud-based services, and no virtualization rights.

7. A, B, C, D. All four answers are advantages of using Windows Server 2012 Server Core. Server Core is a smaller installation of Windows Server and therefore all four answers apply.

8. A, C. Windows Remote Management and Windows PowerShell allow an administrator to configure a Windows Server 2012 machine remotely. The command prompt is used locally on a Windows Server 2012 Server Core system, and there is no application called Microsoft Remote Admin (MRA).

9. B. Windows Server 2012 Features On Demand allows an administrator not only to disable a role or feature but also to remove the role or feature's files completely from the hard disk.

10. D. The Get-WindowsFeature cmdlet allows an administrator to view a list of available and installed roles and features on the local server.

Chapter 2: Domain Name System

1. B. Because of the .(root) zone, users will not be able to access the Internet. The DNS forwarding option and DNS root hints will not be configurable. If you want your users to access the Internet, you must remove the .(root) zone.

2. C. Active Directory Integrated zones store their records in Active Directory. Because this company only has one Active Directory forest, it's the same Active Directory that both DNS servers are using. This allows ServerA to see all of the records of ServerB and ServerB to see all the records of ServerA.

3. D. The Secure Only option is for DNS servers that have an Active Directory Integrated zone. When a computer tries to register with DNS dynamically, the DNS server checks Active Directory to verify that the computer has an Active Directory account. If the computer that is trying to register has an account, DNS adds the host record. If the computer trying to register does not have an account, the record gets tossed away and the database is not updated.

4. A. If you need to complete a zone transfer from Microsoft DNS to a BIND (Unix) DNS server, you need to enable BIND secondaries on the Microsoft DNS server.

5. B. Conditional forwarding allows you to send a DNS query to different DNS servers based on the request. Conditional forwarding lets a DNS server on a network forward DNS queries according to the DNS domain name in the query.

6. B. On a Windows Server 2012 DNS machine, debug logging is disabled by default. When it is enabled, you have the ability to log DNS server activity, including inbound and outbound queries, packet type, packet content, and transport protocols.

7. D. Active Directory Integrated zones give you many benefits over using primary and secondary zones including less network traffic, secure dynamic updates, encryption, and reliability in the event of a DNS server going down. The Secure Only option is for dynamic updates to a DNS database.

8. A. Windows Server 2012 DNS supports two features called DNS Aging and DNS Scavenging. These features are used to clean up and remove stale resource records. DNS zone or DNS server aging and scavenging flags old resource records that have not been updated in a certain amount of time (determined by the scavenging interval). These stale records will be scavenged at the next cleanup interval.

9. C. The dnscmd /zoneexport command creates a file using the zone resource records. This file can then be given to the Compliance department as a copy.

10. D. Stub zones are very useful for slow WAN connections. These zones store only three types of resource records: NS records, glue host (A) records, and SOA records. These three records are used to locate authoritative DNS servers.

Chapter 3: Active Directory Planning and Installation

1. B, C, D. The forest and function levels have to be Windows 2003 or above to install an RODC.

2. B. A domain controller can contain Active Directory information for only one domain. If you want to use a multi-domain environment, you must use multiple domain controllers configured in either a tree or forest setting.

3. D. NTFS has file-level security, and it makes efficient usage of disk space. Since this machine is to be configured as a domain controller, the configuration requires at least one NTFS partition to store the SYSVOL information.

4. A, D. To convert the system partition to NTFS, you must first use the CONVERT command-line utility and then reboot the server. During the next boot, the file system will be converted.

5. B, E. The use of LDAP and TCP/IP is required to support Active Directory. TCP/IP is the network protocol favored by Microsoft, which determined that all Active Directory communication would occur on TCP/IP. DNS is required because Active Directory is inherently dependent on the domain model. DHCP is used for automatic address assignment and is not required. Similarly, NetBEUI and IPX/SPX are not available network protocols in Windows Server 2012.

6. A, C. The SYSVOL directory must be created on an NTFS partition. If such a partition is not available, you will not be able to promote the server to a domain controller. An error in the network configuration might prevent the server from connecting to another domain controller in the environment.

7. B, C. You need to run the ADPrep.exe command when installing your first Windows Server 2012 domain controller onto a Windows Server 2008 R2 domain. ADPrep /rodcprep actually gets the network ready to install a read-only domain controller and not a GUI version.

8. A. You'll need to use Active Directory Federation Services (AD FS) in order to implement federated identity management. Federated identity management is a standards-based and information technology process that will enable distributed identification, authentication, and authorization across organizational and platform boundaries. The ADFS solution in Windows Server 2012 helps administrators address these challenges by enabling organizations to share a user's identity information securely.

9. B. The HOSTS file is a text-file-based database of mappings between hostnames and IP addresses. It works like a file-based version of DNS. DNS resolves a hostname to an IP address.

10. A. You only need to give them rights to the stellacon.com zone using the DNS snap-in. If they do not have any rights to the stellatest.com zone, they will not be able to configure this zone in any way.

Chapter 4: Administering Active Directory

1. A. A computer account and the domain authenticate each other by using a password. The password resets every 30 days. Since the machine has not connected to the domain for 16 weeks, the computer needs to be re-joined to the domain.

2. C. Checking the box Account Never Expires will prevent this user's account from expiring again.

3. D. The dsadd command allows you to add an object (user's account) to the Active Directory database.

4. A. Distribution groups are for emails only, and distribution groups cannot be assigned rights and permissions to objects.

5. A. Inheritance is the process by which permissions placed on parent OUs affect child OUs. In this example, the permissions change for the higher-level OU (Texas) automatically caused a change in permissions for the lower-level OU (Austin).

6. B, E. Enabling the Advanced Features item in the View menu will allow Isabel to see the LostAndFound and System folders. The LostAndFound folder contains information about objects that could not be replicated among domain controllers.

7. A. Through the use of filtering, you can choose which types of objects you want to see using the Active Directory Users and Computers tool. Several of the other choices may work, but they require changes to Active Directory settings or objects.

8. A, C. You can easily move and rename OUs without having to promote domain controllers and make network changes. This makes OU structure much more flexible and a good choice because the company may soon undergo a merger. Because security administration is important, delegation can be used to control administrative permissions at the OU level.

9. A, B, C, D. All of the options listed are common tasks presented in the Delegation of Control Wizard.

10. D. The Delegation of Control Wizard is designed to allow administrators to set up permissions on specific Active Directory objects.

Chapter 5: Managing Group Policy Objects

1. A, B. If you want your clients to be able to edit domain-based GPOs by using the ADMX files that are stored in the ADMX Central Store, you must be using Windows Vista, Windows 7, Windows 8, Windows Server 2003/2008/2008 R2/2012.

2. D. If you assign an application to a user, the application does not get automatically installed. To have an application automatically installed, you must assign the application to the computer account. Since Finance is the only OU that should receive this application, you would link the GPO to Finance only.

3. C. The Resultant Set of Policy (RSoP) utility displays the exact settings that apply to individual users, computers, OUs, domains, and sites after inheritance and filtering have taken effect. Desktop wallpaper settings are under the User section of the GPO, so you would run the RSoP against the user account.

4. B. The Enforced option can be placed on a parent GPO, and this option ensures that all lower-level objects inherit these settings. Using this option ensures that Group Policy inheritance is not blocked at other levels.

5. A. If the data transfer rate from the domain controller providing the GPO to the computer is slower than what you have specified in the slow link detection setting, the connection is considered to be a slow connection and the application will not install properly.

6. D. To disable the application of Group Policy on a security group, you should deny the Apply Group Policy option. This is particularly useful when you don't want GPO settings to apply to a specific group, even though that group may be in an OU that includes the GPO settings.

7. A. GPOs at the OU level take precedence over GPOs at the domain level. GPOs at the domain level, in turn, take precedence over GPOs at the site level.

8. B. The Block Policy Inheritance option prevents group policies of higher-level Active Directory objects from applying to lower-level objects as long as the Enforced option is not set.

9. A, B, C, D. GPOs can be set at all of the levels listed. You cannot set GPOs on security principals such as users or groups.

10. D, E. Administrative templates are used to specify the options available for setting Group Policy. By creating new administrative templates, Ann can specify which options are available for the new applications. She can then distribute these templates to other system administrators in the environment.

Chapter 6: Configuring Active Directory Infrastructure

1. B. The NTDS settings for the site level are where you would activate and deactivate UGMC.

2. A. By decreasing the Replication interval for the DEFAULTIPSITELINK object, you will decrease the replication latency for all sites using the DEFAULTIPSITELINK.

3. D. In the Active Directory Sites and Services console, the Server NTDS settings are where you would activate and deactivate global catalogs.

4. D. Preferred bridgehead servers receive replication information for a site and transmit this information to other domain controllers within the site. By configuring one server at each site to act as a preferred bridgehead server, Daniel can ensure that all replication traffic between the two sites is routed through the bridgehead servers and that replication traffic will flow properly between the domain controllers.

5. C. By default, Connection objects are automatically created by the Active Directory replication engine. You can choose to override the default behavior of Active Directory replication topology by manually creating Connection objects, but this step is not required.

6. B. The Knowledge Consistency Checker (KCC) is responsible for establishing the replication topology and ensuring that all domain controllers are kept up-to-date.

7. D. Site link bridges are designed to allow site links to be transitive. That is, they allow site links to use other site links to transfer replication information between sites. By default, all site links are bridged. However, you can turn off transitivity if you want to override this behavior.

8. B. The Simple Mail Transfer Protocol was designed for environments in which persistent connections may not always be available. SMTP uses the store-and-forward method to ensure that information is not lost if a connection cannot be made.

9. D. The Directory Service event log contains error messages and information related to replication. These details can be useful when you are troubleshooting replication problems.

10. A, D. By creating new sites, Christina can help define settings for Active Directory replication based on the environment's network connections. She can use Connection objects to define further the details of how and when replication traffic will be transmitted between the domain controllers.

Chapter 7: Configuring Active Directory Server Roles

1. B. One of the main certificate validation methods is called Online Certificate Status Protocol (OCSP). When certificates get revoked, your certificate server needs to make sure that these certificates don't get used again. You can perform this validation in many ways. The most common validation methods are CRLs, delta CRLs, and OCSP responses. Using Network Load Balancing ensures fault tolerance.

2. A. With the Certificate Authority Web Enrollment Service, users can easily request certificates and retrieve certificate revocation lists (CRLs) through a web browser. It is a good practice to load this service on a member server and not a domain controller. This machine can issue certificates to web users, and for security reasons, you do not want a domain controller talking to web-based users.

3. D. Key archival allows a key to be stored for later recoverability if necessary. The private key portion of a public-private key pair is archived and can be recovered when needed.

4. B. The Network Device Enrollment Service allows network devices (such as routers) to obtain certificates even though they do not have an account in the Active Directory domain.

5. C. The Authority Information Access extension specifies where to find the up-to-date certificates, and this will allow ServerA to support the Online Responder.

6. A. RODCs do not store account credentials by default. They allow for authentication through credential caching, but not all accounts have to be cached. You can decide which accounts (or all accounts) to cache on an RODC by using a password replication policy. This policy allows an administrator to determine which user groups will be allowed to use the RODC credential caching.

7. A. Enterprise root CAs and stand-alone root CAs are the two main types of CAs. Enterprise root CAs (automatically integrated with Active Directory) are the top-most trusted CAs of the hierarchy. They hold the certificates that you issue to the users within your organization. The stand-alone root CAs hold the certificates that you issue to Internet users.

8. A, B. GPO enrollment automatically issues a certificate to a user through the use of a Group Policy object (GPO). Web enrollment allows users to request certificates and retrieve certificate revocation lists (CRLs) through the use of a web browser. Auto enrollment automatically issues a certificate to a user after either the user or an administrator configures a setting on the user's computer.

9. A. Active Directory Federation Services (AD FS) provides Internet-based clients with a secure identity access solution that works on both Windows and non-Windows operating systems. AD FS also gives users the ability to do a single sign-on (SSO) and access applications on other networks without needing a secondary password.

10. C. AD CS allows administrators to configure services for issuing and managing public key certificates. Companies can benefit from AD CS security by combining a private key with an object (such as users and computers), device (such as routers), or service.

Chapter 8: Using Virtualization in Windows Server 2012

1. B, D. Hyper-V can be installed on the Standard, Enterprise, or Datacenter Editions of Windows Server 2012. Itanium, x86, and Web Editions are not supported.

2. C. The external virtual network type will allow the virtual machine to communicate with the external network as it would with the Internet, so A is wrong. The internal-only network type allows communication between the virtual machines and the host machine. Because the question says that only communication between the virtual machines should be allowed, the only valid answer is private virtual machine network. The last option, public virtual machine network, does not exist in Hyper-V.

3. A. This question focuses on the fact that you cannot change the memory if the virtual machine is running, paused, or saved. The only valid answer is to shut it down and then change the memory.

4. A. The only virtual hard disk that increases in size is the dynamically expanding disk. Thus this is the only valid answer to this question. The fixed-size disk creates a disk of the size you specify, the differencing disk is a special disk that stores only the differences between it and a parent disk, and the physical disk uses a physical drive and makes it available to the virtual machine.

5. C. Physical hard disks cannot be configured using the Virtual Hard Disk Wizard, the Edit Virtual Hard Disk Wizard, or the New Virtual Machine Wizard. You can configure and attach a physical disk only by using the virtual machine's settings.

6. B. Hyper-V is not supported on Itanium-based systems, thus he cannot install it.

7. A, B, C. The minimum CPU requirement for running Hyper-V is a x64-based processor (Itanium is not supported), hardware Data Execution Protection must be enabled, and hardware-assisted virtualization must be enabled. There is no minimum requirement for a dual-core processor.

8. C. This question relates to the setup command used to install the Hyper-V server role on a Windows Server 2008 Server Core machine. It's important to remember that these commands are case sensitive, and that the correct command is start /w ocsetup Microsoft-Hyper-V, which is option C. All of the other commands will fail to install Hyper-V on a Server Core machine. If you were using a Windows Server 2012 machine, you would use the DISM command.

9. A, D. The Hyper-V Manager is available only for Windows Server 2008, Windows 7, and Windows 8. There is no version available that runs on Windows Server 2003 or on Windows XP SP3.

10. C. The virtual network type in which the machines communicate with each other and with the host machine is called *internal only*. In a private virtual network, the virtual machines can communicate only with each other, not with the network or the host machine. The external network type defines a network where the virtual machines can communicate with each other, with the host machine, and with an external network like the Internet.

Chapter 9: Configuring TCP/IP

1. D. To calculate the network mask, you need to figure out which power number (2^x) is greater than or equal to the number you need. Since we are looking for 1000, $2^{10} = 1024$. You then add the power (10) to the current network mask (53 + 10 = 63).

2. A. When you look at an IPv6 address, the first sections tell you the IPv6 address space prefix. Fd00:: /8 is the unique local unicast prefix, and this allows the server to communicate with all local machines within your intranet.

3. C. The unique local address can be FC00 or FD00, and it is used like the private address space of IPv4. Unique local addresses are not expected to be routable on the global Internet, but they are used for private routing within an organization.

4. A. A Class B address with a default subnet mask of 255.255.0.0 will support up to 65,534 hosts. To increase the number of networks that this network will support, you need to subnet the network by borrowing bits from the host portion of the address. The subnet mask 255.255.252.0 uses 6 bits from the host's area, and it will support 64 subnets while leaving enough bits to support 1,022 hosts per subnet. The subnet mask 255.255.248.0 uses 5 bits from the hosts and will support 32 subnetworks while leaving enough bits to support 2,046 hosts per subnet. 255.255.252.0 is the better answer because it leaves quite a bit of room for further growth in the number of networks while still leaving room for more than 1,000 hosts per subnet, which is a fairly large number of devices on one subnet. The subnet mask 255.255.254.0 uses 7 bits from the host's area and will support more than 120 networks, but it will leave only enough bits to support 500 hosts per subnet. The subnet mask 255.255.240.0 uses 4 bits from the hosts and will support only 16 subnetworks, even though it will leave enough bits to support more than 4,000 hosts per subnet.

5. A. The network mask applied to an address determines which portion of that address reflects the number of hosts available to that network. The balance with subnetting is always between the number of hosts and individual subnetworks that can be uniquely represented within one encompassing address. The number of hosts and networks that are made available depends on the number of bits that can be used to represent them. This scenario requires more than 35 networks and fewer than 1,000 workstations on each network. If you convert the subnet masks as described in the chapter, you will see that the mask in option A allows for more than 60 networks and more than 1,000 hosts. All of the other options are deficient in either the number of networks or the number of hosts that they represent.

6. A. The subnet mask 255.255.255.192 borrows 2 bits from the hosts, which allows you to build four separate networks that you can route through the Windows server. This will allow you to have 62 hosts on each segment. A mask of 255.255.255.128 would have been even better, with two subnets of 126 hosts each, but that wasn't an option and this solution gives you room for growth in the number of subnets. The subnet mask 255.255.255.224 borrows 3 bits from the hosts. This allows you to create 8 networks, which you don't need, and it leaves only enough bits for 30 hosts. The subnet mask 255.255.255.252 borrows 6 bits from the hosts. This allows you to create more than 60 networks, which you don't need, and it leaves only enough bits for 2 hosts. The subnet mask 255.255.255.240 borrows 4 bits from the hosts. This allows you to create 16 networks, which you don't need, and it leaves only enough bits for 14 hosts per subnet.

7. B, C, D. When you add up the locations that currently need to be given a network address, the total is 3,150, and the maximum number of hosts at any one of these

locations is fewer than 1,000. The subnet masks need to support those requirements. Assuming that you choose the Class A private address space 10.0.0.0/8, the subnet masks given in options B, C, and D will provide the address space to support the outlined requirements. The subnet mask 255.255.240.0 supports more than 4,000 subnets and more than 4,000 hosts. The subnet mask 255.255.248.0 supports more than 8,000 subnets and more than 2,000 hosts. The subnet mask 255.255.252.0 supports more than 16,000 subnets and more than 1,000 hosts. Although each of these subnet masks will work, at the rate that this company is growing, 255.255.252.0 is probably the best mask to prepare for the future. It's unlikely that there will ever be more than 1,000 hosts on any given network. In fact, that number would probably cause performance problems on that subnet. Therefore, it's better to have more subnets available to deploy as the company grows. The subnet mask 255.255.224.0 supports more than 2,000 subnets—an insufficient number to cover the locations. The subnet mask 255.255.254.0 supports more than 32,000 subnets, but only 500 hosts per subnet, which are not enough hosts to cover all of the locations.

8. C. The CIDR /27 tells you that 27 1s are turned on in the subnet mask. Twenty-seven 1s equals 11111111.11111111.11111111.11100000. This would then equal 255.255.255.224.

The network address 192.168.11.192 with a subnet mask of 255.255.255.224 is perfect for Subnet A because it supports up to 30 hosts. The network address 192.168.11.128 with a subnet mask of 255.255.255.192 is perfect for Subnet B because it supports up to 62 hosts. The network address 192.168.11.0 with a subnet mask of 255.255.255.128 is perfect for Subnet C because it supports up to 126 hosts.

9. A. Microsoft's jetpack.exe utility allows you to compact a JET database. Microsoft JET databases are used for WINS and DHCP databases.

10. B, D. If the first word of an IPv6 address is FE80 (actually the first 10 bits of the first word yields 1111 1110 10 or FE80:: /10), then the address is a link-local IPv6 address. If it's in EUI-64 format, then the MAC address is also available (unless it's randomly generated). The middle FF:FE is the filler and indicator of the EUI-64 space, with the MAC address being 00:03:FF:11:02:CD. Remember also the 00 of the MAC becomes 02 in the link-local IPv6 address, flipping a bit to call it local.

Chapter 10: Managing DHCP

1. D. The Conflict Detection value specifies how many ICMP echo requests (pings) the server sends for an address it is about to offer. The default is 0. Conflict Detection is a way to verify that the DHCP server is not issuing IP addresses that are already being used on the network.

2. A. Microsoft's `jetpack.exe` utility allows you to compact a JET database. Microsoft JET databases are used for WINS and DHCP databases.

3. B. An exclusion just marks addresses as excluded; the DHCP server doesn't maintain any information about them. A reservation marks an address as reserved for a particular client.

4. A. When the DHCP server crashed, the scope was effectively deactivated. Deactivating a scope has no effect on the client until it needs to renew the lease.

5. B. `ipconfig/all` is still the command to display the IP configuration on Windows machines. The `/all` switch is needed to show the details that include the DNS server address. The `winipcfg` command is used for Windows 9*x* workstations. The other commands are not valid.

6. B. TCP/IP is the standard protocol of choice, but it also increases the complexity of configuring Windows XP operating systems. Because of this complexity, Microsoft has implemented Automatic Private IP Addressing (APIPA). When an APIPA IP stack is configured for DHCP and a server isn't located, the stack is automatically configured with an address in the 169.254.0.0/16 range. This allows an IP network to be set up fairly easily. The other options are incorrect for the following reasons: DHCP servers can support any number of subnets or scopes, within reason. A DHCP server doesn't validate the scope information while clients are communicating with it. Finally, a user cannot bring a DHCP server online because the user needs administrative capability to add the service.

7. B, C, E, F. The key word to remember is *DORA*. IP lease *discovery* is used when a DHCP-enabled IP stack is initialized to locate a DHCP server with this specialized broadcast. When a DHCP server receives the discover packet, it sends out an IP lease *offer* containing an available address. The client *responds* to the DHCP offer with an IP lease acceptance message showing that this address is acceptable. Finally, when the DHCP request is received, the server sends out an IP lease *acknowledgment*, which contains configuration options for the IP stack and adds the information to the DHCP database.

8. B. Manual settings override DHCP options.

9. D. During lease renewal, the client gets all configuration information offered by the server not a subset of that information.

10. B. When you install a DHCP server using Windows Server 2012 and Active Directory, the server won't be permitted to provide DHCP services until it has been authorized. When you authorize a server, you are actually adding its IP address to the Active Directory object that contains a list of DHCP servers. If the address of the server isn't on the list, the DHCP service will fail. The other options are incorrect for the following reasons: DHCP relay agents are used to send DHCP requests across routers that don't support BOOTP. Windows Server 2012 computers don't need to be rebooted after DHCP has been installed in order to start the service.

Chapter 11: Managing and Maintaining Servers

1. D. All of the applications that are running on the Windows Server 2012 machine will show up under the Details tab. Right-click the application and end the process.

2. A. If you use MBSA from the command-line utility `mdsacli.exe`, you can specify several options. You type **`mdsacli.exe/hf`** (from the folder that contains `Mdsacli.exe`) and then customize the command execution with an option such as /i*xxxx.xxxx .xxxx.xxxx*, which specifies that the computer with the specified IP address should be scanned.

3. B, E. You can set the Registry key `HKEY_LOCAL_MACHINE\Software\Policies\ Microsoft\Windows\WindowsUpdate\AU\UseWUServer` to 0 to use the public Windows Update server, or you can set it to 1, which means that you will specify the server for Windows Update in the `HKEY_LOCAL_MACHINE\Software\Policies\Microsoft\ Windows\WindowsUpdate` key. The `WUServer` key sets the Windows Update server using the server's HTTP name, such as, for example, `http://intranetSUS`.

4. C. Server Manager is the one place where you install all roles and features for a Windows Server 2012 system.

5. C. All options are valid steps to complete the configuration except option C because SERVERB cannot automatically draw updates from whichever sources are on SERVERA.

6. B, D, F. Option A schedules the updates to occur at a time when the computers are generally not connected to the corporate network. Options C and E require more user interaction than would be considered minimal. By setting updates to occur with no user interaction at noon, you satisfy the requirements.

7. D. You can recover system state data from a backup, which always includes the Active Directory database. In this case, Event Viewer and System Monitor wouldn't help you recover the database, but they might help you determine why the hard drive crashed in the first place.

8. D. By using the Network Monitor, you can view all of the network packets that are being sent to or from the local server. Based on this information, you can determine the source of certain types of traffic, such as pings. The other types of monitoring can provide useful information, but they do not allow you to drill down into the specific details of a network packet, and they don't allow you to filter the data that has been collected based on details about the packet.

9. A. Microsoft Baseline Security Analyzer is a free download that you can get from Microsoft's website.

10. C. The Update Source And Proxy Server option allows you to specify where you will be receiving your updates (from Microsoft or another WSUS server) and your proxy settings if a proxy server is needed.

Chapter 12: Configuring Network Access

1. C. The correct syntax for the route add command is as follows: route add *destination mask subnetmask gateway metric cost*. In option A, the destination and gateway addresses are reversed. Option B uses incorrect metrics. Option D uses gateways that are not on the host's subnet.

2. A. The only way to accomplish all of the goals is to use RIPv2. OSPF and EIGRP cannot be used in Windows Server 2012 RRAS. Area border routers are simply special versions of OSPF routers.

3. A. RIP is optional; you can use static routes on a remote dial-up router to avoid dealing with dynamic routing protocols.

4. B. RIP route filters allow you to configure your routers to either ignore or accept updates from specific network addresses or a range of addresses. TCP/IP filtering is configured at each individual host to control the traffic at a granular level, such as a specific address, UDP port, or TCP port. IP packet filtering is used on the router inter-face to control IP traffic based on subnet masks, IP address, or port. RIP peer filtering is used to control communication between individual routers rather than control the entire network address.

5. C. The route print command can show you all or part of the routing table from the command line. Just typing **route print** into a command window will give you a complete dump of the entire routing table.

6. A, B, D. RIP neighbors are optional. If no routes are arriving, or if there is no static default route, the router may not be able to route traffic.

7. A. RIP is a distance-vector protocol that periodically broadcasts routes to the other servers. It's useful for a very simple routed network. Your environment is much too complex to configure static routes. Every time something changes, you would need to modify all the routing tables manually. OSPF cannot be used in Windows Server 2012.

8. B. IP packet filters are applied at the RRAS server and can control access based on rules that act on source and destination addresses and ports. For example, you could build a rule that specifies the IP address of all acceptable Web destinations while drop-ping all other requests, or you could create a rule that would use IP addresses to pre-vent requests from reaching specific sites.

   TCP/IP filters are configured at each workstation; although they can control specific communication, the administrative overhead is unacceptable for a broad-based policy. Configuring each browser through global policies is not a valid option. Using static routing tables applies only to communication between routers; it wouldn't involve the ultimate destinations of the packets.

9. D. Any of these factors could prevent traffic from flowing, and therefore all should be checked.

10. C. An IP-in-IP tunnel encapsulates IP datagrams inside other IP headers. This allows you to send packets that are not supported—such as multicasts—to other locations that are supported. Multicast boundaries use the multicast scope, rate of traffic, or IP header to control the forwarding of the traffic, but this does not allow that traffic to flow across a section of the network that does not support it. This is also the case for multicast heartbeat, which is used to look for multicast support connectivity on the network. RIP is a routing protocol that manages the tables that locate routes through the network. It is not involved in the support or lack of support of multicast traffic.

Chapter 13: Understanding Security

1. C. To create multiple password policies, you would use ADSI Edit (or `adsiedit.msc`).

2. D. Universal security groups, global groups, and domain local groups are all available when you are running a Windows 2003 and 2012 domain functional level.

3. B, E, G, H. The Active Directory Users and Computers tool allows system administrators to change auditing options and to choose which actions are audited. At the file system level, Isabel can specify exactly which actions are recorded in the audit log. She can then use Event Viewer to view the recorded information and provide it to the appropriate managers.

4. D. The Delegation of Control Wizard is designed to assist system administrators in granting specific permissions to other users.

5. C. Delegation is the process of granting permissions to other users. Delegation is often used to distribute system administration responsibilities. Inheritance is the transfer of permissions and other settings from parent OUs to child OUs. *Transfer of control* and *transfer of ownership* are not terms applicable to OUs.

6. B, C, E. The Account Lockout Duration states how long an account will be locked out if the password is entered incorrectly. The Account Lockout Threshold is the number of bad password attempts, and the Account Lockout Counter is the time in which the bad password attempts are made. Once the Account Lockout Counter reaches 0, the number of bad password attempts returns to 0.

7. B. The best practice is to add users to global groups and apply permissions to the domain local groups where the resources reside.

8. D. When resources are made available to users who reside in domains outside the forest, Foreign Security Principal objects are automatically created. These new objects are stored within the `Foreign Security Principals` folder.

9. B. Account logon events are created for domain account activity. For example, you have a user who logs on to a server so that they can access files; the act of logging on to the server creates this audit event.

10. B, E, F. The first step is to enable auditing. With auditing enabled, Alexis can specify which actions are recorded. To give permissions to the Audit user account, she can use the Delegation of Control Wizard.

Chapter 14: Managing File and Print Services

1. C. You need to publish shares in the directory before they are available to the users of the directory. If NetBIOS is still enabled on the network, the shares will be visible to the NetBIOS tools and clients, but you do not have to enable NetBIOS on shares. Although replication must occur before the shares are available in the directory, it is unlikely that the replication will not have occurred by the next day. If this is the case, then you have other problems with the directory as well.

2. A. The Sharing tab contains a check box that you can use to list the printer in Active Directory.

3. A, C. A printer may not show up within Active Directory if the printer has not been shared or if the client does not have permission to view the printer. The printer will appear as an object in Active Directory even if it is offline or malfunctioning.

4. B. Offline files give you the opportunity to set up files and folders so that users can work on the data while outside the office.

5. A, B, C, D. Improved security, quotas, compression, and encryption are all advantages of using NTFS over FAT32. These features are not available in FAT32. The only security you have in FAT32 is shared folder permissions.

6. E. By giving Moe Modify on the NTFS security setting, you're giving him just enough to do his job. You could also give Sales or Finance the Modify permission, but then everyone in those groups would be able to delete, change, and do more than they all need. Also, Moe does not need Full Control to change or delete files.

7. B. Disk quotas allow you to limit the amount of space on a volume or partition. You can set an umbrella quota for all users and then implement individual users' quotas to bypass the umbrella quota.

8. C, E. The Admin group needs Full Control on the NTFS security and shared permission settings in order to do their job. To be able to give other users permissions, you must have the Full Control permission.

9. B. The Distributed File System (DFS) Namespace service in Windows Server 2012 offers a simplified way for users to access geographically dispersed files. DFS allows you to set up a tree structure of virtual directories to allow users to connect to shared folders throughout the entire network.

10. D. File servers are used for storage of data, especially for users' home folders. Home folders are folder locations for your users to store data that is important and that needs to be backed up.

Chapter 15: Managing Remote Access Services

1. B. The boot threshold for an interface controls how long the relay agent will wait before forwarding DHCP requests it hears on that interface.

2. B. Multilink PPP has nothing to do with encryption of data. Multilink is easy to set up, relatively low in cost, and it makes the connection faster.

3. C, E. MS-CHAPv2 provides encrypted and mutual authentication between the respective RRAS locations. MPPE works with MS-CHAPv2 and provides encryption for all of the data between the locations. CHAP provides encrypted authentication, but MS-CHAPv2 is needed for MPPE to work. PAP is the lowest level of authentication providing passwords, but it sends passwords in cleartext, which is not the most secure solution. L2TP needs to team up with IPsec to provide the data encryption for the secure transfer of information between the locations.

4. B. MS-CHAPv2 authentication allows you to create VPN connections with a stand-alone server using PPTP and MPPE. MPPE employs keys that are created via MS-CHAPv2 or EAP-TLS authentication. EAP-TLS is not the correct answer because only domain controllers or member servers support EAP-TLS. Stand-alone servers support only MPPE. Neither PAP nor CHAP is supported with MPPE.

5. A, C. L2TP connections can be used to authenticate both sides of the VPN. L2TP needs IPsec to provide the encryption for the connection. These two together will provide the secure and authenticated transmission of data across the Internet between the two sites. PPTP connections provide encryption only using MPPE, but they don't provide authentication between the machines. RADIUS is a service that provides dial-in connectivity. MS-CHAPv2 is an authentication protocol for clients accessing the network.

6. B. L2TP and IPsec each has its own negotiation procedure for making a connection. If you remove the IPsec portion of the connection and the problem is alleviated, it is likely that IPsec is the problem, and you can then focus on IPsec. If the problem remains, you can work on the L2TP portion of the connection. IPsec has two modes: tunnel mode and transport mode. But because L2TP is a tunneling protocol, there is no sense in using IPsec tunneling. IPsec transport mode is used with L2TP and should be set aside for troubleshooting, as discussed. The L2TP implementation in Windows Server 2012 doesn't support MPPE.

7. C. The default configuration for RRAS supports 5 PPTP ports and 5 L2TP ports. There are up to 150 sales reps trying to connect to the server, but only the first 10 will be able to connect. You can increase the number of ports available, up to 1,000, by using the Ports Properties dialog box. The Windows 8 clients are, by default, ready to support VPNs; they will first try L2TP and then switch over to PPTP if ports are unavailable.

8. C, E, G. Because the communication is not a continuous or frequent occurrence, it doesn't make sense to have the line always available, so RRAS with demand-dial will be less expensive than ISDN, which is always up. MS-CHAPv2 provides encryption and a mutual authentication process. The MPPE provides the encryption of the actual data that travels across the connection. PAP is a cleartext authentication method, and CHAP provides only one-way authentication. L2TP doesn't provide any encryption by itself.

9. C. When you use Windows accounting, the local Windows account logs are found in the *systemroot*\System32\LogFiles folder. These logs can be stored in one of two formats for later analysis—Open Database Connectivity (ODBC) or Internet Authentication Service. The Performance Monitor utility that came with Windows NT has been replaced with the system event log. This keeps track of global service errors such as initialization failures and service starts and stops. There is no RRAS authentication log. You do have RADIUS logging available; when it's used, the log files are stored on the RADIUS servers. This is useful when you have multiple RRAS servers because you can centralize RRAS authentication requests. Active Directory is not used to log events from the various services in Windows Server 2012.

10. B. The Server Status node in the RRAS snap-in shows you a summary of all the RRAS servers known to the system. Each server entry displays whether the server is up, what kind of server it is, how many ports it has, how many ports are currently in use, and how long the server has been up.

Chapter 16: Configuring High Availability in Windows Server 2012

1. B, D. Only the Standard and Datacenter Editions of Windows Server 2012 can participate in a failover cluster.

2. B, D. Only the Standard and Datacenter versions of Windows Server 2012 can have NLB.

3. D. A Windows Server 2012 cluster consisting of servers running the x64 version can contain up to 64 nodes.

4. B. Drainstop is the function that allows the current session to end before stopping the cluster on the node. Evict is used to remove a node completely from a failover cluster. Pause is used to keep resources from failing over to a failover cluster node. Stop will immediately end the cluster service on the NLB cluster node, not allowing the current sessions to complete.

5.   D. A Windows Server 2012 NLB cluster can contain up to 32 nodes.

6.   A, C. SQL Server and Exchange Server are supported only on failover clusters. Websites and VPN services are network-based services, so they are better suited for NLB clusters.

7.   B, D. Websites and Terminal Services are all designed to work with NLB clusters. Database servers like SQL Server do not work on NLB clusters.

8.   B. To use unicast communication between NLB cluster nodes, each node must have a minimum of two network adapters.

9.   B. Up to two votes can be lost before quorum can no longer be achieved. These votes can come from the file share witness or a cluster node.

10. B. In a three-node cluster, only one node can be offline before quorum is lost; a majority of the votes must be available to achieve quorum.

Chapter 17: Configuring File and Storage Services

1.   A, B, C. Windows Server 2012 supports only software RAID levels 0, 1, and 5. Other types of RAID, such as RAID-1+0, are available with hardware RAID controllers.

2.   B. Round robin uses all available paths, and all paths will be active. Failover, Dynamic Least Queue Depth, and weighted path will not load-balance across the paths.

3.   C. The minimum number disks required in a RAID-5 set is three.

4.   B. The minimum number of disks required in a RAID-1 set is two.

5.   D. The iSCSI default port is TCP 3260. Port 3389 is used for RDP, port 1433 is used for MS SQL, and port 21 is used for FTP.

6.   B. The largest available partition available with MBR is 2 terabytes.

7.   D. MBR supports only four primary partitions, but the fourth partition can be made into an extended partition where many logical partitions can be created.

8.   A. Fibre Channel HBAs use the WWN (World Wide Name) to identify itself from other HBAs in a Fibre Channel fabric. An iqn is used by an iSCSI initiator to identify itself. MAC addresses are used with NICs. A UNC (Universal Naming Convention) is used to designate file locations on a network.

9.   B. When you're creating a RAID-5 volume set, a basic disk will be converted into a dynamic disk.

10. D. To calculate RAID-5 disk space, add the total available space across all disks and subtract the space of one disk.

Chapter 18: Implementing Disaster Recovery

1. A. Using images allows you to back up and restore your entire Windows Server 2012 machine instead of just certain parts of data.

2. C. If you need to get a stalled computer up and running as quickly as possible, you should start with the Last Known Good Configuration option. This option is used when you've made changes to your computer's hardware configuration and are having problems restarting but have not logged into the machine. Last Known Good Configuration will revert to the configuration used the last time the computer was successfully booted.

3. A. You have to run the Disk Cleanup utility to delete the previous versions and then run Shadow Copies in System Protection. There is no Keep Only Last Shadow Copy option.

4. B. To create a restore point manually or to restore your computer to a previous restore point, you use the Shadow Copies tab of the System Properties dialog box. Although System Restore uses restore points, you do not use the System Restore utility to create a restore point.

5. B. You should start with the Last Known Good Configuration option. This option is used when you've made changes to your computer's hardware configuration and are having problems restarting. The Last Known Good Configuration will revert to the configuration used the last time the computer was successfully booted. Although this option helps overcome configuration errors, it will not help when there are hardware errors.

6. C. When you enable boot logging, the file created is \Windows\ntbtlog.txt. This log file is used to troubleshoot the boot process.

7. C. To repair the system files quickly, you can use the Startup Repair tool. You can restore an image by using the Backup and Repair Center, but it is faster to use the Startup Repair tool. Additionally, you will not lose any personal files by using the Startup Repair tool. Alternatively, you could try to use System Restore to go back to a previous checkpoint.

8. B. When you run your computer in Safe mode, you simplify your Windows Server 2012 configuration. Only the drivers that are needed to get the computer up and running are loaded.

9. C. The Backup Once link allows you to start a backup on the Windows Server 2012 system.

10. D. If you need to back up and restore your Windows Server 2012 machine, you need to use the Windows Server Backup MMC.

Appendix
B

About the Additional Study Tools

IN THIS APPENDIX:

- ✓ Additional Study Tools
- ✓ System requirements
- ✓ Using the Study Tools
- ✓ Troubleshooting

Additional Study Tools

The following sections are arranged by category and summarize the software and other goodies you'll find from the companion website. If you need help with installing the items, refer to the installation instructions in the "Using the Study Tools" section of this appendix.

The additional study tools can be found at www.sybex.com/go/ mcsawin2012. Here, you will get instructions on how to download the files to your hard drive.

Sybex Test Engine

The files contain the Sybex test engine, which includes three bonus practice exams, as well as the Assessment Test and the Chapter Review Questions, which are also included in the book itself.

Electronic Flashcards

These handy electronic flashcards are just what they sound like. One side contains a question, and the other side shows the answer.

Videos

For many of the hands-on exercises, we have also included video-walkthroughs. Look for the video icon for exercises that include video walkthroughs.

PDF of Glossary of Terms

We have included an electronic version of the Glossary in .pdf format. You can view the electronic version of the Glossary with Adobe Reader.

Adobe Reader

We've also included a copy of Adobe Reader so you can view PDF files that accompany the book's content. For more information on Adobe Reader or to check for a newer version, visit Adobe's website at `www.adobe.com/products/reader/`.

System Requirements

Make sure your computer meets the minimum system requirements shown in the following list. If your computer doesn't match up to most of these requirements, you may have problems using the software and files. For the latest and greatest information, please refer to the ReadMe file located in the downloads.

- A PC running Windows 8 or older
- An Internet connection

Using the Study Tools

To install the items, follow these steps:

1. Download the `.ZIP` file to your hard drive, and unzip to an appropriate location. Instructions on where to download this file can be found here: `www.sybex.com/go/mcsawin2012`.
2. Click the `Start.EXE` file to open up the study tools file.
3. Read the license agreement, and then click the Accept button if you want to use the study tools.

The main interface appears. The interface allows you to access the content with just one or two clicks.

Troubleshooting

Wiley has attempted to provide programs that work on most computers with the minimum system requirements. Alas, your computer may differ, and some programs may not work properly for some reason.

The two likeliest problems are that you don't have enough memory (RAM) for the programs you want to use or you have other programs running that are affecting installation or running of a program. If you get an error message such as "Not enough memory" or "Setup cannot continue," try one or more of the following suggestions and then try using the software again:

Turn off any antivirus software running on your computer.   Installation programs sometimes mimic virus activity and may make your computer incorrectly believe that it's being infected by a virus.

Close all running programs.   The more programs you have running, the less memory is available to other programs. Installation programs typically update files and programs; so if you keep other programs running, installation may not work properly.

Have your local computer store add more RAM to your computer.   This is, admittedly, a drastic and somewhat expensive step. However, adding more memory can really help the speed of your computer and allow more programs to run at the same time.

Customer Care

If you have trouble with the book's companion study tools, please call the Wiley Product Technical Support phone number at (800) 762-2974. 74, or email them at `http://sybex .custhelp.com/`.

Index

Note to the Reader: Throughout this index **boldfaced** page numbers indicate primary discussions of a topic. *Italicized* page numbers indicate illustrations.

Numbers

6to4 prefixes, 445
802.1X enforcement, 754

A

A records, 36, 64–65, 439
AAAA records, 36, 64–65
AAS (application assignment scripts), 227
ABE (Access-Based Enumeration), 683
access control. *see* Routing and Remote
    Access Services (RRAS)
access control entries (ACEs), 150, **620–621**
access control lists (ACLs), **620–621**, *620*
Access-Based Enumeration (ABE), 683
account operators, 614
ACEs (access control entries), 150, **620–621**
ACLs (access control lists), **620–621**, *620*
Activate Scope, **477–478**, *478*, **482**, *482*, **493**
Active Directory
    account integration in, 816
    administration of. *see* administering
        Active Directory
    audit policies for, **639**
    backing up. *see* Backup for Active
        Directory
    Backup for. *see* Backup for Active
        Directory
    Best Practices Analyzer in, **345**
    data store in, 835
    DNS and, *51*
    infrastructure of. *see* Active Directory
        infrastructure
    installing. *see* installing Active Directory
    Integrated zones in, **51–52**, *51*
    Management Pack in, **345**

planning. *see* planning Active Directory
recovery of. *see* disaster recovery (DR)
Recycle Bin in, **842–843**
replicating. *see* replicating Active
    Directory
roles in. *see* Active Directory roles
security in. *see* security, in Active
    Directory
Sites in. *see* Active Directory Sites
Users and Computers in. *see* Active
    Directory Users and Computers
WSUS and, 523
Active Directory Administrative Center
    (ADAC), **184–185**, *184–185*, 345
Active Directory Application Mode (ADAM),
    112
Active Directory Certificate Services (AD CS)
    Administrative Center in, 345
    Authority Information Access in, 338–339
    Auto Enrollment of certificates in,
        334–335, *334*
    backing up CA servers in, 341
    Best Practices Analyzer in, 345
    BitLocker in, **344**
    CA server settings in, **339–342**
    certificate templates in, **335–337**, *336–337*
    configuring, generally, **324–326**
    defined, **2**, **6**
    enrolling user/computer certificates in,
        333–335
    Hyper-V in, **345**
    installing, **326–333**
    managed service accounts in, **345**
    Management Pack in, **345**
    Offline Domain Join in, **345**
    overview of, **342**
    PowerShell cmdlets in, **344–345**

Active Directory Certificate Services (AD CS)
(*continued*)
  read-only domain controllers in, 343–344
  read-only SYSVOL in, 343
  Recycle Bin in, 344
  revoking certificates in, 337–339
  security in, 342
  system key utility in, 344
  Web Services in, 345
  Windows Server 2012 and, 342, 344
Active Directory Delegation (AD Delegation),
  212
Active Directory Domain Services (AD DS),
  2, 6, 120–123
Active Directory Federation Services (AD FS)
  claim mapping in, 350
  configuring, 349–350
  custom claims in, 350
  group claims in, 350
  identity claims in, 350
  installing, 346–349
  introduction to, 6, 346
  planning, 112
  trust policies in, 349–350
  Web Agents in, 349
Active Directory infrastructure
  authentication scenarios in, 285–286
  bandwidth and, 257–258
  bridgehead servers in, 262, 279, 279–280
  changing environments and, 282
  connection objects in, 276–277, 277
  constraints on networks and, 257–258
  costs and, 258
  domain controllers in, adding, 300–301
  domain controllers in, cloning, 283–284
  domain controllers in, demoting, 301–302
  domain controllers in, placing, 280–281
  domain operations masters in, 304
  Domain Services connections in, 277
  domain trees in, creating, 294–300
  domain trees in, generally, 290, 291
  domain trees in, joining to forests, 300
  domains and sites in, 260
  event logs in, 285
  exam essentials on, 314–316

exam objectives on, 255
firewall configurations in, 285
forest operations masters in, 303
forests in, generally, 290, 308
forests in, planning, 290
forests in, promoting, 294
forests in, using, 292–294, 293
global catalog servers in, 281–282, 281,
  310–311
Internet and, 257
intersite replication in, 272–274, 273
intrasite replication in, 272
introduction to, 256
local area networks and, 257
moving server objects in, 277–278, 278
multiple domains in, 287–290, 303
network connectivity in, 285
network planning overview and, 256–258
operations masters in, generally, 303
Repadmin commands in, 286
replication in, configuring, 271
replication in, distributed file system, 263
replication in, generally, 258–259, 261
replication objects in, 265
review questions on, 317–319
router configurations in, 285
server topology in, 279–280
service requests in, 260–261
single-master operations in, 303–305
site links/site link bridges in, 274–276, 274
sites and domains in, 260
sites in, configuring, 270–271
sites in, creating, 266–268
sites in, generally, 258–260
sites in, implementing, 264–265
sites in, planning, 261–263
subdomains in, 294–300
subnets in, 264, 268–270
summary of, 313
synchronizing information in, 285
System Monitor for, 284
topology in, 286
trees in, creating, 294–300
trees in, generally, 290
trees in, joining to forests, 300

trees in, planning, **290**
trees in, promoting, **294**
trees in, single, **291–292**
trusts in, **305–309**, *306*
types of networks and, **257**
Universal Group Membership Caching in, **283, 312**
user principal name suffixes in, **310**
wide area networks and, **257**
Active Directory Lightweight Directory Services (AD LDS)
  authentication stores in, 351
  configuring, **351–354**
  defined, **6**
  installing, generally, **350–351**
  installing on Server Core, **354**
  introduction to, **350**
  in LDAP, 350
Active Directory Migration Tool (ADMT), 148, **170**
Active Directory Rights Management Services (AD RMS)
  administrative roles in, 355
  Auditors in, 356
  defined, **2, 6**
  Enterprise Administrators in, 355
  installing, **356–359**
  Internet Explorer and, 356
  introduction to, **355–356**
  Microsoft Office and, 355
  Service Group in, 355
  templates in, 356, **360**
Active Directory roles
  Certificate Services in. *see* Active Directory Certificate Services (AD CS)
  defined, **323**
  exam essentials on, **361**
  exam objectives on, **321–322**
  Federation Services and, **346–350**
  introduction to, **323**
  Lightweight Directory Services and, **350–354**
  review questions on, 362–364
  Rights Management Services in, **355–360**

Server Manager for, **323–324**, *324*
summary of, **360**
Active Directory Service Interfaces (ADSI), 130, 631–633, **846**
Active Directory Sites
  configuring sites in, 271
  creating sites in, 266–268
  moving server objects in, 278
  replication in, generally, 266
  site links/site link bridges in, 275–276
  specific servers in, *278*
  subnets in, 269–270
Active Directory Users and Computers
  in administering AD, **176–177**, *177*
  Advanced Features in, 176–177, *177*
  creating OUs in, 151–155
  Filter Options in, 176–177, *176*
  finding objects in, 183–184
  moving objects in, 177–178
  resetting computer accounts in, 179
  RSoP in, 243
  schema information in, *127*
  shared folders in, 182
Active Directory Web Services (ADWS), **345**
AD CS (Active Directory Certificate Services). *see* Active Directory Certificate Services (AD CS)
AD Delegation (Active Directory Delegation), 212
AD DS (Active Directory Domain Services), **2, 6, 120–123**
AD FS (Active Directory Federation Services). *see* Active Directory Federation Services (AD FS)
AD LDS (Active Directory Lightweight Directory Services). *see* Active Directory Lightweight Directory Services (AD LDS)
AD RMS (Active Directory Rights Management Services). *see* Active Directory Rights Management Services (AD RMS)
ADAC (Active Directory Administrative Center), **184–185**, *184–185*, **345**

ADAM (Active Directory Application Mode), 112

Add Exclusions, **481**, *481*

Add Exclusions And Delay, **473–474**, *473*

Add IP Filter, *594*

Add Roles And Features Wizard, *5*

additive security, 661

address formats, *438*

Address Management utility, **447–451**

address pools, **464**

Address Resolution Protocol (ARP), **404**, 788

addressing concepts, **438–443**

adjacency, *563*

adjunct policies, 741

administering Active Directory

    AD Administrative Center for, **184–185**, *184–185*, **345**

    AD Migration Tool in, **170**

    AD Users and Computers tool in, **176–177**, *177*

    Advanced Features for, **177**, *177*

    command prompts in, **185–186**, *186*

    Computer object properties in, **171–172**

    exam essentials on, **187–188**

    exam objectives on, **143**

    Filter Options for, **176**, *176*

    group properties in, **175**

    group strategies in, **175–176**

    groups in, creating, **176**

    groups in, generally, **174**

    introduction to, **144**

    objects in, availability to users, **180**

    objects in, creating, **165–170**

    objects in, deleting, **178**

    objects in, finding, **183–184**

    objects in, importing from files, **170**

    objects in, managing, **171–179**

    objects in, moving, **177–178**

    objects in, overview, **162–165**

    objects in, properties of, **171–174**

    objects in, publishing, **179–185**

    objects in, renaming, **178**

    offline domain joins in, **170**

    organization of AD in, **163–164**

    OUs in. *see* organizational units (OUs)

    Overview screen for, *185*

    printers in, **180–182**

    querying AD in, **183–184**

    resetting computer accounts in, **179**

    review questions on, **189–192**

    shared folders in, **182**

    summary of, **187**

    System folder in, *177*

    templates in, **168–169**

    User objects in, **171**

    user principal names in, **167–168**

Administrative Center, **184–185**, **345**

administrative roles, 340, 343–344, *355*

Administrative Templates, 197

administrative tools, **126–127**

administrators, on computer SERVER1, *245–246*

Administrators groups, 614, 616

ADMT (Active Directory Migration Tool), 148, **170**

ADMX Central Store, 198

Adprep, **113**, 300

ADSI (Active Directory Service Interfaces), 130, 631–633, **846**

Advanced (Custom) Settings, in RRAS, **728**

Advanced Boot options

    boot logging in, **852–854**, *853*

    in disaster recovery, **850–855**

    introduction to, **850–851**, *851*

    menu modes in, **854–855**

    in safe mode, **851–852**

Advanced Features, in AD, **177**, *177*

Advanced Security snap-in, *819*

Advanced tab, for printing, 691–692, *691–692*

advertising, 226–227

ADWS (Active Directory Web Services), **345**

AGDLP acronym, 175

aging, **81**

AIA (Authority Information Access), **338–339**

alerts, **535**

alias records, 36, **65**, 439

allocate-on-write transactional models, 102

analysis tools, **535, 635–637**
Anonymous Address, 442, *443*
anycast addresses, 441–442, *443*
Appearance tab, 534, *534*
application assignment scripts (AAS), 227
application clustering, **765, 776–781,** *779–780*
application data partitions
  creating, **129–131**
  introduction to, **129**
  ntdsutil for, **132–134**
  replicas in, **131–132**
Application layers, **404,** *405*
Application Server, **6**
application virtualization, 368. *see also* virtualization
applications, in GPOs
  assigning, **229, 232–233**
  categories of, **238–239**
  deploying, **228**
  installing, **225**
  publishing, **229, 232–233**
AppLocker, **231**
architecture, of Hyper-V, **370–371,** *371*
Archive attributes, 833, *833*
area border routers, 563, *564*
areas, in OSPF, 563
ARP (Address Resolution Protocol), **404,** 788
ASCII files, 37
attributes, defined, **113**
audit policies
  for AD objects, **639**
  audit logs in, **640**
  auditpol.exe in, **640–641**
  implementing, **638–639**
  overview of, **638**
  for security, **637–642**
  in Windows Server 2012, **641–642**
auditing tasks, in AD CS, 340
Auditors, 356
auditpol.exe, 203–204, *204,* **640–641,** *641*
authentication
  in AD LDS, 351
  in AD replication, **285–286**

authenticators, defined, **733**
  CHAP for, **703**
  EAP for, **733**
  in IP routing, *577*
  Kerberos for. *see* Kerberos
  PAP for, **733**
  RADIUS for, **718, 734, 752–753**
  RRAS for, **733–734, 745–746,** *746,* **752–754**
  selective vs. forest-wide, 307
  smart card, **633–634**
  Windows, **753–754**
Authentication Mechanism Assurance, 326
authoritative restores, **841–842**
Authority Information Access (AIA), **338–339**
authorizing servers, in DHCP, **470**
Auto Enrollment of certificates, **334–335,** *334*
autoconfiguration, 435–436
automated installations, 226
automatic certificate enrollment, **217–219**
Automatic Updates, **509, 511–512,** *512,* *522–523*
autostatic update mode, 563
AXFR (full zone transfers), 55

B

Background Intelligent Transfer Services (BITS), 511
background zone loading, **58**
backing up
  Active Directory. *see* Backup for Active Directory
  Backup Operators for, 615
  CA servers, **341**
  databases, 340–341
  virtual machines, **392–397**
backup domain controllers (BDCs), 114
Backup for Active Directory
  ADSI Editor in, **846**
  Archive attributes in, 833, *833*
  authoritative restores and, **841–842**

Backup for Active Directory (*continued*)
  Bare Metal Restore in, 835–836, *836*
  compacting directory databases in, **845**
  database mounting tools in, **844**
  defragmentation in, 845
  GPOs in, **837**
  introduction to, 831–832, *832*
  nonauthoritative restores and, **842**
  ntdsutil. exe in, 844–845, *844*
  offline maintenance in, 843–845
  overview of, 833–837
  Recycle Bin and, 842–843
  Repadmin utility in, 845–846
  replication in, 845–846
  Restartable Active Directory Services in, 842–843
  restoration and, 841–842
  scheduling backups in, **836**
  setting up, 837–841
  System State data backups in, **835**
  System State data recovery in, 836–837
  types of backups in, 833–834, *833*
  wbadmin commands in, 846–847, *846–847*
bandwidth, in AD, 257–258
Bandwidth Allocation, in RRAS, 711
Bandwidth Allocation Protocol (BAP), 747
Bare Metal Restore (BMR), 830, 835–836, *836*
baselines, 535
basic disks, **797–799**
BCD (Boot Configuration Data), 816
BDCs (backup domain controllers), 114
Berkeley Internet Name Domain (BIND), 41, 91–92, *92*
Best Practices Analyzer (BPA), **345**
BGP (Border Gateway Protocol), 564
bidirectional trusts, 306
BIND (Berkeley Internet Name Domain), 41, 91–92, *92*
BitLocker Drive Encryption
  in Active Directory Certificate Services, **344**
  defined, **2**
    in file services, **666–671**, *669*
    Full Volume Encryption in, **668**
    introduction to, **666**
    Network Unlock in, **668**
    passwords in, 667–668
    PINs and, 667–668
    provisioning in, **667**
    Used Disk Space Only encryption in, **667**
    in Windows Server 2012, **668–671**, *669*
BITS (Background Intelligent Transfer Services), 511
Block GPO Inheritance, 212–213, *213*
Block Policy Inheritance, 201
BMR (Bare Metal Restore), 830, **835–836**, *836*
Boot Configuration Data (BCD), 816
boot files, 835
boot logging, 852–854
boot options. *see* Advanced Boot options
boot records, 796–797
booting from VHDs, **816**
Border Gateway Protocol (BGP), 564, 713
border routing, **564–565**, *565*
BPA (Best Practices Analyzer), **345**
BranchCache
  defined, 2–3
  distributed mode in, **672–674**
  in file services, **671–678**
  firewall configurations in, **672–674**
  hosted mode in, **674–675**
  installing in Windows Server 2012, **675–676**
  introduction to, **671–672**
  PowerShell and, **676–677**
  in Windows Server 2012, generally, **677–678**
bridgehead servers
  in AD infrastructure, *262*, **279**
  defined, 262–263
  in replicating AD, *279–280*
Built-In containers, 164
built-in domain local groups, **614–616**, *614*, *616*

C

cache locking, **60**
caching, defined, **47**
caching-only server configuration, **70–71**
Callback Control Protocol (CBCP), **703**, 734, 737
caller ID, 735, 737
canonical name (CNAME) records, 65
CAs (Certificate Authorities). *see* Certificate Authorities (CAs)
CAU (Cluster-Aware Updating), **786**
CBCP (Callback Control Protocol), **703**, 734, 737
CCP (Compression Control Protocol), **703**, 711
CDPs (CRL distribution points), 338
Cert Publishers group, 325
Certificate Authorities (CAs)
    in AD CS, generally, **326**
    certificate templates and, 336
    Enterprise Root, 326
    introduction to, 217
    server settings in, **339–342**
    Stand-Alone Root, 326
    Subordinate, 326
Certificate Authority Web Enrollment Role Service, 325
certificate auto enrollment, 333–335, *334*
Certificate Mapping, 326
Certificate Publishers, 217
certificate revocation, 337–339
certificate revocation lists (CRLs), 338
Certificate Service DCOM Access, 615
Certificate Services. *see* Active Directory Certificate Services (AD CS)
certificate templates, 218, **335–337**, *336–337*
Certification Authority MMC, 339
Certification Practice Statement (CPS), 325
chained installations, 510
CHAP (Challenge Handshake Authentication Protocol), **703**
child domains, 291, 294–299. *see also* parent-child relationships

CIDR (Classless Inter-Domain Routing), 409, **431–434**, *431*
circular logging, 535
claim mapping, 350
Class A networks, **411**
Class A subnets, **430–431**, 434
Class B networks, **411**
Class B subnets, 422–423, **428–430**, 433
Class C networks, **411–412**, **426–428**, *428*
Class C subnets
    creating, *424*
    eight-subnet networks of, **426–428**
    hosts per, 423
    introduction to, 421
    in TCP/IP, **423–426**, **432–433**
    values for eight-subnet networks of, *428*
Class D addresses, 494, *565*
Class D networks, 412
classes, in DHCP, 490, **492**
classes, in DNS, **62**
Classless Inter-Domain Routing (CIDR), 409, **431–434**, *431*
client computer certificates, 336
clients
    in AD installations, **127–134**
    in DHCP scopes, 490
    in DNS, **41–42**
    multicast addresses for, **494–495**
    in RRAS, **723–730**
    in Windows Deployment Services, **21–22**
    in WSUS, **521–524**
CLR (common language runtime), 24
cluster nodes, 776
cluster quorums
    dynamic quorum management in, **769–770**
    in failover clustering, 768, *769*
    witness configuration and, **769**
Cluster Shared Volumes (CSV), 397, **786**
Cluster-Aware Updating (CAU), **786**
clustered applications, defined, 765
clustering. *see* failover clustering
cmdlets, *25–26*, 344–345, **786**
CNAME (canonical name) records, 65

CNG (Cryptography Next Generation), 335
COM (Component Object Model), 130
COM+ Class Registration databases, 835
command prompts, in AD, **185–186**, *186*
common language runtime (CLR), 24
communities, *548*
compacting directory databases, **845**
Component Object Model (COM), 130
compression, **657**, *657*
Compression Control Protocol (CCP), **703**,
    711
Computer and User Sections, **199–200**
Computer Management, 105–106
Computer Network Options, 216
Computer object properties, **171–172**
Computer objects, 164
Computer Section Only, **199**
Computer Selection pages, 243–244, *244*
Computers containers, 164
conditional forwarding, **79**
Configure DHCP Options, **474–478**
configuring
    AD Federation Services, **349–350**
    AD infrastructure, **271**
    AD LDS, **351–354**
    AD replication. *see* replicating Active
        Directory
    AD roles. *see* Active Directory roles
    AD sites, **270–271**
    AD with command prompts, **185–186**
    application data partitions, **129–134**
    automatic updates, **235**
    DNS. *see* configuring DNS (Domain
        Name Service)
    file servers. *see* configuring file servers
    GPOs, *198*
    high availability. *see* high availability
    Hyper-V, **375–385**
    IP routing, **573**
    IP-based connections, **711–713**, *711*, *712*
    offline folders, **653–656**, *654*
    ports, **715–716**, *716*, *723*
    printing services, *688–692*
    security, **635–637**, **751–755**

    shadow copies, **848–849**
    TCP/IP. *see* configuring TCP/IP
    user access, **736**
    user principal names, **167–168**
    virtual machines, **385**, **388–389**
    VPNs, **715–718**
    Windows Server 2012. *see* configuring
        Windows Server 2012
    WSUS, **509**
configuring DNS (Domain Name Service)
    AD integration in, **134–136**
    aging in, **81**
    caching-only server configuration in,
        70–71
    conditional forwarding in, **79**
    delegating zones for, **77–78**
    external forwarding in, **79**
    forwarding in, **79**
    General tab in, **72**
    introduction to, **67**
    load balancing in, **70**
    manually creating records in, **79–80**
    Name Servers tab in, **74**
    round robin in, **70**
    scavenging in, **81**
    Start Of Authority tab in, **72–73**, *73*
    WINS tab in, **74**
    zone properties in, **71–75**
    Zone Transfers tab in, **74–75**
    zones for dynamic updates in, **75–77**
configuring file servers
    BitLocker in, **666–671**
    BranchCache in, **671–678**
    DirectAccess in, **678–680**
    disk quotas in, **680–682**
    Distributed File System in, **682–685**
    File Server Resource Manager in, **664–665**
    introduction to, **649–650**
    NTFS and shared permissions in, **661–663**
    NTFS in, generally, **657–659**
    offline folders in, configuring, **653–656**
    permissions in, **656**
    publishing AD objects in, **651–653**

Share and Storage Management in, **663–664**

shared permissions and NTFS in, **661–663**

shared permissions in, generally, **659–660**

sharing folders in, **650–653, 656**

Volume Shadow Copy Service in, **656**

configuring TCP/IP

  CIDR in, **431–434**

  Class A networks in, **411**

  Class A subnets in, **430–431, 434**

  Class B networks in, **411**

  Class B subnets in, **428–430, 433**

  Class C networks in, **411–412,** *428*

  Class C subnets in, **423–428,** *424,* **432–433**

  configuring Windows Server 2012 and, **1**

  dual stacks in IPv6 in, **444**

  exam essentials on, **452**

  exam objectives on, **403**

  hierarchical IP addressing in, **407–408**

  host addresses in, *415*

  information commands in, **446**

  integration of IPv6 in, **443–447**

  IP Address Management in, **447–451**

  IP addressing in, generally, **407–412,** *409–410*

  IPv6 addressing in, **438–443**

  IPv6 in, generally, **434–438**

  migration of IPv6 in, **443–447**

  network addresses in, *415*

  network classes in, **409–412**

  overview of TCP/IP in, **404–407**

  Properties window in, *440*

  quantities of subnets/hosts in, **434**

  review questions on, **453–455**

  structure of IP addressing in, **408–409**

  subnet masks in, **416–418,** *416–419,* *431*

  subnets, calculating number of, **418–419**

  subnets, hosts per, **421–423**

  subnetting, easy application of, **420,** *420*

  subnetting, implementation of, **413–416,** *414–415*

  subnetting, traditional application of, **423**

  subnetting networks in, generally, **412–413**

  subnetting requirements in, **413–414**

  subnetting with IPv6 in, **446–447**

  summary of, **452**

  tunneling in IPv6 in, **444–446**

configuring Windows Server 2012. *see also* installing Windows Server 2012

  70-410 exam objectives on, **1**

  70-411 exam objectives on, **1–2**

  exam essentials on, **29**

  exam objectives in, **1**

  Features on Demand in, **27–28**

  PowerShell in, **23–27**

  remote management in, **22–27**

  review questions on, **30–32**

  summary of, **28–29**

  WDSUTIL command-line utility, *20–21*

  WinRM in, **22–23**

Connection Manager, **751**

connection objects, **276–277,** *277*

connection-level security, **734–735**

Constraints tab, **745–746**

Contact objects, 164

containers, OUs as, 163–164

copy backups, 834. *see also* Backup for Active Directory

copy on write, 102

costs, **258**

counter logs, 535

counters, **527,** *528, 529*

CPS (Certification Practice Statement), 325

CRLs (certificate revocation lists), 338

cross-forest trusts, **307**

Cryptographic Operators, 615

Cryptographic Service Provider (CSP), 326

Cryptography Next Generation (CNG), 335

CSP (Cryptographic Service Provider), 326

CSV (Cluster Shared Volumes), **397, 786**

custom claims, 350

Custom Views, 544, *545*

D

DAC (Dynamic Access Control), **627**

daily backups, 834. *see also* Backup for Active Directory

Data Protection Manager (DPM), 850

Data tab, 533, *533*

Database Backup and Restore, 340–341

database files, 500–501

database mounting tools, 844

database zones. *see* zones in DNS

Datacenter, 9

deactivating DHCP scopes, 493

default routes, 559

Default Routing and Remote Access, 492

defragmentation, 845

delegating control
    of AD users, 625–627
    of GPOs, 211–212
    in OUs, 149–150, 159–162, 163

delegating zones, 77–78

Delegation of Control wizards, 159–162

demand-dial routing, 567

demand-dialing, 574, 576–581

demotions, 132

Dependency Viewer, **781–783**

Deployment Services. *see* Windows Deployment Services (WDS)

deprovisioning, 174

desktop virtualization, 368. *see also* virtualization

Details tab, *247*, 540

DFS (Distributed File System), **682–685**, *685*

DFS Management console, 685, *685*

DFS Namespaces, 684

DFSR (Distributed File System Replication), **263–264**

DHCP (Dynamic Host Configuration Protocol)
    address pools in, 464
    advantages of, 460–461
    authorizing for Active Directory, **468–469**
    authorizing servers in, 470
    classes in, defined, 461

defined, 3

disadvantages of, 461

DNS and, 43–45, *45*

DORA process in, 459

enforcement in, 754

exam essentials on, 502

exam objectives on, 457

exclusions in, 463

installing, 464–468

introduction to, 458

`ipconfig` lease options for, 461–462

lease release in, 460

lease renewal in, 459–460

Options in, *475*

overview of, 458–464

relay agents in, 464

request messages in, 460

reservations in, 463

review questions on, 503–505

scopes in. *see* DHCP scopes

snap-ins in, 467–468, *468*

summary of, 501

superscopes in, 462

unauthorizing, 469–470

DHCP scopes
    Activate Scope for, 477–478, *478*, 482, *482*
    activating, generally, 493
    Add Exclusions And Delay for, 473–474, *473*
    Add Exclusions for, 481, *481*
    classes in, 492
    Configure DHCP Options for, 474–478
    creating in IPv4, 471–479
    creating in IPv6, 479–482
    database files and, 500–501
    deactivating, 493
    Default Routing and Remote Access in, 492
    defined, 462
    DHCP Options for, *475*
    DNS tabs for, *498*
    Domain Name And DNS Servers for, 476, *476*

in Dynamic DNS, **497–499**
exclusions in, **487–488**, *488*
introduction to, **471**
IP Address Range for, **472**, *473*
IPv4 options for, **490–492**, **497–499**
IPv4 server properties in, **484–486**
IPv6 server properties in, **486–487**
Lease Duration for, *474*
lease duration for, **474**, **481–482**, *482*
MADCAP and, **494–495**
multicast scopes in IPv4, **494–497**, *496–497*
multiple DNS servers and, **499**
New Scope Wizard for, *472–482*
option assignments in, *490–492*
properties of, **483**, *483*
reservations in, **488–489**, *489*
Router configuration for, **475**, *475*
Scope Prefix for, **480–481**, *480*
screen names for, **472**, **479**, *479*
server properties of, **484–487**, *484–487*
superscopes for IPv4, **493–494**
user class options in, **492**
WINS settings for, **476–477**, *477*
Dial-in tab, *736*
Dialing Options, **726**
dial-up access restrictions, **745**
Dial-Up Connection Properties, **723–730**
Dial-Up Networking (DUN), **700–704**, **725–726**
differencing virtual hard disks, **383**
differential backups, **834**. *see also* Backup for Active Directory
DirectAccess, **678–680**
Directory Services Restore Mode (DSRM), **835–836**
Disable settings, 196
Disabled OUs, 174
Disallowed (software is not allowed), 231
disaster recovery (DR)
    AD recovery in, **831**, **841–842**
    Advanced Boot options in, **850–855**, *851*
    Backup in. *see* Backup for Active Directory

Boot options in, **850–855**
Data Protection Manager in, **850**
exam essentials on, **857**
exam objectives on, **829**
introduction to, 300, **762**, **830**
protecting systems in, **830–831**
review questions on, **858–860**
shadow copies in, **847–850**
Startup Repair tool in, **856**
summary of, **857**
vssadmin.exe in, **849–850**, *849–850*
disconnected network configurations, **521**
Disk Management, 105–106, **383–384**, *383*
Disk Mirroring, **801**, *802*
disk quotas, 102, **680–682**
Disk Striping, **800–801**, *802*
Disk Striping with Parity, **801**, *802*
DiskPart, *815*
DiskRAID, 815
Distributed File System (DFS), **682–685**, *685*
Distributed File System Replication (DFSR), **263–264**
distributed mode, **672–674**
distribution groups, 175, **611**
DMS Install, *807*
DNS (Domain Name System)
    Active Directory Integrated zones in, **51–52**, *51*
    AD integration in, generally, **134–136**
    advantages of, **58–62**
    aging in, **81**
    alias records in, **65**
    background zone loading in, **58**
    BIND Secondaries in, *92*
    cache locking in, **60**
    caching in, **47**
    caching-only server configuration in, **70–71**
    clients in, **41–42**
    conditional forwarding in, **79**
    configuring, generally, **67**
    database zones in, **48–57**
    defined, **3**
    delegating zones for, **77–78**

DNS (Domain Name System) (*continued*)
    DHCP for, *45*, *498*
    DNS devolution in, **61**
    DNSCmd in, **90**, *90*
    DNSLint in, **88–89**, *89*
    DnsUpdateProxy in, **62**
    Dynamic Updates in, **44–45**, *44*
    Dynamic vs. Non-Dynamic, **42–44**
    Event Logging tab in, *74*
    exam essentials on, **93–94**
    exam objectives on, **33**
    external forwarding in, **79**
    forwarding in, **79**
    General tab in, *72*
    GlobalName zones in, **54**, **57**
    hierarchy of, *40*
    host records in, **64–65**
    HOSTS files in, *37*
    installing, **67–70**
    integrated zones in, **51–52**
    introduction to, **35–36**
    inverse queries in, **47**
    IP addresses in, **36–41**, **58–59**
    ipconfig in, **89–90**, *89*
    iterative queries in, **45**
    load balancing in, **70**
    local databases in, **49–50**
    log files in, **91**
    mail exchanger records in, **66**
    manually creating records in, **79–80**
    monitoring, **81–84**, *82*
    name server records in, **64**, *64*
    name servers in, **41**, **74**, *74*
    netmask ordering in, **61**
    non-Microsoft DNS servers and, **91–92**
    Notify in, *53*, **55–56**
    nslookup in, **84–88**, *87*
    pointer records in, **47**, **65–66**
    primary zones in, **49–50**
    process of, **42**
    Properties dialog boxes in, *71*, *74*, *82*
    queries in, **42**, **45–47**, *46*
    read-only domain controllers in, **59**
    record types in, **62–67**

    record weighting in, **61**
    recursive queries in, **45–47**
    replication scopes in, *56*
    resolvers in, **41–42**
    review questions on, **95–97**
    Root Hints tab in, *71*
    root zones in, **91**
    round robin in, **70**
    scavenging in, **81**
    secondary zones in, **50–51**
    Security Extensions in, **60**, **61**
    Server logs in, *544*
    servers in, **41–42**
    service records in, **66–67**
    set command in, *86*
    snap-in, **81–84**
    socket pools in, **59**
    SRV records in, *67*
    start of authority in, **62–63**, *63*, **72–73**, *73*
    stub zones in, **53–54**, *53*
    summary of, **92**
    time to live in, **47–48**
    top-level domains in, *39*
    trees in, **291**
    troubleshooting. *see* troubleshooting DNS
    trust anchors in, **60–61**
    WINS tab in, **74**
    zone properties configuration in, **71–75**
    zone transfers in, **54–55**, *56*, *57*, **74–75**
    zones for dynamic updates in, **75–77**
DNSCmd, **90**, *90*
DNSLint, **88–89**, *89*
DNSSEC (Security Extensions), **60–61**
DnsUpdateProxy, **62**
domain controllers (DCs)
    adding, **300–301**
    backup, **114**
    cloning, **283–284**
    demoting, **301–302**
    flow of information between, *256*
    placing, **280–281**
    planning for placement of, **302**
    primary, **114**
    read-only, **100**

Domain Controllers OU, 164
domain functional levels, **109–110**, *110*
domain local groups, 175, 612
Domain Name And DNS Servers, **476**, *476*
Domain Name System (DNS). *see* DNS
    (Domain Name System)
Domain Naming Masters, 303
domain operations masters, **304**
Domain Profile, 816, *817*
Domain Services connections, *277*
domain trees, 290, *291*, **294–300**. *see also* trees
domain users/groups, 610–611
Domains for GPOs, 200
DORA (Discover, Offer, Request,
    Acknowledge), **459**
DPM (Data Protection Manager), **850**
DR (disaster recovery). *see* disaster recovery
    (DR)
DSRM (Directory Services Restore Mode),
    835–836
dual stacks, **444**, *444*
Dynamic Access Control (DAC), **627**
dynamic disks, **797–799**
Dynamic DNS (DDNS), **42–45**, **497–499**
Dynamic Host Configuration Protocol
    (DHCP). *see* DHCP (Dynamic Host
    Configuration Protocol)
dynamic least queue depth, 806
Dynamic Memory, 369
dynamic quorums, **769–770**
dynamic routing, **560–564**, *561*
Dynamic Updates, *44*, **75–77**
dynamic volumes, 103

E

EAP (Extensible Authentication Protocol),
    706, 733
Easy Print Driver, **693**
Edit tool, 631–633
Edit Virtual Hard Disk Wizard, 384–385,
    384–385
Editor, **846**

EFS (Encrypting File System), **657**,
    658
elevated privileges, 226, 241
elevation-of-privileges attacks, 307
Enabled settings, 196
encapsulation, 704, **707–708**, *708*
encrypted tunnels, 705
Encrypting File System (EFS), **657**, *658*
Encryption, in RRAS, **748–749**, *748*
Enforced option, 202, *213*
enrolling user/computer certificates, **217–219**,
    333–335
Enrollment Agent, 325
Enterprise Administrators, 355
Enterprise Root CAs, 326
Essentials version, Windows Server 2012, **10**
EUI-64 (Extended User Interface 64-bit),
    441, *443*
Event Logging tab, 74
event logs, **285**, **722**
Event Viewer
    audit logs in, 640
    installing AD and, **124–126**
    for server management, **541–545**,
        542–545
eviction, 776
exclusions, **463**, **487–488**, *488*
export policies, in Firewall, **824**
exporting virtual machines, **392–393**
Extended User Interface 64-bit (EUI-64),
    441, *443*
Extensible Authentication Protocol (EAP),
    706, 733
Extensible rights Markup Language (XrML),
    356
external forwarding, **79**
external trusts, **307**
external virtual networks, 379
Extranet enrollment, 333

F

failback configurations, 805

failover clustering. *see also* high availability
  application clustering in, **776–781**, *779–780*
  cluster nodes in, **776**
  cluster quorums in, **768–769**, *769*
  Cluster Shared Volumes in, **786**
  Cluster-Aware Updating for, **786**
  creating clusters in, **775**
  defined, **3**, **6**
  Dependency Viewer in, **781–783**
  dynamic quorum management in, **769–770**
  geoclustering in, **774**
  installation of, **770–771**
  introduction to, **765–767**
  multisite clusters in, **774**
  PowerShell cmdlets for, **786**
  Print Services role in, **777–779**
  requirements for, **767–768**
  resource properties in, **783–785**, *783–785*
  role clustering in, **776–779**, *777*
  service clustering in, **776–777**
  SQL Server and, *766*
  Validate a Configuration Wizard in, *767*, **771–774**, *772, 774*
  validating cluster configurations in, **770**
  in Windows Server 2012, **786**
  witness configuration in, **769**
failover configurations, **805**
fault tolerance, **259**, **300–301**. *see also* RAID (Redundant Array of Independent Disks)
Features on Demand, **27–28**
federated identity management, **112**
Federation Services, **346–350**
Fibre Channel, *369*, **813–814**
File and Storage Services, **6–7**
File Server Resource Manager (FSRM), **3**, **663–665**, *665*
file services
  BitLocker in, **666–671**, *669*
  BranchCache in, **671–678**
  compression in, **657**, *657*
  configuring servers for. *see* configuring file servers
  DirectAccess in, **678–680**

  disk quotas in, **680–682**
  Distributed File System in, **682–685**, *685*
  Encrypting File System in, **657**, *658*
  exam essentials on, **694**
  exam objectives on, **647–648**
  File Server Resource Manager in, **664–665**
  file servers in, defined, **649**
  introduction to, **649**
  NTFS in, **657–659**, *660–662*, **661–663**
  offline folders in, configuring, **653–656**, *654*
  permissions in, **656**, **660–662**
  PowerShell for BranchCache in, *676–677*
  PowerShell for FSRM in, *665*
  printing. *see* printing
  publishing AD objects in, **651–653**
  review questions on, **695–698**
  security in, **658–659**, *659–660*
  servers in, generally, **649–650**
  Share and Storage Management in, **663–664**
  shared permissions in, **661–663**
  shared permissions in, generally, **659–660**
  sharing folders in, **650–653**, **656**
  summary of, **693**
  Volume Shadow Copy Service in, **656**
file storage. *see* storage configuration
file system encryption, **103**
File System verification, **101–105**
FileHash switches, **264**
filename extension mappings, **238**
Filter Options, in AD, **176**, *176*
filtering GPOs, **209–210**, **212–213**
fine-grained password policies, **630–633**
Firewall
  in AD replication, **285**
  Advanced Security snap-in for, **818**, *819*
  in BranchCache, **672–674**
  Domain Profile in, *817*
  exam essentials on, **825**
  GPOs for, **824**
  import/export policies for, **824**
  inbound/outbound rules in, **820–821**, *820–821*

introduction to, **816–820**
IPsec in, *818–819*, **824**
Monitoring section for, **824**
Private Profile in, *817*
Public Profile in, *818*
review questions on, **826–827**
summary of, **825**
in Windows Server 2012, **821–823**
flat addressing, 407–408
Flexible host isolation, *755*
folder redirection, **219–221**
Force Policy Inheritance, 202
foreign security principals, 164, **618**, *618*
forests
    in Active Directory, **111–112**, *308*
    in cross-forest trusts, 307
    in forest-wide authentication, 307
    introduction to, 290
    operations masters in, 303
    planning, **290**
    promoting, **294**
    trees joining, **300**
    using, **292–294**, *293*
format options, *101*
forwarding, in DNS, **79**
Foundation version, Windows Server 2012, **10**
FQDNs (fully qualified domain names), 39–40
FSRM (File Server Resource Manager), **3**, **663–665**, *665*
full backups, 834. *see also* Backup for Active Directory
full installation mode, **373–375**
Full Volume Encryption (FVE), **668**
full zone transfers (AXFR), *55*
fully qualified domain names (FQDNs), 39–40
FVE (Full Volume Encryption), **668**

G

GC (Global Catalog). *see* Global Catalog (GC)

General tab
    in DNS, **72**
    in LAN interfaces, *575*
    in Performance Monitor, 532, *532*
    in printing services, 688, *688*
    in RIP interfaces, **581–583**, *582*
    in RRAS, **724–725**, *724*
Generic Routing Encapsulation (GRE), *595*, 707
geoclustering, **774**
geographically-based structures, *152*, **774**
Global Catalog (GC)
    AD forests in, 293–294
    introduction to, 111
    servers in, **281–282**, *281*, **310–311**
    trees/forests in, 290
global groups, 175, 612
global unicast addresses, 441, *443*
GlobalName zones, **54**, *57*
glue host records, *53*
GPMC (Group Policy Management Console). *see* Group Policy Management Console (GPMC)
GPOs (Group Policy objects). *see* Group Policy objects (GPOs)
GPPs (Group Policy Preferences), 197
gpresult.exe command, **247–248**, *248*
GPT (GUID Partition Table), 796
Graph tab, **533–534**, *534*
Graph view, **529–530**, *530*
Graphical User Interfaces (GUIs)
    in ADSI, 130
    introduction to, 11
    in MBSA, **546–547**
    in Windows Server 2012, **14–17**
GRE (Generic Routing Encapsulation), *595*, 707
group claims, in AD FS, 350
Group Policy
    configuration options in, *198*
    defined, **7**
    introduction to, **195–196**
    Management Console for. *see* Group Policy Management Console (GPMC)

Group Policy (*continued*)
    objects in. *see* Group Policy objects
        (GPOs)
    for security, **634**
    security settings in. *see* Group Policy
        security settings
    settings for, **196–199**
Group Policy Management Console (GPMC)
    assigning applications in, 232–233
    automatic certificate enrollment in,
        218–219
    creating GPOs in, 203–206, *205*
    delegating administrative control in,
        211–212
    folder redirection settings in, 220–221
    introduction to, 196
    linking GPOs to AD in, 207–208, *208*
    offline folders in, configuring, *654*
    PowerShell and, 221–222
    publishing applications in, 232–233
    removing programs in, 239–241
    removing software in, *240*
    security filtering in, 209–210, *209*
    software restriction policies in, 231
    software updates in, 234
    WSUS and, 523–524
Group Policy objects (GPOs)
    administrators in, *245–246*
    application categories in, **238–239**
    application deployment in, **228**
    application installation in, **225**
    AppLocker for, **231**
    assigning applications in, **229**, 232–233
    auditpol.exe in, *204*
    automatic certificate enrollment in,
        217–219
    in Backup, **837**
    blocking inheritance in, *213*
    Categories tab in, *239*
    Computer and User Sections of, **199–200**
    Computer Section Only of, **199**
    Computer Selection pages in, *244*
    configuration options in, *198*
    configuring automatic updates in, **235**

    creating, **203–206**
    defined, **200–201**
    delegating administrative control of,
        211–212
    deploying software, implementation of,
        229–235
    deploying software in, generally, **222–229**,
        236–242, *236–237*
    Details tab in, *247*
    Enforced option for, *213*
    enrolling user/computer certificates in,
        217–219, 333
    exam essentials on, **249–250**
    exam objectives on, **193–194**
    filename extension mappings in, **238**
    filtering of, **209–210**, **212–213**
    in Firewall, **824**
    folder redirection settings in, **219–221**
    gpresult.exe command for, **247–248**,
        248
    Group Policy in. *see* Group Policy
    implementing, generally, **203**
    inheritance in, **201–202**, **212–213**, *213*
    introduction to, **195–202**
    linking to AD, **207**, *208*
    Loopback Policy in, **215–216**
    managing, **207**
    Merge mode in, **216**
    MSI package files in, *228*
    network configurations in, **216–217**, *216*
    offline folders in, **653–655**
    package defaults in, **236–238**
    planning strategies for, **202–203**
    PowerShell cdmlets for, **221–222**
    Properties dialog boxes for, *247*
    publishing applications in, **229**, **232–233**
    removing programs in, **239–241**
    removing software in, *240*
    Replace mode in, **216**
    Results Wizard in, **243–245**, *244–245*
    review questions on, **251–253**
    RSoP in logging mode for, **243–246**
    RSoP in planning mode for, **246–247**
    script policies in, **214–215**

scripting options in, *214–215*

security groups for, **210**

security in, generally, **627–633**

Security Settings for, **199–200, 209–210,** *209*

Share option for, **230–231**

Slow Link Detection in, **231–232**

Software Installation Properties in, **236–239,** *236, 237, 239*

software management life cycles and, **223**

software restriction policies in, **231**

software updates in, **233–234**

Startup/Shutdown Scripts for, *214*

summary of, **248–249**

Summary Of Selections pages in, *245*

troubleshooting, **242–248**

User Selection pages in, *244–245*

verifying software installation in, **234–235**

Windows Installer for, **224–228, 241–242,** *241*

Windows Update for, **224**

WMI for, **208–209**

WSUS and, **524**

Group Policy Preferences (GPPs), 197

Group Policy security settings

applying, **629–630**

fine-grained password policies in, **630–633**

introduction to, **627–629,** *628–629*

for smart cards, **634**

groups

creating, **176, 622–624**

delegating control of, **625–627**

introduction to, **174**

in OUs, *145,* **151, 164–165**

properties of, **175**

scope of, **611–614,** *613*

strategies for, **175–176**

guest operating systems, **369–370,** *369–370*

Guests, 615–616

GUID Partition Table (GPT), 796

GUIs (Graphical User Interfaces). *see* Graphical User Interfaces (GUIs)

H

hardware, **372,** *372,* **536**

hash algorithms, 326–327

HBAs (host bus adapters), 808, 813–814

hierarchical IP addresses, **407–408**

hierarchy of DNS, *40*

high availability

achieving, generally, **763–765**

components of, **762–763**

exam essential on, **791**

exam objectives on, **761**

failover clustering for. *see* failover clustering

foundation for, **764**

introduction to, **762**

Network Load Balancing for, **787–791**

patch management in, **764–765**

ratings of, *763*

review questions on, **792–793**

summary of, **791**

Windows Server 2012 for, **786**

Histogram view, 530, *531*

Hobbes' Internet Timeline, 435

home folders, 650

host (A) records, 64

host addresses, **409,** *415*

host bus adapters (HBAs), 808, 813–814

host records, **64–65**

host routes, *559*

hosted mode, **674–675**

HOSTS files, 37–38, *37*

Hyper-V. *see also* virtualization

in Active Directory Certificate Services, **345**

architecture of, **370–371,** *371*

configuring, **375–385**

defined, **3, 7**

Dynamic Memory in, 369

Edit Virtual Hard Disk Wizard in, *384–385*

features of, **368–370**

Fibre Channel in, 369

full installation mode in, **373–375**

Hyper-V. *see also* virtualization (*continued*)
  guest operating systems in, **369–370**, *369–370*
  hardware requirements in, **372**
  installation warning windows in, *372*
  installing, **373–375**
  Manager for. *see* Hyper-V Manager
  Offline disks in, *383*
  overview of, **367–373**
  quick migration in, 368
  requirements for, **372–373**
  resource metering in, 368
  in Server Core, **375**
  in Server Manager, **375–376**, *376*
  settings for servers in, *377*
  software requirements in, **373**
  virtual hard disks in, **381–385**, *382*
  virtual network cards in, *381*
  virtual switches in, **378–380**, *379*, *381*
Hyper-V Manager. *see also* Hyper-V
  configuring existing VMs in, **387–388**
  configuring new VMs in, **388–389**
  creating virtual machines in, **386–387**
  deleting virtual machines in, **389**
  differencing hard disks in, 383
  Edit Virtual Hard Disk Wizard in, **384–385**
  exporting virtual machines in, **392–393**
  importing virtual machines in, **392–393**
  Inspect Disk in, 384
  Integration Services in, **391–392**
  internal virtual networks in, **380–381**
  overview of, **376–377**, *376*
  server settings in, **377–378**
  settings for servers in, *377*
  Smart Paging in, 389
  snapshots in, **394–396**
hypervisors, defined, **372**

I

IANA (Internet Assigned Numbers Authority), 71, 406
ICANN (Internet Corporation for Assigned Names and Numbers), 40, 71

ID records, 264
identity claims, 350
IGMP (Internet Group Management Protocol), 566
import policies, in Firewall, **824**
importing virtual machines, **392–393**
Inbound Filters, *593*
inbound/outbound rules, **820–821**, *820–821*
incremental backups, 834. *see also* Backup for Active Directory
incremental zone transfers (IXFR), 55
InetOrgPerson objects, 165
information commands, **446**
Infrastructure Masters, 304
inheritance
  in GPOs, **201–202**, **212–213**, *213*
  in OUs, **148**, 150, 163
initialization files, 227
initializing disks, **796–797**
Inspect Disk, 384
installing
  Active Directory. *see* installing Active Directory
  AD CS, **326–333**
  AD FS, **346–349**
  AD LDS, **350–351**, **354**
  AD RMS, **356–359**
  BranchCache, **675–676**
  DHCP, **464–468**
  DNS, **67–70**
  failover clustering, **770–771**
  Hyper-V, *372*, **373–375**
  server components in WDS, **20–21**
  Windows Server 2012. *see* installing Windows Server 2012
installing Active Directory
  AD DS in, **120–123**
  administrative tools and, **126–127**
  Adprep for, **113**
  application data partitions in, **129–134**
  clients testing, **127–134**
  DNS integration in, **134–136**
  domain functional levels in, 100
  Event Viewer and, **124–126**
  exam essentials on, **137–138**

exam objectives on, **99**
introduction to, **100**
joining domains, **128**
LDP tool for, 130
LDP tool for checking, *130*
local domain controllers and, *134*
naming contexts in, *134*
ntdsutil for, **132–134**, *132–133*
planning for. *see* planning Active
    Directory
process of, **114–123**
promoting domain controllers in, **114–120**
replicas in, **131–132**
schema information in, *127*
on Server Core, **120–123**
Users and Computers tool for, *127*
verification of, **124–128**
installing Windows Server 2012
  70-410 exam objectives on, **1**
  70-411 exam objectives on, **1–2**
  Add Roles And Features Wizard in, *5*
  exam essentials on, **29**
  exam objectives in, **1**
  with GUIs, **14–17**
  Installing Windows screens in, *16*
  keyboards, *17*
  planning for, **4**
  review questions on, **30–32**
  selecting operating systems in, *15*
  with Server Core, **17–18**
  server features in, defined, **2–8**
  server features in, migrating, **8–9**
  server roles in, defined, **4–8**, *5*
  server roles in, migrating, **8–9**
  summary of, **28–29**
  types of installation in, **11–14**
  upgrade path recommendations, *10*
  versions of Windows Server 2012 in, **9–10**
  Windows Deployment Services in,
    18–22
instances, **527**
Integrated Services Digital Network (ISDN),
  567, **702**
integration
  of DNS zones, **51–52**

Integration Services for, *391*
of IPv6, **443–447**
ISDN for, *567*, **702**
Interactive Mode, **85–86**
internal routing, *564*
internal virtual networks, **380–381**
Internet, *257*
Internet Assigned Numbers Authority
  (IANA), *71*, *406*
Internet Corporation for Assigned Names
  and Numbers (ICANN), *40*, *71*
Internet Explorer, *356*
Internet Group Management Protocol
  (IGMP), *566*, **788**
Internet layers, **404**, *405*
Internet multicast backbone, *566*
Internet Protocol (IP), *257*, **704**
Internet Protocol Security (IPsec). *see* IPsec
  (Internet Protocol Security)
Internet service providers (ISPs), *257*, *430*
Internet Small Computer System Interface
  (iSCSI), **808–810**
Internet Storage Name Service (iSNS),
  810–813
internetworks, *556–557*
intersite replication, **272–274**, *273*
Intra-Site Automatic Tunnel Addressing
  Protocol (ISATAP), *437*, *444–445*
intrasite replication, **272**
inverse queries, **47**
IP (Internet Protocol)
  addresses in. *see* IP addresses
  datagrams, *707*
  defined, **704**
  introduction to, *257*
  in ipconfig. *see* ipconfig
  IP-in-IP interfaces/tunnels in, *567*
  in IPsec. *see* IPsec (Internet Protocol
    Security)
  routing in. *see* IP routing
  in RRAS, **711–713**, *711*, *712*, *747*
  in TCP/IP. *see* TCP/IP (Transmission
    Control Protocol/Internet Protocol)
  version 4 of. *see* IPv4
  version 6 of. *see* IPv6

IP Address Management (IPAM), **3**, **447–451**
IP addresses
    Class A networks in, **411**
    Class B networks in, **411**
    Class C networks in, **411–412**
    in DNS, **36–41**
    hierarchical scheme of, **407–408**
    network classes in, **409–412**, *409*
    Range for, **472**, *473*
    special network addresses in, *410*
    structure of, **408–409**
    in TCP/IP, **407–412**
IP Control Protocol (IPCP), **703–704**
IP routing
    configuring, generally, **573**
    demand-dial interfaces in, **576–581**
    interfaces in, generally, **573–574**, *573*
    LAN interfaces in, **574–576**, *575*
    Logging tab in, **587–588**, *587*
    managing, **597–601**
    managing protocols in, **589**
    monitoring, **598**
    in network access. *see* IP routing
    Preferences Levels tab in, **588**, *588*
    properties in, generally, **587**
    RIP in, **581–586**, **589**
    `route add` in, **590**
    `routeprint` for, **598**
    RRAS for, *568–572*, **590–591**
    static routes in, **590–592**, *591*
    troubleshooting, **598–601**
`ipconfig`
    in DNS, **89–90**, *89*
    interface identifier for, *446*
    IPv6 interfaces in, **446**
    lease options in, **461–462**
    in planning AD, **107**, *107*
IPCP (IP Control Protocol), **703–704**
IPsec (Internet Protocol Security)
    enforcement in, **754**
    in file services, **678**
    introduction to, **437**
    L2TP/IpSec tunneling in, **709**
    policies in, **824**

    Settings in, **818**, *818–819*
IPv4
    DHCP scope options in, **490–492**
    IPv6 vs., *438*
    RRAS and, **711–712**, *711*
    server properties of, **484–486**
    Static Route dialog boxes in, *591*
    subnetting in, *420*
IPv6
    address format in, *438*
    Address Management in, **447–451**
    addresses in, generally, **36**, **438–443**
    concepts in, **435–438**
    configuring from command prompts,
        440
    defined, **36**
    in DNS, **58–59**
    dual stacks in, **444**, *444*
    history of, **435**
    information commands in, **446**
    integration of, **443–447**
    interface identifier in, *446*
    IPv4 vs., *438*
    known addresses in, *443*
    migration in, **443–447**
    need for, **435**
    prefixes in, *443*
    Properties window in, *440*
    RRAS and, **712–713**, *712*
    server properties in, **486–487**
    subnetting with, **446–447**, *447*
    in TCP/IP, generally, **434–435**
    tunneling in, **444–446**
ISATAP (Intra-Site Automatic Tunnel
    Addressing Protocol), **437**, **444–445**
iSCSI (Internet Small Computer System
    Interface), **808–810**
ISDN (Integrated Services Digital Network),
    567, **702**
iSNS (Internet Storage Name Service),
    810–813
ISPs (Internet service providers), **257**, **430**
iterative queries, **45**
IXFR (incremental zone transfers), *55*

J

JET (Joint Engine Technology), 500–501
joining domains, **128**
Joint Engine Technology (JET), 500–501

K

KCC (Knowledge Consistency Checker), 131,
   265, 274
Kerberos, **3**, 616, 734
Key Archival tasks, 340
Key Distribution Center Service, 616
Key Recovery Agent, 340
key-based renewals, 342
keyboards, *17*
Knowledge Consistency Checker (KCC), 131,
   265, 274
known addresses, *443*
krbtgt accounts, 616

L

L2TP (Layer 2 Tunneling Protocol), 597,
   706–707, **709**
Label Distribution Protocol (LDP), 130, *130*
LANs (local area networks), 257, 574–576,
   575
Launch NPS, *739*
Layer 2 Tunneling Protocol (L2TP), 597,
   706–707, **709**
LDAP (Lightweight Directory Access
   Protocol)
   AD LDS in, 350
   defined, **6**
   DNS and, 66
   LDP tools for, 130, *130*
LDP (Label Distribution Protocol), 130, *130*
leases
   duration of, **474**, *474*, **481–482**, *482*
   release of, **460**
   renewal of, **459–460**
Lightweight Directory Access Protocol
   (LDAP). *see* LDAP (Lightweight
   Directory Access Protocol)

Lightweight Directory Services (LDS). *see*
   Active Directory Lightweight Directory
   Services (AD LDS)
linear logging, *535*
Link Control Protocol (LCP), **703**, 711
Link layers, **404**, *405*
linked value replication, 111, 261
linking to Active Directory OUs, 207,
   208
link-local addresses, 441, *443*
link-state maps, 563
live migration, **396–397**
load balancing, 50, **70**. *see also* Network
   Load Balancing (NLB)
load balancing and failover (LBFO),
   791
local area networks (LANs), **257**, 574–576,
   575
Local Computer Policy Tool, 203
local databases, 49–50
local domain controllers, *134*
Local File, in RRAS, 719–722
Local GPOs, 200
Local Security Policy, *334*
local security principals, **610–611**
local users/groups, 610–611
logging mode, RSoP in, 243–246
Logging tab, **587–588**, *587*
logical grouping of resources, **146–148**
logs
   in DNS, *74*, **91**
   event, **722**
   in Performance Monitor, *535*
   in RRAS, **719–722**, *721*
   in server management, 535
   in WSUS, **521**
Loopback Policy, **215–216**

M

MAC (Media Access Control), 787–788
MADCAP (Multicast Address Dynamic
   Client Allocation Protocol), **494–495**
mail exchanger (MX) records, **66**

maintaining software, 223–224
Managed By tab, *158*
managed service accounts, **3**, 164, **345**
Management Pack, **345**
Mandatory Upgrade, 234
manually creating records, 79–80
mapping business organizations, *147*
masked vs. unmasked bits, 418
masks, defined, 417. *see also* subnet masks
Master Boot Record (MBR), 796–797
MBone, 566
MBR (Master Boot Record), 796–797
MBSA (Microsoft Baseline Security
    Analyzer), **546–547**, *547*
mbsacli.exe, **547**
mean time between failures (MTBF), 763,
    831
mean time to recover (MTTR), 763
Media Access Control (MAC), 787–788
menu modes, **854–855**
Merge mode, **216**
Microsoft Baseline Security Analyzer
    (MBSA), **546–547**, *547*
Microsoft CHAPv2 (MS-CHAPv2), 733
Microsoft Device Specific Module (Microsoft
    DSM), 805
Microsoft Management Console (MMC)
    AD replication in, generally, 266
    creating OUs in, 151–155
    defined, **126**
    for GPOs. *see* Group Policy Management
        Console (GPMC)
    installing AD FS in, 346–349
    installing AD LDS in, 350–351
    installing AD RMS in, 356–359
    introduction to, 11
    moving server objects in, 278
    Server Manager in. *see* Server Manager
    site links/site link bridges in, 275–276
    sites in, configuring, 271
    sites in, creating, 266–268
    subnets in, creating, 269–270
Microsoft Multipath I/O (MPIO), **805–807**
Microsoft Office, 230, 355

Microsoft Patch (MSP) files, 227
Microsoft Point-to-Point Encryption (MPPE),
    708
Microsoft Transformation (MST), 227
Microsoft Windows Installer (MSI)
    for GPOs, **224–228**, **241–242**, *241*
    issues addressed by, 225
    packages in, 227, *228*
    troubleshooting, 226
migration, 351, **443–447**, 693
mixed mode networks, 734
MMC (Microsoft Management Console). *see*
    Microsoft Management Console
    (MMC)
modems, defined, **702**
modulator-demodulators, 702
monitoring
    AD replication, **284–286**
    DNS, **81–84**, *82*
    in Firewall, **824**
    IP routing, **598**
    networks, **536–537**
    performance. *see* Performance Monitor
    in RRAS, **722**
mount points, **804–805**
mounted drives, 103
moving server objects between sites, **277–278**,
    278
MPIO (Microsoft Multipath I/O), **805–807**
MPPE (Microsoft Point-to-Point Encryption),
    708
MS-CHAPv2 (Microsoft CHAPv2), 733
MSI (Microsoft Windows Installer). *see*
    Microsoft Windows Installer (MSI)
MSIMaging-PSPs containers, 165
MSMQ Queue Alias objects, 165
MSP (Microsoft Patch) files, 227
MST (Microsoft Transformation), 227
MTBF (mean time between failures),
    763, 831
MTTR (mean time to recover), 763
Multicast Address Dynamic Client Allocation
    Protocol (MADCAP), **494–495**
multicast addresses, 442, *443*

multicast routing, **565–567**, *565*
multicast scopes, **494–497**, *496–497*
multihomed computers, 566
multihomed routers, 416
Multilink And Bandwidth Allocation
　　Protocol (BAP), 747
multilink extensions, **704**
multimaster replication, 262
Multipath I/O (MPIO), **805–807**, *807*
multiple DNS servers, **499**
multiple domains, **287–290**, 303
multiple server types, 649–650
multisite clusters, **774**
MX (mail exchanger) records, **66**

N

name server (NS) records, 53, **64**, *64*
Name Servers tab, **74**, *74*
naming contexts, *134*
NAP (Network Access Permission), 737
NAP (Network Access Protection). *see*
　　Network Access Protection (NAP)
national access points (NAPs), 564
negative cache TTL, 47
neighbor discovery, 438, 442
Neighbors tab, **584–585**, *584*
.NET Framework, 24
netmask ordering, **61**
network access
　　border routing in, **564–565**, *565*
　　dynamic routing in, **560–564**, *561*
　　exam essentials on, **601–602**
　　exam objectives on, **555**
　　introduction to, 556, *557*
　　IP routing in. *see* IP routing
　　L2TP packet filters in, **597**
　　multicast routing in, **565–567**, *565*
　　Network Access layers in, **404**
　　Open Shortest Path First in, **563–564**,
　　　　564
　　PPTP packet filters in, **595–597**
　　review questions on, **603–605**
　　routing in, generally, **556–559**

routing in Windows Server 2012 for,
　　567–568
Routing Information Protocol in, **561–563**
routing tables in, **559**
in RRAS, **568–572**, **738–744**, *739–741*
static routing in, **560**
summary of, **601**
TCP/IP packet filters in, **592–595**
VPN packet filters in, **595–597**
Network Access Permission (NAP), 737
Network Access Protection (NAP)
　　DHCP scopes and, 485, *486*
　　introduction to, **7**
　　RRAS and, **754–755**
Network Address Translation (NAT), 435,
　　567–568
network attached storage (NAS), 796, **814**
Network Device Enrollment Service
　　(NDES), 325
NetWork Discovery, 108
Network File System (NFS), 663
Network Interfaces nodes, **573–574**, *573*
Network Load Balancing (NLB)
　　creating clusters in, **788–789**
　　defined, **7**
　　introduction to, **787**
　　managing clusters in, **790**
　　modifying cluster properties in, **789–790**
　　Network Load Balancing Manager
　　　　for, 790
　　NIC Teaming in, **791**
　　requirements for, **788**
Network Monitor, **536–537**
network operating systems (NOSs), 102,
　　149, 608
Network Policy and Access Services, **7**
Network Time Protocol (NTP), 304
Network Unlock, **668**
Networking tab, **729**, *729*
networks
　　access in. *see* network access
　　addresses of, *415*
　　classes of, **409–412**, *409*, **426–428**
　　configuring in GPOs, **216–217**, *216*

networks (*continued*)
  connectivity in, **106–109**, *285*
  constraints on, **257–258**
  features in, **3**, **7**
  internetworks, *556–557*
  load balancing in. *see* Network Load
    Balancing (NLB)
  planning, generally, **256–258**
  private, 768
  public, 768
  routes of, *559*
  RRAS protocols for, **704**
  services for, **20**
  virtual, *378–381*
  virtual private. *see* virtual private
    networks (VPNs)
New Mirrored Volume Wizard, *802–804*
New Scope Wizard
  activating scopes in, *478*, *482*
  Add Exclusions And Delay in, *473*
  Add Exclusions in, *481*
  creating new scopes in, *478–480*, *479*
  DHCP Options in, *475*
  Domain Name And DNS Servers in, *476*
  IP Address Range in, *473*
  Lease Duration in, *474*, *482*
  Router in, *475*
  Scope Prefix in, *480*
  welcome page in, *472*
  WINS Servers in, *477*
New Technology File System (NTFS). *see*
  NTFS (New Technology File System)
NFS (Network File System), 663
NIC Teaming, **791**
No Override, 202
non-active directory networks, **522–523**
nonauthoritative restores, 842
Non-Dynamic DNS, **42–44**
Nonmandatory Upgrade, 234
non-Microsoft DNS servers, **91–92**
normal backups, 834. *see also* Backup for
  Active Directory
NOSs (network operating systems), 102, 149,
  608

Not Configured settings, 197
Notify dialog boxes, *53*, **55–56**
NPIV (N-Port Identification Virtualization),
  814
N-Port Identification Virtualization (NPIV),
  814
NS (name server) records, *53*, **64**, *64*
nslookup
  on command line, **85**
  error messages in, **87**, *87*
  in Interactive Mode, **85–86**
  responses in, **86**
  troubleshooting DNS with, generally,
    84–85
  using, **87–88**
ntdsutil. exe
  in AD infrastructure, *281*
  in Backup, **844–845**, *844*
  in installing AD, **132–134**, *132–133*
  using, 133–134
  viewing naming contexts in, *134*
NTFS (New Technology File System)
  file services in, **657–659**, *660–662*
  in planning AD, **102–104**
  self-healing, 103
  shared folders in, *660–662*
  shared permissions in, **661–663**
  support for, 101
NTLMv2, 734
NTP (Network Time Protocol), 304

O

objects, in AD
  availability of, **180**
  creating, **165–170**
  delegating control of, **626**
  deleting, **178**
  finding, **183–184**
  importing, 170
  managing, **171–179**
  moving, **177–178**
  in organization units, 144
  overview of, **162–165**

properties of, **171–174**
publishing, **179–185**
renaming, **178**
objects, in GP. *see* Group Policy objects
    (GPOs)
objects, in OUs, 165
OCSP (Online Certificate Status Protocol),
    338
octets, 407
offline conversions, 398
Offline disks, *383*
offline domain joins, **170, 345**
offline folders, 221, **653–656**, *654*
offline maintenance, **843–845**
one-way trusts, **306**
Online Certificate Status Protocol (OCSP),
    338
online conversions, 398
Online Responder, 325, 338
Open Shortest Path First (OSFP), 557,
    563–564, *564*
Open Systems Interconnection (OSI), 558
operations masters, **303**
option assignments, *490–492*
Options tab, **725**, *725*
organizational units (OUs)
    administering properties of, **157–158**
    benefits of, **146**
    creating, **151–155**
    delegating administrative control in,
        149–150, 163
    delegating custom tasks in, **160–162**
    deleting, **156**
    geographically-based structures of, *152*
    GPOs and, 201, 207
    group policies in, **151**
    groups in, *145*
    inheritance in, **148**, 150, 163
    logical grouping of resources in, **146–148**
    Managed By tab for, *158*
    managing, **155**
    mapping business organizations to, *147*
    modifying structure of, **156–157**
    moving, **156**

naming, 148
objects in, 165
overview of, **144–146**
planning structure of, **146–151**
Properties dialog boxes for, *158*
purpose of, **145–146**
renaming, **156**
troubleshooting, **163**
users and, *145*
OSFP (Open Shortest Path First), 557,
    563–564, *564*
outbound rules, **820–821**, *820–821*
Overview screens, *185*

P

package defaults, **236–238**
PAP (Password Authentication Protocol), 733
parent-child relationships
    in Hyper-V, *371*
    in OUs, 150
    in trees, 291, 294
partial attribute sets (PASs), 311
Password Authentication Protocol (PAP), 733
passwords, 343, 666, **667–668**
PAT (Port Address Translation), 435
patch management, **764–765**
PDCs (primary domain controllers), 114,
    304
Performance Monitor. *see also* performance
    tools
    ActiveX Control in, *527*
    adding counters in, *529*
    alerts in, **535**
    analyzing data in, **535**
    Appearance tab in, *534*
    Data Collector Sets in, *527*
    Data tab in, *533*
    deciding what to monitor in, **528–529**
    General tab in, *532*
    Graph tab in, *534*
    Graph view in, *530*
    Histogram view in, *531*
    introduction to, **527–528**

Performance Monitor (*continued*)
  logs in, **535**
  MMC version of, *527–528*
  performance objects in, **527**
  properties in, **532–535**, *532–534*
  Report view in, *531*
  saving data in, **535**
  Source tab in, *533*
  System Stability Index in, *527*
  viewing performance information in,
    529–531
Performance tab, in Task Manager, **538**
performance tools
  Event Viewer, **541–545**, *542–545*
  introduction to, **524–526**, **536**
  MBSA, **546–547**, *547*
  Network Monitor, **536–537**
  Performance Monitor. *see* Performance
    Monitor
  SNMP, **548–549**
  Task Manager, **537–541**, *538–541*
periodic update mode, in RIP, **562–563**
permissions
  in AD security, 609, **619–620**, *620*
  in file services, **656**, **660–662**
  in shared folders, *660–662*
persistent routes, *590*
personal identification numbers (PINs), **4**,
    667–668
personnel, *258*
per-user access, **749–750**
physical requirements, *256*
physical-to-virtual (P2V) conversions,
    397–399
ping commands, *108*
PINs (personal identification numbers), **4**,
    667–668
PKIs (public key infrastructures), **2**, **217–218**,
    325
PKI-savvy applications, 218, 325
Plain Old Telephone Service (POTS), **702**
planning
  Active Directory. *see* planning Active
    Directory

domain structures, **112–113**
GPOs, **202–203**
in RSoP, **246–247**
rule of thumb for, *525*
sites, **261–263**
trees in, *290*
Windows Server 2012 installation, **4**
planning Active Directory
  domain functional levels in, **109–110**, *110*
  exam essentials on, **137–138**
  exam objectives on, **99**
  File System verification in, **101–105**
  forest functionality in, **111–112**
  format options in, *101*
  introduction to, **100**
  network connectivity in, **106–109**
  NTFS in, 101, **102–104**
  planning domain structures in, **112–113**
  Resilient File System in, **101–102**
  viewing disk configurations in, **104–105**
pointer (PTR) records, 47, **65–66**, **498–499**
Point-to-Point Encryption, **708**
Point-to-Point Protocol (PPP)
  DUN and, *701*
  frames in, *707*
  overview of, **703–704**
  in RRAS, **710–711**, *710*
  VPNS and, **706–707**
Point-to-Point Tunneling Protocol (PPTP)
  introduction to, *567*
  network access in, **595–597**
  RRAS and, **708–709**, *716*
pools, defined, **458**
Port Address Translation (PAT), **435**
port numbers, *406–407*
ports
  for printing services, 690, *690*
  in RRAS, **715–716**, *716*, **722**, *723*
  in TCP/IP, **406–407**
POTS (Plain Old Telephone Service), **702**
power numbers, *447*
PowerShell
  Active Directory Module for, **126**,
    344–345

for BranchCache, **676–677**, *676–677*
CA servers and, 342
cmdlets in, *25–26*, **221–222**, **344–345**, 786
configuring, **23–27**
for FSRM, *665*
starting, **27**
in Windows Server 2012, **23–27**
PPP (Point-to-Point Protocol). *see* Point-to-Point Protocol (PPP)
PPTP (Point-to-Point Tunneling Protocol), *567*, **595–597**, **708–709**, *716*
Preboot Execution Environment (PXE), 21, 461
predefined global groups, **616–618**
predefined options, 490
Preferences Levels tab, **588**, *588*
prefixes, in IPv6, *443*
presentation virtualization, 367. *see also* virtualization
primary domain controllers (PDCs), 114, 304
primary zones, **49–50**
printing
    in AD administration, **180–182**
    configuring printers for, **688–693**, *688–692*
    creating printers for, **686–688**
    Easy Print Driver for, **693**
    exam essentials on, **694**
    exam objectives on, **647–648**
    introduction to, 7, 649, 686
    migrating print servers for, **693**
    Print Operators for, 615
    Printer objects in, 165
    printer servers for, **686**
    publishing printers for, **686–688**
    review questions on, **695–698**
    summary of, **693**
private networks, 768
Private Profile, 817, *817*
private virtual networks, 379
Processes tab, 537
profiles, defined, **736**
promotions, 114–120, **114–120**, 290

properties
    of DHCP scopes, **483**, *483*
    in DNS, *71*, *74*, *82*
    in Event Viewer, *543*
    for GPOs, *247*
    in IP routing, 587
    in IPv6, *440*
    of OUs, *158*
    for Performance Monitor, *532–534*
    in server management, **532–535**
    in software installation. *see* Software Installation Properties
Protect Container From Accidental Deletion, 178
protecting storage. *see* Firewall
protecting systems. *see* disaster recovery (DR)
provisioning, **667**
proxy mode, in IGMP, 566
PTR (pointer) records, 47, **65–66**, **498–499**
public key infrastructures (PKIs), 2, 217–218, 325
public networks, 768
Public Profile, 818, *818*
publishing AD objects, 180–182, **651–653**
PXE (Preboot Execution Environment), 21, 461

Q

quads, 407
queries in DNS
    caching, **47**
    defined, **42**
    introduction to, 45, *46*
    inverse, **47**
    iterative, **45**
    recursive, **45–47**
    time to live in, **47–48**
querying AD, **183–184**
quick migration, 368, 397
quorums, **768–770**, *769*

R

R&D (Research and Development), 156
RADIUS (Remote Authentication Dial-In
    User Service)
    authentication in, **752–753**
    introduction to, **718**
    in RRAS, 734
RAID (Redundant Array of Independent
    Disks)
    Disk Mirroring, 801, *802*
    Disk Striping, 800–801, *802*
    Disk Striping with Parity, 801, *802*
    DiskRAID, 815
    introduction to, 103
    sets in, **802–804**, *802–804*
    storage in, **800–802**
    volumes in, 799, *804*
RAID-5, 799, *804*
RAS/VPN client configuration, **723–730**
read-only domain controllers (RODCs), 13,
    59, **343–344**
read-only SYSVOL, 343
realm trusts, **307**
record types, in DNS, **62–67**
record weighting, **61**
recovery passwords, 666
recovery point objectives (RPOs), 763
recovery time objectives (RTOs), 763
recursive queries, **45–47**
Recycle Bin, 344, **842–843**
Redialing Options, **726**
Redundant Array of Independent Disks
    (RAID). *see* RAID (Redundant Array of
    Independent Disks)
ReFS (Resilient File System), **101–102**
Registry, *522–523*, 835
Relative ID (RID) Masters, 304
relay agents, **464**
remote access. *see* Routing and Remote
    Access Services (RRAS)
Remote Authentication Dial-In User Service
    (RADIUS). *see* RADIUS (Remote
    Authentication Dial-In User Service)

Remote Desktop Services, **3–4**, **7**
Remote Installation Services (RIS), 18
remote management, **22–27**
Remote Procedure Call (RPC), 272
Remote Server Administration Tools (RSAT),
    222
remote storage, 103
removing software, **224–225**, **239–241**
renaming organizational units (OUs), **156**
renewals, 342
Repadmin utility, 286, *286*, **845–846**
Replace mode, **216**
replicating Active Directory
    authentication scenarios in, **285–286**
    Backup and, **845–846**
    bridgehead servers in, *262*, **279**, *279–280*
    changing environments and, **282**
    configuration of, generally, **271**
    connection objects in, **276–277**, *277*
    DFSR in, **263**
    domain controllers in, cloning, **283–284**
    domain controllers in, placing, **280–281**
    Domain Services connections in, *277*
    event logs in, **285**
    firewall configurations in, **285**
    global catalog servers in, **281–282**, *281*
    installing AD and, **131–132**
    intersite replication in, **272–274**, *273*
    intrasite replication in, **272**
    introduction to, **258–259**, *261*
    monitoring, **284–286**
    moving server objects in, **277–278**, *278*
    network connectivity in, **285**
    Repadmin commands in, *286*
    replication objects in, *265*
    router configurations in, **285**
    schedules for, *273*
    server topology in, **279–280**
    site links/site link bridges in, **274–276**,
        274
    synchronizing information in, **285**
    System Monitor for, **284**
    topology in, **286**
    troubleshooting, **284–286**

Universal Group Membership Caching
   in, **283**
replication scopes, in DNS zones, *56*
Replicator group, 615
ReplState switches, 264
Report view, 530, *531*
Requests for Comments (RFCs), 38
Research and Development (R&D), 156
reservations, **463**, **488–489**, *489*
resetting computer accounts, **179**
Resilient File System (ReFS), **101–102**
resolvers, **41–42**
resource metering, 368
resource properties, 783–785, *783–785*
resource records (RRs), 48
Restartable Active Directory Services,
   842–843
restoring
   Active Directory, **841–842**
   databases, 340
   virtual machines, **392–397**
Restricted Groups, 200
Resultant Set of Policy (RSoP), **243–247**
Results Wizard, *244–245*
revoking certificates, 337–339
RFCs (Requests for Comments), 38
RID (Relative ID) Masters, 304
right-click options, *387*
Rights Management Services. *see* Active
   Directory Rights Management Services
   (AD RMS)
RIP (Routing Information Protocol)
   Advanced tab in, **585–586**, *585*
   defined, **561–562**
   dynamic routing in, 560
   General tab in, **581–583**, *582*
   interfaces in, **581–586**
   introduction to, 557, **581**
   Neighbors tab in, **584–585**, *584*
   network access and, **561–563**
   periodic update mode, 562–563
   properties in, generally, **581**
   protocols in, **589**
   Security tab in, **583–584**, *583*

RIS (Remote Installation Services), 18
RODCs (read-only domain controllers), 13,
   59, **343–344**
role clustering, 776–779, *777*
root (.) designation, 38, 40, **91**
root domains, 290
Root Hints tab, *71*
root servers, 41
round robin, **70**, 805–806
route add, 590
routeprint, 598
router mode, in IGMP, 566
routers
   in AD replication, **285**
   area border, 563, *564*
   for DHCP scopes, **475**, *475*
   discovery of, 560
   introduction to, 258
   multihomed, 416
routing
   border, 564–565, *565*
   dynamic, **560–564**, *561*
   IP. *see* IP routing
   multicast, **565–567**, *565*
   in network access, generally, 556–559
   Open Shortest Path First in, 563–564, *564*
   Routing Information Protocol in, 561–563
   RRAS installation in, **568–572**
   static, **560**
   tables in, **559**
   in Windows Server 2012, **567–568**
Routing and Remote Access Services (RRAS)
   access control in, **735**
   Advanced (Custom) Settings in, **728**
   Authentication Methods options in,
      745–746, *746*
   Callback Control Protocol in, **703**
   CHAP in, **703**
   Compression Control Protocol in, **703**
   configuring servers for, **710–713**
   Connection Manager in, **751**
   connection-level security in, **734–735**
   Constraints tab in, **745–746**
   Dial-in tab in, *736*

Routing and Remote Access Services (RRAS)
    (*continued*)
    Dialing Options in, **726**
    dial-up access restrictions in, **745**
    Dial-Up Connection Properties in,
        723–730
    dial-up networking in, **700–704**
    encapsulation in, **704**, **707–708**, *708*
    Encryption in, **748–749**, *748*
    event logs in, **722**
    exam essentials on, **755–756**
    exam objectives on, **699**
    General tab in, **724–725**, *724*
    installing, **568–572**
    introduction to, *556*, **700**
    IP Control Protocol in, **703–704**
    IP in, generally, **704**
    IP routing in, **590–591**
    IP settings in, *747*
    IP-based connections in, **711–713**, *711*,
        712
    ISDN in, **702**
    L2TP/IpSec tunneling in, **709**
    Launch NPS in, *739*
    Link Control Protocol in, **703**
    logging in, **719–722**, *721*
    managing, **718–723**
    multilink PPP in, **704**
    network access policies in, **738–744**,
        739–741
    Network Access Protection in, **754–755**
    network protocols in, **704**
    Networking tab in, **729**, *729*
    Options tab in, **725**, *725*
    per-user access in, **749–750**
    Plain Old Telephone Service in, **702**
    Point-to-Point Protocol in, **703–704**,
        710–711, *710*
    ports in, configuring, **715–716**, *716*, **723**
    ports in, monitoring, **722**
    PPTP tunneling in, **708–709**
    RADIUS in, **718**, **734**, **752–753**
    RAS/VPN clients in, **723–730**
    Redialing Options in, **726**
    remote access policies in, **744–751**

review questions on, **757–760**
security in, configuring, **751–755**
security in, generally, **732–735**
Security Options group in, **727–728**
Security tab in, **726–727**, *727*, *752*
Select Condition in, *739*
server logging in, **719**
Settings tab in, **746–749**, *747–748*
Sharing tab in, **730**, *730*
SSTP tunneling in, **709**
summary of, **755**
troubleshooting VPNs in, **716–718**
tunnels in, *705*, **709**
Typical (Recommended) Settings in,
    727–728
user access in, configuring generally, **736**
user authentication in, **733–734**
user profiles in, **736–738**, **745**
VPN Connection Properties in, **724–730**
VPNs in, configuring, **715–718**
VPNs in, generally, **705–709**, *705*
VPNs in, installing, **714–715**, *714*
Windows Authentication in, **753–754**
wireless access and, **730–732**
Routing Information Protocol (RIP). *see* RIP
    (Routing Information Protocol)
RPC (Remote Procedure Call), **272**
RRAS (Routing and Remote Access Services).
    see Routing and Remote Access Services
    (RRAS)
RRs (resource records), **48**
RSAT (Remote Server Administration Tools),
    222
RSoP (Resultant Set of Policy), **243–247**

S

Safe mode, **851–852**, **854**
saving data, **535**. *see also* Backup for Active
    Directory
scavenging, **81**
Schannel SSP, **4**
scheduling, *273*, **836**
Schema Masters, **303**
schemas, *127*, **293**, **303**

scopes. *see* DHCP scopes
screen names, **472, 479,** *479*
script policies, **214–215,** *214–215*
Scripting Syntax, 24
secedit.exe., **636–637,** *636–637*
secondary zones, **50–51**
Secure Sockets Layer (SSL), **4**
Secure Sockets Tunneling Protocol (SSTS),
   709
security
   in Active Directory. *see* security, in Active
     Directory
   analysis tools for, **635–637**
   auditing for, **4, 637–642**
   auditpol.exe in, *641*
   configuration tools for, **635–637**
   defined, **7**
   of domain services, 342
   exam essentials on, **643**
   exam objectives on, **607**
   in file services, **658–659,** *659–660*
   GPO filtering for, **209–210,** *209*
   GPO settings for, **199–200, 627–633,**
     628–629
   Group Policy for, **634**
   groups, 175, **210,** 611
   introduction to, **608**
   principals, 164
   review questions on, **644–645**
   in RRAS, 727–728, 732–735, 751–755
   secedit.exe. in, **636–637,** *636–637*
   in Server Core, **13**
   in shared folders, **658–659,** *659–660*
   smart card authentication in, **633–634**
   summary of, **642**
security, in Active Directory
   access control entries in, **620–621**
   access control lists in, **620–621,** *620*
   account operators in, 614
   Administrators group in, 614, 616
   audit policies in, **637–642**
   Backup Operators in, 615
   built-in domain local groups in, **614–616,**
     614, 616
   Certificate Service DCOM Access in, 615

computer accounts in, 610
Cryptographic Operators in, 615
distribution groups in, 609, 611
domain local group scope in, 612
domain users/groups in, 610–611
Dynamic Access Control in, **627**
foreign security principals in, **618,** *618*
global group scope in, 612
group scope in, **611–614,** *613*
groups in, creating/managing,
   622–624
groups in, delegating control of,
   625–627
groups in, generally, **609**
groups in, using effectively, **621**
Guests in, 615–616
implementing, generally, **622**
introduction to, 608
krbtgt accounts in, 616
local users/groups in, **610–611**
managing, **619–620,** *619*
objects, delegating control of, **626**
overview of, generally, **609**
permissions in, **619–620,** *620*
predefined global groups in, **616–618**
Print Operators in, 615
Replicator group in, 615
security groups in, 609, 611
security principals in, generally, **609–610**
universal group membership caching in,
   612
universal group scope in, 612
user accounts in, 609
user templates in, **624–625**
Users group in, 615, *616*
users in, creating/managing, **622–624**
users in, delegating control of, **625–627**
Security Configuration and Analysis,
   635–637
Security Extensions (DNSSEC), **60–61**
security identifiers (SIDs), 174, 178, 609
Security tab
   for printing services, 692–693, *692–693*
   in RIP interfaces, **583–584,** *583*
   in RRAS, **726–727,** *727, 752*

Security Templates, 198, 635–636
Select Condition, *739*
Select Disks page, *802–804*
Select The Operating System That You Want
    To Install screens, *15*
selective authentication, 307
self-enrollment, 355
self-healing NTFS, 103
Server 2012. *see* Windows Server 2012
server certificates, 336
Server Core
    installing AD LDS on, **354**
    installing AD on, **120–123**
    installing Hyper-V on, **375**
    installing Windows Server 2012 with,
        11–14, 17–18
server licensor certificates (SLCs), 355
server logging, **719**
server management
    alerts in, **535**
    analyzing data in, **535**
    Baseline Security Analyzer in, **546–547**
    deciding what to monitor in, **528–529**
    in DHCP scopes, **484**, *484–487*, 490
    in DNS, **41–42**
    Event Viewer for, **541–545**, *542–545*
    exam essentials on, **550**
    exam objectives on, **507**
    hardware in, *536*, **536**
    in Hyper-V, **377–378**, *377*
    in installing Windows Server 2012, **2–8**
    introduction to, **508–509**
    logs in, **535**
    MBSA in, *547*
    migration in, **8–9**
    Network Monitor in, **536–537**
    Performance Monitor in, **527–536**, *529–
        534*
    performance monitoring in, generally,
        524–526
    performance tools in, generally, **526, 536**
    properties in, **532–535**
    review questions on, **551–553**
    saving data in, **535**

SNMP in, **548–549**
summary of, **549–550**
Task Manager in, **537–541**, *538–541*
topology in, **279–280**
viewing performance information in,
    529–531
Windows Automatic Updates in, *512,
    522–523*
Windows Deployment Services in, **19**
Windows Update in, *511–512*
in WSUS, **513–521**
Server Manager
    for Active Directory roles, **323–324**, *324*
    creating subdomains in, **295–299**
    Hyper-V in, **375–376**, *376*
    installing AD FS in, **346–349**
    installing AD LDS in, **350–351**
    installing AD RMS in, **356–359**
    installing DFS Namespaces in, **684**
    installing DHCP Server in, **464–467**
    installing DirectAccess in, **680**
    installing Hyper-V in, **373–375**
    installing RRAS in, **568–572**
    installing WSUS servers in, **514–517**
server roles, **4–9**, *5*
Server Status, in RRAS, **719**
Server Update Services. *see* Windows Server
    Update Services (WSUS)
server virtualization, 367. *see also*
    virtualization
service (SRV) records, **66–67**, *67*
service clustering, **776–777**
Service Group, in AD RMS, 355
service principal names (SPNs), **3**
service profiles, 751
service requests, **260–261**
service-level agreements (SLAs), **762–763**
Services tab, **540**, *541*
set command, *86*
Settings tab, in RRAS, **746–749**, *747–748*
shadow copies
    configuring on volumes, **848–849**
    Data Protection Manager in, **850**
    in disaster recovery, **847–850**

introduction to, 847
vssadmin.exe in, 849–850, *849–850*
Share and Storage Management, **663–664**
Share option, for GPOs, **230–231**
shared folders
in administering AD, **182**
BitLocker in, **666–671**, *669*
BranchCache in, **671–678**
compression in, **657**, *657*
DirectAccess in, **678–680**
disk quotas in, **680–682**
Distributed File System in, **682–685**, *685*
Encrypting File System in, **657**, *658*
File Server Resource Manager in, **664–665**
in file services, **656**
introduction to, **650–653**
on networks, **651–653**, **656**
NTFS in, **657–659**, *660–662*, **661–663**
offline, **653–656**
permissions in, **656**, *660–662*
PowerShell for BranchCache in, *676–677*
PowerShell for FSRM in, *665*
in printing services, **165**
security in, **658–659**, *659–660*
Share and Storage Management in,
663–664
shared permissions in, **659–663**
Volume Shadow Copy Service in, **656**
shared permissions, **659–663**
Sharing tab, **689**, *689*, **730**, *730*
shortcut trusts, **307**
SHV (System Health Validator), 755
SID Filtering on External Trusts, **307**
SIDs (security identifiers)
for objects, **174**, 178
trusts and, 307
of user accounts, 609
Simple Mail Transfer Protocol (SMTP),
272–273
Simple Network Management Protocol
(SNMP), **548–549**
single sign-ons (SSOs), 346
single-master operations, **303–305**
site links, **265**, **274–276**, *274*

sites
Active Directory. *see* Active Directory
Sites
in AD infrastructure, **258–260**
creating, **266–268**
defined, **260**, **264–265**
GPO settings for, 200
implementation of, **264–265**
moving server objects between, **277–278**,
278
planning, **261–263**
SLAs (service-level agreements), 762–763
SLCs (server licensor certificates), 355
Slow Link Detection, **231–232**
smart cards, 4, **633–634**
SMTP (Simple Mail Transfer Protocol),
272–273
snap-ins
Advanced Security, *819*
DHCP, **467–468**, *468*
DNS, **81–84**
snapshots, **393–396**, *395*, 847
sneakernet, 195
SNMP (Simple Network Management
Protocol), **548–549**
SOA (start of authority), **62–63**, *63*, **72–73**, *73*
socket pools, **59**
software
deploying, **222–229**
in Hyper-V, 373
installation properties of. *see* Software
Installation Properties
life cycles in management of, **223**
maintaining, 223–224
providers of, 814
removing, 224–225, **239–241**
restriction policies, 200, **231**
updating, **233–234**
verifying installation of, **234–235**
Software Installation Properties
application categories in, **238–239**
file extension mappings in, **238**
in GPOs, **236–239**, *236, 237, 239*
package defaults in, **236–238**

Software Restriction Policy, 200
Software Settings, in GPOs, 197
Source tab, 532, *533*
special multicast addresses, *565*
special network addresses, *410*
SPNs (service principal names), **3**
SQL Server, *766*
SRV (service) records, **66–67**, *67*
SSL (Secure Sockets Layer), **4**
SSOs (single sign-ons), 346
SSTS (Secure Sockets Tunneling Protocol),
    709
Stand-Alone Root CAs, 326
Standard version, Windows Server 2012, **10**
start of authority (SOA), **62–63**, *63*, **72–73**,
    73
Starter GPOs, 198–199
Startup Repair tool, **856**
Startup/Shutdown Scripts, *214*
stateless autoconfiguration, 435–436
static routing, 560, **590–592**, *591*
storage configuration
    basic disks in, **797–799**
    booting from VHDs for, **816**
    DMS Install in, *807*
    dynamic disks in, **797–799**
    exam essentials on, **825**
    exam objectives on, 795
    Fibre Channel in, **813–814**
    initializing disks in, **796–797**
    introduction to, **796**
    ISCSI in, **808–810**
    ISNS in, **810–813**
    mount points in, **804–805**
    Multipath I/O in, **805–807**, *807*
    network attached storage in, **814**
    protection of. *see* Firewall
    RAID in, generally, **800–802**
    RAID sets in, creating, **802–804**,
        802–804
    review questions on, **826–827**
    summary of, **825**
    Virtual Disk Service in, **814–815**, *815*
    volume sets in, **797–800**

in Windows Server 2012, generally,
    796
stub zones, **53–54**, *53*
subdomains, 40, **294–300**
subnet masks. *see also* subnets
    CIDR and, *431*
    in configuring TCP/IP, **416–418**, *416–419*,
        431
    default, 417, *417*
    in ISPs, **430**
subnets
    addresses of, **413**, *419*
    calculating number of, **418–419**
    Class A, **430–431**, **434**
    Class B, **428–430**, **433**
    Class C, **423–428**, **432–433**
    in configuring TCP/IP, generally,
        412–413
    creating, **268–270**
    defined, **262**, **264**, **412**
    easy method for, **420**, *420*
    implementation of, **413–416**,
        414–415
    with IPv6, **446–447**, *447*
    masks in. *see* subnet masks
    network addresses and, *415*
    number of hosts per, **421–423**
    requirements for, **413–414**
    sample of, *414*
    TCP/IPv4, *420*
    traditional method for, **423**, *424*
Subordinate CAs, 326
Subscription Properties, 545, *545*
Summary Of Selections pages, *245*
superscopes, **462**, **493–494**
synchronization, **285**, **521**
system backups, 834. *see also* Backup for
    Active Directory
System folder, *177*
System Health Validator (SHV), **755**
system key utility, **344**
System Monitor, **284**
System State data, **836–837**
SYSVOL, **343**, *835*

T

Task Manager, **537–541**, *538–541*
TCP/IP (Transmission Control Protocol/
    Internet Protocol)
    Add IP Filter in, *594*
    configuring. *see* configuring TCP/IP
    in DNS, generally, 35–36
    in Dynamic DNS, 44
    Inbound Filters in, *593*
    IP addressing in, **407–412**
    ipconfig and, *107*
    layers communicating in, **405–406**, *405*
    model of, **404–405**, *405*
    overview of, **404–407**
    packet filters in, **592–595**
    port numbers in, **406–407**, *406–407*
    subnets in. *see* configuring TCP/IP
TCP/IPv4 subnetting, *420*
Telemetry, 7–8
templates
    in AD RMS, 356, **360**
    Administrative, 197
    certificate, 218, **335–337**, *336–337*
    in security, 198, **624–625**, 635–636
    for users, **168–169**, **624–625**
Teredo, 437, 443, 445
test labs, 525
testing updates, **521**
time to live (TTL), 42, **47–48**
TLS (Transport Layer Security), **4**
TLS/SSL (Schannel), **4**, 734
top-level domains (TDLs), 39–40, *39*
TPM (Trusted Platform Module), 666–667
TRACERT commands, 108
Transfers tab, *56*
transitive trusts, **306**
Transport Layer Security (TLS), **4**
Transport layers, **404**, *405*
Transport Level Security (TLS), 733
transports, defined, **279**
trees. *see also* forests
    creating, **294–300**
    introduction to, **290**

joining to forests, **300**
planning, **290**
promoting, **294**
single, **291–292**, *291*
troubleshooting
    AD replication, **284–286**
    DNS. *see* troubleshooting DNS
    Event Viewer for, **125**
    GPOs, **242–248**
    IP routing, **598–601**
    of OUs, **163**
    VPNs, **716–718**
    Windows Server 2012, **125**
troubleshooting DNS
    DNS snap-in for, **81–84**
    DNSCmd in, 90
    DNSLint in, 88–89
    introduction to, 81, 84
    ipconfig in, 89–90
    log files in, 91
    non-Microsoft DNS servers and, 91–92
    nslookup in, 84–88
    root zones in, 91
trust anchors, **60–61**
trust policies, 349–350
Trustbridge, 112
Trusted Platform Module (TPM), 666–667
trusts, **305–309**, *306*
tunneling
    in IPv6, **444–446**
    in ISATAP, 437, **444–445**
    in L2TP, **597**, **706–709**
    in PPTP, 567, **595–597**, **708–709**, *716*
    in RRAS, *705*
    in SSTS, **709**
two-way trusts, **306**
Typical (Recommended Settings), **727–728**

U

UGMC (Universal Group Membership
    Caching), **283**, **312**, 612
unauthorizing DHCP, **469–470**

unicast addresses, 441–442, *443*, 494

unidirectional replication, 343

unique local addresses, 442, *443*

Universal Group Membership Caching (UGMC), **283, 312,** 612

universal groups, 175, 612

unreachable, defined, **574**

Unrestricted (software is allowed), 231

update sequence numbers (USNs), 263

updates
    Automatic, **509, 511–512,** *512, 522–523*
    Dynamic, *44,* 75–77
    Windows Update for, 224, 509–510, *511–512*
    in WSUS. *see* Windows Server Update Services (WSUS)

upgrade path recommendations, *10*

upgrading applications, 234

UPNs (user principal names), **167–168**

Used Disk Space Only encryption, **667**

User
    certificates, 336
    containers, 164
    Network Options, 216
    objects, 165, **171**
    Selection pages, 243–246, *244–245*

user principal names (UPNs), **167–168,** 310

users
    access of, 736, 749–750
    in AD Users and Computers. *see* Active Directory Users and Computers
    authentication of, **733–734**
    class options for, **492**
    delegating control of, **625–627**
    domain, 610–611
    local, 610–611
    OUs and, *145*
    profiles for, **736–738, 745**
    security and, 615, *616,* **622–624**
    in Task Manager, 538, *539–540*
    templates for, **168–169, 624–625**

USNs (update sequence numbers), 263

V

V2V (virtual-to-virtual) conversions, **398–399,** *398*

Validate a Configuration Wizard, 767, **770–774,** *772, 774*

Variable Length Subnet Masking (VLSM), 47, 562

VBScript (Visual Basic Scripting Edition), 130

VDS (Virtual Disk Service), **814–815,** *815*

verification
    of AD installations, **124–128**
    File System, **101–105**
    of network connectivity, **106–109**
    of software installations, **234–235**

versions of Windows Server 2012, **9–10**

VHDs (virtual hard disks). *see* virtual hard disks (VHDs)

viewing disk configurations, **104–105**

viewing performance information, **529–531**

virtual devices, defined, 372. *see also* virtual machines

Virtual Disk Service (VDS), **814–815,** *815*

virtual Fibre Channel, 369

virtual hard disks (VHDs)
    creating, **382–384**
    differencing, **383**
    in Hyper-V, **381–385,** *382*
    introduction to, 28
    managing, **384–385**
    types of, **382**

Virtual Machine Connection, **390–391,** *390–391*

virtual machines. *see also* virtualization
    backing up, **392–397**
    configuring, generally, **385**
    configuring existing, **388–389**
    creating, **385–388**
    deleting, **389,** *389*
    exporting, **392–393**
    Hyper-V Integration Components in, **391–392**
    importing, **392–393**

live migration in, 396–397

managers for, 345

quick migration in, 397

restoring, 392–397

right-click options in, *387*

snapshots in, 393–396, *395*

Virtual Machine Connection in, 390–391, *390–391*

virtual networks, 378–381, *381*

virtual private networks (VPNs)

client configuration in, 723–730

Connection Properties for. *see* VPN Connection Properties

enabling RRAS as, **715**

enforcement in, 754

introduction to, 257

IP routing and, *576–577*

packet filters in, 595–597

in RRAS, 705–709, *705*, **714–718**, *714*

in Windows Server 2012, **706**

Virtual Switch Manager, 379

virtual switches, 378–380, *379*, *381*

virtualization

defined, 367–368

domain controller cloning and, 283

exam essentials on, 399–400

exam objectives on, 363–364

Hyper-V in. *see* Hyper-V

introduction to, 367

physical-to-virtual conversions for, 397–399

review questions on, 401–402

summary of, 399

virtual machines for. *see* virtual machines

virtual-to-virtual conversions in, 398–399, *398*

virtual-to-virtual (V2V) conversions, **398–399**, *398*

Visual Basic Scripting Edition (VBScript), 130

VLSM (Variable Length Subnet Masking), 47, 562

Volume Activation, **8**

volume sets, **797–800**, *804*

Volume Shadow Copy Service (VSS), **656**

Volume Snapshot Service (VSS), 847

VPN Connection Properties. *see also* virtual private networks (VPNs)

Advanced (Custom) Settings in, **728**

Dialing Options in, **726**

General tab in, **724**

Networking tab in, **729**

Options tab in, **725**

Redialing Options in, **726**

RRAS, **724–730**

Security Options group in, **727–728**

Security tab in, **726–727**

Sharing tab in, **730**

Typical (Recommended) Settings in, **727–728**

VPNs (virtual private networks). *see* virtual private networks (VPNs)

VSS (Volume Shadow Copy Service), **656**

VSS (Volume Snapshot Service), 847

vssadmin.exe, **849–850**, *849–850*

W

WAN Miniport (PPTP) dialog boxes, *716*

WANs (wide area networks), 51, 257

wbadmin, **846–847**, *846–847*

WDS (Windows Deployment Services). *see* Windows Deployment Services (WDS)

WDSUTIL command-line utility, *20–21*

Web Agents, 349

Web enrollment, defined, **333**

Web Enrollment Role Service, 325

Web Server (IIS), **8**

Web Services, 345

weighted path configurations, 806

WEP (Wired Equivalent Privacy), 731–732

wide area networks (WANs), 51, **257**

Windows

Authentication in, 753–754

Automatic Updates in, **509**, **511–512**, *512*, *522–523*

Windows (*continued*)
  Deployment Services in. *see* Windows
      Deployment Services (WDS)
  Firewall in. *see* Firewall
  Installer in. *see* Microsoft Windows
      Installer (MSI)
  Network Load Balancing in. *see* Network
      Load Balancing (NLB)
  NT File System in. *see* NTFS (New
      Technology File System)
  Server 2012 in. *see* Windows Server 2012
  Server Backup in, **8**
  Server Migration Tools in, **8–9**
  Server Update Services in. *see* Windows
      Server Update Services (WSUS)
  Settings in, 197
  System Resource Manager in, **8**
  Update in, **224, 509–510,** *511*
Windows Deployment Services (WDS)
  clients in, **21–22**
  defined, **4, 8**
  network services in, **20**
  preparing, generally, **19**
  server components in, **20–21**
  server requirements for, **19**
  in Windows Server 2012, **18–22**
Windows Internet Name Service (WINS)
  for DHCP scopes, **476–477,** *477*
  in DNS, **74**
  introduction to, **42**
Windows Management Instrumentation
    (WMI), **208–209**
Windows Remote Management (WinRM),
    22–23, *23*
Windows Script Host (WSH), 214
Windows Server 2012
  Active Directory Certificate Services and,
      344
  audit policies in, **641–642**
  BitLocker in, **668–671,** *669*
  BranchCache in, **677–678**
  Certification Authority server settings in,
      342
  clustering features in, **786**

configuring. *see* configuring Windows
    Server 2012
Event Viewer for, **541–545,** *542–545*
failover clustering in, **786**
firewall configuration in, **821–823**
for high availability, **786**
Hyper-V in, **345**
installing. *see* installing Windows Server 2012
MBSA in, **546–547,** *547*
Network Monitor in, **536–537**
Performance Monitor in, **527–536,**
    529–534
performance monitoring in, generally,
    524–526
performance tools in, generally, **526, 536**
SNMP in, **548–549**
Task Manager in, **537–541,** *538–541*
virtualization in. *see* virtualization
VPNs in, **706**
Windows Server Update Services (WSUS)
  Active Directory networks and, **523**
  advantages of, **512–513**
  approving updates in, **521**
  client configuration in, **522–524**
  client requirements in, **521–522**
  configuring, generally, **509**
  defined, **8**
  disconnected network configuration in,
      521
  GPO configuration for, **524**
  Group Policy and, 235
  inbound/outbound rules in, *821*
  non-active directory networks and,
      522–523
  Registry keys in, *522–523*
  server configuration for, **517–521**
  server installation for, **514–517**
  server requirements for, **513**
  synchronization logs in, **521**
  testing updates in, **521**
  using, generally, **512**
  Windows Automatic Updates in, **509,**
      511–512, *512, 522–523*
  Windows Update in, **509–510,** *511–512*

WinRM (Windows Remote Management), **22–23**, *23*
WINS (Windows Internet Name Service). *see* Windows Internet Name Service (WINS)
Wired Equivalent Privacy (WEP), 731–732
wireless access, **730–732**
witness configuration, **769**
WMI (Windows Management Instrumentation), **208–209**
workflows, **24**
World Wide Name (WWN), 814
WSH (Windows Script Host), 214
WSUS (Windows Server Update Services). *see* Windows Server Update Services (WSUS)
WWN (World Wide Name), 814

X

XrML (Extensible rights Markup Language), *356*

Z

zones in DNS. *see also* DNS (Domain Name System)
Active Directory Integrated, *51*
configuring properties for, **71–75**
defined, **41**
for dynamic updates, **75–77**
GlobalName, **54, 57**
integrated, **51–52**
local databases in, **49–50**
Notify, **55–56**
primary, **49–50**
replicating, **54–55**, *56*, 57
secondary, **50–51**
signing, 60
stub, **53–54**, *53*
transfers of, **54–55**, *56, 57*, 74–75

Free Online Study Tools

Register on Sybex.com to gain access to a complete set of study tools to help you prepare for your MCSA Windows Server 2012 Certification

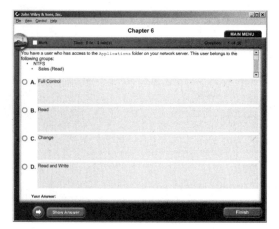

Go to www.sybex.com/go/mcsawin2012 **to register and gain access to this comprehensive study tool package.**

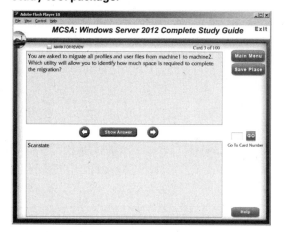

Comprehensive Study Tool Package Includes:

- **Assessment Test to help you focus your study to specific objectives**
- **Chapter Review Questions for each chapter of the book**
- **Three Practice Exams to test your knowledge of the material**
- **Electronic Flashcards to reinforce your learning and give you that last-minute test prep before the exam**
- **Over an hour of companion videos of many of the exercises presented in the book**
- **Searchable Glossary gives you instant access to the key terms you'll need to know for the exam**